FORD AHEAD

A HISTORY OF

The Colonial Motor Company Limited

ROGER GARDNER

FRASER BOOKS

Published by The Colonial Motor Company Ltd
in association with Fraser Books,
Chamberlain Road, RD8, Masterton
First published December 2004

ISBN: 0-9582521-1-4

Editing and Production: Diane and Ian Grant
Formatting: Graham Kerrisk, Printcraft, Masterton
Distribution: Nationwide Book Distributors,
P O Box 4176, Christchurch
Printed by Publishing Press Limited,
31 William Pickering Drive, Albany, Auckland

CONTENTS

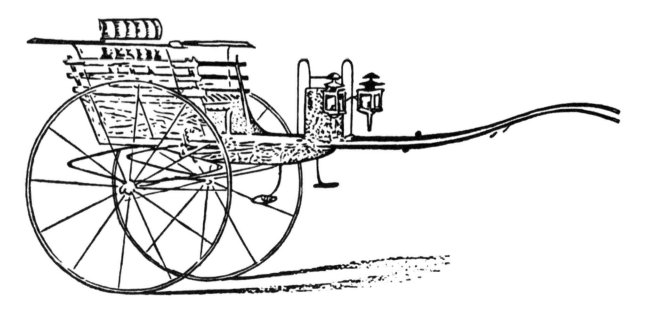

Rouse & Hurrell Catalogue drawing of a gig from 1885.

FOREWORD

Since 1859, The Colonial Motor Company Limited (CMC to most) and its forebears have been in the transport business – horses, carts and carriages, then cars, trucks and tractors.

CMC has been in the 'Ford' business since 1908. For the first quarter century the company represented Ford Motor Company of Canada as the New Zealand distributor and, from 1936, as a holding company for a group of Ford franchised dealerships. In this, the bigger part of CMC's history, the real heroes have been the management and staff of the dealership subsidiaries, spread from Kaitaia to Invercargill, who have been the company's face to the public.

Since 1918, Hope Gibbons, his four sons Hope, Alf, Robert and Norman, daughter Elsie, and their descendents, have been the cornerstone shareholders

In motoring times, CMC has always been with Ford and this partnership has been the basis of a long term relationship, akin to marriage, that has stood the test of time and seen both the 'Ford' brand and CMC, through good times and bad, overcome challenges and adapted to circumstances in an industry and marketplace that has never stopped changing.

In 2000, Roger Gardner proposed setting about the challenge of combining the CMC Group's history into a single book expanding on the previously recorded history in the company's in-house magazine *Impact* during the 1970s and 1980s. The original aim was to publish the book as part of Ford's centenary year in 2003, but the vast array of recorded history and the uncovering of much previously unpublished information proved a bigger and far more interesting challenge than he ever envisaged. At every turn there was another interesting lead to follow.

As the research evolved, CMC's history became Roger Gardner's story of the evolution of a country, a company and the people that contributed to its life and times. Each dealership subsidiary has a story of its own, its managers, staff and customers' characters and the evolution of the business, along with the town it is located in.

Time tends to reveal a reflective honesty on events and actions taken, which at the time were dealt with on the reality and pressures of the day. No business is all a 'bed of roses' but longevity and ongoing success reflect upon the creativity, character and tenacity of those involved.

For each generation of people the products of their childhood became the – often overrated – cars of their dreams. For my generation Lotus Cortina, Ford GT40, Escort RS, Falcon GT. For our parents Model A's, Ford V8s, Fordson Tractors, for their parents the Model T. For the children of today, we hope there is a Ford in their future dreams.

The 'product' is the passion that attracts and keeps the people in our business. The car as we know it has evolved for over a century now and the evolution will go on. The personal liberty the motor car has brought to our lives has become an expression of the freedom of life.

From all of us in the company our thanks to Roger Gardner for his determination in bringing this history to fruition.

Graeme Gibbons
CEO
The Colonial Motor Company Limited

This Rouse & Hurrell Easy Gig from 1882 cost just £33.

PREFACE

This history is about the people associated with 89 Courtenay Place in Wellington since 1859; what they did, what they accomplished, and the factors that affected them. It includes the story of one of the longest partnerships in motoring times between Colonial Motor Company and Ford Motor Company. To a lesser extent, it is a roadside view of wheeled transportation in New Zealand since its beginnings 150 years ago, together with some of the social aspects.

The Colonial Motor Company is a pioneer company that has survived, not by chance, but through the efforts of its management and staff, for more than a century in a tough industry. It grew from a coachbuilder into a countrywide motor group, and is listed on the New Zealand stock exchange. The company has had a remarkable number of long serving staff members, with more than 10 working for CMC for 50 years. My start working for them was in 1960, yes 'them' – Mr R B, P C and then Graeme Gibbons. It is still very much a family business.

During research, it was my good fortune to find people wanted to help me. Discussion and interviewing has been time consuming and I was not able to get to everyone so, inevitably, some important people have been missed. No history will ever be complete. Peter Gibbons, whose memory is legendary, has lived with the company since birth, been its managing director and chairman. We have spent hours discussing aspects of the company and its people, and P C has helped me to get it right in a number of ways. Thank you Peter, your help and contribution has been very significant. Thank you also Graeme Gibbons, for giving me the opportunity and support to assemble this history.

Most of the records after 1902 are still in the vault, which has been there nearly as long, together with hundreds of photographs. The subsidiary companies have considerable differences in their photographic collections, and it looks as if a 'clean out' has occurred at some. A great pity, resulting in some inferior quality images being used. In the course of research different versions of the same 'event' have been found. My solution has been to check the very good records as far as possible and make a judgment, but there will surely be errors, which is regrettable and the reader is invited to let me know their own version.

People have asked me if Ford Motor Company is criticised, and the answer is no. Ford is a huge multi-national with a turnover greater than New Zealand's gross national product and, like all companies should be, it is there to make a profit. Ford has, and continues to provide, a vast array of exceptionally good products, which have benefited millions of people. It would be difficult for me to sell or own any other make. However, from time to time, some of Ford's servants have handled matters in a manner that probably did not produce the best result, in my opinion.

History is a never-ending journey, and like a journey, if you do not know where you have come from, it is hard to work out where you are actually heading. The Colonial Motor Company has a very long and proud history, experiencing turbulent, as well as good times, competition, loyalty and satisfaction, both to the receiver and giver. Transportation is a cyclical business, affected by governments, people and products. CMC has survived, one of the very few to have done so. It is a great story, and if it helps people to recognise some of the signposts on the way, and for the staff and management, their contribution to its success, then my aspirations will have been achieved.

Roger Gardner
October 2004

ACKNOWLEDGEMENTS

The first *New Zealand Guide* of 1867,
Wellington – advertising William
Black, coachbuilder.
*The New Zealand Illustrated Tourist
Guide* of 1925, Richard Wedderspoon
– advertisements.
The *Wairarapa Daily* of 1879 and 1880,
Greytown – William Black
advertisements.
The *NZ Freelance* – information on
Rouse & Hurrell and William Black.
The *NZ Mail* – as above.
The *NZ Spectator* – as above.
The Evening Post – HB Gibbons, RB
Gibbons obituaries.
The Dominion – HB Gibbons, RB
Gibbons obituaries.
The Wanganui Chronicle – Hope
Gibbons obituaries.
Family archives:
Hope Gibbons Family
Peter C Gibbons, Wellington
Mrs A Page, Waikanae
Petherick Family
Graham Petherick, Wellington
Haworth Family
Mrs R Ryan, Masterton
Hurrell Family
Don G Smart, Lower Hutt
Meadows Family
Jeremy Busck, Whangarei
Deidre Macken, Wellington
Gordon Hughan Ltd
W J Worsfold, Carterton
Larmour Family
Mrs K J Macleod, Scotland
Lyttle Family
Graeme Lyttle, Masterton
Dorothy Campbell, Masterton
Lewis Family
Janette G Lewis, Christchurch
Phillipps Family
Phillip B Phillipps, Masterton
Wilkinson Family
A J Wilkinson, Cambridge
Alexander Turnbull Library – printed
materials and photographs.
Auckland War Memorial Museum – use
of Olaf Petersen's photograph.
Wellington City Archives – photographs
and plans.
Wairarapa Archive – information and
photographs.
Archives New Zealand – W B Black
insolvency papers.
Statistics New Zealand Yearbooks and
various statistics

NZ Statutes
McLean Motor-Car Act 1989
Motor Cars Regulations 1902
Apprenticeship Act 1923
Main Highways Board Act 1924
Motor Industries Commission
Report 1981
The Colonial Motor Company Ltd –
archives, letters, minute books,
photographs and published material.
Ford Motor Company – archives,
correspondence and publications in
New Zealand, Canada, USA,
Australia and England.
NZ Automobile Association Inc. – maps,
photographs and archives.
NZ Retail Motor Trade Association –
handbooks of annual statistics and
related motor regulations.
NZ Emergency Management and Fire
Service Reports of 1946.
Graham Stewart Photographic
Collection.
Peter Childerhouse at Te Aroha
Historical Society.
King and Dawson Architects –
photographic archives.
Denis LeCren's history of Nelson Ford
dealers.

Dictionary of New Zealand Biography
Vol 3 (1901-1920) – Hope Gibbons
(Diana Beaglehole).
New Zealand Encyclopedia,
Department of Internal Affairs, 1969
(NZ Government).
Ford - The Men and The Machine,
Robert Lacey.
Tin Lizzie, Philip Van Doren Stern.
100 years of Motoring in NZ,
John McCrystal.
The First Fifty Years, Ian J Main.
Coachbuilders in New Zealand.
End of the Penny Section, Graham
Stewart.
The Veteran Years, Pam MacLean and
Brian Joyce.
100 Years in New Zealand, Tony
Nightingale.
Our Motoring Heritage, T T N
Coleridge.
On the Road - The Car in NZ,
Graham Hawkes
Carapace, M H Holcroft.
To all the many others who have
corresponded, talked and discussed
aspects with me, thank you.

PART ONE –
89 COURTENAY PLACE

BOSS OF THE ROAD

The Latest and Best

THIS new light touring car fills the demand for an automobile between a runabout and a heavy touring car. It is positively the most perfect machine on the market, having overcome all draw-backs such as smell, noise, jolt, etc., common to all other makes of Auto Carriages. It is so simple that a boy of 15 can run it.

The FORDMOBILE with detachable tonneau, *$850*

For beauty of finish it is unequaled—and we promise **IMMEDIATE DELIVERY.** We haven't space enough to enter into its mechanical detail, but if you are interested in the **NEWEST** and **MOST ADVANCED AUTO** manufactured to-day write us for particulars.

FORD MOTOR COMPANY

689 Mack Avenue   **Detroit, Mich.**

The first Ford advertisement which appeared in the Saturday Evening Post, *June 27 1903.*

The first changes to the Model T in 1911 included front door.

The road between Tirau and Rotorua over the Mamaku Range was notoriously bad. This Model T has chains on the rear wheels and, although the clay surface looks remarkably good, there was little room for passing.

NZ Post Office built special mail collection and delivery vans for their GPOs in 1915.

CHAPTER ONE
THE CARRIAGE BUILDERS

On August 15 1911, history was made at an extraordinary general meeting of shareholders of The Rouse and Hurrell Carriage Building Company Ltd. Wellington's earliest and most prominent coachbuilder quit its core business, declaring a final move to motorcars by changing its name. The meeting was held at the company's offices at 89 Courtenay Place, Wellington. There were six shareholders and the general manager/secretary present, and proxies, or voting rights, were received from another 11 shareholders. Chairman, Charles Boyd Norwood (later Sir Charles), put the motion, seconded by Alexander Veitch, that the company change its name to 'The Colonial Motor Company Limited' (CMC). The motion was unanimously approved. For some months, directors had debated the names suggested by general manager, Charles Larmour: National Motor Company, Royal Motor Company or

Colonial Motor Company. Checks were made with the registrar of companies, Charles Larmour held out for Colonial, directors and shareholders agreed, and so it has remained. The last vestiges of coach building were now removed, and so ended the company's 52 years in that line of business and its forerunners. It might be a change of mode, but they were still in transportation!

Early settler William Bishop Black founded his American Coach Factory at 89 Courtenay Place in Wellington, in 1859. It was adjacent to the central depot of Cobb & Co. He lived on the premises, making and repairing coaches for the expanding market in New Zealand. Black had one employee, a boy to operate the bellows for the forge.

At the time roads were few and far between, and some of those were only bridle tracks or semi-charted walking tracks. New Zealand was covered in dense

In the 1850s, Wellington's Te Aro area consisted of one acre small farm blocks. Looking east towards Mt Victoria, Te Aro Pa is right of centre, Manners Street runs diagonally through the photograph and leads to Courtenay Place. By 1860 the population had grown to 7,000 people.
[Photo 1857; ref: F-1395-1/, Alexander Turnbull Library]

Militia formed most roads along strategic routes in the 1850-60s, giving quick access to trouble spots during the land wars. This is the unusually wide Great South Road from Auckland to Waikato. Soldiers guard the workmen at Williamson's clearing, and the bridge over the stream was built, with faggoted approach ramps, to stop erosion. [Photo 1863 by Lt Col Wm Temple ref F-663-1/2, from Urquhart Album, Alexander Turnbull Library]

A typical road with deep ruts 4ft 8in apart cutting into the surface. Poor drainage meant the surface held water, resulting in a quagmire in winter, and a very rough surface in summer. Fixing a broken axle was not a five minute job, even if you could find someone to help. [Photo 1909 from James McAllister Collection, ref: G-8148-1/1, Alexander Turnbull Library]

bush, scrub and swamps, and there were very few large cleared areas. Most of the access to towns and districts was by boat when sailing past, or by horse or on foot. Roads, built by contractors with hired gangs of helpers, were developed for the provincial governments as strategic access roads for militia, as well as for settlement. Much of the North Island was on a war footing with Maori.

The road to Paekakariki had been started in 1846 but was not finished until 1849. The road through the Hutt Valley, and on across the Rimutaka range, was started about 1843 and finished in 1856 for the huge cost of close to £40,000. At the same time, the Great South Road out of Auckland was steadily moving south. With the constant attacks on travellers, it had been nicknamed 'The Khyber Pass', where British soldiers had served before their New Zealand engagement. In 1868 the East Coast Road from Wellington through to Napier was completed, and also along the West Coast to Wanganui. A year later the West Coast Road reached New Plymouth.

Formed by men with picks and shovels, wheelbarrows and carts, the roads were clay tracks, little more than two metres wide, a nightmare by today's standards. It was backbreaking work, and progress was slow. When wet they reverted to a muddy bog that was slippery and treacherous, with little space to pass anywhere. Carts usually had a 4ft 8in (1.42m) track, and they cut deep ruts with their narrow wheels. In

Left: The Rimutaka hill road had a reputation for strong wind, with vehicles often blown off the road. Most coaches had roll-up leather sides that allowed the wind to pass through. [Photo 1870 from James Bragge Collection ref: PA7-30-03, Alexander Turnbull Library] Below: This 1901 road building gang had changed little from its 1860s counterpart. [Photo: James McAllister Collection ref: G-9471-1/1, Alexander Turnbull Library]

summer the road dried out to a very rough, dusty potholed surface with deep fissures. Rivers had to be forded, or a flat bottomed punt used to cross them. Travel was not for the faint hearted.

Wellington, in 1859, was only a small town of 7,000, established by the New Zealand Company in 1840. It grew quickly, and people needed transport to go about their business. From William Black's small start it was soon evident there was a big demand for vehicles built to suit the local needs. Orders for farm carts, wagons and traps, the favourite vehicles of the pioneers,

Crossing the Buller River in the 1880s. The punt was attached to the cable by pulley, and a type of rudder was set against the current to push it across. [Photo: Tyree Bros collection ref: G-619-10x8, Alexander Turnbull Library]

Rouse & Hurrell,

WELLINGTON
PRICE LIST

	£ s d
Pair-Horse Landau .. .. .. From	180 0 0
Circular-Fronted Brougham	110 0 0
Pair-Horse Brake to carry 10 persons	90 0 0
Holiday Brake	75 0 0
Family Wagonette to carry 8 persons	80 0 0
Small Family Wagonette to carry 6 persons	85 0 0
Ladies Park Phaeton	50 0 0
Physicians Phaeton	40 0 0
Denmark Phaeton	50 0 0
Parisian Phaeton	40 0 0
Two-Seat Jersey	45 0 0
Our Cut-Under Double Buggy	47 10 0
Double-Seated Commercial Buggy ..	44 0 0
Station Waggonette .. ·	35 0 0
Single-Top Buggy .. (without top, £31)	38 0 0
Piano-Box Buggy .. (without top, £23)	33 0 0
Stick-Boby Road Wagon (without top, £25)	35 0 0
The Easy Gig .. (without top, £23)	33 0 0
Our First Prize Dog Cart	40 0 0
Ralli Cart	35 0 0
Grosvenor Cart	37 0 0
Boulevarde Cart	35 0 0
Rustic Cart	35 0 0
Whitechapel Cart	28 0 0
Battlesden Cart	33 0 0
Gentlemen's Cart	24 0 0
Bradley Cart in Quartered Oak	22 0 0
Our Morning Cart	23 0 0
Bradley Cart	20 0 0
Our Best All Round Roadster	26 0 0
Physician's Gig	37 0 0
Yankee Gig	12 0 0
Eureka Car	14 0 0
Three-Spring Express Waggon	35 0 0
Farmer's Cart	22 0 0

as well as for coaches, several of which afterwards rolled for years over the famed Rimutaka Road and along the beach to Foxton, began to come in steadily, while the staff was kept busily with alterations and repairs.   Such was the quality of the vehicles he manufactured, that Black's business prospered and expanded. Demand from outside Wellington soon created an even bigger market.

In 1865 Wellington became the country's capital and seat of government, which boosted its importance. Although not the largest city (population by now was about 20,000), it was certainly developing and moving ahead quickly.

Black's business had also grown and now employed 25 men, in wood and corrugated iron premises covering 11,500sq.ft. By 1874 he had started a sales and repairs branch at Greytown.

Henry Arthur Hurrell grew up in the English village of Banham, Yorkshire, where his father was a blacksmith and master mechanic, servicing many of the machines in the industrial areas nearby. Life was not easy for the family, as his father had a health problem. When he was 18 years old, Hurrell decided to emigrate to New Zealand, and seek his fortune. The *Dallam Tower* left Plymouth with 257 emigrants and arrived at Wellington in 1875.

Henry Hurrell was apprenticed to William Black and learned the trade of coach building. He soon settled into the city and, being an energetic and active citizen, with an excellent singing voice, also found himself frequently on the concert platform entertaining local residents. Music was in his genes, his grandfather a prominent bass fiddle player at the Wesleyan Chapel in Banham.   In 1879, Henry Hurrell married Maria Milner, a Wellington spinster.

While the American Coach Factory was renowned for producing quality vehicles, it was at a cost. Financial disaster struck William Black and, unable to control ballooning debt, he filed for bankruptcy on March 31 1880, with liabilities of £6,406. At the time, this was a huge amount as his average coach could be bought for less than £40. A year later only about three shillings in the pound had been realised from assets. The Colonial Bank was principal creditor and lost over £5,000.

The period from 1875 to 1883 was one of severe world economic depression, with high external trade deficits. A credit squeeze in New Zealand during 1878 and 1879 caused high unemployment and many businesses folded. Wool was the country's main export until the first shipment of frozen meat in 1881, soon followed by dairy produce after the cream separator was invented; slowly New Zealand recovered.

Frederick Rouse had his own Empire Coach Building business in Thorndon Quay, and quickly assessed the opportunity. Rouse took over Black's business after negotiations with the Colonial Bank, invited Henry Hurrell to become his partner, and transferred to 89 Courtenay Place. Rouse had arrived in New Zealand aboard the *Soukar* in 1874,

having already qualified as a carriage builder with George Edgeley, at Walworth in London, before working at the Great Eastern Railway Workshops at Stratford, England.

At the Wellington Exhibition of Trade and Industry in 1885, Rouse & Hurrell received the Silver Medal for New Zealand against all competitors and two first prizes for their manufactures. They had a reputation for turning out buggies, officers' dogcarts, gigs, landaus and many other styles of vehicles. The partnership worked well, the business expanded greatly, and in 1886 substantial, new, three storey brick premises were constructed in front of the factory, at the Courtenay Place site. Wellington had not seen a carriage builder on this scale before.

Opposite top: Advertisement for William Black's American Coach Factory, in the first New Zealand Guide of 1867.

Opposite bottom: Rouse & Hurrell 1886 price list.

This page top: Impressive Masterton to Wellington VR Mail coach of 1879, ready to depart from James Macara's Cobb & Co depot at the Council Chambers in Queen Street. Made by William Black, to the Concord design, and used by Cobb & Co agencies in NZ. [Photo: Wairarapa Archive, Masterton]

Left: Finishing and painting section of William Black's American Coach Factory in Courtenay Place. [Photo 1909 from James McAllister Collection ref: G-8141-1/1, Alexander Turnbull Library]

A Rouse and Hurrell cut-under double buggy of 1885, priced at £47 10s. The buggy featured a cross mounted semi elliptic front axle spring and full elliptic rear springs, with foot operated friction rear brakes.

Wellington's famous Kelburn Cablecar. Rouse & Hurrell's Gripcar No 3, built in 1903, is being restored for the Kelburn Museum. [Photo 1904 by Muir and Moody ref: F-3716-1/2, Alexander Turnbull Library]

The firm also fitted a steam boiler and engine that supplied power to operate the saws, drills, shapers, planers and finishing machines. The steam engine was connected to overhead drive shafts that drove the machines by pulleys and belts. The partnership name was altered to The Rouse & Hurrell Empire Steam Carriage Works.

The blacksmith's forge still operated, making and repairing springs, axles, tyres and brackets and all manner of harness items. The heat and open fire often caused small fires to start, and with so much wood and shavings about the fires sometimes spread quickly, causing the fire brigade to be called.

Henry Hurrell hadn't forgotten his family back in England, and kept writing, urging them to emigrate to the colony, with promises of work and assistance. With the exception of his father they eventually all came to New Zealand.

In April 1892, Frederick Rouse, then aged about 50, retired from the partnership and left for England on an extended holiday. Henry Hurrell took in Arthur William Petherick and Edward Young Crawley, a recent arrival, as partners. Arthur Petherick had served his apprenticeship with the firm, and was backed by his father Edward Wade Petherick, the first white child born on Petone beach, the day after his parents arrived on the first NZ Company ship *Aurora* in 1840.

The partnership was well established and had successful standard lines that sold through agents in many parts of New Zealand. They exhibited at trade fairs and exhibitions around the country. For as little as £12, a 'Yankee Gig' could be purchased, or if you had £180, you could buy a top of the line 'pair-horse landau', with over 40 other choices available. Customising to your own needs was quite common.

Trams were introduced to Wellington and other cities in New Zealand from about 1865. They were a very popular conveyance with hundreds being constructed, many by Rouse & Hurrell. At first they were horse drawn and, when on steel rails, they could get along at about six mph. From about 1875, steam engines were often hauling three or four tram cars behind them. Much larger electric trams came into use from about 1890. Wellington introduced electric trams in 1901, with many double deckers made by Rouse & Hurrell. They arrived in New Zealand as engine and chassis and municipal corporations tendered the

bodybuilding out to coachbuilders. The tenders for constructing these relatively straightforward, mainly wooden bodywork trams gave a large boost to the industry at the turn of the century.

Motorcars, or 'horse-less carriages', were still a novelty and very few were to be seen anywhere in New Zealand before 1900. William McLean, an elected member of the House of Representatives for Wellington, visited Europe in 1897 and purchased two cars. However, he found on his return that their use was illegal in New Zealand. The traffic laws of the day had no provision for horse-less carriages and McLean tried unsuccessfully to persuade the Wellington City Council to adopt similar measures to those allowing motorcar use in London and Paris.

There was strong lobbying against the legalisation of motorcars, but the McLean Motor-Car Act was introduced in 1898 and allowed use of a motorcar under very stringent conditions. The legislation cost the considerable amount of £200 to introduce, and the draft included McLean's right to charge

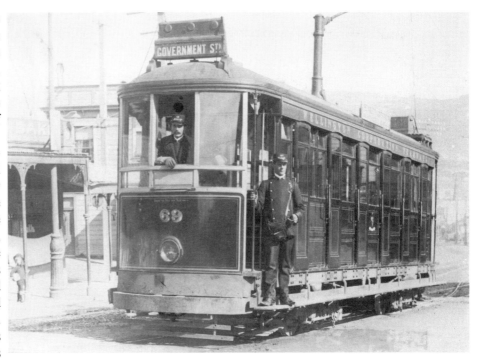

anyone wishing to use a car £3 for a licence. The Act was finally passed without giving McLean monopoly rights to charge a licence fee.

At this time, other new laws were introduced, regulating business and industry, and many partnerships decided to formalise their business structures by registering limited liability companies. This allowed more capital flexibility for shareholders to come and go, and it also protected an individual shareholder's risk and liability to the amount of the registered capital they held. The Rouse & Hurrell partners, knowing the

Electric trams were an important source of work from 1901. The 'Palace' had full width compartments with entry from either side. The conductor walked along the 'running board' collecting fares. [Photo: Graham Stewart collection]

This crowded 'workers only' 'Big Ben' double-decker shows how efficiently large numbers of people could be moved in 1907. [Photo: Graham Stewart collection]

Below: Edward Wade Petherick was the first white child born to NZ Company settlers on Petone beach, just after the Aurora *arrived in 1840. He formed the 'Limited' company, and he, brother-in-law Francis Sidey and son Arthur, were three of the first six shareholders of Rouse & Hurrell. [Photo: Graham Petherick collection]*

difficulties of changing partners and getting new ones, decided to register as a company, obtaining in the process, additional capital to further expand their operations.

A meeting of the subscribers to the new Rouse & Hurrell Carriage Building Company Limited took place on August 12 1902 at Courtenay Place, Wellington. Subscribers were Francis Sidey, chairman, Henry Arthur Hurrell, James Ranson, William Murphy, Arthur William Petherick and his father, Edward Wade Petherick. Francis Edward Petherick of Messrs Bell, Gully, Bell and Myers, Solicitors, reported that the company had duly been registered. Those subscribers attending were appointed interim directors, until the statutory meeting of shareholders was held.

Directors held a meeting immediately afterwards and resolved that Edward Petherick would be secretary, Henry Hurrell general manager and Edward Crawley foreman. The National Bank of New Zealand were appointed bankers, and Bell, Gully, Bell and Myers their solicitors. The registered office of the company was to be on the premises at 89 Courtenay Place.

Henry Hurrell must have reflected with some satisfaction on the achievements of the former partners over the previous 43 years. He could hardly have imagined where the company would be in another 100 years, or even what would happen within the next 10.

The company's coach

building business kept growing and a further director, Alexander Veitch, was appointed with Edward W Petherick becoming chairman. A loan of £5,000 at $4^1/2\%$ was raised and property purchased for a workshop at Pahiatua and a showroom was leased there also. A branch factory and workshop already existed in Feilding and adjoining land was bought for £150. At the end of 1902 a call of one shilling a share was made, increasing the capital to £10,000, the money to be used to re-build the old portion of the Courtenay Place factory.

People were starting to realise the potential of motorcars and, despite their cost, more were being used. The Motor Cars Regulation Act, 1902, gave rights to local authorities to further control motorists with local by-laws. Some local authorities had draconian by-laws which all but prevented car use. The horse transport industry was a very powerful lobby, employing large numbers of people, and it was clearly in their interests to keep the 'horse-less' monsters at bay. On the other hand, some local body councils took a pro-active view, and started developing their roads and bridges on which they charged tolls. This raised further monies that were spent on more improvements, though not always on roads.

Directors realised changes were occurring because of the motorcar, and asked Henry Hurrell to investigate 'the motor car trade' in 1903. He was the wrong person to ask, and he later reported back that he had been advised "to leave it alone".

At the 1904 annual meeting, the company's capital was increased to £15,000, and the next year the balance of unpaid capital was called up at 10 shillings per share.

Alexander Veitch was elected chairman. Michie's Horse Hospital next door in Courtenay Place was purchased, the directors still thinking coach building was going to expand.

The motorcar became more established, with about 500 then registered in New Zealand and, in parallel, the coach building industry was now starting to slide downhill. Rouse & Hurrell found its stock did not move as quickly as it had, and as things slowed down profits fell and pressures increased. Meetings with the National Bank became more frequent and more difficult. The Courtenay Place premises were put up for sale at £11,000, but never quite sold. Staff came and went with increasing speed as new methods and solutions failed. Directors finally decided that if they couldn't beat the motorcar, they had better join in and sell them.

Henry Ford formed the Ford Motor Company in 1903 at Detroit, making and selling his first production motorcar, the Fordmobile Model 'A'. The cars he made were competitively priced at $US850, and simple to use. His partners wanted bigger, more expensive cars, and Ford tried to resist these pressures, believing low cost transport would appeal to the masses. He made a Model C, and later Model F both modified Model As. To appease his shareholders he made a Model B in 1904 costing $2,000, which didn't sell, and a huge six cylinder Model K in 1905, which wasn't a big success at $2,800. The Model N was getting near his

ideal, and finally in 1908 he produced the first Model T that proved so successful.

Over the Rimutakas at Carterton, Gordon Hughan, a blacksmith and cycle agent, realised the future potential of motorcars and decided to try to get the Ford agency, as he thought Henry Ford made good cars. By purchasing a Ford Model N to demonstrate with in 1907, he was granted the Ford agency for that area, by the Automobile Company of New Zealand in Wellington.

Frederick Robert Nathaniel Meadows, export agent for Trengrouse & Co, dairy product importers, Tooley St, London, owned one of the first Locomobile cars in Wellington, but didn't like it. He later bought a Cadillac and a Ford, and in 1906 formed the Automobile Company of New Zealand, to become the first Ford distributor. Later, realising he couldn't run two businesses, he offered it to Rouse & Hurrell. A sub-committee of Norwood, Veitch and Pearson recommended the company's purchase. This was done by exchanging 590 Rouse & Hurrell shares and allowing Fred Meadows to become a director. Rouse & Hurrell ordered the first 12 Model T cars through Peabody's, the New York Ford agents, in 1908. Meadows' contacts through Tooley Street in London stretched worldwide.

Henry Hurrell did not like the new arrangements and, later that year, after discussion with directors, he retired from managing the company, became head of the Central Missions, and stood for the city council.

1903 Model A Fordmobile

Photo: Geo E A Nikolaison

FORD No. 486

The Colonial Motor Company purchased this historic car for £100 plus a new Ford Prefect in 1957. The car was imported in 1904 by John J Boyd, a Wellington builder who lived at Kilbirnie. Mr Boyd bequeathed the car to a relative and it deteriorated to a very bad state, having sat for years in a damp garage amongst rubbish. When found, the wheels were rotted down to the hubs.

The car was put on some old Model T wheels and used from time to time to entertain and sometimes terrify children at staff Christmas parties. At best it could be described as an old banger, complete with rotting seats, and it was a source of amusement.

After it had lain about for some years, the late Gordon Darnell, then service manager at Stevens Motors and a vintage enthusiast, rescued the car. In the early 1970s, after offers from Sir Len Southward, it was decided to restore the car at Gordon Hughan Ltd, New Zealand's oldest Ford dealer, under the watchful eye of the late Rex Porter, a renown vintage car buff. Both he and Hughan's had had a long association with CMC.

It was a labour of love, as the car was re-conditioned from top to bottom. Bernie Cheer of Carterton worked at Hughan's and pulled the car down in any spare moments, completing most of the mechanical and chassis restoration. A new crankshaft was made by Lambert's in Masterton, using a single billet of steel. The front brass reins rail was missing and Rex Porter made patterns and had another caste and polished. Three new brass hub caps were made by Brian Billing of Masterton to match the original. New 30 x 3½ wheels were made to the original specifications by Ian Clarke of Carterton. Surprisingly, most of the 1903 car was still intact. New trim was made using old materials from CMC's body building company, Standard Motor Bodies at Ebor Street Wellington. Bill Bell, the upholsterer in Masterton, had served his time there, and knew where to look.

Finally the wooden body was painted by Athol Ross of Greytown, with multi coats of duco, matched to the original carmine red colour, with the original transfer labels masked out. and left intact. Bernie Cheer took over when Rex Porter became ill, and finished the project. After a final inspection and ride with Rex Porter just before he died, Bernie Cheer delivered the car back to CMC in 'mint' condition. Today 486 is displayed in its special garage next to the lift well of the nine storey CMC Building at 89 Courtenay Place, where people can gaze at it through the glass front. On special occasions it goes on tour, and in 2003, it was out and about celebrating its 100th birthday.

THE SPECIFICATIONS

Engine -	Petrol 2 cylinder horizontally opposed
	Bore 4 inches Stroke 4 inches
	Capacity 100 ½ cu.in. (1,649cc)
	Power 9 bhp at 800 rpm
	Water cooled jacket and radiator
	Ignition by double trembler coil
	Float feed spray carburettor
	Crankcase draft pressure lubrication
Transmission	planetary 2 speed forward, 1 reverse
Steering	Direct link/lever, ½ turn lock to lock
Drive Chain	to open differential
Springing	Fully elliptical front and rear
Braking	Contracting band drum on rear axle
Body	2 seater wooden frame and panels
Colour	Carmine

Wheels	30 inch clincher rim (beaded edge)
Tyres	30x3½ with clincher beads pneumatic
Pressure	55 – 65 p.s.i
Wheelbase	72 inches (1821mm)
Track	55½ inches (1410mm)
Tare	11cwt18lb (568kg)
Options	Detachable 2 seater rear tonneau body; Kerosene lights; bulb horn
Fuel	Gasoline gravity fed from 5gal(US) tank
Top speed	30mph (50kph) approx @ 900rpm
Range	about 135 miles (220km.)

F N R Meadows at the wheel of his Ford Model F about 1906. Fred Meadows had the Ford distribution rights, through Peabody & Co in New York, and formed The Automobile Co of NZ Ltd in 1906. He sold the rights to Rouse & Hurrell in 1908 and became a director. [Photo: Jeremy Busck collection]

It was quite a change from building and selling carriages to selling the new Model T Ford motorcars. One of the staff from the Automobile Company of NZ was employed to run a motor department at £4 a week and a commission of 5% of the profits. Other business people were now very interested in getting a Ford sub-agency, and most of the motor department manager's time was spent negotiating sub-agency arrangements, rather than selling motorcars. By then the company had taken on other agencies, Belsize and Itala cars, as well as Ford.

However, the coach building was not going well, the motorcars were not selling quickly, and the bank kept pressing to reduce the overdraft of £3,000. Things were not good, and losses now began piling up as Rouse & Hurrell lost its way. In 1909 the directors decided they needed to act, and act they did – firing the motor department manager.

A new general manager and secretary, Charles Corden Larmour, appointed in May 1909 at £7 a week, proved to be a key factor in subsequent changes. Larmour liked the new Ford cars, and was keen to get them sold.

Larmour quickly realised that sub-agency commissions were too high, some as much as 20%, and reduced commission rates to a more affordable 10%. Supplies of Ford Model Ts were inconsistent, and Larmour wrote to Peabody's in New York, asking for guarantees of a regular supply of Ford cars in future. When Ford discovered New Zealand was part of the British Empire, this improved the relationship and the arrangements!

In November 1909, the company received notice that Gordon M McGregor, the very powerful head and founder of Ford Motor Company of Canada, would visit New Zealand. McGregor, a young wagon maker from Ontario, had forged a deal with Henry Ford in 1904, giving him the rights

Gordon Hughan had the earliest Ford dealership in New Zealand from 1907. Hughan and family, are pictured while touring in their Model N Ford of 1907. Harry, seated beside his father, took over the Carterton dealership in 1927. [Photo: W J Worsfold collection]

The first Model T was built in late 1908, but very few were sold until 1909. The engine block was one of the first to be cast in one piece, with a detachable cylinder head, and used a flywheel magneto to trigger high-tension trembler coils. A three point suspension and two transverse elliptical springs allowed it to negotiate the incredibly rough roads of the day, twisting, turning and getting through where other larger and heavier cars became bogged. The Model T was revolutionary because it was the first to used vanadium high tensile steel where toughness was required, keeping the weight of the car down. Henry Ford took the first production car on a reliability test run of 1,357 miles, averaging 20 mpg. The only trouble was one puncture. Relatively small, the Model T cost only $US850, about £NZ250, enabling many average income people to own a car. (Ford Motor Company photo)

to sell Ford Motor Company's products to the British Empire, but not including Britain, where Percival Perry (later Sir Percival) had sold Ford Model Bs for use as London taxis. McGregor had a great vision and plenty of drive, and he wanted Fords sold in numbers throughout the Empire, including New Zealand.

McGregor and Larmour met and got on well. New supply arrangements were confirmed through the Ford Motor Company of Canada. No doubt McGregor shared his vision about Rouse & Hurrell's future, and recommended a course of action to Charles Larmour.

Larmour convinced directors that the company's future lay in motorcars. He saw coach building was a thing of the past, and debt was killing the operations. The company needed to be rid of both to survive. Some of the directors were hostile, but Larmour backed up his claims with financial analysis from the auditor, C D Morpeth. The board told Larmour to come up with solutions.

Car numbers in New Zealand had risen to about 3,500 when, in 1910, further reconstruction steps were mooted for the company. These included a decision to reduce the capital by the amount of the debt. This effectively meant shareholders stood the losses. Directors also voted to get out of coach building entirely, concentrate on the motor business and change the name to suit. It was a majority decision and by no means unanimous.

An offer of £1,350 was accepted from J Bett and Company Palmerston North, for all the carriage building equipment and stock.

Then, on August 15 1911, the name was changed from The Rouse & Hurrell Carriage Building Company Ltd to The Colonial Motor Company Ltd.

It must have been very hard for some directors to leave behind all their previous associations with an industry in which they had been a leader for 53 years. However, times had changed, and the company had the foresight to move on.

CHAPTER TWO
THE LARMOUR YEARS

After Rouse & Hurrell Ltd sold all its coach building equipment and remaining stock in 1910, profits turned the corner straight away. General manager, Charles Larmour and auditor, C D Morpeth had been right. From a tentative beginning, with 12 Model T Ford cars ordered in 1908, the company was now ordering Ford Model Ts through Ford Canada in monthly lots of 12 at a time. They would have imported more, but the bank was still nervous, and wouldn't allow more credit without substantial personal guarantees.

When the company's name was changed in 1911 to The Colonial Motor Company Ltd (CMC), there were 73 orders for Model Ts sold forward. In February 1912, R J Durrance, Ford Canada export field manager, met with Charles Larmour and discussed the New Zealand operation. No doubt he would have been pleased with the changes made to the company. All vehicles and spare parts were now supplied monthly through Ford Canada, a much more consistent arrangement than before.

Larmour was still having problems with some of his directors who, it seems, still lived in the horse age, and did not totally understand cars were different to coaches. He was not allowed to own shares, so received no direct reward for his results. This worried Ford Canada, which would only deal with the principal person in the business. Charles Larmour, in Ford's eyes, was the business. Ford would also only issue an agency and supply contract for one year at a time, and that worried directors, who thought this too short a period.

After several loss years and mounting debt, the profit of £1,166 0s 3d for 1911 was welcomed at the annual meeting in March 1912, and Alexander Veitch, by rotation, took over as chairman from Charles Norwood. Showing a profit made the bank much happier and, in April, 54 new Model T cars were ordered.

There was soon sufficient money to pay off £3,000 from the mortgages and the bank relaxed. Charles Larmour received a £50 bonus and was finally allowed to purchase shares in the company. In September, Ford issued a supply contract for 1912, to be reviewed in January. Each month more and more Model Ts were ordered. Charles Larmour had a shrewd sense of timing, he was doing a good job, results were good, and he asked for his contract to be reviewed.

In October 1912, C C Larmour was offered a new five year contract as managing director, at a salary of £800, with commission of 10% of net profit, subject to the Ford contract being retained, and his "behaving satisfactorily". Larmour then started buying shares to increase his holding, finally becoming principal shareholder.

Few people today could comprehend

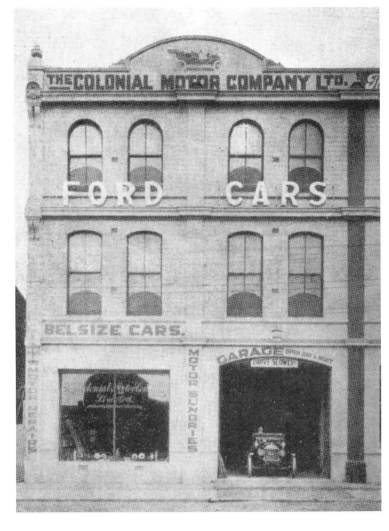

89 Courtenay Place in 1912. The Model T is coming from the service garage, at the rear. The Belsize agency was surrendered about 1912.

Charles Corden Larmour was appointed general manager and secretary of Rouse & Hurrell in 1907. He managed the transition to The Colonial Motor Company and retention of the Ford distribution franchise for New Zealand. [Photo: S P Andrew 1915 ref: G-14246, Alexander Turnbull Library]

Charles Boyd Norwood (later Sir Charles) a shareholder in 1903, and chairman in 1908, before resigning in 1913, after starting Dominion Motors to sell Morris cars. With William Morris (later Viscount Nuffield). [Photo ref: G-48883-1/4 Alexander Turnbull Library]

the difficulties encountered in travelling by motorcar in those times. Roads deteriorated in many areas after the railway was built, with little money spent on them by local authorities. Tollgates, put in by many local authorities to raise money for roads, were effective, but motorists hated them. Taranaki had a number, and roads were better, which resulted in more cars being sold.

The company loaned Arthur Chorlton a Model T Roadster in November 1912, and sponsored the first journey from Wellington to Auckland through the central North Island. Chorlton chose the time, thinking it would be dry, and there would be less likelihood of striking mud. The journey through the central highlands and King Country had never been attempted by car before, and there were no mapped roads from Taihape through Taumarunui to Te Kuiti, just tracks, many used to form the main trunk railway a decade before. Chorlton and his two companions, Richards the driver, and Gilling the photographer, succeeded in an epic 8 1/2 day marathon, enduring the most amazing and arduous conditions on 'roads' described by Chorlton as "execrable".

Few cars, other than a Model T Ford, were as light, tough, reliable and durable, making it very suitable for this journey, and the accolade of 'Car of the 20th Century' is rightly deserved. It is remarkable that such a car also cost less than almost all others, and it is no wonder that Henry Ford sold so many. Chorlton wrote a 72 page account of the journey in 1913. A shorter article, written by him in 1947, with Gilling's photographs, begins on page 25.

One of the major difficulties with travel was the type of tyre fitted to cars. The white pneumatic tyres had no tread for grip and were very slippery in mud. Motorists wrapped rope, chains and sometimes rawhide covers around the tyres to give more traction. The tyre walls were very flimsy by today's standards, and punctures were common from horse nails, sticks and sharp stones. To compound the problem, wheels were not detachable, and spare tyres and tubes were not always carried. Delays were frequent, time consuming and frustrating. After repairing a tyre it had to be inflated to 60–80 PSI with a hand pump. A semblance of tread was added to the rear tyres about 1915, and corded tyres and detachable wheels about 1919.

Things were moving quickly for the company, and sales had increased dramatically. In January 1913, 100 cars were ordered for February delivery. In 1912 sales had increased to 637 for the year, 27% of the 2,344 national sales.

At the annual meeting in 1913 a greatly increased dividend of 25% was declared, which certainly pleased the shareholders. Not all was well in the company though, and discussions took place in August, about the newly formed Dominion Motor Vehicles Ltd, and the conflict of interest of its principal shareholder, Charles Norwood.

In the event, Charles Norwood had been acting in the interests of shareholders of The Colonial Motor Company, trying to secure another business opportunity, and not for his own personal gain. He knew Ford wouldn't agree to it, because other vehicle makes were involved, so used a different name to protect the interests of the company. Shareholders were not happy, so he decided to resign from CMC, his loyalty to the company untarnished, and keep and concentrate his efforts on Dominion Motors, which he did very successfully.

More space was required, especially for servicing vehicles, and it was decided the

Charles Larmour, managing director CMC; Hayes, Hutt agent; Arthur Brett, Auckland Star; E N and J W Souter, Auckland agent; R J Durance, Ford Canada export manager, Auckland 1913.

There were 27 Ford agents in New Zealand in 1914 and over 40 dealers and sub-agents a year later.

FORD AGENTS IN NEW ZEALAND

Ashburton	G H Carson
Auckland	W Souter & Co
Blenheim	Edward Parker
Cambridge	W Souter & Co
Carterton	Gordon Hughan
Christchurch	Henry J Ranger
Dannevirke	Wakeman Bros.
Dunedin	W J P McCulloch
Eltham	Ira J Bridger
Feilding	Wackrill & Stewart
Gisborne	Anderson & Sons
Greymouth	Mark Sprot & Co
Hawera	Norton & Caplen
Invercargill	G W Woods & Co
Lower Hutt	Hayes & McKeage
Milton	Marshall & Summers
Napier	R H J Hamlin
Nelson	W G Vining
New Plymouth	M L Holah
Oamaru	F R Dennison & Co
Palmerston Nth	Wackrill & Stewart
Stratford	L R Curtis
Taihape	Wakeman Bros.
Temuka	Wm. Hally
Timaru	H H Kingham
Wairoa, H.B.	J Corkhill
Wanganui	C H Chavannes, Snr.

sole New Zealand Agents
THE COLONIAL MOTOR COMPANY, Ltd

FORD DEALERS IN NEW ZEALAND

Ashburton	G. H. CARSON
Auckland	W. SOUTER & CO.
Balclutha	BUNTEN & CLARK
Blenheim	EDWARD PARKER
Cambridge	W. SOUTER & CO.
Carterton	GORDON HUGHAN
Christchurch	HENRY J. RANGER
Dannevirke	C. L. NIELSEN & CO.
Dunedin	W. J. P. McCULLOCH
Eltham	IRA J. BRIDGER / WM. THORPE
Feilding	WACKRILL & STEWART
Gisborne	ANDERSON'S MOTOR GARAGE
Gore	G. W. WOODS & CO.
Greymouth	MARK SPROT & CO.
Hawera	N. H. C. CAPLEN
Heriot	TODD BROS. & CO., LTD.
Invercargill	G. W. WOODS & CO.
Lawrence	D. R. JONES
Levin	J. C. MILNES
Martinborough	EVANS & WOODLEY
Marton	NIELSEN BROS.
Masterton	J. H. LYTTLE
Napier	R. H. J. HAMLIN
Nelson	W. G. VINING
New Plymouth	M. L. HOLAH
Oamaru	F. R. DENNISON & CO.
Opotiki	A. J. ANDERSON
Pahiatua	ARNOLD WESTON
Palmerston North	ADAM BURGES
Roxburgh	TODD BROS. & CO. LTD.
Southbridge	C. V. ROI
Stratford	IRA J. BRIDGER
Taihape	WAKEMAN BROS.
Tauranga	F. N. CHRISTIAN & CO.
Te Awamutu	J. M. SPEAR
Temuka	WM. HALLY
Timaru	H. H. KINGHAM
Waimate	F. R. DENNISON & CO.
Wairoa (H.B.)	J. CORKILL
Wanganui	C. H. CHAVANNES, Senr.
Whangarei	THE WHANGAREI ENGINEERING CO.
Westport	J. W. HARKER

Sole New Zealand Agents:
The Colonial Motor Company, Ltd.

Top left: New Plymouth had a smart new Model T fire appliance in 1914.
Top right: Model T delivery van.
Middle: Cambridge Trade Fair display by W Souter & Co in 1913.
Bottom: The Masterton mail service contract was awarded to Roy Tankersley in 1913. He was one of the first to use a Model T car and trailer, licensed to carry five passengers and mail to outlying post offices.

main building fronting Courtenay Place would be extended. J M Dawson, architect, was asked to arrange for another matching double brick three-storeyed portion to be added to the eastern end, covering ground that had previously been Michie's Horse Hospital. This was done in late 1913 at a cost of £2,250.

The Colonial Motor Company profits were now very considerable as the public were clamouring to buy the amazing Model T Fords. Few other motorcars were able to cope so well with the arduous conditions in many country areas of New Zealand. In May 1913 303 Model Ts arrived, at the time the biggest ever single shipment of cars into the Southern Hemisphere.

In October 1913, the company paid a phenomenal 250% dividend of £2 10s on every £1 share held.

Michael (later Sir Michael) Myers, barrister and solicitor, was appointed to replace C B Norwood as director. His firm, Bell, Gully, Bell and Myers had acted for the company since 1902 and he brought a new professional dimension to the boardroom.

Charles Larmour drove over to visit Carterton's Gordon Hughan, who had now been a Ford dealer for six years. Larmour wanted to discuss new sub-agencies to be set up at Masterton, Eketahuna and Martinborough. Gordon Hughan had recently purchased a Model T that had been submerged under seawater in the wrecked *Devon,* which had gone aground at Wellington Heads on August 25 1913, and

together they set off to 'check' this car, returning 24 hours later having travelled 320 trouble free miles to Napier and back.

R J Durrance, from Ford Canada, arrived for the annual visit on January 26 1914 at Bluff, and departed on February 6 from Wellington after meetings and inspections with Charles Larmour. Durrance had responsibilities to see Ford was properly represented in New Zealand, and the Ford agency contract for 1914 was signed off. Durrance was pleased with the way CMC was performing. In February, the company paid another 250% dividend on shares held.

SS Indrabarah ran aground at the Rangetikei River mouth in 1913. Arthur Chorlton borrowed a Model T car and got the first news picture, travelling cross-country through swamp from Bulls.

Model T cars and equipment loading supply ship A25, 1st NZEF, at Wellington.

This prototype ambulance was sent to the training camp at Tauherenikau near Featherston in 1915. [Photo: A Levy collection]

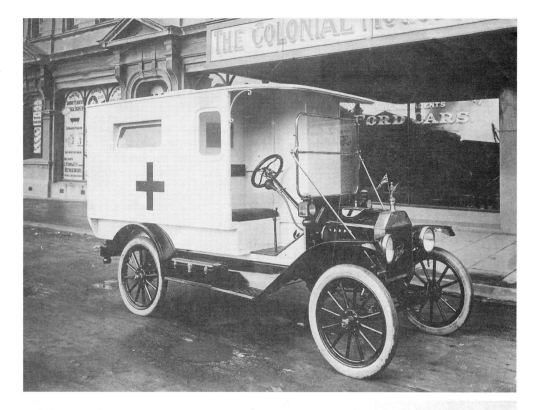

A large number of Model T ambulances and cars were sent with the NZ Expeditionary Force in 1915.

The First World War was declared on August 5 1914, and the directors suspended further orders of new cars. English cars dried up as their industries geared to war. The demand for the Model T was still just as strong; the car had caused a paradigm shift in the cost of travel, both in time and money. Backblocks New Zealand was no longer quite so isolated, and new opportunities kept emerging. In December the directors met and rescinded their previous decision, ordering 100 new Model Ts for delivery in January 1915. The company supplied a number of Model T chassis/cowl units to build ambulances and cars for the war, as the 1st NZEF contingent left for France.

Ford business was very strong and directors were now looking at expansion plans. By now, there were over 40 Ford dealers in New Zealand and many more sub-dealers and service agents. Car registrations were increasing by 30-50% every year, and had reached 17,000, with Ford cars accounting for over one third.

To expand, the company needed space, and when 65 Taranaki Street came up for sale in January 1915 it was purchased for £2,700. The property was on the corner of Taranaki and York Streets and included two dwellings and a shop on Taranaki Street and cottages at 2 and 4 York Street. More adjoining land was bought in York Street when it was available. The original coach-building factory, behind the showroom and offices in Courtenay Place, also had access directly to York Street, so the company had close to two acres available to build on.

The new land on the south side of York Street was for a large Ford service depot and J M Dawson, architect, was engaged to design this. The company had also decided to set up branches in Auckland and Timaru and C C Larmour was authorised to find suitable managers. The directors approved plans to purchase land at Sophia Street, Timaru and Fox Street in Parnell, Auckland, so Dawson was kept busy designing buildings. All these properties were intentionally close to their ports and railways, so vehicles could be shifted quickly from boat to company warehouses and vice versa. Dealers in many parts of New Zealand, still received their new vehicles, petrol, and freight by coastal boats and train.

Michael Myers was given special power of attorney to act for the company, and leave to visit Ford Canada at Windsor, Ontario, for negotiations regarding expansion of the company. Myers subsequently reported back on his discussions and plans for an increase in capital.

Dr W E Collins, a director, was called up for military service in June 1915 and given nine months leave. A total of 124,211, over half of New Zealand's young men of eligible age, were sent overseas to fight during the First World War. Nearly half of them were killed or wounded, an appalling loss to the country. John Grendon Phillips, who started in the office in 1907, was also given leave to join up and the company paid for his uniform.

J G Phillips was married in June 1916, before entering the army. On his honeymoon, the bridal party toured around the North Island during winter, in two Model T cars. At the time this was notable because many roads were regarded as impassable in winter. Largely the original coach roads, they were narrow, little more than clay tracks, and a nightmare when wet and reverted to muddy bogs. (See article beginning page 29.)

There was a decided visual change to the Model T when the distinctive brass radiator disappeared, brass now being required for artillery shells and bullets.

Top: The Ford Service Depot was built in 1915, to J M Dawson's design for £6,496, on the southern corner of York and Taranaki Streets. It was then 'written off', allowable in 1916. [Photo: King and Dawson architects]

Bottom: In 1913 the three storey building had another 33ft section added, with a ground floor showroom and verandah. [Photo: Ian R Bonny collection]

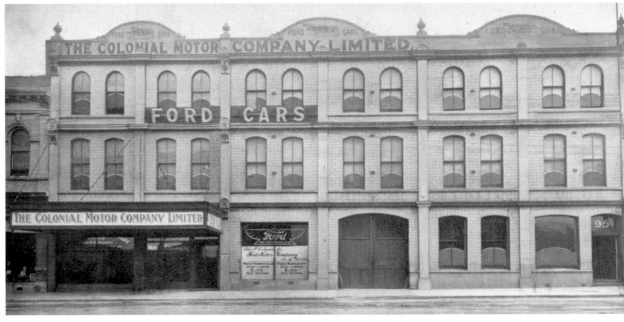

The modern new, rounded steel version changed the car's character, but sales became even stronger.

When Charles Larmour needed to travel overseas on business for five months, Thomas Alexander Low was appointed interim manager in February 1916. Hope Gibbons had made approaches about buying into Colonial Motor Company, and Larmour needed to establish the position with Ford.

In August 1916 Larmour cabled from Vancouver that new lower prices of £160 for Runabouts and £170 for Tourers would apply. In those days Ford Canada set the price of vehicles and the company was paid a commission. The board cabled back asking if Ford Canada would sanction an additional £10 for each model, payable to the company, but this did not happen. Charles Larmour returned in September and the next month the company leased buildings for offices at a weekly rental of £3 10s in Chancery Street and Bacon Lane, Auckland.

T A Low, who had stood in for Charles Larmour, was now given responsibility for the Auckland branch.

Of particular interest to the motoring public at this time, was the 1917 Parliamentary Tour organised by Colonel Allen Bell, chairman of the North Auckland

Development Board. This tour was planned primarily to show the 130 invited guests that the 'roadless north' was not, as many apparently thought, merely a quagmire of gum fields and clay – but rather that the 'winterless north' (the epithet coined by Colonel Bell for this tour), had potential of its own.

Northlanders felt, at the time, that although the rest of New Zealand was being opened up with substantial and passable roads, the needs of the north were largely being ignored. The roads were particularly bad, in places little more than tracks and with bad bridges. It was considered that any efforts to upgrade the roads would be of no avail to the public since nobody ever went to the far north except by sea to its magnificent harbours.

The Parliamentary Tour, which included four ministers of the Crown, 40 Parliamentarians, 30 southern farmers and 60 members of the Auckland Automobile Association, was devised to correct these erroneous views, and particularly to emphasise the need for adequate roading. This it probably did. The 800 miles took 16 gruelling days to complete and was so gruelling that, of the 33 cars that left Auckland, only 10 completed the tour and the 130 passengers were reduced to a hardy 50

The Parliamentary Tour of Northland in 1917 reached Kaitaia and the locals had never seen so many cars in one place before.

persons. Generous hospitality greeted the road-weary travellers at every stop. With so many politicians aboard, many social functions and public welcomes were arranged in little local halls where the visiting speakers strove manfully to paint a glowing picture of Northland opportunity.

But it was not all plain sailing. It rained sub-tropical torrents for several days as the tour turned south from Kaitaia and AA member Mr Wynyard described how the motorists had to roll up their trousers and dig cars out of a sea of mud in the Manukau Gorge. Over 100 motorists arrived unexpectedly at Herekino where the little hotel could only provide accommodation and meals for nine people, with the rest of the party eating biscuits from the local store and bunking down in the local hall on bales of straw. "Early in the evening, however, a number of local Maoris and gum-diggers arrived for a dance in the hall, so the recumbent figures rose up and joined in the revelry until an argument ended in a stand-up fight and put a stop to the merrymaking." So much for Parliamentary dignity on the grand tour.

On another occasion, in fact, two eminently respectable MPs, both later Ministers of the Crown, shared a bottle of beer and then put it in the middle of the road and danced a haka around it. This caused great astonishment to a carload of local people who appeared unexpectedly around a corner.

In 1919, E E Bradbury's travel book, described the area. "Kaitaia, one of the most progressive towns north of Auckland, is situated in the western portions of the Mangonui County. It is the centre of a rich and extensive agricultural district, and has important roads converging on it from all directions." Despite Bradbury's confident words about the roads, he nevertheless described "the easiest way of reaching Kaitaia is by steamer to Awanui, thence 4^1/$_2$ miles by level road".

The reality of the situation is probably more honestly described by another writer who felt compelled to tell the travelling public: "The three best months for motoring over the northern roads are January, February and March. The roads may be quite good enough in December and in April – everything depends upon the weather."

Subsequently, the fight for improvement built up considerably when the tour members were back in circulation and in 1922 the Main Highways Act became law.

Top: Colonel Allen Bell, public relations manager at Kaitaia, engineered the Parliamentary Tour to highlight the appalling road conditions in the Far North.

Middle: The Model T was one of the few cars to get through, and offered the less fortunate a tow. [Photo: MacLean collection]

Bottom: Big heavy cars got into trouble when it rained and roads turned to gluey mud. [Photo: New Zealand AA collection]

An impressive line up of Model Ts outside Wackrill & Stewart, Feilding, where the first meeting of the Garage Proprietors' Assn. of NZ was held in 1917.
[Photo: Ian R Bonny collection]

Model Ts were shipped, one to a case, until 1921 and assembly was often done on the roadside. This 1915 model outside early Auckland Ford dealer, G A Haydon & Co.

During the war shortages showed up with imports of tyres, petrol and parts, and prices escalated to match demand, with petrol peaking at 4s 2d, and some tyres costing as much as £10. The opportunist pricing caused dealers and the public a lot of concern, with variable qualities of petrol causing even more problems, but no rationing or sale restrictions were imposed.

In April 1917, a group of garage proprietors held a meeting at Wackrill & Stewart's office, the Feilding Ford agents, to set up a national body. This was finalised a week later, and the Garage Proprietors' Association of New Zealand was born with the purpose of protecting their interests. It was later re-named The NZ Retail Motor Trade Association. Despite approaches for support, Charles Larmour would have

nothing to do with the new organisation as he believed the company should stick to its core business of distributing and marketing Ford cars. The association went ahead quickly with over 200 members signed up in the first year.

H W Hale, Ford Canada's new export manager, arrived in April 1917 for the annual review, and visited Auckland, Wellington, Dunedin, Timaru and Christchurch. While in Wellington Hale met directors and, at his departure from Auckland, told Larmour he was "very well pleased with the organisation" and the Ford contract was renewed for another year. T A Low, however, decided he would not renew his contract as Auckland branch manager and John Grendon Phillips transferred to replace him in this important sales area.

Charles Larmour's contract was renewed in December at £1,500 per annum, 10% commission and 12 months notice. Plans for reconstructing the company were agreed in principle and handed to the lawyers to draft.

Despite the war, profits were good and the company made £58,800 for 1917, after writing property and stock back substantially. Staff received one extra week's wages at Christmas, and shareholders received a 500% bonus dividend.

A licence agreement was signed between the company and patent holders A J White Ltd and H J Wigzell for the use of their patent no. 36864. This was a spring cushion fitted to the front seat of the Model T, greatly improving comfort, and one

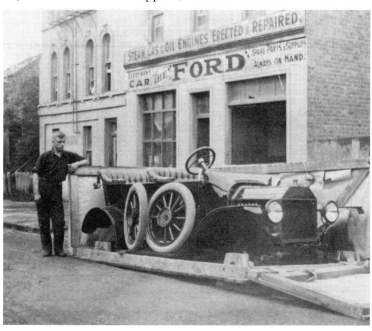

The Model TT truck introduced by Ford in 1919 was designed to carry 1 ton, and had a low ratio rear axle. This truck also had solid rubber rear tyres, to avoid having to unload the whole load with punctures. Ford shipped just the basics – chassis, bonnet, seat and front guards. The cab and body were built locally.

shilling royalty was paid for every one fitted. There were a great number of accessories and modifications available for the Model T, including electric lights, self-starters, and a chassis adaption converting it to a truck. Most were available as aftermarket options; very few made it as original equipment, as Henry Ford kept the base price low, hence more affordable.

On April 10 1918 Charles Larmour declared he was selling his interests in The Colonial Motor Company to Hope Gibbons, and gave 12 months notice of his resignation. The first transfer of his shares was made to Hopeful Barnes Gibbons who was appointed general manager and board secretary, at a salary of £800 per annum. The next month he was made a director and a further 700

shares were transferred to the Gibbons family.

Hope Gibbons of Wanganui was a very successful businessman who was looking for new opportunities. His business

Fordson tractors first became available in 1918, made by Henry Ford & Son at Cork, Eire but, soon after the end of the Great War, were distributed through Ford Canada.

A typical Ford garage layout at C H Chavanne's, Wanganui. The round wooden circle in the foreground is a turntable to swivel cars easily.

interests had expanded into a share of J B Clarkson & Co which imported a range of cycle and motoring related products. After discussion with his family, it was decided to purchase the controlling shares from Charles Larmour in 1916, but the transfer was delayed because of military service call-ups. Robert Barnes Gibbons took his discharge from the NZ Army in England, after war service in France, and travelled to Ford Canada and Detroit for discussions on expansion, particularly related to assembly.

Larmour was given five months leave of absence to travel to Canada and the US to advise Ford Motor Company of the reconstruction plans and change of principal shareholder to Hope Gibbons and his family.

In September 1918 Larmour returned and tabled a comprehensive report to the board of his discussions with Ford Motor Company which was quite happy with the transfer of control. The report included ideas from Ford of ways to save money on exchange transfers and insurances. Shipping had become very difficult in the Pacific due to the loss of many ships on the Atlantic routes during the First World War.

Stock was now prioritised with trucks and the new Fordson tractors taking precedence as essential goods. Ford used influence to arrange new routes through San Francisco to alleviate some of the problem, but it was thought likely that cars numbers would drop by 66% in the next year through lack of space.

Frederick Hills Johnston was employed as acting general manager in October 1918, having previously been a senior manager with the Bank of New South Wales. H B Gibbons reported that the extensions to the Ford service depot in Taranaki St were proceeding well, but it was not possible to estimate the final cost due to alterations.

The board appointed Hope B Gibbons as managing director in December, on the same terms as C C Larmour, who now retired to Scotland. Charles Larmour had very successfully seen the company through its critical transition from coach building to motorcars. Profits had been outstanding for the last eight years, and the company was in a strong financial position and ready for the changes to come.

The Model T had firmly established Ford in New Zealand, with a good dealer representation and predominant share of the market. The new 1 ton trucks were selling well and Fordson tractors were shortly to revolutionise farming. In Ford Canada terms, New Zealand was the most successful overseas market, with approximately 40,000 vehicles registered, over one third of them Fords.

Going on holiday about 1919. Fred Lewis, his wife and three children, all packed up to drive 80 miles, much on tracks, from Timaru, across Burke's Pass to Lake Alexandrina in the Mackenzie Country where they owned the first crib. [Photo: Janette G Lewis collection]

BLAZING THE MOTOR TRAIL TO AUCKLAND IN 1912

BY ARTHUR CHORLTON (IN 1947)

When the Main Trunk railway was opened, towards the end of 1908, the motor-car was already in New Zealand, but it had not, in the special sense yet 'arrived'. That time did not come till nearly twenty years later with a general improvement in the roads.

Having done the journey between Wellington and Auckland, first by rail and steamer, and then by the Main Trunk, I became interested in the possibilities of a motor trip between the two cities through the

Highway No.1 at summit of Paekakariki Hill.

King Country.

There was only one car for a job like that – the old Ford Model T. It was not old then – 1912– and it was by no means "The Universal Car" Henry Ford claimed it to be, at least not in New Zealand.

The Colonial Motor Company fell in with my proposal, provided the car, a three-seater, with full equipment and sponsored the expedition.

The party of three comprised Harold Richards, a first-class driver, the late Ernest Gilling, press photographer, and myself as manager and guide.

The start was made on Friday, November 22, 1912 from opposite the old entrance to the G.P.O.

Taihape was reached at 4.15 p.m. that day, after

an uneventful run of 142 miles at an average speed of 22 miles an hour, which was not bad with the old Paekakariki hill and roads as they were then.

From now on to Te Kuiti we were in totally unmotored country, except for a doctor's single-cylinder De Dion in Taumarunui, landed by train and marooned there ever since. People, horses, cattle, and dogs were scared at the sight of the horseless carriage and, outside Raetihi, a woman wheeling a pram upset it with the baby in a panic stampede.

After a night encamped under a fly by one of the Main Trunk viaducts near Pokako, the motor pioneers, jubilant at their progress, pushed on over the plateau at Waimarino and down past the Spiral at Raurimu.

All was going well, and it was a lovely Sunday, with prospects of being in Taumarunui in the early afternoon.

But the unexpected happened. At Oio, one of the service bridges over a creek built for the railway construction out of timber from the bush had rotted away and collapsed. This looked like the end of the

Crossing the broken bridge.

Arriving in Taihape.

Bullocky Bill and his team at Raurimu Spiral Road.

adventure. It was only a little stream in no deep gully, but Model Ts are not tanks and there seemed little chance of getting across.

Fortunately, there was some new timber for a new bridge handy to the spot, and the pioneers, reinforced by timber-workers from a nearby bush sawmill, off work for the Sabbath, in a few hours erected a sort of Bailey bridge and Taumarunui actually was reached after all that evening.

But beyond Taumarunui there was a blank, and when the motor pioneers set out again for the north on Monday, the fourth day out from Wellington, it was a genuine

Fording river at Ohakune.

Camping the night before Taumarunui.

adventure into the unknown.

There was no road up the Ongarue Valley, only a grass – grown track on the wrong side of the river, which sooner or later would have to be crossed to get to Ohura and the Waitewhena. To cap it all, it had begun to rain and the day looked ominous for a deluge. But there was no going back and the pioneers pushed on.

It was here they struck their greatest piece of good luck of the whole trip.

At Okahukura (Te Koura it was called then) they found Public Works men, on the Stratford Main Trunk railway construction, had built a service road over the hill to Matiere and a bridge over the Ongarue!

The road was rough and the climb high, but the Ford, in heavy rain, made nothing of it, and the party were in Matiere for lunch.

In the boarding-house a local celebrity led the party into taking a supposed 'short cut' to Aria, quite off the intended route via Ohura and Waitawhena.

Less than a mile from Matiere and in full sight of the township the motor travellers were so hopelessly bogged that they could make no

Packing and checking before breaking camp.

Passing road builders on Te Koura Road.

Twixt cliff and chasm.

headway with the block and tackle and had to call on a nearby farmer for horses.

It took four of them to pull the Model T out of the quagmire and over the hill.

The next two days were sheer misery. Without horse traction, in the papa mud and rain, corduroying patches and using greasy block and tackle, the pioneers could only make four miles the first day. Even tanks would have been bogged under such conditions. It was a job for 'ducks', if there had been any then, if not for horses.

So horses it was when at last they could be procured, and for all the next day the pathfinders worked in convoy with an escort of two stout draught horses and their owner; running the car, under its own steam, whenever possible, and waiting for the horses when halted by a morass of mud.

The seventh day involved much road-making and cross-country running in the upper Waitewhena, hitherto untouched by wheeled vehicles of any kind. The settlers went on horseback or used sledges and packed their cream to the factory.

A narrow shave-slips in the Waitewhena.

Emerging from the Waitewhena at Aria.

Auckland at last – 1.30 Saturday 30th with interested spectators outside the GPO.

Finally home, GPO Wellington, E Gilling, H Richards, A Chorlton, G F Hendry.

But the weather was fine at last and, after some close shaves in the wilderness, over punga bridges, and on narrow tracks, crowded by slips to the edge of precipices, the pioneers emerged from the bush at Aria and reached Hamilton at the end of the eighth day.

Thence to Auckland took only half a day, and the battered, mud-stained Model T ran down Queen Street, crowded with staring people just off work, and pulled up at the G.P.O. at 1.20 p.m., Saturday, November 30, 8 days 13 hours from Wellington.

It is of some commentary on the time taken, to add that the same car, stripped of all impedimenta, made a racing run home to Wellington, via Taupo, Napier, and the Wairarapa, in 2½ days (22 hours running time).

It was years before this record was beaten or the pioneering journey through the King Country was repeated.

AROUND THE NORTH ISLAND IN WINTER

A SAGA OF THE MODEL T IN 1916

A tour around the North Island by car in winter causes no comment today, but in 1916 it was considered not only foolhardy, but by some as downright impossible. The state of the roads in many places was appalling, but these intrepid motorists battled through in a light hearted fashion. They had no heaters; canvas hoods and side curtains were the only weather protection.

Newly married Mr & Mrs J G Phillips in a 2-seater Ford and four ladies – Mrs F S Phillips, the bridegroom's mother, Mrs G Cooper, Mrs Potter and Miss M Cooper, the last 'at the steering wheel' of a Ford 5-seater – set off from Wellington after the wedding on June 24 1916, a wet Saturday afternoon. We take up their account:

Although the roads were heavy through mud and ruts, good progress was made, and soon the cars were safely housed for the night at Palmerston North.

Next morning an early start was made, the intention being to reach Hastings. The run through the romantic Manawatu Gorge, with mountains towering above and river surging and roaring below was an enjoyable beginning for the day – but trouble lurked ahead!

After lunching at Dannevirke the party set off under a steady downpour of rain, and as evening approached the heavens seemed to dissolve in a deluge. All hope of getting to Hastings was abandoned. It poured so heavily when darkness came down that the headlights became useless for illuminating the road. One could not see more than a few yards in front. The cars had to creep and crawl, or be brought to a standstill while Mr Phillips climbed out to find the way.

At last, after a tedious and trying experience the cars drew up at Takapau Hotel, where the cold, hungry passengers found rest for the night. On the following day our party were speeding in the direction of Napier, and after an uneventful journey found themselves in the interesting and progressive capital of Hawkes Bay.

So far the trip had been more or less a picnic, and everyone felt that the excellent start made augured well for the rest of the circuit. Many experienced motorists shook their heads when they learned that our party intended to push on by road to Taupo. "That can only be done with safety in summer" was asserted repeatedly. But "never trouble trouble till trouble troubles you" seems to have been the motto of our

Through Marshall's Crossing.

pioneers, and on a clear crisp morning both Fords went humming over a cracking, cutting frost-bound road, shaking down the snowy powder from the trees and shrubs by the wayside.

Soon they were plunging through twelve inches of water at Marshall's Crossing and, after speeding over many switchback miles the cars scaled Titiokura whose summit stands about 2,500 feet above the level of the sea. The descent on the other side was easily negotiated and Mohaka Bridge was quickly left in the rear. The road, which had up to this point been of good metal surface, turned to clay and pumice. The going thereafter was very stiff, especially over the highest point – Turangakumu – estimated to be

Taking a side track.

about 2,700 feet above sea-level. But struggling and panting the Fords fought their way to Tarawera.

After a hasty lunch, the cars moved off again and went scampering across the small plain known as 'The Nunnery'– so-called by the Colonial troops engaged in the Maori Wars, because the native rebels left their women there for safety. But progress was now hampered by rough roads and dangerous corners or 'devil's elbows,' and it was not till late in the day that our pleasure-seekers pulled up at the Terraces Hotel,

Churning through mud, Tarawera.

about two miles from Taupo.

Refreshed by a good night's rest and a delightful sulphur bath, the party set off for Wairakei. A stop was made to view the Huka Falls, appropriately named by the Maoris as 'signifying white foam'. Then there was sight-seeing at the thermal cauldrons of Wairakei, the excitable Champagne Pool and the strongly flowing Waikato, with its blue-green waters, clear as glass, the azure reaches and white freshets giving prismatic colour reflections when the sunshine laps the water.

We now sped on to Rotorua. An hour was spent at Waiotapu, where the impressive labyrinth of mudspurs and craters was hurriedly explored. Back to the road again –

Up to the axles in mud.

off over desolate country and frightful roads – and at seven in the evening Rotorua was tendering its most cordial hospitality to tired and mud-stained motorists. A few days were spent visiting the showplaces there.

On Tuesday morning the Fords left Rotorua for Cambridge after the party had been duly warned that the road was impassable in many parts. To be prepared for the worst, Mr Phillips purchased a spade and an axe, and the cars had not gone far before he had to make free use of both.

Covering 50 yards in 90 minutes.

The execrable road through Mamaku Bush is shunned in winter by every motorist, the usual practice being to rail one's car to Tirau. But the Fords battled through what unquestionably would have been the grave of any other auto. So deep was the mire in places that no progress whatever could be made. Then it was necessary to 'jack' the rear wheels out of the sticky mud, build up the deep ruts with logs, and corduroy the path with manuka in order to give the tyres a grip on the soupy slippery ground. Horse-traction was not resorted to, although several Maoris hovered on the roadside and made tempting offers of 'a tow'.

After mud came holes – deep and treacherous. Nothing could save the cars from occasionally slipping into them. When that

occurred every member of the party had to join in a vigorous push.

Out of the holes into the ruts – that was the next stage in this fierce road-warfare. A four-mile stretch had been deeply ploughed. Along the furrows plunged and swayed the hardy Fords. Skilful driving backed by the sterling qualities of the cars themselves carried the day, and at last our intrepid autoists touched smooth, firm soil. Then no time was lost in rolling through Tirau and on to Cambridge. But so shockingly bad had been the greater part of the road that the traversing of 56 miles had consumed nearly eleven hours!

Next morning rain fell heavily as the cars left Cambridge for Auckland. When Huntly was reached it was deemed prudent to put chains on the rear wheels.

In winter no motor cars travel between Hamilton and Auckland as the roads bear the most sinister notoriety. That they well deserve the worst that has ever been said of them was the unanimous opinion of our sextette as it found itself held fast in a bottomless patch near Rangiriri. This portion of the highway was so unspeakably dangerous and difficult that only fifty yards were covered in one and a half hours. Both Fords were so far down in the sticky, gluey clay that the differential dragged behind, while the front axle pushed the mud before. But the Ford endurance triumphed again. Once the first car succeeded in getting over, a good start on the low gear and a quick rush brought the second through on the tracks of the other. Only those who have attempted this sort of motor-driving can appreciate what demands it made on Miss Cooper's skill and nerve. The slightest deviation from the track would have bogged the Five-seater, and the whole painful, arduous performance of digging her out would have had to be gone through. No wonder three cheers were given as the cars resumed the journey to Auckland.

The climb over the Razorback, which is generally considered to be a fair test of an automobile's stamina, was thought lightly of after the experiences at Rangiriri. Shortly after six in the evening the cars bustled into Auckland, and the party rose with one accord and hastened its steps to a cheerful, comfortable restaurant. Hardly had the tasty, tempting fare been placed upon the table than an irate policeman darkened the scene. This guardian of the law somewhat imperiously directed the famished travellers to remove their cars which, he said, were causing an "obstruction." Outside, a crowd of wondering spectators had clustered round the mud-laden 'Fords'. Mud covered the number back and front; mud was coated deep over body and hood; mud formed a thick crust round every wheel.

The following day, however, the mud was gone. Both cars were thoroughly washed, greased and oiled. But no repair work whatever was done – for none was required. Every part of each battle-scarred Ford was in perfect running order.

What the party did and saw in Auckland is no concern of ours. We join it again on the day the cars left the Queen City on their homeward run.

Of the journey from Auckland back to Hamilton there is nothing new to relate. It was almost a repetition of the trials and struggles of the northward trip.

Next day the cars were splashing on to Te Awamutu, lauded by its proud inhabitants as ' Garden of the Waikato.' Rain was steadily falling. The roads

A dangerous slip.
Grounded in a hole.

At Government Hostel, Waitomo.

the underworld – Waitomo, Ruakuri and Aranui Caves – stern duty cries "forward" so back to the cars we must come.

The road-battles already recounted, especially those in Mamaku Bush and Rangiriri, though severe, were merely preliminary trials of Ford Strength and Ford Dependability. The crucial test was now approaching.

Mr. Phillips and his lady companions decided to attempt what no other motorist had ever done in winter, namely, to travel from Te Kuiti over the Mokau and Mount Messenger, to New Plymouth. This road is one of the most delightful motor trips in New Zealand. The scenic grandeur of forest, river and mountain gorge form an unforgettable panorama. The trip, however, has always been regarded as strictly a summer one. "The roads," remarks *The Motorist's Guide,* "are only passable for motors during summer and autumn." This statement will now have to be modified in view of the great achievement of the two Fords, whose astonishing exploits we have been following.

Our adventurous party received little encouragement at Te Kuiti when its intentions became known. A liveryman said that he would not take £50 to attempt to motor over the road. As for a woman being able to perform the feat, the idea was absurd. He would guarantee that the cars would have to turn back or be towed. However, with stout hearts and bright faces, the enterprising six went off over an undulating, un-metalled road, and on past Pio Pio to Mahoenui, where some youthful Maoris gathered around the cars and amused themselves with putting their cold hands on the hot radiators.

After a brief stay in Mahoenui, a vigorous attack was begun on Taumatamaire Hill, a long climb of seven miles. It proved indeed a long, long climb for the cars had only travelled two or three miles when the discovery that the supply of benzine was insufficient to propel them much farther brought both Fords to a dead stop. A search showed that though benzine had been ordered at Te Kuiti none had been placed in either car. Darkness had now fallen. Mahoenui was six miles away, without even a track to walk on. To tramp back to that township for motor spirit would have been a fool's errand.

Over the hill one would probably have had to travel many miles before striking a farm with a shearing-plant and a surplus stock of benzine. Besides, the cars were now axle deep in mud and could not be moved one way or another. There was no sensible alternative to spending the night on the hillside, so the party set about making itself as comfortable as possible. A stocktaking of the commissariat revealed that there was an allowance of two thin sandwiches to each person. It was therefore unanimously decided to eat one for tea and supper combined, and to reserve the other for breakfast. When this 'substantial' repast had been disposed of, each tired

were miry and pierced with holes. Although from Te Awamutu to Hangatiki no motor cars travel during the winter season, that was no reason why the Fords should turn back. Their drivers had confidence in their cars' ability to carry them to the Waitomo Hostel and they were not disappointed. The highway was simply a channel of grey slippery mud, as inviting in appearance as Tikitere – that abomination of desolation' near Rotorua. But even the worst road has an ending – and in this instance, the conclusion was a bright, warm welcome at the Hostel for visitors to the famous and fascinating Caves.

Greatly as we should enjoy accompanying the party in its inspection of those glistening halls of

Following in the tracks.

and hungry traveller made ready to sleep. The hours crept slowly on until 10.30 p.m. when everyone awoke, thinking that morning had arrived. But the clear light was from a big-orb'd moon. The disappointment banished sleep and the succeeding hours passed at a snail's pace.

A lifetime had gone – or so it seemed to six grey-faced, shivering humans – when at last Dawn streaked the skies and the longed-for day came stealing in. Daylight brought renewed Hope and Courage – and a meagre meal of a sandwich apiece. When the tanks were examined it was found that each contained a small quantity of spirit. From the Two-Seater the benzine was drained into a Thermos flask and transferred to the other car, which was in front. Mr. Phillips then 'jacked' up the Five-Seater out of its mud-bed and started off to reach the hill-top, with the five ladies following as best they could over the slippery mire. The ascent was a searching test of the Ford. Owing to the tremendous road strain the engine was simply 'eating-up' the benzine. Luckily there was a plentiful supply of water by the roadside, so that it was easy to keep the engine cool.

When the summit of Taumatamaire was attained, a magnificent scene was presented for the admiration

Felicitations from the roadmen.

of the motor pioneers. But their thoughts were more concerned with benzine and the hapless car left behind. The whole party was now on board the Five-Seater, which went downhill, passing a dray drawn by five horses. At sight of the Ford the driver dropped his reins and exclaimed "Good Heavens, where did you come from?" To say he looked aghast is no exaggeration. He was amazed that any auto should be in that neighbourhood in winter. No car had been driven that way, he said, since April. That particular car was a Ford with a Scot at the wheel – surely an ideal combination of pluck and endurance!

After a brisk run of some four miles the Five-Seater arrived at Mr. Bignal's homestead where they received a cheery welcome and a supply of benzine. With the tin on his shoulder, Mr. Phillips left the five ladies to push on at their pleasure, and set off to bring the Two-

Seater over Taumatamaire. He caught up on the dray which, by dint of plodding, soon brought him and the precious petrol to the mud-gripped Ford.

Having stood for eighteen hours on the one spot, the car had sunk down so far that the differential rested on the ground. However, with the aid of the driver of the dray and another Good Samaritan, the Ford was soon prized up and pushed on to a patch made firm by logs and branches. Then the engine was started and off she went, snorting and panting up-hill.

It was now, after 1,700 miles of rough travelling, that Mr. Phillips had his first puncture. The slight damage caused by a chain was soon repaired, however, and the Ford 'plugged away' until it was over the hill crest. Downhill it ran as sweetly as ever. About three or four miles from Awakino it caught sight of the Five-Seater ploughing through the mud, every turn of the wheels sending up streams of the evil, glutinous stuff.

When the Fords splashed into Awakino they were warmly greeted by a crowd waiting to cheer the first motor cars to reach that township in the winter months. The news of their coming had been telephoned and farmers for miles around stopped work and rode in to meet the party. It was remarked that what had been accomplished was all the more notable as the roads had been soaked by rains heavier than any experienced for twenty-three years. Special admiration was bestowed on Miss M. Cooper – the pilot of the Five-Seater. Everybody said she was "the gamest of the game".

From Awakino the cars set off next morning for Mokau. The going was very rough for the roads were of papa and clay. But the Fords never shirked their work. They never faltered or failed. Mokau was crossed in a punt. Then a halt was called owing to a shortage of benzine. Mr. Phillips rowed down the river to a boatshed

Near Tongapurutu.

and was fortunate to procure from the owner of an oil launch sufficient to carry both cars to Tongapurutu where the night was spent in comfort. The arrival of the two Fords was the talk of the countryside. Miss Cooper was again the recipient of many compliments, for no lady had ever driven a car to Tongapurutu at any time. Even in summer almost nine out of every ten cars on that road fail to complete the journey under their own

power and have to be 'towed.'

Shortly after eight next morning Mount Messenger was tackled. "Absolutely impassable in winter" says the Road Book. But the Fords went on undaunted, with something of the courage and confidence of the statesman who cried "I trample on impossibilities." In summer a mail and passenger motor service runs between Waitara and Tongapurutu, but during the winter season the 60 h.p. car used stops at the Uruti Flats, and the remaining part of the trip is covered by a coach and five horses. When Mr. Phillips asked the coach-driver at Tongapurutu about road-conditions he was assured that the Fords would be buried before they had travelled far.   "There is no bottom to the road" said the pessimistic Jehu, who added "I will pick you up before we get to the top of Mount Messenger and tow you along to Uruti." However, his evil forebodings did not materialize – fortunately for our party.

Mount Messenger, though a formidable obstacle, proved less difficult to ascend than Taumatamaire. It is true that the road was execrable – its badness could not be exaggerated. It did its utmost to prevent progress by mud, boulders, ruts and holes. But the top was reached and the Fords stopped to allow their occupants to exchange congratulations. Some roadmen working at this altitude added their felicitations. They explained that they were startled by the sound of the approaching cars. They believed that nothing but a flying machine could ride over Mt. Messenger at that time of year. After a cheerful chat with the roadmen the Fords picked their way downhill and set off with a will to conquer four miles of wretched road – a quaking, splashing, slippery stretch of clay, pitted with deep holes. At first it seemed as if the doleful prediction of the coach-driver was to be realized and that the Fords would indeed be 'buried.' But though wallowing hub-deep in mire, the cars struggled on and won a signal victory. Yard by yard they forced a way over ground of the consistency of soup and glue. Nearly three hours were occupied in traversing four nightmare miles – a record that reveals more vividly, perhaps, than would pages of description the extraordinary difficulties overcome by the two hardy, fearless Fords.

Now came a brief respite of fairly good road, and at this stage the cars were overtaken by the coach from Tongapurutu. In front, however, there was a slough of three hundred yards in length. it was perhaps the worst bit of quagmire encountered that day. The coach driver renewed his offer of 'a tow – an offer that was gently, but firmly declined.   The Fords with a plunge went into the mud, and bucking, splashing, slipping and snorting, they succeeded in reaching terra firma. Then our motoring braves shook hands all round for their troubles were over and gone.   They could now bid good-bye to bad roads.

The final part of this eventful trip will have to be summed up in a very few words. The cars travelled from New Plymouth via Mt. Egmont, Wanganui, Palmerston and over the Rimutakas to Wellington. This portion of the journey was, as everyone agreed "just like heaven." The Fords romped along as if they had never been tested to the utmost limit of motor endurance. In crossing the Rimutakas one car went right over on high gear, and the other more than three parts of the way 'on high'– a truly remarkable performance considering that neither engine had been cleaned since the party left Wellington.

After covering some 2,300 miles each, and passing successfully over roads that have always proved fatal to other cars, both Fords arrived in Wellington sound in every part and fit to win again in the same ordeal. Despite the bumpings, twistings, and wrenchings they endured, the cars required no mechanical repairs whatever at any stage of their 'gruelling' itinerary. The only troubles met with were those presented by the highway. The cars themselves never once refused to do their duty. Every mile of the road they lived up to the Ford reputation for strength, stamina and reliability. Even the 'Fisk' Tyres on their wheels proved that only the best is good enough for a Ford. Although Mr. Phillips had an awkward puncture on the breast of Taumatarnaire, it is noteworthy that the Five-Seater under Miss Cooper's guiding hand, reached the home garage without a single tyre mishap.

When the engine of the Two-Seater was taken down and examined in Wellington, the bearings were found to be absolutely as good as new. The back axle, too, when taken apart was equally satisfactory, the bevel gears being none the worse for having helped to accomplish what is perhaps the greatest motoring feat to the credit of any car in New Zealand.

On top of the Rimutakas.

CHAPTER THREE

THE EXPANSIVE TWENTIES

Hope B Gibbons' immediate priority in 1919 was to set out plans for the future, in consultation with his father, Hope Gibbons, and brothers. In 1904 Hope Gibbons had called a family conference and suggested they combine their resources and work together in business. They became a very successful team, and owned or had interests in breweries, flax mills, farms, quarries and a majority shareholding in wholesaler J B Clarkson and Company, later re-named Hope Gibbons Ltd. Hope Gibbons had enormous business capability, was a strategic thinker, had intellect, drive, strength of purpose, and above all he instilled a loyalty to each other into his family.

F H (Toddy) Johnston, as general manager, was the first of a number of key people who were brought into the company because of their knowledge and skill, to boost and strengthen the management base. Johnston was made secretary to the board and sat in on most of the changes.

Share capital was a high priority for reorganisation, as the company's capital base was now too small, and Michael Myers and Hope B Gibbons set out to change this.

Planning for assembly of cars was also a priority and was driven by two factors. Firstly, cubic space drove shipping costs, and by packing disassembled components instead of completed cars, savings would be considerable. A shortage of ships in the Pacific often meant stock ran short, requiring buffer stock of one extra month that also added cost. It was decided a larger central assembly plant would be built, with smaller plants in Auckland and Timaru.

J M Dawson, prominent Wellington architect, was appointed company architect, and was given plenty to start on. He enjoyed the art deco look, and many of the buildings designed by him for the company, were in this classical style. Extra buildings were needed in Auckland and Timaru, but Wellington required a major

Chairman Hope Gibbons, (seated at right) with his four sons, left to right: Hope, Norman, Robert and Alfred.

Frederick Hills (Toddy) Johnson, general manager.

building for car assembly and it was estimated it would cost in the vicinity of £50,000. This would take time to build, and needed to be close to the port.

Michael Myers recommended the company liquidate and reform with a capital of £200,000 in 4,000 shares of £50. Robert B Gibbons had returned from the First World War and was appointed liquidator and assistant managing director to carry out the reformation. Shareholders approved the proposal, and the new articles of association giving very wide powers to the company were filed with the Companies Office.

On December 16 1919 the new company was incorporated. Hope Gibbons was appointed chairman, Hope B Gibbons managing director, Robert B Gibbons assistant managing director, and Alfred Barnes Gibbons, Michael Myers, Frederick N R Meadows, and Arthur Warburton became directors. Many of the 1902 shareholders, 44 in total, transferred to the new company, with the Gibbons family collectively holding 45%. The company had £93,000 on call at the National Bank of New Zealand.

In Auckland, The Universal Motor Company Ltd took over the assets of Carlaw and Jones, which had been operating as Ford agents in Chancery Lane, after Souters closed down in 1916. There had been difficulty in appointing new agents, so the Gibbons family had formed

The first motor assembly plant was a cube 100ft high and 100ft square. Built of pre-cut punched shell steel riveted together, with reinforced concrete floors and brick infill walls, it was the highest building in Wellington when finished in 1922. [Photo taken Aug 13 1921 by King & Dawson Architects]

Universal Motors themselves.

A N Lawrence, a new export manager from Ford Canada, arrived for the annual inspection and when the board met him on July 17 1920, he reported he found things in New Zealand very satisfactory.

Ford Canada cabled soon afterwards to say they were taking over control and sales of the new Fordson tractor from Henry Ford and Son Ltd, on August 1 1920. They indicated an intensive sales campaign would be necessary, together with a new sales agreement. New Zealand was allotted 720 tractors for the first year, a number the board regarded as "a long way too large for New Zealand's requirements".

This news necessitated some serious work to establish new sales and service outlets and a campaign to introduce tractors to farmers. Not all dealers were interested initially and took some convincing about the merits of Fordson tractors. The company decided it was important for them to lead the way and country areas needed targeting.

The directors approved planning for the erection of a nine-storey building facing York Street, and backing directly onto the Courtenay Place building. The new building was based on Ford's Windsor Plant

design in Canada, with administration on the top two floors, assembly starting on the seventh floor and progressing down, adding components until vehicles were driven away at ground level. Ford obliged by making drawings, designs and expertise available.

The building would be a 100ft high steel-framed structure, a first for New Zealand, using ready to assemble pre-cut lengths of steel imported from Canada, with reinforced concrete floors and brick in-fill walls added. It was the first high rise building to be erected in Wellington.

Architect J M Dawson prepared plans to the Ford design criteria, together with city council compliance details and tender documents for the work. Ford insisted it be built exactly to their design, facing south, despite protests that this was back to front for the Southern Hemisphere sun.

Tenders for the new nine-storey building came in and a contract was let at £39,447, jointly to Hansford and Mills, and Mitchell and King. This was 20% under estimates and the board gave the go ahead, despite the windows being back to front for the sun. While the tender price may not sound expensive, the cost of erecting a similar building today would be $10-15 million. Cars were then only £165, so 245 cars approximately equated to one nine-

The assembly plant was built facing south to York Street, back to front for the Southern Hemisphere sun, but Ford Canada insisted it be this way.
[Photo 1922 ref: PA1-q-144-057 at Alexander Turnbull Library]

storey building. A similar equation might apply today.

At the end of 1920 the company had increased its performance substantially under Hope B Gibbons' guidance, ably assisted by his father and brothers and the new management team. For two years, profits before tax were in excess of £100,000, more than 50% return on the new capital, an exceptional result.

The board gave H B Gibbons a vote of thanks for his leadership over the two years, and leave to visit Ford Motor Company of Canada. The managing director's agenda no doubt included more discussion about the allocated 720 tractors. His father, Hope, said it was important to develop personal contacts with Ford management as this would produce better outcomes.

On his return, Hope B Gibbons said relations with Ford had never been better, outlining some observations from his travels about the current business climate. The world economy had taken a setback after the war, and New Zealand exports to England were not in high demand, creating a severe balance of payments deficit, but this position was not expected to last for long.

The company reduced some of its ordering for a period and judiciously managed to get through 1921 without loss. It also maintained all the building projects without any cut-back, thus preparing itself for the recovery.

The new nine-storey assembly plant opened in 1922 and, as well as being the highest building in Wellington, was the first full vehicle assembly operation in New Zealand, drawing a lot of public attention.

Parts were delivered to each floor by a vehicle sized lift starting with chassis components on the seventh and sixth floors.

Trim components were made on the fifth floor, body assembly was on the fourth floor and painting on the third floor. Completed bodies were lowered on to the finished chassis on the second floor, and

The assembly line 1920s style.
Above: An army of clerks on the top floor kept check on activities.

Right: Assembly started with trim and components on the eighth floor.

Top: At work in the trim department.

Middle: Chassis assembly on the seventh floor.

Left: Engines, axles and springs, guards and radiators were added on the sixth floor.

the finished product parked on the ground floor, ready to be driven away. Cases of completely knocked down (CKD) parts were stored in the light well.

The site was deliberately close to the Taranaki Street wharves, only 400 metres away. One hundred unit case lots of vehicle parts were received and loaded from the ship's hold directly onto CMC trucks, getting around the normal delays with stevedoring. A bond was required by the Harbour Board against any claims that might arise through using the ship's cranes, and stevedoring dues had to be paid as if the Harbour Board was unloading.

However, the time of four minutes from ship's hold to assembly plant was much faster, and less costly, than the usual procedure. When the CMC trucks were not carting goods, they were hired out and used as company demonstrators.

H B Gibbons told the board he had arranged a possible sale of the recently built Ford service depot, and a lease of some of the York Street bulk store after the opening of the nine-storey building. The board authorised the managing director to confirm arrangements, and Dunlop Rubber Company purchased the Ford service depot in Taranaki Street for £18,000, taking

Other views of sixth floor activities.

Left: The bodies were dropped on at the second floor.

Middle: Electrics and paint followed.

Bottom: Finally, cars were driven away on the ground floor, ready to be sold.

the prescribed Ford way, paint was literally poured onto the bodywork from a 4 inch nozzle hose out of a 44 gallon overhead drum. The result, when the paint dried, had sags, blisters and runs in many places, quite unlike Canadian-built vehicles. During a visit to Windsor Plant, Canada, Robert B Gibbons discovered that the poor finish was caused by the paint being too cold. Unlike Canada, Courtenay Place assembly was not at a controlled temperature. Getting the paint at the right temperature made all the difference and resulted in a sag-free lustre. Later, of course, paints were sprayed on, with several coats required.

Below: H J Tutschka's dance orchestra was the first to broadcast live on radio in 1922. Charles Forrest began broadcasting in early 1922 as 2YK, then merged with the Hope Gibbons organisation to form Wellington Broadcasts Ltd, with a studio on the top floor of the Ford Building which gave better signal strength.

possession in September 1922. Alex Harvey and Sons leased the bulk store for three years.

At the same time an arcade was built from Courtenay Place through to the assembly plant. Vehicle sales for the whole of Wellington were being conducted adjacent to this in the ground floor of the Courtenay Place building.

Wellington service facilities were a problem, without the Ford service depot, so new service workshops were built in Ebor Street. With their classical Art Deco style, the frontages are now protected heritage buildings. More Ebor Street land was purchased when available, and further buildings erected.

Painting cars was also a problem. In

One of the people interviewed for company training in July 1920 was Ormond Hutchinson, just returned from Europe, where he served in the artillery during the war. He was accepted and despatched to Timaru branch for training in customs entry, collection, assembly, despatch and marketing of vehicles. Orm Hutchinson became the first Colonial Motor Company road organiser for the South Island, with a territory from Kaikoura to Bluff. It was his responsibility to keep dealers up to the mark and ensure they were adequately stocked and making the most of the opportunities, if necessary showing them how to do things.

Driving around the South Island, attending

farmers' meetings and tractor demonstrations was quite an adventure for Orm Hutchinson. It was also done in all weathers, accompanied, depending upon the season, by dust or mud, the repair of countless punctures, usually dressed in a suit, and fording many rivers or streams in his Model T.

In those days, tractors were a totally new concept for farmers who still used horses to do their ploughing, cropping, and carting work. Occasionally a traction engine would come in to do chaff cutting, threshing, or even hauling wagon trains, but only contractors had these. The same arguments used before occurred again, but this time it was tractors versus horses. Change did not happen without effort.

The work done in converting from horses seemed endless and very slow for a start. Once a tractor had been sold, the farmer then needed to be taught how to use it. However, after someone had owned a tractor for a short time, the whole district quickly knew what the new novelty was capable of. The first sale usually bred further sales rapidly. Orm Hutchinson's hard work paid off handsomely, and his techniques were taught to all salesmen. After a slow start, tractor sales multiplied quickly to about 500 per year and still increasing. (The tractor story is told in detail in Chapter 31.)

When Walter Ingle resigned from

Opposite top: A 1925 Wellington taxi owner, W Baldwin said: " I have owned and driven a Ford for nine years. During that time it has covered 300,000 miles and is going as well as ever. My car has a landaulet body; I have done 34 miles to the gallon on a straight run. It is still in commission and giving satisfactory service."

Left: Ormond Hutchinson, first road organiser, then Timaru branch manager.

Colonial Motor Company Timaru branch sales meeting at Timaru, August 23 1924. Most South Island dealers were there with their salesmen and sales managers. Dealers on the West Coast, Nelson and Blenheim were serviced from the Wellington branch.
Back left: Eckroyd, Rangiora; Broom, Christchurch; Anderson, Dunedin; Holmes, Ashburton; Baker, Dunedin; Sheldon, Christchurch; O'Neil, Temuka; Tonecliffe, Dunedin; Tripner, Christchurch. Third row: Wilson, Rangiora; Daniels, Dunedin; Pringle, Milton; Brown, Timaru; Ching, Christchurch; Harvey, Dunedin; McLay, Dunedin; Smither, CMC; Hally Jnr, Temuka; Box, Timaru. Second row: Carson, Ranfurly; Smith, Ranfurly; Farquhar, Balclutha; Laurence, Timaru; MacDonald, Gore, Brown, Dunedin; Henry, Christchurch; Gemmell, Oamaru; Sinclair, Oamaru; Hally, Temuka. Front: Phillips, Dunedin, Cassells, Christchurch; Kersley, Christchurch; Hutchinson, CMC; Duncalf, CMC; Chatwin, CMC, Stevenson, Balclutha; Wood, Timaru; Bennetts, Christchurch. Dealer principals' are underlined

Timaru branch, George Duncalf was appointed manager in July 1922. Orm Hutchinson became his assistant manager, and they organised sales training for all the South Island dealers and their sales staff.

Directors decided the sales operation should be separated from the main distributing company as Ford Motor Company had issued a policy directive against distributors being involved in retail. Ford Sales and Service Company Ltd was set up to retail Wellington sales and service in March 1923, but no suitable dealer could be found with enough capital. H B & R B Gibbons declared their interest in the company and put the bulk of the capital in, appointing Col H E Avery as manager, who put up his own capital share.

Todd Brothers held the Ford agency for most of Otago, and wanted to take on other franchises, but this was not allowed under the Ford franchise agreement demanded by Henry Ford, so they dropped the Ford agency. Getting another dealer who had the capital and ability was a problem. After discussing it with the board, the Gibbons family decided they would have to put in personal capital to get Dunedin started, as this was the only way around the Ford policy.

Ford Motors (Dunedin) Ltd was set up in May 1923. John Grendon Phillips resigned his Auckland branch manager's job, and put up his share of capital to become the Dunedin dealer. The Board congratulated J G Phillips "on his rise in the ranks, from an office boy when he

An impressive Trackson conversion kit was available to fit the Fordson, making it competitive with the Caterpillar 2 ton, but the ordinary Fordson sold better at half the price. Ormond Hutchinson demonstrates Alan Grant's crawler and plough at Levels, "after six months of uninterrupted service".

John Andrew's daughter, Mary Andrew, was involved in the Ford business, teaching many women to drive the Model T. She turned her hand to ploughing with considerable success, and is shown at the Pukekohe A & P Show demonstrating to farmers the simplicity of using a Fordson tractor.

Top left: W G (Bill) Taylor, Auckland branch manager.

Top right: W A (Bill) Fraser, Wellington branch manager.

entered the company 16 years ago, to Auckland branch manager, which he ably conducted, and now to take over one of the best Ford dealerships."

Eight other country Ford dealer points were signed up for different areas of Otago, to replace the Todd Brothers territory. Alf Kingston was transferred to Auckland as manager, and J Rickard was appointed Wellington manager.

At Palmerston North, Ford Motors Manawatu Ltd was started, again with the help of capital from the Gibbons family. The manager, Jesse Selwyn, put up his capital as well.

The Apprenticeship Act came into force on August 29 1923, after recommendations from the Motor Trade Association. This opened the way for a consistent, fair and structured training scheme, to bring new tradesmen into the industry. Over the years many thousands of apprentices have had their training at CMC subsidiaries, and have made their contributions to the success of the company.

During 1915, Gordon Hughan had started a sub-agency in Masterton, with J H (Jim) Lyttle and his brother Ted, at the north end of Queen Street. In June 1919 Gordon Hughan's Carterton premises burnt down one night in a disastrous fire that destroyed the blacksmith's shop, cycle shop and garage, including all the plant, records and 33 cars. Not to be dismayed, and despite being inadequately insured, Hughan rebuilt the garage section immediately.

After the fire, he needed more capital to finish rebuilding, and H B and R B Gibbons stepped in with financial help, taking a share in his business, which then became a limited liability company. The Carterton premises were rebuilt and extended, and the Masterton Ford branch was sold off in 1923 to MacDonald, becoming a separate agency, after the Lyttles preferred to relocate and sell Maxwell cars.

F C (Fred) Facer, national sales manager.

New Prices are Lower than ever before in History

PRICES AGAIN REDUCED

Effective January 2nd, 1923

	Price 18 Months Ago	Present Price	Reduction
Chassis with 4 fixed rims and tyres	£223	£125	£98
Runabout ,, ,, ,,	255	156	99
Touring Car ,, ,, ,,	265	173	92
Touring Car with starter, demountable rims, spare rim, tyre and carrier - - -	315	204	111
Truck Chassis with demountable front rims and pneumatic rear tyres - - -	260	180	80
Sedan with starter, demountable rims and spare rim, tyre and carrier - - -	415	298	117

Prices are F.O.B. Wellington and are subject to alteration without notice.

The Colonial Motor Company Limited

Representing The Ford Motor Company of Canada Ltd.

Ford prices AGAIN Reduced

Effective 1st December, 1924

Touring Car with demountable rims, spare rim and tyre carrier	...	**£158**
		Elec. Starter £17 extra
Runabout, with demountable rims, spare rim and tyre carrier	...	**143**
		Elec. Starter £17 extra
Truck Chassis, with demountable rims & **pneumatic** or **solid** rear tyres		**151**
		Elec. Starter £17 extra
Sedan-Tudor, with starter, demountable rims, spare rim and tyre carrier		**257**
Sedan-Fordor with starter demountable rims, spare rim and tyre carrier		**284**
Coupe, with starter, demountable rims, spare rim and tyre carrier	...	**234**
Light Delivery Runabout. with demountable rims	...	**147**
		Elec. Starter £17 extra

Prices subject to change without notice.   Above Prices F.O.B. Wellington

FULL Balloon Tyre Equipment (4 Tyres) optional at £12 extra

British Manufacture! The Ford Car is completely made in Canada, with the exception of parts to the value of £3 10 0.

A B Gibbons was given leave to visit Ford in Canada and America and reported back in December that the meetings had gone well and relations were only improved by the visits. In those days it took up to 12 days to get to Ford Canada head office at Windsor, Ontario, and 12 days to return. Henry Ford and Ford Motor Company, Detroit, were only 10 miles away from Windsor, northwest across Lake St Clair.

In June 1922 the board voted £25,000 to set up a Ford finance facility to assist dealers with sales, along similar lines to the government's NZ Guarantee Corporation. This was extended to £35,000 two months later. By then, financing was a very useful tool to sell both new and the used vehicles that were now available in large numbers. In January 1924 the board increased the allotment to 'Ford Finance Company' to £50,000, and Michael Myers cautioned about the use of the name 'Ford' Finance Company, instead of CMC Finance and it was resolved to look at this aspect. By the end of the decade the company had £200,000 in the finance subsidiary.

There is no doubt that the Parliamentary Tour of Northland of 1917 had a great deal to do with the Main Highways Board being established on April 1 1924, under Hon J G Coates. Although road construction was now being planned on a national basis, funding had to be found and who better to fund it than the motoring user.

The first census of June 1925 to include motor vehicle details showed New Zealand had:

Population	1,401,000
Cars	71,000
Trucks	11,000
Motor cycles	22,000
Buses	1,030

Road funding was voted by government from: taxes on tyres (collected from 1917), licence fees on registered vehicles, (introduced from November 6 1926), and petrol tax a year later at 4d per gallon, taking the cost to 1s 8d.

New Zealand's roads were still in a very poor state, and particularly bad in Northland and the King Country areas. Taranaki had the best roads, using tollgates to raise money that was then directly funded back to roads. However, under the new 1925 Motor Vehicles Act, tollgates were not allowed and were removed.

NEW ZEALAND ROADS LTD

The Gibbons family decided roads were an important opportunity, and set up New Zealand Roads Ltd in 1925, the main purpose being to promote the sale of Fordson tractors and Model T trucks, as tools for road construction.

Early graders were high, cumbersome and operated by 'Heath Robinson' remote controls. Hidden underneath were comparatively small Fordson tractors, working their hearts out! Road rollers were developed, and excavator scoops. Tractors were also very convenient mobile power plants to drive stone crushers, air compressors, water pumps, and all sorts of ancillaries such as elevator belts.

The first front-end loaders were built, often with cable controls, and ingenious trip devices, to lift and release their loads. Later, some were converted to clip on a bulldozer blade, another first.

Model T trucks were used for a myriad of tasks, and were the first mobile concrete mixer trucks in New Zealand.

Several significant roads were built by NZ Roads, including the Waioeka Gorge road north of Gisborne to Opotiki, and the Great North Road out of Auckland, one of the first concrete roads. The Devonport north road and the road between Napier and Hastings were other concrete roads built. Road making was one of Colonial Motor Company's few non-motor ventures, and was probably influenced by the chairman's vision of an ideal New Zealand served by a first class highway from Wellington to Auckland, flanked by generous plantings of native trees on the western side and deciduous trees on the other side, funded from road taxes.

W J S (Bill) McCurdie, tractor sales manager, was at the NZ Roads construction contract on the Paekakariki Hill road for a period, and remembered it well: "I went out there to get some experience of equipment under everyday working conditions. Unfortunately it was mid-winter and each morning 50 Fordson tractors had to be started up. I don't need to go into the difficulties involved – but I can assure you that getting those tractors going each morning was a fact of life!" (The heavy crankcase oil used, almost solidified overnight in the winter, making hand-cranking near impossible, unless you were a superman.)

NZ Roads was liquidated at the end of 1927 while building the difficult stretch of highway south of Paraparaumu. The Paraparaumu peat and some poor design calculations resulted in financial difficulties that were beyond the company's resources.

Although NZ Roads did not make any profit, it certainly showed how Fordson tractors and Model T trucks could be adapted to other uses and valuable sales and conversions followed. In 1925, 1,058 Fordson tractors were sold, which further enhanced the Ford partnership.

An early cable operated pivot loader.

Fordson powered Acme 8 ton roller, with 7ft grader blade mounted in the middle.

Fordson Miami 20 cubic ft earth scoop.

Ripping up the old surface with a Fordson.

The Fordson-Wehr one man grader.

Fordson-Schramm air compressor operating a rock drill.

Concrete aggregate batching plant using a Fordson and 1 ton Model T truck.

Portable stone crushers, driven by Fordsons, pounded rocks into aggregate on the job.

Fordson-Lessman bucket loader.

Fordson driven Rees Rototurbo pump could lift 5,000 gals per hour to 100ft.

Model T portable concrete mixer, the first in New Zealand.

The prototype concrete paving machine which built the Devonport borough roads in the 1920s, driven by Fordson tractors, hidden underneath.

*W J S (Bill)
McCurdy.
CMC tractor
manager.*

*The Universal
Motor Company
premises built in
1926, on the corner
of Symonds Street
and Glenside
Crescent, was an
icon of the Southern
Hemisphere, and
'quite the best car
dealership of the
day'.*

Meanwhile, the Auckland Automobile Association had been actively helping all motorists, and progressively introduced the black and yellow signposts, later adopted by all associations and spread throughout New Zealand in the 1920s.

Taihape was a small but important service point on the main highway north, and difficulty was experienced in getting a dealer established. The company purchased premises and leased them to J W Etevenaux, who became the Ford agent for Taihape in 1925.

For some time there had been a need to have suitable retail premises in Auckland instead of the usual converted stables. J M Dawson designed a superb, new, purpose built facility, in classical Art Deco style, and this was erected on the Symonds Street and Glenside Crescent corner for The Universal Motor Company Ltd. It became an icon building, attracting attention not only from customers, but from Ford people around the world. Ford Canada proclaimed it to be "the finest retail premises handling our products".

R B Gibbons was welcomed back in December 1924 having spent time overseas and with Ford. Hope Gibbons emphasised the importance of building the relationship and frequent visits to Ford Motor Company. Robert Gibbons replied that the factory was more than pleased with the company, and "the New Zealand organisation was miles ahead of any other overseas Ford organisation under their control".

At their next meeting in February 1925,

the managing director reported that he and R B Gibbons had met P W Grandjean, secretary of Ford Canada, in Auckland, accompanied by Hubert C French and R A Macfarlane who were on their way to set up Ford Motor Co of Australia. The representatives assured the Gibbons brothers that there was no possibility of any interference with the franchise in New Zealand as the relationship could not be better.

Discussions took place about increasing the company's capital base as still greater expansion was required, and in March 1925 it was resolved to increase the capital to £300,000 by creating 2,000 new £50 shares. After shareholders met and agreed to the increase, the Gibbons family took up their proportionate 1,133 of the 2,000 shares.

CMC decided a standard price would operate throughout New Zealand in 1925, equalising freight. Prior to this, when provincial customers went on holiday to a city they often found the price of cars cheaper. With this strategy, the company was the first of any Ford affiliates in the world to equalise pricing. Now Kaitaia and Invercargill were not penalised for being so far away from the assembly factory.

Timaru staff, under their new branch manager, Ormond Hutchinson, moved into new building extensions in Sophia Street in May 1925. With the assembly operations, staff now exceeded 50 people. Shortly after this, W Stanley Smart, the nephew of coachbuilder Henry Hurrell, was appointed branch service manager, advising dealers on their service needs. CMC now had over 240,000 sq ft of assembly buildings at three locations: Auckland, Wellington and Timaru.

In May 1925 Ford Motors (Canterbury) Ltd was incorporated and commenced trading with George Duncalf, transferred

from Timaru, as manager. Christchurch city required a much more substantial operation than was operating with Jay and Wright, who had inadequate service facilities and poor sales. Again, a new dealer was sought but, after a lack of interest, the Gibbons family supplied the capital.

Standard Motor Bodies Ltd started up at Ebor Street in September 1925, with John Hunt as manager. J H L Hunt was a master coachbuilder, who emigrated to New Zealand in 1895, and was the foreman bodybuilder at Munt Cotterill, a large carrying company that also built bodies for trucks and drays. He was fair but tough, and could organise or build anything. The company was formed by the Gibbons

family to build 'standard' bodies for Model T car and truck chassis. For £30 you could have a truck deck, or, for £40, a van. They also built specialist bodies, like school buses and fire engines to order.

CMC staff generally were recognised for their support in producing the great 1925 result, and the following minute was passed:

"The directors recognised that the success of the year's trading was to a great extent due to the efforts and loyalty of the individuals in its employ and it was resolved:-

"That a bonus be paid to all the company's employees as a token of appreciation, viz:- One day's pay for every employee, plus one day's pay for every three months of completed service. The maximum bonus, to

Top: The Auckland assembly plant at Fox Street, Parnell in the mid 1920s. This was a support plant to Wellington, on a smaller scale for the local area, saving freight by being close to the market.

Bottom: Inside the Auckland assembly plant at Fox Street. The 'knocked down' pack was a cheap and compact method of shipping Fords around the world.

Ford Motors Canterbury started in 1925 in Tuam Street.

The 'New Beauty' Model T was welcomed in Christchurch with a vast street parade, led by a veteran Ford Model F of 1905.

be ten days pay. and the minimum £1".

This sort of recognition was not new. However, the increase in the scale of the bonus and sent an important message to staff. Further discussion took place at the same meeting about setting up a superannuation fund for staff at some time in the future.

Bulk petrol storage was introduced in January 1926 by British Imperial Oil Company (Shell), at Miramar where they were able to fill 12,000 'flimsies' (4 gallon tins) a day. These were then normally stored in warehouses, with the occasional disastrous fire. Petrol was normally bought by the case, containing two 4 gallon tins. Hand pumps for each brand appeared, usually on the footpath in front of dealerships from the early 1920s. Made by J Bowser & Co in Australia, the pumps

quickly became known as 'bowsers'. You could buy Shell, Voco, Texaco or Big Tree petrol at a cost of 1s 4d per gallon and get it hand pumped directly into your tank. In remote country areas it was still sold by the case. Petrol tax became a government revenue earner on November 1 1927, with 4d (25%) of the retail price going to the Roads Board.

There was great competition between the CMC assembly operations in Auckland, Wellington and Timaru over which branch could assemble a Model T 'New Beauty' phaeton the fastest. There were many claims and counter claims so it was decided a competition would take place, and teams from each assembly branch were selected. Rules were laid down, with the principal criterion that the car had to be driven around the block after assembly.

An official timekeeper was at each plant as the frenzied task started. Chassis brackets were fitted, then springs, axles, wheels, engine and transmission. The body was lowered on before the radiator, guards, running boards, windscreen, electrical fitting and wiring went on. Timaru stopped the clock at 52 minutes, and the car was fired up. Bill Leeney, Timaru's test driver, tightened the last wheel nut before driving out, amidst cheers. At the first corner all four doors flew open, but around the block the ragged rascal ran.

On return the car was stripped and rebuilt. The chassis was found to be only half completed with over 100 rivets

missing, but these minor inadequacies of a Friday morning were overlooked, and CMC managing director, Hope B Gibbons, cabled congratulations to the Timaru team. Orm Hutchinson sent each man home with a pound of bacon and a dozen eggs as a bonus for beating Auckland and Wellington.

Timaru finished a slender 60 seconds ahead of Wellington and 90 seconds ahead of Auckland. The North Island cars were unlikely to have been any better than Timaru's. (A Model T normally took three hours to assemble with all the rivets!)

On July 7 1926, RM4, the first railcar went into service and ran for many years between Wyndham and Edendale in Southland. Built at the Petone Railway Workshops on a Model T truck chassis, the 'rail motor' could reach 50kph and carry 11 passengers. This was followed shortly afterwards by RM5, a slightly lighter version, but this was withdrawn in 1931 as it was too light for the job.

By now, the considerable retail interests of the company and dealers were requiring attention to ensure they kept operating profitably and reported results correctly. Already some of the New Zealand operations were struggling. Ford Motor Company had been discussing the need to keep dealers 'on

Left: Petrol hand pumps known as 'bowsers', were first introduced in the early 1920s. You could buy Plume, Shell, Voco, Texaco and Big Tree, with most service stations multi-branded. Previously petrol was sold by the four gallon tin, two to a case.

Above: The RM4 railcar, nicknamed 'The Pie Cart', was originally a Model T truck and carried 11 passengers. It was built by NZ Railways and the first went into service between Wyndham and Invercargill. This exact replica was photographed by Bill Richardson on the 'Kingston Flyer' line north of Invercargill.

Left: This was the first time School Bus No.1 took children home after school, on March 31 1924, at Pio Pio, 15 miles south from Te Kuiti. The Model T chassis with its newly built bus body could carry 30 children, and cost £226.
[Photo: Education Department]

track' financially, because they were handling large amounts of money, with some unable to control what was happening, and consequently 'going bust'.

Consequently, the company employed Henry Neil Scrimshaw, as part of head office, to set up a management accounting system, so all dealers could report in a way that highlighted areas of their business and enabled managers to better understand what was happening in service, parts and sales. 'Scrim' was a very astute judge of people and what they were up to, and set to work developing a very good accounting system. He then engaged a number of bright young accounting graduates, and they travelled

New Zealand, setting dealers up with proper management systems. Often one of his team would be left behind for several months to make sure the job was done properly.

Amongst other things, Scrim formalised the finance instrument to enable secure delivery of vehicles. These were set up as a debenture over undertakings with the dealer's bank. With this guarantee in place, the dealer did not have to wait until funds were cleared, thereby speeding up delivery and lowering costs.

The company had now expanded substantially from its 1919 reformation, and employed nearly 1,000 staff. It had no trouble attracting good people, as it had an excellent reputation for good work practices, and as an employer which looked after its staff.

When Michael Myers retired from the board at the annual meeting in 1926, as he wished to travel overseas for an extended period, the board placed on record its esteem and thanked him for his valuable advice and services over 12$^{1}/_{2}$ years as a director. Myers later went on to become Chief Justice of New Zealand and was knighted. The board nominated Norman Barnes Gibbons, Hope Gibbons' fourth son, to take his place. Norman Gibbons was involved in the family's farming operations and other businesses, and more recently in Ford Motors Manawatu.

In December 1926, the board approved taking over and writing off the £1,226 13s 10d losses MacDonald had incurred operating Masterton Ford Motors. They transferred stock, plant and debtors of the agency, to Francis Robert Bridges to operate. MacDonald would not sell to Bridges directly, so H B Gibbons brokered the transaction. Bridges had been a sales manager at Ford Sales and Service, Wellington.

Meanwhile, the business climate in New Zealand was not good. Farming had been suffering from low commodity prices and low sale volumes for a number of years. This was affecting all sectors of the economy, and unemployment was climbing. The government was now holding talks with a number of parties about how trade could be increased between New Zealand and other countries.

Over 80% of New Zealand's exports went to Britain, which was not receiving the support that it expected for its own exports. There was talk of a proposed new tariff giving preference to British products, and there was discussion about what 'British' meant; did it mean British Empire countries? The current tariff was 20% on

Michael Myers, later Sir Michael and chief justice, a director from 1913 to 1926, updated CMC's financial structure and articles. [Photo: S P Andrew ref: F-18601-1/1, Alexander Turnbull Library]

Below: The rural postal service started in 1915, with delivery of the Timaru Herald *newspaper, using Model T cars. [Photo: Timaru Herald]*

*The 'New Beauty'
Model T was a
stopgap measure,
when Henry Ford
finally realised he
had to develop a
new model to keep
pace with the
competition. Prior
to 1926 this
attractive 'Colonial'
runabout body was
produced by CMC.*

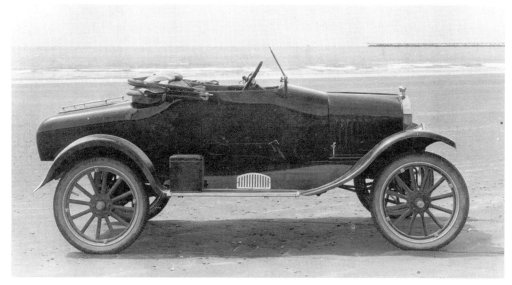

*The JWA Special
was built from
Model T parts by
Stan Andrew, son of
John W Andrew. It
held the
Australasian speed
record of 93.26mph
in 1924 recorded at
Muriwai Beach,
north west of
Auckland, and was
second in the 50
mile NZ Cup race.
Foreign parts
included a
streamlined radiator,
overhead valve
cylinder head,
counterbalanced
crankshaft,
aluminium pistons,
the flywheel
(reduced 3/4 in), two
carburettors,
magneto and 3:1
crown wheel and
pinion. Stan Andrew
is at the wheel with
mechanic Jack
Broun (later service
manager of CMC,
then Ford NZ).*

CIF values.

A target of the trade talks were motor vehicles, which had a large effect on trade balances. At that time, the predominant sources of vehicles were United States (50%), Canada (36%), and England (12%). Over 30% of vehicles registered were Fords originating from Canada, so naturally, anything related to tariffs was of vital interest to The Colonial Motor Company.

By now, the Model T was nearing the end of its life, with sales becoming more difficult, despite the 'New Beauty' body. Ford prices were set from Canada and kept reducing to match competition, but other car manufacturers were introducing innovations that were more exciting to some buyers. Nevertheless, the Model T was still a force to be reckoned with and had the high market penetration of 26.9% in 1926.

Ford Canada requested The Colonial Motor Company to increase dealer commissions, and reduce retail prices to meet demand. This would mean a squeezing of the

company's margin. CMC cabled back that they wished to retain their margin.

CMC was aware that the impending change of model, involving a shut-down at Highland Park, Detroit, would mean there would be a period with no new vehicles available from Ford Canada, and there was real concern about how dealers would survive the transition.

In January 1927, John W Andrew merged with Universal Motor Company in Auckland, at the instigation of CMC and because of the likely supply shortages. The company became John W Andrew & Sons Ltd, including Gibbons' shareholding and capital. New vehicle sales were now conducted from Universal Motors' building in Symonds Street and used cars were sold at New North Road.

Hope B Gibbons left on February 1 1927, for the annual director's visit to Ford in Canada and Detroit, and also to hold discussions in England. During March he cabled back from Canada that Ford had

*Left: Hope B
Gibbons about 1927.*

'flagship' building on the corner of Upper Symonds Street and Glenside Crescent at a cost of £46,175. It was leased to John W Andrew and Sons Ltd, on March 24 1927, thereby freeing up working capital.

Concurrently, Ford Motors (Dunedin) Ltd was purchased in total, land at valuation, assets and liabilities at book value, from the Gibbons family. Subsequently, as opportunities arose, other dealerships would be purchased from the Gibbons family.

On September 16 1927, Ford Sales and Service Ltd, Wellington, was purchased on the same basis. By that stage it owned most of Ebor Street, plus a link section into Jessie Street.

In August 1927, Edsel Ford, Henry's son, drove the 15 millionth Model T off the production line at Dearborn and announced it was to be replaced by a new car. Production ceased and sales of Model Ts slowed, finally running out completely before the end of 1927.

At a directors' meeting, Arthur Warburton, a 1908 shareholder from Rouse & Hurrell days, and director since 1913, said: "The Colonial Motor Company shareholders should consider themselves lucky in having the Gibbons family who had looked after the company's interests, and in their masterly way, had established and financed the main city dealerships, using their own money. This was the only way the strong network could have been made, knowing the Ford Motor Company's views. The company was indebted to the family for carrying the load for so long." His remarks were seconded by F N R Meadows, the other director and shareholder from Rouse & Hurrell days.

Below: Wallace R Campbell was born and grew up in Windsor, Ontario. He started with Ford Canada in that city in 1905. He was a friend of Edsel Ford and was promoted to president of Ford Canada in 1929, after holding other important positions. He told H B Gibbons in 1927 that there wasn't enough money in the world to persuade him to accept a position at Ford Motor Company in Detroit.

agreed to increase dealer commissions without reducing the company's margin.

He also had discussions at Ford Canada about the new car to replace the Model T. However, Henry Ford was playing his cards very close to his chest, and there were still no details, even to Canadian management. Ford Canada thought the new car might be available in August, but Henry Ford had had a nasty accident and this was likely to cause delays.

Hope Gibbons cabled in March 1927 that Ford had changed its position regarding distributors being involved in dealerships, and it was now in order for the company to be directly involved. The previous directive had been brought about by a South African distributor who had acquired practically all dealerships in his territory, effectively tying Ford's hands and forcing it to start its own operation there. Now Ford was more interested in the amount of product a distributor could move, and anything that improved volume was considered worthwhile.

To assist the struggling Auckland merger, directors decided to buy the

Hope Gibbons had written to the board from Detroit that Edsel Ford, Henry's son, had stated that all overseas distributors selling more than 3,000 cars a year should be owned by Ford. Ford Canada said they did not want that arrangement in New Zealand, because CMC, the best performing export distributor in the world, was doing a good job. In July, the company received a letter from W R Campbell, president of Ford Canada, saying that at some time Ford might have to take over

A novel Christmas package Model T offer at Universal Motors showroom in 1927. The car was the first Model T built in the world since 1913 that wasn't black. The colour 'Neutria', chosen by Mrs R B Gibbons, was a marketing ploy, to help bridge the year long production gap between the Model T and Model A in New Zealand.

Below: Edsel Ford driving his father Henry away in the 15 millionth Model T in 1927.

assembly, but not immediately. Forewarned, directors said they could only await developments.

The last shipment of Model T components had arrived and the intention was that New Zealand would get a few sample new cars by December. In any event The Colonial Motor Company needed to buy built-up new model cars for at least six months, until assembly packs could be restarted. With the expected delay in assembly of the new model, plant managers were told to run down their staff after the last Model Ts were roadworthy.

Following a British survey of the New Zealand car market, during 1926, the British Society of Motor Manufacturers and Traders (SMMT) arranged a £2,000 advertising programme in 1927 promoting British cars, aided by articles 'placed' in the Auckland AA journal *New Zealand Motor Life*. Tariff changes made by the government in August 1927 favoured small British cars by allowing a 5% advantage to New Zealand assembled vehicles under £200. The shape of the market began to change but, with the only other eligible car, the Model T being phased out, this didn't show up until later.

The Abingel Concrete Company was contracted to build garage premises at Lower Hutt and the building was started in March 1928. Architect Dawson had now taken in two partners, King and Cook, and the building was designed by Keith Cook. Although Cook worked in the firm's Brandon Street office, he lived in Lower Hutt and could keep an eye on progress. The company would set up a new dealership in Lower Hutt as soon as the building was completed.

The first new Model A vehicles were left hand drive, and six were despatched to New Zealand by ship to provide samples for customers to view and order from. Stock followed, arriving in late July 1928, with everything pre-sold.

In preparation for the new Model A, the company set up a special service department under Jack Broun that organised an education programme, detailing all the changes and 'new features'. These were presented to special new service schools for dealer personnel. Jack Manning and two others were instructors at the school. Jack Broun had been service manager at John W Andrews in Auckland, and Stanley Smart, CMC South Island service manager transferred to Andrew's to replace him.

At the beginning of October 1928, Ward and Rawnsley were appointed dealers at Lower Hutt, in the new premises on the corner of Queen Street and Main Road. Ivan Edward (Jack) Rawnsley had been a pilot/engineer in the Royal Flying Corp in the First World War. Returning home, he

Publicity to counter British SMMT advertising in New Zealand, shows cars outside the Timaru branch in 1927, with 'Fords are British' windscreen banners.

Below: Under service manager Jack Broun, three service instructors – Neil Small, Jim Power and Jack Manning – were key people, providing much needed rapid instruction for all the Model A changes.

Get Behind the Wheel and Experience for YOURSELF*

The Amazing Performance of The New Ford Car

THE NEW FORD, you must keep in mind, is an entirely New Car, and you can have no conception of its amazing performance except by your own personal experience—*from behind the wheel!* Then, and only then, can you really understand why already 2,000,000 of the New Ford Cars have been produced—and still the demand is greater than the supply.

On the road you have doubtless noticed the attractive, compact, and entirely modern appearance of the New Ford Car—its smart steel-spoke wheels, its bumpers back and front, its snug roomy seats.

Now, test the *performance* of the New Ford Car. Feel the thrill of the New car's ample horse-power, the astonishingly smooth running of the engine —even at forty or fifty miles an hour. Experience its "live" flashing pick-up, its amazing hill-climbing ability. Observe how comfortably the Car rides, how it holds the road even at high speeds, and when cornering fast. Notice the extraordinary ease and confidence with which you handle the Car; and the absolute control that its unique Six-Brake system gives you.

And remember, that with all these outstanding features, you still obtain the most outstanding economy and Low Maintenance Cost. More, you can obtain this completely-equipped Car at a price so modest that it represents unparalleled value. Then the network of 82 fully equipped Ford Service Stations from one end of New Zealand to the other, gives the final assurance of always getting the best possible service.

Motor Out of Income

Begin the enjoyment of owning and driving a Ford NOW! For a small initial outlay you can begin to motor out of income. Ask your dealer for full particulars of the Ford deferred payments plan.
Prices from £205

Tudor Sedan
As Illustrated
£245

★ One Hour's FREE Driving Tuition

Take this Unique Opportunity!
Whether you are thinking of getting a new Car or not, present this Coupon to your nearest Ford Dealer, either in person or through the post—or telephone him, and he will send a New Ford Car, and let you drive it for an hour or more. If you cannot drive a car, an expert will gladly give you an hour's Tuition FREE!

The Ford Motor Company of Canada, Limited, whose policy is one of continuous improvement, reserves the right to change specifications and prices without notice.

Tear this Out

FORD FREE DRIVING COUPON.
To the Authorised Ford Dealer (see address below)
I will be pleased to accept your invitation for an hour's Free Tuition driving the new Ford Car. Kindly let me know the date and time at which you will send a Car for me
Name ....
Address ....

LADIES! This Coupon offers an excellent opportunity for YOU!

There's a New Ford Car Waiting for YOU to step into the Driver's Seat! WHEN will you?

THE COLONIAL MOTOR COMPANY LIMITED
WELLINGTON · AUCKLAND · TIMARU

F.Z.—6

Above: First New Zealand advertising for the Model A featured free driving tuition for ladies who clipped and mailed a coupon.

D McL Wallace, Ford dealers at Te Aroha, took delivery of this impressive train load of new Model A cars and trucks in December 1929. They drove in convoy up the main street in Te Aroha, stopping the traffic.

climbed Mt Cook, and later became a road organiser and then production manager with Colonial Motor Company.

In 1928, Chevrolet registered 2,341 cars against Ford's 2,043. It was the first time Ford had been beaten in the New Zealand market. However, Ford did not register a new vehicle until August, as dealers anxiously waited and waited for the acclaimed new Model A to arrive. The Model A was an immediate success, much to nervous Ford dealers' relief, selling over 500 vehicles per month. Ford sales in 1929 were 5,392, comparing favourably with Chevrolet's 4,280, but the competition had also made gains with their new National model.

On February 12 1929, the government set up the Transport Department separately from the NZ Police for traffic law enforcement. A special third party insurance, with compulsory premiums added to annual vehicle licence fees, was introduced to prevent claims for negligent driving accidents being uninsured. Claims were equalised each year and premiums adjusted to suit.

The Christchurch property of Williams, Stephens and Co, carriers at Tuam and St Asaph Streets, came up for sale in 1929 and, being well located, was bought to allow Ford Motors Canterbury Ltd to relocate.

Top: A late 1920s photograph looking up Taranaki St before it was widened. Colonial Motor Company on the left, and Hope Gibbons on the right were the tallest buildings in Wellington, and the 'Ford' sign could be read from the Hutt Rd. The four storey Dunlop Tyres building was originally the Ford service depot in 1915, and later had two more storeys added. Most buildings in the photograph, other than the two tallest, have now been demolished, failing to meet seismic standards.
[Photo 1928 S C Smith collection, ref: G-45208-1/2 Alexander Turnbull Library]
Below: A bustling 1929 Commerce Street scene at Kaitaia – a hive of activity on farmers' sale day – with Northland Motors on the immediate left.

Henry Ford and son Edsel, pose with a client, at the Model A introduction in 1928, Madison Square Gardens, New York.

1929 STATISTICS

Licensed cars 152,609 - Ford 25%, Chev 9.9%
Trucks   13,667 - Ford 43%, Chev 14%

The car population had more than doubled in five years, and the number of commercial vehicles nearly trebled. Ford's market penetration dipped with the Model T run out.

Statistics show 1,470,654 men, women and children lived in New Zealand in 1929, and their uptake of cars was very high:

USA	1 car for	4.9 people
	1 vehicle	5.6 people
NZ	1 car for	9.6 people
	1 vehicle	7.9 people
Canada	1 car for	10.3 people
	1 vehicle	9.1 people
Britain	1 car for	47.0 people
	1 vehicle	34.3 people
Australia	1 car for	14.8 people
	1 vehicle	13.2 people

The ratio in country areas was much higher than cities served by public transport. Taranaki invested their tolls in good roads and had one car to every 5.5 people, nearly a car per household; Hawke's Bay was one for every 6.1.

In the 1929 year the motor industry collected:
Customs duty tax, tariff, fuel, etc   £2.63million
Of this, spent on Main Highways   £1.54million
Transferred to Consolidated Fund   £1.09million

WHERE CARS CAME FROM

The sources of cars shifted as small English cars became more popular and price competitive.

Source %	1925	1926	1927	1928	1929
UK	15.3	11.5	19.5	14.5	17.4
Canada	44.0	35.5	21.5	29.0	46.0
USA	38.3	50.5	56.5	55.5	36.5
Europe	2.3	2.5	2.5	1.0	0.1

The change from Model T to Model A shows clearly.

WHAT CARS COST IN 1930 IN £S

Austin 7 Tourer	189	Austin 7 Saloon	217
Model A Roadster	198	Model A Saloon	238
Model A Fordor	280	Ford Town Sedan	298
Morris Minor Tour	210	Morris Minor 2D	232
Chev Roadster	230	Chev Coach	249
Singer Junior	235	Whippet 4 Tourer	235
Rugby 4 Roadstr	240	Plymouth Sedan	292
Standard 10	295	Clyno 11hp	300
Essex Challenger	355	Rover 10 Tourer	345
Erskine 6 Sedan	370	Nash Standard 4D	385
Graham-Paige 612	385	Durant 63 Sedan	385
Oldsmobile Sedan	398	Armstong-Siddeley	440
Chrysler 66 Royal	455	Marmon Roosevelt	489
Hudson 8 Standard	525	Studebaker Victoria	565
Oakland Sedan	525	Morris Isis 6cyl	549
Buick 8 Empire	540	Willys Knight 70B	565
Velie 50 de luxe	545	Wolseley 21/60	595
Fiat 521C sedan	595	Crossley 6 Aero	720
Austin 20/6Carlton	775	Vauxhall Richmond	785

CHAPTER FOUR

THE TREACHEROUS
THIRTIES

The 'Slump', or world depression, was triggered by the New York Stock Market collapse in October 1929. Initially, this had little apparent effect in New Zealand, but surely and steadily, the financial cancer spread worldwide. By the end of 1930, the 'Slump' was affecting most businesses in New Zealand.

Farming, the backbone of our economy, withered under the numbingly low commodity prices. Wool was 4d a pound; lamb and beef demand was almost non-existent and realised similar returns – all was being sold under the cost of production. Farmers 'shut the gate' and their chequebooks. A number of farmers walked off their land, unable to pay their mortgages. Many of these disillusioned farmers had been assisted onto farms, mostly in the New Zealand back-blocks, under the government rehab(ilitation) scheme for returned soldiers after the First World War. Fortunately, the Mortgage Relief Act was passed on April 17 1931, saving at least a further 4,000 farmers and countless house owners. The country was in a financial mess, export income fell 40% in two years, and the coalition government struggled.

Politically it was a busy period, with all western-style governments around the world under pressure to find solutions to the international unemployment crisis. By September 1932 73,240 men were on unemployment relief in New Zealand, with 16,000 more on 'special work' schemes. This totalled 14% of the workforce, but men under 20 and unemployed women were neither counted nor provided for. In effect, 20% of New Zealand's workforce had no work. It was serious.

One of the 'special work' schemes was to construct and repair roads; and between 1930-35 3,500 miles (5,700km) of new roads and 1,000 new bridges were built, often using work gangs with picks, shovels and wheelbarrows. The Roads Board spent nearly £10 million in this period, the money coming from petrol and tyre taxes.

Trade tariffs were due to be re-negotiated, and there was support for a reciprocal trade treaty with England, with cars featuring strongly in this. Britain wanted to supply more cars to New Zealand; they were taking over 80% of all our exports, but only getting 17% of our car imports.

Public demand in New Zealand was for

The Great Depression was a heart breaking time for many. Unemployed men in 'special work' gangs carved out roads, which could have been built with machines. Construction on part of the Akatarawa Road from Upper Hutt to Waikanae. [Photo ref: G24537-1/1 PCColl-5348 Alexander Turnbull Library]

American cars, as they were more robust and better able to negotiate the country's poor roads. English cars were built for flat roads and had poor power to weight ratios, driven by a cranky domestic RAC horsepower tax which was based upon piston area, instead of developed power, or even cubic capacity. Cylinder wear with the long stroke engines was high, resulting in high maintenance.

However, the attitude of the private buyer had changed with the arrival of the low re-priced small English Austin 7, Morris Minor, Hillman and Singer cars, which had good petrol consumption, and were said to be economic to run. This, of

Top: A Standard Motor Bodies Model AAC fire engine, one of many built at the time. This Feilding Fire Board engine remained in service for over 50 years.

Right: This new Model A van home delivered bread daily, except Sundays.

Below: Ford Sales and Service Wellington used this smart breakdown truck built on a Model AAC chassis by Standard Motor Bodies.

course, was a fallacy as petrol consumption is only part of the running cost, but many private car owners only travelled 3-5,000 miles a year, and had no real idea of the expenditure per mile to run a vehicle, not understanding depreciation as a cost. Business, which understood this, also understood the bigger American and Canadian cars had lower running costs because they needed fewer repairs. Fanned with propaganda spread by British manufacturers, the small cars got a hold in the market and became fashionable, achieving nearly half the diminished 1932 new car market.

From The Colonial Motor Company's viewpoint, supply from Canada was still the only source of Fords. Every time the government talked of introducing preferential British tariffs, the company referred to 'British Empire' tariff, rather than British, trying to protect its Canadian source and keep the government away from classifying Canada as 'foreign'. The company held discussions with highly ranked customs officers and government ministers on the effects of tariffs.

Meanwhile, sales declined rapidly as unemployment increased. New cars were still being sold, but trade was poor, and used car sales dipped alarmingly as they fell drastically in value. This was a major problem for dealers, many of whom delayed cutting prices as they waited for the market to turn. Instead, it continued to get worse.

The weak used car market was exacerbated by hire purchase finance defaults. The average New Zealander could not afford to keep a car while his children went without essentials. Dealers were liable for any shortfall on repossessions. A car may have a finance value to clear of, say, £75, but its market value might only be £15; result: the dealer loses £60. Membership of the Motor Traders' Association, now supported by CMC, declined from 1,296 members in 1930, to 404 in 1934, due to 'financial stringency' and gives an idea of the devastation being felt by retailers. CMC was providing much of its own dealer finance and wrote off many of these debts to keep its dealers solvent.

The banks moved, stopping credit for many dealers until their accounts were in order. This made things worse because it strangled trade. CMC had put secured debentures in place with all Ford dealers,

in order to speed up the delivery of new vehicles. Any other delivery method required funds to be cleared first, which slowed down deliveries.

CMC then issued specified credit guarantees with the affected Ford dealer's bank to try to help them trade out of the situation. Unfortunately, this worsened the situation in some cases, and the banks then appointed receivers. Fortunately the company had large reserves and it absorbed and wrote off many of the losses, getting its dealers back in operation again.

Most Ford dealers survived, but some did not. Where possible, another party was found to take over the business, but the risks of starting a motor business were unattractively high in the early 1930s. In these cases CMC had few options but to take over the dealership, or lose their debenture completely. Most of the companies that failed became subsidiaries, while remaining available to suitable buyers.

H N Scrimshaw, the company's internal auditor, was very busy, with a skilled team who travelled to dealers, assessing their position, and helping to put them back on track. The earlier work, started in 1926, now paid big dividends, helping most Ford dealers to survive. There is no doubt the financial management systems put in place by Neil Scrimshaw were superior and the envy of every non-Ford dealer. Financial systems used today by CMC are very similar.

The Colonial Motor Company had to make many cut-backs to survive; directors were pragmatic, facing up to what was needed quickly, and getting on with planning ahead. The company had been managed conservatively and had substantial reserves which were used when needed. Directors were mostly concerned that their prized dealer network survived, to be ready for the upturn, and higher Ford sales.

The year 1930 began routinely in New

DEPRESSION VEHICLE SALES

Year	All makes	Ford sales(share)	Market change	Fordson Tractors
1929	26,694	5,365 (20.1%)		
1930	19,309	5,135 (26.6%)	down 27.7%	194
1931	8,299	1,988 (23.9%)	down 57.0%	38
1932	5,111	1,015 (19.9%)	down 38.4%	44
1933	4,974	1,279 (25.7%)	down 2.7%	47
1934	12,417	2,674 (21.5%)	up 149.6%	88
1935	19,844	4,772 (24.0%)	up 59.8%	88

THE VISIONARY: H N SCRIMSHAW

H Neil Scrimshaw, chief clerk of Clarke, Menzies and Co, a public accountancy practice in Wellington, joined Colonial Motor Company to set up a dealer accountancy system throughout New Zealand. This included the management principles and practices so necessary for a viable enterprise, and was operating prior to 1930.

Travelling continuously throughout the country, he gave guidance and inspiration to accountants and Ford dealers in the implementation of this practical system. Many of the CMC Group managers had a period training with 'Scrim', who had a practice of posting people to Ford dealers temporarily, to assist in all manner of management and accounting functions. Physical fitness is all the rage today, but this sort of thing was nothing new to Neil Scrimshaw. In the early 1930s he kept himself and his staff fit by regular use of a medicine ball. This he would throw at any given time; from say 7-7.30am, or even skipping morning tea for 20 minutes, much to the disgust of some of his staff, who soon found it was useless to argue!

Arrival at a dealership was often timed at about 5pm, when 'Scrim' would suggest that they all went for a beer. By the next morning he knew practically everything about the dealership, and where to start.

'Scrim' was a devoted golfer and had a book by Bobby Jones, the world-famous golfer of the time. However, he disagreed with Bobby's theories and used to demonstrate the correct way on the hotel carpet. The next time at the golf course Bobby invariably proved he knew something about golf, much to 'Scrim's' disapproval.

Auditing and accounting functions were carried out with little observance of weekends but wherever 'Scrim' and his team happened to stop, the golf clubs would appear.

Getting about New Zealand was quite difficult in the 1930s and travelling to the West Coast from Canterbury meant a train trip through Otira tunnel with the car on a railway wagon. The road over Arthur's Pass was impassable in winter and the Lewis Pass had not been formed as a road. Westport was a place they enjoyed and had some great tales to tell.

The foresight and planning of H N Scrimshaw is a legend, and he saved many Ford dealers from bankruptcy in the Depression. Ford dealers were the envy of other dealers because they knew what was going on in their businesses. Many people who 'Scrim' trained later became Ford dealers.

Neil Scrimshaw died in 1953, but the system he developed is still used today by CMC Group dealers, as it is considered to give the best picture of a dealership's finances.

Both Neil Scrimshaw's sons were involved with CMC Group; Len Scrimshaw was branch manager of Hawke Motors Te Aroha, and Don Scrimshaw was credit manager of Avery Motors.

Travelling through the bush at Otira Gorge in 1932 in their new 1932 Ford V8. 'Scrim' and Bob Gower (later accountant for Stevens Motors).

Top left: Westport breakwater about 1933. 'Scrim', Spencer Allen (later dealer at Manurewa, Papatoetoe and Howick), Phil Phillipps (later m-d Phillipps Motors New Plymouth), Jack Kilkenny then over 80, m-d Kilkenny Motors and former mayor of Westport.

Top right: Don Mullan and Neil Scrimshaw along the road. Don Mullan joined CMC in 1929 as cashier, and completed his accountancy exams. He then served on the road with 'Scrim' on audit and advisory functions before going to Timaru as manager in 1932 and, in 1962, becoming a director of CMC.

Middle: Visiting Patea in 1932 by Model A. Left to right: Don Mullan, 'Scrim', Bert Wedde (later went to GM), Jim Power (later service manager Avery's).

Bottom left: A golfing four: Rear, Bob Gower, 'Scrim'. Front, Bert Wedde, Bill Taylor, later Ford sales manager.

Bottom right: At Goose Bay near Kaikoura: Don Mullan, H N Scrimshaw and Bob Gower. Don Mullan regularly went to Goose Bay for years afterwards.

Zealand and, encouraged by CMC, Morley Smith, a sales promotion specialist from Canada, toured dealers with R S Milliken, the new export sales manager of Ford Canada. Declaring the New Zealand organisation in better shape than its Australian counterpart, which they had just visited, they gave sales promotion lectures to dealers, but the market did not change for the better, in spite of their advice.

From being on a par with sterling, the NZ pound was depreciated 10% by the government in 1930, to help exports and slow imports. There was little in the way of monetary policies then, and changes were made on an ad hoc basis with little planning, but the move certainly slowed vehicle sales.

Amidst all the chaos, the Model A Ford led sales in the New Zealand car market, again reinforcing Henry Ford's engineering genius, and son Edsel Ford's styling influence. The Model A differed in key design areas from the Model T. The transmission was changed from an epicyclic band-driven system to a clutch and three-speed slide gearbox. Ignition was by a high-tension coil instead of trembler coils, and steering and four-wheel brakes were much improved. It was the first Ford fitted with a laminated safety windscreen. The sedan body was a welded steel structure, significantly stronger than the Model T, and similar in style to the Lincoln. The Model A led the market because of its style and quality; it drove much better than most cars, was tough, reliable, and significantly cheaper.

When Norman B Gibbons visited the Ford Canada factory in June 1930 he had detailed discussions with Detroit engineers about premature main bearing wear, causing ovality and crankshaft rumble. He observed that the alignment seemed to be fine. The bearings were machine burnished and this packed metal onto the shoulders of both the cap and block. When the cap was removed and the half bearing tested using a reamer, it took metal from the shoulders first, indicating that if the bearing cap was now round, then the block was certainly not. When the crankshaft was re-fitted and the bearings attached with shims, the bearing would be oval. They all agreed, but were mystified as to why it should be this way. N B Gibbons had to depart, and the engineers were left to solve the problem. The process was later changed, the factory advising, without explanation, it was now OK.

On June 27 1930, Arthur Warburton died suddenly. Directors missed his wise counsel and recorded the contribution he had made over 28 years, as one of the founding shareholders of the company and its coach-building forerunner, and as a director since May 26 1913. J M McLean was appointed to the board. Formerly general manager of the National Bank, he had personally supervised the company account for many years.

The 1930 financial year ended with a reasonable profit, despite changing conditions, with reserves now £150,000. Brodie Motors Ltd began business on August 1 1930, taking over from sub-agents Dalgety and Co, at Kaikohe, with Hector Brodie as manager. Kaikohe had expanded from a village in 1918 to a centre for the Far North, with the rail link from

Colonial Motor Company sponsored an Auckland to Wellington non-stop journey (except for fuel), with the gear lever sealed in top gear, to illustrate how flexible the Model A Ford was. It was an ambitious enterprise given the state of the 'razor back' Bombay Hill, Mt Messenger pass near New Plymouth and the Paekakariki Hill. However, in April 1931 Ken Wilkinson drove the 471 miles in 10 hours 49 minutes elapsed time, at an average speed of over 43mph and raised a number of eyebrows.

Whangarei. Dawson King and Cook designed new garage premises which were built for £1,189, by Dudley Builders of Kaikohe.

Meanwhile, the United Party government was failing to cope as the depression intensified, and a deal was brokered with the Reform party to operate a coalition government after the 1930 elections. They passed legislation cutting wages by 10%, but people were still losing their jobs.

In May 1931, the coalition government regulated that all salaries and wages be cut a further 10%, with every wage earner to also pay an unemployment tax to help with relief schemes. This meant many families could not now meet their basic budgets, and still more people lost their jobs. Riots were quelled in Auckland, Wellington and Christchurch. The government claimed communists were responsible for the riots, but most were ordinary people, incensed at the way the country was being run. The average New Zealander resented the government deeply.

In June 1931 the bank put Dunnett and Downey Ltd, Timaru Ford agents into receivership. This triggered a flood, and in the next few months more receivers were appointed to:

W B McAdam Ltd at Te Kuiti,
F R Bridges Ltd at Masterton,
Te Awamutu Motors Ltd at Te Awamutu,
Taylor and Macdonald Ltd at Pukekohe,
Callanders Ltd at Waimate,
F R Furminger Ltd at Waipawa,
Kingston Motors Ltd at Feilding.

Timaru Motors Ltd was formed on June 15 1931, with Sid Enting as manager, buying out the assets of Dunnett and Downey. Jim Thornton started Northland Motors Ltd, on July 31 1931, taking over the business of Holder & Johnston at Kaitaia. Fagan Motors Ltd started trading in Masterton under manager Pat Fagan, on Armistice Day, November 11 1931, buying the assets of F R Bridges Ltd. With the intention to buy out and own their business, all had assistance from CMC. Jim Craik was sent into Te Awamutu Motors to manage for the receiver, and Percy Ferguson went to Taylor and Macdonald at Pukekohe to keep accounts, after a share buyout.

Conditions were critical for many dealers, and the Company wrote off £45,962 in bad debts to dealers, and recorded its first loss of £15,956. A 5% dividend was paid from reserves.

On a brighter note, CMC sponsored Cambridge dealer Ken Wilkinson's Model A journey from Auckland to Wellington. To show how good the car was, it was also locked and sealed in top gear. The *Auckland Herald* was delivered the 471

The welcoming party at Wellington GPO were left to right: Bill Fraser, G C Boys, Col Avery, N B Gibbons, Arthur Dotchin, Ken Wilkinson, R B Gibbons and F H (Toddy) Johnson.

Gangsters 'Bonnie and Clyde' stole Ford V8s for getaway cars. Bonnie Parker pictured with her revolver and a stolen car. Clyde Barrow sent this photo and note to Henry Ford: "I have drove Fords exclusively when I could get away with one." They were ambushed and died in a Ford V8 riddled with 107 bullets in 1934.

miles from Auckland to Wellington via Taranaki in a record 10 hours 49 minutes elapsed time, including fuel stops, and on unsealed roads. This certainly made Ford dealers smile, particularly if their opposition was jealous.

Despite the worldwide financial chaos, British motor manufacturers were still lobbying and spreading propaganda about buying British cars. What they didn't say was that they took New Zealand's export produce because it was so cheap compared to other sources. Ford of Britain's new plant at Dagenham started in October 1931, but initially could only produce right hand drive versions of the Detroit vehicles which the Canadians had been doing for years.

Sir Percival Perry, chairman of the British Ford Company, advised Henry Ford they faced certain disaster unless they could bring out a bantam car to compete in the British market. Ford agreed, and the Detroit design team, under E T (Bob) Gregoire, produced a new baby design of the US 1932 V8 in three months. Amidst wide acclaim, the 8hp Model Y car was shipped to Britain and launched at the Royal Albert Hall, on February 12 1932. This was the first Ford designed by Detroit to meet specific foreign laws, and saved Ford of Britain.

H B Gibbons outlined in detail to CMC's September board meeting, the steps taken to help and finance dealers through the 'Slump' and the resultant enthusiastic dealer organisation which, in most cases, had come through the worst, and was ready to handle the future trading of Ford products.

R B Gibbons reported at the same meeting that the new Ford V8 and B4 had both been enthusiastically received by dealers and public at Auckland, Wellington

and Timaru. The Ford V8 Roadster at only £264 (£26 more than a B4) suddenly projected Ford dealers into a totally new performance field and a different market, hitherto the province of the elite and wealthy. There were very few cars that could accelerate faster than a Ford V8, and those that could cost a fortune. US gangsters found it particularly suitable; John Dillinger, and Clyde Barrow ('Bonnie and Clyde') both wrote to Henry Ford endorsing the speedy V8.

CMC definitely needed a small car to keep market share, and finally negotiated buying the new 8hp British car through Ford Canada. The first 200 of the new Model Y were shipped in late 1932, with great expectations. However, when they arrived, it was found they had been shipped with the chassis frames in an open hold under 200 tons of newsprint, fortunately with the body panels and mechanicals boxed separately. There were no assembly instructions or parts manuals. All the chassis arrived in bent condition, and had to be re-built. Nearly all had initial rear axle problems because of the damage, but despite the poor start, they sold to eager buyers who found it was a spacious and comparatively perky small car.

Assembly was now a good deal more complex for CMC, highlighting the need for a new plant to cope with the diverse new models and new all-steel construction. Directors decided more land near the Courtenay Place plant should be purchased, and negotiations for the two acre area near the Wesley Church started. Research indicated that at least 80,000sq.ft. of floor

The Model Y 8hp prototype at the Albert Hall, London in 1932. This car, built from scratch in three months by Henry Ford's design crew in Detroit, was the first Ford designed for a specific market, and it was a great success.

space was needed which, with equipment, was likely to cost over £100,000.

Business did not pick up to any degree by 1933, due mostly to the coalition government depreciating the exchange rate by 25%, and a new 5% sales tax, introduced to raise money for the government coffers. Farmers welcomed the exchange alteration which improved their income, but the move was highly controversial because it effectively increased the cost of all imported goods, and reduced demand. New Zealand actually had good overseas reserves at the time, and needed market stimulation, not suppression.

In June 1933, the government spent £12,000 on a 'Buy NZ Made' campaign, and the Reidrubber factory opened at Penrose. Import substitution, with the obvious benefits of more jobs and less money spent outside New Zealand, was encouraged. At the same time, the Associated Motorists Petrol Company formed in 1931, by Todd Brothers and South Island Motor Union in response to high petrol prices, started importing Europa 77 octane petrol from Russia. Within 10 days it was sold at outlets around New Zealand, starting a price war that saw petrol come down 21% in price to 1s 7d in 1933.

The government moved to stop the discounting with the Motor Spirits Regulation of Prices. An oil company was quoted as saying that the government stopped the price war because the NZ Associated Motorists Petrol Company was not robust enough to take on the major oil companies. Perhaps, but petrol prices remained under control until 1988.

There were now two petrol grades available, 69 octane and leaded 77 octane. For some time, knocking had been evident in many cars, causing premature engine failure and over heating. By adding tetra ethyl lead, the octane rating was increased, and in most cases knocking ceased. Manufacturers continued to increase engine compression ratios to improve performance, but durability suffered unless octane rating increased.

The motor industry was now targeted by the government which indicated it wanted to increase the local content in cars by using differential tariffs. This would encourage assembly using New Zealand labour and completely knocked down (CKD) parts. British cars would be encouraged, and submissions were invited. At the time, only CMC and General Motors were assembling cars, mostly from semi-knocked down (SKD) components. CKD was an unknown area for government, which did not specify the term exactly, trying to encourage participation before setting limits.

New Zealand had a number of trade treaties with different countries, including Canada, due for renewal in 1934. Canada was in a unique position: on one hand it was a Dominion of Britain and expected favourable treatment; and on the other hand, it was New Zealand's only source of American Ford cars.

CMC became heavily involved with government officials in an effort to determine what was meant by the term CKD. What percentage of the vehicle had to originate from the supply source? Could parts come from different countries? There were a number of other questions.

In April-May 1934, H B Gibbons visited Ford Canada. Relations were very good and the Canadians reinforced this

1932 V8 poster.

The new 'baby' Ford had initial teething problems. When the first shipment of 200 arrived with badly bent chassis, it meant a chassis straightening as well as assembly job. When the Model Y went into service, CMC had to supply one and a half rear ends per car, because 50% gave trouble. As one wit said: "All babies have back end troubles – the Ford baby is no different."

The car was a great success and sold 554 in 1934 alone, a very considerable portion of the New Zealand market.

The Model Y paved the way for the Model C 10hp and later the Prefect, which was one of the most successful models, the chassis continuing in production for nearly 20 years.

A Ford V8 hearse built by Standard Motor Bodies on an extended chassis. It was smooth and quiet.

confidence by changing the credit arrangements, from the normal letters of credit with bank order, to an open monthly trading account. CMC remained their most successful overseas distributor, achieving the highest market shares.

Over the three weeks Hope Gibbons was at Windsor, discussions covered details about a new assembly factory in New Zealand, and the local content levels of production sought by the New Zealand government. British preferential tariff was mooted, but would this also mean British Empire? Who would control the new factory – Ford, CMC, or joint ownership? The new V8 engine had exhibited excessive oil consumption, but a fix of square, instead of diagonal-cut, piston rings was now in

production. There were some hefty topics, quite apart from the usual detailed Ford trading matters.

Car radios were beginning to make an appearance, and H B arranged with Stewart Warner in the US for a number of radios to be shipped to New Zealand where they were fitted as 'added value' to slower moving vehicles, helping to clear them. This was significant at a time when not many homes had a radio. The promotion worked well and more radios were ordered.

Hope Gibbons then went on to Dagenham in England where he saw the new 10hp Model C Ford and told Ford England this was likely to be more successful than the Model Y 8hp because of its better power output and larger body.

The 1933-34 V8 Roadsters designed by Bob Gregoire were a hit, and spawned car racing everywhere. A ready made racer, it looked great and didn't cost the earth.

When it arrived in New Zealand, the rounded sides 10hp C, or 'Preggy C' as it was known, sold well. There was still a large demand for the Canadian Ford V8, but the smaller British Fords were very popular, and certainly competed successfully in their market slot against British Austin, Morris, Standard and Hillman cars, increasing Ford's market share.

After H B Gibbons returned from England and Canada, he tabled his reports about the factories to the board. While there was an obvious need for a new factory, after discussions with Ford in Canada and Dagenham, it was decided to hold off until it was clear where tariffs would lie, and trade negotiations had been finalised as the new factory's needs were getting more expensive and more complicated.

Assembly of steel bodies needed special jigs and spot welding guns. Ford considered it unsatisfactory to have steel bodies assembled outside their own factories, and Britain was not at all organised for CKD methods of production for export.

The board thought it logical for Ford Canada to set up the new assembly plant in New Zealand. Directors were not unhappy with Ford owning and controlling the assembly; it did, after all, mean CMC would not have to put up an estimated £125,000. The company would continue to take all product, vehicles and parts, from the factory and distribute this through its very successful dealer network, ensuring Ford's market domination. But there was unease in the boardroom. CMC had to prove that the partnership would work better than Ford going alone.

The Society of Motor Manufacturers (SMMT) in Britain was demanding a bigger slice of the import cake and exerting considerable political pressure. The New Zealand government had its own agenda, wanting fewer built-up vehicles and more assembly of CKD components in the country to help unemployment. Ford Canada, on the other hand, wanted things to stay as they were, distrusting SMMT and government motives.

In August 1934, the government

Beach and dirt track racing developed quickly, drawing huge crowds around the world.

announced changed tariff rates, giving British vehicles a clear preferential advantage, and, a 10% advantage to completely knocked down (CKD) cars. CKD was not defined, other than that it related to cars imported with the body and chassis dismantled. Canadian sourced vehicles were given an intermediate rate between British and foreign rates. This applied from January 1935, but government also said rates would be reviewed again at trade talks that year.

Ford Canada's W R Campbell wrote expressing concern at the attitude of NZ Customs, which appeared to be anti-Canada and pro-Britain. In fact, the government was looking to do three things: encourage employment in assembly, improve trade with Britain, still our principal export market, and increase dairy exports to Canada.

King George V was due to celebrate his 25th Jubilee in June 1935, and prime minister Forbes would be there. Trade negotiations were set to take place afterwards, when J G Coates, minister of finance and customs, would also be in Britain.

It was a better year for CMC and its dealers in 1934. Because of British imports, market share dropped to 22%, but volumes more than doubled. Final arrangements were made with most of the dealers who had failed to cope, and new companies were to be set up in Invercargill, Lower Hutt, Feilding, Dannevirke, Otorohanga, Te Kuiti, Te Awamutu,

Hamilton and Pukekohe.

CMC tried to finance dealers into their own businesses, but this did not always work out, and some fell back on the company. George Duncalf retired at the end of June 1934, and Ormond Hutchinson took over as manager of Ford Motors Canterbury in Christchurch. R U (Bob) Macaulay shifted from Auckland branch to take over Timaru branch. J V (Jack) Stevens was appointed manager of a new subsidiary company Stevens Motors Ltd, and took over from Ward and Rawnsley at Lower Hutt on June 15 1935. Ward then became the Ford dealer at Marton, while Rawnsley started a flying school in Wellington.

A Christmas bonus was given to all staff – a half day's pay for each month worked during 1934. The board minutes record that "this came as a complete surprise and was most welcome."

In March 1935, both Alf B and R B Gibbons left to visit Ford factories and suppliers in the US, Canada and England. R B Gibbons was also to advise a New Zealand Customs party leaving for tariff and trade negotiations in Britain. In addition, Auckland branch manager, W G (Bill) Taylor and his wife left in April 1935 to visit Ford Canada and Britain so he could advise the board about some assembly needs.

R B Gibbons and A B Gibbons briefed Ford Canada president W R Campbell, sales manager R S Milliken and export sales manager George H Jackson in April-

Ambulances based on the V8 light trucks got to their destinations much more quickly than before. This extended 1934 one ton truck conversion from SMB cost £401.

Westland Hospital Board Hokitika.

May about the current trade agreement negotiations, and the likely new assembly tariff changes that differentiated between 'Set Up' (Built Up) cars and knocked down (CKD) cars. This would necessitate a different short-term approach until a new assembly factory was built in New Zealand. They discussed many of the factory's requirements, but its control was left open. As far as Ford was concerned, CMC was still looking for a suitable site.

Ford Canada wanted to be party to negotiations with the SMMT and the British and New Zealand government officials. It was agreed that W R Campbell, or R S Milliken, would be in London at the time of British-New Zealand trade negotiations in June and July 1935.

There were a number of factors to consider in planning New Zealand vehicle demand in 1936:

1. Any trade treaty negotiated with Britain or Canada might be temporary, as both the New Zealand and Canadian governments were likely to change at the end of 1935. When, then, would any trade treaty be likely to become operational?

2. From discussions with the British trade delegation and SMMT, it seemed knocked down and British cars were going to be favoured. The difference in tariff rate was going to be the key. There may still be a carrot for Ford Canada if they could reach 75% local content for export. They were then achieving about 65%.

3. There was likely to be a time difference between any treaty becoming effective and the date when a new assembly plant would be built. How long would this period be?

Decisions about 1936 vehicle orders needed to take all contingencies into account. The new British Ford 10 hp model would be introduced in October, with the first cars arriving by the end of 1935. The Canadian Ford V8 was due to change model about the same time.

A new factory in New Zealand would not be ready to start production until at least August 1936. Because of the parliamentary elections, and a likely change of government, any new trade treaty was unlikely to be ratified until at least February 1936.

If CMC ordered a large shipment of the new models to arrive in December, it should attract tariff at the current rate. After February, imports were likely to attract the

R B Gibbons was in Canada in 1935 not only to help Ford Canada with British vehicle trade and tariff negotiations, but to assist the New Zealand government publicise the need for Canada to sell its milk and cream in the US and import New Zealand butter to help the Canada-NZ trade treaty negotiations.

new tariff. It was thought the change in tariff would be between 10-20%. Stocks of set-up (Built Up) vehicles needed to be on hand to carry through until CKD production started in September. A total of 3,500-4,000 built up vehicles would cost £1.5 million, a huge sum, but possible to borrow.

On Saturday July 6 1935, R B Gibbons was penning these strategies from his London hotel room to his brother in Wellington. The previous night he had met Bill Taylor and his wife at 1.15am at Waterloo Station, as they arrived in London, and taken them to their hotel. Dr Craig, Comptroller of NZ Customs, was in London and telephoned to discuss their meeting the next day, Sunday July 7, and his meeting afterwards with Lord Rootes of the SMMT, at the unusual time of 9pm, to discuss the New Zealand trade treaty prior to the formal talks.

After an initial meeting with Dr Craig, it was established that SMMT would accept that Canada could not be forced above 65% (Empire) local content, but British tariff at 5% and Canada at 12.25% for CKD components was unlikely to be agreed to by SMMT.

Dr Craig and Mr Lawrence of NZ Customs were to meet SMMT on Monday July 8, and a further meeting with minister Gordon Coates on July 13 to try to reach final agreement. After that, Coates was committed to other meetings.

R B Gibbons knew Canada could get to 75% content if pushed and suggested the following table for negotiating a compromise:

PROPOSED TARIFF TABLE

Empire Content	CKD		Set Up	
	UK	Canada	UK	Canada
At 75% + surtax	5%	10% 2.25%	15%	25%
At 65% + surtax	5%	12.5% 2.8%	15%	25%
Foreign + surtax	50% 11.25%		60% 13.5%	

At the Monday conference were Lord Rootes and SMMT secretary Toohey, R S Milliken and R B Gibbons, Dr Craig, and secretary Lawrence from NZ Customs.

R B Gibbons reported the meeting was heavy going but agreement was reached for 75% Empire content while conceding Canadian 2.5% on CKD, with everyone pleased at the result. To the SMMT, which had never reached any agreement before, the offer of 75% Empire content suited them very well as a basis for other negotiations. R B Gibbons commented that few in the group had negotiating skills and kept taking

positions and sitting pat. Simply by offering alternatives, a compromise was reached.

Now that the British-New Zealand trade treaty had been agreed, a political letter from Coates accepting the agreement was required. This was the final outcome announced on July 15 1935:

"New Zealand mutton, lamb, beef, and pork will continue to be imported into Britain with no levy, while British goods will receive preferential import tariff into New Zealand."

The details of duties were not publicised!

DUTIES ON MOTOR VEHICLES

	Britain	Canada	General
CKD 75% content	5%	10%	50%
+surtax 9/40ths		2.25%	11.25%
CKD 65% content	5%	12.5%	50%
+surtax 9/40ths		2.875	11.25%
Set Up (BU)	15%	25%	60%
+surtax 9/40ths		5.625	13.5%

There were further detailed definitions of what was allowed for CKD; this included 'shells' (body shells welded together but not finished), which were very difficult to assemble without special positioning jigs.

As the new assembly factory in New Zealand had been put on hold until the trade treaty was finalised, R B Gibbons sailed on the *MS Berengario* to New York and then flew to Windsor for further talks with W R Campbell about the new factory. There had been hypothetical discussions previously;

now there was a real situation to debate.

Campbell found it difficult to conceive a large factory in New Zealand assembling Ford vehicles not controlled by the company. R B Gibbons had anticipated this and let the argument flow. He agreed there were a number of factors why Ford would want control: it was an established practice for Ford to control all major assembly; Ford regarded control of manufacture as its absolute sphere, or obligation; Ford wanted to control profit from any plant, achieving as much as possible, and controlling inter company billing; and finally, security of the New Zealand market for Ford, and also for Ford Canada, was paramount.

However, R B Gibbons was able to cable from Windsor on July 29 1935:

"GIBBONS COLMOCO
WELLINGTON
FORDCANADA WILL ESTABLISH ASSEMBLY FACTORY GEORGE JACKSON APPOINTED MANAGER BOB"

Manufacture was one thing, but distribution was another. As R B Gibbons said, it was, logically, only a flow on process from manufacture with nothing else changed. Orders, service, dealer finance, advertising, stocks of vehicles and parts,

Aloha Baker's round-the-world run in the 1936 Centrepoise V8 drew crowds everywhere. In Christchurch, she was welcomed by Orm Hutchinson, with Bill Taylor, Ford NZ left, George Jackson m-d, Ford NZ right, and sales manager Bill Henry far right.

Below: Hawke Motors was set up to take over from D McL Wallace at Te Aroha in 1936, with Roy Hawke as m-d. The used car division with R & G (reconditioned and guaranteed) cars on display, at the former Dodge dealer premises in Bridge Street.

were all a function of distribution. However, although CMC activities and capital were inextricably tied to Ford, Campbell felt there was no Ford precedent for the proposed CMC relationship as Ford Canada would now have wider responsibilities in New Zealand: to protect its invested capital; a manufacturer must also see its products serviced well; there was a responsibility to see its image advertised, and the need to build a good name. No finality was reached in the discussion before R B Gibbons flew to San Francisco, carrying a letter from Campbell detailing why Ford would set up the new factory. By the time he arrived home, he had been away for an exhausting six months.

Because of the difficulty in getting long-term compliance with the trade treaty due to the likely change in government in November, to get the factory started it was agreed the treaties would apply for six months, effectively binding any new government to the treaty and to Ford's factory establishment terms.

Ford Motor Company of New Zealand Ltd was incorporated in late 1935, and dealers and public were informed a new factory would be built. The government was keen to see this established in the Hutt Valley where an industrial park was being developed with manpower for industry being encouraged to the area by low cost housing.

In November 1935, the government was defeated and Michael Savage's Labour party swept into power, with 53 of the 80 seats. Soon after, Bob Semple, the new minister of works, drove a bulldozer over a wheelbarrow, signifying that road construction would now be done by machines, not dole gangs.

Market conditions were now much improved with 1935 volumes close to those achieved before the Depression. Despite all the distractions during the year, Colonial Motor Company had kept their dealers busy, and included value added offers, achieving a market leading 24% share of the 19,844 new vehicle sales.

After considerable work by R B

Gibbons, and negotiations with a number of government parties, a suitable factory site was located at Seaview in the Hutt Valley where it was central for distribution, near government and CMC. In November 1935 an option was taken on three industrial sites, and George H Jackson signed in December to purchase the total of 13.25 acres for £13,125 on January 31 1936. This gave enough room for assembly but not sufficient for a parts warehouse, and an adjoining section was bought in 1937 for parts distribution.

The Seaview industrial area was once the site of a Maori pa, abandoned long ago because of heavy flooding by the multi-stranded Hutt River. The river was contained between stop banks in the 1920s, and the river mouth was stabilised at Port Road in the late 1930s. The area to the east was now regarded as suitable for industry, and the Railway workshops had been shifted from Petone to Woburn.

The new factory, designed by Ford Canada in classical Art Deco style, was similar to factories in Australia, Africa and Canada. The plans were drawn up in New Zealand by King, Cook and Dawson. Unlike the earlier multi-storeyed design, this building was largely on one level. Local consulting engineer, Ian McCallum, was retained and did considerable work in relation to the site requirements and foundations.

In the process of starting a trading bank account for Ford New Zealand, two Ford Canada executives, George H Jackson and secretary Tom B Cavaghan, arrived at the chosen bank, which shall remain nameless, to set up the company's accounts, to find both the manager and accountant out at lunch. It was a very costly lunch because, miffed at their absence, the two Ford executives simply went next door, where the manager of the Bank of New South Wales greeted them and opened their trading accounts which have remained there ever since.

Meanwhile, CMC was busy planning how the new distribution and retail organisation would work. Those companies still in the Gibbons family ownership would need to be brought back under CMC.

Left: T B (Tom) Cavaghan, first secretary, Ford NZ.

Below: Macaulay Motors had all the latest models at 1936 Southland A & P Show. Left to right: Model 68 V8 Standard £317, Model Y 2dr 8hp £229, Model C 10hp £289, Model 68 V8 deluxe £345.

Bottom: Northland Motors staff in 1936. From left; M Waddell, apprentice; R Northwood, painter; L Masters, mechanic; Jim Thornton, owner; G Carstens, service manager; Cedric Harrison, salesman; B Renton, accountant; Hilda Moore, parts/ office; I McKinnon, F Cresswell, mechanics; R Perkins, assistant accountant; F Sands, Cliff Maria, A Perkins, J Short, mechanics; and W Thornton, lubrication.

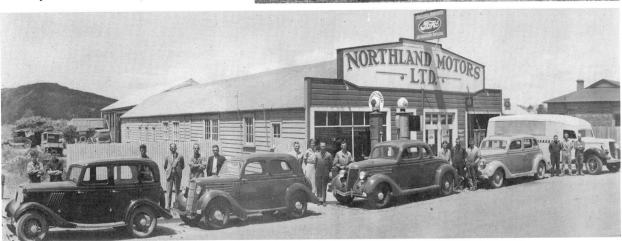

The classic 1936 Ford V8 Coupe with rear rumble seat, a lot of car and great style for £319.

Subsidiary companies would have to be re-named without 'Ford' in their title, adequately capitalised, brought into line with reporting dates and any tax losses utilised. All other Ford dealers who used 'Ford' in their name, would have to remove this to conform with policy.

There was other tidying up to do. The Fred Baker Motors franchise in Hamilton was terminated and Armstrong Motors Ltd appointed with assistance from CMC. G W Woods did not want to develop their premises at Invercargill so Macaulay Motors Ltd was formed by CMC to take over and R U (Bob) Macaulay transferred from Timaru branch manager to be manager. Similarly, H Derby and Co in New Plymouth was still in financial difficulty, so Len Nicholls Motors was formed as a subsidiary to take over there,

Orm Hutchinson negotiated an innovative deal to replace 52 Whippet Gold Band taxis – and delivered all the replacements to the Gold Band stand in Cathedral Square, painted in fleet colour at CMC's assembly plant in Courtenay Place. No cash changed hands; the vehicles were all on hire purchase, with the 52 Whippets as a deposit. The cars operated 24 hours a day in shifts with drivers receiving about 33% of the takings. The cars all covered an average 300,000 miles before being replaced in 1938 by 52 Ford V8s that ran right through the war, and were, in turn, replaced by 52 1947 V8s. This pioneering replacement deal forged the way for others.

with Len Nicholls as manager.

In March 1936, F N R Meadows retired from the board, having served 28 years. Instrumental in the transition from coach building to motor vehicles, Fred Meadows had been appointed a director as part of the 1908 merger with the Automobile Company of NZ Ltd, which Meadows had started and owned. F H Johnston, retiring general manager, was appointed director at the annual meeting to replace Meadows.

Negotiations for leasing the 'Cathedral site' in Taranaki Street, Wellington had finally been agreed in early 1936. Although the original intention had been to build the new factory there, directors decided the land was still necessary for the future, and Millers West Australian Hardware Company continued to occupy the site until March 1937.

At the directors' meeting on June 5 1936, managing director H B Gibbons announced that, out of the blue, Ford Motor Company of NZ Ltd had written to say it would be taking over all aspects of distribution at the same time as assembly started. This was a total bombshell and over a number of days' discussion the extent of the changes were outlined. CMC's operations would be reduced to the sale of cars through their own retail subsidiaries, finance operations, and certain manufacturing.

The board immediately gave H B, R B, and N B Gibbons power to negotiate with Ford and make the best arrangements possible. It was not an easy assignment, after all the assurances from Ford Canada that the Colonial Motor Company was making an excellent job of distribution, and had long been lauded for getting the best results anywhere overseas.

Below: Model C 10hp van came as a chassis, bonnet and windscreen, with the rest made by SMB. Complete cost £256.

Bottom: A typical 1935 V8 service car built by Standard Motor Bodies, carried nine fare paying passengers, mail and half a ton or more of freight. The chassis was £311, and body £420.

Right: Ford Canadian V8 trucks arrived as a chassis cowl, with cabs and rear tip bodies built by SMB. They were excellent value for money in 1935, especially when they could be overloaded and still perform. This 2¹/2 tonner had done 52,000 miles on bush tracks without trouble by 1937. Cost: chassis £296, cab £43, body £19, hoist £32. Total cost £390 10s.

A cable was sent to W R Campbell, their 'friend' at Ford Canada, expressing surprise and disappointment at the action.

"JACKSON HAS COMMUNICATED ESSENCE OF YOUR CABLE AND WE ARE COMPLETELY TAKEN BY SURPRISE STOP WE HAVE BEEN FULLY OCCUPIED DEVELOPING ORGANISATION FOR HANDLING TREMENDOUS INCREASE OF BUSINESS DURING RECENT MONTHS WITH NO OTHER THOUGHT BUT DEVELOPMENT OF FORD INTERESTS IN NEW ZEALAND STOP THIS PREVENTED ANY VISIT TO CANADA THIS YEAR STOP WE ARE AND HAVE ALWAYS BEEN WILLING AND ANXIOUS TO COOPERATE UNDER YOUR NZ ORGANISATIONS CONTROL IN HANDLING FORD PRODUCT HERE STOP WE WILL BE DISAPPOINTED IF YOUR DECISION TO UNDERTAKE THE DISTRIBUTING OPERATIONS IN NEW ZEALAND IS FINAL BUT IF THIS IS SO WE MUST ACCEPT THE POSITION STOP THE FORD LINE HAS HAD OUR WHOLEHEARTED SUPPORT FOR MANY YEARS AND WILL CONTINUE TO HAVE THAT SUPPORT IN THE FUTURE GIBBONS."

Campbell cabled back two days later:

"GREATLY APPRECIATE YOUR CABLE EIGHTH STOP SINCE WRITING YOU JULY 29TH LAST WE HAVE GIVEN THE SUBJECT OF ASSEMBLY AND WHOLESALING FUNCTIONS CONSIDERABLE THOUGHT AND HAVE CONCLUDED THAT THESE FUNCTIONS ARE LOGICALLY AND ECONOMICALLY INSEPARABLE STOP THAT BEING SO WE CONSIDER IT BEST FROM STANDPOINT OF ALL CONCERNED TO MAKE CHANGES COINCIDENT WITH COMMENCEMENT OF PRODUCTION STOP WE GREATLY APPRECIATE THE SPLENDID EFFORTS OF COLONIAL MOTOR COMPANY IN MERCHANDISING FORD PRODUCTS IN NEW ZEALAND AND ARE HAPPY TO HAVE YOUR ASSURANCE OF A CONTINUATION OF THAT SUPPORT IN THE FUTURE CAMPBELL."

Directors were shattered at Ford's change of tack; they had thought their distribution was safe. However, it is fair to reflect that CMC had, for the previous seven years, been the last remaining distributor of any consequence worldwide, and changes were inevitable. Edsel Ford had decreed in 1927 that any distributor selling more than 3,000 cars should be owned by Ford. Ford Canada also saw it had a huge investment in buildings and plant in New Zealand, and needed the security of having their own control over distribution. Directors were deeply hurt, but swallowed hard and got on with negotiating the future.

An extraordinary meeting of shareholders was called on July 31 1936, where the changes were outlined:

• Retail sales through subsidiaries and associates would continue, accounting for about 50% of all Ford vehicles sold;

• Financing at retail and wholesale would continue where directors considered it prudent;

• Manufacturing would continue: building commercial bodies; reconditioning engine units and other smaller units; manufacture of fire engines and pumps; manufacture of hoists;

• Land and buildings would remain a capital investment to be leased or disposed of;

• Staff would get the opportunity to join Ford, although some might wish to stay and join retail and manufacturing operations.

All staff and dealers were then advised of the impending changes. Many dealers

Left: A formidable businessman, Wallace R Campbell, president of Ford Canada, cabled the bad news. Until trying to do the job itself, Ford Canada did not realise how effective Colonial Motor Company was at achieving top market share.

Opposite middle: The first British Fordson 'heavy' trucks, the Sussex and Surrey were potentially good, but in reality a disaster. They were heavy, badly geared and, with the smaller underpowered British 60hp V8, they could barely maintain top gear on a flat road with no load. Cost: chassis £535, cab £45, 15ft 6in x 7ft deck in white pine or kauri £25, total cost £605. The 6 x 4 was £40 more.

Opposite bottom: The 1937 4 door Ford 10hp replaced the Model C 10hp, with more seating and headroom, finding great market favour in New Zealand. Cost £298.

The Colmoco trailer pump prototype built in 1936, using a 90hp V8 to drive the axial pump, delivered 400 gallons of water per minute. It was much more manoeuvrable than a fire engine, and could be towed to where it was required.

Below: The first trailer pump was built by Colonial Motor Company engineering department (Colmoco) in 1936. The Ford 90hp V8 engine proved ideal for pumping water at high pressure, and could be used for fire fighting or dispersing flood waters. There are records of units pumping out flood water continuously for three to 21 days at a time. The development team at Colmoco in Ebor Street next to Standard Motor Bodies.

wrote to say they were shocked but expressed their admiration and thanks to the directors who had helped their businesses so much with advice and finance through troubled times. "Things would not be the same without the Gibbons touch." Indeed, the Ford market penetration obtained by CMC has not been equalled since.

Also on July 31 1936, the Motor Vehicle Amendment Act was passed, legislating a 30 miles per hour speed limit in built up areas. There were no national speed limits until this point, although local by-laws existed in many places.

Many other things changed in 1936. The government took over the Reserve Bank; a state housing plan was launched; guaranteed prices for dairy products were introduced; inter-island trunk air services began; compulsory union fees were deducted from wages, and the working

week was reduced from 44 to 40 hours; Jack Lovelock won New Zealand's first Olympic gold medal; and Jean Batten flew from England to New Zealand in record time. Everything it seemed, was open to change.

Meanwhile the new factory was being built. With a floor area of 183,000 sq.ft. (17,000 sq.m), it was a large project in 1936, and an army of contractors was involved. All the surrounding area was fully levelled and paved. The 2¼ acres in front was laid down in lawn and gardens, and when finished it was a landmark marvel in the Wellington area. Five hundred new jobs were on offer and many of the Colonial Motor Company staff members transferred. The railways laid a special track into the area, capable of holding 24 wagons at one time.

The splendid new £160,000 factory was opened at Seaview in October 1936 with a

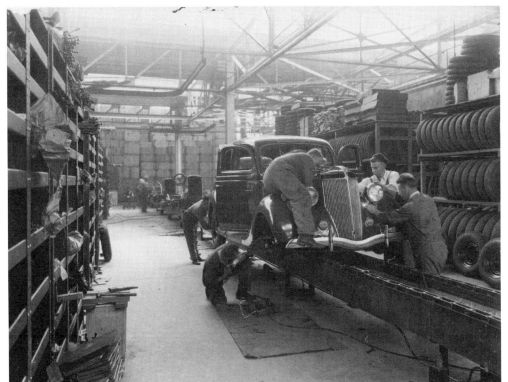

George H Jackson, first managing director of Ford New Zealand and formerly sales manager of Ford Canada. The offices, lined in mahogany ply, became known as 'mahogany row'.

Middle: Ford V8s on the Seaview assembly line.

Bottom: The new 183,000 sq.ft. Ford factory, on 14 acres at Seaview, made a considerable impression when it opened in October 1936. Colonial Motor Company staff were given the opportunity to transfer to Ford. The Ford factory was the first industrial building of any consequence in the Seaview area, and could be seen from Wellington. At first the offices used internal blinds to try to control the fierce afternoon sunlight; later external awning blinds were erected. Seaview Road, where staff cars were parked, was literally by the sea. After the Hutt River mouth was stabilised, dozens of acres of land were reclaimed for bulk fuel storage and industrial use.

CAR IMPORTS		1929	%	1936	%
Britain	BU	4,064		8,661	
Britain	CKD			4,660	
British	total	4,064	17.4%	13,321	55%
Canada	BU	10,740		3,051	
Canada	CKD			1,520	
Canadian	total	10,740	45.9%	4,571	19%
USA	BU	8,529		920	
USA	CKD			5,415	
USA	total	8,529	36.5%	6,335	26%
Other sources		28		1	0%
TOTAL	BU	23,361		12,633	52%
TOTAL	CKD			11,595	48%
TOTAL		23,361		24,228	

The first Ford dealer conference at the new Seaview factory in November 1936. It was a momentous occasion for Colonial Motor Company executives, as they handed over control to Ford New Zealand.

great deal of fanfare, and the Ford Motor Company held their first dealer conference. Invitations went to Hope Gibbons, H B Gibbons and R B Gibbons, and other directors, although they were not now recognised as Ford dealers. The transition had gone smoothly on the surface, thanks to the immense amount of work done by the CMC executives, and particularly R B Gibbons, who got on well with people and wanted to see the new arrangement work for "his staff", many of whom transferred to Ford.

Among those who transferred were W G

(Bill) Taylor, who became sales manager; Jack Broun, service manager. Harold Peron Ralph later became parts manager, and then managing director in 1961. Harold Ralph had started a world journey in 1924 from his home in Argentina, but stopped at his first port, Wellington, where he remained, working for Colonial Motor Company, and then Ford.

There was yet another blow when Ford wrote advising directors that all retail hire purchase business had to be arranged through Alliance Finance Corporation, the only company approved to arrange Ford dealer business.

In 1936 there was another jump in new vehicles with 24,228 being imported, but also a considerable shift in the source and from assembled (BU) to CKD cars. (See table.)

There were at least two satisfied parties – Britain and the New Zealand government, which now had a large assembly industry, nearly all in the Hutt Valley, producing half the cars. The Canadians and American suppliers were not happy, having lost a sizeable share of their exports to New Zealand, and CMC, who had built the first proper motor vehicle assembly plant in New Zealand, now had to close it down.

Standard Motor Bodies was busy and

the CMC manufacturing division was shifted next door at Ebor Street, where they continued to make fire engines and pumps, truck hoists, plus recondition car components, with Jack Manning supervising. There were over 100 men working at Ebor Street.

Warrant of Fitness regulations were introduced in 1937 to ensure the safety of motorists and public, and all cars had official safety checks every six months at government testing stations in cities, and certified agents in country areas.

Auckland's Fox Street Parnell operation, no longer in use, was sold to International Harvester Company.   In Timaru the

Top: The new 8hp Anglia was introduced in 1938, some time after the Model Y was no longer available. This car was sold at £265, providing basic robust motoring, and still sold as the 'Popular' in the 1950s.

Middle: Wellington Tramways bought 10 of these 'pay as you enter' 25 seater Ford V8 185in. wheelbase omnibuses built at Petone by NZ Motor Bodies.

Bottom: A few of the huge Lincoln Zephyr V12 limousines were imported, but the high £775 price tag kept sales low.

This 2¹/₂ ton V8 truck could haul an 8 ton payload on Class IV roads. It used an Abingdon tandem axle compensating rocker which gave smoother running and spread the loading. Truck £296, trailer £235, and a total of £531.

warehouse and assembly building were empty, with Timaru Motors using a part. The three storey 'front' building at Courtenay Place and York St despatch depot were used by Avery Motors. In April 1937 Avery Motors started building on the two acre 'Cathedral' site with a petrol station and lubritorium. The bulk of the land was used for car parking at one shilling per day until agreement could be reached with the city council, which was talking of extending Ghuznee Street through to Tory Street, about positioning of buildings and permits. The workshop and sales buildings, begun in 1938, were finished as the Second World War started.

With industry concentrated in the Hutt Valley, the new government instituted the first state housing scheme, with an ambitious building programme of 5,000 houses per year, in an effort to attract labour for the factories. In 1938 the Social Security Act was passed, guaranteeing a wide range of benefits: universal superannuation; age, widows, orphans, invalids, miners and family benefits; invalid, sickness and emergency benefits; and the basis of a national health service.

The company decided to split its £50 shares into £1 shares, and removed the restriction on share transfers. A number of the early shareholders had died and their estates could not be wound-up because private shares were not easily traded.

In April 1938 Ford Motor Company advised it was withdrawing the tractor franchise from Ford dealers and transferring it to Booth McDonald Ltd, Christchurch agricultural machinery dealers. (Later it moved to Gough Gough and Hamer, also at Christchurch.) It was claimed that Ford dealers had poor sales volumes, and were not focussed on tractors. Ford wanted better results, but did not get them. The Fordson was a good tractor but, as with the Model T, it was now 20 years old.

H M Basil Orsborn was appointed receiver for J L Braithwaite Ltd at Waipukurau and, after attempts to sell, an

auction was set down for November 14 1938. Colonial Motor Company bought the business after it was passed in at auction, and Cordery Garage Ltd was formed, with F M Cordery appointed manager.

Ford Motor Company brought in new policies regarding dealer representation, which it said were designed to create more competition, and were based on Canadian experience. Many former sub-dealer points were given full dealer status over the next 20 years, thereby weakening their neighbours. These were chosen on geographical location in some cases and took no account of population or volume. Dealers needed volume sales that come

Top: A closed type 15cwt V8 van built by Standard Motor Bodies from the windscreen back, with pressed steel side panels. It cost £315. Bottom: This 1939 V8 de luxe cost £361.

Top: In Wanganui, Merewether Motor Company's, approach to wartime rationing. Left to right: Eric Merewether, dealer; C A Smith, sales manager; C F Lomas, secretary; and Mos Bignell, manager, 'on their bikes'. Both Eric Merewether and Mos Bignell lost sons in action during the war.

Bottom: *Henry Ford explains the 1932 V8 design to his son Edsel. Once again Henry had proved his mechanical genius and got the market going at the depth of the Depression. Edsel Ford was in charge of all body design.*

with population to achieve financial strength for growth, so they could withstand the economic swings brought by New Zealand's dependence upon primary product exports.

When Len Nicholls in New Plymouth wanted to sell his shares in Len Nicholls Motors and was bought out, New Plymouth became a subsidiary, Phillipps Motors Ltd, with Phil Phillipps, one of H N Scrimshaw's team, taking over as manager.

R B Gibbons proposed that managers of subsidiary companies be paid commission based on the net profit achieved by the company under their control. The board agreed. He also proposed, and it was agreed, that managers could buy shares in CMC provided purchase money was not borrowed, and that any sales were made back through the CMC. This gave the managers a proper stake in the business under their control. Before Ford came to New Zealand, CMC often started businesses, with the appointed manager putting in capital and subsequently buying out control. The risks in the early thirties were greater, and managers often could not afford the money, so many subsidiary companies were later 100% owned by CMC.

The Courtenay Place nine-storey building was casually let on a floor by floor basis, and then finally leased to the Crown, as offices for the Inland Revenue Department, on November 30 1938. The lease was for up to 21 years, with three yearly rights of renewal, or outright purchase, at the 1937 valuation of £150,000.

In December 1938 import control regulations were introduced, together with exchange controls, to try to stem the flow of capital out of New Zealand. The country could not spend more than it was earning and, with farming still not receiving realistic returns, government had to control expenditure.

In just a decade motor vehicles had developed rapidly and became much more reliable, with huge technical advances and radically changed appearances. More and more New Zealanders bought new or used cars, many on hire purchase, and discovered freedom to travel where they wanted to, despite the stringencies of the early 1930s.

Edsel Ford was responsible for body design at Ford, and Ford cars had become very stylish through the work of designer Bob Gregoire and Edsel's artistic influence. There was however, a lag in chassis design as Henry Ford blocked changes.

Hope Gibbons said at the annual meeting in March 1939:

"You would all probably like me to forecast the future, but at this time that is a little beyond my powers. If it could be done by accepting business and economic conditions, I might arrive at some

WHERE CARS CAME FROM

Source%		1930	1936	1939
UK	BU	23.9	35.7	19.7
UK	CKD		19.2	41.2
Canada	BU	55.4	12.6	0.1
Canada	CKD		6.2	33.9
USA	BU	20.6	3.8	2.3
USA	CKD		22.4	2.4
Europe	BU	0.1	0.004	0.02
Europe	CKD			0.4

1939 STATISTICS

Cars registered   215,210 - decade change up 39%
Trucks registered   62,790 - decade change up 79%

New Zealand had a population of 1,640,000 people, with the second highest world vehicle density.

USA	1 car for	5.6	people
	1 vehicle for	4.9	people
NZ	1 car for	7.6	people
	1 vehicle for	5.9	people
Canada	1 car for	9.5	people
	1 vehicle for	8	people
Australia	1 car for	12.5	people
	1 vehicle for	9	people
Britain	1 car for	24	people
	1 vehicle for	18	people

TRAFFIC DENSITY PAST A TALLY POINT:
Auck – Ham (Tamaki)   1934/5   2,698;   1937/8   4,217
Wgton –Paekak (Porirua)   1934/5   959;   1937/8   1,854
Chch – Timaru (Tinwald) 1934/5   542;   1937/8   558

TRACTORS IN USE IN 1940 TOTALLED 11,278
1940 number holdings with tractors was   10,435
1940 number holdings with only horses   50,451
1940 holdings with no horse or tractor   25,418

IN THE 1939 YEAR THE MOTOR INDUSTRY COLLECTED:

Customs duty tax, tariff, fuel, etc	£6.18million
Of this, spent on Main Highways	£3.43million
Transferred to Consolidated Fund	£2.75million

Ngauranga Gorge was a tight winding road (middle), built in the 1850s, which few people used. In 1938 it was closed for a year while the new road was carved in two huge 's' bends (top), ready for the 1940 centennial. [The 1912 photograph, A P Godber collection ref: F-1395-1/2, Alexander Turnbull Library. The 1938 photograph is from the New Zealand AA collection]

reasonably definite conclusions, but politics both here and abroad will most likely play an important part, and to forecast the future of politics is difficult. If any of you gentlemen can assist us in that we will be pleased." The world scene was now quite unstable, and when the Second World War was declared on September 3 1939, it was not a great surprise. The thirties had been a turbulent decade that had bruised and battered many people's lives and, with prospects of more to come, optimism was in short supply.

A centennial show-off, this over-bridge, one of the first in New Zealand, is still in use today. The ships are very different, the trains belch smoke, and there are very few high rise buildings. [Photo: S C Smith collection ref: G-45295-1/2, Alexander Turnbull Library]

CHAPTER FIVE

THE CHALLENGES OF WAR: RATIONING & SHORTAGES

After months of anxious speculation, Britain declared war on Germany on September 3 1939. New Zealand followed suit the next day when a very tired prime minister Michael Joseph Savage announced with due rhetoric that Britain was at war, and "where she stands, we stand".

Quite apart from the horror of another world conflict only 21 years after the First World War, New Zealand was still a British Empire outpost, with the 'home' country reliant on New Zealand for food and help. As a Dominion, New Zealand stood with Britain and again offered to send armed forces, albeit with some conditions after the Great War fiascos that had caused unnecessary loss of life. For the New Zealand government, it was an economic godsend after the balance of payments difficulties of the previous three years, as Britain guaranteed to buy everything farmers could produce at good prices.

Despite the war the Centennial Exhibition went ahead, celebrating New Zealand's 100th anniversary of the signing of the Treaty of Waitangi on February 6 1940. Staged from November 8 1939 until May 4 1940, it had been planned for a number of years. In the special buildings constructed at Rongotai, Wellington, and opened by Governor General, Lord Galway, Ford Motor Company had a massive stand with 21 staff and exhibited all manner of 'new' technology: stroboscopes, brake reaction testers, paint fade testers and cut away displays. There were also service teams dissembling and reassembling engines and a special visitors lounge, the 'in' place to meet your friends for a cup of tea. Ford dealers previewed the exhibition during their conference in late October 1939. Amazingly, by the time it closed in May 1940, two thirds of New Zealand's population or 1,056,417 people had officially visited the Ford stand.

Vehicle stocks were quite high in 1939 as importers had over-estimated demand, following the changes to tariff in 1935. For three years factories had tried to get maximum throughput to cover their investment costs, importing far too much completely knocked down (CKD) stock, and dealers had been pushed and cajoled to sell and overtrade on new vehicles, with the predictable result of large stocks of both new and used cars.

On October 4 1939, the government passed the Emergency Regulations Act rationing petrol and soon afterwards, many food and clothing items. Fuel was very tight and rationing allowed about 150 miles per month.

Fuel was rationed on car size: 7hp cars were allowed 4 gallons per month; 10hp-19hp cars received 6 gallons; and 20hp+ cars 8 gallons per month. When the government requisitioned 1938 and 1939 used cars from dealers, for war use, the pressure on used car stocks was relieved, but dealers were left with the older, less desirable cars. However, much of the new vehicle stock was also requisitioned, and

It was the 100th anniversary of the Treaty of Waitangi on February 6 1940, and New Zealand celebrated with the Centennial Exhibition in a specially built venue at Rongotai, Wellington.

Ford had a large exhibition and invited all Ford dealers to attend at the time of the annual conference. Colonial Motor Company board members had a special invitation and Hope Gibbons is accompanied by R B, H B and N B, with George Jackson and staff.

The Governor General, Lord Galway opened the Centennial Exhibition and parties of guests were invited.

when total import restrictions came into force, dealer stocks quickly depleted.

On March 27 1940, Prime Minister Savage died. He had been in indifferent health for two years, exacerbated by dissident Labour MPs and then the worry of leading a country into war. Many other New Zealanders were called up in a different way to serve their country. This included over 350 men and women from the Colonial Motor Company and subsidiaries, nearly half of all staff.

CMC had just got its feet on the ground again after the Depression, followed by Ford's take-over of assembly and distribution. War meant the company now faced a new and different set of challenges: high contingent liabilities from hire purchase, lack of manpower especially technical, and a lack of vehicles to sell. The challenge was going to be how to break even.

In May 1940, Jim Thornton, principal owner of Northland Motors, died suddenly at Kaitaia. The company had financed him into the business and was asked to take it over by his family. CMC bought out his shares at par and Northland Motors became a subsidiary, but it was still available for sale to a suitable buyer.

The managing director's eldest son, 2nd Lt Hopeful Hope (Bun) Gibbons was killed in action in 1941, and far too many other staff members were similarly lost or seriously injured during the war. The impact these tragedies had on those left at home was immense. Hardly anyone was spared from the loss or maiming of a near relative or friend.

Retail sales and business in the subsidiary companies fell away very quickly, particularly after petrol was rationed, and, of course, profits fell. On the other hand, with staff being enlisted, there was a smaller wage bill. With turnover halved by the end of 1940, management was asked to focus on reducing contingent liabilities, stocks of used cars and debtors as quickly as possible. Within a year these items were less than a third and rapidly reduced.

Despite the uncertainty in dealerships, CMC's manufacturing department and Standard Motor Bodies were now busy making war goods. As the NZ Expeditionary Forces geared up, the government's Munitions Department issued contracts to make Air Force fire engines and 'crash wagons', ambulances,

Air Raid Precaution (ARP) fire pump trailers, stationary fire pumps, special steel bodies for army trucks, ammunition containers, first aid boxes, stretchers, aiming targets, and a variety of leather goods.

Most of the fire pumps were for the armed forces, but a number were also for New Zealand's protection, and were supplied under the Emergency Precautions (EPS) Scheme to public works, forestry and fire boards, upgrading much of their

Top: V8 4 x 4 Army fire tender for desert use.
Middle: Small rural volunteer fire board unit built from a 1938 V8 car.
Bottom: Special CMC Civil Aviation crash tender with Ford F12 Marmon Harrington 6 x 6 and 250hp V8 engine, fog and foam sprayers.

Army base fire tender with front mounted pump on one ton V8 chassis.

A CMC V8 crash tender with foam tanks and fog sprayers for RNZAF.

Two 4 x 4 forest fire units specially developed for NZ Forest Service, based on a military forward control rear engined V8 4 x 4 'Beaverette' chassis. A massive water tanker with pumping gear driven off the PTO, could be controlled by one operator (opposite bottom). The fire tender (right) used a high pressure water or fog hose through the roof hatch. These highly manoeuvrable units performed well over difficult terrain, climbing 1 : 3 hills.

equipment.

Meanwhile, New Zealand was worried about an enemy attack, especially from Japan. It was thought likely that such an attack would be from the sea with cruiser-size guns and would be on main ports using incendiary shells aimed at starting fires and disabling local services. Emergency planning took place using the 1931 Napier earthquake as a model.

All major ports were provided with heavy gun-emplacements, and the New Zealand Home Guard was mobilised with personnel not able to serve overseas, providing fire watches and readied for emergency help. New Zealand had a strict blackout. Blackout curtains had to be installed, there were no streetlights, and driving was difficult at night as masks were placed over headlights.

More and more work was commissioned by the Munitions Department, and both Standard Motor Bodies and CMC were declared 'essential

Home guard practising with the V8 trailer pump in central Wellington in 1941. The unit could lift large volumes of water up to 100ft high.
[Photo: The Dominion *]*

industries'. Ford Motor Company was in the same category, making hand grenades plus a large variety of war goods in addition to assembly of some war vehicles, and later making armoured bren gun carriers, and refurbishing damaged vehicles.

By now it was impossible to get a normal supply of spare parts for vehicle maintenance and repairs unless they were 'essential' for war use. Shipping was restricted, and after Japan attacked Pearl Harbour in December 1941, arrivals were spasmodic as they often waited to travel in convoys.

New Zealand was pleased when US training bases were established at Wellington and Auckland for training, and in the Far North at Waipapakauri where Pacific and Tasman ocean reconnaissance flights were based. As US troops moved to the front, others came for training, and later many were sent back to New Zealand for rest and recreation.

American industries were quickly geared up to mass production of vehicles, guns, tanks, ships and aeroplanes. Shipbuilding was reinvented and new all steel 'Liberty', K Class for cargo and P Class for personnel, and freighter ships were mass-produced in the US with welded hulls, saving both time and materials.

Many of these ships were rushed into service to protect the North Atlantic freighters from German U-boats, and were very basic, with no fire fighting equipment. The P and K ships very soon appeared in the Pacific, and with the higher ambient temperatures there was a much higher fire risk. In the Battle of the Coral Sea, the fire from one incendiary shell could destroy a whole ship. When the US Navy found it could get fire pumps fitted very quickly by CMC, ships en route for the invasion of the Solomons and Tarawera, or servicing the New Hebrides, would arrive in Wellington to have the equipment fitted. CMC would install two, sometimes three, two-stage Sulzer fire pumps and hose equipment, often in 24 hours. These were driven by 100hp Gray marine diesels, as the US Navy would not use petrol engines because of fire risk.

Many ships arrived with deck cargo of boxed Gray engines – maintenance spares for landing craft (LCTs) – and then had the pumps and equipment built and fitted by CMC, which got the pumps cast and machined all over New Zealand, wherever engineers had spare capacity. It was quite an achievement by the staff to build and install fire-fighting equipment, and to despatch a ship so quickly.

CMC settled into a new pattern, and subsidiary Ford dealer companies tried to eke a living from servicing vehicles, but it

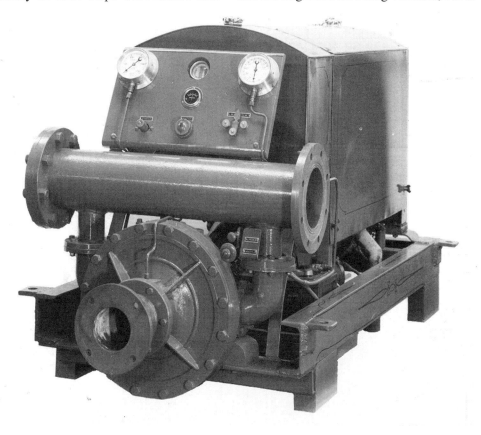

This large fire-pumping unit for ships used a Gray marine diesel.

was a difficult period. Vehicle sales were almost non-existent by 1942. Rather than having four departments, business was condensed by most dealers into two areas – workshop and everything else. Skilled mechanics were in very short supply, and many women took up the challenge of repairing and servicing vehicles. Most of the mechanics still at dealerships were older and were only certificated, so it was not possible to train apprentices. It was a challenge for dealerships to break even, and many could not.

Despite the difficulties, lateral thinking 'No. 8 wire' solutions were common. If you couldn't get petrol, why not use coal gas? Hutchinson Motors built a monstrous frame over the roof of an Anglia and mounted a huge sack of gas to drive the engine. The coal gas was not very efficient, but at least you could drive around. With a range of 20 miles it was limited by the location of gasworks, and not much use to country people.

When gas producers were invented – coal was burnt and separated into gas – they gave a little more range. This apparatus was mounted on a special bracket hung on the back of the vehicle and, more often, on the running board, or cut into the front fender. When a vehicle was going along the road belching smoke it was hard to tell if it was using a gas producer, had caught fire, or was about to blow up. Sometimes it was all three!

Kerosene was more plentiful than petrol, and once an engine was hot, you could switch a low compression motor over from petrol to kerosene, but woe betide the person who forgot to switch back to petrol before stopping. There really were no successful alternatives to petrol for private motoring and most people got about on foot or bicycle, or on horses in the country, keeping their precious petrol for special days.

Repairing vehicles became an art form when spare parts and tyres were not available, with many vehicles fitted with parts from wrecks of entirely different makes. Lateral thinking, innovation and Kiwi ingenuity were the order of the day.

Ebor Street, in contrast to dealerships, was a hive of activity. Standard Motor Bodies was turning out hundreds of steel bodies each month for army trucks, in addition to building more specialised fire and crash tenders. The CMC manufacturing department was committed to building ARP

fire pump trailers, plus other specialised equipment. Often they would be waiting for engines or parts to arrive and have to part-process trailer pumps, ready to assemble and despatch. Pumps were cast in foundries at Dunedin, Wanganui and Wellington, and then mated, machined, built up and tested by specialists at Ebor Street. Some of the work had to be sub-contracted to companies with spare capacity in Auckland, Wellington and Christchurch. Long hours were worked to meet shipping deadlines and maintain production schedules. Many production staff averaged over 50 hours work a week when the pressure went on.

In August 1942, the Munitions Department asked CMC to supply 600 extra fire pump trailers, at the rate of 100 per month, with further orders to follow. The US Forces and Allied Eastern Supply Group had seen and wanted them. Expanding production four times over was quite a feat when resources were so scarce. A further 324 engines were made ready for shipment, with a £10,000 deposit paid to Ford, and the next 300 ordered, which seemed to be standard. Large quantities of raw materials were needed so continuous production could be maintained, and some Standard Motor Bodies staff members were shifted around to help fill the orders. Trailer pumps were as expensive as cars, costing £378 each, plus there was additional equipment – 400ft of hoses, standpipes, branches, nozzles and filters, sometimes costing an extra £100 per unit. Accurate records with serial numbers had to be kept.

After Ford took over assembly and distribution in 1936, the nine-storeyed building in Courtenay Place was rented

A coal gas sack mounted on a light steel frame, would give a range of 20–30 miles on this Anglia, and saved precious petrol rations of 4 gallons (18 litres) per month.

floor by floor for two years until December 1938, when Inland Revenue took a lease for 21 years, with three year reviews, including an option to purchase at £150,000 at any review. The Auckland Fox Street assembly buildings were sold in 1938 to International Harvester Company. Timaru Motors leased a portion of its old assembly plant to the army, and Avery Motors' new building was leased for army stores – both for the duration of the war plus six months. Extensions planned for Stevens Motors were postponed.

Many of CMC's subsidiaries were occupying inferior premises, so company managers were briefed to look out for suitable premises – several opportunities came up during the war years. Craik Motors, Te Awamutu purchased an adjacent house property that enabled later expansion, and the large J G Ward Estate building in Dee Street, Invercargill was purchased in 1941 for £15,000. Macaulay Motors was located in the lane immediately behind this building, and the newly acquired premises gave a much better sales presence in the main business area. D McL Wallace's garage premises at Te Aroha

A standard wartime trailer pump used a 100hp Mercury Ford V8 engine. Not only could it be used for fire fighting but also to disperse flood waters, and on occasion operated continuously for weeks at a time.

Below: A group of 75 trailer pumps ready for despatch to the Western Front.

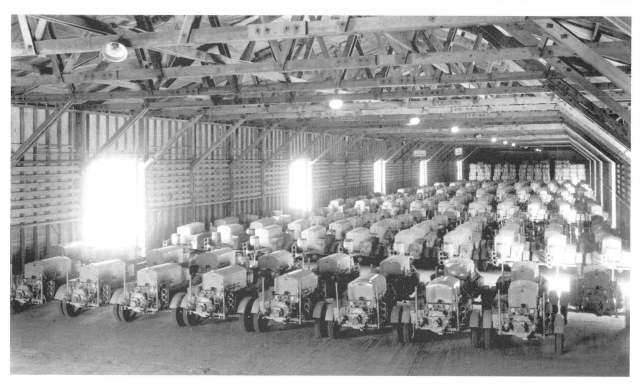

EDSEL BRYANT FORD
1893 - 1942

Edsel Bryant Ford, president of Ford, died at his home on May 26 1942. He was a very capable, sensitive and artistic man who had responsibility for all styling at Ford and Lincoln. There has been little said but, in his 1986 book *Ford*, Robert Lacey claims Edsel Ford died from cancer, or undulant fever, or ulcers. Many said it was due to the stress his father Henry placed him under. The family will tell you he died from a broken heart. He had worked tirelessly, and since 1938 in great pain, to keep Ford Motor Company functioning, despite the endless interference of his father. Henry Ford made his only son Edsel, president of Ford Motor Company in 1919, then proceeded to undermine and interfere with his decisions over the next 22 years.

Edsel Ford's death was a tragedy that threatened the very existence of the Ford Motor Company. The graft-ridden board voted Henry Ford as president again, but he was living in an orbit of the past, and not capable of running the vast company.

Dismayed, the family recalled Edsel Ford's son Henry II from the navy, to take over their interests. Somehow the company stayed together until September 21 1944 when, persuaded by his wife Clara, 81 year old Henry resigned in favour of his grandson, Henry Ford II. Ford Motor Company, although not out of the woods, was safe again.

Henry and Clara Ford with their grandson Henry Ford II.

were purchased for £3,500, then leased to the army for the duration of the war plus six months.

Hutchinson Motors leased their Bowling Rink premises for military use in Christchurch and Neal's Garage at Otahuhu was purchased for £4,100 by John W Andrew and Sons. Northland Motors was hit by a tropical cyclone in August 1942, which demolished most of the premises, but there was only one minor staff injury and the buildings were temporarily restored. A section in York Street was sold off and the leased garage premises at Waipukurau were purchased. In New Plymouth, two shops in Devon Street, adjoining the dealership were bought for £5,500.

By 1944, some troops had returned home, helping to relieve the skills shortage. Some were back in their old jobs, others by choice or circumstances were in different jobs. A few did not return to work and had difficulty settling down. Rehabilitation was not easy and often took time. Many with injuries were never the same again.

CMC staff superannuation became a reality from April 1 1945, with most of those eligible joining. The benefits of the scheme included: instant life insurance cover, organised savings for retirement, with a company subsidy added to contributions, and a tax deductible saving. Although discussed as far back as 1926, there had been inhibiting factors preventing an earlier introduction. It was an important step forward in the good staff/company relationship, but did not guarantee continued employment.

W A (Bill) Fraser, managing director of Avery Motors, died suddenly in September 1945, the first beneficiary from the full life cover of the superannuation scheme. He was only 45. H B Gibbons said the organisation had lost both a man of fine business ability and judgment, and a loyal and strong friend. Bill Fraser had been Wellington branch manager, taking over Avery Motors when Col Avery went to Army Headquarters before the outbreak of war.

Victory in Europe finally came on May 8 1945, but the war against Japan in the Pacific and South East Asia continued until August 15 1945. The record shows that the company made a large contribution to the war effort:
• Over 350 staff members were enlisted

in the NZ Armed Forces, and at least 10 were killed.
• Over 3,500 fire pump trailers were manufactured, 1,811 supplied to NZ Forces and over 1,600 more sent overseas to the allied forces. Many more were supplied to local authorities.
• Over 5,000 steel truck bodies were built for the NZ Armed Forces.
• Over 113 fire engines and crash tenders were built, and another 28 for New Zealand fire boards and the forest service.
• A large volume of hydraulic gear and pumping equipment and smaller equipment was made for the NZ and US Armed Forces.
• £65,000 was contributed to War Loans.

Peace was wonderful, but normality was not as it had been. Normal was rationing, as were import restrictions, building restrictions, controlled land sales, and power cuts; normal was take this or nothing; normal meant shortages and frustration. And as far as new cars were concerned, most people had to wait over 25 years to get a real choice.

To New Zealand troops who had been to war, coming home was often a disappointment. Many had been to exciting places and had extraordinary experiences. Others had learned to drive, and some to fly. Settling down, with all the accompanying shortages, was a very humdrum affair.

Import licences were announced in June 1945, to the value of 75% of the CIFE (cost including freight and excise) of car licences allowed in the base period of January to June 1938 from Britain only. This could only be used for CKD unless there were extenuating circumstances. It was likely many New Zealand factories would be short of assembly staff. Trucks chassis could be imported from Britain to 100% of the base period Jan-June 1938. Supplementary licences were granted in January 1946 for cars from Britain, Canada and US of 35% of the 1938 base period for CKD and 25% for BU. Similarly, trucks were increased to 50%. More cars were allowed from Britain the next year if they were CKD, but fewer from Canada and USA. Trucks fared much better and doubled in volume.

The armed services were disbanded quickly, and most war vehicles sold off. Cars and trucks were keenly sought, and

commanded huge prices compared to their pre-war worth. When released by the Munitions Department, George Jackson, managing director of Ford NZ, left for Canada and Dagenham to arrange new vehicle supplies.

Assembly at the Seaview plant started again, firstly for trucks, in October 1945. Ford were still re-conditioning US General Purpose vehicles recovered from the Pacific war zones. "Jeepers creepers," US Major General Lynch had said when he first saw one demonstrated on rough ground; and so it became a jeep. The drab olive colour going down the line contrasted sharply with the brightly coloured new civilian trucks. New forward control V8 bus chassis were imported from Canada, to have bodies built by NZ Motor Bodies at Petone; the first went to Auckland and Christchurch City Councils.

At 11.00am on Thursday May 16 1946, George Jackson received the keys from production manager Ted Signal for the first civilian car to be assembled since 1940 –

an English Prefect 'Ten'. The first Canadian V8s arrived soon afterwards, and Ford made their first, pitifully small, vehicle allocations to dealers.

Government legislators ensured cars remained in short supply. For every car imported there were 20 buyers, despite prices rising by 50% in many cases. Waiting lists were normal, as were 'incentives' offered to salesmen and managers, to jump the queue. Some dealers took the bait and lived to regret it, losing not only their integrity, but also their jobs. Neither Ford nor CMC would tolerate 'back handers' and came down heavily on those who took them. Ford dispensed with two dealers and CMC with two dealer principals.

The Fordson tractor franchise, taken away in April 1938, was given back to Ford dealers again in February 1946. The 20hp Model N Fordson had not changed much in 30 years, but in 1947 the new model E27N or, as it was affectionately known, 'Cast Iron Clarice', was a step up from the

George Jackson, Ford NZ managing director, accepts the keys of the first post-war Prefect, from production manager Ted Signal, at 11am on May 16 1946. It was the first private car to be produced since early 1940.

Model N. Even though it had the same base kerosene engine, options included a higher performance 27hp petrol engine, and a 6 cylinder Perkins diesel for the first time. A lot of development had been done during the war, and hydraulic rear lift arms were available, together with a choice of alternative gear ratios to suit different needs. It ran on cleated steel or low-pressure rubber tyres.

This was great news for Ford dealers, as New Zealand was starting serious farm development. Soon afterwards, the new light 18hp Ford Ferguson tractor was introduced, giving another perspective and opportunity. It was, though, to be short-lived, due to an argument with Harry Ferguson over who owned the hydraulic patents.

As farming developed, new uses were

Top: "What'll she do", they wonder as they gaze at the features.

Middle: Ploughing with the 18hp Ford Ferguson, Bob Macaulay (right) supervising.

Bottom: A typical Canterbury field day with farmers arriving early to see the new E27N Fordson.

found for tractors. Much of New Zealand's hill country farmland was still covered in manuka 'scrub', preventing grass growth. Hundreds of Fordson tractors were fitted with extra width steel wheels and 'scrub' bars, which literally pushed over the manuka trees and crushed them. Later these areas were 'burnt off' and sown with pasture grass.

Hope Gibbons was 90 when he died on June 25 1947. He had been a director of the company for over 28 years, and chairman since December 1919, quietly having a huge influence, not only on CMC, but also Hope Gibbons Ltd. He was treated

Top: John W Andrew's Otahuhu showroom in 1946, showed a large selection of vehicles: a Fordson N tractor costing £386, V8 coupe, £670, V8 Fordor, £723 and Prefect, £520. But only the tractor was 'available'. Shortages of cars were to be a problem for the next 25 years.

Bottom: Ford NZ tractor manager, Bill Toomey, introduced a sales competition for five coveted tractor banners amongst dealers in 1948. Tractors were one of the few vehcles in free supply to dealers, and sales took off. Field days were a feature, with ploughing demonstrations, fuel consumption tests and equipment displays drawing large crowds of farmers, few of whom had driven a tractor before.

HENRY FORD 1863 - 1947

Henry Ford was 83 when he died at his home, 'Fair Lane', Dearborn (pictured below) on April 4 1947. Henry Ford's mass production methods revolutionised industry. He had given the world affordable transport on the roads, and released people from their farm drudgery with tractors, creating a new sense of freedom and wealth for many. Edgar A Guest said in a stirring radio tribute: "We are all his debtors now. There is none of us, rich or poor, in humble or high place, whose life has not been bettered by his labour. He came into this world when the backs of men were weary and heavy-laden. By the dreams he had, pursued and achieved, the burdens of drudgery were taken from the shoulders of the humble and given to the steel and wheel."

Henry Ford was a remarkable man who contributed hugely to the world in many ways. One hundred thousand queued to walk silently past his bier at the pillared hall in Greenfield Village on April 9 1947. Twenty thousand stood in the rain outside St Paul's Cathedral next day, and Detroit stopped to honour his funeral at 2.30pm. Henry Ford put the world on wheels.

HOPEFUL GIBBONS 1856 - 1947

Hopeful Gibbons was the sixth of 12 children born to shipbuilder Robert Gibbons and his wife Sarah at Tasmania on October 4 1856. The family sailed to Dunedin in 1862, but later moved to Wellington, Nelson and Onehunga. Hope Gibbons left school at 13, after taking exception to a remark by his teacher, and worked selling clothes, as a handy boy on the wharf, on coastal ships, and later in a brewery and sawmill. He worked in a shipping business at Gisborne, where he obtained his ship's engineer certificate in 1876 and took charge of a lightering business, destroyed by floods in 1878.

After helping his brother establish a brewery at Napier, Hope, aged 23, purchased his own brewery at Patea. He married Jessie Barnes in 1881 and they lived on a small farmlet at Patea. A keen sportsman, he played representative rugby for Taranaki West Coast. The family moved to Wanganui in 1895 and bought the Wanganui Brewery for £3,000.

Hope and his sons agreed in 1904 that they would work together as a business team. They purchased 50% of J B Clarkson & Co, cycle importers at Palmerston North, opened a Wellington branch in 1910, and later took over fully, renaming it Hope Gibbons Ltd. The company was one of the largest importers of motor vehicle accessories and parts, motorcycles and motorcars, as well as cycles. Later they imported the first refrigerators and radios, and were involved in early radio broadcasting. The family built up extensive farm holdings, and shares in other businesses – Southern Cross Biscuits in Wanganui, flax mills at Shannon, an engineering business at Palmerston North, salt mining, road building and quarry ventures. Controlling shares in their largest venture, Colonial Motor Company Ltd, were purchased in 1918, with Hope Gibbons remaining chairman for 28 years until his death.

All four sons moved to Wellington, but Hope stayed in Wanganui, involved in public affairs, and serving on many committees including those for

Queen Victoria's Jubilee, South African War Memorial and Cook's Gardens sports ground. He chaired the Wanganui fund raising effort in the First World War, raising £68,000 in 10 days and later constructing the Durie Hill War Memorial Tower. Awarded the MBE for his war work, he was elected to the Wanganui Power Board in 1923, and was Mayor of Wanganui from 1924-27, a period in which it became New Zealand's fifth largest city. He was involved in the Peat Park Trust, the purchase of the Corn Market Reserve, Kowhai Park, the city abattoirs, construction of the airport, the Alexander Museum, and many parks and reserves.

Hope and Jessie Gibbons raised funds to revive the Wanganui Horticultural Society and the local Plunket Society and, in 1921, bought and donated a soldiers' convalescent home, which later became the Jessie Hope Gibbons Maternity Hospital. In 1936 they gave a site for the Children's Health Camp. Hope Gibbons also assisted the St John Ambulance Association and was made Commander of the Order of St John.

Hope and Jessie Gibbons travelled extensively, and were known for their hospitality to many, including governors-general, at Hikurangi, their home on Bastia Hill. Jessie Gibbons died in 1936.

Alfred Hemingway, chairman of the Wanganui Education Board, wrote of Hope Gibbons:

"We know him by his work – work that will cause him to be remembered when all present have passed .... We can with truth say of him that his life was gentle and the elements so mixed in him, that nature will yet rise up and say to all the world – this was a man."

Ford F100 pick up set new standards for light trucks.

Rhys Sale became president of Ford Canada after W R Campbell died suddenly in 1949. He met New Zealand dealers soon afterwards and is seen here talking to Orm Hutchinson.

with the greatest respect by everyone who came in contact with him. People admired his fair dealing, good advice, leadership and foresight. His grandson, Frederick Norman (Bill) Gibbons, managing director of Selwyn Motors, Palmerston North, was appointed director and Hope B Gibbons became chairman. Les Clarke was shifted

to Te Aroha to manage Hawke Motors in 1948 and Merv Dineen to manage Te Kuiti Motors. Director, J M McLean died in May 1947, having been on the board since 1931, contributing much of his extensive financial experience in banking to advise wisely through the critical early thirties and during the restructuring after Ford took over in 1936. Ormond Hutchinson was appointed a director in May 1947, bringing his vast knowledge of market retailing to the board. After he returned from the army, R W (Pat) Stewart was appointed secretary. Jack Chapman had acted as secretary while Pat Stewart was overseas.

The subsidiary companies needed to become independent to fit in with Ford's policies, and the capital of each was increased so they could own their own land and buildings. This was approved in October 1947, and CMC sold the properties to them. From then, dividends were paid to shareholders, instead of rent. They could then be properly compared financially with other Ford dealers and with like companies in the CMC Group.

Following the unexpected death of W R Campbell, Rhys M Sale was appointed president of Ford Canada, and toured New Zealand in January 1949. After visiting a number of Colonial Motor Company's subsidiaries and meeting dealers, he congratulated the company on its organisation.

Henry Ford II was now fully at the helm of Ford in Detroit and, knowing his own business shortcomings, he hired a team of high achievers to get Ford going again. The

'Whiz Kids' initial appraisal, under the guidance of Ernie Breech, showed that during the 1930s, Ford had made very few mechanical changes to the V8 chassis, and while the car was very sound and stylish, it had been left behind by other American models.

On March 14 1949, Ford introduced a brand new model, the Forty-Niner. The car was a radical departure for Ford. The V8 Forty-Niner changed everything; with its independent front suspension and two semi-elliptic leaf spring rear suspension, replacing the single transverse spring. Passengers rode in luxury between the axles. There was a host of mechanical refinements, with 'Magic touch' brakes, and a major styling change, the full width body doing away with separate mudguards and running boards. The car was a stunner, and an instant hit everywhere.

Ford dealers reported 60,000 people visited the dealerships to see the cars the first day, and people came for miles to see the new Ford. Within three days, 148,000 had been to Ford showrooms. Good as 'The Car of 1949' was, only a handful arrived, making their allocation a nightmare for dealers. New import regulations meant very few cars could be bought from dollar countries with most being imported from England.

John Andrew died in early 1949. He had been a high profile, enthusiastic Auckland Ford dealer since January 1917. He used to doff his hat to customers as they passed by in their Fords. How did he know they were his customers? Quite simple really; he trimmed off one corner of the number plate of the cars he sold. When beach racing began at Muriwai he supported his son Stan's participation in highly modified and stripped down Model Ts.

Four years after the war's end CMC was still unable to start improvements to subsidiary company premises because war regulations were still in place, restricting building and land sales. Petrol was still rationed. The public was angry about

The Forty-Niner Ford V8 was an instant hit across the world, providing new standards of ride and comfort; braking, performance and styling. Henry II's 'Whizz Kids' had succeeded in getting Ford back on track in three years. It was a snip at £1,021; on the 'black market' it cost £1,500.

1949 STATISTICS

Cars registered   230,227,   decade change 7%
Trucks registered 119,792,   decade change 26%
70% of cars registered were over 10 years old
3% of cars registered were over 20 years old

NZ POPULATION WAS 1,892,100 IN 1949:

Density NZ	1 car for	8.2 people
	1 vehicle for	5.4 people

TRAFFIC DENSITY DAILY PAST A TALLY POINT:

Auck-Hamilton	(at Tamaki)	7,825
Wlg-Paekak	(at Porirua)	2,742
Chc – Timaru	(at Tinwald)	1,198

TRACTORS IN USE WERE 27,447, UP 143% IN DECADE

1949 number holdings with tractors was -	24,416
1949 number holdings with only horses -	37,057
1949 holdings with no horse or tractor -	25,684

IN THE 1949 YEAR THE MOTOR INDUSTRY COLLECTED:

Customs duty tax, tariff, fuel, etc	£9.11million
Of this, spent on main highways	£0.97million
Transferred to Consolidated Fund	£8.14million

inflation and impatient with controls. The Labour government liked controls, and the bureaucratic power that went with them. Left wing unions were supported, and they created industrial unrest, particularly on the waterfront. There were suggestions that international communism was linked with the extreme left. Not all New Zealanders agreed with the government's approach and Labour was defeated in the 1949 elections.

It had been a turbulent decade and, although there had been triumphs, it had been an unhappy time for many.

CHAPTER 6
PLANNING AHEAD

After the war, refugees arrived from Europe together with larger numbers from Britain and the Dutch settlements in Indonesia. New Zealand's new immigration policies attracted people from England and, with the assistance of the Dutch government, from Holland, and shiploads of 'Ten Pound Poms' and 'Dutchies' arrived on specially chartered boats. The majority were single and in their twenties. They were charged a nominal £10 (normally £100) for their passage, when they signed a two year 'work where directed' contract. Most quickly adapted and took up citizenship.

Apart from boosting New Zealand's population and creating a demand for housing, immigrants supplied the country with new skills and a ready-made workforce. Many new government projects were started, particularly the building of hydro-electricity dams and distribution systems, and new roads. New industries were given protection from import competition, allowing secondary manufacturing to develop.

Road improvements had begun in the 1920s with the introduction of the Main Highways Board, but they were fairly haphazard as Depression work schemes and the Second World War stymied most plans. Besides, traffic volumes were still at low levels. 'Sealed roads' were often only a 10-12ft strip of tarseal and chips on the centre portion of a road with gravel verges, making passing quite difficult. With mostly poor foundations, roads quickly reverted to potholes.

After the war, there were new bigger trucks that could carry much greater loads. However, bridges were the most inhibiting highway factor. Initially these were built in timber, with larger spans using steel frames and some in reinforced concrete. Virtually all rural bridges were single lane, many not able to carry more than 10-15 tons gross weight. A number actually failed. Highway No.1 still had a great deal of unsealed road and many single lane bridges in the central North Island, and the Far

North was still immersed in dust or mud. Roads were becoming wider, but were categorised by axle loadings into Class I, II, III and IV, restricting vehicles according to maximum bridge loading and road capabilities.

Amendments to the Public Works Act in 1947-48 designated new motorways, limiting access to motor traffic only with

Dealers sold farmers many Fordson tractors with steel wheels and a 'scrub bar'. They pushed over manuka and gorse and then disced the flattened scrub, to be fired when dry.

no cross traffic. This was the first sign there might be a future plan. The National Roads Board was established in 1954, with the task of supervising all construction and maintenance of state highways. Local authorities and municipalities were still in charge of their own roads, but funding revenue was allocated from the National Roads Fund, and collected from road users via petrol tax, tyre tax, mileage tax, plus registration, licence, and heavy traffic fees. In addition, there was a start-up £1 million from government. Gradually expenditure increased and highways improved, many being re-aligned from the early winding coach tracks, with proper foundations and drainage.

The government also designated and constructed new highways, giving access to areas they wished to develop – the Haast Pass, Western Taupo, and the southern Coromandel Peninsula from Kopu to Hikuai. All roads took time and money, but at least there was now some sort of planning and priority.

Post Second World War farming receipts jumped with the application of super phosphate. Available in the 1930s, it hadn't been widely applied until after the war. Aerial fertiliser application was starting, and science began to play a major part in farm development. There were a

The English Pilot V8 cars were a carry over design of the 1930s US V8 but on a smaller scale. They were snapped up by a starved market, but at £864 were underpowered, old, and not a car to rave about.

The Prefect, introduced in 1936, had a facelift in 1952, with streamlined headlights. Cost £579.

large number of new backblocks farmers as a result of more rehab(ilitation) loans to returned servicemen, and the Lands and Survey Department was developing large, rough, land blocks in many remote districts, to later subdivide into economic farm units.

The first commercial aerial fertiliser applications were made at L E Daniell's Wairere Station near Masterton in 1948, using a Grumman Avenger torpedo bomber. The torpedo housing was filled with fertiliser and, when in position, the doors were opened, allowing the fertiliser to fan out over the farm. Now the thinking caps went on. Tiger Moth aircraft, used by the air force to train war pilots, were being disposed of. Cheap, manoeuvrable and adaptable, they could land and take off anywhere. The second cockpit was removed and a chute built with release vents.

Very soon a huge industry developed, applying fertilisers to previously inaccessible hill country farms. Highly productive pastures developed which increased sheep and cattle numbers dramatically, making farming viable in the hilly backblocks.

However, New Zealand still had major problems with its balance of payments and there were extremely tight Reserve Bank currency controls. Import restrictions were severe and new cars remained nearly impossible to buy. People travelling overseas had to apply for travel funds,

based on meagre New Zealand daily allowances, often finding they could not stay in reasonable hotels or eat at good restaurants, because they did not have enough money. Still, pastoral farming continued to be the main income earner and boosted the economy for a time with the 1951 wool boom.

In 1950 the 'No Remittance Licence' scheme was introduced, allowing the importation of vehicles using private funds held outside New Zealand. This meant that if assets or shares were held in another country, these could be sold overseas and the money used to pay a deposit for a new car, which could then be imported. This move quickly made the new car market a very competitive one for people with overseas assets. There were then two classes of new car buyer, a first class buyer with overseas funds and a third class one without; salesmen had to quickly assess which type of buyer they were talking to!

When George Jackson, Ford NZ managing director, left for Canada on promotion to vice president, overseas sales in May 1950, Ralph K Johnson arrived

Ralph K Johnson was briefly managing director after George Jackson.
Below: Ford Thames trucks arrived in the early 1950s; this one converted for Mataura Fire Brigade. Although better than the Sussex, they were small, 2 and 3 tonners, with a gutless 4 cylinder petrol tractor engine. The chassis/cab cost £851.

The new Five Star Zepyhr and Consul were an instant success in 1951, and arrived at the same time as 'No Remittance'. During the wool boom many were imported built up. A Zephyr 6 cost £905 and Consul 4 £815.

from Canada as his replacement. Welcomed by dealers at their conference, Ralph Johnson said he was very aware of all the shortages, but pleased to see dealers had sold record numbers of new Fordson tractors the previous year for good profit, and that there were excellent opportunities for No Remittance sales.

Meanwhile, both H B Gibbons and N B Gibbons were in semi-retirement and poor health. The effects of the Depression, Ford's takeover and the losses of the war, as well as age, were taking their toll. In their absence much of the work fell particularly to R B Gibbons, and A B, who was managing director of Hope Gibbons Ltd. H B retired as managing director in 1950 but remained chairman, and R B took over as managing director and deputy chairman.

Additional help was required in head office, and L H (Les) Clarke, manager at Hawke Motors Te Aroha, was appointed general manager in May 1950. In October 1950, Norman B Gibbons died after a long illness, and Alfred Barton Gibbons (A B Junior) was appointed to the board.

Petrol rationing was finally removed in June 1950. The National government was determined to "free the country from socialism, inflation, bureaucracy and high taxation." The government got tough with unions and there was a standoff between the militants who were mainly watersiders,

freezing and transport workers, allegedly with communist connections. After the Waterfront Strike in 1951, a snap election increased the government's majority.

From CMC's view, the vehicle shortages were very frustrating because there was a market out there that could not be satisfied. To make matters worse, Ford NZ continued splitting territories and adding new dealers. Dealers were making inadequate profits which inhibited planned improvements, but CMC decided to push ahead regardless, as their dealer staff could not work effectively under inadequate conditions.

When the Korean War boosted demand for wool in early 1951, farmers were receiving up to 240 pence (£1) per pound for super fine and 160 pence for fine wools, a huge increase on the 12 pence received during the Second World War. While the price soon came down, it settled at about half the peak, a much better level. Farmers were quickly in the market settling debt and buying new cars, tractors and trucks, with many exotic and expensive cars sold if they were available.

Car licences were initially granted in proportion to the six month history of imports measured in 1938. Post war licences were first allowed for a two year period on the basis of 75% of the six month 1938 base – $37^{1}/_{2}$% of that year. This was changed with ad hoc supplementary

licences, but dollar sources were reduced, and then 'deferred' from the US in 1948. In 1951, with the wool boom, car import licences were lifted for a short period from 'soft currency' areas (UK effectively), but restricted to lump sum grants from 'hard currency' dollar countries. Unfortunately, a number of firms, Ford included, could not use all their licence money quickly, because factories, mainly British, were locked into production 12 months ahead. Relatively few US and Canadian cars were imported in the post war period, Canada achieving more than the US, because of the British Commonwealth link. Licensing complexities continued throughout the 1950s, and the numbers of cars failed to meet demand. On the other hand, trucks and tractors for production fared well.

At a Ford NZ dealer conference on September 26 1951 sales manager Harold Ralph revealed the new Consul 4 and Zephyr 6 from Ford of Britain. Heralded as the new 'Five Star' cars, they were designed with five key new factors: overhead valve oversquare engines, within-the-wheelbase comfortable seating for six, independent front suspension, all steel integrated chassis and body, and all round hydraulic brakes. Dealers were ecstatic about the new models, a smaller version of the very modern Forty-Niner.

Public acceptance was stunning and dealers couldn't get the cars they wanted and needed. More licences were granted in November and greater numbers of cars did come in, but not nearly enough. No Remittance sales rocketed with these totally new vehicles, and many were imported built-up from Britain. The Consul 4 had a 1508cc engine, and Zephyr 6 a 2262cc

engine, and both performed well. They had 3-speed column change gears. The New Zealand versions had basic equipment, coming without heaters or radios, which were both protected imports and had to be made locally, but these cars were modern, setting standards for the decade. The Zephyr 6 was a great performer, and the Transport Department got an early share. Both Consul and Zephyr were popular in motor sport.

Following the Ford dealer conference, CMC held a two-day meeting to discuss future planning needs. On the first evening all CMC managers were invited to dinner at Mr and Mrs R B Gibbons' home and the first gold Omega watches, in recognition of 25 years continuous service (including any military call up), were presented to nine managers: R E (Ray) Clarke, L C (Les) and W G (Wilf) Gladding, Auckland; P L (Phil) Phillipps, New Plymouth; P F (Pat) Fagan, Masterton; John Hunt, Standard Motor Bodies; Orm Hutchinson, Christchurch; A C (Mac) McPherson, Dunedin and R B Gibbons.

The presentations were quite unexpected and enthusiastically received. In turn, the managers were asked to present 17 more gold watches to their own staff members who qualified. Although only a token, to many staff it was a prized possession, and this tradition has been carried on since then, usually with a ceremony at a special occasion, and has helped to preserve the very good staff and management relationship.

By the end of 1951, Macaulay Motors had delivered 300 new Fordson tractors, an average of more than one each week since

The 1952 Fordson Major took a big jump ahead, with new 40 hp diesel and petrol engines, a dual range gearbox, lift arm hydraulics and power take-off; thousands sold at £520. Hawke Motors' A & P Show stand in 1953 featured a Fordson Major tractor revolving in a manner likely to contravene today's OSH standards.

With manpower shortages in the 1950s, labour saving devices were in demand. Max Snook (above) developed the Pelican loader which unloaded a railway wagon of bulk material quickly, using one man. A further adaptation, with a slewing hydraulic boom, sped up the whole process.

Ford dealers began selling them again in 1946. Tractors had become a major profit centre for all dealers, not only for sales but also for parts and service. However, tractors needed space, nearly four times the workshop space occupied by a car and, of course, trucks were similar.

The 'all new' Fordson Major tractor range was introduced to very excited dealers in July 1952. Here was another coup: a redesigned tractor with a new Ford 40hp diesel engine, enhanced performance, improved hydraulics and a host of other refinements. There was little opposition in the medium tractor market at the time, and Ford dealers capitalised as much as they could.

The new tractors created new opportunities, with many dealers finding new applications for them. Max Snook at Hutchinson Motors, developed a clamshell loader for handling grain and coal, and Pelican loaders were soon appearing at railyards all over New Zealand. Max later developed a hydraulic chain bucket

trencher for drain and cable laying. John Holder at Northland Motors built a rear scoop loader, which mounted to the three point linkage.

In December 1952, when his health meant he could not cope with the pressures of the job, Ralph Johnson resigned as managing director of Ford NZ and returned to Canada after introducing his successor, Brock F Jamieson, to dealers. Brock Jamieson had been with Ford Canada and

Top: Queen Elizabeth II's first tour of New Zealand in late 1953 and early 1954 included a visit to Ford at Seaview. She inspected the Mk I Zephyrs on the assembly line.

Ford Malaya. He had been a prisoner of the Japanese for three and a half years, at Changi, Singapore, before rejoining Ford Canada.

In 1952, Charles D Morpeth, auditor to the company since 1909, died suddenly. H Neil Scrimshaw, still internal auditor, took over as temporary auditor but resigned following the annual balance in 1953, and died a month later. Both men had made important, but different, CMC contributions over a very long period. Neil Scrimshaw's management accounting system principles, introduced in the late 1920s are still in use today, modified for modern computer methods. J E (Jack) Haisman, a former associate of 'Scrim', was appointed auditor.

Because of the pressure tractors had put on facilities, extra land was purchased at all CMC dealers. In many cases this was on the outskirts of the towns and cities, with separate tractor and truck operations planned. However, war regulations were still in place with many local authorities controlling land sales and building restrictions delaying the process.

Northland Motors, largely destroyed by a cyclone in 1942 had approval to rebuild. A new workshop was started in 1952, followed by parts, administration and showroom gradually replacing temporary structures, and the very smart, almost totally new dealership was completed in 1955.

Queen Elizabeth was on her first royal tour of New Zealand when she paid a visit to the Ford plant at Seaview in January 1954. New Zealand was a strongly patriotic Dominion, pleased to see its Queen and her visit was enthusiastically received, people turning out in thousands to cheer and wave. The Queen shared New Zealand's grief at the Tangiwai rail disaster, Christmas Eve 1953, with the loss of 151 people.

Meanwhile, CMC was actively looking for more land near Auckland, where the population expanded rapidly after the war.

Bottom: The Ford trim cutters held particular interest.

With the new motorways foreshadowed, it was possible to work out potential sites for future development, and land was bought in key locations at New Lynn, Panmure, Wiri (later Manukau City), Otahuhu, Howick and Royal Oak. Agreement about future dealerships was reached with Ford in 1954 but, because of vehicle supply, no start-up dates for new dealerships were decided.

With all the capital demands more money was required and shareholders approved a one for one bonus issue on January 19 1954, taking capital from £300,000 to £600,000, paid out of reserves. In turn, subsidiaries were re-capitalised as needed.

In May 1954 government authorised 6,000 new vehicle licences, 1,200 from North America. To obtain North American licences, it was necessary for 'essential business users' to put their case in writing to the Board of Trade. Dealers were quickly advised of the opportunity, and a large number of the licences were granted for Canadian V8 Ranch Wagons. Many applications were fairly 'thin' in 'essential

business' terms, but were granted. This system was repeated the next year, and Ford dealers again quickly secured a good share of cars. It was apparent the squeaky joint often got the oil and later, if a good case presented itself, an application to the Board of Trade often produced a licence.

Ford NZ appointed a number of new dealers in June 1954, making full dealers of some who were only sub-agents. One large new dealer, Lewis Motors at Takapuna, was appointed without any discussion with, or warning to, John W Andrew's, taking a large portion of their prime market area and precious car allocation. This action shocked CMC whose directors thought the action unethical. There were now 80 fully-fledged Ford dealers, with no sub-agents.

When Ford came to New Zealand in 1936, one of their prime objectives was to increase market penetration, and they thought the best way to achieve this was the same as in North America – add more dealers and make them fight for market share. But New Zealand was too small, with a fragmented and scattered population.

A fair cop! Microwave speed detectors were first used by the Transport Department in 1955. Notice how, to save money, the road had a sealed centre portion and metalled sides.

Top: The new Anglia, and 4 door Prefect, had Zephyr styling and a perimeter frame floor pan, instead of a chassis, with 1172cc engine and 3 speed gearbox. An Anglia cost £612, a Prefect £638 and the 100E Van £631.

Middle: The Mark II Consul and Zephyr had larger bodies and engines. Consul cost £884, Zephyr £988 and Zodiac, shown here, £1077.

Bottom: The bus version of new Thames Trader.

*South Auckland
Motors began in
1954, at Ford's
request, taking over
John W Andrew's
Otahuhu branch on
Great South Road.*

Increases in dealer numbers simply made existing dealers weaker financially. At that time, there were North American cities with more people than the whole of New Zealand, but with fewer dealers. This attitude was to cause difficulties in New Zealand for the next 50 years. In defence against another dealer encroaching or being appointed within a territory, CMC devised a branch strategy. If a border was vulnerable, form a branch and put up an outpost to defend the territory. Despite the expense, this worked well, and in some cases the branches were made into separate dealerships to appease Ford.

In 1954 South Auckland Motors was formed at Otahuhu with CMC capital, to take over the John W Andrew's branch on Ford's insistence, and Les Gladding, previously branch manager, was appointed

to manage the new company. Although Otahuhu had been a small rural town, industrial development in the area was creating rapid expansion.

By early 1955 CMC had planned developments at subsidiary companies estimated to cost £250,000 just for the buildings. Additional new dealership premises were being planned at Auckland, Wellington, Christchurch and Dunedin, meaning projects had to be prioritised and staged, to protect cash flows. New car volumes were very difficult to predict, because licensing kept changing up and down in volume.

To try to offset the lack of new car profit, CMC's used vehicle sales operations were strengthened, and outside display areas set up at most dealerships. Used cars were restored to prime condition and, with the

*Right: Macaulay
Motors shifted into
the main business
area of Dee Street,
Invercargill in 1954,
and had a showroom
for the first time. The
Queen stayed next
door at the Grand
Hotel.*

*Opposite bottom:
Hutchinson Motors'
stand at the Royal A
& P Show 1955,
Christchurch, with
everyone in their best
outfits. It was a big
occasion, with the
Governor General in
attendance. The
Pelican loader won a
gold medal.*

HOPE BARNES GIBBONS
1882 - 1955

Hope Barnes Gibbons died on December 9 1955, at the age of 73. One of Wellington's best known business men, he led the company as managing director for over 32 years until 1950, and as chairman from 1947 until his death. His intellect and keen analytical ability to see new business directions made him the key driver in the Gibbons family team, and CMC prospered and expanded to a large organisation under his tutelage.

H B started work with J B Clarkson and Co in Palmerston North in 1905 but moved to Wellington with the business in 1910, became managing director in 1918 and changed its name to Hope Gibbons Ltd in 1921.

H B was the largest shareholder in CMC, held the Ford Agreement for New Zealand from 1919 until 1936, and was praised by Ford for having the 'best overseas performance'. In the Depression H B, and brother R B, salvaged many dealers from bankruptcy, and encouraged and staked them, thus keeping the dealer group intact, with market shares not equalled since.

Disillusioned with Ford's actions in 1936, when they cut CMC out of distribution, finance and reconditioning, he found it difficult to deal with them, and withdrew.

Prominent in the NZ Wholesale Motor & Cycle Trade Federation until its dispersal in 1934, he was first president, and then chairman of the new Motor Trade Federation (later NZ Motor Trade Assn). For many years a board member of Scots College, and finance committee chairman, he did much to stabilise the college's financial position.

An enthusiastic horticulturist, he created prize-winning gardens at Lyall Bay and Eastbourne and was a member of the Royal Institute of Horticulture which awarded him its highest accolade – Associate of Honour (AHRIH [NZ]). He was a past president of the NZ Alpine and Rock Garden Society, and a past president of the Rotary Club of Wellington.

The Johnsonville saleyards were purchased in 1955 after the Wellington northern motorway was designated. Avery Motors built a branch, and this became Newlands Motors in 1966.

Below: Avery Motors, Taranaki Street in 1958. Standard Motor Bodies occupied the low white buildings on the right, and Nos. 4, 3, 2 and 1 bay workshops run on down Ebor Street. The nine storey Ford building can be seen on the left.

shortage of new cars, were fetching really good prices. For example, a low mileage 3-year-old Zephyr still fetched the new price. Previously, apart from Auckland and Christchurch, where separate subsidiary used car companies had been formed in the 1930s, used cars had been stored in the workshop overnight and just parked anywhere during the day until they were 'cashed up'. Now used cars were a good profit centre developing consistent cash flows. Used tractors and trucks were much slower with seasonal demands affecting turnover.

In August 1955 Peter Craig Gibbons joined the CMC head office. Peter Gibbons shadowed his father, R B, from a small boy, learning an immense amount about the company, its people, and locations. He enlisted in the Royal NZ Navy on his 18th birthday, and was mainly based at Rosyth, Firth of Forth, Scotland on cruisers. After being commissioned sub-lieutenant, he returned home in January 1946 and

completed a Bachelor of Engineering degree at Canterbury University College, graduating in 1949. He then joined H N Scrimshaw's audit team before going to Timaru Motors as accountant in 1954. His first head office job was as assistant to the general manager, Les Clarke. Peter Gibbons' engineering knowledge was immediately useful on all the building projects, especially when technical difficulties occurred, as happened at Stevens Motors, Johnsonville and later in New Lynn. After a disastrous fire in the early hours of May 3 1956 at Standard Motor Bodies, he helped to settle claims disputes and refined the rebuilding design needs.

In the course of acquiring land in Lower Hutt, Pearce Holdings Ltd, a land developer, was bought, complete with land in the city's CBD. This purchase of a company in financial difficulty was cruicial to getting a large enough area amalgamated

for Stevens Motors' further development. Its tax losses provided ongoing debate with the IRD and consultants for years.

The new motorway north out of Wellington from Johnsonville to Porirua was announced and, seeing Johnsonville as a future distribution centre, 20 acres at Broderick Road, Johnsonville were purchased for Avery Motors, when put up for sale for £16,750 in July 1955. This area had been the stock saleyards and holding paddocks for the Wellington abattoir before being included in an urban development plan.

In response to its new activities, the board increased its size from seven to eight members, nominating Gordon Hope (Don) Gibbons and Peter Craig Gibbons, who were appointed at the 1956 annual meeting.

In 1957 the Mark II Consul and Zephyr 6 were introduced. The cars were a definite improvement, slightly larger with sharper styling and with refined mechanicals. The government reduced 1957 car import licences 21%.

No Canadian trucks had been imported since 1948 except for a few multi-axle heavy-duty chassis up until 1953. They had been tough

The new Thames Trader with forward control cabs in 3, 5 and 7 ton load capacities, and a bus chassis, offered a new profit opportunity for Ford dealers with its wide range of possible applications. Many farmers bought trucks to cart their own stock, because of the 30 mile rail restriction.

and popular trucks. However, government licensing favoured English trucks and the Ford Thames 2 and 3 tonners had come in, but they were small and not very popular. Late in 1957, the promised new Thames Trader 2, 3, 5 and 7 ton forward control models arrived with petrol and diesel engines. Ford was catching up on the market and becoming competitive again. The new trucks provided an opportunity to take up the slack of reduced car licences and dealers re-established Ford trucks quickly and in numbers.

Aerial topdressing expanded, and new Fletcher aircraft were able to carry much larger loads more quickly. Ingenuity remains a New Zealand characteristic and A J (Jim) Wilkinson, of Cambridge, designed a long boom half ton front end loader for the Fordson tractor, able to deal with bulk fertiliser and load aircraft in one action. This was fitted to a Fordson tractor

The first aircraft loaders were built on modified tractors, but they were very slow travelling between jobs. H John Holder, diesel mechanic and then salesman for Northland Motors, redesigned the loader to fit on the rear of a Thames Trader, with rear cab and dual controls to operate from front or rear. It became the industry standard and is still used today.

by Northland Motors for Advance Aviation, a subsidiary of James Aviation. The machine did a great job but was cumbersome and took too long travelling between jobs.

John Holder at Northland Motors devised a way of mounting the loader on a Thames Trader 55 truck. He helped James Aviation develop the idea with a rear-mounted loader and dual front and rear driving controls, using the Wilkinson loader boom. The Trader 55 could travel a great deal faster than a tractor, carry aircraft fuel and was far more efficient.

One of the most serious problems encountered with aerial topdressing was corrosion of equipment when the fertiliser mixed with rainwater. Truck cabs were not then treated for corrosion and were particularly vulnerable. The rear loader, tank and controls were mounted on a sub-frame which could be easily detached, reconditioned and shifted to another truck. This became the industry standard and hundreds have been built, remaining almost identical 45 years later.

A new 28hp Fordson Dexta tractor was introduced in 1958 and was well received. For many farmers, the Fordson Major tractor was bigger than needed and dairy farmers, especially, bought the smaller Dexta. Ford introduced the live PTO (power take off) on both tractors, which gave added versatility when using implements. Fordson tractors were a key factor to dealer profitability, and thousands were sold.

CMC now had over £1 million invested in 15 Ford dealer subsidiaries, plus equities in John W Andrew Ford and other associate companies. Subsidiary companies returned over 15% on their capital which had expanded 60% in 12 months. Service and parts were still the most profitable departments, followed by used cars, new and used tractors and trucks. The poorest return was, and still is, from new cars.

The motor industry reeled when the 'Black Budget' of 1958 changed sales tax on motor vehicles from 20% to 40%. The amount of sales tax collected remained about the same as 1955, but individuals were paying significantly more, because since then the numbers of car licences issued had dropped by 42%, and the budget reduced licences yet again. Petrol was taxed another 6d per gallon, taking it to 3s 9d per gallon, and the extra £8.8 million collected from petrol did not go to roads, but straight into the Consolidated Fund. There were already finance restrictions before the budget, which meant that a new car had to have a 50% deposit and be paid off within 18 months. New commercials and used cars were allowed 25% deposit and 24 months terms. None of these actions diminished the demand for new cars; motorists just had to pay more.

The Crown lease of the nine-storey 'Ford' building in Courtenay Place was due to end on November 30 1959, and the board was very concerned the government might exercise its right to purchase the building at its 1937 value of £150,000. Directors waited with bated breath for the deadline to pass. It did, and the building could now be restored to provide economic income.

CMC had ambitious development plans in a number of areas, but few had been completed because of delayed planning approvals and building permits. It was a very frustrating process, with government deliberately hobbling the industry because exports were poor and the country's overseas reserves were seriously depleted.

Top: Ford introduced the small 30hp Dexta tractor in 1958, with live hydraulics, dual range gears and 3cyl diesel motor. It was a perky machine and suited many farmers who did not need a large tractor.

Bottom: Show day at Timaru in 1958, with the new Fordson Power Major driven by office boy Ken Mullan.

1959 STATISTICS

Cars registered   492,847   - decade change   + 114%
Trucks registered 198,198   - decade change   + 65%
39% of cars registered were over 10 years old.
25% of cars registered were over 20 years old.

NZ POPULATION WAS 2,359,700 IN 1959:

| Density NZ | 1 car to | 4.8 people, |
| | 1 vehicle | 3.4 people |

TRAFFIC DENSITY DAILY PAST A TALLY POINT – 1961:

Auck-Hamilton (Greenlane)	15,690	12yr inc.	+100%
Wgton-Paekak (Paekakariki)	3,980	12yr inc.	+45%
Chch – Timaru (Rakaia)	1,828	12yr inc.	+53%

TRACTORS IN USE 75,291,   DECADE INCREASE 274%

*1952 number of holdings with tractors was 38,434.
*1952 number of holdings with horses only, 25,357.
*1952 holdings with no tractors or horses, 26,497.
*1952 was the last time this statistic was taken.

IN THE 1959 YEAR THE MOTOR INDUSTRY COLLECTED:

Customs duty tax, tariff, fuel, etc	£30.6million
Of this, spent on main highways	£19.8million
Transferred to Consolidated Fund	£10.8million

To be fair, the government had, on the other hand, made large strides with main roads. There were now 8,963 bridges over 25ft. long. A total of 1,229 new reinforced concrete or steel and concrete bridges had been built in a decade, with the most famous the Auckland Harbour Bridge. Many single lane wooden bridges were rebuilt as dual carriageway concrete and steel bridges. In total, 3,000 miles of new roads were formed, and sealed roads doubled to 14,692 miles. £150 million was spent on New Zealand roads by the National Roads Board. A good start, but still more was needed.

Still New Zealand's largest roading project, Auckland Harbour Bridge, was opened on May 31 1959, and traffic queued like lemmings to get across. Photo by Olaf Petersen was taken half an hour after the bridge opened. It was later widened with 'Nippon clip-ons'.
[Photo Alexander Turnbull Library, with consent from Auckland War Memorial Museum, which holds Petersen's collection. Ref: F-66931]

CHAPTER SEVEN

GOING AHEAD

In 1960 New Zealand was still totally reliant on sales of primary produce overseas, with sickening swings in overseas returns dictating what goods could be imported the next year. Primary produce was largely sold in its raw state and New Zealand took what it could get on world markets, often not receiving true value. Productivity on farms increased steadily for 30 years after the Second World War by 1% per annum as new farming methods and refinements were adopted. Farm labour kept reducing as mechanisation increased. Swampy land was drained, scrub cut back and pasturelands developed to feed more cattle and sheep. Despite the development of secondary industries, nearly all raw materials used, other than labour, wood and cement, were imported, thereby negating many of the gains.

On the other hand, we had very high living standards in relative terms, full employment, plenty of good food, cheap housing and money in our pockets, but we were very much "rugby, racing and beer". Restaurants were few and far between, and evening entertainment was limited to movie theatres and weekend dances, as the pubs closed at 6pm. There was a good ratio of cars to people because there were few public transport options, but the age of the cars was extraordinary. In 1958, 85% were more than two years old, 39% were over 10 years old and 15% were pre-war rusty relics more than 20 years old.

Because of the scarcity of new cars, a nearly new car was worth more than a new one, creating an obsession among many to own a brand new vehicle. There were many ways of 'acquiring' overseas funds, and No Remittance provided opportunities for the less scrupulous. However, the scheme did provide a genuine way for New Zealand to import cars without using up reserve funds.

To make matters worse, the 'desperate to own a new car' buyers were prepared to

The 105E Anglia was launched in 1959 but there were few on the road before 1960. Costing £858, it was roomy and distinctive with 'the pram' rear window, a free revving 997cc engine, 4 speed gearbox and good handling. The 105E engine was the base design for a whole series of engines – 997cc, 1,198cc, 1,298, 1,340cc, 1,498cc, 1,598cc, and 1,798cc – that spawned car club, rally and formula racing enthusiasts.

bribe dealer sales people, and were abusive when turned down, claiming dealers were discriminating. For every customer who had a new car allocated, another 10 were unhappy.

In 1960 roads were improving, but the process was expensive and slow. The Far North had few sealed roads; Napier to Taupo had treacherous sections and was largely unsealed; and apart from the main arterial highways, roads were rough and very secondary, with little seal. Nearly all the raw material for roads was locally produced, apart from the machinery, fuel and emulsion used for 'tarsealing'.

Meanwhile, there were other important developments: New Zealand joined the International Monetary Fund, started television broadcasts, laid the Cook Strait power cable, built the Marsden Point fuel refinery in 1964, abolished capital punishment, negotiated the NAFTA trade agreement with Australia, ended the 6 o'clock swill, brought in decimal currency, piped natural gas to Auckland and opened Auckland International Airport at Mangere. New Zealand was definitely going ahead.

The Colonial Motor Company had identified that its 934 strong staff were aging and a number of replacement management positions would occur through retirements. There were a number of suitable staff replacements, but not sufficient. A recruitment programme was initiated throughout the country and about 20 young 'executive trainees' were employed over the next five years. Training was initially in company accounting

The Consul 315 in 1961 was the first Ford with disc front brakes.

functions, followed by sales. Some accounting graduates from the auditors were also taken into the programme. When a vacancy occurred at a group dealership, a trainee was shifted in and, as most were single, this was a fairly simple process. A small contingent of young hopefuls were moving around the CMC Group.

The lease expired on the nine-storey 'Ford' building in Courtenay Place on November 30 1959. But the Crown did not exercise its option to purchase the building at its 1937 valuation of £150,000, now considerably less than its market value. The building was vacated, but needed considerable maintenance work. The IRD had moved out some time before, and under the 'alternative occupancy rights', the Crown had sub-tenanted a number of other parties, who had altered the building, adding a wooden mezzanine floor and a number of partition walls, plus 70 toilets on various floors, and a 3,000 gallon water supply on the roof, which damaged the roof membrane, and caused leaks. It was a mess.

Now new tenancies were negotiated with the Crown for three floors. The wooden mezzanine and partitions were dismantled, and the roof water storage, which created a 14 ton seismic loading, was removed. New automatic lifts were installed. The building was unusual with its floor loading of 150lb per square foot, compared to 30lb per square foot for the average office. The Alexander Turnbull Library occupied two floors because they needed high floor rating for storing books.

Lane Walker Rudkin leased one floor, H A Tuck another, and soon the building was returning a realistic income.

New building was under way in 1960, after all the delays with planning and permits, but the ambitious programme still had a long way to run before completion. Northland Motors, Kaitaia had been completed in 1955, but Otahuhu, Invercargill, New Plymouth, Sockburn, Dunedin and Lower Hutt had only started, and were by no means finished. Building restrictions were still in place for transactions over £30,000 and with inflation now increasing costs, delays were still happening. A number of tenders were broken into stages so they were under £30,000 and thus able to continue.

Several more properties were purchased in Lower Hutt, in what seemed to be a never ending process to acquire enough space, but a new road was planned to the rear of High Street, and until this was finalised the administration and sales building had to wait. Further properties were identified at dealership locations as desirable and were purchased when offered for sale.

General manager Les Clarke resigned to go to John Burns in Auckland at the beginning of 1960, and Peter Gibbons took over most of his roles. At the end of 1960

Above: Northland Motors on the day in 1961 when Brock Jamieson came to visit. All the new models were there: Consul II, Galaxie, Zodiac, Anglia, Consul 315, Fairlane, and 107E Prefect.

CMC Group management meeting 1961. Left: Pat Fagan, Masterton; Les Gladding, Otahuhu; Lofty Henderson, Lower Hutt; John Livingston, Palmerston North; John Holder, Kaikohe; Percy Ferguson, Kaitaia; Ray Clark, Auckland; Bill Gibbons, Palmerston North; Don Gibbons, Waipukurau; Peter Cederman, CMC; Colin Cliff, New Plymouth; Frank Perkins, CMC; R B Gibbons, CMC; Peter Gibbons, CMC; Merv Dineen, Te Kuiti; Jack Rogers, Morrinsville; Orm Hutchinson and Hutch Hutchinson, Christchurch; Bob Greenfield, Auckland; Jim Ambler, Te Awamutu; Ian Lyons, Wellington; Bob Macaulay, Invercargill; Ellis Smith, Te Aroha and Don Mullan, Timaru.

Opposite bottom: Falcon XL was only available on 'No Remittance' and cost £1,240, with 3 speed gearbox, drum brakes and 2,360cc 6 cylinder engine.

The Colonial Motor Company board in 1962. Clockwise from front left: F N (Bill) Gibbons, G H (Don) Gibbons, Gerald B Gibbons, L C (Les) Gladding, R B (Bob) Gibbons, A B (Alf Jnr) Gibbons, Orm Hutchinson, Peter C Gibbons, D S (Don) Mullan, Jim Flannery, secretary, Peter V Cederman, general manager.

R W (Pat) Stewart resigned as secretary, moving to Hastings, where he had interests in a bakery. H Frank Perkins, who had just completed a review of the group accounting system and written an operating manual, was appointed secretary. In 1961 Peter V Cederman was appointed CMC group manager. Peter Cederman had started at Stevens Motors and been accountant there before a short period as assistant manager at Avery Motors.

Chairman Alf B Gibbons died on November 16 1961, after a short illness. He had been a director since 1919 and chairman for the last five years, and his 42 year contribution was acknowledged with grateful thanks. Although not in the front line as an executive, he had played a significant role as a director. He and his brothers had always worked together as a team in their collective business interests.

Ford Motor Company had now been in New Zealand 25 years and, in typical Ford style, found a way to celebrate by announcing a new model, this time the Consul 315, the first Ford with disc front brakes. A year earlier the greatly changed Anglia 105E model, with its robust free revving 997cc oversquare engine, had arrived. They both had reverse sloped rear windows which raised styling eyebrows and were distinctively different.

In February 1962 directors appointed managing director Robert B Gibbons as chairman, and Les C Gladding a director.

F H (Tod) Johnson retired from the board after 44 years with Colonial Motor Company in May 1962, the board expanding when Gerald B Gibbons and Don S Mullan were appointed directors.

The Mark III Zephyr 6 was introduced during 1962 and took the market by storm, together with the Zodiac and Zephyr 4. They had 4 speed column change gearboxes, front disc brakes and a larger body. Ford Australia started building the US Falcon XL model soon afterwards, to compete with the Holden, but the early US design was not rugged enough for Australian conditions until modified, when it became a strong seller. The only way you could buy a Falcon was with a No Remittance licence, making them a scarce, 'premium' used car, often fetching more than the new price. As Ford would not sanction dealers selling at over list prices, the only way a used Ford could reach its real market price was by giving the buyer an artificially low trade-in. By 1964, the company had introduced a covenant for all new car sales, preventing their resale for two years, and the government a one year covenant for No Remittance vehicles.

Brock Jamieson, managing director of Ford NZ, retired in June 1962, moving back home to Canada and leaving many friends in New Zealand. His successor was Harold P Ralph, who had been employed by CMC in 1924, on his arrival in New Zealand from

Top: 1962 Zephyr and Zodiac had 4 speed column change, bench seats and disc front brakes. Zephyr 4, £1,126; Zephyr 6, £1,228; Zodiac with heater/radio £1,413.

The first Cortina arrived in October 1962 with 1198cc engine and 4 speed gears. Cost: 2 door £923, 4 door £989. Simple, spacious, good performance and handling.

Harold P Ralph replaced Brock Jamieson as Ford NZ managing director in 1962.

Cortina Super arrived with a 1,498cc engine and then, a popular Cortina wagon costing £1,098. The cars did everything well and were soon joined by a performance GT model (No Remittance only.)

Argentina, before transferring to Ford in 1936. H P Ralph had worked for a period at Windsor, in overseas sales at Ford Canada, before returning.

Ford Detroit bought the controlling interests in Ford Canada and other world affiliates in the 1950s, and management of overseas operations now reported to Ford International. This was part of the rationalisation brought about by Henry Ford II, and the 'Wizz Kids' he employed in 1946. Ford of Europe was established in 1958 as part of this change.

New Lynn Motors was given the Ford green light to start in 1962; plans were finalised and tenders called. Colin J Cliff was appointed manager in March 1962, having been manager of Phillipps Motors New Plymouth. He had the daunting task of starting up from scratch, with no staff and no buildings. He moved to Auckland, bought a house for his family, bought a caravan for an office, parked it on the building site in mid-winter, and started selling vehicles.

Foundation difficulties meant excavation of the site to a depth of five metres was necessary in places, plus the removal of ancient rotted kauri stumps which had plasticised. This changed the design and a two storeyed building resulted. By the end of 1962, the first building stage was finished and Colin Cliff had 22 staff.

Stages 2 and 3 followed. At the end of 1965, New Lynn Motors had sold 2,000 vehicles and had 71 staff members.

No Remittance sales increased steadily, directly improving profits, aided by the new Cortina model, released in 1962. A 'Plain Jane', the Cortina was rushed to market by Ford International because it was cost efficient to produce compared to the Consul 315. It was a straightforward design that did everything well. Within a year Cortina had set new sales records worldwide with model variants introduced to suit buyers. One of the desirable models was the perky Built Up Cortina 1,500cc GT. The first GT arrived off a ship from Britain in 1963, drove straight to Pukekohe, and competed, with no preparation, in the Benson & Hedges 500 mile production saloon car race, winning handsomely. Everyone wanted one and No Remittance orders climbed quickly. Soon after this, the famous high performance Lotus Cortina was launched, winning races and rallies all over the world.

In 1962, a new Dividend Retention Tax was applied to unlisted companies which did not pay out 40% of tax paid profits. Colonial Motor Company wished to use some of the profits to pay for its building programme, and found the only way this could be done without paying the new tax was to go public. The company applied to the NZ Stock Exchange for listing in 1962, implementing changes to the Articles of Association, and reporting dates to comply. The year was a better one, with sales of £8.4 million, up 10% and profits up 17%

By Christmas 1963, New Lynn Motors had an upstairs showroom with mezzanine offices, and workshop and parts underneath, on the corner of Titirangi Rd and Great North Road Auckland.

Craik Motors knocked down the old corner lubritorium and got a whole new main road frontage in 1964.

A big day in 1964 for Macaulay Motors, Invercargill; opening of new showroom and consolidation of operations at Avenal.

Above: Panmure Motors began in a caravan in 1964 but had spectacular new premises operating in 1965, right on the busiest roundabout in Auckland.

with greater expense control. Staff numbers were now over 1,000.

Sockburn buildings were completed for Hutchinson Motors in May 1963, a new truck service and lube bay were built at Te Awamutu, and new staff amenities for Kaikohe. New workshops were planned at Invercargill, Dunedin, Lower Hutt, Masterton, Te Kuiti, and New Lynn. After discussion with Ford, planning for three new dealerships began.

A very large amount of building was

now underway and more capital was needed. Shareholders approved increases in share capital from £600,000 to £950,000 in 1963 and then to £1,350,000 in 1964. The board's actions were justified when profits increased 584% in the decade, despite the shortage of new cars.

Panmure Motors started in 1964 when Trist Atkins shifted from Te Kuiti to start up, like his neighbour Colin Cliff, from a caravan office on site at the Panmure Roundabout. Originally to be a branch of

South Auckland Motors, Ford wanted it to be separated. The landmark building was ready in early 1965, and was soon busy expanding with more service buildings.

Late in 1964, a group of New Zealand tractor dealers was invited to attend the World Ford Tractor Convention in New York and England where the new Ford tractor range was presented by Ford International with all the usual American razzle-dazzle. The new tractors were all world models and went from 25 hp to 100 hp in a range of 10 models. The tractors were all newly designed and incorporated excellent new features, including a revolutionary Select-O-Speed 'shift on the go' transmission with no clutch. All you did to change gears was click the gear lever quadrant to the next one of the 12 positions and off the tractor went, even under full power.

It was a hot seller when it arrived in 1965 until the problems started. The Select-O-Speed had gremlins inside it and almost every transmission had to be stripped down and a variety of parts changed and re-assembled – until it happened again. Eventually every transmission was re-worked with modified parts and some semblance of reliability was achieved. The manual change ordinary gearbox model was a complete contrast, and performed well without all the problems. Select-O-Speed was a disaster for customers and dealers, both losing confidence in the process. Warranty costs were borne by Ford in theory, but dealers suffered as they could not meet warranty time schedules and this affected their financial performance.

Henry Ford II paid an official visit to Ford New Zealand in April 1965, accompanied by a large retinue including security guards. While here he met New Zealand Ford dealers at a memorable luncheon. Henry Ford II was an icon, and every dealer in the country who was not a Ford dealer was extremely jealous. Henry Ford was pleased to receive an attractive painting of a part of the Southern Alps from

Opposite bottom: The new Ford tractors launched in 1964 were completely redesigned with purpose built diesels and 6 x 2 manual or 10 speed Select-O-Speed transmission. They were excellent performers but the S-O-S was just that, and nearly broke dealers. The Macaulay management team in 1964, left to right: Henry Holden, tractor service manager; unknown; Bill Maclaren, managing director; Dave Miller, salesman; Dave Jackson, business manager; Peter Tait, tractor service manager; Gerry Soulsby, truck sales manager; and Paul Drummond, salesman.

Tom Marshall, tractor foreman at Craik Motors, brought a wealth of valuable experience and skills to tractor servicing when he emigrated from England in 1962 after becoming a qualified toolmaker and gaining experience in servicing a large Massey Ferguson fleet. When all Select-O-Speeds had to be modified he invented his own test rig. This rig, using an old pre war electricity stand by generator engine, could fully test the transmission before it was installed.

Henry Ford II visited NZ in 1965 and met dealers for lunch, where he was presented with an oil painting of the Southern Alps. Orm Hutchinson, Christchurch and Doug Johnstone, Taupo, making a presentation speech, R B Gibbons, CMC, Henry Ford II, Harold Ralph, FNZ and Tom Lilley, FMC.   Henry Ford II replied and admired the picture.

local Ford dealers. He was not told the common name of the peak because of his recent divorce; it was 'The Nun's Veil', and was chosen for its artistic merit. Whether it was a poor flight into Wellington on an aged DC3 aircraft, or some rough wine that got him out of sorts, we may never know, but the visit was not a success for Ford NZ and Mr Ford did not consent to the proposed capital expansion.

Sockburn Motors Ltd, at Christchurch, was created as a separate dealership in 1965 with W A (Bill) Goss as manager, and the initial staff nearly all coming from Hutchinson Motors.

The Mark IV Zephyr V6 was launched in 1966, a truly advanced car after the very popular Mark III. With larger body, independent front and rear suspension, disc brakes all round, and a V6 2,500cc (3,000cc

on Zodiac), it was a huge step forward technically, and despite the 15% increase in price, offered value for money.

New Zealand still had 83 and 86 octane rated petrol in the 1960s, but many of the new vehicles had been designed for a much better quality fuel, or higher octane. The Mark IV Zephyr had a short stroke high compression engine designed for 95 octane unleaded fuel and, of course, did not appreciate being fed low octane, poor quality fuel. This resulted in excessive knocking ('pinking' or pre-ignition), especially under heavy loads at low speeds. All sorts of engine problems occurred, such as overheating and premature wear, and with them came customer disenchantment. It was a brilliant car, but ahead of its time in New Zealand. Fortunately, Ford introduced NZ Falcon assembly in 1966,

at their upgraded plant, which had a much greater tolerance for the country's poor fuels.

In 1966, the Thames Trader truck was phased out and the D Series range introduced, firstly with 3, 5 and 6 ton fully forward control cabs. They were a modernised Trader chassis with a smart new cab that tilted for servicing. Soon afterwards, a 7 and 8 ton 130 hp diesel arrived with heavier components. The trucks sold well as the country developed, and in the late 1960s light tandem trucks

Rhys Sale, president of Ford Canada, made a farewell visit to NZ as Ford International, Detroit, took over world control. From left, Hutch Hutchinson, Harold Ralph, Ford NZ, Orm Hutchinson and Rhys Sale. Sockburn Motors opened in 1965, on the high traffic Main South Road at Blenheim Road roundabout. The buildings are still in use today although heavily disguised behind the new Ford identification, and the dealership is named Avon City Ford. On the corner nearest the roundabout is the old store which served as sales offices and parts department for a period, and further up the side road an old house was used as staff room.

Top: The new Zephyr V6 and Zodiac were launched in 1966, setting new standards in space, quietness and handling. Zephyr V6 cost £1,417 and Zodiac £1,748. They also challenged dealers with technical problems that took a lot of time, money and patience to solve.

Middle: Panmure Motors' office 1,300cc Escort competed in the Benson & Hedges 500 mile race from 1968-70, winning its class each year.

Below: The Escort replaced the 105E Anglia in 1968 and was available in 2 door Deluxe 1,098cc and Super 1,298cc. Costing $1,523 and $1,586, they were soon seen hotted up and racing to success.

D Series trucks were launched in 1966 and the new fully forward control, tipping cab was much easier for drivers to get into and see out from. At first these were in 3, 5 and 6 ton versions but then 7 and 8 ton models, and light tandems arrived. Here a 5 tonner with Standard Motor Bodies' all steel body and tip.

with 150hp turbo and 185hp V8 Cummins diesel, a long wheelbase 150hp bus chassis and 130hp fire engine were introduced. Ford dealers now had a large and competitive range of mid sized trucks available and operations really started to expand, with still more service capacity needed. CMC Group was fortunate to have the large new service workshops built during the 1960s at New Lynn, Panmure, Otahuhu, Te Awamutu, New Plymouth, Masterton, Lower Hutt, Sockburn, Dunedin and Invercargill. All were variations of a design by structural engineer Martyn Spencer, of Wellington, and have stood the test of time as they are still used today.

Part of the Seaview Ford plant expansion included New Zealand's first full cathodic paint anti-rust dip process. Previously, serious rust problems started as early as three years, and kept panelbeaters in business. There were also signs that the plant might not be able to cope with the increasing diversity in vehicles, which required more space, so the area formerly used for the parts warehouse was converted to truck and tractor assembly, but still the plant was crowded and inefficient.

New Zealand roads continued to improve considerably during the 1960s, with much more use by motorists.

Traffic density had nearly doubled in a decade as New Zealanders went to the beach or lake, or even skiing at the

Below: The XR Falcon 500, built locally from 1966, and popular with No Remittance customers. The Falcon Sedan cost £1,240 and Wagon £1,333.

CMC Group Management met in 1968. Left to right front: Alex Trail, Kaitaia; Barry Wisneski, Kaikohe; Ian Morgan, Morrinsville; Alan Hodges, Johnsonville; R B Gibbons, CMC; Peter Gibbons, CMC; Don Mullan, Timaru; Mac MacPherson, Dunedin; Colin Cliff, New Lynn; Max Caigou, Wellington; and Lofty Henderson, Lower Hutt. Rear: Merv Dineen, Te Awamutu; Trist Atkins, Panmure; Peter Cederman, CMC; Don Gibbons, Waipukurau; Jim Flannery, CMC; Phil Phillipps, New Plymouth; Bill Goss, Sockburn; Bruce Harvey, Auditor; George Daniel, Christchurch; Basil Orsborne, CMC; Ellis Smith, Te Aroha; Randal Thomson, Masterton; Hutch Hutchinson, Christchurch; Bill Blackburn, Dunedin; Bill Maclaren, Invercargill; John Emery, Otahuhu; Norm Shorter, Te Kuiti; and Royce Cox, New Plymouth.

1969 STATISTICS

Cars registered	847,935	- decade change	+ 72 %
Trucks registered	279,256	- decade change	+ 142 %

42% of cars registered were over 10 years old
6% of cars registered were over 20 years old

NZ POPULATION IN 1969 WAS 2,804,000:

Density

US	1 car to	2.3 people
	1 vehicle to	1.9 people
NZ	1 car to	3.3 people
	1 vehicle to	2.5 people
Canada	1 car to	3.3 people
	1 vehicle to	2.7 people
Australia	1 car to	3.4 people
	1 vehicle to	2.7 people
UK	1 car to	4.7 people
	1 vehicle to	4.0 people

TRAFFIC DENSITY DAILY PAST A TALLY POINT IN 1969:

Auck-Hamilton (Greenlane)	35,750	(228% of 1961)
Wgton-Paekak (Paekakariki)	7,260	(182% of 1961)
Chch-Timaru (Rakaia)	3,520	(193% of 1961)

TRACTORS IN USE WERE 95,421, DECADE INCREASE + 27%

IN 1969 YEAR THE MOTOR INDUSTRY COLLECTED:

Customs duty tax, tariff, fuel, etc	$102.5 million
Of this, spent on National Roads	$ 66.3 million
Transferred to Consolidated Fund	$ 37.2 million

weekend. Many families hooked caravans onto their cars and had their holidays far from home. The Napier-Taupo road had large re-alignments and was sealed in time to transport truckloads of timber from the Taupo area to the Napier port. The Haast Pass road was finally opened after 10 years of building.

In July 1969 McMillan Motors, a continuous import licence holder for Rover and Morgan cars, changed franchise and became a Ford dealer at 428 Greenlane Road, Auckland. This was a shock to South Auckland Motors and John W Andrews, who had no prior indication their territories would be split by Ford in this manner.

The winds of change were ruffling the new vehicle market at the end of the 1960s, and the transition to free supply was now occurring, although not as quickly as many people thought. An economist will say the difference between under supply and over supply is one unit, but in the case of New Zealand's car market other factors were involved, shortages from suppliers because of labour strikes prolonging the changeover.

The Colonial Motor Company had had a momentous two decades of expansion and rebuilding right through New Zealand, and now had the strongest dealer group in the country, staffed with 1,300 people working in top class facilities. The expansion, costing over £1 million (CPI equivalent to $40 million in 2002), had been generated from within the company and dividends were now starting to flow to shareholders. Robert B Gibbons decided after 50 years in the day-to-day management of the company, and having overseen the development of the CMC Group, it was time to retire. His son, Peter C Gibbons was appointed managing director from January 1 1969, with R B remaining as chairman.

CHAPTER EIGHT

THE SHOCKS OF THE SEVENTIES

Commercial conditions were more buoyant in 1970, and business was cautiously expanding, but New Zealand was facing an uncertain future with its primary exports because it was likely the United Kingdom would join the European Economic Community. The EEC was producing surplus agricultural produce it was already dumping in England. Most of our meat and dairy exports were still being exported to England, so a trade pact with the EEC was likely to have serious consequences in New Zealand. Wool, our other main export, was on an international market with Australia the only other main producer. Forestry and fishing were still in their infancy. Builders had just started using treated pine timber to construct houses.

The NZ motor industry fared better than expected as governments phased out the No Remittance scheme in the late 1960s. It had done its best with an over supply of cars that removed the distortions and made it a buyer's market. Add finance regulations to keep money tight and it was bound to happen. By the early 1970s the market had virtually freed up, and many cars became available 'off the floor', but there were still periods of shortages for other reasons.

There was some relief in 1971 when New Zealand secured continued access for butter and cheese to the United Kingdom, but there was dismay in 1973 when the UK joined the EEC, and there were clear signs of them abandoning their faithful ally. Primary exports had a roller coaster ride all through the decade. By 1976, the EEC had imposed quotas on NZ agricultural exports.

Natural gas was now being piped to Auckland and soon Wellington and Napier were on line from the Kapuni field in Taranaki, together with many intermediate centres. When more gas was discovered at the offshore Maui field the experts worried how the huge volumes could be used.

The first 'oil shock' in October 1973 was a major disruption to New Zealand life. Exploration was stepped up in the search for fuel self-sufficiency. New Zealand pioneered the previously untried 'Gas to

A re-enactment of the first Wellington-Auckland car journey in 1912 that tackled the King Country was held in 1971. Vintage buffs Ray Ivin and Pam McLean followed the original route as far as possible and met a number of the people who witnessed the original run 59 years before. Here they cross a river in a 1915 Model T Runabout loaned by Sir Len Southward.

Gasoline' (GTG) plant at Waitara, converting gas to synthetic petrol fuel.

With the abundance of natural gas, the government subsidised motorists for the next decade, as cars were converted from petrol to compressed natural gas (CNG) or liquefied petroleum gas (LPG). Both fuels were cheaper than petrol, but this move also saved the country overseas currency, which was now under pressure from lower export returns.

Roads continued to improve and many large deviations, such as those between Mangaweka and just north of Taihape, were finished. The cost of imported fuel was a powerful incentive for government to improve roads – better roads used less fuel and less overseas funds. It is said the government approved lowering the crest height of the road deviation north of Mangaweka by a further 20 metres to achieve annual calculated savings of $15 million in fuel.

Tiwai Point aluminium smelter near Invercargill started production in 1971. New Zealand's population reached three million people, and the metric system of weights and measures was introduced in 1976. The country became regulation driven with the change of government in 1975, as attempts were made to control agricultural production with incentives and financial clamps to control inflation and demand. The government embarked on a series of 'Think Big' projects, aimed at making the country self sufficient in fuel and energy.

The second 'oil shock' of 1979 was accompanied by 'carless days', when motorists nominated which day a car would not be used, as New Zealand struggled to cope with fuel rationing again.

The Licensed Motor Vehicle Dealers Act, passed in 1976, set new trading standards to protect consumers and put disciplines in place, preventing much of the 'horse trading' that had existed, and making dealers responsible for their own actions.

It was a turbulent decade where outside influences had considerable effects on our lives.

The Colonial Motor Company was still busy with its building programme in 1970, and buying any property that was available near Avery Motors in Taranaki Street, Wellington. The city council was pushing ahead with plans to bring the motorway further into the city, tunnelling under the Terrace, into and down Ghuznee Street, and was planning to take part of Avery Motors' site. The whole motorway project was messy and had not been finalised because of considerable public opposition to the proposed route that cut through historic housing and a pioneer cemetery.

The proposed motorway plan meant Avery Motors might need to re-locate, or demolish part of its present facility, which was on Diocesan Trust lease land. More properties were purchased in Jessie and Ebor Streets, behind Avery Motors, as a precaution.

At the same time the city council was proceeding with its seismic rating code on all buildings in the central business district. The nine-storey 'Ford' building in Courtenay Place was caught in the

Takapau Fire Board's new D1212HE fire appliance was delivered by Ruahine Motors in May 1969. Costing $22,000, it had all the latest gear and an alloy body.

compliance net. It became a substantial exercise to work out the economics of compliance versus demolition. The building was a valuable asset earning considerable income, but was it worth the cost of compliance? J M Dawson was architect for the original construction, and his successors, King and Dawson Architects in Wellington, were asked to do the study.

In 1970 new vehicle supply was expected to be about the same as 1969, despite production problems in the UK. Ford had a substantial fire at the Dagenham export plant, followed by strikes at Ford suppliers and then a dock strike. Similar strikes were occurring in New Zealand and R B Gibbons remarked at the annual meeting "that it was disturbing to see the excellent relationship built up between employers and employees in New Zealand over a period of many years, in danger of being eroded by industrial disputes."

It was now evident that the Seaview Ford plant was unable to cope with the new volumes expected and the reason for Henry Ford's visit in 1965 was, in part, to provide the investment for this expansion. However, strikes in the United Kingdom opened the door for Australian built up product, which was highly sought in the New Zealand market. No Remittance had virtually ceased as the government had planned, and extra shipments of 5,000 BU cars were licensed, helping to slow buyer demand.

Colin J Cliff, managing director of New

Lynn Motors, was made a director in 1970, the second dealer director to come from the important Auckland area, which had a third of New Zealand's population.

In the greater Auckland market, CMC was busy acquiring more sites, with new branches established at Massey, Henderson and Avondale for New Lynn Motors. South Auckland Motors opened branches at Mangere, Penrose and Papatoetoe. They also wanted to start a branch at Wiri, but Ford would not allow this. Panmure leased a 3,000 sq.ft. workshop nearby until expanded facilities at the site were completed. Christchurch was busy extending Papanui branch and established Sydenham as a branch, while Sockburn expanded further. Wellington was of continuing concern as the city council still could not make up its mind about Ghuznee Street extensions. Another site was bought in Adelaide Road for used cars and commercials, and the Johnsonville workshop was extended to take

Colin J Cliff was appointed a CMC director in 1970.

Blue Bus Services took delivery of this impressive 45 seat R226 coach in 1971 from Fagan Motors. Cost $23,000.

Henry Ford II in Wellington in 1971. Left to right: Joe Auton, sales director FNZ; Orm Hutchinson, Christchurch; Bill Gibbons, Palmerston North; Herby Dyke, Hamilton; Henry Ford II; Harold Ralph, managing director FNZ; Bill Bourke, president Ford Australia.

Below: Ralph B Fawcett started at Ford NZ in 1949. He transferred overseas, later heading Ford Rhodesia, and then Ford Singapore.

commercials.

The purpose of establishing branches was to protect territories. Ford still had the idea that another dealer in the market would produce a greater market share, so a strategically placed branch might stop this from happening. With Auckland developing so rapidly it was also not clear when a substantial suburb might end up as a future city, in which case a branch could be made a separate dealership, like Panmure.

Regarded as akin to royalty, Henry Ford II returned in 1971, this time with his company jet and retinue, which toured the country by air while Henry Ford was occupied in talks. The aerial touring produced some flack from Civil Aviation which wanted flight plans in advance, whereas the plans kept changing as Mrs Ford found something new and interesting to view! Ford NZ management was determined to achieve their expansion, and no expense was spared to entertain Henry Ford with the best, including his favourite Dom Perignon champagne. Again Ford dealers met him for lunch, giving him New Zealand books and an antique Cellini silver bowl that Mrs Ford loved. In the end, the new component manufacturing plant and assembly line at Wiri were approved.

Ford had bought 70 acres at Wiri in 1964, and established the National Parts Centre there in 1965. A new transmission and chassis manufacturing plant was opened in 1972. Government export arrangements enabled Ford NZ to gain export credits for component manufacturing for other affiliates, and to apply these to import licences for Built Up cars, thereby achieving a greater share. This effectively meant Ford could import Built Up vehicles at will from any NAFTA source. The Seaview plant expanded with a second commercial assembly line after parts had shifted to Wiri. A second assembly plant for Falcon only was built and opened in 1974, giving Ford the largest assembly operation in New Zealand.

In mid 1971 Harold Ralph retired, having worked for CMC for 12 years and for Ford the last 37 years. He was succeeded by Ralph P Fawcett, a New Zealander who had started at Seaview, and worked for Ford overseas including managing Ford Rhodesia until the plant closed down. H F O'Brien (Brien) Reeve transferred back home from Ford's Thailand office, which also closed. He became sales and marketing director, taking over from J G (Joe) Auton, who was posted to Ford Singapore as managing director.

By mid 1972 the car market was in free supply and there were large stocks of new vehicles. The last of the Mark IV Zephyrs had been assembled in 1971, but there were still a number in stock around the country.

Used car prices dropped away quickly when supply freed up, and Colonial Motor Company held strategy meetings to discuss the market implications.

An interesting market factor was the buyer preference for Built Up vehicles, mainly because the standard of assembly was so much better and heaters and radios were not 'extras'. Dealers also noticed the difference between BU and CKD vehicles in the amount of rectification work needed before delivery. There was pressure on the Seaview plant for both deliveries and better standards, but the two did not seem to go together. Industrial unrest increased as unions exercised their powers with confrontational bargaining and stop work meetings. The early 1970s heralded the

Avery Motors, one of the last multi-branded service stations, was open seven days in the late 1960s. During the oil crisis restrictions in 1979, it had to close from midday Saturday until Monday morning.

ROBERT B GIBBONS 1899 – 1973

Robert B Gibbons died in July 1973 at the age of 85, after a short spell of indifferent health. He was the third son of Hopeful and Jessie Gibbons. R B received a university scholarship, and studied law for a year, before deciding to become an apprentice engineer with Jas J Niven and Co at Napier. After completing his apprenticeship he joined Scott, Niven Engineers in Palmerston North, and then became warehouse manager for J B Clarkson & Co. In 1916 R B left with the 1st NZEF for France, serving as a commissioned officer in the trenches. He took his discharge in 1919 in England, visiting Ford Canada on the way home.

Appointed assistant managing director in 1919, he acted as liquidator of the old Colonial Motor Company, and secretary of the new re-formed company. R B assisted the government with trade negotiations in Britain and Canada in 1935, helping to safeguard Ford's

position in New Zealand. He smoothed over many of the difficulties with the Ford takeover in 1936, and kept communication going with his personable style. His engineering background and interest helped develop the fire engine, trailer pump and other engineering projects, which secured the company financially through the late 1930s and 1940s.

Recognising the path ahead for Colonial Motor Company, after the Second World War, R B drove the rebuilding of dealerships and saw the fulfilment of his work in the CMC Group, arguably the best automotive retail group in New Zealand.

Robert Gibbons was a Dominion president of the NZ Motor Trade Association, and for many years a board member of Marsden Collegiate School, and the Wellington Savage Club.

Outside business and his family, he relaxed fishing, especially from his launch *Veca* in the Marlborough Sounds, and in Wellington waters.

CMC Group Management in 1972. Standing from left: Roger Gardner, Waipukurau; Max Caigou, Wellington; John Emery, Otahuhu; Trist Atkins, Panmure; Bill Blackburn, Dunedin; Bill Maclaren, Invercargill; Jim Flannery, CMC; Barry Wisneski, Morrinsville; Bob Tunley, Standard Motor Bodies; David Bodley, Te Awamutu; Wattie Faloon, Timaru; Royce Cox, New Plymout; Len Scrimshaw, Te Aroha; George Daniel, Sockburn; Michael Gibbons, CMC; Hutch Hutchinson, Christchurch; Ian Lambie, Kaikohe; Peter Craig, Te Kuiti; Alex Trail, Kaitaia; Peter Wood, Auditor. Seated: Lofty Henderson, Lower Hutt; Colin Cliff, New Lynn; Peter Cederman, CMC; Peter Gibbons, CMC; Marjory Pierard, CMC; Basil Orsborne, internal auditor; Norm Shorter, Johnsonville; and Randal Thomson, Masterton.

Right: Cortina MkIII came in 1974, with new models including the peppy 2000 GT.

start of Japanese car assembly in New Zealand, with their higher quality standards. Suddenly there were other factors for consumers to consider.

No one was prepared for the 'oil shock' in late 1973, when fuel oil increased in price from $US2.21 to $US5 per barrel for crude. Petrol at the pump went from 48¢ per gallon for premium grade to 55¢, and then 79¢ a year later. Far worse than the cost hike was the prospect of rationing, and the open road speed limit was cut from 55mph to 50mph (80kph) in December 1973, making a significant difference to fuel consumption. Petrol sales were banned from midday Saturday until Monday morning.

Ford had Escort 1,100 and 1,300cc small cars and Mark II Cortina 1,300 and 1,600cc medium cars, so dealers were well placed to get a good share of the downsizing car market. There was no small luxury model and Ford introduced a New Zealand Cortina 'Executive' model, which also helped fill a gap. Falcon was still a

major player in the rural market and was also the most suitable for natural gas conversion.

In 1973 Gerald B Gibbons was elected chairman of the board. D S (Don) Mullan retired, and C L (Lofty) Henderson, managing director of Stevens Motors, was appointed to replace him. In March 1975, secretary C J L (Jim) Flannery retired after 50 years with the CMC Group, and M L (Max) Caigou was appointed secretary. Max Caigou had been managing director of Avery Motors but, after a major heart attack, it was hoped his new role would be less stressful.

A bonus issue of 1,300,000 fully paid shares was made from reserves, on a 1:2 basis, in July 1974. Sales and profits had been steadily increasing together with accelerating inflation, and this was having a considerable effect on trading as people decided to buy now and not pay more later. However, hire purchase regulations were becoming impossible for cars, with 50%

C J L (Jim) Flannery retired in 1973 after 50 years with CMC Group. Bob Macaulay (left) spoke at his farewell.

Middle: Gerald B Gibbons, the new chairman and new director C L (Lofty) Henderson.

Ford opened the Wiri assembly plant in 1974. John Emery spoke at the opening watched by Alf King, production manager, the mayor of Manukau, and Ralph Fawcett, Ford NZ managing director. The new plant gave Ford the largest production capacity in New Zealand and, with it, market leadership.

Top two photos: New Plymouth operations were consolidated in 1975 and included a magnificent central sales showroom. The site, bordered by three streets, was the result of negotiations over 20 years. The 1958 workshop is at right rear, administration and parts back left, with sales in the centre foreground.

Bottom: Napier Motors converted an adjacent factory for its sales and administration in 1976.

deposit and 12 months terms.

Vehicle financing was becoming increasingly difficult due to government regulations which restricted the supply of money available to finance companies, in addition to the straightjacket hire purchase regulations for new, and, later, used cars. The board decided to register Tara Services Ltd as a subsidiary finance company, to keep flexibility for its dealers. The company advised all staff that a cash deposit scheme was available offering excellent returns, and many took up this opportunity. A consultant was hired by the board to advise on the effects of the Stabilisation of Prices Regulations.

The Mark III Cortina arrived in 1974, an enhanced model range with 1,600 and

Con Berry, parts manager Napier Motors, Len Morrison, new car foreman Avery Motors, Les Gladding, managing director South Auckland Motors and Orm Hutchinson (below) all celebrated 50 plus years service in 1974.

Below: Ormond Hutchinson retired in 1975 and his son Ormond Alexander Hutchinson became managing director.

The MkIV Cortina was a winner and strengthened its No.1 position in New Zealand. Wagon sales accounted for 10% in 1977.

At the time when Escort was a world leader, British champion rally driver Russell Brookes met and discussed his Masport BDA Escort with Ford enthusiasts at Panmure Motors prior to the 1978 Motogard International Rally.

2,000cc engines in a larger body. There were also 2000GT and 2000E models in the range. Cortina became No.1 seller as production increased, driving Ford to No.1 market share spot as well.

In 1975, in an effort to get motorists away from large cars, the government introduced differential registration charges depending upon engine sizes. Although the charges only ranged from $32 for under 1,300cc to $100 for over 4,000cc, this move effectively choked the sale of cars over

2,601cc, as New Zealanders flocked to do the right thing and downsize.

Again Ford dealers were well placed with the Cortina range and Ford added a base 1300cc model which, despite its size, had the correct rear axle ratio and performed well. The new Escort II arrived with more room and was immediately in demand with 1,100cc and 1,300cc engines. Falcon, along with its competitors, was hit badly and this sector shrank from 40% to about 15%.

Motor and power cycles, on the other hand, expanded in use from 45,079 licensed in 1970 to 95,730 in 1975. Also of interest was the change in farming methods from using tractors to motorcycles, which were very much faster getting about farms. Tractor sales peaked at 6,171 in 1973 then declined as farmers cut costs, shed labour and used contractors. In 1978 only 2,811 tractors were sold.

Heavy commercial vehicles had become very large operations for many dealers. The

NEW MOTOR CAR REGISTRATION CHARGES 1975

Engine cc	0-1,300	1,301-2,600	2,601-4,000	4,001+
Regn. fee	32.00	48.00	60.00	100.00
License fee	20.00	20.00	20.00	20.00
ACC levy	14.20	14.20	14.20	14.20
Insurance fee	5.00	5.00	5.00	5.00
Label	.10	.10	.10	.10
TOTAL	71.30	87.30	99.30	139.30

Ford D Series trucks introduced in 1966, with 100bhp diesels, were very popular in the market. The Ford DT2418 Cummins V8 engine 200hp light tandem, introduced in 1973, had become a preferred truck for many rural carriers, carting loads far larger than it was designed for. Overloading had consequences, of course, and workshops were busy keeping them on the road.

The Wellington Motorway extensions were re-prioritised to Grade 8, effectively putting the project on hold, and Avery Motors still did not know what was happening. Nevertheless, more properties were bought in Jessie and Ebor Streets.

Electronic L8000 punch card mini computers were installed at five volume subsidiaries, replacing the old Burroughs Sensematic machines which were obsolete and cannibalised to keep other subsidiaries' machines going. Later in 1978, a computer bureau leased the seventh and eighth floors of the nine-storey building, after the NZ Motor Corporation head office moved out.

In November 1975 four staff members – Orm Hutchinson, m-d Hutchinson Motors, Les Gladding, m-d South Auckland Motors, Con Berry, parts manager Napier Motors, and Len Morrison, pre-delivery foreman Avery Motors, met the board to celebrate their 50 years of service. Orm Hutchinson resigned and retired after 55 years service, and his son Ormond Alexander ('Hutch') Hutchinson was appointed to the board.

A change in the collection of sales tax, from payable at point of wholesale delivery from Ford to after the retail sale, was made in February 1976 and had a very beneficial effect on cash flows. Following this, Bruce G Harvey, the company's auditor, presented a study analysis of the financial position in March 1976, including implications and effects of the rapidly increasing inflation of the NZ dollar. Inflation became the key problem for the whole of the country. A year later he presented a further report detailing medium and long-term strategies for finances.

Hutchinson Motors' major refit in 1978 greatly enhanced the showroom and reception areas. The new showroom opened up the building front to customers, barely recognisable from its late 1800s beginnings.

Top: Transit received a facelift and 2,000cc OHC Cortina engine in 1978 – and was a very effective van.

Middle: D Series trucks remained popular throughout the country. Part of Transport Wairarapa's Ford fleet delivers stock to the saleyards early in the day.

Below: The R226 Series Ford bus chassis – here transformed into a Blue Bus 45 seater – was very popular and performed well.

In July 1977 Ford introduced the Mk IV Cortina range into New Zealand, further strengthening its hold on the market. The car fitted the moment and had new 'European' styling that further enhanced its market position, complete with a luxury Ghia 2.0 model. By now Cortina wagons were predominant in the market, accounting for 10% of Cortina sales.

Many company representatives were taken out of 6 cylinder cars and made to drive 4 cylinder vehicles. Stock agents, who drove many miles on back country roads, resented the move and saw their safety and image downgraded even though the times dictated change. One stock agent, who had threatened to 'kill' his Cortina, had the grace to return after a very hard 90,000 kms and say "You know, this is not a bad car."

Most of the major subsidiaries' rebuilding had now been completed, but new branches were still being opened near Auckland. Wellington remained a problem as decisions on the motorway extension were shelved. At Timaru the old assembly buildings were sold to the city council for a car park, and a new

dealership was built on the corner of Sophia and Cannon Streets. Invercargill had shifted from lower Dee Street out to Avenal, and the old building was sold. Hutchinson Motors undertook a major refurbishment, with the complete frontage of the building re-modelled.

Ralph P Fawcett retired in May 1978, and J G (Joe) Auton returned from Singapore as managing director of Ford NZ. Ford revised allocations to a 'key control' system which took account of resident population in market areas, plus consideration for fleet and parts volumes. A new range of Cortina models was introduced, built up from Australia, with unique Falcon-engined 6 cylinder models. Although looking similar, these cars were very different in the chassis and suspension.

In 1979 the second 'oil shock' struck and the government regulated with 'carless days'. Every car had to have a sticker nominating which day it was not to be used. This further increased conversions to either CNG or LPG as those cars received an 'X' label (exempt) and could be used every day. Certain occupations such as doctors were also exempted.

Top: The 1978 XD Falcon launch in Sydney was attended by Henry Ford II, and re-launched big cars. It cost $7,800.

Below: A 60 year re-enactment of the 1917 'Parliamentary Tour' stopped at Fairhall Motors, Kaikohe in 1977.

Top left: Michael H Gibbons was appointed a director in 1979.

Top right: In 1978, Joe Auton returned to New Zealand as managing director of Ford NZ.

Below: 'Carless days' were introduced with the second, 1979 oil crisis. The windscreen label showed the nominated day the car was to remain garaged. Doctors and some others were exempted with an 'X' label. Natural gas powered cars were exempt.

Les Gladding retired from the board on May 31 1979 after serving more than 50 years, 17 as a director. Michael Hume Gibbons, who had worked at New Lynn and Stevens Motors, was appointed to the board. Later that year, Peter Cederman, who had poor health, resigned as general manager, as did Bruce Harvey, auditor, who was replaced by Peter M Wood. At the annual general meeting, the chairman, Gerald Gibbons, noted that the rate of inflation at more than 15% exceeded the rate of retained earnings after tax, presenting a significant problem.

1979 STATISTICS

Cars registered   1,260,057 - decade change of + 48%
Trucks registered   357,664 - decade change of + 28%
   40.1% of cars registered were over 10 years old
   0.7 % of cars registered were over 20 years old

NZ POPULATION IN 1979 WAS 3,163,900:
Density NZ   1 car to   2.51 people
            1 vehicle to   1.95 people

TRAFFIC DENSITY DAILY PAST A TALLY POINT:
   Auck-Hamilton (Redoubt Rd)   31,810 (new place)
   Wgtn-Paekak   (Paekakariki)   11,000 (151% of 1969)
   Chch – Timaru (Tinwald Sth)   3,820 (new place)

RETAIL PRICE FOR STANDARD FUEL	**1972**	**1979**
Cents per litre	10.12¢	41.50¢
Cents per gallon	48.0¢	189.0¢

TRACTORS IN USE – 90,252; DECADE DECREASE 3.2%

IN THE 1979 YEAR THE MOTOR INDUSTRY COLLECTED:
Customs duty tax, tariff, fuel, etc $565.4 million
Of this, spent on State Highways $159.5 million
Transferred to Consolidated Fund $405.9 million

CHAPTER NINE

THE EIGHTIES REVOLUTION

The decade started with New Zealand tightly regulated under a government determined to control inflation. 'Think Big' was here; we were going to make our own steel, and our own synthetic petrol from natural gas, and massive projects were embarked on. The government managed to do a deal with the EEC for butter, but special police were needed to stop riots during the South African rugby tour in 1981. More regulations in 1982 imposed a 12 months wage, price and rent freeze to try to stop price rises, and this was extended for another 12 months, trying to control imported inflation. An impossible task, this created difficulties with international economic rating agencies. Industrial relations were in chaos, with poor productivity, a situation which was exacerbated by the wage freeze.

A snap election overturned the government in 1984 and the Labour party proceeded on a deregulation binge never seen here before as New Zealand became a trading, and traded, commodity. Everything was questioned for its monetary worth, and many people found they were not very highly valued as unemployment soared.

Farmers reacted very quickly to the removal of their subsidies and simply stopping spending, as they had done in the 1930s. Farm labour declined and contractors were used, sheep and beef numbers dropped after 1985, causing rapid changes to the rural farm service and meat industries which, in many cases, withered to extinction.

The government also withdrew many services, made state departments into corporations, and sold a number off to the highest bidder. Most regulations were reviewed and were either modified or removed. The NZ dollar was floated, bobbled along, and has been an international pawn since. Following the share market crash in 1987, New Zealand was in a depression and 100,000 people were out of work, with more to come.

Money spent on roads increased with the traffic volume, with $171 million spent by the National Roads Board in 1980, mainly on motorway and bypass roads around cities. Road design became more expansive and major realignments were undertaken to make motoring safer, speed traffic up, shorten distances and help use less fuel. Expenditure accelerated each year and $787 million was spent on roads in 1989.

Australia and New Zealand signed the Closer Economic Relations (CER) Agreement in 1983, ushering in trans-Tasman free trade. Australia had design rules (ADR) which effectively prevented used cars being imported and protected its motor industry; New Zealand's

Henry Ford II died on September 29 1987 having devoted his life to the Ford Motor Company, which he began rescuing from the financial wilderness in 1943. He made it a global giant and became the industry's leader. His views, often forthright, were respected by all.

Reg Day, the CMC building caretaker, raises the flag for a royal visit in 1981. Hope Gibbons building is behind.

With the changes made to 'Baggage Car' rules, New Zealand became the largest importer in the world of used Japanese cars (Jap Imports). Values kept falling for both new and used vehicles over a sustained, lengthy period. A number of dealers did not survive as rationalisation took place, and the new policies changed the motor industry forever. The industry employed one in every six working New Zealanders in 1980, compared to one in five in the US. By 1987, the ratio was changing.

New Zealand was a small player in a big world, and it became a case of sink or swim with the new currents, which carried people on to new destinations, not necessarily their chosen ones.

Carless days, regulated in 1979, were still in force and people put up with it, but not willingly. The legislation became a bureaucratic nightmare, and was repealed in May 1980. Gas conversions to CNG and LPG fuels were big business, and were being fitted by many dealers. Gas use meant people could drive their car when and where they pleased. Open road speed was still only 80kph.

Conversion costs were subsidised by government with a grant of $1,500. LPG was a premium fuel and cars performed well, often better than on high-octane petrol. The cheaper CNG contained more impurities and was less efficient, causing some cars to perform below expectation. In general the larger the engine, the better they went. Both conversions took up space in the luggage boot and CNG cylinders were much heavier, needing re-rated rear springs. Experiments using CNG in public transport buses were less successful because of additional weight and space imposed by gas cylinders, and their poor range, and the idea was not pursued.

Branches were still vitally important to main city dealers. Extensions were made at Papatoetoe, to incorporate additional service as well as sales, for South Auckland Motors, together with a new service facility and sales outlet at Mangere. The Sydenham branch of Hutchinson Motors was extended and a 4-bay workshop constructed to give added service to sales.

Dealers needed big workshops to prepare new cars after poor assembly, and pre-delivery averaged about four days or more as faults were made good. In the cities the cost of land meant branches were an effective and lower cost way to expand

governments could have followed suit but chose not to.

From 1983 the motor industry changed more than at any time in the previous 50 years. New Zealand had a British preferential tariff system based upon now out of date trading relationships. Our exports to Australia, Japan and the US were each more than double our exports to the United Kingdom. The 1981 Industries Development Commission (IDC) recommended de-regulating the NZ motor industry, and the Motor Industry Plan was finally adopted after the government fiddled with changes in 1984.

Transport licensing was phased out between 1983 and 1986, so that road transport could cart goods in competition to the railways for the first time in 50 years. In 1933 licensing prevented road transport from carting goods more than 30 miles in competition to rail. In 1961 this was increased to 65 kilometres, and 150 kilometres in 1977. From 1986 heavy road transport expanded dramatically.

The motor vehicle market was in turmoil with the changes and deregulations.

workshop capacity, in addition to their defence of border role.

Alf B Gibbons reached the age of 70, and according to Article 76 incorporated into changes to the Articles of Association in November 1979, he retired, after 33 years with the company, during some of which he was secretary of the subsidiary companies. He was joint managing director of Hope Gibbons Ltd for many years with his brother G B. Alf's place on the board was taken by C John Emery, then managing director of South Auckland Motors.

The Japanese car industry was now affecting world markets. Twenty years earlier their cars and trucks were regarded as a joke, but this was no longer the case. American W Edward Deming had been shunned at home, with his quality management methods, but found the Japanese people eager converts who became fanatical about his principles. Japanese cars achieved high production quality, had lots of extras built in, and were relatively low cost to buy. Japanese designers refined and incorporated many good ideas from US and European competitors.

In the US, the motor industry was in turmoil with Ralph Nader, the consumers' crusader, who labelled some vehicles as 'lemons', and worse, claiming some models caused accidents. He assisted court actions over liabilities, causing the industry to spend millions on compensation, recalls and safety. The United Auto Workers Union in the US was very active and, while workers had been laid off when sales declined in the past, it was no longer that simple. In the United Kingdom there were supply problems with prolonged strikes and union unrest, and many Ford factories relocated to Europe where favourable labour union deals were struck.

In February 1981 Ford NZ introduced dealers to the Ford Courier Utility, which had a twin, the Mazda B1800. In spectacular style, O'Brien Reeve, Ford sales & marketing director, slashed his way with a sword through a bamboo curtain to the new utility. There was a reluctance to accept Japanese sourced product, but the reality was there; a tough 1 tonne economical utility, already proven by Mazda, assembled in New Zealand, but with a Ford badge. Ford talked about the Mazda-based Ford Econovan, due to arrive later, and a new small car from the same source.

Ford commenced assembly of the Ford Laser at the Seaview plant in early 1981. Based on a Mazda 323, the car quickly caught the attention of production staff as it could be assembled perfectly, with doors and other panels coming together just as they should do. It was a dream to work with after some of the English cars; if you could get the left rear door to fit and close, then the boot would not, or vice versa. Everything in the Laser was precisely laid out, and would interchange exactly with any other similar model Laser.

When Ford introduced Laser to dealers in Gisborne, "the first place in the world to see the rising sun each day", they too were astonished at its quality, and even more surprised with the performance and space this small car provided. Within a month of the public launch on April 9, Laser became New Zealand's top selling car model. Dealers found they spent very little time on pre-delivery, and even less on warranty. Importantly, the car looked different from a Mazda 323, which shared the same platform, similar mechanicals and many other components.

There was a great deal of confused logic. Many people would not buy a Japanese product, because of past associations, but a Laser was not Japanese, because people thought of it as a Ford. The Ford Laser changed people's thinking because of its quality and price. The Ford marketing team, under manager Brent Cederman, had succeeded.

C Lennox Henderson retired from the board in 1981 and W D (Bill) Maclaren, managing director of Macaulay Motors, Invercargill, replaced him at the annual meeting.

CMC received a final ultimatum for both the nine-storey building and three-storey building at 89 Courtenay Place; either modify to comply with the seismic code or demolish by

C John Emery, managing director of South Auckland Motors was elected a CMC director in 1980.

W D (Bill) Maclaren, managing director of Macaulay Motors, Invercargill was elected director in 1981.

Above and opposite: Laser was launched as 'The Star Car of the Eighties'. Ford's first front wheel drive car, it had excellent handling and performance, good looks, and minimal warranty . It was top seller in a month, and came in three body styles: 4 door sedan, 3 and 5 door hatchback. There were 4 engines: 1100cc, 1300cc, 1500cc and 1500Sport. Prices started at $8,990.

The first Courier 1 tonne wellside utility was already proven as a Mazda B1600. Ford dealers were surprised how well it sold; rugged and reliable, it did everything asked of it.

1988. There were few options with the 1886 three-storey double brick building as it was not economic to fix. The 1921 nine-storey assembly building was different, having used concrete and steel, but needed new seismic shear walls and substantial changes to the foundations to comply. In addition, new off-street parking requirements were imposed; it was going to be expensive, but less than the increased value of the building.

Other Wellington CBD building owners had received seismic requisitions, and one of those, Wright Stephenson and Co, made the decision to sell its four buildings on the corner of Taranaki and Jessie Streets. The 97 Taranaki Street five-storey double brick building was not economic to fix, and the adjoining three-storey building on the corner of Jessie Street was doubtful. The two and three-storey warehouse buildings were adjacent in Jessie Street. However, here was

an opportunity for Avery Motors to aquire land next to Standard Motor Bodies' panelbeating shop, which could be used for service bays. After more than a year of negotiations it was purchased for $550,000, with the idea of modifying the two- and three-storey buildings and demolishing the five-storey building.

Work commenced on conversion and seismic strengthening using structural engineer Martyn Spencer, of Spencer Holmes Miller. The old five-storey building was demolished to give display space along Taranaki Street. The three-storey building on the corner of Jessie Street was reduced by one floor and converted to provide a ground floor parts and petrol merchandising operation with a flat roof. The adjacent three-storey warehouse was reduced by one floor and connected to the two-storey building in Jessie Street. These adjoined Standard Motor

Business managers met Lex Wallace and the new LINC computer system in 1982. When implemented, it used too much memory and had to be abandoned. The Magix system replaced it and worked well with ordinary PCs.

Above: Avery Motors was still waiting for a council town planning decision on the Ghuznee Street extension, so built a branch at Adelaide Road to relieve some of the space pressure at Taranaki Street.

Below: A map of Te Aro about 1985 showing company properties, and the likely route of Ghuznee Street extension.

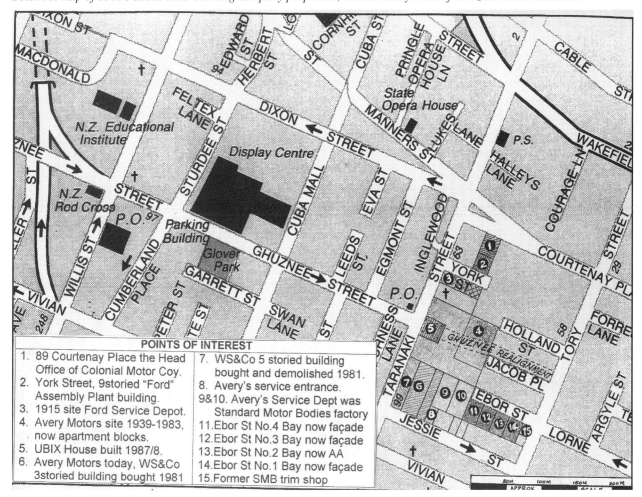

POINTS OF INTEREST

1. 89 Courtenay Place the Head Office of Colonial Motor Coy.
2. York Street, 9storied "Ford" Assembly Plant building.
3. 1915 site Ford Service Depot.
4. Avery Motors site 1939-1983, now apartment blocks.
5. UBIX House built 1987/8.
6. Avery Motors today, WS&Co 3storied building bought 1981
7. WS&Co 5 storied building bought and demolished 1981.
8. Avery's service entrance.
9&10. Avery's Service Dept was Standard Motor Bodies factory
11.Ebor St No.4 Bay now façade
12.Ebor St No.3 Bay now façade
13.Ebor St No.2 Bay now AA
14.Ebor St No.1 Bay now façade
15.Former SMB trim shop

Bodies' panel shop. The upper floors were strengthened and a vehicle ramp added to allow vehicles to be stored above the new sales operations, and ramped across to the roof of the altered corner building. The end result was the very attractive city dealership of Avery Motors, opened in 1983. Adelaide Road branch closed, staff transferred back to Taranaki Street and the building was leased.

After prolonged negotiations with the Diocesan Trust Board over Avery Motors'

old leased site, a sale to Colonial Motor Company was made in June 1983 of Town Acres 243 and 244, originally planned for the construction of the Wellington Cathedral. The new cathedral had been built in Molesworth Street, and planned changes to it necessitated a sale price of $1.25 million. The ownership gave CMC control of the land once the Ghuznee Street extension issue was resolved. The company now owned over six acres at Te Aro,

Top: Avery Motors found a new home when Wright Stephenson's sold their buildings on the corner of Taranaki and Jessie Streets. The five-storey building was demolished and next door's three-storeys reduced to two and strengthened to meet the earthquake code. Next door, Standard Motor Bodies panel shop became the workshop.

Below: This 1989 aerial view shows the buildings more clearly. It is very different today.

Highland Park Motors, built at East Tamaki in 1983 as a service station, quickly became one of the largest in Auckland. Used cars were then added and it was a logical franchise site, but Ford did not agree, and it was leased.

providing large-scale development opportunities.

Computers were now a business reality, and a decision was made to use the new Burroughs LINC system to replace the punch card system and worn out Sensematics. The LINC system was a promising new 'real time' system. A mainframe B1955 Burroughs was installed costing $198,840 plus software of $83,000 and a specialist engineer was employed to maintain and enhance the programmes. CMC Group was the first in the world to use the system in the motor industry.

LINC worked very well and steadily increased capability until it ran out of memory space. The 'real time' aspect was brilliant, but the memory requirements had not been fully appreciated. Motor industry applications need huge amounts of information storage for random access. It soon became apparent that the LINC system, although good, was going to cost far too much to operate, and an agreement was reached with Burroughs to abandon the project. Computer Bureau Ltd (later Datacom), now tenants in the Courtenay Place 'Ford' Building, 'number crunched' information until a suitable alternative was found.

As a result of the IDC Motor Industry Plan, released in 1981, Ford was now planning to expand production capacity and enlarge the Wiri assembly plant. To make this viable, they required a minimum vehicle volume annually. They wanted CMC Group to guarantee to take a large fixed volume of their output for a long period ahead. CMC knew profits dropped when car manufacturers pushed volumes too high and reluctance led to a decision not to sign.

CMC bought and leased a nine acre farmlet on Great South Road at Wiri in 1963. The land was finally re-zoned in 1982 and the company subdivided, roaded and sold part to Cable Price Downer, but kept the three acre prime site for the proposed Manukau City dealership. Shareholders found this worthwhile, receiving a tax free dividend from the $479,000 profit.

Land bought near Howick in the Highland Park area in 1976 was finally developed in 1983 after 10 years of zoning applications to sell petrol, CNG and LPG. In a key location, the operation was leased and was soon selling over 4 million litres per year. Service bays were added and a used car display area set up for a newly formed subsidiary, Highland Park Autos Ltd.

Ford launched the Telstar car and hatchback in August 1983, further expanding its link with Mazda. Again these 'new' 1.6 and 2 litre Fords filled the bill as the last of the very popular Cortinas was assembled. Cortina's European replacement was the more expensive Sierra. At the time New Zealand's dollar value did not support vehicle purchases from Europe, the yen providing better value. Fortunately, Ford NZ was able to obtain the base model new Sierra wagon, as no Telstar wagon was then available. Wagons were a large and important sector of the 1.6–2 litre market, needed by commercial users.

The English D Series trucks had also run out, and the replacement Cargo range did not stack up. Ford NZ formed a new joint venture 'first' with Hino Trucks in Japan. Hino models were re-labelled as Fords, but the arrangement took nearly 18 months to come to fruition, causing severe dealer pain. The new Hino Fords found ready acceptance with customers. They performed very well and service warranty and repairs reduced substantially.

At the end of 1983, board chairman, Gerald B Gibbons resigned for health reasons. Involved directly and indirectly with the company for 47 years, first in 1936 with auditor H N Scrimshaw, then after war service, he was joint managing director of Hope Gibbons Ltd with his brother A B Junior. For a period secretary of the subsidiary companies, he was appointed to the CMC board in 1961, and was chairman

Above: Ford assembled the English Sierra Wagon in New Zealand in 1983. It cost $17,995 with 1.6 litre engine, and $18,890 with 2.0 litres.

Ford introduced Telstar when Cortina was phased out in 1983. At first only a four door sedan, 1.6L cost $16,795 and 2.0GL $18,995. There was soon a five door TX5 hatchback at $21,032. Ordinary looking, they performed and handled well and customers liked the performance and extra gadgets and 'gizmos'. The drop in warranty made dealers happy too.

Above: N Series Ford trucks arrived from Hino in 1983, after 18 months with no medium trucks. They were very good, almost indestructible trucks.

Ford Trader 2, 3 and 4 tonners were introduced and became a very popular tough truck. D Series went out at the same time and the Mazda sourced Trader warranty was much lower.

from 1973. A keen boatie, G B sailed his launch in awful conditions on April 10 1967 to rescue survivors from the sinking *Wahine*, and was awarded the George Medal for his actions.

Gordon Hope (Don) Gibbons was appointed chairman, and John Greville Gibbons, G B's son, was appointed to the board. A year later, F N (Bill) Gibbons reached board retirement age, and John A Wylie, a nephew resident in Auckland, was appointed in his place.

Seismic alterations of the nine-storey CMC Building at 89 Courtenay Place commenced in August 1983. New expanded bell piles were driven to more than 40ft below the building and the ground and first floors were converted to three car-parking decks. A new seismic tower, incorporating lifts, stairways and toilet blocks for each floor, was added to the former light well on the north side, with a new glass curtain wall with spectacular views over Wellington. A new penthouse was added to the top of the building. This light-well change added considerably to the available area on each floor, and provided more than 90,000 sq ft of space in total. During the four years of conversion, the building was fully leased, due mainly to the skill of secretary Max Caigou and patient tenants who gradually took over their new greatly enhanced spaces. Having cost $4.7 million, the seismic coded structure had a new value of $9.7 million. The exercise

was a triumph.

Inflation was now running at 1¹/₂% per month, and profits from motor trading were unable to keep pace, despite cost cutting. There simply was not enough margin to cope with inflation and taxes and maintain cash flow. Fortunately, the company's land acquisitions were appreciating quickly with inflation and masking the motor trading results. Between 1981 and 1985 the government valuations of company properties increased from $16.7 to $30.7 million. Fifty percent of the balance sheet land assets were property not used for motor trading. In 1985, Colonial Motor Company recorded its highest ever profit after tax of $7.15 million, a return of 19.8% on shareholders' funds. Shareholders received a 1 for 5 bonus, taking issued capital to $17,160,000. Trading profit after tax was 2.28 cents per dollar sold. Land development was profitable, and outside investment companies saw opportunities.

When the IDC Report was adopted in 1983, motor assemblers thought they now had the surety of direction they needed. Ford NZ committed $50 million to upgrading the Wiri assembly plant and production of world quality vehicles using computer controlled gantry and welding robots. Ford NZ thought they would be able to export some models to Australia and receive built up Falcons in exchange, thus benefiting both parties under the new CER arrangement.

Many aspects of the Motor Industry Plan were either modified or changed to try to stop distortions that occurred when ingenious New Zealanders found their way around the new regulations. One of the most significant changes was the alteration to 'Baggage Car' rules. Introduced to assist in attracting defence and government personnel to sign up for overseas tours of duty, it allowed them to bring back cars they had used for more than 12 months without duty and only paying nominal taxes, provided they were kept for two years. Now, both the use period before importation, and holding period after

John G Gibbons, Hope Gibbons' great grandson, was elected to the board in 1983.

Left: John A Wylie, great grandson of Hope Gibbons, was appointed director in 1984.

The nine-storey building, now earthquake compliant, was a great rebuilding success. The glass fronted sheer wall created spectacular views over the city and harbour. The rebuilding saved millions while adding to its total value.

Below: The board in 1985. From left back: Orm Hutchinson, John Gibbons, Bill Maclaren, John Wylie. Front: Michael Gibbons, Peter Gibbons, Don Gibbons (chairman), Max Caigou (secretary), Colin Cliff. Absent: John Emery.

arrival, were abolished.

Tendering for imports became chaotic as used car dealers sought licences, and then commenced importing used cars, particularly Japanese, which suffered an artificially high depreciation, and exotic cars from other areas of the world. Import tendering introduced penalties but was later abolished. Buyers, by the planeload, were flown overseas to anywhere for 24 hours, and their prearranged 'baggage cars' returned later. "Buy a used car and get a free overseas holiday", the advertisements said. Pilots and aircrews on international routes had instant access to a new, lucrative occupation as unlicensed car importers.

Ford NZ managing director J G (Joe) Auton transferred to be president of Ford Lio Ho manufacturing operations in Taiwan, and Australian W A (Bill) Hartigan, replaced him on September 1 1985. A forceful character, Hartigan was blunt, but got things done, although not in the way New Zealanders were used to, or necessarily liked.

The public began to lose confidence in 1986 and new car registrations dropped as changeover costs soared. Manufacturers had over-ordered vehicles and discounted their products, trying to get more from a reduced market. This squeezed dealer margins as it had 50 years before. With GST being introduced on October 1 1986, the public rushed to buy new cars for the two months before. However, on October 1, when sales tax was removed and GST of 12.5% went

REGISTRATION OF CARS IMPORTED INTO NEW ZEALAND			
	NEW CARS	USED CARS*	M.CYCLES
1970	66,546	3,738	5,529
1975	80,043	4,863	20,838
1980	75,666	2,701	29,957
1981	89,453	1,907	24,571
1982	83,657	1,812	22,306
1983	74,077	1,766	16,938
1984	83,657	2,019	15,975
1985	81,516	2,918	13,425
1986	76,075	3,946	13,372
1987	77,499	12,129	12,609
1988	71,212	17,372	8,968
1989	83,862	50,966	5,796
*prev.registered o'seas (NZ Dept Stats & Motor Ind. Yearbooks)			

on, cars actually dropped in price. When Jap imports increased and New Zealand became the world's largest importer of used Japanese cars alarm bells sounded within the industry.

On the night of August 8 1985, Stevens Motors' showroom and administration building was razed, in a fierce fire, considered to have been arson. Fortunately, nobody was on site at the time. Cars in the showroom literally exploded as their fuel tanks reached flash point, setting off a chain reaction to the next car. However, all company records, kept in a fire delay strongroom, as in all CMC companies, were salvaged intact. After the fire, Stevens Motors' sales and administration were consolidated across the road in the parts and service building. Current and forecast needs did not justify the same facility.

After considerable delay in settling the insurance claim, the old Stevens site, now worth $3.25 million, was re-developed as office and retail complexes with joint venture partner Government Life. The first building, Colonial House, three floors totalling 57,000 sq ft, was fully leased to Inland Revenue and sold on completion at the end of 1987, while the adjacent Fairmont House, of three floors totalling 27,000 sq ft was being built and leased.

Brierley Investments Ltd made a takeover offer to CMC shareholders on April 29 1986, to buy their ordinary shares for $3.50 cash. Directors met and, after receiving advice, wrote to shareholders asking them to reject the offer as the shares were worth much more. Brierley's were after the valuable property held by CMC Group which, with inflation, was certainly worth more than the offer. Eventually the offer was withdrawn, but

W A (Bill) Hartigan came from Australia to be Ford's managing director. He was abrasive but got things done, and succeeded in getting Mazda assembly under VANZ.

Brierley's now held 13.8% of the company's shares. When they requested a board seat, directors refused.

South Auckland Motors' new building, at Great South Road, Manukau City, was opened on October 30 1986, for a total cost of $4.7 million. Garry Jackson, former vehicle sales manager of Ford NZ, was appointed dealer principal, with John Emery managing director. Other South Auckland Motors' properties were rationalised; Neilsen's Road was sold; part of the land and buildings at King and Gordon Streets, Otahuhu were sold; branch premises at Mangere, East Tamaki and Papatoetoe were leased.

Computer operations, using Magix software which utilised networking power,

were set up under Peter Kohnke, who formed Alpha Centauri Systems (ACS) with Steven Grant and contracted to CMC. System development was relatively fast and soon had all the CMC Group on line with dedicated data lines. Enhancements eventually linked into Ford via X25 network, using an emulator, devised by Peter Kohnke and Steven Grant, to 'talk' to Ford's system. The software, written by ACS, integrated all accounting of individual and group companies, cross-referenced sales, parts and service, and incorporated management reporting and forecasting. The Magix system reduced many tedious accounting functions and arguably became the industry's best practice.

After buying the two acres of Diocesan

land at Te Aro in June 1983, CMC engaged Fletcher Building to design Te Aro Square business park and submit a building application to the council. After further town planning delays, the council were obliged to grant a building permit in February 1986, following a High Court order, and building started on a six-storey office block of 55,000 sq ft opposite the end of Ghuznee Street. Before completion, U-Bix Corp had taken the lease for two floors and naming rights. This established a new potential for Te Aro Square.

Te Kuiti Motors Ltd closed down on March 31 1987, after more than 50 years operation with the CMC Group. Sadly, the operation which had trained 15 group managers and 18 accountants was no longer viable. The rural town was in severe strife due to the farming recession, and 25% of the town's residents were registered as unemployed, with many more too proud to do so.

High profile Auckland Ford dealer McMillan Motors decided to become dual franchised and, despite warnings from Ford, went ahead with Toyota on a separate site at Royal Oak. Ford NZ unceremoniously cancelled their franchise in April 1987. The territory remained open for many years, as Ford failed to find another dealer.

Graeme Durrad Gibbons was appointed general manager of CMC in September 1987. After graduating from Otago as a Bachelor of Commerce and Associate Chartered Accountant (CA), he had spent five years at Ford NZ in finance and distribution, then nine months at New Lynn Motors, before starting at CMC on February 1 1984 where his financial skills were used to establish parameters for the Magix computer system. Graeme Gibbons' immediate role as general manager was to assist in restructuring as the CMC Group came to terms with the

Below: With the changing vehicle market there was less need for service and parts, and a decision was made to redevelop Stevens Motors in the former parts and service building across High Street.

Above: Graeme D Gibbons, another of Hope Gibbons great grandsons, became general manager in 1987. He championed CMC Group restructuring.

economic changes that were occurring.

New Zealand's sharemaket crashed, along with western world markets, in October 1987. All of New Zealand was now in an economic downturn, not just the rural areas. CMC Group's main concern was to institute change and lower expenses in line with current sales which had fallen significantly. New vehicles remained at similar levels but fell in value with tariff changes. Used car values also fell drastically and continuously during the next four years, due to Jap imports and tariff changes. CMC Group lost about $2 million on used car trading in 1988, but maintained a strict policy of keeping stocks in line with sales, culling any over-age units. Branches were leased out to other parties, surplus land and buildings were sold and rationalisation of premises and staff occurred.

Ford NZ, under Bill Hartigan, negotiated and merged assembly with Mazda, the new company called Vehicle Assemblers of NZ Ltd (VANZ), producing both Ford and Mazda vehicles for New Zealand. Ford's 1936 Seaview plant closed in 1988, and all Ford NZ operations transferred to Wiri, now called Manukau City. With Mazda's Sylvia Park plant, VANZ had a production capacity of 155 units per eight hour day, the country's largest, which gave it the necessary economy of scale.

From April 1 1988 the price of motor spirits (petrol) was deregulated, thus ending 55 years of government control over both the purchase and selling prices. Petrol selling margins could now be set by individual retailers. Most large petrol stations were leased by the four petrol distributors who controlled prices to suit their market volumes.

In 1988, Ford Australia introduced a new EA Falcon range, after a great spiel about its superior quality. The quality of the early cars was appalling, due in part to assembly methods which inhibited the car's progress. New Zealand assembly at Manukau City was actually better than the Australian built cars, and production teams had to suffer the ignominy of being sent to New Zealand to find out how to build their own car.

The New Zealand retail motor trade was

Ford celebrated 50 years in New Zealand in 1986 and Red Poling, world president, dropped into Avery Motors during a flying visit. Here he tries out the driver's seat in 'Pamela', a 1934 Ford Y, with tuition from Avery's managing director, George Daniel.

over-crowded but adjusted each month as dealers liquidated or went broke. Ford finally agreed 71 dealers were too many, but little happened, except in tractors and heavy trucks. Ford sold out of tractors internationally to New Holland. New Zealand Ford tractor distribution was handled by CB Norwood Distributors, and tractor dealers were reduced to 19. Heavy truck dealers were also reduced – to 18 and then seven dealers. This rationalisation strengthened the remaining dealers, but although the very important profit centre of parts and service remained, the changes

removed a number of provincial dealers, depleting rural market share.

W (Bill) Hartigan returned to Australia in December 1988, having achieved a great deal with the assembly merger with Mazda and formation of VANZ. J E (Jim) Miller was appointed managing director from January 1 1989. Jim Miller came from Detroit and his softly spoken approach, and new quality ideas and methods for production and customer service, brought out the best in people. Dealers responded well to his smiling approach and ideas.

Liquidity problems in New Zealand's

Top: South Auckland Motors' impressive new dealership at Manukau City was opened on October 30 1986.
Bottom: Following town plan changes, Te Aro Square development started very quickly with a six-storey office block of 55,000 sq ft opposite the Ghuznee Street intersection.

Top: A new baby Ford Festiva arrived in 1988, filling a gap in the small car lineup at $16,995.

Bottom: EA Falcon was launched in 1988 by Ford Australia. A great concept which promised much for dealers, it delivered considerable challenges. Cost: $33,290.

commerce and banking, with insolvencies and redundancies, put pressure on all business activity. Despite this, new vehicle sales went ahead in 1989, with 83,862 sold, and the decade average, close to 80,000 cars per year, was the highest ever.

In 1989, W D (Bill) Maclaren retired from the board and P A (Pat) Cody, managing director of Timaru Motors, replaced him. The Fairmont House property development was completed and leased to NZ Insurance, but the U-Bix Centre had been delayed with foundation difficulties.

Times were very tough for all franchised dealers, and many quit, but CMC Group was resilient, changed with circumstances, and soon bounced back. Property development had helped the group remain viable and in profit all through the turmoil. Rationalisation of the industry after the huge changes was inevitable, and those who remained would be stronger financially, or would they?

There was intense competition in the market and, when this happens, profit suffers. Rural dealers had started to recover a little, but now city dealers were in difficulty, and Ford was giving substantial quarterly bonuses for achieving

targets. For a city dealer, the last sale, sometimes on the last day of the quarter, might be worth incentives of $100,000. The amount of money at stake caused huge problems for neighbouring dealers, and often put Ford dealers head to head with each other, instead of the opposition brand dealers.

1989 STATISTICS

REPORTING CHANGED SO COMPARISONS ARE DIFFICULT IN SOME AREAS

Cars registered   1,430,806   - decade change   + 13.6%
Trucks registered   308,258   - decade change   − 13.8%
  48% of cars registered were over 10 years old (last kept 1986)
  3% of cars registered were over 20 years old (last kept 1986)

NZ POPULATION IN 1989 WAS 3,384,600:

1 car: 2.3 people;   1 vehicle: 1.77 people
New cars and station wagons registered   83,862
Ex overseas cars and wagons registered   50,966

TRAFFIC DENSITY DAILY PAST A TALLY POINT, NOT AVAILABLE

TRACTORS IN USE − NO LONGER KEPT

RETAIL PRICE FOR STANDARD FUEL FROM NOV 1 1989

Cents per litre petrol   107¢
Included is Excise Tax   26.4¢
Goods & Services Tax   11.9¢

FROM 1989 YEAR THE MOTOR INDUSTRY COLLECTED TAXES DIFFERENTLY, NO LONGER EASILY ANALYSED

State Highway expenditure $404 million*
Local authority roads expenditure $292million*
Total public roading expenditure $696 million*
* 15 month expenditure due to change of period
(NB: Statistics collection altered after June 30 1986, with many details now no longer available.)

J E (Jim) Miller came from Michigan to be managing director of Ford NZ with new quality ideas and culture. A great tonic, at a very depressed time, he got on well with dealers, getting them going again.

Colonial House was built on the Stevens Motors' fire site as a joint venture with Government Life, leased to IRD and sold. Later, the adjoining Fairmont House was similarly built, leased and sold.

Peter Gibbons retired as managing director and became chairman of the board in 1990. Colin Cliff presented a salver and tea service at Faith and Peter Gibbons' farewell.

Johnsonville petrol marketing was redeveloped and leased to Caltex in 1990. Peter Gibbons cuts the ribbon with Caltex managing director Bernie Stevenson and watched by the board.

Graeme Gibbons took a study group to the United States to look at new ideas in 1990. Left to right: Grant Daniel, New Plymouth; Graeme Gibbons, CMC; Peter Kohnke, ACS; Alan Gilmour, Ford International president; Alan McElroy, Invercargill; Russell Lange, Christchurch; and John Blyth, Panmure.

CHAPTER TEN

LIVING WITH CHANGE

New Zealand was having great difficulty in coming to terms with the rush of reforms. The Labour government of 1984 and its 1990 National successor changed the country's way of life in some fundamental ways. Many government departments were 'corporatised' and then 'privatised' and some struggled to exist in the real world. Education, health and social welfare, which New Zealanders took for granted as basic rights, were straight-jacketed in an effort to make them more efficient. On the other hand, the removal of most economic activity restrictions produced a new group of entrepreneurs.

Employment Contracts were legislated in 1991, helping to change employees from pawns to business team members prepared to be more flexible and helpful to the cause of satisfying customer needs. A wave of new legislation came in during the early 1990s, aimed at consumer protection including the Fair Trading Act, Consumer Guarantees Act, Commerce Act, Building Act, Human Rights Act, Privacy Act, Companies Act, Health & Safety Act, and Resource Management Act. Compliance became a business nightmare, and litigation levels increased dramatically as 'examples', often minor breaches, were found, tried in court, and punished with huge fines.

Some things, however, seemed to be studiously ignored by government. Jap import used cars came in by the boatload, bringing with them all sorts of bio-security problems – painted apple and Asian gypsy moths, mosquitos, spiders, insects, snakes, pests and diseases. The under-funded Customs did not have the physical capability to check what was happening, nor the wit to stop it. Bizarre examples, such as refuse trucks complete with rotting household rubbish, were imported. Re-built wrecks written off and ordered for destruction, and stolen vehicles, reappeared in New Zealand. Japan contrived special tests, to artificially depreciate their cars to zero in five years and make them cheap in real terms, to foster Japanese automotive

manufacturing. In 1989 50,966 used imports arrived. In 1990 there were 85,324, and, despite intense lobbying by the motor industry spelling out the inherent dangers, governments did nothing of consequence to change things. Used import cars are now around 100,000 per year.

The writing was on the wall for the motor assembly industry; it could not survive against the tide of export subsidised Jap imports, and new lowered tariffs. General Motors was first to close its Trentham plant in November 1990 and eight years later all assembly plants had gone. Few of the component manufacturing industries could survive without assembly, and closed down, despite export sales of components to Japan, the US and Australia. Ford tried to export New Zealand built models to Australia under the CER agreement, but the Australian government, protecting their own automotive industries, would not have a bar of it. Thousands of motor industry workers, about 10% of the New Zealand labour force, lost their jobs. Every other country with automotive assembly has some form of protection, the industry perceived as being good for training in diverse skills, as well as employment. The New Zealand government chose to abandon assembly of new vehicles, a major employer of New Zealanders, in favour of an imported used car industry using overseas workers, predominantly from Japan.

Chief executive officer, Graeme Gibbons took a CMC Group of six people to study selected US dealers, visit Detroit and attend the North American Dealers Association (NADA) annual conference. The study tour opened the group's eyes to new ideas on how another country operates its motor industry, their systems, people handling and operating methods. The NADA convention offers multiple workshops on most aspects of retailing vehicles, and their keynote speakers are outstanding. In a normal year between 15,000 and 25,000 US dealers attend.

At the end of June 1990 Peter C Gibbons retired as managing director and Graeme Durrad Gibbons, P C's son, was appointed chief executive officer on July 1 1990. P C had joined CMC Group after completing his Bachelor of Engineering in 1950, working in the audit office and then at Timaru, before returning to head office in 1954. P C became managing director in 1968, bringing a great inner strength and loyalty to the company and to the people and their families who served it. He had a remarkable memory and attention to detail renowned from Kaitaia to Invercargill; a vision for town planning futures, property acquisition and its eventual fulfilment; and a continuing loyalty to the Ford flag. P C became board chairman when Don Gibbons stepped aside after 16 years in the position, at the annual meeting in 1990. When Colin Cliff turned 70 and retired as a director John A Blyth, dealer principal of East City Ford, replaced him.

The work done by CMC from 1988 on change management, restructuring and removing costs from their rural and provincial subsidiaries had, in most cases, paid off, and they were now trading profitably. The computer systems were connected to Ford's system using an emulator via X25 pacquet switching, enabling the paperless selection and ordering of parts, submission of warranty claims, and later ordering of vehicles.

Meanwhile, the city and metropolitan companies were being seriously affected as the effects of the depressed primary economy spread more widely. Trading was difficult in the early 1990s with new vehicle prices dropping after tariff changes, used car prices still falling, the market flooded with new and used cars, and new car discounting rife. The discounting caused great antagonism amongst dealers, who fought for sales to 'their customers', often finding that 'their customers' were being picked off by a neighbouring 'Friendly Ford' dealer. This infighting seriously debilitated all dealers financially, a number closed down, and further collapses were likely.

Ford believed that the best way forward was for dealers to improve customer care quality by lifting standards and achieving greater customer satisfaction and loyalty, thereby creating a competitive difference. Ford NZ managing director, Jim Miller, was in his element when he introduced a new annual premier dealer competition. Customer feedback was measured from questionnaires, together with Ford market requirements, and four dealers emerged with elite President's Awards. In the first awards, Hawke Motors, at Morrinsville and Te Aroha, received one of the four awards; and dealer principal Ken Mullan and his wife Ann went to exclusive Huka Lodge to receive this from the president of Ford Asia Pacific.

By 1992 CMC Group had achieved three of the four awards – Team Hutchinson Ford, Fagan Motors and Ruahine Motors

The Laser MkIII came in 1990, and was larger with 1,600cc and 1,800cc engines. The very popular 3,4 and 5 door models seemed to be almost indestructible.

No. 89 Courtenay Place changed when the 1886 double brick building, no longer complying with the seismic code, was pulled down. It was replaced with a double storey building to match the nine storey office tower.

– and Timaru Motors and Avon City Ford had received runner-up Distinguished Achiever's awards. CMC Group has consistently won the President's and Distinguished Achiever's awards ever since with positive staff attitudes permeating dealerships and producing a true customer service ethic. The two Christchurch dealers, Team Hutchinson Ford and Avon City Ford have taken a lead, both winning many times.

Ford instituted dealer workshops aimed at changing attitudes to circumstances and people, and promoting team attitudes within dealerships. Jim Miller said: "Make change your friend", and those who did, succeeded in turning around their businesses. The workshops were similar to those started by CMC Group in 1988 when the going was tough for rural dealers. CMC focussed on 'what you can do for yourself', Ford focussed on 'changing the culture within your business', and dealer staff learned to eat an elephant, one bite at a time.

Meanwhile, property development went ahead. At Te Aro the U-Bix Centre was fully leased, with the new National Educational Qualifications Authority occupying the top four floors. Stevens Motors shifted further up High Street in Lower Hutt and the old site was redeveloped, saving Stevens huge amounts of property rent. At Johnsonville, a new multi fuel service station was built and leased to Caltex, and a part of the lower land was sold to the joint venture extending the shopping centre. Negotiations were still going on with parties for the development of the rest of the two acres at Te Aro. The old 1886 three-storey double brick building at 89 Courtenay Place was pulled down, and the present two-storey building and arcade was built to match the front of the nine-storey CMC building, completing the seismic requisition needs.

Profits were poor in 1991 with motor trading showing a loss for the first time for 60 years. This was caused by the shakedown in restructuring, and further recession in the city markets. CMC Group staff fell from 900 in June 1990, to 764 a year later, considerably down on the 1,350 employees of the early 1970s. Office clerk numbers reduced over a 20 year period by more than 50% as computer systems took over their repetitive, often boring jobs. Much better information was now readily available from a computer, making management decisions more informed.

After an agreement was reached with

two key parties to develop a major supermarket and large retail outlet at Te Aro, a resource management application was made to Wellington City Council for consent under the new act. However, after waiting an interminable period for answers, the deal fell through and soured the project. Interestingly, the objections made were not from neighbours, but from competing supermarket operators, thus making an ass of the new act's processes.

In 1992 G H (Don) Gibbons retired, under Article 76. Don had worked for the company for over 50 years, been dealer principal at Kaikohe and Waipukurau, a director since 1956, and chairman for 16 years, taking a key part in the significant changes in that time. J P (Jim) Gibbons, dealer principal of Energy City Ford, was appointed in his place. A G (Grant) Daniel was appointed general manager in September 1992, having been dealer principal at Phillipps Motors in New Plymouth.

Five subsidiaries changed their trading names after Ford lifted the ban on using 'Ford'. Napier Motors Dunedin became Dunedin City Ford; Sockburn Motors, Christchurch, became Avon City Ford; Phillipps Motors New Plymouth became Energy City Ford; Panmure Motors became East City Ford; and New Lynn Motors

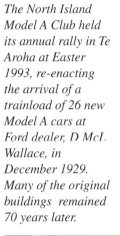

The North Island Model A Club held its annual rally in Te Aroha at Easter 1993, re-enacting the arrival of a trainload of 26 new Model A cars at Ford dealer, D McL Wallace, in December 1929. Many of the original buildings remained 70 years later.

Maidstone Motors in Upper Hutt was purchased and combined with Stevens Motors' management. The staff with their dealer principal Malcolm Davison.

became West Auckland Ford. The Auckland name changes reflected the expanded areas of operation. Trading profits recovered in 1992 and in 1993 profit doubled to $6.2 million after tax, although it was still below the board's objective of 10% return on shareholders' funds. In 1994 profits increased again to $7.71 million,

returning 11.5%.

At the end of 1993, Ford managing director Jim Miller was shifted to European Operations as the Eastern German and Soviet markets opened up. He had made a significant mark in the five years, not only in helping dealers introduce quality, but turning around attitudes in the VANZ

East City Ford at Panmure expanded its territory and took over Otahuhu for a period.

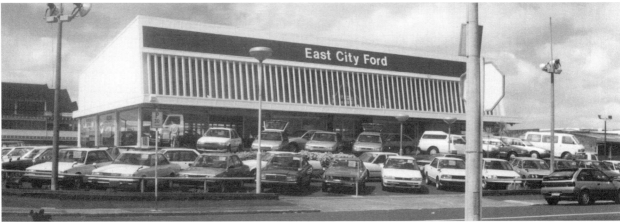

Top: Philippe Mellier came from Ford France to be Ford NZ chief executive in January 1994, and soon departed to become president of Ford Mexico.

Below: In 1994, A W (Tony) Brigden arrived from England to become Ford's managing director and begin the dealer rationalisation.

assembly plant to produce world quality vehicles and improve efficiencies. VANZ was awarded Ford's 'Q1' rating in February 1994, one of only a very few awarded in the world, signifying the quality processes were the best.

Realising that Jap imports were an Achilles heel for assembly, 'Mr Quality', Jim Miller, lobbied government, and tried to develop new vehicle trade with Australia, to keep our assembly industry open. Unfortunately, neither Australian nor New Zealand governments would co-operate for their very different reasons. Australia wanted to keep its motor industry and protected it; New Zealand wanted to get rid of trade barriers, and lower the Consumer Price Index (CPI).

Philippe Mellier from Ford France succeeded Jim Miller as managing director of Ford NZ, but dealers found he did not understand many key aspects of the New Zealand market, making autocratic changes, and losing many good staff. After a relatively short period of 10 months he departed to be president of Ford Mexico, and dealers and Ford staff sighed with relief.

Tony Brigden became managing director of Ford NZ on November 21 1994. Coming from England, he fitted more comfortably into New Zealand life.

Ford Louisville extra heavy trucks became available from Australia in 1992, and four New Zealand dealers were appointed, including three from CMC Group – South Auckland Motors, Avery Motors, and

Avon City Ford. Heavy truck dealers had been rationalised in the late 1980s and, after Ford announced in 1993 that the contract with Hino was not going to be renewed, there were no new Hino Ford trucks after March 1994. Despite Ford NZ's good intentions to find a replacement, it did not look hopeful; Ford Cargo was only produced in US in left hand drive; Iveco already had Ford affiliation in the UK, but there were problems with the franchise.

Good as the small Ford Trader trucks from Mazda were, they were only for loads of 1.5 to 4 tonnes. The prospect of no mid-range heavy trucks presented a major problem for many CMC Group dealers who had built up large operations in trucks sales, service and expertise.

Happily, quite by chance, New Zealand distribution for PACCAR trucks became available. Colonial Motor Company registered its interest; Graeme Gibbons advised Ford and received the green light to go ahead, provided the business was totally separated from, and did not affect, Ford business. Economic projections showed extra heavy truck use was expanding.

Southpac Trucks Ltd was formed with 87.5% Colonial Motor Company capital, and 12.5% from M G (Mike) Corliss, who became chief executive. Southpac took over the franchise and stock from South Pacific Trucks and set up at Wiri Station Road, Manukau City as New Zealand PACCAR distributor of Kenworth and Foden extra heavy premium trucks on January 1 1994. Three CMC Group members formed separate truck companies: South Auckland Trucks Ltd, Fagan Trucks Ltd, and Timaru Trucks Ltd. The business mushroomed beyond projections and was profitable.

In February 1995 CEO Graeme Gibbons took a second study group of CMC managers to the US, visiting selected dealers in five cities, Ford Motor Company in Detroit and the NADA Annual Convention at Dallas. It was a difficult year in the US and only 14,000 dealers attended. The opportunity was also taken to visit Detroit Diesel and Cummins truck engine plants at Detroit and Indiana, and the huge Louisville truck plant. Again the group was exposed to good ideas and methods which could be applied in New Zealand.

Government had previously indicated a new takeover code proposed by the

Top: Southland
Tractors began
trading in 1993,
selling the New
Holland, Fiat, Ford,
and Kubota tractors
at Invercargill. John
Scott, operations
manager, at right.

Left and below: The
modernised Hawke
Motors' premises at
Morrinsville and Te
Aroha serviced Piako
County in the
Waikato.

Securities Commission would be brought in, but now decided to defer this indefinitely. CMC directors needed to comply with NZ Stock Exchange requirements, in terms of a takeover code. At the board meeting of September 12 1995, it was recommended that changes to the Articles of Association be put to shareholders at the annual meeting. Chairman Peter Gibbons was due to retire under Article 76, and directors decided O A (Orm) Hutchinson was the most suitable person to become chairman elect.

If a bomb had dropped on CMC head office on October 18 1995, it could hardly have caused more fallout. As the 1995 annual report to shareholders stated:

"Before 7am on Wednesday 18 October 1995, Guinness Peat Group PLC's (GPG)

sharebrokers began to phone shareholders of the Company with a verbal offer for up to 49.9% of the shares. The Directors (except Michael and John Gibbons who had accepted and were associated with the offer) issued a 'don't sell' notice and followed up with a letter to shareholders dated 18 October 1995 urging shareholders not to sell until a report from SBC Warburg had been received as to the value of the shares. In that letter, the Directors pointed out the underlying asset value of the shares and the current trading position for the first quarter. Directors wrote again on 23rd October with information for shareholders, and on 25 October received the SBC Warburg report which confirmed the Directors' preliminary view that the offer price of $2.55 was inadequate and did not

Auckland CMC Group dealers John Blyth of East City Ford, Jim Robb of West Auckland Ford and Matthew Newman of South Auckland Motors admire the new 3.0 litre Taurus from the United States. A great car, but Falcon was cheaper.

Stevens Motors shifted further up High Street to new premises after their old site was sold for a supermarket development. This move reduced the site rental significantly.

Stan Watson's retirement from Ruahine Motors was celebrated with a reunion of former managers. At rear: Ken Mullan, Roger Gardner, Jim Gibbons, David Bodley and John Blyth. Front: Jim Robb, Stan Watson and Don Gibbons.

represent fair value. The Directors resolved to implement an ongoing plan to maximise value for all shareholders including:

• a special interim dividend of 28.75 cents per share payable immediately in an endeavour to save imputation credits that would be lost if GPG's shareholding had exceeded 34%,

• a change in dividend policy to include distribution of up to 75% of net profit after tax, subject to specific circumstances,

• rationalisation of the Company's property holdings and other assets,

• repayment of surplus funds to shareholders,

• focus the Company on its core motor trade activities."

In 1904 Gibbons family members had decided to stick together in all their commercial undertakings, which they did very successfully over many years, building substantial family investments. The jewel of their investments was CMC, and it seems hard to understand why Michael and John Gibbons took the risks

CMC directors in 1995. From left: Michael Gibbons; John Blyth; Peter Gibbons, chairman; Jim Gibbons; Orm Hutchinson, chairman elect; John Gibbons; John Wylie; Pat Cody; and John Emery.

Top: Southpac Trucks began in 1994 as New Zealand Kenworth and Foden distributors. Mike Corliss CEO, second from right, with his staff, outside their Wiri Station Rd premises at Manukau City.

Middle: In 1994, Timaru Motors delivered 20 new Ford LTS800 Louisville trucks with 5cu.m. concrete bowls to Allied Concrete, Invercargill.

Below: Telstar third generation TX5i was released in 1993 and cost $35,995. The V6 XRi model was $45,295.

they did, and put the company in jeopardy. Had GPG gained their objective of 49.9%, CMC could well have been divided up, sold off, and ceased to exist.

Directors took charge of the situation, and put a plan into action to stabilise the company. Shareholders were advised not to sell, as the offer was too low, and GPG did not increase their stake from the 33.9% shareholding gained on October 18. An agreement was made with GPG over immediate operational issues, in order to minimise damage.

With the resignation of Michael H Gibbons and John G Gibbons, and the retirement of Peter C Gibbons and P A (Pat) Cody from the board, A I (Tony) Gibbs (GPG), and Graeme D Gibbons were elected directors at the AGM and directors appointed Maurice W Loomes (GPG) and Gary H Weiss (GPG) to fill the two remaining vacancies after the AGM.

The sharemarket and GPG thought Colonial Motor Company was under-performing, as it was achieving returns in the area of 12%, when motor retailing normally performed at 15%. CMC Group had secured prime real estate locations in the 1950-90 period, to ensure their motor dealership development throughout New Zealand. Many Auckland sites were now in use as motor dealerships, having been leased to third parties, until development and town planning caught up. Te Aro sites in Wellington had proved slow to develop with the new planning and resource consent processes, and the decision was now made to sell these, and other non-motor sites which realised a large pool of money that was returned to shareholders. The company's land 'portfolio' was achieving 'normal' returns of about 8%, but this effectively lowered motor returns from 15% to 12%.

By the time GPG directors reached the boardroom, there was very little for them to do. They received a cash payment of $1 per share as did all shareholders, and the value of shares increased by 20%. After 18 months GPG sold their shares to two Malaysian companies, MBM Resources Berhad and Central Shore SDN Berhad, which were involved in motor vehicle assembly and sales and wanted an outside association. The sale was beneficial for CMC. New directors were appointed after the three GPG appointees resigned in July 1997. They were Dato' Rahim Hallim from MBM Resources and Chee Kwan Poh from Central Shore. C K Poh resigned in July 1998, with Peter D Wilson, of Napier, appointed in his place.

Fairhall Motors' tractor sales and service team at Kaikohe. From left: John Jenkinson, John Field and Russell Foote.

In 1995, Team Hutchinson Ford was officially opened by Orm Hutchinson and Tony Brigden. Refurbished showroom bottom of page 187.

Below: CMC Group managers in 1997. From left standing: Ian Duncan, Wellington; Matthew Newman, Manukau City; Ian Lambie, Dunedin; David Tobin, Waipukurau; Roger Gardner, Masterton; Neville Goldsworthy, Far North; John Flanagan, Avon City; George Smith, CMC; Russell Lange, Christchurch; Jim Robb, West Auckland; John Luxton, Invercargill; Visteurs Altments, secretary; Ken Mullan, internal auditor; Russell Marr, Timaru; Alan McElroy, Southland Tractors. Seated: John Blyth, Panmure; Graeme Gibbons, CMC; Grant Daniel, CMC; Jim Gibbons, New Plymouth.

Property had insulated CMC in a business that is notoriously cyclical. With the new dividend policy, the trick was going to be managing the lean years without significant reserves. Directors held a number of strategy meetings, identifying strengths and weaknesses for the future. Sticking with your core business is fine, but would it stick with you?

Max Caigou had been working for CMC Group for 45 years when he retired as secretary at the end of 1996. He started with CMC and served at Te Awamutu, Lower Hutt, Masterton, Waipukurau and Invercargill, before becoming managing director of Avery Motors in 1964. Ten years later he was appointed CMC Group secretary. As the annual report says, "Max

Shareholders at the 1998 annual meeting were introduced to the exciting Ford Ka with 'new edge' styling, in the CMC Building arcade at 89 Courtenay Place.

has been the cornerstone of support and loyalty to the company." A new company secretary, Visteurs Altments was appointed to take over but, after two years, decided to leave the city for family life in Nelson. The new secretary, J G (Jack) Tuohy was appointed in 1998. B C (Barry) Wisneski, who had been internal auditor for 20 years, retired, and K S (Ken) Mullan was appointed in his stead.

In response to Ford NZ's market representation plan, CMC agreed to changes:

• Craik Motors at Te Awamutu closed down in 1996, after 62 years, and the franchise shifted to Fairview Motors Hamilton;

• Hawke Motors at Morrinsville and Te Aroha closed down in 1997, after 61 years, again shifting to Fairview Motors Hamilton;

• Fairhall Motors at Kaikohe closed down in 1998, 67 years after it opened, and was absorbed into Pacific Ford at Whangarei;

In 1995, Team Hutchinson Ford refurbished its showroom using large historic murals of the dealership in earlier days. It was officially opened by Orm Hutchinson and Tony Brigden.

Right: European cars were finally making a comeback. Focus has set new benchmark standards for class C cars, winning new customers and rave reports. Here a Focus Zetec 2,000cc 5-door in the city.

Below: Southpac Trucks added two drive through preventive maintenance bays, with inspection pits, to improve customer service.

Opposite top: Nigel Wark, formerly sales director of Ford NZ, became managing director in 1997.

Opposite middle and bottom: A major redevelopment of Timaru Motors was made in 1997, consolidating operations at Washdyke, after selling their city site in Sophia Street. This spectacular facility combined Ford, Mazda, Extra Heavy Trucks, Shell Washdyke and Elite Transport Refinishers, alongside Highway 1 on the outskirts of Timaru city and port. At the opening: Ian Dewsnap, Ford Credit; Orm Hutchinson, CMC chairman; Russell Marr, dealer principal; Nigel Wark, Ford NZ; and Graeme Gibbons, CEO CMC Group.

• Northland Motors closed at Kaitaia in 2000, after 68 years in business, with Pacific Ford at Whangarei taking over;

• MS Motors at Nelson, and Marlborough Ford at Blenheim were acquired in 1998, and now operate as MS Motors (1998) Ltd;

• In 1997 Stevens Motors, Lower Hutt, Maidstone Motors, Upper Hutt, and Newlands Motors were placed under the management of Avery Motors as a single retail group, to reduce costs. This subsequently split into Avery Motors and Stevens Motors, which share a number of administration functions.

Tony Brigden was transferred to Ford Australia in September 1997, and Australian Nigel Wark, director of sales and marketing since 1995, was appointed CEO. Tony Brigden had realised that Ford's market representation policy was weakening dealers and started the dealer rationalisation programme. During the 1940-60s period, Ford made a number of small sub-agents into main dealers and added new dealers in areas where they thought competition would result in extra market share. While this might have produced short-term gains when times were good, it weakened dealers financially, causing failure in tough times.

VANZ closed its assembly plant in December 1997. It was one of the last to go, and gradually all component manufacturers went. Today, the motor industry is almost entirely in retail

servicing. Once it employed 1 in 6 of the working population; today it is 1 in 20.

In 1998, Ford NZ announced the formation of a Retail Joint Venture (RJV) for Auckland, involving eight Ford dealers, including West Auckland Motors, East City Ford and South Auckland Motors from CMC Group. Seven of the dealers joined the RJV, selling their operations to the new company, Auckland Auto Collection. They were later joined by three Mazda dealers; the whole operation was owned by Ford NZ 41.98%, Mazda NZ 16.04% and CMC 41.98%. The new company merged all staff and some operations were closed or amalgamated. Today AAC is operated as three dealers – North Harbour, John Andrew, and South Auckland, all operating Ford and Mazda.

Mazda franchise changes also took place, and were taken up at Timaru Motors and Avery Motors, operating from Wellington Mazda, and Stevens Motors. At first Mazda resisted giving the franchise to Ford dealers as they were seen as competitors, but since Ford became the chief shareholder in Mazda the alliance has grown.

The representation changes have been immense, taking time to

absorb and shake down. In 1973 there were 84 Ford dealers. Today there are 34, and this number may well change again as small dealers opt to become service dealers. The financial stringencies on dealers are increasing year after year as new technology becomes a mandatory part of the business. Recent examples of this have been the Fordstar training tool, connecting dealers to a satellite transmission costing $40,000; the WDS computer-based diagnostic analysis system, a marvellous tool costing over $30,000; the Dealer Identification and Appearance (DIAP) Programme is going to cost $50,000 to $200,000 or more per site. A dealer must earn enough tax-paid profit to invest in these requirements, often a difficult task.

Nigel Wark continued to rationalise Ford NZ market representation until he returned to Ford Australia in January 2000 when Nigel Harris returned from Europe to become managing director. A graduate employed by Ford NZ in 1981, Nigel Harris spent time as a field manager, then was head of business management before transferring to Ford Europe in 1993 and becoming managing director of Ford Greece. Later he became

MS Motors Ltd at Nelson was purchased by CMC in 1998, together with a branch at Blenheim, formerly Marlborough Ford, and parts and service agent West End Motors at Kaikoura.

sales director of Jaguar. Although in a different role on his return, he still knew most dealers, and how New Zealand operated.

In late 1996 Ford USA introduced a completely redesigned Louisville HN80 large truck range, to rave reviews from customers and dealers, but the paint was hardly dry before the sale was announced of the extra heavy duty Ford HN80 truck line to Freightliner Corporation. This caused consternation amongst Louisville dealers in Australia and New Zealand because Freightliner and Paccar were arch rivals, neither sanctioning the other's presence, let alone dual franchise dealerships.

In 1997 the New Zealand truck market was seriously affected by the so-called Asian crisis, falling 24% as logging declined sharply in response to the virtual cessation of log exports to Asia. Hundreds of heavy trucks, which are mainly financed, were suddenly 'for sale' as their owners could not meet finance payments. The market could not absorb them and used trucks depreciated heavily.

CMC rationalised their representation, with Southpac Trucks taking over the Rotorua and Masterton operations in 1999. Paccar bought DAF Truck Operations at Eindhoven, Holland, and Southpac gained the franchise. This gave Southpac a vital leg into European source trucks with more

MS Motors also has four BP service stations run as a cluster by Kate Motley, pictured with John Flanagan, dealer principal.

Team Hutchinson Ford had three of the 10 qualified Ford master technicians in New Zealand in 2002. From left: Craig Foster, Alan Cross and Daniel Reeve.

Ford introduced 'Registered Technician Programmes', and in 2000, Gavin Henwood, of Fagan Motors was awarded the first Ford master technician rating by Ford Service Training Institute, Detroit. He is using the Worldwide Diagnostic System (WDS), plugged into the vehicle electronics, allowing extensive diagnosis of the increasing complexity of vehicle management systems, watched by Keith Allen, parts and service manager.

favourable pricing and a range of smaller trucks. After detailed discussion with DAF engineers, a number of specification options were made available to suit New Zealand conditions, and when the new DAF trucks were launched in New Zealand, they were an instant success, although the market continued at a low level. In 2000 the market recovered and grew, with Paccar trucks taking a predominant share. Southpac took over retailing in the South Island at Christchurch, when Timaru Trucks decided to continue with Mercedes Benz and Stirling (formerly Louisville) trucks through their renamed Trucks South company. The rationalised truck operations have been profitable.

On October 1 2000 chairman Ormond A Hutchinson died suddenly, a few weeks before he was due to retire, at age 70. An accountant at Hutchinson Motors when he started in 1953, 'Hutch' later became dealer principal, taking over from his father Ormond in 1966. Hutch was made a director of CMC in 1975, and later was one of the instigators of the Ford Dealer Council in the late 1970s. Hutch became chairman of the board in 1995 and chairman of Auckland Auto Collection in 1999. Ormond Hutchinson worked for the company for 52 years, his son, Hutch, for 47, and his grandson John has been working at Team Hutchinson Ford for more than 10 years, an extraordinary family dedication to one company in today's world. We salute them!

John A Wylie, great grandson of Hope

Gibbons, has been chairman since 2000. When John Emery retired in 2002, having reached the compulsory retirement age, after working 50 years for CMC Group, Ian D Lambie, dealer principal of Dunedin City Ford was elected a director. In May 2003, Dato' Rahim Hallim sold his 6.93 million shares in Colonial Motor Company to

Top: In 1999, the Fordstar network across Australasia allowed live interactive broadcast for communication and training. Paula Newton conducts training session in Wellington.

Above: Bruce McCoubrey, service manager, and Phil Hayes, training manager, of Avon City Ford take a Papanui High group in special classrooms where students gain NEQUA training credits.

Far left: Nigel Harris returned as Ford NZ managing director in 1999, following a number of overseas assignments for Ford.

Left: Richard Matheson, the new managing director of Ford NZ, was previously with Ford area sales at Boston in the United States.

Southpac Trucks completed major refurbishment of Wiri Station Road premises, greatly enhancing the workplace and improving efficiency.

The Ford dealer group introduced new premises' standards in 2003. They were trialed at Avon City Ford and Team Hutchinson Ford in Christchurch, before being progressively adopted by all dealers.

In 2001, Nigel Harris, Ford NZ managing director, reveals the new Mondeo to the dealer group.

The Ford dealer group celebrated Ford Motor Company's centenary at Detroit in 2003. Outside Henry Ford's home, Fair Lane in Detroit are: Edsel Ford II, Graeme Gibbons, Jim Gibbons and Stuart Gibbons.

Below:All New Zealand Ford dealers, including the past and present CMC dealers photographed, were invited to a reunion in November 2003, to celebrate the Ford centenary.

other parties, bringing to an end the beneficial association with MBM Resources Bhd and, on July 1 2003, he resigned from the board.

In July 2002 Nigel Harris was promoted to managing director SAMCOR Ford/Mazda South Africa. After an inter-regnum period with treasurer Randall Lewis as acting chief executive, Richard Matheson from Boston in the United States, transferred to become managing director. During Nigel Harris' time in New Zealand, Ford sold off their alloy wheel die-cast manufacturing plant at Manukau City, lowering Ford NZ's grading and it is now only a sales operation.

Today, there are nearly 180,000 first time registrations of new and imported used cars each year and, with the escalating number of vehicle imports, our roads are increasingly choked. Auckland has a chronic problem and is spending vast amounts on a new motorway grid, being paid by all motorists from a surtax of 4 cents on every litre of petrol. The highway between Auckland and Hamilton will soon be a separated twin lane north and south carriageway. Wellington has serious traffic problems with its narrow main access routes.

Expenditure on roads has increased to nearly $1 billion each year to try to keep pace with the increase in traffic. An interesting road completed recently was the reconstruction of the road between Arthur's Pass and Otira, where a treacherous 900m section has been made

In 1999, Mike Corliss, chief executive Southpac Trucks (right), shakes hands to finalise a deal with fleet manager Peter Spooner, of NZ Dairy Group, for 62 Foden Alpha trucks.

safer with a 440m viaduct, concrete roofed, and with a cantilevered bridge section. This $39 million engineering triumph now protects motorists from falling boulders. However, nothing in New Zealand road engineering has yet come close to the scale of Auckland Harbour Bridge.

Above: Ford sold its heavy trucks to Freightliner in 1998 who re-badged the Louisville range as Sterling. Bill Richardson, of H W Richardson, Invercargill, takes delivery of his 100th Louisville/Sterling truck from Russell Marr, dealer principal of Trucks South (formerly Timaru Trucks).

Left: Director John Emery, with his wife Jan, completed 50 years service and celebrated his retirement at the annual meeting in 2002.

Below: Team Hutchinson Ford had new signage in Christchurch.

Ford Territory has redefined family motoring standards for comfort, handling and performance on or off all roads. At home in the hills, this Ghia model is at the beach.

CMC's 1903 Model A Fordmobile celebrated its 100th birthday with Bill Richardson. It visited his truck museum in Invercargill, later moving around other Ford centenary gatherings in New Zealand, winning many more friends.

2000 STATISTICS

REPORTING CHANGES AND COMPARISONS ARE NOW DIFFICULT IN SOME AREAS

Cars registered 1,912,592, a decade change of 32%
Trucks registered 381,021, a decade change of 31.7%
56.6 % of cars registered were over 10 years old
8.9 % of cars registered were over 20 years old
The mean age of cars was 11.42 years.
The mean age of trucks was 12.25 years.

NZ population in 2000 was 3,825,800:
  1 car :   2.03 people
  1 vehicle: 1.61 people

OECD SELECTED COMPARISON OF PERSONS PER CAR

Germany	1.92	Australia	1.97
New Zealand	2.03	United States	2.15
France	2.16	Canada	2.20
United Kingdom	2.39	Japan	2.47

New cars and station wagons registered   57,618
Ex overseas cars and wagons registered   116,124

TRAFFIC DENSITY DAILY PAST A TALLY POINT, NOT AVAILABLE

TRACTORS IN USE NO LONGER KNOWN

RETAIL PRICE FOR STANDARD FUEL
  Cents per litre 105¢ + Auckland tax 4¢   total 109¢
  Included is Excise Tax   26.4¢
  Plus Goods & Services Tax   12.1¢

State Highway expenditure $593 million
Local authority roads expenditure $291 million
Total public roading expenditure $884 million

Road user charges collected $532 million
Petroleum fuel excise collected $810 million
Direct motoring taxes $1,342 million

PART TWO –
THE SUBSIDIARIES

THE "COMPLEAT" Ford SALESMAN

Trist Atkins, of Panmure Motors Ltd, knew a skilled cartoonist who depicted the joys of being a salesman.

THE SUBSIDIARIES

Part two of this history is about the main trading subsidiaries which are largely Ford dealers. Many of these companies have operated for more than 50 years, and are widely scattered across New Zealand. All have their own stories, some because of their unique locations, others for the way they have developed and the particular products they specialise in. Ten have now closed down or been absorbed into other operations. Together they form the CMC Group, the oldest and still the most significant motor group in New Zealand.

Fordson tractors have made a major contribution to New Zealand's farming and industry, as well as the trading success of the CMC Group. Fordson is no longer with us as Ford has sold its tractor and heavy truck operations world-wide. Because of their special place in history, tractors are covered in Chapter 31, using a tractor study article in the CMC Group staff magazine, *IMPACT*, published in 1974.

To give the reader a perspective of the CMC Group, the locations of companies and branches are shown on the map below.

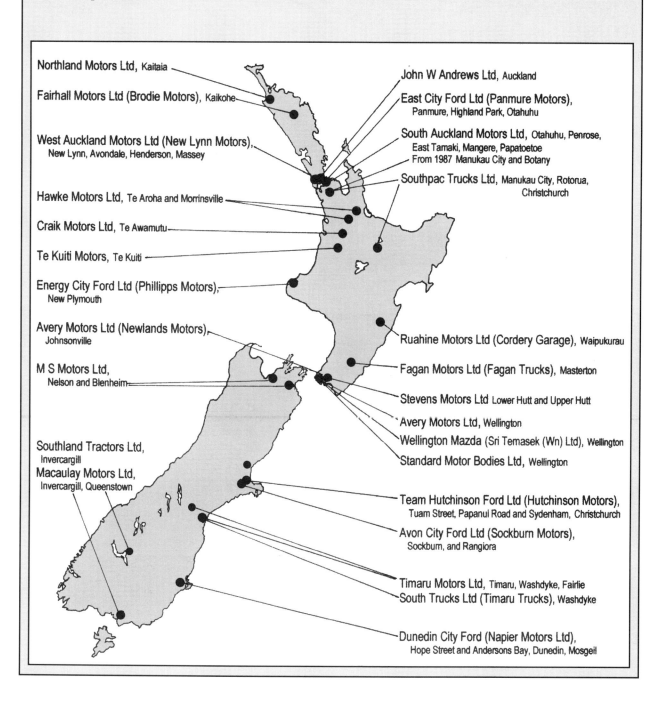

Northland Motors Ltd, Kaitaia

Fairhall Motors Ltd (Brodie Motors), Kaikohe

West Auckland Motors Ltd (New Lynn Motors),
New Lynn, Avondale, Henderson, Massey

Hawke Motors Ltd, Te Aroha and Morrinsville

Craik Motors Ltd, Te Awamutu

Te Kuiti Motors, Te Kuiti

Energy City Ford Ltd (Phillipps Motors),
New Plymouth

Avery Motors Ltd (Newlands Motors),
Johnsonville

M S Motors Ltd,
Nelson and Blenheim

Southland Tractors Ltd,
Invercargill
Macaulay Motors Ltd,
Invercargill, Queenstown

John W Andrews Ltd, Auckland

East City Ford Ltd (Panmure Motors),
Panmure, Highland Park, Otahuhu

South Auckland Motors Ltd, Otahuhu, Penrose,
East Tamaki, Mangere, Papatoetoe
From 1987 Manukau City and Botany

Southpac Trucks Ltd, Manukau City, Rotorua,
Christchurch

Ruahine Motors Ltd (Cordery Garage), Waipukurau

Fagan Motors Ltd (Fagan Trucks), Masterton

Stevens Motors Ltd Lower Hutt and Upper Hutt

Avery Motors Ltd, Wellington

Wellington Mazda (Sri Temasek (Wn) Ltd), Wellington

Standard Motor Bodies Ltd, Wellington

Team Hutchinson Ford Ltd (Hutchinson Motors),
Tuam Street, Papanui Road and Sydenham, Christchurch

Avon City Ford Ltd (Sockburn Motors),
Sockburn, and Rangiora

Timaru Motors Ltd, Timaru, Washdyke, Fairlie
South Trucks Ltd (Timaru Trucks), Washdyke

Dunedin City Ford (Napier Motors Ltd),
Hope Street and Andersons Bay, Dunedin, Mosgeil

CHAPTER ELEVEN

THE FAR NORTH

Today, the far north of New Zealand is a place of long, glistening white beaches, clear blue sea and sky, warm temperatures and a relaxed life style. The name Kaitaia means abundant food, but the milk and honeyed overtones we associate with the district today have been made possible only by the hard and often back-breaking work of early settlers.

The far north was associated with the Church Missionary Society and mission stations were set up from 1815, prior to the Treaty of Waitangi, at a number of settlements, including Kaitaia in 1834. Before this, the area was widely known for the kauri tree and gum. The Bay of Islands and Far North were amongst the earliest parts of New Zealand to be settled by Europeans. Russell, or Kororareka as it was originally known, in the Bay of Islands, was the first capital. Sailing ships visited from the late 18th century to cut kauri spars, masts and timber, and discovered the gum could be dissolved to make an excellent varnish.

During the 1850s, large areas of Crown land were made available for purchase and settlement and in the 1870s the Homestead Act provided for free grants of 50 acres of first class, or 75 acres of second class, land, conditional on survey costs being paid and improvements being made within specified times.

At the same time as the area was being opened up for farmland, gum-diggers, saw-millers and flax-millers were also swelling

Below: Loading gum onto a lighter boat at Ahipara in 1910. Bullock teams hauled a dray out to the lighter, which ferried the load to the ship in deep water. (Photo Northwood Collection, Alexander Turnbull Library)

Left: R A Johnston's new Kaitaia store about 1918. Commerce Street was good compared to most roads, with side drains and crowned centre.

the population. It is estimated that for many years during the peak of the kauri gum trade, there were between 3,000 and 5,000 diggers in the far north fields. The privations endured by the early settlers, many of them single men from Dalmatia, were very severe and most made little more than a subsistence living.

In 1900, the Kaitaia Co-operative Dairy Company began, but the condition of the roads was crucial in deciding the opening and closing dates of the dairy season. All manufactured butter was carted to Awanui by bullock team, and shipped to Auckland.

Roads, by and large, were just mud

tracks and, until well into the 20th century, ships provided the best access to the district. For example, R V Johnston used the river in preference to the road when he brought supplies the six kilometres from Awanui to his store in Kaitaia.

Often farmers spent hours cutting lengths of 'teatree' manuka, laying them on tracks before they could get their wagons through. This process, known as 'corduroying' was common in many parts of New Zealand, and was particularly necessary after the arrival of the horseless carriage which inevitably became stuck in mud at the first sign of rain or swamp.

A substantial proportion of farms were self-supporting by 1904, but their owners talked of earlier days when they felled the bush in winter, worked on the gum fields in summer, burned the dried out trees and scrub, and sowed grass seed in the autumn. All of this contributed to the rigours of early farming in the area. Rail, of course, was still a dream and, although a few cars had ventured through the area with exploring pioneers as early as 1904, those who possessed such luxuries had to do their own repairs.

KAITAIA -
NORTHLAND MOTORS LTD

About 1915-16, a Mr Tremaine started a small garage, about 20x20ft, in Commerce Street where Northland Motors later built in the 1950s. He also held a Ford sub-agency from the Whangarei Engineering Company although there would have been very little repair work to do as it appears there were only six cars in the whole Mangonui County.

As the only Ford sub-agency in the Far North, Tremaine had to take delivery of two cars a year, at a cost of about £200 each. To sell them would have been very difficult so, dissatisfied with this venture, he sold the business to Stan Holder who, with his father, bought the garage as a going concern for £800. One of Stan Holder's staff was Cedric Harrison who was apprenticed in

1924, and stayed with the firm all his working life. He later became a salesman and service manager of Northland Motors.

To supplement his finances, Stan Holder operated a small moving picture show he took to Peria, Kaingaroa and Lake Ohia on a horse-drawn wagon. His assistants were Charlie Bray and Sonny Watts whose daughter later married Percy Ferguson.

Model Ts were shipped to Mangonui from Auckland as deck cargo on small coaster boats. Unloaded at the wharf, they were driven 25 miles to Kaitaia, which took 1-1^1/2 hours, depending on the condition of the road.

In 1926, R A Johnston went into partnership with Stan Holder in the Ford agency. Ray Johnston's father, Roy, had established a general store in the days of the gum-diggers, at Larmers Corner, the navigable limit of the Kaitaia River. Ray Johnston later built a new store in Commerce Street.

Stan Holder and Ray Johnston sold vehicles in Kaitaia until 1929, shortly after the Model A Ford arrived, Holder sold his shares to Jim Thornton and returned to farming.

On November 12 1930, Northland Motors Limited was formed with a share

STANLEY HOLDER

Phone
12

P.O. Box
40

Licensed FORD Agent
ALL ACCESSORIES STOCKED
Repairs in all Branches at Shortest Notice

———

KAITAIA

*Opposite top:
Digging kauri gum at
Houhora in 1910 was
very hard work under
trying conditions.
Many gum-diggers
came from war torn
Dalmatia on Europe's
Adriatic coast.
[Photo: Northwood
Collection, Alexander
Turnbull Library]*

*Opposite bottom:
Gum-diggers' abode
1910. Cleaning the
gum in front of their
sacking tent with sod
cooking chimney.
Note tools and spears
for prod searching
swamps for gum.
[Photo: Northwood
Collection, Alexander
Turnbull Library]*

*Left top:
Advertisement from
an early tourist
magazine.*

*Left bottom: At the
Kaitaia A & P Show
in 1923. The Model T
cars and Model N
Fordson tractor were
'hot property'.*

Jim Thornton bought out Holder and Johnston and set up Northland Motors in 1930, had all the pain of the Depression and died in 1940. CMC bought his shares from the estate.

capital of £3,000, divided equally between J O Thornton and R A Johnston. Johnston later sold his shares to Thornton.

The arrival of Jim Thornton also brought Miss Hilda Moore, who was his parts assistant in Warkworth. Hilda Moore, or Miss Moore as she was always known, is one of the clearly remembered dealership staff. In 1980, Hilda Moore (then Mrs Millar) talked about those years at Northland Motors.

"Mr Thornton went to Kaitaia by car in early November 1930. Mrs Thornton and the children followed later, travelling from Auckland by a small plane and landing on the south end of Ninety Mile Beach. Their pet bulldog 'Bill', was sent up by boat (two days voyage), and arrived very ill from being over-fed and very black with grime from the coal. The boats had just stopped taking passengers, but cargo still continued to go by boat.

"I travelled to Kaitaia by train to Whangarei, and then by service car via Kaeo to Kaitaia, a long trip (220 miles), leaving Auckland about 8 am and arriving in Kaitaia just on dark. I had been reading all I could find about the district which was described as a very progressive area with a good town and a sealed main street. However, when I arrived I found a very rough metal road. It transpired that the street had been sealed, but the previous summer had been very hot and the seal had melted, causing havoc in the shops. So the locals had got together and chipped all the seal up.

"A spare parts man from John W Andrew's arrived at the same time as I did. We worked from daylight to dark the first few days sorting out parts and putting them in some sort of order. They were all loose in boxes, over-stocked in some parts with no stock of others.

"In the workshop we inherited Ian McKinnon and Cedric Harrison from the previous owner, and they and Mr Thornton were the workforce for some time. This was during the 1930 Depression and work and money were hard to come by. For quite a period of weeks Ian and Cedric came to work full time but only got paid one week's wages. Things picked up and they both stayed and gave good service over many years. Ian eventually moved to Whangarei. Cedric, of course, stayed in Kaitaia.

"The workshop built up till it was very busy and gradually people from a distance learned to book in for repairs. They found if they booked in they could rely on their job being started at once and finished at the appointed time and usually for a pre-determined price. This policy brought us many good and reliable customers."

The early thirties also saw the return home of Cliff Maria after he had completed his motor apprenticeship in Auckland. In 1933 he joined Northland Motors as a mechanic, supposedly for six weeks, but

stayed 35 years until his retirement in 1968. In those days a lot of the work was servicing engines that generated power for milking machines and electric light.

Northland Motors had two diesel generators and a two-cylinder Model T engine, Jim Thornton's brainchild, that used only the front two cylinders and gave good service.

Cedric Harrison recalled: "It was virtually a full time job servicing milking machines and we often had to work into the night. There was no question of knocking off and coming back in the morning, because the cows would be due to be milked in a few hours.

"We used to have a go at everything, even repairing machinery in the paddock. I remember doing a valve-grind on a model N tractor where the roof was the sky – at least it didn't rain that day." Cedric Harrison's transport was a Harley Davidson, and sidecar which carried all his gear.

Cedric Harrison became a salesman in 1932. "Jim Thornton was a tough man, but a fair boss, and in his book, you had to sell something every day.

"Whenever we sold a new car which wasn't very often during the Depression days we used to think we had done pretty well. But as far as Jim was concerned the deal wasn't done (no commission was paid) until the trade-in was sold; and so sell it we did."

He remembers visiting a sheep farmer and staying there a fortnight, finally selling him a new car and truck, which in those days was a tremendous achievement. "The old boy had every intention of buying, but wanted company. Whenever we got near to the pen-signing stage, he would hold off on some pretence or other and leave me dangling. I had no inkling what he was up to at the time and it was a bit unsettling. In

the end he bought the vehicles and made me a very happy salesman." Salespeople who are taught to stay with the prospect 'until he buys or dies' will be pleased to know it is not a new concept.

At this time, Kaitaia had a regular shipping service from Auckland, operated once weekly by the Northern Steamship Company. The ships called at Russell and Mangonui. All cars, spare parts, petrol and oil were shipped through Awanui. After 1936, when Ford took over distribution from CMC, vehicles were railed to Kaikohe and driven over to Kaitata. Used car re-conditioning was done on site and painting was done by hand with two people, one brush and a tin of paint each side – starting at the front and finishing at the centre of the rear panel.

The Depression times were very difficult financially. Northland Motors Ltd struggled from the beginning and was finally partially sold to the Colonial Motor Company in 1935. Bruce Renton was sent up by H N Scrimshaw ('Scrim') to be accountant in 1935 and to establish the full management accounting system.

In 1938, Percy Ferguson arrived as accountant. He had started work with H N Scrimshaw at audit and had been seconded to Taylor & Macdonald at Pukekohe, where he stayed until Stan Andrew took over the business. He then worked with Scrim in Wellington, until he was literally 'dropped off' by Scrim for a month to have a look at the Kaitaia dealership, where he remained for 28 years until his death in 1966.

When electric power was finally turned on in Kaitaia in 1939 everyone danced in the street that night. War was declared shortly afterwards; amongst staff called up was Cedric Harrison who had become service manager after Gordon Carstens retired. Cliff Maria took over the workshop

Opposite bottom: Hulme's 'Faith in Australia' Vildebeast plane landed on Ninety Mile Beach, often used on pioneering flights as a re-fuelling point before tackling the long haul to Australia across the Tasman. It was also used by Kingsford-Smith.

Northland Motors 1936 staff. From left: M Waddell, apprentice; R Northwood, painter; L Masters, mechanic; Jim Thornton, owner; G Carstens, service manager; Cedric Harrison, salesman; B Renton, accountant; Miss Hilda Moore, parts and office; I McKinnon, mechanic; F Cresswell, mechanic; R Perkins, assistant accountant; F Sands, mechanic; Cliff Maria, mechanic; A Perkins, mechanic; J Short, mechanic; and W Thornton, lubrication. In front: Model Y 8hp, Model C 10hp, 1936 V8 coupe, V8 fordor, and V8 2 ton van.

Right: Percy Ferguson dressed as a bridegroom at a 1939 carnival in Kaitaia to celebrate the arrival of electric power.

Below: Cape Reinga lighthouse, Cliff Maria's wartime port of call. The upper photo shows 'the meeting of the tides' at the Cape where, according to Maori legend, the souls of the departed go to their resting place.

while he was away.

In late 1940, after a prolonged illness, Jim Thornton died. The Colonial Motor Company bought his shares at Mrs Thornton's request and Percy Ferguson was appointed manager. Percy married Sylvia Watts in 1942, after first being seconded to the army area office, and their eldest son Gary was born in 1945. Sylvia's father, Sonny Watts, was borough foreman and, earlier, had been one of Stan Holder's assistants in the 'movie' business.

The Marine Department took over the lighthouse maintenance contract using a Ford V8 van, but Cliff Maria rescued this twice when it was stuck in sand.

Rescuing vehicles off the beach was a regular occurrence and Cliff Maria said he recovered at least 30 stuck in the sand, from a baby Austin to a Rolls Royce. Often, by the time they got there the vehicle was well and truly stuck to the seabed. They were often write-offs because once under water they were literally flattened with the pressure of the sea.

The war years saw dramatic changes in Kaitaia, particularly with the influx of army and air force personnel. Ken Crene, who was cost clerk then, said that at times there were more than 11,000 extra people in the district, resulting in many of the town's facilities being stretched to the limit.

Fighter-bombers were doing enemy submarine patrols from the air base at Waipapakauri, and much of Northland Motors' time was spent servicing army vehicles. Ken Crene recalled the time when a mechanic handed in a job time card with 12 hours 'filing' logged up. When questioned, it transpired that the 'filing' consisted of modifying, because of shortages, a Plymouth part to suit a Ford.

In 1941, the lighthouse was transferred from Motauapoa Island, off Cape Maria van Diemen, to its present position on Cape Reinga, and it was Cliff Maria's job to service the pumps used in the lighthouse every six weeks. On one early occasion, after he had serviced the pumps, he was

apprehended by the Home Guard for turning on his car lights while driving back to Kaitaia along Ninety Mile Beach. They thought he had been signalling to the Japanese! Cliff Maria recalled: "Two of us used to go up in a little Singer (one of the few vehicles not taken over by the Army), and if the tides were unfavourable we had to stop the night and return next day. Because of blackout restrictions, we had to drive along the beach without lights, before cutting inland up the streambed to Te Paki Station. Then it was another 10 miles to the lighthouse. It took us about five hours. The blackness on the beach seemed to close right in, leaving you with an eerie sense of isolation. It wasn't a very pleasant feeling. On top of this you had to try and see where you were driving, but after a few trips you got used to it."

The cyclone of August 1942 was vividly remembered by all those there at the time. The event was widely noted, with *The Northland Age* of August 27 1942 reporting: "....Striking the northern edge of Kaitaia at about 10.20 am on Wednesday, a cyclone of tremendous intensity carried on its path of destruction through the main street, causing damage estimated at many thousands of pounds before it finally abated. One child was fatally injured while nine other people were hurt .... One of the most extensively damaged business premises was that of Northland Motors Ltd., and here there were some remarkable escapes from injury. Workmen engaged at the rear of the building just managed to vacate before the building fell. One heavy truck standing in the yard adjacent to the premises was turned over and lay on its

The 1942 cyclone did a lot of damage, as these Northland Age *photos show.*
Left: The old workshop was patched up by the Army and, with building restrictions, had to suffice for 13 years.
Below: The Singer car used on workshop jobs is at right, partly obscured by the salvage truck.

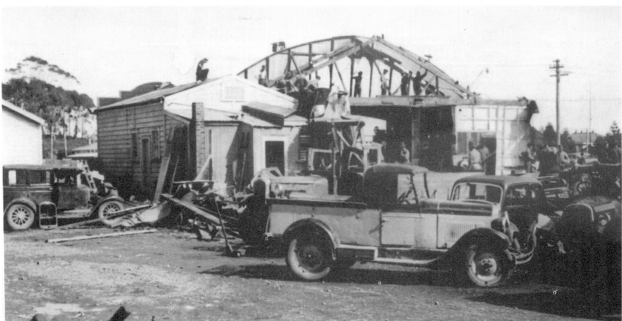

After the cyclone the butcher's old shop became the office and parts department.

side. Fortunate indeed were the members of the office staff of this company, for here too much damage was done…."

Dwellings at the rear of Northland Motors came in for their share of the cyclone's destructiveness, although the paint and panelbeating shed close by suffered no ill effects.

On August 30 1942, Hilda Moore wrote to H B Gibbons, managing director of the Colonial Motor Company….

"….the storm flattened the workshop portion, and took the roof off most of the store and office and left the office wall all twisted and that had to be demolished for safety….

" The new Anglia and demo Anglia are both damaged, but neither extensively. A used Singer that we use for going out to small jobs etc had glasses broken, but very little damage. Our salvage truck was in the yard and escaped untouched….

"The old butcher's shop had the veranda and a good portion of one side torn off the roof. The roof has now been repaired and we have moved all our office records into there."

Almost 40 years after the event, Hilda Moore remembered…. "My recollection of the cyclone is of being battered on the head with a water pipe that fell from the ceiling and caused many small cuts on the top of my head. It bled profusely but was not serious.

"The army was a big help in cleaning up the mess. Each morning a gang of young fellows would arrive and do whatever was required. They had a machine that they ran the old roofing iron through and flattened and re-corrugated it. In a few days every business had some sort of shelter. The panel shop at Northland Motors was not damaged and we moved into the 'butcher's shop' with store and office equipment.

The old butcher's shop was crowded with parts and records, leaving very little space for four people to work in.

George Horsford bought this Model A Phaeton from Cedric Harrison on May 23 1930. He was back in 1946, 16 years later, getting his 100,000 mile check. From left: George Horsford, Bill Thornton (Jim's brother), Ian McKinnon and Cedric Harrison. George Horsford came back 20 years later, to get Cedric Harrison to do the 125,000 mile check.

Left: Percy Ferguson demonstrates a Perkins diesel Fordson halftrack and giant discs in 1946.

Below: At the 1949 A & P Show: John Holder, Percy Ferguson, Cliff Maria and Don Gibbons.

Some invoices from the office were found in Broadwood, over the ranges in the Hokianga".

Following this disaster, a building programme was commenced. The bare essentials were provided immediately, but because of war restrictions and the lack of building materials for quite a long period afterwards, new buildings were not completed until 1955, 13 years later.

Hilda Moore recalls other events that occurred about this time. "One of the first trucks we sold in Kaitaia was to a Maori family (Mutu Kapa). They were so proud of their new possession that they invited the staff to a celebration at the Bluff (Ninety Mile Beach), and we were guests of honour at a hangi with everything imaginable in it. The whole proceedings were done with due courtesy on both sides.

"I remember the sale mostly because it fell to my lot to read aloud the full details of the hire purchase agreement. The old Maori man was sitting in the office with a blank look on his face, but I think he understood a lot more than he let on."

Early in 1943, a temporary building replaced the previous workshop. The only available material was fibrolite from which the walls and roof of the building were made. Partly burnt trusses from the hospital were also used in this construction. Later a tractor shop was built with re-rolled roofing iron.

Hilda Moore remembered: "Dixon Perry worked in the panel shop, at times the only one doing that work during the war. Knowing he would want time off to plant his kumara, I asked him to give us some idea when he would be away. 'I don't know, I just get up one morning look out at the weather and know this is the day. So I keep the children home from school and we all plant kumara,' he said. So we never

*In 1955, the new
buildings were
completed, making
a huge difference to
working conditions.*

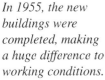

did get any notice when kumara planting would be, but judging by the end result, he certainly chose the right day. Dixon had a useful sized family of 16 children to help him."

Hilda Moore left in 1948 to get married and subsequently lived at Warkworth. Ray McKeown shifted from Kaikohe to be accountant and Ken Crene was cost clerk.

The construction of a substantial open-sided workshop with lift-up doors was started in 1952. By 1955, new offices and a showroom had been completed. The showroom had plate-glass windows tilted at 20 degrees to give visibility without reflection, and vehicles were displayed in front, together with the petrol pumps.

In 1958 the whole of Kaitaia was engulfed in a massive flood caused by the simultaneous flooding at the confluence of two rivers. The new workshop and offices were swamped and needed a huge cleanup. This had happened before in 1936. Water streamed through the town, causing such damage that new stop-banks were raised in the hopes of preventing future flooding.

Business in the Far North went ahead rapidly after the Second World War, assisted by the government land development schemes that converted thousands of acres into productive farmland. Northland's economy greatly benefitted from this and the new aerial topdressing industry which was started in the 1950s.

During the late 1950s, Stan Holder's son, John, known by some as Hori, worked for Northland Motors as a salesman, after farming with his father at Kaeo. They built a 40ft yacht on the farm, and when John Holder had completed his diesel

certification in 1952, they sailed to Fiji and back. Even if Northland Motors couldn't get many new cars, they sold lots of tractors and trucks at this time. John Holder became sales manager in 1959.

When the Thames Trader trucks arrived in 1958, John Holder saw big opportunities to work with the aerial topdressing industry. It was his ingenuity which overcame one of the problems with loading fertiliser into aircraft. Jim Wilkinson, of Cambridge, designed an excellent loader using a modified Fordson tractor. However, it took a long time to transfer from one job to another, and was also over-width on the road. John Holder convinced Arthur Langman, local manager for Ossie James' Advance Aviation Ltd, that this loader should be mounted on a Trader truck chassis, with a rear dual control operation. The prototype was a huge success and many similar trucks were commissioned. Today the same loader and rear dual control cab arrangement remains the industry standard.

John Holder was appointed manager of Fairhall Motors, Kaikohe in 1961 and later Colin Moore, from the workshop, became salesman.

Northland Motors had a succession of accounting trainees from CMC Group companies who were ably taught in the ways of the north by Alex Trail. Alex Trail had started as cost clerk at Fairhall Motors in 1948, and took over as accountant in 1957. He transferred to Northland Motors as accountant in 1960, when Ray McKeown moved to Avery Motors.

Among his trainees in the early 1960s were Don Hodgson, Robin Astridge, Roger

Trucks became big business after the Thames Trader arrived in 1957. The new county fleet.

Gardner and Ken Mullan, all later senior CMC people.

The Far North was certainly very different. Driving from Wellington to Kaitaia was a very long journey. Once you got to Auckland you were still only half way to Cape Reinga. At Kawakawa, where the railway ran through the middle of the street, the pub had a hitching rail and horses. Then the dust started.

The dusty roads seemed endless and, in the Hokianga, were some of the roughest in New Zealand. You could tell a car was coming by the column of dust which was visible far ahead of the vehicle. When wet, these roads were treacherous and slips were common with many a vehicle having to be recovered from over the bank at the side of the road. The 'wrecker' was kept busy, pulling vehicles back on to the road and also recovering them when stuck on Ninety Mile Beach.

The first topdressing loader was cumbersome and slow. John Holder worked out how it could be fitted to a new Trader with rear controls.

The 1954 Thames, 'Cost Cutter' model, had a 4 cylinder tractor engine, and with geared winches, pulleys and anchors, was a slow but quite efficient machine for recovering cars.

New car assemblers did not consider corrosion until Ford began providing some protection in 1966. Certainly, the sub-tropical humidity and salt-laden climate of the Far North was an open invitation to rust. Standard treatment for a new car in Kaitaia was to spray underneath with 'seachrome', and then with underseal. Finally, 'fishelene' was sprayed inside all the door panels and everywhere underneath. 'Fishelene' was a potent-smelling, varnish type product, which took days to dry, and was made from fish oil. If you took a vehicle on the beach, you washed down the underside immediately afterwards, and many people sprayed on used engine oil as well. Cars from the Far North had a distinctive odour, but survived remarkably well with this treatment. If not treated, they would have rust appearing within a year.

Underseal applicators seemed to find the job dehydrating, and you would often see them in the pub at the end of a hot day. This was 'six o-clock closing' time, when the pubs stopped serving at 6pm and you were out 10 minutes later. On Friday nights, a number of the staff would discuss the week, or more likely the coming weekend, over a few beers, at the Kaitaia Hotel. For some reason, the underseal man was always late, probably because he was scrubbing off all the paint and 'fishelene'. He would finally arrive about 5.30 and go straight up to the bar to get eight 12 oz. glasses of beer in a milk bottle crate, consume these in no time flat, and then join in with the rest.

In the 1960s, New Zealand was closed at the weekend, and Saturdays and Sundays were given over to sport and, in the north,

The staff in 1964. From left: Percy Ferguson, Grant Anderson, Reg King, Cliff Maria, Alex Trail, Cedric Harrison, Dixon Perry, Pat Harrison, David Jones, Frank Mahalovich, Elaine Leyland, Bevin Beazley, Dennis Hewitt, Murray Harrison, Don McDonald, Ron Durney, Bob Scotney, Jim Crene, Colin Moore. In front: Spencer Tattersal, Lee Notton, Brian Lane, and Eddie Wells.

Left: Dixon Perry received his 25 year gold watch in 1964 from managing director Percy Ferguson. He started in 1939 as a handyman, built the first panel shop and became the panelbeater.

PERCY FERGUSON 1912 – 1966

Percy Ferguson died unexpectedly in 1966. He had seen the company through difficult times during the war, and led its post-war development.

Born in Hamilton, he went to school in Pukekohe and started accounting work with Taylor & Macdonald, Pukekohe's Ford dealer in 1932. He transferred to CMC audit staff when the business was sold to Stan Andrew, and auditor H N Scrimshaw dropped him off in Kaitaia to "see how it looked". He stayed, and became manager in 1940 after Jim Thornton died. He married Sylvia Watts in 1942 and they had two sons, Gary and Ross.

Always fair and polite, his quiet efficiency and keen intellect resulted in Northland Motors' high standing in the community. He received his CMC Omega gold watch in 1964.

Two 25 year watch holders who are also great fishing mates. Cedric Harrison (right) started work with Stan Holder in 1924 as an apprentice. He transferred to Northland Motors in 1930, became a salesman in 1935, service manager in 1940 and retired in 1968.
Cliff Maria served his apprenticeship in Auckland, and returned to Northland Motors in 1933. During the war he was service manager then, in 1947, parts manager, handing over to Reg King in 1966. He retired in 1968.

fishing. Everywhere, there were beautiful beaches, with lots of fish and shellfish to be taken.

Some shellfish, like toheroa, were a protected species, and only available at certain times of the year, and even then in limited numbers. This did not worry some, and stories of people being caught with sugar bags full of toheroas were common.

One hapless fellow was caught and jailed, stupidly ploughing them out of the beach with his tractor.

There were still a number of the original Dalmatian gum-diggers around in the 1960s, who kept to themselves, speaking very broken English, like a sort of 'pidgin'. Many had been locked up as aliens during the First World War so it was little wonder

they mistrusted the authorities and kept to themselves. One day a conversation was heard, but could not be seen, at the parts counter, where a fellow was being served:

"I vant ze rubba ring," croaked a voice.

"I see," said Reg King, "what size?"

"I vant ze big rubba ring!" he said.

"Just a minute, I'll get you one."

The writer's mind was exploding with curiosity, when past the open door came a little wizened old man, wheeling an 11 x 38 tractor tyre, exactly ze rubba ring he wanted, and nearly as tall as he was. A chat to Reg King revealed that understanding some 'Dalis' was often difficult, but if you knew their vehicle and understood sign language, it was easier.

When Percy Ferguson died suddenly in 1966, much to everyone's shock, Alex Trail was appointed manager.

Colin Moore, who had started as an apprentice in 1956, transferred to sales in 1964, and later became sales manager. His forte was selling trucks and the new D Series gave him the scope to deal with a new range of customers. Reg King became parts manager after Cliff Maria stepped down in 1966 and retired in 1968 after 33 years with the company. Reg King was also a very good operator and knew his parts. Cedric Harrison also retired in 1968, having been with Northland Motors since its inception in 1930, and with the Kaitaia Ford dealership for nearly 44 years.

Over the years, there have been a number of families providing new generations of staff for the company. Jim Thornton's son Jim served part of his apprenticeship before going off to Italy with the Army Service Corps during the war. His brother Bill retired after the war, having spent 20 years maintaining vehicles. Bill's son, Bill, came to the parts department from school, having already spent time pumping petrol and assisting. He left to go into a dairy business in the late 1950s.

Cliff Maria's daughter, Noeline, worked in the office for six years, from 1952, until she went farming at Motutangi. His granddaughter, Gaylene, worked in the office for a short time after she left school.

Cedric Harrison's father, Pop, retired from the dairy factory and, for a short time, Northland Motors was able to boast of three generations working there at the same time. Cedric's son, Murray, completed his apprenticeship, and daughter Pat worked in the office for some years before getting married.

The Crene family were settlers in the Houhora district as early as 1878 and a number worked in the dealership. Ken Crene joined the company in 1939 as cost clerk and was there when the cyclone struck in 1942. He became accountant and then shifted to Wellington in 1949. He left the group in 1953 and spent 16 years working in Auckland. In 1973 he returned to become accountant again, when Alex Trail was dealer principal. Ken Crene's wife Irene, worked in the office in 1951-52, and Gary Crene, a cousin, was a tractor mechanic in the 1960s. Jim Crene, another cousin, completed his apprenticeship and was later service manager before buying his own dairy.

Alec Trail's son, Darrel, left school and started in the office where he spent seven years before being transferred to Te Kuiti Motors as accountant. Gary Moore, Colin's son, started as an apprentice and qualified as a mechanic.

Later in the 1970s a number of the Lands and Survey development farms were converted into forestry blocks. Some land had not successfully adapted to pastoral farming; it either started slipping when saturated with rain, or became too dry to sustain pasture. Trees have stabilised the land and large areas have been planted in pinus radiata forests. These have now provided a new timber industry, with many new jobs and opportunities. The planting of trees, however, signalled changes in employment patterns, with fewer people in work and less money being spent while the trees grew. Tourism

Alex Trail receiving his Omega watch for 25 years service from chairman Gerald Gibbons in 1974.

After Ford sold the tractor franchise to Norwoods, Northland Motors retained the agency. Bevan Beazley, service manager in the 1980s, selling tractors at an expo day in 1994.
The company moved to new premises in 1993, completing the shift in a weekend. Staff from left: Bob Wilson, Ted Baker, Robert Emery, Neville Goldsworthy, Vicky McDonnel, Eddie Wells, Les Olsen, Graeme Masters, Bevin Beazley, Greg Hodgson. Front: Glen Ashton, Doug Ashworth.

The staff fishing trip, held most years, has produced great hauls. From left: Eddie Wells, Carey Moore, Bill Bradford, Grant Hammond, Bob Wilson, Fred Gardiner, Colin Moore, Gavin Chapman, Bevan Beazley, Terry Lamb, Graham Masters, Wayne Masters, the fishing organiser and son (on bonnet).

helped fill this gap and, with better roads, tourist numbers steadily increased in this exotic area.

Another ingenious member of the staff was Bill Wilson, tractor serviceman, who developed a tractor side-mounted hydraulic fencepost rammer after people told him it wouldn't work. He was successful and has patented the machine which uses a 450lb hammer, and is able to drive in about 700 posts a day with one man, operating on gradients up to 1:2.

Eddie Watts became parts manager in 1975, and Bevan Beazley returned from the aviation industry in 1976, where he had been an aircraft technician, to become service manager until he retired in 1992. Eddie Watts was made parts and service manager in 1992, finally retiring in 2001 after 41 years with the company.

In 1988, Alex Trail retired, having spent just on 40 years with the CMC Group, the last 27 years in Kaitaia, where he still lives, enjoying golf and fishing.

Neville Goldsworthy, who started work at Phillipps Motors in 1960, and later became manager of Te Kuiti Motors, was then appointed dealer principal of both Northland Motors and Fairhall Motors. He had a hard task as the winds of change had started blowing.

Progressive de-regulation of the motor industry from 1987, allowing used car imports from Japan, and removal of new vehicle tariffs, had a profound effect on all dealers. Heavy trucks stopped in 1992 when Ford went out of the business; service needs were steadily declining as new vehicle needs changed. The pressure went on to break even. Added to this, the farming community had been hit by government changes in 1985 that removed all subsidies, and government services were steadily being dismantled. Restructuring became inevitable.

In 1993, Northland Motors relocated premises, still in Commerce Street, but to a more modern, compact facility further north. The whole transfer was accomplished in a weekend, and represented a considerable achievement in planning and organisation.

Neville Goldsworthy remained dealer principal until Northland Motors became a Ford sub-dealer, to Pacific Motor Group, Whangarei, in July 2000. Neville Goldsworthy is retired and lives back in his hometown New Plymouth after also serving 40 years with the CMC Group.

Northland Motors continues to serve the Far North in a different, but still very important way. The wheel has turned full circle and the dealership is now under the guidance of Hamish Sheard, dealer principal of Pacific Motor Group at Whangarei. He started in the motor industry at Fairhall Motors, now also part of the new group.

Colonel Bell, Kaitaia's public relations manager in 1916, would be pleased with today's roads in the 'Winterless North', and with the tourists who come in ever increasing numbers to visit. Each day, busloads are transported from various parts, as far away as Auckland, on journeys to Cape Reinga. There they watch the meeting of the tides, and drive 60 miles down part of Ninety Mile Beach, which still evokes all the stories and legends from the past.

KAIKOHE - FAIRHALL MOTORS LTD

Kaikohe was a small Maori village in the very centre of Northland. The name came from an incident where a raiding tribe forced local Maori to hide in the kohekohe trees on Kaikohe Hill, where they survived by eating the berries. The name was at first Kai Kohekohe (kohekohe food) and later shortened.

The village remained isolated until 1914 when the railway was pushed through from Whangarei and stopped at Kaikohe. As a consequence it became the hub of Northland. If you wanted to receive or send goods by rail, then you went to Kaikohe. After the First World War, returning servicemen took up many ballot farms available in the area.

Despite the increased settlement, roads were still appallingly bad, and access to Northland was by ship or rail, each to a limited area. Colonel Allen Bell of Kaitaia, was chairman of the North Auckland Development Board, and never ceased agitating for improved roads for the North, without which the area would not develop. He succeeded in arranging the Parliamentary Tour of Northland in 1917, which led to the formation of the Highways Board in 1922. From that point onwards, the roads gradually improved.

Ngawha Hot Springs nearby are famed for their soda mercury spring waters, with supposed curative properties for skin and rheumatic disorders. From 1928–34 a British company mined about 20 tonnes of mercury there, but abandoned New Zealand after a supply contract was signed with Spain.

On Kaikohe Hill there is a monument to Hone Heke who cut down the British flagpole at Russell in 1844, and nearby, at Lake Omapere and Ohaeawai, are famous battle sites where Maori and British troops fought from 1845.

Today, there is a grasslands research centre nearby and Northland Agricultural College.

In 1930, The Colonial Motor Company decided to set up a full Ford dealership at Kaikohe. The roads had finally started to improve in the late 1920s and Kaikohe was showing growth as an agricultural farming centre and, with the railhead, it was regarded as the gateway to the north. Dalgety and Company had been sub-agents until then.

Brodie Motors Limited was incorporated in July 1930. Tenders were called for a new building, 33ft deep and 66ft wide, designed by the company's architect J M Dawson. Dudley Builders was successful for £1,189. It was described by the town council as "an attractive and pleasing design – in fact a credit to the town." The original specifications called for the building to be connected to the town water supply and drainage. However, there was to be a 35 years wait for these amenities in Kaikohe. Brodie Motors had to use an artesian bore for water, but there was one unique plumbing feature in the building – a flush toilet, the first in Kaikohe.

Hector Brodie wrote a letter to R B Gibbons on July 7 1930: "I would suggest that the firm be described as the Ford Service Station because I hope the business will be somewhat in advance of the general idea of a Garage. The word 'Service' should be prominent because there are a great many Ford users in this territory who do not know what service means, and we hope to prove to them that Ford service is second to none."

Brodie Motors took over from Dalgety's on August 1 1930, buying all the Ford parts and all new vehicles on hand – one Tudor and one Phaeton Model A. R U(Bob) Macaulay, manager at Auckland branch of CMC (later m-d of Macaulay Motors, Invercargill), made arrangements for stocktaking and changeover. One paragraph in the letter of instruction from CMC dealt with 'demonstrators':

"Dear Mr Brodie,

....The most important item to assist you in sales, is the running of a demonstrator car that gives a good demonstration. This must be a 'New' Model A. We think that a Tudor (2 door) is probably better for this purpose than a Fordor (4 door)....

Yours truly,

R B Gibbons."

The premises were completed in 1931 and it was quite an imposing structure in the town at the time. Unusual features included a vented roof with quite a high pitch and a clear floor area without any internal pillars. A hydraulic hoist was installed in front of the building for lubrication, together with new petrol 'bowsers' (pumps) selling Big Tree petrol, the brand named after the magnificent local kauri trees.

A S Paterson and Co was distributor of Big Tree petrol until the late 1920s when they sold out to Shell Oil Company. CMC imported its own oils and Valvoline was universally used in Ford cars because of its premium quality. With the advent of bulk petrol and petrol bowsers it was common for service stations to be multi-branded until the 1960s when single branding became normal. Fairhall Motors was the last company in the CMC Group to operate a Big Tree pump.

Everything was ready for the 'booming' tourist traffic that was said to be coming to see the giant kauri trees in the Waipoua Forest and Trounson Park. A court house and local government offices were also established about this time, but the anticipated rush of tourists took years to arrive.

Bob Macaulay decided Brodie Motors needed a service manager and asked Ted Williams, who worked at the Fox Street, Parnell, assembly plant if he would like to go to Kaikohe.

"I asked Mr Macaulay how long that would be for," said Mrs Dorrie Williams, "and he said about two years. However as it turned out, those two years stretched to 15, but that's life isn't it?"

Driven up to Kaikohe by Bob Macaulay, they arrived on a dark, rainy night. It was something she would never forget, Mrs Williams recalled in 1970. The first thing she saw were flickering lights in the street, and was told they were torches. There were no street lights in Kaikohe – in fact there was no power until 1939. If you wanted to find your way safely at night you took a torch.

After dropping their bags at the hotel, Bob Macaulay drove them up to one end of the main street and back again, and said, "Well, you've seen it."

"I had little sleep that night wondering what the next day would bring," said Mrs Williams. "The next morning confirmed my worst fears. Here I was, fresh from Auckland city, and all I could see were 15 shops strung out along the street, with plenty of empty sections.

"That night we moved into an old house. There was no ceiling in the lounge, all the rafters were exposed and there were mice, lots of them. I sat down on a packing case and started to cry; I was cold and I was miserable.

"Ted bustled around and tried to cheer me up by saying he would find the gramophone and give me some music. No transistors in those days!

"There we were in our old house, the rain coming down, the furniture all piled up, no floor coverings and just benzene lights to see by, with music coming from a wind up gramophone.

"If you wanted to go to the toilet, you

Brodie Motors opened for business on August 1 1930 in new premises. The lubrication was done under an external roof in the front of the building. An oil bar had engine oil on tap, and four new bowsers pumped Big Tree, Shell, Plume and Voco. Big Tree petrol was named after the kauri trees nearby.

had to go 50 yards down the backyard!

"Yes, those were real pioneering days.

"Nevertheless, I soon got over my homesickness for Auckland and we often look back on those times with real affection, recalling the many friends we made in Kaikohe. It was a really wonderful community, and its true worth was certainly shown during the war years."

Ted Williams remembered the Depression in detail: "When we arrived at Kaikohe in 1931 the Depression was well and truly upon us. They were tough days.

"About every 12 months we would hold an auction and try to get rid of some of our old vehicles and various bits and pieces. In time this collection became 'Rotten Row'.

"Of course with money so short, we didn't do too well out of it. At an auction in 1932 I remember a Model T going for 17s 6d and a 1929 Studebaker – which would have cost about £300 two years before – for 30s and a Model T back end for 5s.

In those days I was on £1 10s a week and on call 24 hours a day. The money may not sound much today but it was good going then. And you also have to remember that a great many men were out of work and anyone holding down a job was very lucky indeed."

Ted Williams remembers Hector Brodie as a fair but exacting boss and particularly strict on giving service to customers. This made a deep impression on one young apprentice, who soon got his chance to impress customers.

"Up bowled a Model T one day, with two very prim and proper ladies. After filling up with petrol – both ladies had to get out as the tank was under the front seat – the young man put everything back in place. Then, conscious of Mr Brodie's exhortations on service, he turned to the driver and said; 'And how's your water, Madam?'

"We had other moments too; an apprentice had been told to clean and polish a new Ford V8 for a customer. It was our pride and joy, the first 1936 model to come to us, and we were out to make an impression.

"After he had washed and 'leathered' it off, it was left outside. The apprentice, about to climb into the front seat for a final check, was horrified to notice black spots on the white woollen upholstery, so came in for some cleaning fluid. We were all busy at the time and nobody realised what he wanted the cleaner for.

"Well, when I caught up with him I nearly had a fit. He had nearly rubbed through the upholstery without making the slightest impression on the spots. The answer was simple. There were some drops of water on the windscreen, and the sun shining through reflected them as black spots on the seat!

"Another day an old Overland came in with the differential 'cut out'. The mechanic put a new crown wheel and pinion in and the customer came in to collect his car. Starting up, he went to move off but instead of first gear, he found himself in reverse. Fortunately, he managed to stop before hitting anything."

The mechanic had put the new gears in back to front and, in effect, given the car three speeds in reverse and one forward. You can't do that with many cars, and the Overland just happened to be one of them.

Hector Brodie continued to run the business from 1930 until 1937 when, because of ill health, he retired and Harry Fairhall was appointed manager and the company took his name, as was the custom at that time. 'Fairy' as he was affectionately known, was one of the people enticed to the General Motors franchise before the war, joining Ebbett Motors in Hamilton, and later becoming managing director.

In 1937 the workshop was extended a further 35ft behind the original structure to cope with the increasing amount of vehicle maintenance and repair work. The Depression was over and things were looking up.

George Fraser was appointed manager in 1937, until he went into camp in 1940. At that point Bruce Renton, who had been accountant in Kaitaia, managed the business until he too was mobilised in July 1941, when Ellis Smith arrived.

Ted Williams organised a very successful staff social club on behalf of the firm, which for a number of years ran the Fairhall Motors Ball.

"This was not just a dance," said Ellis Smith in 1970, "but a ball with formal dress and regarded as the social event of the dancing season. There must be many matrons now who made their entrance into society at the Fairhall Motors Ball.

"During the war period, quite substantial amounts of money were raised

at the balls and donated to patriotic funds. I can recall the young ladies with their individual 'basket suppers' for which the men bid with spirit to share the supper dance, and to augment the patriotic funds.

"Nor did the absence overseas of the local young men cause the Ball to be discontinued. I remember one year placing a call to the officer in charge at Waipapakauri Air Force Station, eight miles north of Kaitaia and over 60 miles away, and importing a large busload of willing Air Force partners."

Mrs Williams and all the wives of Fairhall Motors staff prepared the supper. "We used to cook, and how we used to cook! We used tea wagons to distribute the supper in the hall, savouries on top and cakes on the bottom."

Ted Williams recalled that New Zealand's first casualties in the Second World War came from Northland. "Buster Marshall, a taxi driver, and Horrie Longworth, Fairhall Motors' accountant at the outbreak, both enlisted on the same day and went overseas in the 1st Echelon. They were taking cover in a shell hole in the Middle East when a shell came over and killed them both."

One of the important aspects of garage servicing was the ability to heat, bend, straighten and weld metals, a job that had been done by the village blacksmith. Early motorcars used acetylene lights. Garages used carbide generators to produce acetylene. Mixed with compressed oxygen, brought in by boats, garages were able to do their own repairs. Straightening axles was a common job because of the deep ruts and holes in the notorious Northland roads. Many of the early drivers were in the notorious category as well, driving their cars the same way as their horses, riding roughshod across country with inevitable results. Fairhall Motors had its own carbide generator for acetylene until the late 1960s.

Northland was the nearest landing point for possible Japanese invasion, and in early 1942 became an area of intense military activity. New post offices were erected in Kaikohe and Kaitaia, and large airfields built at Waipapakauri and Kaitaia. From that time, Kaikohe became a busy thriving area, a large hospital was erected, and the only hotel had a large clientele.

Ted Williams and his wife left Kaikohe in 1945 to take over the Opononi Hotel where they remained for another 12 years. During this time, Opo, the world-famous dolphin appeared.

"We had tremendous crowds, especially on Sundays. We used to have three meal sittings for casuals, but oh, it was hard going. Just when everyone was about to sit down, some ass would call out, there's Opo, and there would be a rush to get outside, which messed up the menu no end. But Ted had a word to the launch man who managed to keep Opo occupied further out in the harbour during lunch."

Not long after Opo died, Ted and Dorrie Williams bought the Kaukapakapa Hotel

'Opo' the dolphin was cruising the Hokianga wooing crowds. Ted Williams, former service manager, then the proprietor of the Opononi Hotel, giving Opo a gentle scratch as swimmers close in.

Ellis Smith built his house next to the garage and, when he left, the company bought and extended it.

Fairhall Motors staff in 1950, from left back: Joe Begbie, Ron Hogan, Vic Pearson, Ernie Walker, Ray McKeown, Geoff Dickeson, Bill Wilson. Front row: Bill Hogan, Alex Trail, Charlie Sloan, Norm Hudspith, Frank Robertson, and Ellis Smith, who was transferring to manage Te Aroha.

and moved there for five years before retiring at Te Atatu in 1962.

They both looked back on their time at Fairhall Motors with affection. "Kaikohe has changed a lot from when we first knew it. But the many friendships we made never changed."

Fairhall Motors progressed with the district. Tractors had been taken away from Ford dealers in 1936, when the Ford Motor Company arrived, and were handed back after the war. In 1947 the Fordson E27N tractor was introduced and it was a big step ahead. 'Cast Iron Clarice', as it was known, had a double-range gearbox, with kerosene,

petrol and diesel motors. The Fordson E27N was sold successfully and Ellis Smith, single-handedly, sold over 35 in one year.

Ellis Smith built his own house in Clifford Street in 1947, which backs on to the company premises from a rear section. The house had only one bedroom, because of the building restrictions and the fact that 'Smithy' lived alone.

Soon afterwards, a new lubrication building went up at the rear of the workshop, to replace the single hoist in front of the dealership that could no longer cope with the volume of work.

The lubrication bay was rebuilt behind the garage with more space.

Ellis Smith was transferred in 1951, to manage Hawke Motors in Morrinsville and Te Aroha, and the company bought his house.

His replacement was Don Gibbons who had been working at Hawke Motors in Te Aroha. Don married Florence Barclay, the Kaikohe bank manager's daughter, and they settled down and enlarged the manager's house as each of their daughters arrived.

Don Gibbons continued on with tractor sales, as few cars were now allocated, and Kaikohe would have received only about six a year. He was transferred to Cordery Garage, Waipukurau, in 1956 and Jack Harland took over.

Fairhall Motors was now recognised as a training dealership for new managers. It was much easier for a 'new' manager to learn and understand how a small dealership operated than be swamped by a large business.

Jack Harland had been accountant at Macaulay Motors, Invercargill, and was used to large volume tractor sales. He managed the business until transferring to Wellington in 1961.

In November 1961, H John Holder moved down from Kaitaia, where he had been sales manager, to take over as manager. With his knowledge of trucks, tractors and diesel engineering, Fairhall Motors made further rapid strides. In 1965 he transferred to New Lynn Motors as sales manager and Barry Wisneski, who had recently married Evelyn, was made manager. Barry Wisneski said that by the time he got to Kaikohe the service manager had taken over the manager's house, so he ended up buying his own. He was there until 1969, and was then shifted to Hawke Motors to take over from Ellis Smith who was retiring from Te Aroha.

Ian Morgan, who was branch manager, at Hawke Motors, Morrinsville, was appointed manager, and took up residence with his family in the manager's house, now empty in Clifford Street. Ian Morgan liked the area, resigned and bought the Opua General Store.

In 1972, Ian Lambie, who had been accountant at Te Kuiti Motors, and then had a year in vehicle sales at South Auckland Motors, was appointed manager. He and his wife Sue spent the next five years in

Fairhall Motors about 1960. The 1947 V8 'jail bar' wrecker can be seen inside the workshop entrance. Parts on the right, the lube hoist was behind the building, petrol pumps on the right, and a new Fordson Dexta on show with a 107e Prefect and Mark II Zephyr.

Bruce Ellis spent a period at Kaikohe as accountant, before transferring to Christchurch where he still works as accountant for Team Hutchinson Ford.

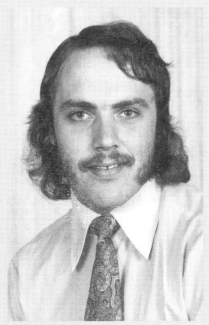

Kelvin Horsford started as apprentice motor mechanic and shifted to parts in 1970. He completed his parts trade certificate, qualifying first in his class for three years. He was also a Kaikohe senior rugby player.

Ian Morgan was manager in 1969.

Alby Franklin was appointed sales manager in 1971.

Ian Lambie was manager from 1972.

Neville Goldsworthy became manager in 1987 and, as at Te Kuiti earlier, had the job of closing the company down in 1998.

Above: The workshop was a happy place in 1971. From left: Sid Lyon, Ray Underwood, Bill Pou, Colin Hurst, Fred Roberts, Moka Watling, Dave Coss and Ron Dixon.

Left: Keen rallyers, Fred Courtenay, service manager, and his wife won many car club events. He successfully led a service crew in the 1974 Heatway national rally.

Below left: Sue Brown and Averill Poa ran the office in 1971.

Below: Stuart Holm came to manage the business in 1977, with his wife Ivy.

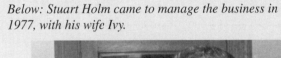

Kaikohe before moving to Avery Motors, Wellington, and later, becoming general manager at Newlands Motors and dealer principal at Napier Motors, Dunedin in 1980.

Stuart Holm, who had been sales manager at Craik Motors, Te Awamutu, was appointed manager in 1977, but resigned in 1979 and moved to Hamilton.

Richard J Kilkenny spent a period at Fairhall Motors as manager until Peter J Lloyd arrived with his family in 1980, spending the next four years learning the business. Peter Lloyd then shifted to take over Phillipps Motors at New Plymouth.

Grant Daniel, son of George Daniel at Avery Motors, was appointed manager in December 1984. He had been at Hutchinson Motors in Christchurch, and enjoyed the warmth and relaxed lifestyle of the 'Winterless North', and was reluctant to return to Christchurch.

Economically, the Far North became a backwater with the radical changes made by the government in 1985. When subsidies were removed, much of the north could not sustain pastoral farming, and more pine forests were planted. Many of the original farms were very small dairy holdings and these were steadily amalgamated into larger units. The effect of these changes was a reduction in jobs and increase in unemployment. All government back-up services declined with the changes.

At this stage, Alec Trail and Barry Wisneski, who was now internal auditor for the CMC Group, used to manage the place by remote control. Barry Wisneski would arrive each month to make sure all the accounts were up to date and, with his great capacity for work, could complete most things in a day.

Neville Goldsworthy, who had been manager at Te Kuiti Motors, arrived in 1987 and jointly managed both Kaitaia and Kaikohe dealerships until Fairhall Motors closed down in 1998.

Government policies have directly dictated the economic viability of many rural communities and the operation of businesses. During its time Fairhall Motors had been a considerable asset to Northland, providing excellent service, employment and training for many people. Those fortunate enough to have been there will remember Kaikohe as Ted Williams did; it may have changed, but the people there were, and still remain, their great friends.

Today Kaikohe is serviced from Whangarei, where The Pacific Motor Group's dealer principal is Hamish Sheard, whose motor industry experience began in the office of Fairhall Motors, Kaikohe.

Fairhall Motors Ltd staff, March 1986. Rear from left: Colin Hurst, Neil Davis, Toby Beazley, Paul Edwards, Russell Foote, Hugh Pepper. Front: Hamish Sheard, John Field, Don Nisbet, Grant Daniel, John Jenkinson, Mike Haywood, Donna Gibbons.

GREATER AUCKLAND FORD DEALERSHIPS

Auckland area has had a very changeable history in terms of Ford Dealers. It is the largest vehicle market in New Zealand, accounting today for nearly 40% of the country's total. For an overall picture, the following chronological changes will give readers a quick perspective.

1907   W Souter & Company of Cambridge, granted Ford agency from Automobile Co of NZ Ltd for Auckland Province and, over a period, established dealerships at Cambridge, Fort Street, Auckland and later Whangarei.

1908   The Colonial Motor Company Ltd obtained New Zealand agency for Ford from Automobile Co of NZ Ltd.

1909   John W Andrew, grain and produce agent, granted a sub-agency from Souter's at £5 per car.

1914   CMC appointed G A Haydon, engineer in Hobson St, opposite Farmers' Trading Co, as additional city dealer.

1917   W Souter & Co relinquished franchise. CMC purchased Fox Street, Parnell depot to assemble and distribute vehicles from. Carlaw & Jones, stable proprietor, Chancery Lane appointed dealer.
       John W Andrew, Eden Terrace, appointed dealer Jan 9, and ceased grain and produce business.
       Auckland area from Wellsford to Mercer, declared a common territory for the three dealers.

1919   Carlaw & Jones bought out by CMC and renamed The Universal Motor Company Ltd.

1922   John W Andrew started a branch at Pukekohe. CMC started full assembly at Fox Street.

1927   Universal Motors and John W Andrew merged. Henry Ford stopped making Model T.

1934   Pukekohe bought by Stanley Andrew and named Stan Andrew Ltd, now independent dealer.

1936   Ford Motor Company set up at Seaview, CMC finished at Fox Street, Parnell.

1937   Lees Brothers Papakura Ltd appointed dealer at Papakura, Stan Andrew conceded territory.

1938   John W Andrew purchased land to build a branch at Otahuhu, started branch in Great South Road.

1942   Neal Motors sold premises to John W Andrew on corner Great South and Gordon Roads, Otahuhu.

1953   Ford Motor Company set plan for new dealers in Auckland area at Takapuna, West and Panmure. CMC purchased land at New Lynn, Panmure, Howick. John W Andrew bought land at Royal Oak.

1954   Lewis Motors started at Takapuna to cover North Shore to Waiwera.
       John W Andrew sold Otahuhu branch to South Auckland Motors Ltd at Ford's request.

1960   Lees Brothers started a separate company, Lees Industries Ltd, to make industrial product.

1962   New Lynn Motors started and built at Titirangi Great North Roads intersection.
       Lewis Motors Ltd taken over by Lyon Motors Ltd at Takapuna.

1963   CMC bought 9 acre farmlet at Great South Road, Wiri.

1964   Ford Motor Company purchased 70 acres industrial land at Wiri and set up NZ parts distribution warehouse.

1964   Panmure Motors started and building commenced on Panmure roundabout.

1966   John W Andrew started branch at Greenlane.
       Stan Andrew Ltd at Pukekohe sold to D & W Motors Ltd, previously dealer at Dargaville.

1967   New Lynn Motors set up branch at Avondale.
       John W Andrews started selling used cars at Pt Chevalier site.

1968   South Auckland Motors established branch at Papatoetoe.

1969   South Auckland Motors established branch at Penrose.
       MacMillan Motors Ltd appointed Ford dealer at Greenlane.

1970   Lees Brothers set up a used car outlet at Gt South Rd, north of Papakura.

1971   New Lynn Motors set up branch at Henderson.

1972   New Lynn Motors set up a branch at Massey.

1973   Lyon Motors set up a branch at Birkenhead.
       John W Andrew set up a branch at Gt North Rd, Grey Lynn.
       South Auckland Motors started new branch at Mangere Centre, and another at East Tamaki.
       Brian Cotter Motors Ltd appointed dealer at Albany, in Lyon Motors' territory.

1974   Ford Motor Company constructed a new assembly plant at Wiri to build joint Mazda/Ford product.

1982   D & W Motors re-formed shareholding and Gerry Davies son of D P took over.

1983	John W Andrew Ltd sold out company to Neville Crichton (ARNCO Holdings), t/a John Andrew Ford.
1986	South Auckland Motors new Manukau City site opened on Oct 30.
1987	John Andrew Ford - Crichton sells to Stuart W Bowater.
	MacMillan Motors franchise cancelled April, because they dual franchised with BMW and Toyota. SAM Penrose Branch sold, East Tamaki branch leased, Papatoetoe branch leased. New Lynn sell Avondale.
1988	Ford NZ forms joint venture VANZ with Mazda NZ to assemble Ford and Mazda vehicles.
1988	Brian Cotter sold interests to Goudie Motors Ltd, from Thames, who set up at Silverdale.
	Panmure Motors changed name to East City Ford, New Lynn Motors changed to West Auckland Motors.
	D & W Motors Ltd sold out to Barry Holdaway Motors Ltd.
1989	Ford Motor Company re-located head office and all operations to Wiri closing Seaview plant.
1991	Lyon Motors sold out to North Harbour Ford.
1993	Lees Bros sold to Peter Rees Ltd t/a Papakura Ford.
	Barry Holdaway Motors sold out to Brent Greig t/a Pukekohe Ford.
1995	Trevor Walmsley appointed D P John Andrew Ford.
1997	North Harbour Ford collapsed and later taken over by John Andrew Ford.
1998	Stuart Bowater died Feb 21.
	Ford Motor Company proposed RJV dealer, Auckland Auto Collection Ltd, owned 50/50 with CMC and bought out Goudie, John Andrew, West Auckland, East City, South Auckland and Pukekohe Ford, on Mar 1 1999, leaving Papakura Ford as the only independent in Greater Auckland.
2000	Mazda dealerships added to AAC, shareholding changed to 41.98% Ford NZ, 41.98% CMC, 16.04% Mazda NZ.
2003	Papakura Ford terminated Feb 28 2003. AAC now operating as North Harbour, John Andrew and South Auckland.

Auckland was still surrounded by country towns in the 1910-40 period, all with annual A & P shows. Haydon's show stand in 1915, shows two Model Ts and, behind, a Paige on Dexter and Crozier's stand. British Imperial Oil Company later became Shell.

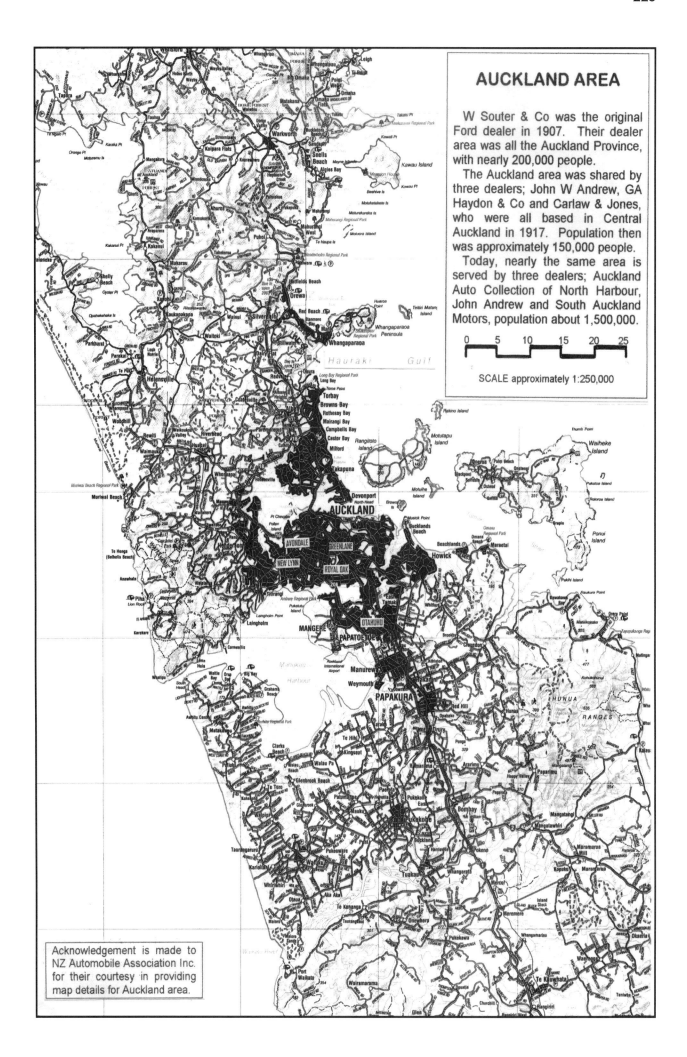

AUCKLAND AREA

W Souter & Co was the original Ford dealer in 1907. Their dealer area was all the Auckland Province, with nearly 200,000 people.

The Auckland area was shared by three dealers; John W Andrew, GA Haydon & Co and Carlaw & Jones, who were all based in Central Auckland in 1917. Population then was approximately 150,000 people.

Today, nearly the same area is served by three dealers; Auckland Auto Collection of North Harbour, John Andrew and South Auckland Motors, population about 1,500,000.

SCALE approximately 1:250,000

Acknowledgement is made to NZ Automobile Association Inc. for their courtesy in providing map details for Auckland area.

W Souter & Co was the Ford dealer representative for Auckland province from 1908 until the end of 1916. Originally in Cambridge, father J W and son E N came to Auckland, setting up in Fort Street. In 1913 sitting in the cars are from left: Charles Larmour, CMC managing director; Hayes, Hutt dealer; E N Souter, Auckland; R J Durance, Ford Canada export field manager; Arthur Brett, Auckland Star; and J W Souter, Auckland.

Model Ts were shipped one per case, and delivered to Souters by horse and dray, as was most freight at the time.

CHAPTER TWELVE

AUCKLAND -

JOHN W ANDREW & SONS

John Watson Andrew was born at Papatoetoe in 1869 and grew up at Otahuhu. He later joined his father Frank Andrew in a grain, produce and chaff cutting business. They were also passenger bus operators, using single and double-decker coaches with up to five horse teams. John Andrew learned how to manipulate the ribbons, controlling team and buses around the streets of Auckland before motor vehicles. In 1900 they had 100 buses and over 300 horses in stables at Chancery and Elliot Streets near the city markets.

John Andrew was keen on machinery, and experimented with a number of early engine types: steam, gas and electricity and, when combustion engines arrived, he tried two and four cycle engines. His first car in 1907 was a single cylinder Cadillac, but he sold this a little over a year later and bought one of the first Model T Fords from W Souter & Company.

Soon afterwards, he badgered Souter's to get an agency to sell Fords, finally becoming a sub-agent at £5 per car commission. John W was granted the Chase truck franchise in 1911 and sold 36 in the five years he held the franchise. Many of these were converted to buses, and in 1916-17 he formed the Chase Sightseeing Company using a charabanc bodied Chase truck, taking tourists around Auckland. John W's eldest son, Stanley, came into the business in 1912 and looked after the assembly and service side until he went overseas with the NZ Armed Forces, driving ambulances in France.

John W used to doff his hat to his customers as they drove past, and people wondered how he knew them. It was simple really; he had cut the corner off their front number plates.

On January 9 1917, Colonial Motor Company made John W Andrew a Ford dealer when Souter's relinquished the franchise. His daughter Mary was driving tutor, and brother-in-law George Gladding

was sales manager. Together with Auckland Ford dealers G A Haydon and Carlaw & Jones, they sold Ford cars in a common territory between Wellsford and Ohinewai. Two years later Carlaw & Jones was renamed The Universal Motor Company, with Gibbons family shareholding.

Stan Andrew returned after the First World War, and the partnership, renamed John W Andrew & Son in 1920, expanded rapidly. A year later John Andrew's younger son Ivan joined the business to concentrate on service and an 's' was added to make John W Andrew and Sons. R E (Ray) Clarke joined the firm as secretary in June 1921.

After the arrival of Fordson tractors in 1919, it was decided to open a country branch at Pukekohe, and tractors, cars and one ton trucks were sold and serviced there from 1922. Tractors were a new concept for farmers, who had always used horses, and demonstrations were held at A & P shows and in groups, with Mary Andrew showing farmers how to plough with a tractor, accompanied by her father John W, with his order book. They sold plenty of tractors.

In 1923 Wilfred G Gladding joined the business, as did Leslie C Gladding a year later. The partnership was made into a limited liability company, John W Andrew and Sons Ltd, with a capital of £30,000, and the Andrews and George Gladding holding shares.

Stan Andrew was keen to try his hand at beach racing. He built up a racer using mainly Model T parts, helped by Jack Broun (later service manager of CMC, then FMC). They raced at Muriwai Beach and, after several attempts, set a new Australasian speed record of 93.26 mph over 5 miles in 1924.

Colonial Motor Company advised John W Andrew that the Model T was going to run out in 1926, and there would not be enough new cars for at least a year. When they proposed a merger of The Universal

G A Haydon, an engineer in Hobson Street, was given the franchise in 1914. The company later expanded its premises, buying an old hotel next door, and rebuilding it for car, truck and tractor sales in the early 1920s.

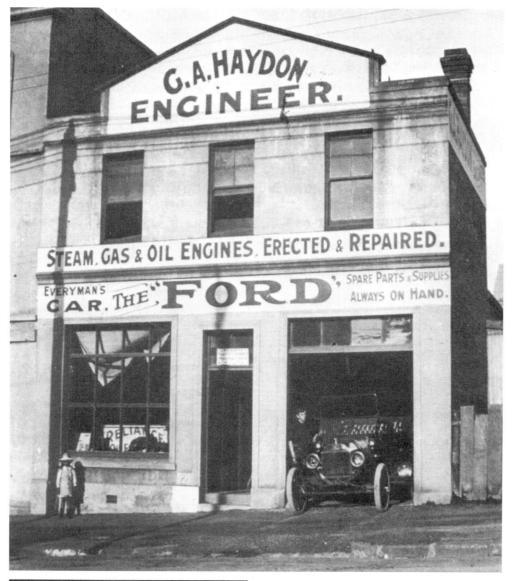

John Watson Andrew started selling Ford cars in 1908 for a commission of £5 per car. He became a Ford dealer in 1917, after the Souters retired.

Motor Company Ltd with John W Andrew and Sons Ltd, John W agreed, provided he retained control. The two companies merged on January 1 1927, with Colonial Motor Company holding just over 30% of the shares, and leasing John W Andrew and Sons Ltd the spectacular Art Deco Universal Motors dealership on the corner of Symonds Street and Glenside Terrace.

When the Model A Ford arrived in 1928, the business became buoyant again, and was back to normal for two years.

John Andrew enjoyed boating and fishing, and owned two launches, the small *Esme A,* which he sold in the early 1920s, then the *Caprice.* John W drew up his own plans for the Andrew Fordson marine engine, the first one powering the *Caprice.* The Andrew family suffered a major setback when Ivan Andrew was tragically killed after a marine outboard motor he was working on disintegrated.

With the growth of Auckland business, and the economic pressure of the

Depression in 1931, Andrews decided to sell the Pukekohe branch to Taylor & Macdonald Ltd. John W Andrew & Sons Ltd suffered just as much as most companies in the slump, but controlled their used car stocks and got through, and in 1933 sales improved quickly.

Taylor & Macdonald at Pukekohe, however, were in receivership, and after attempts by Percy Ferguson from H N Scrimshaw's office, to get them back on track, the business was offered for sale.

Stanley Andrew resigned from Andrew's and bought the company, which traded on as Stan Andrew Ltd from March 1936.

Wilf G Gladding became general manager, and John W, semi-retired and afflicted with arthritis, remained managing director and chairman.

Lees Brothers were appointed Ford dealers at Papakura in 1937, Andrews decided to set up a sales branch at Otahuhu to protect the southern part of their territory. Plans were drawn up for a garage, and

CMC branch operated from Fox Street, Parnell, very close to the port. They stored cars in crates there at first but, in the early 1920s, the buildings were expanded to assemble cars, as was done in Wellington and Timaru. This helped reduce Model T prices.

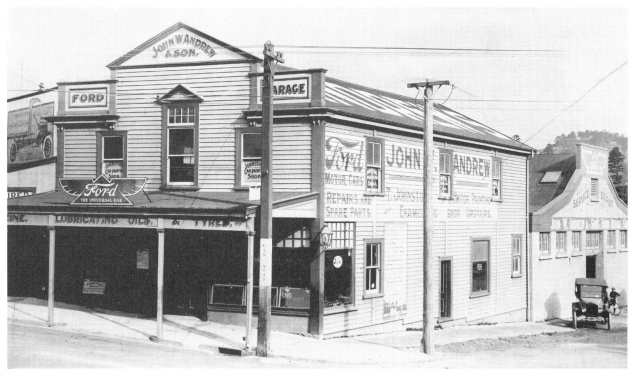

John W Andrew's premises at Eden Terrace. The front was used for showroom and parts sales. The workshop was built down the hill. Below: The 'old' Universal Motor Company premises. Service was down the side street and under the showroom and parts department.

tenders closed the day the Second World War began. Ford still wanted the branch completed, but it was impossible with the wartime restrictions. After Japan attacked Pearl Harbour in 1941, Neal Motors offered their garage business for sale, on the corner of Great South and Gordon Roads. Andrew's bought this and Les C Gladding became branch manager.

The war years were very difficult, with no new cars, government requisitioning all 1938 and 1939 used cars, and petrol rationed. Many staff members served overseas and it was hard to make ends meet. After the war, staff returned, but the restrictions and rationing continued making trading difficult and frustrating.

John Watson Andrew died in 1949 at the age of 80. He had been an Auckland transport pioneer, and associated with Ford for 40 years as head of the largest Ford dealer in New Zealand. Wilfred Gladding took over the helm.

It was a great surprise to Andrew's, when Ford appointed Jack Lewis a Ford dealer at Takapuna in 1954, taking their

North Shore territory without any discussion. After a meeting with Ford and The Colonial Motor Company, where future development of the Auckland market was set out, with new dealer points at West Auckland and East Auckland, Ford then informed Andrews' their Otahuhu branch had to become a separate dealership. Les Gladding resigned as director of Andrew's, and became managing director of South Auckland Motors for CMC while his brother Wilf was appointed managing director of Andrew's.

Land was bought at Royal Oak in 1954, and a branch set up there under Eric Picot in 1957, to provide a service depot for customers, and new vehicle pre-delivery centre. Auckland had started to expand rapidly and there was no longer enough room at Symonds Street. One and a half acres of land was bought at Glen Innes, so another branch with further workshop and

Top: Tractors were on display next to the lubrication bay, and were big business in 1947.

Bottom: Parts sales were available on the Symonds Street level. This up-to-date counter was quite something in 1948.

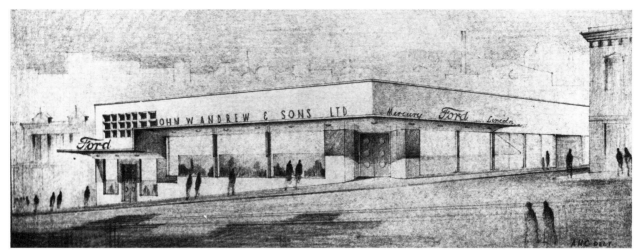

A 1960 concept drawing for new Khyber Pass premises for John W Andrew and Sons Ltd, which was subsequently built and became their headquarters. The Symonds Street building was sold to NZ Truth newspaper.

display space could be formed with W S Chambers as manager.

Wilf Gladding retired at the end of 1961 and R J (Bob) Greenfield, who had been on the staff nine years, was appointed general manager. There were now over 200 people working in the company, and the Foodstuffs property on Khyber Pass was bought when it came up for sale in 1962. More adjacent land was purchased, and it was decided to shift the head office to this site and sell Symonds Street.

Being the largest Ford dealer, and indeed the largest dealer in the country, also brought its problems. On the one hand, you had more customers requiring cars and trucks; and on the other hand, you were the most obvious starting point for Ford if any changes were required. Andrew's might have more than 10% of Ford's distribution channel, but was it a strength or weakness to be so large?

McMillan Motors was appointed a Ford dealer at Greenlane in 1969. Again this was in Andrew's territory, and situated between their head office and branches. At the time Ford said McMillan's appointment brought a direct importing licence holder into the Ford camp, which could improve their market share. There was certainly an increased level of competition between Ford dealers, and branches were set up in defence by all dealers. But it seemed that no matter what Andrew's did, it did not please Ford.

John W Andrew and Sons Ltd sold out to ARNCO Holdings Ltd after a period of negotiations, with Neville A Crichton becoming dealer principal in March 1983. The dealership continued to trade on as John W Andrew Ltd, and relocated to leased premises at 1 Great North Road at Newton, trading much as before.

Neville Crichton sold his shares to Stuart Bowater in 1987, and moved to a new venture in Sydney. McMillan Motors decided to dual franchise with Toyota after a warning from Ford, and had their Ford franchise cancelled in 1987.

Trading conditions kept the heat on dealers to survive, and most of the branches set up to defend territories were sold off. A number of franchise dealers did not survive, and the industry slimmed in numbers. Many dealers started importing Japanese used cars, and some adopted dubious practices such as clocking odometers, rebuilding wrecks and falsifying vehicle details, thereby destroying their integrity and creating the derogatory term 'Jap import' – a used vehicle of doubtful quality and background.

During the 1990s Ford rationalised its dealer group to more sensible numbers, with many changed to service dealers. Stuart Bowater died after a battle with cancer on February 21 1998, and Trevor Walmsley, his chief operating officer, carried on as dealer principal for the Bowater estate.

In November 1998 Ford announced a new retail joint venture (RJV) for the Auckland market, inviting the seven Auckland Ford dealers to sell and become partners as one large RJV dealer, following overseas Ford practices. Later, Mazda NZ and Mazda Auckland dealers were also invited to join.

On March 1 1999 Auckland Auto Collection Ltd was born. Today this company sells Ford and Mazda vehicles from three trading operations: North Harbour, John Andrew and South Auckland Motors. Auckland Auto Collection is owned 41.98% by Ford NZ, 41.98% by Colonial Motor Company and 16.04% by Mazda NZ. D Ross Moore is CEO.

CHAPTER THIRTEEN

WEST AUCKLAND – NEW LYNN MOTORS / WEST AUCKLAND FORD

New Lynn was named in the 1850s by James Utting, the English surveyor, who was struck by the similar topography to his hometown, King's Lynn in Norfolk. New Lynn remained a small country village of 30–40 people for 50 years. Sir Robert Stout, chief justice, proclaimed it a town district, and part of Waitemata County, on June 20 1910.

When the first board met they made application to wrest their town from Waitemata County control, but government declined this, saying more than 500 persons were required for independence. When the 1911 census showed the population at 522, another application resulted in Governor General Lord Islington gazetting its independence from Waitemata from April 1 1911. The 1,392 acre town grew slowly until, after the Second World War, new immigration boosted its population to 10,000 by 1960.

Earlier, Maori had not settled in the area because of the clay soil, which did not grow good kumara, but they hunted bird life in the bush. More significantly, they linked the Kaipara and Waitemata harbours with a portage route for their canoes, known today as Portage Road.

The clay was not all bad though, and early settler Rice Owen Clark, experimented making field tiles to drain his farm. He was soon supplying the local market with tiles and bricks. His grandson, Thomas E Clark, negotiated the merger of local potteries in 1929, creating The Amalgamated Brick and Pipe Company. This became Crown Lynn Pottery, later Ceramco, New Lynn's largest industry, known internationally for its pottery and industrial products.

In August 1962, New Lynn Motors was granted a motor vehicle dealer's licence and

Looking south over New Lynn about 1955, Great North Road runs towards the bottom centre of the photgraph. The lower intersection is Titirangi Road with New Lynn Motors' light-coloured empty site on the top right side. Across the railway opposite New Lynn Motors is the large Crown Lynn Pottery complex.

The corner site in 1962, Crown Lynn's chimney on the skyline. Left of the New Lynn Motors sign is the caravan office.

started trading with a new vehicle allocation of 50 units. The company had one hectare of scrub and weed-covered low-lying land on the corner of Titirangi Road and Great North Road at New Lynn, one four metre caravan as an office, one employee and a sign proclaiming their existence.

The company was the first all new dealership to start from scratch in The Colonial Motor Company Group after the war, and the manager, Colin Cliff, was not one to be put off by any lack of resources; in his words, "these need to be acquired as you go along". His wartime exploits in Italy and Europe had taught him a lot about making the most of opportunities. In May 1962, Colin and Barbara Cliff left their home in New Plymouth and set out for Auckland to establish the new dealership.

Colin Cliff had been manager of Phillipps Motors Ltd in New Plymouth, and his father had worked for Derby and Company, its forerunner. Colin Cliff had literally been born into the motor industry at New Plymouth, in the historic old 'Round House' on the dealership land where his parents lived. The Round House had been home to the armed constabulary during the land wars in the 1850s and had been erected as a pre-fabricated kitset sent from England.

Thinking and planning ahead has been a hallmark of The Colonial Motor Company, and 'West Auckland Motors Ltd' was registered on September 3 1954 and 2 1/2 acres of land purchased for £10,000 on a key road intersection ready for the formation of a new dealership. Vehicle import restrictions meant that CMC had to wait another nine years, until Ford Motor Company would give the go ahead and back the dealership with cars. In the meantime the company and the land were

waiting. Colin Cliff recalls: "Every year the council used to write to Colonial Motor Company, saying the site was covered in noxious weeds, and that something should be done about it. The Company would then write to a local scout group and arrange to get it cleared for a donation."

It was mid-winter when Colin Cliff parked the caravan on the swampy site on a patch of shingle laid by aptly named local contractors, Duck Brothers. "If I needed a telephone, I used the one at the baker's next door. This was handy, and I always had morning tea there." Across the road was Sonata Laboratories, and Colin Cliff found that the principals, the Colemore-Williams brothers, had been customers at Phillipps Motors before they shifted to Auckland after the Second World War. There began a very good arrangement: Sonata needed cars and vans and couldn't get them; New Lynn Motors needed customers and had the vehicles.

Colin Cliff recalls that he only had one new car for sale on the site, plus his demonstrator, "heavily loaded with 'extras'", under the sign announcing the new dealership. "If I managed to sell both, I got my wife to drive down and pick me up."

In the planning stage, after consulting local people, it was decided the name should be changed to New Lynn Motors Ltd, and very shortly afterwards business started from the caravan. Jack Pearce transferred from New Plymouth and started as service manager in October 1962, and was number two on the staff. Charged with the job of creating a service department from nothing, he set up a temporary shelter next to the caravan.

Planning for the buildings was underway but difficulties were encountered putting down foundations in what was a

Building underway. The bakery building had been bought and was now being used as the office.

former kauri swamp. The problem with the old tree stumps, probably thousands of years old, was their stumps had rotted into a type of semi-liquid plasticine which kept moving when anything was placed on top of it. A team of structural engineers and architects, Spencer, Hollings and Ferner, was engaged to assist and design the new dealership. Eventually, after thousands of cubic metres of mud and old tree stumps were removed, solid earth was reached. It was decided a two-storeyed building with an upper mezzanine third floor could be economically designed, with workshop below and sales and administration above at street level. This also saved valuable land. The building was designed to be built in two stages; Stage one was tendered at £54,220 and started in the hole below the road in October 1962.

When vehicles were being received, and pre-delivery and service work needed to be done, Jack Pearce supervised and contracted out to a local garage what he could not do himself. Then he found temporary premises 12 kilometres away at Span Farm, Henderson and started employing service staff to be ready to move into the new building when it was completed.

In the meantime the company was fortunate in leasing an old brick shop next door, and administration and sales were

The workshop was operating while building continued above.

transferred from the caravan. In the early days Colin Cliff and Jack Pearce did everything, and it was very hard work. Jack Pearce remembered, in December 1962, "One day, I flew to Wellington to pick up a new Zephyr, which I drove straight back to New Lynn, ran a pre-delivery check, cleaned it up, and we sold it next day, Christmas Eve. The majority of our cars came by rail in those days and we drove up the urgent ones, but some came by sea. Colin and I caught a local bus service, that wasn't very reliable, down to the wharf to collect the cars from ships."

Workshop equipment arrived at the end of January 1963 and the first mechanics started work. Jack Pearce remembered: "I was surprised when I had a free hand in ordering what I wanted, and we bought the best available equipment. The service

Left: Colin J Cliff, first manager.

Right: W Jack Pearce, first service manager.

Left: Chris Norris, first parts manager.

Right: Leo Dixon, first sales manager.

department became a reality, even if it was temporary and 12 kilometres down the road, but service was inhibited, because the location was out-of-the-way." Cars and staff had to be continuously shuttled back and forth, creating difficulties until the new workshop was finished

Very soon afterwards Chris Norris arrived from South Auckland Motors, Otahuhu, to take charge of a non-existent parts department. He had grown up in Morrinsville, had a period at Waipukurau, and was then sent on a crash course to South Auckland Motors to find out how a large parts operation worked. Michael Gibbons came from Stevens Motors, Lower Hutt, to be accountant. Difficulties were in abundance, but getting trained 'Ford' people was impossible, so the company implemented its own training programmes which proved invaluable over the following years.

Stage one of the building was completed by Easter 1963, and the car workshop was moved back to the ground floor with the builders still working above. Span Farm was still kept going as a satellite workshop, as space was still very short, and as Colin Cliff said, "It was very handy for doing warranty work, out of the public view". Having service people on the same site made organisation and control a lot better, but a wet winter plus builders overhead made conditions very trying. The excitement of the new venture helped keep morale high despite difficulties, and the staff did a great job coping with the conditions.

The site was also on the main water supply route from the Waitakere Reservoir to Auckland city, and this proved to be a hazard over the years. It burst several times with water spouting up to 30 metres into the air. Colin Cliff remembers: "The water blocked the road and caused traffic jams, with the worst blast scouring a hole in the road of three metres diameter. As a result we had to provide a special drainage system to prevent major flooding."

Stage two of the building contract was let for £52,000, but the showroom and administration area progress was slow. It was finally completed and ready for staff to move in on October 31 1963. The first part of the development was now finished.

After one year several major customers were on the books. Waitemata County Council was the largest at the time, taking 100 vehicles a year. Industrial development was expanding in the area and large new businesses such as Reckitt and Coleman, Nestlé and Coca Cola moved in, also needing vehicles.

The expansion in sales volume that took place, and the need to have even more vehicles, especially commercial vans, created continual headaches. Tractors and medium trucks were freely available. Colin Cliff recalls they used to purchase Escort vans from Ford dealers all over New Zealand. Many country dealers were only too happy to accept retail price for their vans and, although it cost New Lynn Motors money to deliver the vehicle, this was more than made up down the line with service and happy customers.

Vehicle deliveries also reached a peak in November 1963, and staff had great difficulty in delivering all the vehicles before the end of the year. There was no pleasure in trying to move into the spectacular new premises with all the other pressures, so the staff decided to hold a Christmas party for their 22 children instead. This annual party carried on, as it did at many of the other CMC Group companies.

The new year arrived all too soon and

Staff children's Christmas party and a ride in the fire engine.

NEW LYNN MOTORS

MERRY XMAS

Staff, Christmas 1965.
Back row from left: J P Groos, C R Rawlings, C W Janes, R Seja, D Urwin, D Downey, D W de Bettencor, W Offen and C W Main. Third row: K Dyer, B Lyon, D B McTavish, R Thomlinson, D Wales, D Henderson, N Risman, D Robertson, M Cooper, K Lee, C Mitchell, R Hunt, W Magowan, C Iwan, J Marriot, K Jordan, R Allen, B Gillbanks, R McLeod, J Paul, L J McQueen. Second row: J Andrew, J Cooper, R Scott, C Morse, L Jennings, B Shaw, R Young, A Halbach, R McCabe, W Withey, J Thomas, D Wadman. Front row: G Duncan, A Ireland, K burrows, R Haythornthwaite, J Andrew, M Ross, A Necklen, L Dixon, W J Pearce, C J Cliff, M H Gibbons, C Norris, H Thomlinson, A Ireland, P Bissett, D Bolton, R Kennedy, J Chapman, R Clarke. Away: F Armfield, P Cater.

staff realised that, good as their smart new facilities were, they were not going to cope with the burgeoning vehicle sales and service. A Stage three workshop and parts extension was required immediately, so planning started, detailing layouts and working through the raft of detail for the new building.

In April, Leo Dixon transferred from Avery Motors, Wellington, to become sales manager. He had spent two years at Te Kuiti Motors Ltd as accountant, and then, like Chris Norris, had been sent on a crash course to Avery Motors, learning about volume sales. He further boosted No Remittance and used car sales.

No Remittance was the peculiar system devised by the government to allow private import of new cars using private overseas funds. Government import licences were still very restricted, and new vehicles were short to the extent that a new Ford Mk III Zephyr, which cost £1,228 to buy in 1964, was worth £1,500 on the 'black market' straight after it was bought. After a year of use, an owner could sell his old car and buy a new one at no cost if overseas funds were used. Needless to say, 'the experts' in the motor industry managed to dream up the most amazing ways to obtain overseas funds. Today, one shudders at the cavalier methods of the time, but people needed transport.

One of the useful by-products of the No Remittance scheme was an incentive offered by Ford Motor Company. For every No Remittance licence obtained, the company got an extra new car allocated as well. Suffice to say, New Lynn's allocation was boosted substantially by No Remittance business.

The old brick shop, which had been used as an office in the early days, came up for sale and was purchased. A little later an adjoining glassworks and house were purchased, cleared out and quickly converted into additional workshop space.

Tenders for the new workshop and parts building were let in October 1964 but it took another 11 months before it was occupied. The workshop was ideal, full of natural light, warm in winter and able to be opened up in summer, allowing good ventilation. Martyn Spencer was contracted to design the building, and parts sales were on the second floor with large open display marketing. It was the most advanced service and parts facility in Auckland at the time.

At the end of 1965, after only three years operation, the dealership had surpassed its targets, 71 people were on the staff, over 2,000 vehicles had been sold and delivered, and parts and service business was at record levels.

Although New Lynn Motors was now completely on site, and booming ahead, there remained significant opportunities in the outlying areas to the north and west and, rather than have Ford Motor Company set up other new Ford dealers, it was decided to establish branches in strategic areas when suitable opportunities arose.

Avondale branch was established in 1967, and a two bay service workshop was built there in the next year. This gave service to the large Rosebank industrial area as well as Avondale. Colin Cliff remembers that they were losing customers in that area: "We found this young mechanic who had bought the land to set up a service station, only to find that he couldn't get a licence to operate it. So we

Top left: The new dealership stood out on the night skyline.

Left: The new workshop and parts building, allowed all staff to come back to the one site.

Below: The showroom was at street level, with a workshop underneath and another across the yard. Some of the offices were upstairs.

main site, where it is still used by the maintenance man." So the Avondale branch was in operation and, sure enough, the customer losses stopped. However, it was short lived as the Auckland City Council re-zoned the land as suitable only for commercial selling purposes. Not to be put off, the corner site was then attractively terraced, fenced, floodlit and converted to sell used cars, still as a branch of New Lynn Motors.

Henderson had started to develop commercially, and in 1968 R B Gibbons told Colin Cliff he should look out for some

Above: The first four apprentices to qualify in 1967. Standing: Roy McCabe and Barry Shaw. In front: Bruce McTavish and Robert Thomlinson.

Top right: Robert Thomlinson won a Rotary International scholarship to study in England in 1968.

Right: Bruce McTavish joined Bruce McLaren's racing team in 1969, becoming his No. 2 mechanic. Here he is 'banging up' Bruce McLaren's car wheel nuts.

said we would buy it from him and sell him a property in Onehunga, which I knew was available. He said 'yes', so we moved him over there. Then we bought the house next door on the corner and shifted this to our

available land there. After approaching Acet Corban, it was arranged that three half-acre sites his family owned were sold to Vineyard Enterprises Ltd, a new company owned by Colonial Motor Company. "They only cost $20,000 each, but at the time it was a lot of money. $60,000 was enough to build the Corbans three really good houses," Colin said, "and whenever I see Acet, I ask him how our houses are."

This was right opposite Corban's Vineyard, one of New Zealand's most prestigious and oldest wineries. New Lynn Motors was now able to give on the spot service to increasing numbers of its horticultural and farming clients at Henderson.

Later in 1970 another opportunity came about in a more unusual way. New Lynn Motors had a large wholesale parts business that extended into the northern country area and, when one of their commercial customers, a country garage at Massey, was put into receivership, it was decided after discussion with the receiver, that New Lynn would take over the land and buildings, realising on the main assets and settling the creditors. The garage was a going concern,

with a multi-brand service station, lubrication bay, workshop and panelshop, all on one and a half acres.

The new Massey branch continued to operate the existing vehicle service operation for local clients and retained the panelbeater as a tenant. Tractors now had a ready made farming base and tractor sales and service, centred on the Massey Branch, were boosted.

Tom Marshall, tractor service foreman at Craik Motors, Te Awamutu, was transferred to re-organise the service. He came to New Zealand in 1962, having trained as a toolmaker and helped service the 15 tractors and machines on his family's farm in Surrey. His 12 years with CMC at Te Awamutu had taught him all about Ford tractors, and he was an acknowledged expert in fixing the infamous Select-O-Speed transmissions.

In addition to Tom Marshall, Massey branch was a little League of Nations with Dave Dobbin in parts, formerly a cabinet maker from Dublin; Steven Fong in the workshop, who arrived from China with his parents; Willem Blom in tractor service, formerly from Haarlemmer Meer in Holland; and Ivan Moloczzij in the

Avondale branch operation.

Henderson branch.

Top: Massey branch.

*Right: The Kumeu
A & P show was a
popular event.*

workshop, whose mother was from Samoa and father from the Ukraine.

Massey had many intensive horticultural and lifestyle blocks around it, and all needed the service and back up that New Lynn Motors provided.

Jack Pearce was made official right-hand man to Colin Cliff, and was promoted to manager, and Herb Bennett transferred from Macaulay Motors Invercargill, to be New Lynn service manager.

An unusual opportunity occurred when Car Haulaways storage yard, at Manurewa, was flooded by water, affecting over 100 new Ford vehicles which the Ford Motor Company could no longer sell. Jack Pearce put a proposition to Colin Cliff, that the company tender for the whole lot, which would make the insurance underwriter's job easier than dealing with many different people. "Colin said 'yes', much to my surprise. When I asked him about the money, he just said he'd fix it, and told me to get on and do it. I was a bit taken aback with his trust, as a lot was involved. We were successful, and set about re-conditioning them. What we discovered

was that the water had not been as deep as we thought, and hardly any damage had occurred. We checked every vehicle thoroughly and put aside a warranty contingency, but barely needed it. The result was great, we fixed anything that happened, even if it wasn't due to water, and we made a lot of money."

In 1975 the Regional Authority dropped another bombshell, announcing it would be widening the road as part of the Avondale by-pass development. This was a horrendous and expensive nightmare for the dealership that took 15 months to complete, and managing director Colin Cliff estimates that it cost New Lynn Motors some $2 million in lost sales.

The dealership lost five metres along its entire frontage covering some 200 metres, and this was over and above the frontage lost when the street was initially re-aligned. It was the third time council had requisitioned land from the company.

"Because of that development, we lost the facility of getting cars in or out of our new car showroom, which was a severe blow to us," Colin Cliff said. "As a result

Left: Dave Wadman, Massey branch manager.

Right: Herb Bennett, service manager.

we had to build a side door into the showroom, but even so, the movement of cars was restricted, as we had a central stairwell leading to the service area below."

To compensate for the loss of land the Regional Authority agreed to construct a display deck able to accommodate the same number of vehicles as had previously been on display. Concrete pillars were positioned, so that a concrete parking slab could be constructed, along the street frontage. It was a significant task and involved one of the largest continuous concrete pours in New Zealand history, with 300 cubic metres of concrete being set down in 36 hours.

But the route to the new display area was a long and hard one. "My estimate of $2 million in lost sales was based on the direct result of the frustrations, inconveniences and contractors' upheavals during the road construction, that affected all parts of the business, from petrol to new car sales," Colin Cliff said.

Left: Jim Syme, business manager

Right: Barry Helleur, heavy commercial manager.

Aerial photograph shows all New Lynn Motors' buildings in position. A total of nine metres of street frontage was taken by council in three stages. When the final five metres of street frontage was taken two concrete platforms were made to give a similar amount of display space, and created extra storage underneath.

Herb Bennett recalled he had complaints from many customers who couldn't find their way into the workshop because of the road works. "What made matters even worse was that we would have days when mechanics were doing nothing for much of the day, and we knew the work was outside waiting to come in. In addition, the general condition of the yard was appalling, with mud and other debris washed down the ramp, with bits of wood and steel lying around everywhere. Fortunately, after work finished, our customers all came back for service."

Jack Pearce said: "For several months you could count the number of people coming in on one hand. The dust permeated everything, buildings, cars and paperwork. And the sales staff realised that the public didn't want to come into the building because of the conditions."

Telephone services were also affected and were often out of action totally for hours at a time. Colin Cliff said: "In one two month period, telephone lines were cut five times, and without a telephone our business grinds to a halt. At the end, we had to get commercial cleaners to go right through the premises to sort out the mess." A couple of staff left with the frustrations, but the rest were loyal despite all the difficulties.

However, although there were restrictions on its service during the alterations, the petrol station gained real benefits. As it had to be re-sited, a new shop displaying accessories and motoring needs was built, with larger fuel storage tanks installed.

New Lynn Motors' 120 staff settled down after the distractions, and the company did very well, and was first in the CMC Group to make a profit of over $1 million dollars after tax in a year. The new vehicle market freed up after 30 years of shortages, with Ford the leading brand and New Lynn was often short of cars.

The Ford Laser, Courier and Econovan made a big impact on the market in 1981, with Laser immediately becoming the top selling car in New Zealand. Soon afterwards, Ford Telstar arrived to replace Cortina, which had been such a mainstay for Ford, and this, too, was a success. When D Series medium trucks ran out in 1983, there was quite a gap for 18 months until the new Ford-Hino N Series truck arrived, which affected commercial profits. Customers were delighted with the quality of these new products, which had very little warranty, and subsequently affected the need for large workshop facilities. Ford said dealers should reduce facilities, but this was easier said than done.

Colin Cliff retired from New Lynn Motors in 1983 after 47 years in the industry, but continued on as marketing director of CMC Group, a special new appointment, until 1990. In his inimitable style, he had created a very large and profitable subsidiary from a swampy paddock, using his skills and unbounded imagination. Jack Pearce became managing director in a seamless transition.

After the new Labour government's policies were introduced in the mid-1980s, the NZ motor industry changed dramatically and CMC Group started re-structuring in 1986 to reduce costs. Computers were introduced, with the new Magix system saving an immense amount of duplication in cross-referencing, helping to locate information quickly, and removing repetitive jobs.

In early 1987 Avondale branch was sold. It was also decided Massey would be closed and sold, and Henderson renovated, with the workshop extended to continue to provide service back-up to the northwest area.

In January 1988 Jim Robb was transferred to New Lynn, to be general manager, with the idea that he would take over when Jack Pearce retired. He had been

Henderson branch was extended and modernised in 1989.

Jim Robb, CEO, started at South Auckland Motors in accounting and then joined sales. In 1987 he was appointed dealer principal of Ruahine Motors, and came to New Lynn in 1989 as manager. He understudied Jack Pearce before taking over in 1990.

dealer principal at Ruahine Motors Waipukurau, and prior to that was in accounting and sales at South Auckland Motors.

When Ford decided to sell out of tractors worldwide, the tractor franchise was relinquished and Norwoods took over distribution. A number of the tractor staff members were made redundant when Massey branch was closed. Tom Marshall bought the tractor contacts and tools and set up his own tractor repair business which he still operates from Dairy Flat.

Jack Pearce retired from New Lynn in May 1990, becoming relieving dealer principal at South Auckland Motors for 18 months. Jim Robb became CEO at New Lynn Motors and completed the restructuring. New Lynn Motors had reduced staff from 120 to 75 over four years.

In 1992 New Lynn Motors celebrated 30 years operation and changed its name to West Auckland Motors Ltd, to better

A 'Service Lane' quick service facility was set up, including panel work, paint oven and tyres, in the building next door, taken over from Motor Traders Ltd.

reflect the Waitakere district it serves.

Ford managing director Tony Brigden was keen for New Zealand Ford dealers to offer a 'fast service quick quote' scheme, along the lines of the UK Rapid Fit. After some time and modification, Service Lane was set up with West Auckland Motors, which had already started down this path, one of the first Ford dealers to offer this type of service.

The neighbouring Motor Traders building, now empty, was purchased, and the rear portion of the building set up as a new panel and paint department with the latest equipment and an air-conditioned bake oven. In the front third of the building, the fast service shop for exhausts, mufflers, brakes and tyres was installed and run as a unit with the service station and panel shop. This opened in 1996 and was an immediate success.

In November 1998 Ford announced its rationalisation of the Auckland market under a single retail joint venture (RJV) dealer. New Lynn Motors and six other Auckland Ford dealers were absorbed into the Auckland Auto Collection on March 1 1999, ending its 37 year history. The company always had an outstanding market share, performing at the top of the class.

CHAPTER FOURTEEN

EAST AUCKLAND –
PANMURE MOTORS LTD /
EAST CITY FORD

Panmure Motors was the second Colonial Motor Company dealership to start from nothing after the Second World War. It is situated on the roundabout at Panmure, one of the highest traffic flow points in New Zealand, with the main arterial routes flowing through the area delivering to significant industrial warehousing and retail shopping nearby. It is also the corridor to the eastern bays suburbs.

In 1951, CMC began a far-sighted programme of land acquisition at strategic locations where business was likely to develop in New Zealand, especially in Auckland which expanded rapidly after the war with new immigration policies bringing many European and English settlers. Panmure was one of the locations identified and a 2^1/$_2$ acre plot was

purchased beside the Panmure roundabout. For another 13 years the leased farmland sat there, and John Emery, manager of South Auckland Motors, collected the rent every month, while Ford Motor Company considered an approval. The original application was for a branch of South Auckland Motors, as the Panmure area was in their territory but, much to managing director Les Gladding's disappointment, Ford insisted it be a new, separate dealership to ensure a greater level of competition between dealers.

In 1964 the Mt Wellington Borough Council published figures showing a traffic count of 4,000 vehicles per hour at peak times, and 30,000 in a day, through the Panmure roundabout – large numbers for New Zealand. The main commuter road to Howick, Pakuranga and points east flowed

Looking southeast across Panmure basin about 1954. Panmure Motors site has been outlined, adjacent to what later became the Panmure roundabout, where five roads intersect. By 1960 it had one of the highest traffic counts in New Zealand as commuters and industry converged from north, west and east to cross the railway.

Trist and Margaret Atkins.

through the northern side of the dealership.

Plans for the new dealership were considered and rejected, until a unique design that naturally moulded with the roundabout and site was chosen. The building designs were tendered and work started in June 1964. Even today the design is crisp, clear and attractive, fully justifying its original purpose and standards that it set. In 1964 it was a clear-cut winner, giving a very high profile to the dealership.

T S (Trist) Atkins was appointed manager of the new Panmure Motors Ltd in October 1964. Trist had been manager at Te Kuiti Motors for the two years before, and had started with CMC Group in 1958 at Fagan Motors, Masterton where he was accountant. Like many other managers at the time, he was given rapid experience and training with CMC Group subsidiaries at

Invercargill and Wellington.

Trist Atkins had many challenges ahead. When he arrived the framework of the building was there, together with the usual worksite shambles. Like Colin Cliff, a neighbouring dealer at New Lynn, he started operating from a caravan. Trist Atkins and his total staff of one, salesman Don Hodgson, moved into the unfinished shell in December 1964, and the caravan was towed away. They had to keep moving, however, as painters, carpenters, and electricians chased them around, completing the new sales and administration building.

Eric Monahan was appointed service manager in February 1965, starting from scratch with no staff and no workshop. He came from South Auckland Motors, Otahuhu, where he was workshop controller, and had earlier served his apprenticeship which he began in May 1944 at the princely sum of 18s 4d per week.

Eric Monahan hunted around the area to find premises to lease until the new workshop was built. He found these at Marua Road, Ellerslie, then had to get equipment and staff organised. He was no stranger to the area, as he had been a student at Panmure Primary School, just across the road from the new dealership.

Trist Atkins remembers hiring staff. "Eric and I had a system for hiring apprentices and when Eric had sorted out the last six or so applicants, we used to ask them to sit a small, written test paper that we had devised. There was nothing complicated about it; it was just a series of

The first sale was made by the dealership from this caravan in 1964.

The spectacular new sales and administration building curved to match the roundabout.

The first workshop beside the main building on left.

Hardly up, the building was used as a pilot for the new 'Ford' blue band dealer identification in 1967.

Left: Griff Harvey, first sales manager. Right: Don Hodgson, used car manager.

Panmure Motors staff in 1967. From front left: Trist Atkins, Ray Haughton, Colin Tutty, Dawn Linder, Carol McLennan, Leewyn Timmins, Neil Hebden. Second row: Keith Harris, not known, Gavin Fortune, Willy Lee, Don Hodgson, Murray Hoare. Third row: Griff Harvey, Eric Monahan, Bob Bassett, Jim Donald, Ken Boakes, Wayne Hedgeman, Wayne Kasper. Fourth row: Brian McDonald, Neil Matheson, Doug Morley, Clyde Sole, Ross Mc Lennan, Ron Maitland. Rear: Roy Brown, Andy Mikkelsen, Doug Wilson, Neville Thompson, Ray Gunn.

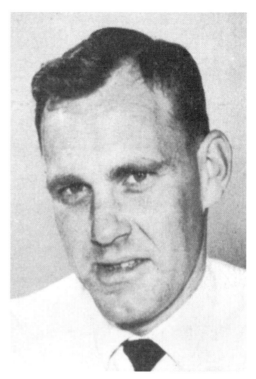

everyday questions. This helped us to get people who were practical and logical. We reckoned that we had the best staff and best workshop around."

Roy Brown was appointed parts manager in August 1965, transferring from Craik Motors, Te Awamutu. He emigrated from England in 1948 after serving with the Royal Navy during the Second World War. He joined Te Kuiti Motors in 1955 having hitch-hiked and worked around both the North and South Islands.

Griff Harvey joined the team as sales manager in July 1965. In the RNZAF during the war, he was, on return, a timber haulage contractor, and then salesman at Matamata Motors.

After Basil Orsborn, at South Auckland

Motors, carried out accounting work for the first 18 months until volumes increased substantially, Neil Hebden took over and completed the management team as accountant in March 1966. He had joined CMC Group 14 years earlier as an office junior at head office in Wellington, later transferring to audit, South Auckland Motors, Timaru Motors and Stevens Motor before going to Kaikohe as accountant five years before.

Work started in January 1966 on the new parts and service building, and in July dealership staff moved in with all of them now on site. Panmure Motors now had 35 staff members operating at full steam, building up customers, market share and profits.

No Remittance was at its height then and Don Hodgson was busy as the specialist in this important area. Trist Atkins, who had seen the start of No Remittance in the early 1950s, ably coached him. In 1951 vehicle licensing was removed and cars flooded in with the wool boom. But licensing was back again in 1952. By chance, Trist Atkin's boss at the time asked him to apply to Customs for a licence using the previous old forms. It was granted and they kept this 'quiet'. In the next year Matamata Motors, who had a vehicle allocation of only 12 cars per year, kept applying and sold 150 No Remittance cars, far outstripping the competition in No Remittance sales.

Panmure Motors enjoyed over 48% of the available No Remittance market, which helped to expand the allocation of vehicles. With Ford's incentive scheme, having obtained a No Remittance licence for a new car, an extra vehicle of the same type was allocated. Today it seems hard to imagine new vehicles being scarce, but in those days, if you didn't have overseas funds you could wait 10–15 years to get a new car.

Motor racing was one of the high profile advertising methods used by Panmure Motors to get its name recognised. A bond was established with Doug Benefield, managing director of Mason and Porter, who started rallying with sponsorship from Panmure Motors. In 1968 they decided to try out the new Escort 1,298cc in the Benson & Hedges Production Car Race at Pukekohe. The Escort was thoroughly prepared by service staff with Trist Atkins insisting that everything had to be done strictly to the rules. Much to their delight, the Escort was the first 4 cylinder car home, winning the 1,001–1,300cc class by eight laps, equal with the winning 1,601–2,500 cc car, and ninth overall.

"After the race the car had to be scrutineered; they literally pulled it to pieces and were measuring everything," said Trist. "Some hours later, after weighing the flywheel, it was pronounced that it had been modified. Our foreman Brian McDonald said it's not, it's the same one that came with the car, and we knew it hadn't been altered in any way. They were using a spring balance, so Brian said we're taking it down to the all night chemist to

The office 1968 Escort 1,298cc was entered in the 500 mile B & H race, coming 1st in class. The exercise was repeated the next two years with the same car and same results. Panmure Motors were top sellers of Escort in Auckland.

Blair Robson, CEO of Masport, went rallying with success in this MkIV Zephyr, winning the Gold Star Rallies in 1967-68. In 1966 Blair Robson with Doug Benefield and Neil Kennedy won in a MkIII Zephyr.

get it weighed properly. So off they went with a scrutineer and weighed it, and, of course, it was alright – what a circus."

However, there were repercussions; Eric Monaghan stormed in one morning saying, "Either those bloody cars go or I'm going – people come in here, and they want to talk all day about racing cars and it's not on, I've got a business to run."

"He was quite right of course," said Trist. "So we started a company called Midnight Motors and rented a workshop near the dealership. All the rally and motor racing work was done there. Jim Donald, our foreman, went down there and took a few of the staff, and everything was kept separate from the dealership. Most of the work done was after hours and was

Blair Robson then used a new XR Falcon in the Gold Star Rally, coming 7th overall.

voluntary. It didn't actually cost the company much, but it brought hundreds of people to us."

Not only did they do well in 1968, but the Panmure team returned in 1969 and repeated the performance. After 500 miles the Escort was only 35 miles behind the winning 3,300cc six and 28 miles behind the 5 litre V8. And they did it again in 1970 with the same car – which had been used

as the office hack in between.

With three consecutive wins in the Benson & Hedges, and three consecutive Gold Star Rally wins in 1966, 1967 and 1968, Panmure Motors was the most successful Ford dealer in NZ motorsport at the time.

And so began a long-term relationship with Mason and Porter, Panmure Motors supplying vehicles and service for all its

The Escort 'twin cam' 1,800 model was a runaway success in rallying worldwide. In 1972 Blair Robson entered in the Heatway International Rally coming 2nd in class, 7th overall.

Jim Donald drove Panmure Motors BDA Escort II in the 1976 Heatway International Rally.

International rally drivers held a meeting at Panmure Motors in 1979. From left: Hannu Mikola, Aya Mikkola, Trist Atkins, Ingbrett Hertz, Arni Hertz and Ari Vatanen share stories.

South African racing driver, Desiré Wilson, won a Formula One race in Britain and competed here in the Escort Sport series in 1980, sponsored by Panmure Motors.

90 vehicle fleet. The association with car racing and rallying continued with Mason and Porter a major supporter of the NZ World Championship Masport Rally Team Ford Escort BDA through the 1970s.

By 1972, Panmure Motors had outgrown its service operation and had to lease additional space at Bowden Road, Mt Wellington, while a new workshop was constructed adjacent to the existing parts and service building. As always, this took

time and the temporary lease was extended until 1974.

Always known as a straight shooter who led by example, Trist Atkins observed a passing horse depositing manure on the workshop driveway, and asked the service manager to find an apprentice to get a shovel and bucket and clean it up. A surprised service manager told Trist his apprentice had said he wasn't paid to do that sort of work. Unperturbed, Trist got a bucket and shovelled up the manure while

Eric Monahan received his 25 year gold watch in 1969. He didn't like rally enthusiasts who wasted so much time talking to his people, so the 'Midnight Motors' rally workshop started in rented premises, open until midnight, or....whenever.

explaining to the wide-eyed apprentice the benefits of doing what the boss asked.

In 1978, Panmure was one of the first companies to get the new Burroughs L8000 'computer' and many were the trials and tribulations experienced. Today this would not be regarded as a proper computer and, in fact, it was only up a step in the transition from the old mechanical Burroughs accounting machine to a solid state microchip PC and was actually a punch card mechanical sorter. Still, the L8000 was an advance on what was previously available even if it broke down with irritating regularity. A lot of the manual work was eliminated and the L8000 could produce a result more rapidly than before – when it was working.

Don Hodgson transferred to manage Te Kuiti Motors in March 1981, and Colin Botherway took over as used car manager. He had started as a junior at Te Kuiti Motors in 1970, working in the office and parts. Later he was a salesman under Tom Nealon, and transferred to Panmure in 1976 as a used car salesman. Colin Botherway became sales manager when Griff Harvey retired in 1986. Roy Brown retired in 1988, after 33 years with CMC Group, and Gordon Binns took over as parts manager. When Eric Monahan retired in 1991, after 47 years, Kevin Prior took over as service manager but, sadly, he died a year later, and

Terry Byrne took over.

Staff is a key element in any dealership, and Trist Atkins was proud of his people. "We built the staff up from zero, and all the departmental heads, apart from Eric Monaghan, were from country dealerships. We tried to run it like a country garage on the side of the city. It was no good trying to make it like Andrews, so we didn't. But people kept coming back and back, and they liked dealing with us, and we tried to look after them the same way as you would in the country. None of the staff really stood out, because they were all good at their jobs and they were a good team.

"We had few very big fleets. South Auckland Motors had kept most of those, but very few big trucks were domiciled in the area anyway. However, one year we had 100% of the tractor market – we sold one to the Council. Overall we were selling cars to people and looking after them, and they came back again.

"The other interesting thing was that the business was steady and we always made a profit."

Trist Atkins decided to retire when he was 59 after working in the motor industry from April 8 1947, the day after Henry Ford died. After an overlap with John Blyth, Trist retired on September 30 1987, coincidentally one day after Henry Ford II died, so he spanned a very significant

Left: Business manager Neil Hebden received his 25 gold year watch in 1977.

Right: Parts Manager Roy Brown clocked up 25 years in 1980.

Below: The L8000 Burroughs accounting machine replaced the Sensematics in 1978. It was a punch card reader, bridging the gap to computers. Trist Atkins had this cartoon done for his Auckland dealer friends.

period of Ford history.

John Blyth transferred from Ruahine Motors in Waipukurau to become the new dealer principal on December 1 1986. He had started with CMC Group in February 1966 at Macaulay Motors, Invercargill, and had been at New Plymouth and Timaru

before going to manage Waipukurau in 1984.

John Blyth found the transition from Ruahine Motors quite difficult, because of the scale of the business. "In Waipukurau, you tend to do things yourself, and it was certainly a hands-on job there. Panmure

had 65 people, and there was a manager looking after each area, and it took me some time to work through what each manager was doing.

"I don't think Ford was that happy about me, as they thought the dealership should be getting a larger market share. In fact, we were in an area where a lot of businessmen lived, and they all had their company cars, which were supplied from their head office in Auckland. We didn't have a lot of fleet business other than Masport and Fisher & Paykel; we just sold cars one at a time. On the other hand we were making money every month, where many others were losing their shirts in 1987."

McMillan Motors took on the Toyota franchise, despite a warning to all dealers from Ford Motor Company's managing director Bill Hartigan who unceremoniously cancelled their franchise. This move sent shock waves through the Ford dealer network.

From November 1987, the territory of Panmure Motors changed to include the eastern areas of Howick, Whitford, Botany Downs and Otahuhu, and Trevor Green became branch manager at the old South Auckland Motors building at Atkinson

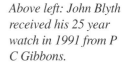

Top: Trist Atkins retired in 1987 after 40 years in the motor industry, and was farewelled at a gathering in Panmure. He was made a life member of the Motor Trade Association, having served a number of branches, on the national executive and as chairman of the MTA finance committee. He started the day after Henry Ford died and retired the day after Henry Ford II died, an extraordinary coincidence.

Above left: John Blyth received his 25 year watch in 1991 from P C Gibbons.

Left: East City Ford management team in 1989: John Blyth, CEO; Neil Hebden, business manager; Trevor Green, branch manager Otahuhu; Gordon Binns, parts manager; and Colin Botherway, sales manager. CMC awards for top financial performance in 1989 and 1991 are proudly displayed.

Following a change in boundaries, Panmure Motors changed its name to East City Ford, with a branch at Otahuhu, the former South Auckland Motors home, managed by Trevor Green.

Avenue, Otahuhu. The Panmure name no longer identified with their customer area, and the name was changed to East City Ford in 1988.

The period of the late 1980s and early 1990s was a difficult period for Ford dealers, with some leaving the industry, but East City Ford continued to make money every month of every year.

Following Colin Cliff's retirement, John Blyth was appointed a director of Colonial Motor Company in 1990, maintaining the company's Auckland interests.

The East City showroom was given a major upgrade in 1993 and the service reception and parts retailing area in 1994.

After Ford Motor Company announced a retail joint venture for the Auckland area market in November 1998, inviting the eight dealers to join together in a single company, on March 1 1999 East City Ford was sold to Auckland Auto Collection, ending 35 years as a CMC subsidiary. Many of the staff members continue to work for AAC, while others have taken up new opportunities.

CHAPTER FIFTEEN

OTAHUHU & MANUKAU CITY - SOUTH AUCKLAND MOTORS LTD

Bishop Selwyn established several churches at strategic points to enable the armed constabulary to worship. One of these was at Otahuhu, beside the Tamaki River, 150 years ago.

Otahuhu became a country town, 12 miles south of Auckland on the Great South Road, and developed as industry established nearby. In 1950 it was a borough of 8,000 people with the nearby meat freezing works, phosphate plant and railway workshops the principal employers. The surrounding area, including Mangere, Panmure and Howick, was mainly devoted to market gardening and farming. New factories were starting to be built in the Otahuhu and Penrose area near the railway and main highway.

After Lees Brothers were appointed a Ford dealer at Papakura in 1937, John W Andrew & Sons decided they should establish a branch to protect their southern boundary, and bought land on the Great South Road to build a service garage at

Otahuhu in 1938. In the interim they leased a property on the corner of Fairburn Road and Great South Road, setting up a small sales operation there. Tenders for the branch buildings closed the day the Second World War started in 1939, and plans were stymied. Ford still wanted a full service garage at Otahuhu because, with petrol rationing, customers would have to travel too far to the city for supplies. With wartime restrictions this was easier said than done.

After the Japanese attacked Pearl Harbour, Neal Motors, the Vauxhall/Bedford dealer on the corner of Gordon Road and Great South Road Otahuhu, decided to close and offered their premises for sale at the beginning of 1942. John W Andrew & Sons bought the garage and equipment for £4,100, sending L C (Les) Gladding to take over.

Les Gladding later recalled: "We opened up a few months after Pearl Harbour was attacked by the Japanese. I was appointed manager, and all I had with me was one mechanic.

"Not only did we have to contend with wartime difficulties – most vehicles had been bought by the government for military purposes – we also had manpower regulations which made staff recruiting a very difficult business indeed as all the best tradesmen were being manpowered. It was a most difficult time, and one black week my only sale was a two and sixpenny tin of rust inhibitor.

"In 1946 men began to return from overseas. At this early stage the original property was already becoming too small and efforts were made to enlarge it, but land was under sales control.

"We finally managed to acquire additional land at £9,300 which was much above the normal value and, indeed, for a comparable area was the highest anywhere in New Zealand at the time."

After the war, restrictions remained in place, petrol rationing continued until 1950, and car imports were severely licensed until *Les Gladding, 1950.*

Right: Showroom in 1947 shows a Model N tractor, Ford V8 coupe, and two V8 sedans.

Below: The parts department was quite small and simple originally, but very soon needed a lot more space.

1970. Ford had given the tractor franchise back to dealers in 1946 so tractors were available. The company made repeated applications to the National Building Controller in Wellington for permission to add to the service building area because of increased demand for service, but approvals were worse than slow. Despite all the building delays, land nearby was acquired whenever it was available, section by section, and by 1960 nearly four acres had been bought along Gordon Road from Great South Road to Atkinson Avenue, including six house properties.

Les Gladding had 24 people working in his team in 1949, with 16 in the workshop, and despite all the difficulties the business expanded quickly. John Emery joined the company in 1951, and remembered his interview with Les Gladding: "Les was busy with someone

The workshop in 1954 shows mostly pre-war cars in for service.

else, so I had to wait, and watched a mechanic splitting a tractor in the showroom corner, as there was nowhere else to do it. There was oil and mess everywhere.

"I went into the office when Les was free, and we talked about the position advertised. We had just got going, and there was a sudden crash and glass was flying everywhere. Eric Monahan had run out of space and accidentally put a half shaft from the tractor he was working on through Les' window. There was silence for a moment, and then Les went on as if nothing had happened and he offered me a position as sales cadet trainee, as I was too young for the other job.

" I remembered wondering afterwards on the way home what sort of an outfit I was going to, but my first impressions mislead me.

"Fordson tractors were in free supply, as they were classed as essential goods, so they represented an opportunity and it wasn't long before we were selling about 60 a year. The area had a lot of farms, and of course many market gardens. We were able to sell ploughs, rotary hoes and loaders. In those days we sold gorse bars to farmers around Whitford to push the gorse over and crush it ready to be burnt off."

The wool boom put further pressure on cars in 1951, and industrial growth around Auckland increased in leaps and bounds, particularly on the north, west and south edges. There were large numbers of immigrants arriving in Auckland from England and Holland, and CMC bought a number of key sites at New Lynn, Panmure, and Howick, anticipating future development.

Trucks were in short supply after the war and, when war surplus trucks were auctioned at Cornwall Park, a number were knocked down to the company. Getting the old trucks back to the dealership was often difficult, especially trying to tow a non-starter behind a Prefect!

Lewis Motors was appointed a Ford dealer at Takapuna in 1954, to cover the area from Waiwera to Takapuna. This area had been John W Andrew & Son's territory, and no prior notice was given to them that this would happen. CMC and Andrew's were very surprised and held a meeting with Ford soon afterward to discuss the future of Auckland. It was agreed that, when vehicle numbers were suitable, new dealers would be set up at West Auckland and Panmure, each likely to become satellite cities within Auckland. John W Andrew's bought land at Royal Oak and later at Glen Innes, for the same reasons, and were looking at other central city sites.

Ford then announced that John W

Les Gladding and staff 1948. Back left: Don Muirson, Neil Mathieson, Jack Westrop, Ross Moore, Snow Davis, Ken Butt, John Coleman. Middle left: Dave Armstrong, Roger Morrison, Bob Scopes, Gordon Cooper, Gus Hansen, Bill Parfit, Eric Monahan, Erle Farrelly. Sitting left: Graham Umbers, Shirley Young, Bill Hastings, Spence Griffin, Les Gladding, Basil Orsborn, Eric Davis, Shirley Jones, Stewart Michael.

Andrew could no longer continue at Otahuhu, but agreed to setting up a separate company with Colonial Motor Company shareholding and Les Gladding as managing director. Les Gladding and his brother Wilf had worked at Andrew's since the early 1920s. Their father George's seed and grain business – Gladding and Hunter at Eden Terrace – was bought by his brother-in-law John W Andrew in 1907, and the Gladding family were shareholders in John W Andrew & Sons Ltd.

South Auckland Motors Ltd (SAM) was registered as a result, splitting from John W Andrew & Sons Ltd on September 1 1954.

After the war the first building work done was an extension to the lube bay, using second hand material, and a staff cafeteria. The workshop was extended by 10,000 sqft in 1953 at a cost of £15,000. It seemed no sooner had one project been finished, than a new one was started. A two-storey block was erected in 1955 behind the showroom to house parts and offices. Tractors now had five service bays, and another lube bay was added. Some of the old houses were cleared and a yard set up for customer vehicles. Another workshop was built, and a service station, further along Gordon Road.

No Remittance new car licences were now being granted to people with overseas funds, and applications for import licences

for special commercial needs were considered by the Board of Trade. These ranged from doctors, undertakers and surveyors, to business travellers and tradesmen who needed dual-purpose vehicles. With allocated cars so short, special licences were an opportunity to increase the numbers, and staff members played their part in identifying people who might qualify.

In April 1957 the adjacent corner of Great South Road and Gordon Road was leased and set up to sell used cars and the new Thames Trader. Truck sales immediately grew rapidly with Ted Holmes as specialist truck salesman, while John Emery found there was never enough space for used cars.

When Les Gladding was hospitalised with a life threatening health problem in October 1959, John Emery was made assistant to the manager to cover for him and deliver his special report on Thames Trader trucks to the 1959 Ford Dealer Conference, although Ford would not initially recognise his presence as dealer spokesman which did not help the dealer cause.

The whole area was still growing rapidly with new housing developing just as fast as industry, and farms disappearing. SAM's commercial business was growing rapidly and, with the shortage of new cars, the need for good used cars was high. Land

was found on Great South Road at Fairburn Road – the same piece used by John W Andrew's branch in 1938 – and was set up as the most modern used car display facility in Auckland at the time. It opened in July 1960, giving an immediate boost to used vehicle sales.

When Mangere Airport was constructed in the early 1960s contractors used a fleet of Thames Trader trucks with a special side-tipping body which South Auckland Motors had developed with Stevens Motors. Ford purchased 70 acres at Wiri in 1962 and relocated the national parts centre there. Once the airport opened, much of Auckland's distribution warehousing was established in the Mangere area.

By now SAM had successfully developed customer partnerships with a number of large companies – NZ Forest Products, Alex Harvey Industries, Wilson Rothery, Fletcher Construction, Dominion Breweries and others who were based in the area, and they formed a significant part of their core business. Getting enough new cars to supply these companies became a major headache with the shortage of car import licences.

In 1962, when Les Gladding's health had recovered, he was appointed a director of Colonial Motor Company, helping to keep an eye on what was happening in Auckland. John Emery was appointed manager in 1963, taking some of the load off Les Gladding, and they had an excellent management team. Basil Orsborn was chief accountant; Graham Umbers, service manager administrative; Ross Moore, service manager technical; Ken Butt, service manager new vehicles; Garth Prichard, sales manager new cars; Ted Holmes, commercial sales manager; Graham Hamilton, used vehicle manager; Gilbert H Gibbons, marine manager and Dennis Davies, parts manager. A short time later Basil Orsborn was appointed internal auditor for CMC Group, and Beville Johnston became administrative accountant. He had been with CMC Group for 15 years, starting at Te Aroha. He then went to audit, and New Plymouth before becoming accountant at Waipukurau.

Gilbert Gibbons, manager of the Marine Department, developed, made and sold marine gearboxes and conversions for various Ford engines, principally the Consul 204E, Zephyr 206E, Tractor 4 and Trader 6 cylinder diesel. Establishing designs and making, testing and marketing these presented a real challenge, particularly the gearboxes. Diversification

This 1950 aerial photo shows the residential area finally acquired by SAM in outline. On the right side Great South Road, and the original Neal Motors site. Over the road, the used vehicle/truck site, then steadily down Gordon Road to Atkinson Avenue all sites were bought. The parts building was built in 1967 at the rear of the Gordon Road property.

with the products available at the time was seen as an opportunity to make money, which it did.

In June 1963 a new Workshop Control System was piloted in conjunction with Ford. A service reception area, with portico and workshop offices, was built to make a welcome haven for customers. Service mechanics had intercom speakers and requested parts which were then delivered to the job. After a number of hiccups and modifications, the service speeded up and was more efficient under a controller, and many NZ dealers adopted the modified system.

New Lynn Motors started in 1962, and Lewis Motors at Takapuna was sold to Gerry Lyon at the same time. SAM had planned to put a branch at Panmure, which was also developing rapidly, and the 2¹/₂ acre Panmure roundabout site was all ready to start, waiting for Ford approval. Ford gave the go-ahead in 1964, but now required the site to be a separate dealership, "to improve competition between dealers", and Panmure Motors was established.

This upset SAM's plans, and they lost a large amount of their dealer territory on the north-eastern side. Soon afterwards, John Andrew's bought a service station at Greenlane and set up a full branch operation there.

John Emery was appointed general manager and dealer principal of South Auckland Motors in August 1966, and Les Gladding became chairman of directors. Les had now worked 42 years in the motor industry, and had pioneered fleet sales. A very skilled strategic thinker and planner, he knew Auckland backwards.

Many of South Auckland Motors' big customers were in the Penrose and Papatoetoe area, and SAM now planned to protect this territory by starting branch operations in the north at Penrose and East Tamaki and, because of the new airport, south at Mangere, and at Papatoetoe.

After a meagre start with two people in 1942, by 1962 staff numbers at South Auckland Motors had grown to 110, and turnover to £1.3 million.

Like many things, it takes some time to find the right location for a branch. Land was bought at Mangere on Coronation Road in 1965, but development was held up waiting for zoning decisions. Eventually a suitable site was found at Papatoetoe and, after planning approval, a new and used sales centre was set up in 1968, with Barry Hughes as manager. The original farmhouse on the property was kept, the front bedroom used as an office, and the kitchen as a lunchroom.

Another strip of land was acquired at Otahuhu, with enough space for a large new truck workshop, which was then built back from Gordon Road. Another area of land fronting on to King Street, which connected through to the new workshop, was bought, and a new, larger, two-storey parts building was built, with access to Gordon Road and fronting King Street. All this was completed in August 1967 at a cost of $88,500, including equipment.

A complete vehicle sales and service operation on half an acre at the corner of Neilsen and Church Streets, Penrose, was finally located and purchased in March 1969. The Penrose branch started operating in May 1969, with Barry Carson as manager. He started with SAM 20 years before as an apprentice, completed his A Grade Certificate, and had started NZIM qualifications. By now new cars licences had started to free up and sales were quickly increasing.

The branch had barely started when McMillan Motors were appointed Ford

Opposite top: South Auckland Motors in 1954, on the Great South Road corner, looking down Gordon Road towards Atkinson Avenue. Used cars and trucks are across the road.

Opposite middle:Fairburn Road used car lot was started in 1959, and proved a very good site. At the time it was very advanced for Auckland.

Opposite bottom: Parts were recorded on a cardex tray system, with a card recording each part (line item). A medium size dealer would have two people looking after this, and a large dealer like SAM, three or four people maintaining the 100,000 plus line items. Today it is all done by one computer which also analyses stock and suggests weekly orders based on rate of sale.

South Auckland Motors premises at night in 1961.

Top: Auckland's Mangere Airport was constructed in the early 1960s and the company supplied a number of Thames Traders, fitted with a special side tipping bodies, which offloaded directly into a special concrete batching plant laying runways.

Middle: The new two storey parts building gave SAM great opportunities to wholesale parts to other retailers because of their good stocks, ability to buy in bulk, and knowledge of what people needed. It was completed in 1967.

Below: The parts sales counter was right up to the mark in the late 1960s.

The 25 year Omega club members in 1971. From left: Basil Orsborn, former chief accountant and then CMC internal auditor; Ken Butt, new vehicle pre-delivery manager; Les Gladding, former managing director and then chairman; Ross Moore, service manager, and Peter Cederman, general manager of CMC and also a gold watch holder.

dealers at Greenlane in July 1970, another surprise. Soon afterwards McMillan's opened a used car outlet across the road from their headquarters at 428 Great South Road, and then acquired an existing garage on Great South Road Penrose for a commercial vehicle sales operation, right on the boundary of their territory with South Auckland Motors.

There were still problems getting zoning approval at Mangere, and the company went into a ballot for other suitable land but this was not successful. Les Gladding decided on direct negotiation, and on September 28 1970, the board approved a 10 year lease of just over 1¹/2 acres, which could be freeholded at the end of the period.

A very good and unexpected offer for the original former Neal Motors building on Great South Road was accepted in February 1970 and the building was vacated. A new sales and administration building was planned, given the go-ahead

in November 1970, and completed a year later costing $150,000. This landmark building was on the corner of Gordon Road and Atkinson Avenue, now the main commercial road at Otahuhu. The building, which gave SAM a very high profile, was opened on November 25 1971.

Construction of Mangere branch started with a similar styled building, but on a smaller scale. The new Mangere town centre was adjacent and the company had a prime site. Housing developments were rapidly transforming the former market gardening and farm area into suburban housing. Trevor Green, appointed branch manager, was born and bred in the area, joining South Auckland Motors from school in 1958. After qualifying as an A Grade mechanic, Trevor Green became service receptionist and taught motor mechanics at night school; then, enrolled at NZIM, he widened his experience with a year in vehicle sales. Mangere branch

South Auckland Motors' main sales and administration building was opened in 1971 at the opposite end of Gordon Road from where the company started. Atkinson Avenue was no longer residential, but was the main commercial street of Otahuhu.

Mangere branch, west near the airport.

Middle left: Trevor Green, Mangere branch manager.

Middle right: Grant Christie, East Tamaki manager.

Below: East Tamaki branch.

opened on August 27 1973 with a staff of four, all from Otahuhu.

Trevor Green remembered in 1979: "I was manager, car salesman, service receptionist and tea lady, all rolled into one." It was his forte, or was it? Dick Garnham, who was also there at the beginning running parts and workshop, remembered: "Trevor never really regarded a cup of tea as the real thing unless you could stand a spoon up in it, and the most popular news of the first year was when he announced that a lady had been employed to do, amongst other things, the tea making for us."

Trevor Green still thought the strength of the tea was important, because: "In the first year 40 new cars and 98 used vehicles

were sold, and more than 2,700 jobs passed through the workshop, and second year volumes were increasing rapidly." More staff members were recruited locally, and eight more had joined the branch after two years.

When East Tamaki branch on the corner of East Tamaki and Preston Roads, covering nearly 3/4 acre and including an existing service station and garage, was bought in May 1974, the service station was relocated to one side, which gave a better vehicle display area. Grant Christie, who began at SAM as a lube bay attendant, decided to complete his adult apprenticeship and was later asked to manage the branch. "There has been rapid development due to industrialisation and urban development in the area, and I see very good potential in this part of the city."

John Emery had, with the help of Les Gladding, completed the branch strategy in an action-packed 10 years. In 1974 Les Gladding celebrated 50 years work with CMC Group, together with several other people, a remarkable achievement. He remained a director of Colonial Motor Company until 1979 and then retired, but kept in touch.

The centre of growth in the south Auckland area was at Wiri, and CMC bought a nine acre farmlet there on the Great South Road in 1971, to provide for South Auckland Motors' re-location. It took 15 years to obtain the required change of use from 'rural' to 'motor vehicle sales and service'.

Ford had now relocated part of its assembly operation alongside the national

Left: Barry Carson, Penrose branch manager.

Below: Penrose branch, the northern and first of the defence outposts.

Top: Papatoetoe branch, south of Otahuhu.

Right: Barry Hughes, Papatoetoe branch manager.

Far right: Graham Hamilton became used car manager and Papatoetoe manager.

Below: Papatoetoe branch was extended in 1976 and became used vehicle conditioning centre, bringing them up to sale condition.

parts centre at Plunket Avenue, a short distance away and, after a meeting in 1972, Ford indicated the area would be reserved for an independent dealer to develop at some later time.

Penrose branch had major service extensions added in 1976, and Papatoetoe was developed to a full branch after new buildings were erected in 1976. Graham Hamilton, used car manager, was stationed there, and recalled in 1980: "One of the advantages of the Papatoetoe operation is that the entire used car stock is processed through the branch within 48 hours of purchase.

"The new yard has just been sealed and

along with display and advertising we hope to carry 30 cars which will give us one of the largest used car activities in South Auckland.

"We hope to have one of the best used car sales-turnovers in the area. With this expansion programme, this should prove to be a reality."

SAM now had a large number of key staff members, who had developed with the company, reaching retirement age. However, when Ross Moore, Graham Umbers, Ken Butt and Dennis Davies, who had all done sterling service, retired there was no shortage of successors for their jobs, with the training policies and excellent working conditions and relations the company had developed. Laurie Nelson and Alan Dance were service managers; Murray Scott, parts manager; Dick Deveraux and Beville Johnston, sales managers; and Paul Sutherland and Mike Halliday, business managers.

By 1980 trading had become tougher with rampant inflation causing rapid escalation of prices. However, with the introduction of Ford Courier commercials, and Laser and Telstar cars in 1981 and 1983, sales volumes increased and warranty reduced significantly. Then the D Series truck range finished in 1983, and after an 18 month gap Ford replaced this

with the Ford-Hino N Series trucks. These were great trucks, and warranty fell away rapidly, coupled with excellent customer reaction. Warranty and build rectification had been occupying over 25% of all service space; when this now reduced to less than 5% it was necessary to rationalise, and Ford agreed that dealers should look at their facilities to see if cost savings could be made.

The Wiri area changed its name to Manukau City, a new retail centre and commercial developments were built, and Manukau City Council was established. Ford now wanted a new flagship dealer facility at Manukau City and agreed to allow South Auckland Motors to develop the site with a number of very specific conditions. Planning commenced in early 1983.

The motor industry was not ready for the new Labour government's market driven policies in mid-1985 which brought major changes to New Zealand and by 1986 re-structuring was essential to reduce costs. The market was stretched to the limit with discounting as manufacturers sought to increase their market shares. All manner of restrictions were lifted or deregulated. Inflation continued at very high levels with 90 day bills achieving rates of 20–30%, and vehicle prices kept increasing.

John Emery was promoted to manager at the management meeting in 1961. Clockwise around the table from bottom left: Barry Wisneski, Ted Holmes, Graham Umbers, Basil Orsborn, John Emery, Les Gladding, Randal Thomson, Dennis Davies, Maurie Benneworth, Ross Moore and Bill Simpson.

South Auckland Motors turned 25 years old in 1979 and O'Brien Reeve, sales and marketing director of Ford, presented a special plaque to John Emery, managing director and Les Gladding now retired managing director, watched by the management team. From left: Laurie Nelson, Beville Johnston, Trevor Green, Ted Holmes, Paul Sutherland, Graham Hamilton, Dick Deveraux, Barry Carson, Grant Christie, Murray Scott and Ken Butt.

Garry S Jackson was appointed dealer principal of South Auckland Motors in May 1985. He had been Ford Motor Company field operations manager and came with wide marketing and motivation skills. It was an unusual move, with Ford keen to see him succeed in the retail sector. John Emery remained managing director, overseeing the new facility development at Manukau City for another year and a half before transferring to a new assignment with CMC Group.

A tender for the new South Auckland Motors was let to R Savory and Co in February 1986, and construction got under way quickly. Completion was expected in six months, and the superb new dealership opened on October 30 1986. With the shift of South Auckland Motors to Manukau City, it was necessary to rationalise other facilities. Papatoetoe branch had been sold in November 1984; Penrose branch was closed in late 1986; and East Tamaki branch was leased in 1987 and then sold. In 1989 Mangere branch was closed and sold to KFC. The Atkinson Avenue property was now in Panmure Motors' territory and this became their branch under manager Trevor Green until it was later sold.

There were more governmental changes and when the share market collapsed, the motor industry's problems increased. Used car imports were liberalised in 1988, allowing Japanese used cars to flood into the country, and the slide in used car prices

turned into an avalanche.

South Auckland Motors came under extreme pressure and, while it was shifting large numbers of new and used vehicles, expenses were high and profit eluded the best efforts of management. In March 1990, after a five year term, Garry Jackson resigned and returned to Ford Motor Company.

W J (Jack) Pearce, who was retiring from New Lynn Motors, was appointed managing director. He said that it was one of his most difficult challenges, but he managed to re-establish the company on a new lower cost path, and was able to fully retire in July 1991. Matthew Newman, who was already on the staff, took over as CEO on August 1 1991.

When the Ford Hino medium truck range, a significant earner for SAM, ran out in 1993, Ford had no replacement truck available in the mid range. However, although the company was still one of four Ford Louisville truck dealers in New Zealand and was able to continue with the profitable extra heavy truck operation, servicing space at Great South Road was a significant problem with these giants, and they were flagged away in 1995.

As the motor industry gradually got going again, South Auckland Motors picked up, winning the Colonial Motor Company's cup for the large dealer group best profit return on shareholders' funds in 1993. Matthew Newman said he was very

The opening of South Auckland Motors at Manukau City was a festive occasion with Garry Jackson, dealer principal, in his element. The new showroom (below) was spacious and modern, allowing an easy transition from outside to inside, with 100 used cars displayed outside.

'Fondle a Ford', devised by Garry Jackson (centre), was a new win-a-car competition. Radio Hauraki ran an elimination process for the right to keep hands on the car, with strict rules of only 10 minutes 'off' each hour. The last person with his/her hands on won the car some 60 hours later. Current receptionist, Crista Donnelly-Dent was one of those selected: "We were all rapt with the opening night hype and all the celebrities arriving, and I remember how shy I felt with the constant buzz of people, arriving from all over Auckland, who stared at me. I lasted 48 hours before dropping off, but I had no chance as it went until the next day."

At the opening of South Auckland Motors, in a prime site across the road from Manukau City shopping mall, many classic Fords were paraded.

Basil Orsborn retired after working 50 years for CMC, and a presentation was made by chairman, Gerald Gibbons. He was the first accountant at SAM in 1948, but had started with CMC in 1929 at head office. He had been to many subsidiaries setting up their accounting systems, and managed Cordery Garage and Te Kuiti for periods. In 1963 he was appointed CMC internal auditor, inspecting accounting records and helping the subsidiary companies accountants keep their methods and results on track. In his spare time he was an electronics wizard and could rebuild amplifiers, radios and even TVs to produce high fidelity results.

pleased with the recognition for his staff, and it was a major turnaround for the company.

SAM qualified for ISO9002 qualification in 1996, recognition for internationally certifiable quality standards.

When Ford Motor Company changed the Auckland Metro market representation in 1998, inviting the eight Ford dealers into a retail joint venture with them, South Auckland Motors became part of the consolidated company, Auckland Auto Collection, thus ending 44 years as a Colonial Motor Company subsidiary.

Auckland Auto Collection, Southern Region, continues today, operating as South Auckland Motors, from the same site. Matthew Newman is CEO, Mike Halliday, business manager; Colin Botherway, Ford sales manager; Mike Tappenden, Mazda sales manager; Andrew Craw, finance and insurance manager; David Yelavich service manager and Jason Stokes parts manager. In 2003, the company was awarded its first President's Award for customer satisfaction, Ford's recognition for top performance, and in 2004 the company celebrated 50 years in business.

Left: Matthew Newman, current CEO, collecting the CMC large dealer cup in 1993, in recognition of achieving the best return on shareholders' funds.

D McL Wallace, an orphaned Scot, emigrated to New Zealand in 1884, and subsequently built a huge group of related engineering and agency businesses, centred at Te Aroha, but with branches covering Piako County. The Ford dealership was started after the First World War, and was very successfully integrated with his other activities, but the group decided to hand back the Ford agency in 1936, to take on Singer cars and Republic trucks – an interesting decision in hindsight. They closed down in Te Aroha, relocating much of their business to Auckland and sold the premises to CMC in 1942.

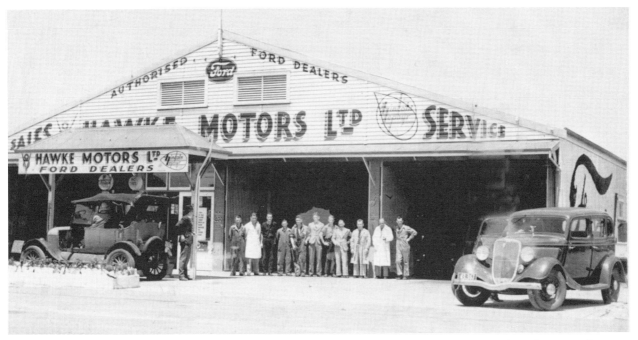

Hawke Motors branch at Morrinsville took over from D McL Wallace in 1937, renting premises from Soanes and Maisey which they later bought. The staff are lined up on the first day. The contrast between the 10 year old Model T, and the four year old Ford V8, illustrates the rapid development in cars.

Better premises became available in Te Aroha in 1938, and the dealership moved to Lipsey Street, which the Farmers Auctioneering had vacated, keeping Bridge Street for used cars.

CHAPTER SIXTEEN

TE AROHA & MORRINSVILLE – HAWKE MOTORS LTD

In the north-east of the Waikato, a long-time rich farming area, are the two towns of Te Aroha and Morrinsville. Both lie on the edge of the Hauraki Plains which were originally accessed by waterways and rivers. Although now rich silt land, early farmers had difficulty with its low-lying and swampy nature. But with development, and the addition of some missing fertiliser elements, it has become one of the most intensively farmed dairying areas of New Zealand.

Te Aroha, a settlement in 1880, was originally known as Aroha Gold Fields Town, sometimes Morgantown. The town district of Te Aroha was established in 1886 when the railway was pushed through from Hamilton. In 1880 gold was found near the town and mining was carried out until 1921. Te Aroha was also a river port from 1880, accessed up the Waihou River from the Firth of Thames. Scows and riverboats would come upstream beyond Paeroa, and much of the dairy produce would be shipped out this way. The town also has hot and cold springs and the government developed the Tourist Domain as a spa, more particularly for mineral drinking waters, in the early 1900s, when it became a fashionable tourist health resort. Immediately behind the town to the east, rises Mt Te Aroha, the first part of the Kaimai ranges.

Morrinsville was originally at the navigable end of the Piako River, and was a holding of 30,000 acres taken up by Samuel and Thomas Morrin. They laid out plans for a village, and the resulting town carries their name. In the economic depression of the 1880s, the farm property fell into the hands of mortgagees and was sold for less than the brothers had spent on development. To make matters worse, sheep capable of resisting the local damp conditions had not been found, and the soils were unable to sustain permanent pastures or yield animal crops. Only one-man farms were able to survive. The establishment of dairy farming in the early 1900s revolutionised farming in the Waikato, and

topdressing has carried this to its present prosperity.

At the end of the First World War, D McL Wallace Ltd took up the Ford agency for Piako County, a territory covering the Thames, Paeroa, Te Aroha, Morrinsville and Matamata districts. D McL Wallace was well established as farm machinery agents and manufacturers, specialists in pumps and milking machinery, foundry casters and engineers, and ideally placed to sell and service Fords to farmers in the area.

The company was a major part of all business in the district and the Ford Model T an ideal vehicle for the times, well suited to the rough swampy roads. Business was excellent until the Depression, the difficulties of the next few years shared with the rest of the country.

D McL Wallace remained Ford agents until March 1936 when it was decided to hand back the Ford agency and change franchises to Singer cars and Republic trucks – an interesting decision in hindsight. Colonial Motor Company took over the agency and some of the DMW motor staff switched as well. Roy Hawke, previously used car manager for DMW, was appointed manager and A G (Mac) McGruer, accountant, took the same position in the new company that was named Hawke Motors Ltd.

Hawke Motors opened in Bridge Street where Arthur Clarke, the Dodge dealer, had been operating. He joined the new company as sales manager. A year later Hawke Motors shifted to Burgess Street, taking over premises from the Farmer's Auctioneering Company while still retaining Bridge Street premises as a used car department.

Used vehicles were a problem in the mid 1930s as people started buying new cars again after the slump. The manufacturers kept pushing for sales of their new cars and imported far too many in their quest for market share, leading to discounting. This left dealers with overpriced used cars for the second time in 10 years, and they were

Roy Hawke took over from D McL Wallace in 1936, and was first manager of the company. Hawke Motors took over the Bridge Street premises of Arthur Clark, the first sales manager, who had closed down his Dodge dealership.

forced to liquidate stocks.

At times there were 80 used cars in stock, when there was only a need for 15. There were auctions on Saturdays to try to move them, and you could sometimes get an older car knocked down to you for a 'fiver' (£5). There was a vast difference in the capability of a new car and one even five years old because of the rapid development in design in those days.

Clive Wishart at Thames continued to operate as a sub-dealer to Hawke Motors until it was made a full dealership by Ford some years later.

In Morrinsville, the D McL Wallace dealership was taken over later in 1936. Percy Petrie was manager until it became a branch of Hawke Motors in 1937, when Norrie Chapman, Roy Hawke's brother-in-law, took over as manager. The first office assistant was Joan McLeod, Arthur Clarke's daughter, who had worked in the Dodge agency office for her father. J L (Jack) Rodgers became the salesman at Morrinsville, shifting from Thames in 1939. The branch operated from new premises leased from Soanes and Maisey in Studholme Street, and this site remained the location for the dealership. Later that year, Norrie Chapman resigned to shift to the Manawatu, and was succeeded by G L (Pete) Petersen who stayed until the end of 1940.

Business ground to a virtual stop in 1939 at the beginning of the Second Word

War. There were no new cars, staff joined up to fight overseas, most of the used cars from 1938 onwards were commandeered for army use and petrol was rationed for emergency use only. Life was difficult, but like many country areas, ingenuity was the order of the day and the business diversified to fit the needs.

Horse transport enjoyed a brief revival, due to petrol rationing, and a saddler and blacksmith joined the staff. Bill Revell was kept busy repairing and renovating saddles and harnesses that had lain idle for years. He did a great job and people were kept mobile, even if it was a bit more restricted on horseback. The horse was great for farmers, and the blacksmith was busy making 'konakies', a part wheel, part sled, horse-drawn vehicle. He was also able to repair all sorts of farming equipment. Many car and truck parts were scarce or unobtainable, and the 'smithy' could often make another, or fix the old one.

Mrs Earle Bailey, now of Wanganui, remembers having to use a horse and trap to take her children about during the war years and also using a konakie to get their cream cans to the gate after milking. Her father bought his first car, a Model T Ford, from Wallace's at Te Aroha after the First World War and had to park it on the road and punt across the Waihou River to their farm, because there was no bridge. She recalls all manner of boats and barges that went up and down the river in the early days, many stopping to pick up or deliver goods if you had a jetty.

The blacksmith and saddler jointly manufactured steel-framed, canvas-covered canopies for army trucks, so the reduced staff numbers at Hawke Motors were very busy, and kept the company viable, as well as helping with the war effort.

In 1941 Jack Rodgers was appointed manager at Morrinsville branch and in 1980 he vividly recalled the difficulties of wartime trading. For a great part of the time he was a one man band handling the administration, responsible for all sales, the parts department, book-keeping, banking, almost everything except service which was Jim Greenslade's preserve.

In 1942, D McL Wallace closed down in Te Aroha and moved its business to Auckland, and Hawke Motors bought the premises under the wartime Land Sales Act. The buildings, on the corner of Whittaker Street and Lawrence Avenue, were

promptly requisitioned by the Army for war use. In 1946, a year after the war ended, the buildings were returned and Hawke Motors began to move to their permanent Te Aroha home.

Most staff returned from the war and rejoined the company and things started to get back to normal. Peter Patton demobilised for the second time, having previously served in the First World War, returned to Stevens Motors in Lower Hutt, and then transferred to be service manager. His friend Charlie Lawrence, who had also returned to Stevens, transferred to Te Aroha shortly afterwards as tractor mechanic. Also demobilised in 1948, Ian Forte joined Morrinsville in the lubrication bay but transferred to parts, and later became parts manager.

Roy Hawke decided to retire after seeing the company through the initial period and the difficulties of the war, and was replaced by L H (Les) Clarke in 1948, who transferred from Te Kuiti Motors where he was manager. Les Clarke, a very strong-minded person who liked things done properly, soon got the branch humming.

Les Clarke set about shaping up the D McL Wallace building at Te Aroha, which was now showing its age, and making it fit the requirements of a Ford dealership. The buildings were originally stables, built with concrete walls and timber trussed iron roof, with a sloping earth floor that followed the natural slope, for good drainage. There were difficulties even though the war had ended, with all sorts of restrictions and building alterations very much regulated.

The Morrinsville branch building was purchased from Soanes and Maisey in 1948

and, only 10 years old, remained the nucleus for later development. In 1953 the premises were re-developed and 3,500 sq ft of workshop was added, giving a total of 9,000 sq ft. Neighbouring property was acquired in 1959, and a used vehicle sales area of 2,500 sq ft developed.

After three years' frustration and waiting, work on modernising the Te Aroha building started in 1949 with the addition of a service station and lube bay. The parts department had a mezzanine floor added in 1950, giving space for bulk storage of parts.

Les Clarke was transferred to Colonial Motor Company head office in June 1950 as general manager, and E P (Ellis) Smith shifted from Fairhall Motors, Kaikohe, to become manager. Trading was still restricted with limited new car imports, but tractors were not affected. Under Ellis Smith, tractor sales became a predominant part of the business in this intensive dairy farming area, and a great success for the company. Hawke Motors were regularly top seller in their group in the newly set up Ford Tractor Banner competitions, with sales in some years of over 100 tractors.

Barney H Gibbons was appointed accountant at Morrinsville in 1952, having started at Colonial Motor Company in 1942 and then transferring to Hutchinson Motors in Christchurch, Macaulay Motors in Invercargill and then Stevens Motors in Lower Hutt.

Ford Motor Company gave Clive Wishart a full dealer status after the war and Hawke Motors lost the northern area of their territory, the first of many incursions initiated by Ford.

In 1954, Len Scrimshaw transferred

After the war, Hawke Motors took over the original D McL Wallace garage on the corner of Whittaker Street and Lawrence Avenue. Prefects were the only cars available initially and, despite the large number on display here, they were in very short supply with import restrictions.

Staff farewell for Les Clarke at Te Aroha, June 1950.
Front row left to right: Ian Forte, Ken Watson, Jack Rogers, Les Clarke, A G McGruer, Jim Greenslade, Tom Hopcroft, Peter Patton.
Centre from left: Ray Peet, Chas Lawrence, A Pickard, Andrew Tildsley, Mort Corrin, Alan Brimblecombe, Ted Revel, Pat Smythe, Claude Hart, Leo Robinson, Roy Baker.
Back, from left: Peter Dons, Cath Cook, Joyce Baker, Noeline Greenwood, Evelyn Hamilton, Jock Harris, Bill Keating, —, Vernon Stuck.

from his father's audit office to be accountant at Te Aroha after Mac McGruer retired. He remained in Te Aroha until his retirement.

During 1966, there was extensive renovation of the Te Aroha building. The lower area over the service station was covered with a translucent fibreglass roof, with stone gardens and steps up to the showroom. Offices were added, plus a large staff room and washroom, all built to a high standard. The outside was carefully co-ordinated to give a unified appearance to the whole building.

Ford appointed another Ford dealer at Paeroa, and Hawke Motors lost a further piece of their northern territory due to Ford wanting to increase competition. In fact, this weakened dealers who effectively lost part of their income, yet still had the same fixed costs.

In 1970, Ellis Smith retired and moved to Auckland to live. 'Smithy' had seen a lot happen over a very difficult time in the industry, and had managed to turn what opportunities there had been to the company's advantage.

Barry Wisneski transferred from Fairhall Motors to become manager. He was based at Morrinsville, because this was now a more central point, and the densest dairying area in the country. Morrinsville area had developed since the war with the draining of swampy areas and increases in soil fertility with fertilisers. Len Scrimshaw was made Te Aroha branch manager.

Ian Morgan, who had been Morrinsville branch manager after Jack Rogers retired in 1963, shifted to Fairhall Motors, Kaikohe, as manager.

Barry Wisneski was well versed in dairy farming having been born on a farm and milking cows before he biked seven miles to school in New Plymouth. Now that most of the problems had been overcome with the revolutionary Select-O-Speed gearbox, tractors were selling well in the Waikato, particularly to the dense farming population around Morrinsville. New car import restrictions were now a little easier, but it never seemed possible to get enough stock, despite selling No Remittance cars.

Ford appointed another dealership at Matamata, further weakening Hawke Motors, by taking territory to the south.

In 1975 Barry Wisneski was transferred to become Colonial Motor Company's internal auditor when Basil Orsborn retired. He had served in many CMC Group dealerships and, with his expert accounting knowledge and capability, he was a logical choice.

Peter Craig, manager at Te Kuiti Motors, transferred to take charge. However, Hawke Motors suffered another set back in April 1979 when the NZ Dairy Company purchased the General Motors dealer at Morrinsville which started supplying trucks and cars for their whole group. They were, of course, using the dealership as a buying discount source, but the large dairy company

Celebrating the 60th Fordson sale for the year in December 1955. Front, left to right: K G Watson, K J Watson, P Childerhouse, I G Lyons, A I Morgan, B H Gibbons, J Rogers, E P Smith, I Forte, C Norris, J Greenslade, —, Helen Fawcet, Nola Williams. Back Row: —, —, L Robinson, —, —, —, P Smythe, L Whitehead.

Middle: Te Aroha had several well attended night street parades at Christmas. In 1957 the team entered Fordson Major in the sweepstakes with salesman Peter Childerhouse as jockey and Keith Watson as trainer.

Below: In the 1959 night parade the Te Aroha branch entered a triple decker: a Prefect on a Thames 800 truck on a Thames Trader truck.

Top left: Peter Patton, service manager at Te Aroha, was the first staff member to receive his 25 year gold watch in 1957, retiring soon afterwards.

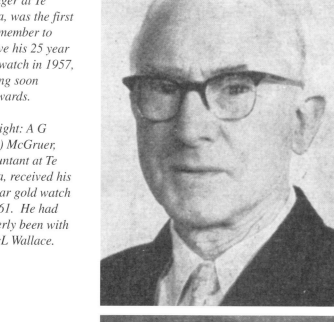

Top right: A G (Mac) McGruer, accountant at Te Aroha, received his 25 year gold watch in 1961. He had formerly been with D McL Wallace.

Middle left: Len Batey, on Te Aroha parts staff, gained top marks for New Zealand in 1965 for his Motor Trade Certification Board parts examination, winning the General Motors prize. He stayed with Ford, and today is working at John Andrew's head office in Auckland.

Middle right: Len Scrimshaw was accountant at Te Aroha, and branch manager of Te Aroha from 1970.

Bottom left: Keith Watson became sales manager at Te Aroha, when his father Ken retired.

Bottom right: Henry Cross was service manager at Te Aroha after Peter Patton retired.

Left: Ted Revell was parts manager at Te Aroha. His grandfather had been on the staff as a saddler

Right: Lou Baker was sales manager at Te Aroha in the 1970-80s. After he helped police to find and apprehend stolen property, through his observation and initiative, he was always known as Kojak.

Long term customers, Albert Stockley Transport at Te Aroha, started in 1923 using solid tyred Model T trucks with a top speed of 12 mph. Albert Stockley's son, Stan, who retired in 1977, maintained that their 12 truck business had been built on Ford general purpose trucks which were good, well-priced units that had helped the company make money.

When Te Aroha was refurbished in 1968 the western side was opened up with a new service station, offices and showroom and staff facilities. There was little left of its stables heritage.

Top left: Ian Morgan was branch manager at Morrinsville, and transferred to manage Fairhall Motors in 1968.
Top right: Barney Gibbons, accountant at Morrinsville.

Lower left: John Ganley, service manager at Morrinsville.

Lower right: Ian Forte, parts manager at Morrinsville.

registrations were a constant pain to Hawke Motors, who were berated by Ford personnel for their apparent poor comparative performance. Ford never acknowledged this distortion.

Colonial Motor Company tried to help the dealership by transferring likely up-and-coming salespeople to Morrinsville, giving them a chance to prove themselves before they were shifted to management around the CMC Group. While the GM dealer was a very distinct challenge, it was also demoralising to be continually undermined by Ford managers who were not paid to see the wood from the trees.

When Peter Craig resigned in 1984 and shifted to Hamilton to become secretary of the Retail Motor Trade Association, Ken Mullan transferred from Ruahine Motors, Waipukurau to be manager.

The government also changed that year and the radical new Labour 'Rogernomics' reforms introduced 'more market' policies. Farmers were the first to be affected, many 'shutting the gate' on expenditure and, with the sharemarket collapse in 1987, trading became very tough. Among the first affected Ford dealerships were Paeroa and Matamata, but instead of giving the territories back to Hawke Motors, Ford amalgamated Paeroa with Thames, and Matamata became a branch of Hamilton.

Above: Morrinsville branch received a major facelift and interior renovations, with upgraded staff facilities in 1968.

Left: Three 25 year watch holders: Charlie Lawrence, tractor mechanic at Te Aroha; Ian Forte, parts manager at Morrinsville; and Len Scrimshaw, accountant at Te Aroha.

In 1988 Ford sold out of tractors to C B Norwood Ltd and Hawke Motors lost their tractor business overnight. Soon afterwards, Ford sold out of heavy trucks, further debilitating their dealers.

The Waikato suffered badly from Ford NZ policies at that time, with Ford dealers fighting one another over the diminished new vehicle market volumes. The Cambridge dealer went into receivership in 1990, and became a branch of Hamilton, and the Tokoroa dealer relinquished the franchise.

Government also rationalised its own departments, withdrawing to major centres in the early 1990s, closing offices and reducing employment in country areas.

When Ken Mullan arrived in 1984, he could not have imagined what was in store. One thing after another attacked most of the business's profit centres and it became a living nightmare. Both branches were severely re-structured to cut overheads. For staff, it was both difficult and demoralising.

However, despite the changes, the company operated efficiently and was the first rural dealership to win the coveted new President's Award introduced in 1989 for looking after its customers better than anyone else in its dealer size group in New Zealand. Ford has no higher measure of dealer success, but being best is sometimes not enough.

Hawke Motors Ltd ceased trading after 61 years on July 31 1997, as part of a New Zealand-wide Ford dealer rationalisation.

The town of Te Aroha, originally the larger of the two, suffered most, as business after business was closed down, amalgamated or shifted after the economic restructuring of the 1980s and 1990s. Morrinsville has a large agricultural tractor and implement distributor and dairy company, but is little more than a dormitory of Hamilton, and Fairview Motors now looks after the interests and needs of Ford customers for the whole Waikato district.

Above left: E P (Ellis) Smith was managing director, with his office situated at Te Aroha. He started working for Colonial Motor Company in 1935, joining H N Scrimshaw's audit staff. In 1937, 'Smithy' was accountant at Fagan Motors, Masterton. Turned down for military service, he was appointed manager of Fairhall Motors, Kaikohe in 1941. When tractors became available after the war, he actively promoted and sold them, and transferred to manage Hawke Motors in 1950. Smithy focussed his team on tractors, and Hawke Motors sold 60 new Fordson Majors in 1955, then topped New Zealand in 1960-61 with Fordson Dexta tractor sales. Respected for fair trading and innovative abilities, Smithy retired in 1969.

Above right: Barry Wisneski, manager between 1969 and 1974, became CMC Group internal auditor after Basil Orsborne retired. He was presented with his 25 year Omega gold watch in 1976 by board chairman, Gerald Gibbons. This is closely watched by Colin Cliff who first employed Barry Wisneski at New Plymouth in 1951. He shifted to audit office, and was then accountant at Waipukurau, Invercargill, New Lynn and Masterton and became manager of Fairhall Motors, Kaikohe in 1965. He had a tremendous, quick ability with figures, and a nose for anything unusual.

Right: Peter Craig was manager between 1974 and 1984 when he resigned to go into an accountancy practice. He had been at several CMC Group companies before being appointed manager of Te Kuiti Motors in 1971.

Service manager at Morrinsville, Rex Nicholson, fitting a safety arch to a new Ford 7000 tractor in 1974. This tractor model used a turbo-charged 5000 engine, increasing output 20% to 105hp, and was excellent for driving power take off implements such as forage harvesters.

Below: At Morrinsville in 1996: Grant Daniel, former sales manager, now general manager CMC, Ken Mullan and Neil Andrew.

Right: Ken Mullan became general manager of Hawke Motors Ltd in 1984. He was instrumental in helping the company to weather the storm of changes in the mid 1980s and 1990s, and had the pleasure of receiving on behalf of the company, the first Ford President's Award in 1989, for being the best dealership in its class at meeting their customers' satisfaction needs. He had the tough task of closing down Craik Motors in 1995, and then Hawke Motors in 1997, as rationalisation took place. Ken Mullan became CMC Group internal auditor, retiring in 2004 after 47 years. Starting as Timaru Motors' office junior in 1957, he moved to Kaitaia, Lower Hutt, Te Awamutu and Timaru, and was appointed manager of Ruahine Motors in 1974.

Sales manager Ken Pearce at Morrinsville, demonstrates some of the features of the new 1989 Laser GL.

Ken Turner, Te Aroha service manager, uses the electronic engine analyser to tune an engine.

CHAPTER SEVENTEEN

TE AWAMUTU – CRAIK MOTORS LTD

Today Te Awamutu is a prosperous country town in the Waikato, surrounded by lush farmland and famous for its rose gardens. It was not always this way. The town started as a Maori settlement with Europeans arriving in 1839 to establish the Otawhao Church Mission Station, today known as Selwyn Park. Across the main road is St John's Anglican Church, built in 1854 by the Church Mission Society, using timber and funds donated by Maori converts.

During the land wars of the 1850-60s, land was confiscated, and the area was one of much dissention. On the south side of the town, Frontier Road, running along the Puniu River, is the edge of the King Country where Rewi Maniopoto, war chief of the Ngati Maniopoto was a prominent leader of the Maori King Movement. It was near here, east of Kihikihi, that Rewi built a pa, the scene of the famous Battle of Orakau in 1864.

Two thousand soldiers, under General Cameron, attacked Orakau Pa but Rewi and his force of about 300, including some women and children, held them at bay. On the third day, Cameron sent a messenger with proposed terms of peace. Nearly out of ammunition and food, Rewi rejected these with his famous *"Kaore e mau te rongo, ake, ake, ake!"* (Peace shall not be made, never, never, never.) An offer made for safe passage for the women and children was also rejected out of hand – *"Ki te mate nga tane, me mate ano nga wahine, me nga tamariki!"* (If the men die, the women and children must also die.) The battle renewed but during the night, Rewi and his followers broke through the British lines and disappeared into the mists and safety of the King Country. The British were left with a hollow victory and an empty pa.

Rewi later mellowed and played a key role in fostering Maori–pakeha relations. In the middle of nearby Kihikihi village he is remembered with a monument and memorial.

The railway from Auckland reached Te Awamutu in 1880 and King Tawhiao made peace the next year at nearby Pirongia, surrendering arms to Major William Mair and ending the land wars.

The town has developed as a bustling, prosperous agricultural trading centre with stock saleyards, dairy factories and other light industrial enterprises.

In 1924, R Gibson was appointed the

Looking southwest over Te Awamutu about 1958. Frontier Road runs across the top left of the picture, and was so named because it was the frontier of the King Country. The road coming in from centre right is from Hamilton; bottom centre is from Cambridge. Leading up from the triangular intersection (today a roundabout) is Arawata Street, a part of Highway No.3. St John's Church is on the left, across the road from Selwyn Park, site of the Otawhao Mission. Beside this is Craik Motors. The new workshop, parts and office are visible. The old boxy structure, with lube bay and sales office was still on the corner of Mahoe Street.

Right: In the 1970s, an invoice book including these 1926 repairs, was found behind a wall during building renovation.

Opposite top: The staff in 1948, from left: Arnold Patterson, John Sherley, Colin Hynd, Sylvia Patterson, Phil Kippenberger, not known, Ray Verity, Bert Jackson, Jim Craik, Pat Hughes, Jim Ambler, Bob Blackwood, Don Paul, Gordon Mills, Bob Quinlan, and John Martin. Jim Craik left shortly afterwards to live in Oamaru and Jim Ambler became manager.

The staff parade in 1936, with Jim Craik, manager, on the right. The office and showroom is behind the petrol bowsers on the right, the lubrication bay by the corner, with the workshop behind, down Mahoe Street.

Ford agent, and the original garage was built on the corner of Arawata and Mahoe Streets. It was a boxy structure that proudly announced the firm was agent for Maxwell Cars, Ford Cars, Harley Davidson Motor Cycles, Pilkington Milking Machines and Alfa-Laval Separators. In 1926 Gibson took in a partner and the firm became Holmes and Gibson, trading on until 1931. Like many motor businesses, they were put into receivership by the bank.

The assets of Holmes and Gibson were taken over by Te Awamutu Motors who operated the Ford franchise with difficulty until 1934, when they also were in serious financial trouble. On December 10 1934, Craik Motors Ltd was formed by the Colonial Motor Company, which bought the assets of Te Awamutu Motors.

The new manager, Jim Craik, had joined CMC in Courtenay Place in 1929 and had been a road organiser until his appointment to Te Awamutu. Trading was still very difficult as the Depression's grip weakened. Soon afterwards Jim Craik enlisted Bob Aiken to help him as the used car specialist. He had been at Ford Sales and Service in Wellington and stayed on working at Craik Motors until he retired about 1961.

Starting from a very low point in 1934, business slowly went ahead, particularly in the service area. Te Awamutu is a closely settled farming area and, although there were only about 3,000 people in the town, there were three or four times as many within a 15 mile radius. Most farmers had their own electricity generators driven by small engines for milking and these were always breaking down so service staff were 'on call' to get things going at all times of the day as the cows had to be milked.

By 1936 sales had picked up considerably and there were 22 on the staff. One of those was Arnold Patterson who

R GIBSON
    Motor Sales and Service
    34 Arawata Street, Te Awamutu

To CASH SALE REPAIRS   *March 1926*
Travel to Kawhia to repair the rear axle of Buick tourer.
Return to procure new crown wheel and pinion and then fit.
    Labour for 4 days   £2 17s 0d
Parts procured   £3 19s 3d
    Hire of Maori's horse to transport mechanic & parts   £1 7s 0d

            TOTAL   £7 13s 3d

started his apprenticeship in 1929 and stayed on to become service manager for many years until his retirement in the mid 1960s.

During the Second World War many of the staff enlisted and the business was mainly repairing farm tractors and machines, if the parts could be found. Petrol was rationed, and cars were seldom used except in emergencies.

Jim Ambler had been on the audit staff of H N Scrimshaw, CMC's internal auditor since 1933 and, after returning from war service, was posted to Craik Motors as accountant.

Craik Motors continued to go ahead with the district as trading returned to normal after the war, although this was hampered by the lack of vehicles under the strict import licensing rules. Additional land was purchased as it became available next to the dealership. CMC had a future vision and was acquiring good commercial land wherever it could.

Confirmed batchelor Jim Craik married May Knight, daughter of the Ford dealer

at Oamaru, and took the opportunity to buy into Knight's Motors Ltd in 1949, shifting to Oamaru.

Jim Ambler, appointed manager to replace him, was a genial giant of a man who loved parties and delighted in practical jokes, some more endearing than others. One of his favourite was to come up to a man with an unbuttoned jacket and button it up. He would then pick his hapless victim up under the armpits and place him on the nearest coat peg, a position quite difficult to escape from. Some of the tales told of him attending dealer meetings, and the reprisals that occurred, cannot be printed here. Don Scrimshaw was sent up by his father H N Scrimshaw to be accountant.

The workshop was considerably extended in 1950 and a new 5000 sq ft area was added. The land behind the premises was quite low lying and the workshop was built above ground with a wooden floor. This made the area much warmer than concrete and gave an extra storage area for parts underneath. On the other hand, the floor was difficult to clean, and heavy vehicles and large tractors could not access it, and were worked on outside in the open.

When Don Scrimshaw was transferred back to Avery Motors, Bill Maclaren shifted from Te Kuiti as accountant in 1956. In a recent interview he said: "We had some hard case customers, and one was a Yugoslav, who was also a partner in the wine and spirits firm that we had sold a new truck to. He came and told me the truck was no good and wouldn't steer, so we went to have a look at it. It was a new forward control Trader, a small one, and was only half loaded up, but with all the

Below: A reunion of staff prior to 1955. From left, back: Murray Blair, unknown, Peter Gibbons, Ackroyd, unknown, Rex Bedford, unknown, Bob Blackwood, Don Scrimshaw, unknown, unknown, Pat Hughes, Ian McGregor. Sitting left: Beverley Steenson, Nita Bedford, Bev Kay, Nancy Yarndley, Jackson, Joy Norman, Ackroyd, Sylvia Woodward.

full crates stacked up behind the cab. Of course all the weight was over the front wheels, and with no power steering, it was hopeless. So I showed them how to load it, and everything was fine again, and from then on he would appear every so often with chillis and other exotic vegetables that he grew in his garden."

When Bill Maclaren was transferred to New Plymouth Alan Davidson was appointed accountant. By the beginning of the 1960s, with the new agricultural methods in use, Te Awamutu district had become a very productive farming centre by world standards. The dealership services an area of only 681 square miles, which had a population of over 30,000 people in the 1960s, giving the unusually high rural density of 44 people per square mile. Major employers included the Waikeria prison and Tokanui mental hospital, apart from dairy factories and support industries.

Transport had become a significant factor in getting produce to the market, and tractors were a very important piece of equipment on every farm. With the dense population, Hodson's Bus Service operated daily buses into Hamilton and school buses all through the district. Hodson's had bought a number of Ford buses and were very good operators. Ford often chartered them to demonstrate new model buses to other operators.

There were numerous agricultural contractors in the area who made hay and silage, planted crops and drained vast areas of swamp land, turning it into productive pasture. Craik Motors was kept busy

selling and servicing, and staff numbers grew.

More land was acquired adjacent to the old mission station for a commercial workshop development. However, Jim Ambler was not to see this happen as, unfortunately, he died in a road accident in 1962.

M W (Merv) Dineen, manager at Te Kuiti Motors, was transferred and appointed managing director in 1962, and for a period ran both businesses. Further staff changes were made at the end of 1962, with Alan Davidson moving to become business manager at Stevens Motors, and Roger Gardner replacing him as accountant.

Merv Dineen quickly set about getting the commercial workshop going and construction was completed in 1963. The workshop had the latest inspection pits with under-floor heating. Trucks had become an important part of the business when the Ford Thames Trader arrived in 1957, and several commercial fleets could now be serviced properly in the new 6,000 sq ft workshop.

Tractors were also a major part of the business, with service repairs being done in an old concrete-floored part of the building by Mahoe Street. The new small Fordson Dexta was an ideal size and found many dairy farmer friends. On-farm servicing, using mobile vans and radio telephones, started; a mechanic could radio in that he was completing a job and be directed to the next one, sometimes less than half a mile down the road. Tractors became more specialised with hydraulic

Staff from 1956 to 1966. From left, back: George Arnell, Fred Boggis, Gordon Gallagher, George Murray, Ken Mullan, Stuart Holm, Barrie Saunders, George King, Noel Harper, Ross Youngson, Dave Lee, Neil Ensor. Sitting left: Ackroyd, Steve Wilson, Jean Dineen, Jocelyn Jefferies, Alan Davidson, Kay Fairweather, Val Youngson, Ian McGregor, Pat Hughes.

Thanks to the skill and enthusiasm of tractor foreman, Tom Marshall, Craik Motors was able to do a running test of Ford Select-O-Speed units before reinstalling them in the tractors. Heart of the test rig was a 10hp Waukesha motor of pre-war origin, used originally as a standby for the air compressor during power cuts in the war and post war period. The motor was mounted on a simple frame with two solid rubber wheels for portability. An old tractor mower driveshaft connected the transmission under test through a built in twin disc clutch, and it took all 10hp to carry out the tests satisfactorily. The benefits of a simulated working test were considerable, allowing a complete check of all operations and a test for internal and external leaks before assembling the tractor, avoiding costly repetitive work. Tom Marshall made many specialised tools for tractors, saving Craik Motors a great deal of money in the process. These included an adaptor tool for testing the breakaway torque limiting clutch; a direct drive clutch pack dismantling and assembly tool, and conversion of gauges for the test rig. Transporting tractors was aided by a special towing 'A frame' mounted to the front axle of the tractor. Tom Marshall transferred to New Lynn Motors in 1972 where he supervised the Massey branch tractor service operations. He now runs his own service business at Dairy Flat.

systems, necessitating dedicated mechanics. When Tom Marshall arrived from England, where he had been a toolmaker and mechanic servicing his family fleet of cropping tractors, he became the tractor service foreman in Te Awamutu.

Car sales grew quickly with the No Remittance scheme and by 1964 the sales department had been re-organised with Roger Gardner now selling vehicles and Stuart Holm, tractors. Ken Mullan transferred from Stevens Motors as accountant. Parts manager Gordon Mills retired and his deputy, Ross Youngson, took over for a short period, but then also left. Roy Brown, who had been parts manager at Te Kuiti, transferred to be parts manager. Arnold Patterson, one of the Omega Club with 25 years service, had health problems and decided to step down from service manager to look after service costing, but still kept an eye on things, and Pat Hughes became workshop foreman. Merv Dineen was surrounded with young people and encouraged them to get ahead and take the business with them.

In 1965, the remainder of the 'funny old boxy building', housing the lube bay and petrol pumps on the corner, was pulled down, and the showroom extended to the full width of the frontage. With the set-back frontage, used vehicles were displayed, and the petrol pumps were housed under a large new canopy. The transformation was a major step forward and business multiplied.

When the new Ford tractors with the revolutionary new Select-O-Speed 'shift on the go' clutchless transmission, were launched in 1965, sales took off. However, when the fabulous new transmissions didn't stand up to customer use every transmission had to be re-worked. Tom Marshall was in his element and devised a special test rig to 'prove' the transmission after re-work before it was reinstalled in the tractor. The customer damage caused by the Select-O-Speed failures took a long time to overcome, but fortunately the manual transmission was a winner.

Above: In 1966, buildings were fully reconstructed with workshops at the rear. The pumps were shifted under the canopy. The new showroom is at left.

Below: Staff, 1966 to 1976, from left: Gary Derbyshire, Kerry Bryan, Steve Wilson, Michael Murray, Henry Holden, John Bates, Howard Frost, Ash Owens. Sitting left: Warren Watson, unknown, Frances Holm, David Bodley, Joanne Johnson, Stuart Holm.

Ken Mullan transferred to Timaru Motors, and Peter Stewart was shifted from South Auckland Motors to be accountant. Later in 1966, Peter Craig transferred from Hawke Motors, Morrinsville to join the sales team. No Remittance was still big business and Craik Motors had over 40% of the local market business and was the major player amongst the dealers. When the new tilt cab D Series trucks replaced the Thames Trader in 1966, more trucks sold.

In 1966 the new Ford Zephyr MkIV arrived with promises of a new standard of motoring. It was a great car to drive, but did not like the low octane NZ fuel, and both ends of the workshop were now hard at work correcting product faults. However, new cars were still in short supply with licensing so the Zephyr sold in spite of the troubles. Fortunately those with overseas funds could choose and bought the very popular new Australian XR Falcons now assembled at Seaview.

In 1968 Peter Stewart resigned to join an accountancy practice and Geoff Atkins was appointed accountant. He had been with CMC Group for 11 years, and was one of 'Scrim's' boys, having been at 12 CMC locations.

John Bates started at Phillipps Motors, New Plymouth, working with Easton Smith in parts for many years, and in 1969 transferred to Craik Motors as parts manager.

Merv Dineen contracted leukaemia and sadly, after a prolonged and often very uncomfortable illness, passed away in late

CRAIK   LTD.

REUNION   1996.

1966 - 76

Left: M W (Merv) Dineen, was managing director from May 1962 until he died on October 1 1969 from leukaemia. He started with CMC at the Wellington assembly plant in 1935, having served his mechanical apprenticeship with Newton King and Co and spending four and a half years as an 'A' grade Ford mechanic at Derby and Company in New Plymouth. He returned after the assembly plant closed, and started with Phillipps Motors in 1938 as service manager. During the war, while Phil Phillipps was overseas in the army, he was acting manager and in January 1948 was appointed manager of Te Kuiti Motors. When Jim Ambler died in a car accident, he ran both companies until Trist Atkins was appointed to Te Kuiti. Merv Dineen had an ability to sense what was happening in the business before it occurred, with both people and products, giving him an uncannily accurate judgement of people and situations. Generous with his praise of staff, he was a good listener and tutor, encouraging many young people who were sent to him for development. Merv Dineen was quietly spoken and well liked; his integrity was absolute and he was appointed a justice of the peace.

Middle left: Bill Smith shifted from being the lube operator to vehicle sales in 1965. He was also a very popular youth worker, helping many people.

Middle right: Henry Holden started at Macaulay Motors, Invercargill, and shifted to Craik Motors as service manager in 1969, later retiring in Te Awamutu.

Bottom left: John Bates started at Phillipps Motors, New Plymouth, shifting to Craik Motors in 1966, and was parts manager until he retired.

Bottom right: Ian Stratford, truck and tractor salesman during the 1970-80s.

David Bodley, and his wife Sally, transferred from Waipukurau where he had been manager, to manage Craik Motors in 1969.

Right: Craik Motors purchased property from Mrs Bonner's estate next to Selwyn Park in 1977, turning it into a very successful used car stand beside the main highway.

Below: A new canopy was added on the north side by the workshop, giving space to do quick jobs under cover.

1969. He started as an apprentice at New Plymouth Ford dealers, Derby & Co, spent a period at Courtenay Place assembly plant, and shifted back to New Plymouth in 1938 as service manager. During the war he acted as manager while Phil Phillipps was serving overseas. In 1948 he became manager of Te Kuiti Motors. In his term with CMC, he had trained many young people, encouraged and counselled them, and then seen them promoted. At a CMC management meeting in the 1970s, half the managers there had worked with him.

In November 1969, David Bodley was appointed manager. He joined Colonial Motor Company in 1964 and worked at four CMC Group locations. In 1968, before he moved to Te Awamutu, he was manager at Cordery Garage, Waipukurau, which became Ruahine Motors with Roger Gardner now in charge.

Shortly afterwards, Henry Holden was transferred from Macaulay Motors, Invercargill, where he had started as an apprentice in 1949, to be service manager. And so another new team was in control at Craik Motors.

In 1974 the building had a substantial refit and additions, taking it to a new standard. Mrs Bonner's house beside the park was purchased from her estate and, after being used as an office during the alterations on the main building, was removed and the area filled and levelled to provide a substantial and picturesque used vehicle display beside Selwyn Park where the Otawhao Mission had been.

The 1960-70s and early 1980s were

very strong years for Craik Motors with used cars, trucks and tractors providing a major part of the sales and servicing. Used vehicle volumes shifted from 14 a month in the 1960s to 40 per month with the new large display.

The reforms of the new Labour government in 1986 seriously affected farming and, after the sharemarket crash in 1987, trading in the Waikato became over competitive. This was made worse by Ford selling out of tractors in 1988 and later heavy trucks, part of the staple needs of country dealers. Added to this, import restrictions were loosened, and used imports flooded in from Japan, causing the floor price of used cars to go into freefall.

Discounting among Ford dealers in the area became rampant, as they fought for diminishing new vehicle shares and the company, along with others in the area, struggled for profitability. Rationalisation in many industries was inevitable but, like many situations in life, it took time and pain to reach a result. Cambridge's Ford dealer, David Watt, was the first Waikato dealer to become insolvent in 1991. Then John Sharplin in Tokoroa decided that he would be better to release the franchise in 1992 and become a simple car seller and repairer.

David Bodley tried everything he could to rationalise the dealership and make it profitable, but sadly could not achieve this, and retired at the end of June 1993. He died a few years later.

The centennial A & P show in 1987 was a big affair for the district.

An opportunity to celebrate 100 years in 1987.

Geoff Atkins, business manager, receiving his 25 year gold watch from CMC managing director Peter Gibbons in 1982.

John Luxton was appointed manager in August 1993, having joined CMC at Hutchinson Motors, Christchurch. However, there had been fundamental shifts in the market and Ford had become very keen to rationalise and reduce the number of dealers. Consequently, John Luxton returned south to manage Macaulay Motors, Invercargill at the end of September 1995, and Craik Motors Ltd closed down, after 64 years of operations at the end of 1995, under the guidance of Ken Mullan, then dealer principal of Hawke Motors, Morrinsville. The territory was combined with the Hamilton Ford dealer, Fairview Motors Ltd.

Craik Motors Ltd had been a very viable business for 61 years, but it suffered seriously with the demise of tractors in 1988 and then heavy trucks in 1991. Both these products had been a vital part of trading in the rich farming community.

Gold watch holders at Craik Motors' reunion in 1996. From left, back: Ken Mullan, Henry Holden, David Bodley, John Bates, Geoff Atkins. Front left: Alan Davidson, Peter Gibbons, Don Scrimshaw.

Wayne Johnson receiving the second R B Gibbons Memorial Award from managing director David Bodley. The award was made to candidates who had shown outstanding ability in their field, and enabled them to further their knowledge in a chosen field. Wayne Johnson travelled for a period in northern Queensland to further his tractor servicing knowledge.

Staff from 1976 to 1986, from left back: Murray Woodham, Peter Kripner, Ian Stratford, Chris Firth, Bryce Roigard, Mark Burnside, Henry Holden, Maurice Hall, Grant Hodgson. Sitting left: Sue Waugh, Geofry Peak, Roger Barron, Mark Buist, Ray Dodds, Glynnis Anderson, Heather Hughes.

Peter Kripner became service manager when Henry Holden retired. He was one of the team which organised the very successful reunion in 1996.

Staff from 1986 to 1996. From left, back: Grant Hodgson, Peter Kripner, Murray Watson, Russell Bayley, Grant McConnachie, Ben Searanche, Conrad Ericson, Henry Holden, Maurice Hall. Sitting left: Carol Hooker, Ian McGregor, Heather Hughes, Leigh Parish, Mark Buist, Bryce Roigard, Ian Stratford, Sue Waugh.

CHAPTER EIGHTEEN
TE KUITI –
TE KUITI MOTORS LTD

Te Kuiti is an abbreviation of 'Te Kuititanga', meaning the narrowing in or closing in, and refers to the strategic constriction of the Mangaokiwa Valley at the Gorge. The Maori village of Te Kuititanga was the home of King Tawhiao, after the Battle of Orakau in 1864, until a formal peace was signed in 1881. During this period the area became known as the King Country, and Europeans entered at their peril.

With the development of the North Island Main Trunk railway, Te Kuiti became a major construction camp in 1887. Today it is a farming centre of less than 4,000 people, servicing the undulating to hilly land that is predominantly sheep grazing country, but with coal, limestone and serpentine being mined nearby, plus a fertiliser works and timber mill.

The area between Te Kuiti and Ohakune was largely unmapped tracks when the first motor journey was made in 1912 from Wellington to Auckland through the King Country, sponsored by Colonial Motor Company. The unmetalled papa clay tracks, formed for the construction of the railway, provided the key to travelling through this notoriously difficult area. The Model T Ford was probably the only car capable of the journey through this area because of its high ground clearance, light weight, strength, reliability and powerful engine. Details of this epic journey are included in Chapter Two.

The first Ford in the King Country district was thought to be a Model T owned by George Hitchcock, a building contractor, in about 1913. There were no service garages in those days, and horses were still the prime transportation in this remote hill country area.

Nothing was done with the roads for many years, but once the roads board was formed in 1922, and when funds were available from about 1926, the main roads were developed. Most of the back roads received a coat of metal during the 1930s, but sealing did not come until the 1970s, and even later for many remote side roads.

In 1915, on the site later to become Te Kuiti Motors, Caley Motors was formed by converting the stables of Henry Free and Company into a motor garage dealing in Rugby and Durrant cars.

McKay & Jones owned the business during the mid-1920s, and became the Ford agents. Hand-operated petrol pumps, or bowsers, were installed when bulk petrol became available from 1926. Passing cars became more common with the growing tourist traffic to nearby Waitomo Caves. This made Te Kuiti a motor servicing point on the route from Auckland to New Plymouth as well as an important rail stop.

W B (Bill) McAdam took over and incorporated the business, becoming the Ford agent in 1929, and operated in conjunction with a garage he had started nearby at Otorohanga in 1925. However, when the Depression, which strangled trade and commerce right through New Zealand, took a severe grip on rural Te Kuiti in 1930, McAdam was seriously stretched financially. When his brother, who was accountant for the company, went into hospital in 1932, Colonial Motor Company tried to help. P L (Phil) Phillipps, then C J L (Jim) Flannery were sent to assist. It was too late, and the bank put the business into receivership on November 3 1932.

Four of the people on the staff at the time were Gordon Burnet, service manager; Bob Edgar, foreman; Tom Nealon, mechanic; and Gordon Goddard who drove the famed Marokopa bus.

Jim Flannery was kept in Te Kuiti to run the business for the receiver until May 1935 when it was put up for auction. The only bid was received from Colonial Motor Company, and Te Kuiti Motors Ltd was formed as a subsidiary, with Jim Flannery as manager.

The Marokopa mail bus was originally started by Bill McAdam to supplement the garage business in 1929, using an extended Model AA Ford truck with a six-seater body and freight compartment. In 1935 this was replaced with a special 17-seater bus built

Top: W B McAdam Ltd was the Te Kuiti Ford dealer, but went into receivership during the Depression. The workshop staff were photographed in 1932. From left: Gordon R Burnet, service manager; Charlie Bray; Jack Paterson; Bob Edgar; Bob Dowdall; and Vernon Adams; with their trusty Model AAC tow wagon.

by Standard Motor Bodies, on a Ford V8 $3^1/2$ ton chassis that met transport regulations. The road to Marokopa was very narrow, rough and treacherous over the Pomarangei Range, and there were many accidents.

Many of the staff were also volunteer members of the fire brigade. The first engine was a Model T Ford one ton truck. Gordon Burnet remembered the Te Kuiti fire-engine.

"One day the fire bell went, and the volunteers rushed off to man the engine and

they set off to the fire. The old truck had great difficulty in keeping up with some of the schoolboys on their bicycles, but they arrived, and made a satisfactory save of the burning property.

"I talked to the deputy fire chief and suggested we do something about the performance of the Model T and give it a 'tune up'. So we planed a spare cylinder head to increase the compression. This was fitted the next night and when we started the motor up it had a much sharper exhaust note. We left and didn't tell the others because we didn't have any authority to do

Right: The Marakopa mail bus was one of the workshop's mainstays during the Depression. With the bus are some of the staff from 1933: Gordon Goddard, bus driver; Les Waugh, mechanic; Jim Flannery, manager for the receiver; Vern Adam, apprentice; and Tom Nealon, mechanic.

THE MARAKOPA BUS

In the period from 1910-1950, when there were fewer vehicles on the roads, service cars were one of the few ways people could get to remote communities in New Zealand. There were about 700 service cars registered throughout New Zealand in 1930, carrying mail, newspapers, freight and passengers on regular timetabled routes. After the Second World War, the need dropped away as more people had access to vehicles; today the rural mail contractor is their equivalent.

The Marakopa bus was typical of the period; in 1929 it was a lengthened Model AA Ford one ton truck with extra seats and a freight compartment. The previous 1927 Chrysler Tourer had external contracting brakes rendered useless with the wet papa clay. The bus was operated by

The original Marakopa bus with Gordon Goddard at the wheel.

W B McAdam to supplement the garage business.

What wasn't typical was the rugged, but picturesque, terrain between Te Kuiti and Marakopa, through bush, with limestone caves and waterfalls. The road was very rough, narrow and tortuously winding. Over much of the 50 miles it was impossible to pass another vehicle. The settlement of Waitanguru was reached after 26 miles. The road then crossed the steeply winding Pomarangei Range to Marakopa.

The bus left Marakopa at 6am each morning, arriving at Te Kuiti four hours later. It was a tough job. When the driver, George Goddard, left the bus at Te Kuiti Motors for any servicing or repairs, he went to sort mail at the Post Office. He then collected groceries, meat, medicines, newspapers and did any personal shopping for clients on the bus run, many of whom could not afford the bus fare to town. The bus left again at 2pm and wound its way back to Marakopa,

delivering mail and goods to people along the route, finally arriving back between 8-9pm. To many along the way, George Goddard was their lifeline to the outside world in those troubled financial times. He was well liked and a very friendly, helpful man.

Jim Flannery, who operated the business for the receiver from 1932 to 1935, remembered the difficulties the bus run presented: "Local residents knew the hour the bus would be passing through and took care not to be on the road at that time.

"The roads were shocking and we were always afraid the bus wouldn't get through. The mechanical team at Te Kuiti Motors, Les Waugh, Vern Adams and young Tom Nealon, did yeoman service in keeping the bus on the road.

"There was always something happening to the bus – breaking a spring after hitting a pot hole; sliding into a bank and bashing a mud guard; even going off the road to avoid crashing into another vehicle. They were always straightening, welding or adjusting something, or replacing springs.

"Another hazard was wandering stock, particularly cattle and wild pigs, that would appear from nowhere on the unfenced roads."

Gordon R Burnet, who was service manager for W B McAdam, remembered one of the many incidents. "One day George Goddard was negotiating a particularly bad piece of the road when the bracket supporting the top of the steering column pulled out of the base of the cowl mounted petrol tank, and all the petrol poured over the driver's legs, through the holes in the floorboards onto the muffler and exhaust.

"It is said that George made his quickest ever exit from the bus, expecting it to burst into flames, which it did not.

"To get the bus going again I sent a mechanic out with a petrol tank from a Hudson, telling him to put it on the roof and tie it down with some wire, and then run a piece of copper pipe down to the carburettor. The bus finished the trip quite successfully, and when it returned to Te Kuiti we located the Hudson tank at the rear of the vehicle and fitted a vacuum tank fuel system. Petrol pumps were not used on many vehicles in those days.

The Marakopa bus on a narrow, rough, and virtually one-way road.

"One day, just before the bus was due to leave, I was giving it a final inspection and, looking underneath, I noticed that the torque tube enclosing the driveshaft had a considerable bend in it. As there was no sign of recent damage under the vehicle, I decided that the driveshaft had been running in this state for some time, and 'cleared' the bus for the trip.

"About half an hour after the bus had left, we received a 'phone call from George to say the transmission had failed.

"We rushed out with the salvage truck and a spare car to get the mail under way. At this stage I felt quite sure the solid steel driveshaft had broken because of the bent torque tube.

"A towrope was attached to the bus and we proceeded to tow it about eight miles back to the workshop in Te Kuiti. We jacked up the rear axle, and somebody rocked a rear wheel and it fell off onto the floor. We had towed the bus eight miles with a broken axle shaft and all that had held that wheel in place had been good luck."

In 1934 a new Ford V8 bus was built by Standard Motor Bodies to comply with new regulations and replaced the now very battered Model A vehicle. The new bus had more space but suffered the same problems with roads that were still terrible.

In 1939 the bodywork had to be strengthened because of the racking caused by the rough roads and when the mail contract was renewed, it was upped from £406 to £445 to cover increased operating costs.

George Goddard became ill in 1940 and could not continue driving the bus. The war had started, petrol was rationed, and the bus ran only three days a week – on Tuesday, Thursday and Saturday. The driver left his home in Te Kuiti on Monday evening at 7pm in his own car, arriving about 10pm and stayed the night with George Goddard. On Tuesday he did the bus run and then, after returning about 9pm, collected his own car and drove home arriving about 1am on Wednesday. On Wednesday evening he started for Marakopa about 7pm to repeat the process. Clearly this could only be a temporary arrangement, as the driver was also running his father's farm on his days off. The contract was ended later in 1940 and was not renewed until after the war because of petrol restrictions.

Ralph Perry, of Perry Motors, Te Kuiti, took delivery of a new Ford D Series bus in 1972. From left: Tom Nealon, sales manager; Ralph Perry, and Peter Craig, manager.

the work, but thought they would like the extra performance.

"Well, we didn't have long to wait as the fire alarm went in the freezing early hours next morning. Pat the driver didn't have time to appreciate the improved performance and arrived at the first corner on full throttle as usual. His efforts to get around the corner were hopeless, tearing the tyre from the rim. They didn't get to the fire, but all the water pipes were frozen solid so they couldn't have done anything anyway.

"Pat said he couldn't understand how it had happened as he always took that corner on full throttle. The engine gave excellent service with the high compression head, but we never told anyone why. When it went up for sale some years later, the Superintendent, who was a carrier, was the highest bidder, and he maintained it was the best 1 ton truck he'd ever driven."

Gordon Burnet, who was a very highly regarded engineer, had done his apprenticeship in Auckland with a company specialising in making parts for rare cars. He could replicate almost any part, often improving on the original. About 1933 he transferred to work with the CMC service manager, Jack Broun, training dealer service people on new models.

After the auction in May 1935, Jim Flannery continued as manager until CMC transferred him to the newly formed Macaulay Motors, and in November, R (Dick) Fox, a road organiser, was sent up as interim manager, with H M B (Basil) Orsborn as accountant. Te Kuiti Motors became a training dealership for accountants and managers from then on.

G F T (Fenn) Hall, also a road organiser at head office, was sent up to Te Kuiti on February 27 1936 to take over from Dick Fox who resumed his previous job. At the end of April 1937, Fenn Hall resigned and was replaced by W J (Bill) Dick. At the same time Basil Orsborn was transferred to set up the new Cordery Garage at Waipukurau, and Les Clarke, who had been at Fagan Motors, Masterton, was made accountant.

Business had slowly started to improve when war broke out in 1939. In 1940 Bill Dick managed to negotiate an increase in the Marakopa mail contract, to £445 for the year, after strengthening work was done on the bus bodywork. However, the contract had to be abandoned later because of petrol

rationing, and the bus was worn out as well as operating at a loss. Te Kuiti Motors never sought the mail contract to Marakopa again.

In March 1940, Bill Dick was called up, together with Tom Nealon. Les Clarke took over as manager, until he was also called up for service in March 1942. Basil Orsborn came back from Waipukurau to look after the company until Les Clarke returned in January 1946.

The workshop was crowded with the increased activity and a Nissen hut was bought, with a five year council permit allowing its use as a temporary workshop – restrictions at the time meant you could not build anything without a permit. This provided immediate relief that actually lasted for 24 years until 1969. The Nissen hut was still in use as the storage shed at a lime quarry many years later.

In 1946 the saddle room of the old coaching stables was converted to an office and a lubrication bay was added to the Esplanade frontage, but the premises were still not adequate.

At the beginning of 1948 Les Clarke transferred to manage Hawke Motors at Te Aroha and Morrinsville, and M W (Merv) Dineen, who had been assistant manager at Phillipps Motors, New Plymouth, shifted to become manager.

When Tom Nealon was given the opportunity by Merv Dineen to become a salesman he grabbed it. Well known and liked in the district, he was a top NZ rugby referee. This was in the days when the Ranfurly Shield was held in Te Kuiti and he refereed the 1949 King Country versus

Tom Nealon was a legend. Starting as an apprentice for W B McAdam, he joined Te Kuiti Motors at the beginning, becoming a salesman and sales manager until he retired in 1977. After six months he rejoined on a part time basis, working when he wanted to. He was an international rugby referee at a time that King Country held the Ranfurly Shield, and refereed the 1949 Australia-King Country game in Te Kuiti. He was a volunteer fireman, including fire chief for five years, and would help anyone in need.

Australia game.

Tom Nealon would often leave in the morning to deliver a new car, returning late in the day with a trade-in and three, four, or even five cheques. When all the paperwork was completed, after the sketchy details were transferred from the back of a cigarette packet, he had invariably done several transactions on the way home, trading and reselling and trading all the way.

He remembered well the keen interest of farmers in the E27N 'Cast Iron Clarice' Fordson tractors: "A Te Anga farmer who had bought one, was so pleased with it that he rang Te Kuiti Motors and said that he would take a second one for £405 – if we could deliver it to his farm.

"This presented all sorts of problems due to an atrocious storm that collapsed the farmer's swing bridge and flooded the river bordering his farm.

"The manager, Merv Dineen, and I set out for the farm, and when we came to the river we picked the quietest spot and dug a track down one side and roughed up the other side so we could broach it. I had to strip down to my underpants to test the river depth, and Merv took a photo of me, which he never handed over, saying he may want to use it against me one day.

"Despite the weather, we made the sale. This was one of about 40 of these tractors we sold near Te Kuiti, a very good record for a small area."

Basil Orsborn, Les Clarke and Merv Dineen and a number of single accountants, lived at the Te Kuiti Club which was very convenient and only a short walk from the dealership. In those days, there were no licensed hotels in Te Kuiti, and the club was the entertainment hub of the district.

Merv Dineen didn't stay at the club for long, however, as he met the district nurse. They got along well and soon afterwards Jean and Merv were married and set up home in Te Kuiti.

The Depression lasted more than 20 years in Te Kuiti, due to the Mortgage and Redemption Act. The Act was passed to defer the foreclosures caused by the strangulation of trade. While the worst effects were avoided, it also greatly slowed recovery, making life in many country areas miserable. In 1951, the wool boom signalled the end of the 1930s Depression, and Te Kuiti got back to normal again.

Bob Edgar lived in Te Kuiti as a boy, and one of his early jobs about 1916 was to swim coach horses in the river. Remembering how difficult this was, he taught his children to swim in the river and they became strong swimmers. He later trained as a mechanic and joined J B McAdam.

In 1951, Len Tinkler, a local identity, rebuilt the north wall of the stables and in the process enlarged the workshop area, adding skylights. The rickety old wooden floor, caused by jacks punching holes through the old timber, was ripped out. The enriched floor of the stables was dug out, no doubt providing great garden compost, tons of it, and a concrete floor was laid that was much more suitable for servicing vehicles.

Accountant George Gay shifted to Avery Motors, and Bill Maclaren was

Bill Maclaren, accountant, delivered the keys for a new Consul in 1954 to D McLeay. Did he trade in his 1927 Model T New Beauty? No, he kept it.

transferred to Te Kuiti to replace him in 1953, just after the wool boom ended. This was at a time when car shortages were extreme, and if you didn't have overseas funds it was almost impossible to buy a new car. This sort of challenge was just what Bill Maclaren liked and he learned, with tuition from Merv Dineen and Tom Nealon, how it could be done. He also married Bob Edgar's daughter, Daphne who, incidentally, became a representative swimmer.

In 1955 the river was bridged behind the dealership in Sheridan Street, which opened up the town's facilities. This was the culmination of work done by Sheridan Street businessmen over 15 years. Basil Orsborn was one of the instigators in 1942 and later Merv Dineen strenuously lobbied the council until it was done.

About this time strong representations were being made to establish a hotel across the road from Te Kuiti Motors, using land partly occupied by Hine and Hetet, solicitors and Maori interpreters, and three other parties. In the process, an agreement between the five parties was nearly finalised, but broke down after one wanted £2,000 more to finalise the transaction.

This set back the hotel project for another 10 years, and it also meant Te Kuiti Motors did not have the land it needed for development.

Meanwhile, the dealership premises were inadequate as the business was still expanding. In 1958 the river flooded, seriously submerging Te Kuiti Motors under waist-high water for three days and badly affecting the foundations. The offices had to be moved across the road to a 60 year old house bought from Mrs Innes Jones. The work needed to restore the old stables building involved reconstruction of one third of it, and took nearly six years to complete.

Soon after the bridge was in place, the company built a new house across the river, for the succession of the mostly married, young accountants, who were arriving for their tour of duty. In 1959, George Daniel and his family were the first occupants. He remembered working with Tom Nealon: "Tom didn't like collecting money or writing hire purchase contracts and always asked me to do it for him. He sold a new truck to a stock transporter who wished to collect it from the Ford plant at Seaview. This meant that I had to go with them to sign up the paperwork.

"We went to collect the contractor from Mangakino and had to wait for him to return, as he had taken a load to Napier. Eventually we set off for Wellington and our customer went sound asleep. It was about 2 am as we were going through Levin, so I suggested that we find a pub and bed and set off again the next morning.

"So we found the only pub still open which had one room left that had one single and one double bed. Tom very quickly jumped into the single bed and I had to share the double bed.

"When I woke up in the morning, our customer sat up and said, 'Let's do the paperwork now', so we did. Fortunately, that's the only time I have signed up an HP agreement in bed with a customer."

Adjacent to the office in Sheridan Street, another property of C J Mullins was bought in 1960 for £12,500. Included in the purchase were an auto electrician's shop, an old peoples' club and a panel beating and trim shop.

This provided extra space, and the future could now be planned. Even though the buildings were 80 year old tin shanties, the auto electrical shop was converted into a showroom with offices and parts department next door.

Merv Dineen transferred to Te Awamutu in 1962 after Jim Ambler was killed in a road accident, and for several months was running both dealerships. George Daniel shifted to Christchurch, and Graeme Lyttle came up from Masterton for a few months as accountant until Leo Dixon arrived in early 1963. Then Trist Atkins was transferred from Invercargill to Te Kuiti and took over as manager.

Norm Shorter, with his wife Jenny, was appointed manager in 1964.

Service manager for many years, Don Vivian, with his favourite wrecker, which he built using this extended 1953 Canadian 5 ton V8. Designing his own lifting and winching gear using a Colmoco hoist, he was able to quickly recover some very large trucks which failed to stay on the very poor district roads. He, Lou James and Eric Martin made up a team of three who would go out at any hour they were needed, mostly at night. Don Vivian was also a fireman and vintage car enthusiast.

Right: Ian Lambie was accountant at Te Kuiti in 1968. The secretary of the Waitete Rugby Club had heard he was a good hooker and called the first day. Next Saturday he played his first game with Colin 'Pine Tree' Meads, the team's captain.

It was clear there was not enough land for Te Kuiti Motors to achieve what was required. The Farmers Auctioneering Company was considering relocating, and a proposal was put to them. Te Kuiti Motors would purchase all their land and buildings and sell them all the property bought in the two Sheridan Street blocks. Agreement was reached just as Trist Atkins was due to be transferred away to start Panmure Motors in 1964, with possession to take place in 1968.

Norm Shorter shifted from New Plymouth where he had been accountant, and became the new manager. He moved in to help the planning team and they also purchased the offices of Hine & Hetet when J M Hine retired. These were demolished to make an open used car display.

Bob Edgar retired in 1966, having started with the company at the beginning and serving 31 years. In that time he served a five year term as fire chief and persuaded Tom Nealon to join the brigade.

After using a Model T fire engine, Tom Nealon explained: "We graduated to an ex army 4x4 Ford V8, and then in 1948 a new Ford V8. If they ever get rid of it, it will be a great buy for someone as it has only done about 20,000 kilometres and it is always kept in perfect nick."

The new service manager was Don Vivian, who was also the breakdown man, and he built up the wrecker, or recovery truck, using a 1953 Canadian V8 truck. There were always accidents that had to be attended, including some large trucks, but they presented no problem to Don Vivian and his able recovery team. He built up a great reputation over the years, saving a valuable racehorse from the flooded river by slinging it out of the water to higher ground – a very dangerous exercise.

Ian Lambie moved up to be accountant just after he was married in 1968. A very keen rugby hooker, he played in Colin 'Pinetree' Meads' team at the Waitete Club.

When the FAC building was taken over in 1968, work started on converting it into a showroom, parts operation and administration offices. In 1970 Tom Nealon had the first sales office ever built for Te Kuiti Motors. The open area in front of the building displayed all the used vehicles and was floodlit at night. The office was a bright and cheerful place and

parts were able to be properly merchandised. Customers and staff were very pleased with the result, even if it had taken 35 years to achieve.

In 1971 Norm Shorter was transferred to Newlands Motors, Johnsonville, and Peter Craig took over as manager. He knew the area well, having grown up in the Taumarunui district, and had worked for several CMC Group companies.

He and Tom Nealon managed to sell a new Ford bus to the contractor for the Marakopa run, continuing the association with the backblocks. The road had improved no end, but it was still quite narrow and tortuous.

In 1971 Ian Lambie moved to South Auckland Motors to further his training in sales, and Richard Kilkenny rejoined CMC after a year off finishing his accountancy studies, and was posted to Te Kuiti.

By now, new vehicle supply had improved, and Tom Nealon and Peter Craig set to work to make the most of it.

In 1974 Peter Craig moved to Hawke Motors in Morrinsville, and Brian Willis was appointed manager. He had been parts manager at Stevens Motors and had had a short spell relieving as manager of Ruahine Motors.

Tom Nealon retired in 1977 after 42 years with Te Kuiti Motors and another six years before that with McAdams. He had seen big changes in that period, and had contributed to the success of the company in a major way. From four people in 1932, the company grew to 17 people in 1977.

After about six months retirement, Tom Nealon was bored, and when Brian Willis arrived at the door one day asking if he would be interested in a part time sales contract, Tom jumped at the opportunity

The new Te Kuiti Motors opened in 1970, after a prolonged land acquisition and swap starting in 1942. The new dealership had good buildings and plenty of space to display vehicles. The 1935 workshop, converted from even older stables, was still in use, across the road on the left.

A horse and rider pulled up at the new dealership in 1970 and, anxious to know if he was trading it in, Tom Nealon went to check. It turned out the horse wanted a drink of water at the service station, and the rider was admiring a new Zephyr.

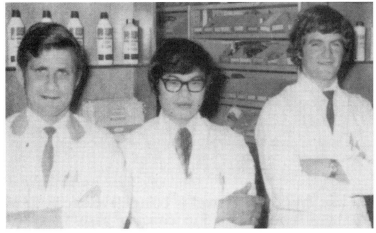

Top: The workshop team in 1971. From left: Eric Martin, Doug Riley, Bill Blackwood, Reg Monk, Jack McLeay, Lou James, George Irvine, Bruce Dunn, Charlie Gordon, and George Whiting.

Above: Parts was well staffed. From left: Robert Ruskill, Young Dong, Colin Botherway.

Right above: Parts manager John Coyle.

Right bottom: Daphne Vivian, Don's wife, was in charge of the office for many years, running this very efficiently, and ensuring a seamless transition between accountants.

Above: Richard Kilkenny was accountant in the early 1970s.

Below: Peter Craig was manager between 1971-74.

and continued to sell, but on a reduced time commitment.

Brian Willis stayed six years and then resigned, moving to live at Taumarunui. Don Hodgson shifted to Te Kuiti from Panmure Motors as manager, but then shifted back to Highland Park Motors in Auckland in 1984. Neville Goldsworthy, sales manager at Phillipps Motors in New Plymouth, was appointed manager in January 1985.

No sooner had Neville Goldsworthy arrived than there were radical changes to government thinking and new, revolutionary free market policies hit home. Te Kuiti reeled with the withdrawal of government subsidies. The farming community were first to feel the effects and stopped spending almost overnight.

By 1987, the effects on Te Kuiti were very serious, with 25% of all residents registered as unemployed and many more were too proud to do so. Business had changed forever.

Te Kuiti Motors was no longer viable and closed down in June 1987. The company had contributed much to the community and had been a vital part of Te Kuiti's business for 52 years. Along with many sectors, the motor industry now needed to rationalise, and the move to larger dealers was starting.

Te Kuiti Motors buildings were sold to David Fagan, world champion shearer, and his brother John, who operate a

farming supplies business. Their uncle, Pat Fagan, was first manager of Fagan Motors, Masterton, where David has won the Golden Shears Championship so often. Te Kuiti will always be a service point for local farmers, but passing traffic barely finds time to blink today.

Brian Willis with service manager Jim Anderson, who was awarded the George Kerr cup in 1977, for merit and qualities of firemanship. The prestigious cup is only awarded when recognition is worthy, not every year. He had been a member of the brigade for five years, continuing a link with Te Kuiti Motors, and remarked: "Ever since the service was inaugurated at least one person from the company has been a volunteer member of the force."

Neville Goldsworthy was appointed 15th manager of Te Kuiti Motors in 1985. The new 'market forces' policies delivered by the Labour government that year, effectively sealed the fate of Te Kuiti which had in excess of 25% unemployment by 1987.
Neville Goldsworthy was transferred to Kaikohe, and Te Kuiti Motors closed down after 50 years, in June 1987.

Lou James received his 25 years gold watch in 1973. He was inducted into the Omega club by two day one stalwarts: Bob Edgar, retired service manager, and Tom Nealon, sales manager.

Former Te Kuiti managers and accountants gathered in Wellington in 1977 to reminisce. From left: David Bodley, d-p Craik Motors; Jim Flannery, CMC secretary; Ian Lamble, d-p Napier Motors; Basil Orsborn, CMC internal auditor; Randal Thomson, d-p Stevens Motors; Bill Maclaren, d-p Macaulay Motors; Peter Craig, d-p Hawke Motors; Norm Shorter, d-p Newlands Motors and Trist Atkins, d-p Panmure Motors. In front Brian Willis, current d-p and George Daniel CEO Avery Motors.

CHAPTER NINETEEN

NEW PLYMOUTH – PHILLIPPS MOTORS LTD / ENERGY CITY FORD

New Plymouth is situated by the sea, near the western tip of the central North Island and at the northern foot of Mt Egmont. Originally a whaling settlement, the town was founded in 1841 by settlers of the Plymouth Company. The rich fertile land in the area, the product of the volcanic ash from Egmont, soon became productive farmland for the urban settlement, with its port connecting it to outside trade.

However, when land troubles between Maori and settlers beset the area, a special constabulary was formed and troops were called in from time to time from Wellington and Auckland. In 1860 the Taranaki War broke out, and a militia garrison was stationed at besieged New Plymouth with many settlers leaving the area. Occasional fighting and unrest persisted until 1881 when a formal peace was made with the Maori people.

The whole district quickly developed into a rich farming area with New Plymouth as the principal market town and port. Rail was connected from New Plymouth to Hawera in 1881 and, with the arrival of refrigeration about the same time, butter production and export became the major industry for Taranaki.

Factories were set up all over Taranaki as the dairying grew, with a myriad of roads and tracks connecting farms to the factories, most no more than a half-day cart journey away because of the quick deterioration of milk.

Oil was discovered in the New Plymouth suburb of Moturoa in 1856, only seven years after the first commercial find in the United States. Although oil promised much for the region, nothing really materialised until natural gas was found on a commercial scale at Kapuni in 1962. Since then, industry has become fully established and New Plymouth has developed from a market town to a provincial and petrochemical centre.

In the early 1900s when motorcars first arrived, Taranaki was one of the most densely populated areas and cars sold very well. The myriad of poor roads presented problems, and local councils set up tollgates, the tolls being ploughed back in developing better roads and bridges. Motorists hated tolls but the roads

Monty Holah was the first Ford agent in New Plymouth in January 1912, using Dumpy West's stable building in Egmont Street. The Model T is about to depart along a remarkably well formed road and footpath. [Photo: Dorothy Campbell taken by father Ted Lyttle.]

improved with Taranaki having the highest density of cars per capita in New Zealand.

The first Ford dealer in New Plymouth was Monty Holah who started selling Model Ts from Dumpy West's stables in Egmont Street in January 1912. Ted Lyttle cut his teeth on Fords with Monty before joining his brother Jim at Masterton in 1916 and becoming Ford sub-agents to Gordon Hughan of Carterton.

In 1913 Monty Holah moved to Liardet Street, and D R McAllum, a local resident, bought his first Model T car there in the first week of 1914. Douglas Lobb, who was a boy in the garage, recalled it also being the town's headquarters for the Model T ambulance, and remembers making many trips in the 'T' during the infamous world influenza epidemic of 1918.

Soon after the First World War, the agency transferred to Harry Derby and Thomas Symons, a farmer financier, and the dealership became known as H Derby and Co Ltd. The Devon Street premises became a distinctive landmark, with the front of a Model T set into the concrete parapet over the verandah.

Monty Holah relocated to better premises in Liardet Street in 1913.

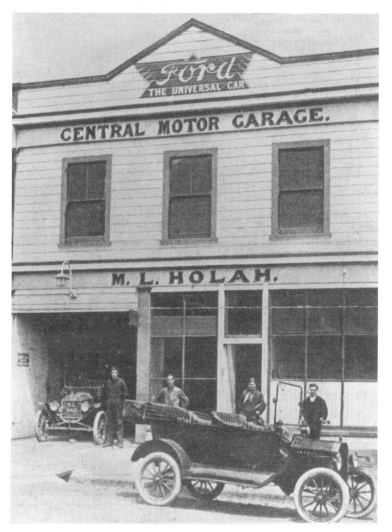

Resourcefulness was the order of the day when, in 1919, Harry Derby needed to get two Model T tourers, and two of the newly released 1 ton Model T trucks, urgently from Wellington to meet an order. Rail or boat was not possible in the time so Harry and son accepted a lift to Wellington with a customer who was going that way. When the Derbys arrived in Wellington, they built a temporary platform out of Ford packing cases on the truck chassis, and mounted the touring cars on top. They then set out for New Plymouth and, after an uneventful journey of 250 miles, the two touring cars and truck chassis were handed over in first class order to the new owners.

The Derbys had property in Courtenay Street nearby, with the historic building known as the 'Round House' and, next door, the 'Square House'. These buildings had been relocated from the centre of town and were originally the garrison headquarters and officers' mess during the Taranaki War in the 1860s. The Round House was a stylish prefabricated building, shipped from England complete and ready to assemble.

Past occupants of the Round House included the parents of aviatrix Jean Batten, Derby's service manager Frank Senter and his family (later service manager at Selwyn Motors, Palmerston North), and Colin Cliff was born there when his father worked as manager of H Derby & Co. Sadly, these historic houses were demolished before the Second World War to make way for new buildings.

The 1920s saw big developments in motoring, led by the Ford Model T, and thousands were built at the three Colonial Motor Company's assembly plants in Wellington, Auckland and Timaru. As the decade ran out, trading became more and more difficult, and the Depression set in from 1930. By 1935 H Derby and Co was in serious difficulties and CMC purchased its assets late that year.

The dealership traded for a period as Len Nicholls Motors Ltd, but changed when Len Nicholls resigned to join Hale at Rotorua.

Phillipps Motors Ltd was formed in December 1938, with Phil Phillipps appointed as managing director. He had worked for Colonial Motor Company since 1926, mostly in the audit team with H N Scrimshaw, but had been accountant at Lucas Brothers, Blenheim before

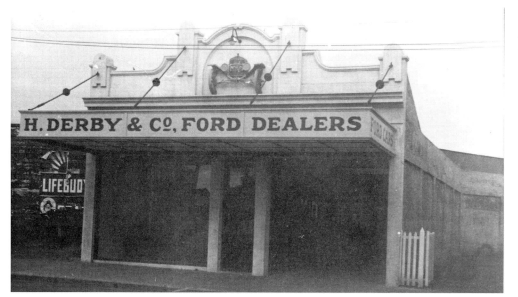

Derby and Co had premises fronting Devon Street in 1920, with a Model T front set into the parapet so that people knew where to find them.

Harry Derby and his son picked up four vehicles in Wellington, two cars and two trucks in 1919. Loading the cars on the truck chassis, using part of their packing cases, they set out on the 250 mile journey, arriving home without incident.

The Round House was a kitset house sent from England about 1850 for the Armed Constabulary to use.

Above: The Square House was built next to the Round House for officers' quarters. Both houses had been shifted there from the central town in the 1920s, and regrettably were demolished before the war.

acting manager and many years ago recalled, to the writer, how difficult it was to manage a business when there were so many restrictions and shortages.

Petrol supply was a nightmare, as rationing coupons were traded on the black market for favours or goods, so people could use their cars. Even if you had the coupons it was a problem, because you weren't supposed to use cars for anything other than 'essential use'. Spare parts were in short supply and often a broken or damaged part had to be repaired or another hand made. Many badly damaged vehicles were cannibalised for parts with nothing thrown away.

By 1946 most of the staff were back from the war, and the company settled down to a steady period of development. This was not without difficulty as New Zealand had to cope with the cost of the war and all the restrictions that remained for the next 50 years. New cars were almost unobtainable, but tractors and trucks were classed as 'economic essential goods' and were more available.

From about 1946 A W (Pic) Pickrang used to work at the dealership as a contract cleaner, always starting very early in the morning and finishing at about 7am. Before anyone arrived he would take a break to read the boss's newspaper carefully before he arrived. He was doing this once, sitting at the boss's desk, when there was a light knock and "Can you tell me where the manager is please?" Pic replied, "He'll be along directly", without looking up. Phil Phillipps replied, "But I *am* the new manager." Despite the

transferring to New Plymouth. Nearly all the staff at the time stayed on, including the service manager Merv Dineen, trim foreman Sam Holden, parts manager Easton Smith, and Colin Cliff and Noel Toomey, both salesmen.

Trading was back to normal by 1938 but this soon changed with the outbreak of the Second World War in 1939. By 1941, many of the staff had enlisted and gone overseas to serve.

During the war, Merv Dineen became

confusion, they became lifelong friends, and Pic joined the company in a full time capacity soon afterwards, working on tractor servicing, and later as parts assistant.

The company set about developing and expanding under Phil Phillipps, but it was a long and tedious business getting sufficient space. As opportunities arose properties were bought, including two adjoining ones in Devon Street, which increased the frontage from 31ft to nearly 70ft. Phillipps Motors then occupied a large property extending right through to Courtenay Street at the rear where used cars and petrol were sold, with the workshops, parts and offices housed between.

In 1946, Noel Toomey went to Ford as tractor manager, and Ford gave the tractor franchise back to dealers, following a lack of marketing success. In 1937 they had taken away the franchise for tractors from dealers and given it to Booth McDonald and Co, and later to Gough, Gough and Hamer. The new E27N Fordson tractors arrived, and they sold very well to farmers who were developing properties using new techniques. Tractor sales expanded and became a major part of the company's business.

With the availability of tractors and trucks, it was obvious a much larger area was required if operations were to be successful. It was decided that the area bounded by Courtenay, Gover and Leach Streets would offer far better long-term prospects, and yet remain close to the city centre. There were many properties to buy.

The nine residential properties took a very extended period of time to acquire and the process was also complicated. A number of families were re-housed. There were also public buildings. A new site

nearer Devon Street was purchased and exchanged for the Women's Rest Rooms.

The New Plymouth City Band, who built their own premises in 1918, were shifted to a new building, and their original foundation stone presented back to them.

Colin Cliff was now sales manager and helping Phil Phillipps with the negotiations, which were long, often tedious and required strength of purpose to see them to a conclusion. Both did amazing work in achieving the satisfactory outcome. Persistence paid off, and 25 years later the land was all obtained, and the company consolidated on one site with boundaries on Courtenay, Gover and Leach Streets.

While all the land acquisitions were proceeding, the pressure was on for space to work in. In 1956, a new 3,500 sq ft workshop and parts department was built in Courtenay Street, and used for truck and tractor sales and service. This was to be the hub of the new development, and was one of the first 'standard' workshop buildings designed for CMC by structural engineer Martyn Spencer.

In case more land was needed for tractors and trucks, 4.5 hectares of newly zoned industrial land was purchased in 1955, at Brown's Road, 10km away at Bell Block.

New Plymouth's industrial expansion was fuelled by the petroleum industry nearby, and both trucks and tractors were a major part of the post-war success of Phillipps Motors. There were 70 staff working there in 1960, and the company could boast full back-up for all facets of motoring with motor trimming, electrical, marine, panel beating and re-conditioning, as well as a petrol station, two service workshops, mobile tractor servicing, a parts

Above: The staff held a family picnic in 1939 before enlisted people went away to war.

Opposite bottom: Phillipps Motors Ltd opened in December 1938, and the whole staff had their photo taken that day. From the left standing: Ian Burke, Jack Holmes, Jack Fenton, Arthur MacKinder, Easton Smith, Colin Derby, Jack Anslow, George Anderson, Laurie Macleod, Colin Cliff, Keith Wighton, Athol Scott, Dick Doughty, Eric Harrison, Lov Hoffman, Jack Broun, Leo Morris, Rupe Kaspar, Norm James, Ern Cubbins, Sam Holden, Ian Okey, Bernie Johnson, Keith Oliver, Tom Hopkins, Cyril Nation. From left, sitting: Jack Right, Lorna Hamilton, Jean Cliff, Bill Toomey, Norm Issacs, Phil Phillipps, Pat Neid, Merv Dineen, Norma Bell, F Appleyard, F Blundel.

Jack Holmes leaning on the front-end loader frame, mounted to a contractor's E27N Fordson. The tractor with dual rear wheels was one of the first diesel engined models, and has mounted discs on the rear. The first loaders were cable operated, and had a removable bucket.

Phillipps Motors rugby team of 1958 challenged and beat Merewether Motors at Wanganui for the 'Ranfordly Shield' of doubtful origin. The exact score is in doubt, but it was a memorable day. Back row left: Ian Sifleet, Alun Evans, Peter Vivier, Henry Green, Bill Jones, David Mayhead, Peter Brennan and Colin Cliff manager. Front row left: Phil Mayhead, Roger Beggs, Trevor Keightly, Debs Copeland, Peter Riley, Tony Powell, Danny Hale, and John Duggan. A women's netball team and a golf team also competed. Herby Dyke took over Merewether Motors in 1963, renaming it Wanganui Motors, and continued the annual challenge, but insisted on playing for a silver cup he donated, instead of the dubious shield.

A 25 years gold watch was an event to celebrate, and Jack Holmes was toasted by members of the Omega club in 1963. Left to right: Easton Smith, parts manager; Merv Dineen, managing director Craik Motors, Phil Phillipps, managing director; Jack Holmes, tractor salesman; Denis Dyer, accountant; Sam Holden, trim foreman; Colin Cliff managing director New Lynn Motors.

department, and a parts and accessories shop in Devon Street.

The success of the company, as always, was largely due to the drive of dedicated staff, many starting their working lives there. Colin Cliff had started sweeping the floor of the lube bay in the early 1930s, and by 1960, was sales and operations manager to managing director Phil Phillipps. There was strong back-up from Denis Dyer, accountant, Easton Smith, parts manager, Sam Holden, trim manager, Gus Craig, service manager, and Royce Cox in sales.

In 1962 Colin Cliff was transferred to Auckland to start up New Lynn Motors Ltd at West Auckland, and Royce Cox became sales manager. Later in 1967 Royce Cox was promoted to assistant manager, when both Denis Dyer and Easton Smith retired. Roy Wellington was transferred from Masterton to be accountant, Trevor Keightley was promoted to parts manager, and Murray Fisher became sales manager.

Gus Craig trained a large number of apprentice mechanics over the years, many winning awards for the high standards they achieved, and he was appointed to the local apprenticeship committee.

Phil Phillipps retired in 1968, after 43 years service to the CMC Group including 31 as dealer principal at Phillipps Motors. He had seen the company develop after the war and been instrumental in getting the land for redevelopment. Royce Cox was made general manager in 1968, and set about further development.

The first task was the re-development

Staff met in 1965 as part of a Ford 'Silver Shoes' programme, aimed at looking after customers.

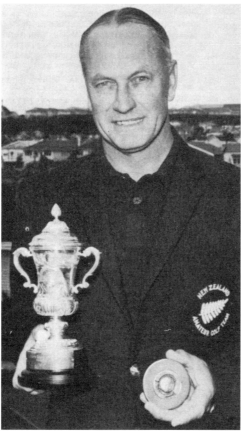

of the showroom on Devon Street, utilising the full width of the frontage. Another innovation was the removal of glass windows so that all the cars were on display 24 hours a day. The effect was dramatic and gave a much larger presence to the company as people could walk in at footpath level. Joe Holden, the newly appointed used car manager, found the new large display helped sales immensely. The parts department and petrol pumps were transferred beside the new workshop area in Courtenay Street, together with the main office.

Gradually over the next five years, as space became available, the full redevelopment of the dealership took place on the Courtenay, Leach and Gover Streets site. Another large section was added to the workshop, increasing it to 20 bays. Then a new two-storey building was added, housing the parts department and service reception areas on the ground floor, and the administration offices above. The buildings now extended along the boundary from Courtenay to Leach Streets, with a large display area on Gover Street.

Finally, the new vehicle showroom was

Top: The Courtenay, Gover and Leach Streets block partly re-developed about 1963. The truck and tractor workshop at back was built in 1958. Used cars are displayed on the lower right corner, and used trucks further left, beside the valet building.

Middle: The new workshop was built between the truck workshop and the new parts and admnistration building.

Below: The new showroom completed the re-development of Phillipps Motors.

Royce Cox became general manager and saw the building programme to a conclusion. He is seen here with his wife, Audrey.

Royce Cox and John Blyth, accountant, looking at results in 1969.

commissioned at the end of 1974. Martyn Spencer designed this unique building, using new construction techniques. It had a five part pre-fabricated roof, 5 x 20 metre sections with timber frames mounted on a steel truss, and structural plywood glued both sides, which was then hoisted and fixed together on top of columns. The roof was covered with a membrane and then glass walls added, to give a spectacular showroom, with 360 degrees visibility. Open display for 75 used cars surrounds the central showroom. The dream of Phil Phillipps and Colin Cliff had finally come true.

Managing director Royce Cox recalls his amazement at how business kept flowing during the difficult construction time: "I don't know how we managed to keep selling motorcars; even cleaning cars for delivery was a problem, by the time they were due to leave they were covered in clay dust again. But our clients seemed to understand that we were working under difficult circumstances, and I think the staff attitude, and the fact that we kept our efficiency up to a high standard, impressed them."

Royce Cox said the layout of the dealership was well designed and would last for years: "The plans are fantastic, and even after a settling in period, there is nothing we would alter now. The amount of planning has finally paid off. The site is big enough and has all the facilities that we envisage we will need in the foreseeable future in the central business district." The company also operated a separate truck and tractor sales division with panel shop and workshop at Waiwakaiho, five kilometres away in the heart of the industrial area.

In 1975, 72 staff were employed and Royce Cox said: "Like all CMC Group companies, we have a hard core of loyal people who make up the company and are responsible for its success." Seven of the staff had 25 year gold watches and Sam Holden had been there 40 years. Royce Cox also noted that nine managers of other CMC Group companies had received part of their training experience at Phillipps Motors.

The Devon Street property, that had served the Ford name so well since 1919, was sold.

John Blyth transferred from Macaulay Motors to be accountant in February 1975, with the idea that he would also get experience in selling used cars. In 1978 Robin Astridge, who was in sales, changed jobs with John Blyth. He had previously been accountant at Ruahine Motors, before trying a sales position. Trevor Keightly was parts manager, Neville Goldsworthy sales manager, and Richard Eagles service manager.

Royce Cox retired in 1984. Having started in the lubrication bay from school, he worked his way up through sales to become managing director, and oversee the shift and consolidation of the company to its new home. New Plymouth had now developed into the petrochemical centre of New Zealand which, combined with the province's rich dairy industry, gave it a

The Omega club had grown in 1975. From left: Barry Clarke, Phil Phillipps (retired), Pick Pickrang, Gus Craig, Royce Cox. Kneeling: Sam Holden, Ted Pentecost and Ray Gunson.

strong economic base for development. Fuel shortages in 1973 and again in 1978 had boosted alternative fuels, which were all nearby, including the world's first 'Gas to Gasoline' plant at Motunui.

Peter J Lloyd was appointed manager of Phillipps Motors, and shifted from managing Fairhall Motors, Kaikohe. The economy was rocked by the government policy changes in 1985, but while farming was set back, petrochemicals continued strongly.

Not long after he had been appointed manager, Peter Lloyd was diagnosed with invasive bone cancer and, after a protracted period of unsuccessful treatment, tragically died at 32, leaving his wife and young family.

Russell J Lange was appointed dealer principal on April 1 1987. Previously general sales manager at Christchurch, he imparted many new ideas on sales presentation and standards. The appointment was only for 18 months, and Russell Lange transferred back to be manager of Team Hutchinson Ford.

Grant Daniel was appointed manager of Phillipps Motors on January 1 1989. It was his second appointment as dealer principal, having managed Fairhall Motors, Kaikohe, for three years from 1984 before returning to Christchurch as general sales manager in 1987.

New Plymouth was still feeling the effects of the government policy changes, which included cutting of government services. Ford's move out of tractors worldwide and truck dealer rationalisation was also affecting sales. Both tractors and trucks had been a very large part of Phillipps Motors' business. The Waiwakaio tractor and truck depot was sold. The St Aubyn Street used cars site was sold and all operations were consolidated at the city site.

Dealer principal Jim Gibbons with his 1996 Energy City Ford management team. From left: Jim Gibbons, John Zittersteijn, Russell Dempster, Stuart Dempster and Richard Eagles.

Staff photo taken in 1986. Peter Lloyd, dealer principal, was away unwell. Front left sitting: Kerry Bridle, Catherine Orr, Jan Martin, Robin Astridge, Richard Eagles, Dave Patten, Trevor Keightly, Ian Berryman, Michelle Rouse, Bev Shotter, and Liz Moyle. Centre left: Gary Bevin, Ted Macolm, Ray Gunson, Stephen Nicholas, Terry Kidd, Ernie Heath, Allan Bonniface, Steve Sutton, not known, Keith Morris, John Rutherford, Phil Mayhead, and Danny Hale. Back left: Wiremu Ruakere, Alan McKay, Brent Bonniface, Stuart Gibbons, Craig Hellier, Kevin Mowat, John Taylor, Paul Maxwell, Andrew Adlam, Alan Krutz, Paul Hanover, Rodney Scouller, Greg Morcock, Ray Hill, Matthew Nield, Alan Sinton, John Wray, Bob McDonald, Greg James, and Grant Downer.

Grant Daniel was appointed manager of Colonial Motor Company in 1992 and shifted to Wellington.

James Picot (Jim) Gibbons became dealer principal in September 1992. Great grandson of Hope Gibbons, he transferred from Ruahine Motors, Waipukurau, where he had been manager for 3 1/2 years. He had worked in the CMC Group since 1973.

In 1993, Phillipps Motors Ltd changed its name to Energy City Ford, reflecting the city's heritage as the petrochemical centre of New Zealand.

With the tractor and heavy truck divisions gone, the company now settled down to marketing new and used cars, and light commercial vehicles. After a period of consolidation, the company is now going ahead with record sale volumes.

Jim Gibbons says: "A successful dealership is one that can strike a balance between the demands of the franchiser to sell more cars at any cost, and the need to be profitable for the shareholders. Energy City Ford does this through its capable staff and staying in contact with its customers."

CHAPTER TWENTY
WAIPUKURAU –
RUAHINE MOTORS LTD

Waipukurau is situated on the edge of the Tuki Tuki River which runs from the foothills of the Ruahine Ranges through the fertile Takapau (Ruataniwha) plains of central Hawke's Bay, and joins the Waipawa River. The settlement was originally a Maori village of the same name, Waipukurau, meaning "a kind of fungus (mushrooms) by the water". A bustling farming town of some 4,000 people, 'Waipuk' was established by station owner H R Russell in 1860, on part of the government land bought by Sir Donald McLean from Te Hapuku on November 4 1851.

Seven kilometres away is Waipawa, a much smaller town of 1,500, established at the same time by another station owner, F S Abbott, and originally known as Abbottsford.

When large stock saleyards were mooted about 1900, Waipawa people did not want them in their town so they were sited beside the railway at Waipukurau. With the large numbers of animals traded, the stock companies and banks expanded in Waipukurau, attracting further commercial development to the town.

Sheep and cattle grazing has always been the main industry, many farmers breeding stock from long established pedigree lines.

A large number of the original central Hawke's Bay sheep and cattle grazing operations of the 1800s, or stations as some are known, were substantial, covering thousands of hectares, and employing large numbers of staff. Over the next 100 years, many of the very large blocks were broken up and split among families, or sold off, with a subsequent drop in labour numbers. However, most central Hawke's Bay farms were still quite sizable compared to the national average.

As well as the predominant farming activity of sheep and cattle grazing, there are meat freezing and packing industries, lime and bentonite quarrying, and farm support industries. Waipukurau's shops attract one of the highest spends per capita in New Zealand. Certainly they have many discerning customers.

Motorcars first appeared early in the 20th century, sold mainly from Hastings and Napier, as many of the large station owners were able to afford vehicles and became keen motorists. A S G Carlyon of Gwavas Station had the first Daimler in New Zealand in 1902, but sold this, at the suggestion of his chauffeur Ernie Waite, for a Darracq 15, and then a 30-40hp Darracq capable of cruising at 50mph in 1906. Carlyon aspired to a Rolls Royce, but the company would not send one to New Zealand because of the rough roads. Undeterred, he went to England, bought a chassis in the Midlands, had a body fitted in London and shipped it home. The 40-50hp laid quite a column of dust at 80mph, a speed not seen on New Zealand roads before. Roads in the area were easier and better than in many places due to the shingle foundations on the expansive plains.

In the 1920s, J L Braithwaite established the Ford agency at Waipukurau, where Ruahine Motors stands today. The main building built by Braithwaite in 1922 was of reinforced concrete, with a rear workshop portion added in 1930. F R Furminger had a sub-agency to Braithwaite at Waipawa.

On September 30 1938, after a protracted financial struggle through the 'Great Depression', J L Braithwaite Ltd went into receivership. The receiver held an auction and Colonial Motor Company, the only bidder, took over the business. Basil Orsborn was sent in from head office to establish the new company and the CMC accounting system and stayed for two years before going to Te Kuiti Motors as manager in 1940. F M Cordery was appointed manager and the new company named Cordery Garage Ltd.

Because of the war, the company virtually stood still from the beginning, and had only a handful of workshop staff. In 1942, a branch called Waipawa Motors was formed, mainly as a service depot, taking

In 1965 Cordery Garage had a butcher's shop and saddler next door on the right.

over F R Furminger. Jim Haworth sold off this business in 1954.

L E (Toby) Dodd was appointed manager on the retirement of F M Cordery in 1942 and became active selling tractors and trucks. Cars were scarce when the wool boom of 1951 arrived, and there was tremendous pressure on dealers to supply cars to newly cash-rich farmers, with the position acute in central Hawke's Bay with its high numbers of wool graziers. The No Remittance Scheme was just starting, and few had the required overseas funds necessary to purchase a new car. The pressure on Toby Dodd was too much and he resigned in August 1951.

Soon afterwards, Colonial Motor Company circularised all their dealers with specific policy guidelines regarding the sale of new cars, and the practices to be observed.

J R (Jim) Haworth became manager in 1952. He had started with CMC Group in 1929, and had been accountant at Macaulay Motors when it began in 1936. After serving in the RNZAF in the war, he was accountant at Timaru Motors from 1946.

In 1951 the next-door property of saddler Alex Blom was bought, together with the butcher and fishmonger. In those days the dealership building fronting the main Ruataniwha Street was the full width of the property, and workshop access was from Russell Street at the rear. The three properties were purchased for vehicle display and access to the workshop.

When Jim Haworth resigned to join an accountancy practice in 1956, G H (Don) Gibbons transferred from Kaikohe and set to work to modernise the premises. The

parts department had a mezzanine floor added for bulk storage and new offices were built within the existing building. Two old houses adjoining the rear of the premises were bought, providing the company with a one acre rectangular block of land. One of the houses was demolished and the other let, long term, to the Waipukurau Bridge Club. Today the Bridge Club has shifted and the house has been removed.

The company also owned six houses in Waipawa and Waipukurau, which were let to staff. Accountants were often sent for a three to four year training period, as the small size of the operation made it possible to see everything happening in the business. Colin Lee was the first in 1950, followed by Max Caigou in 1954; Barry Wisneski in 1956; Geoff Atkins in 1958; Beville Johnston in 1961; Jim Syme in 1964; and Robin Astridge in 1966. After 1971 it was decided to seek a local person who could provide continuity for the trainee managers, but this did not always happen.

In 1967 the old shops were demolished and new areas for vehicle display were set up beside the main street. Large modern sliding doors were added to the front corner of the showroom beside the outside display area, giving pedestrian access, opening up the business and letting much more light into the showroom and offices. The rear area was kerbed and channelled, providing car parks and a sealed driveway through to Russell Street. New grass was sown on the levelled area beside this and a new fence built beside the Bridge Club. The whole yard to the side and rear of the building was paved in hotmix, and the building painted. The transformation was

Top: Cordery Garage became Ruahine Motors in 1968 after the butcher's and saddler's shops were bought and demolished to give display space and access to the workshop. Windows and access doors were fitted to the showroom wall, allowing much more light to enter the building, and planters were incorporated into the display area.

Middle: The workshop had been very dark, so paint and signage lifted everyone's spirits.

Below: The added space visually opened up the business to the public, from the 'hemmed in' Cordery days, giving it an instant street appeal.

Customer Jack Stoddart and his son operated two D Series spreader trucks which were converted to 4WD.

remarkable and the business looked very smart and up to date.

Don Gibbons had indifferent health and was medically advised to retire from day to day operations, so while the renovation was under way, David Bodley arrived in April 1968 to take over, starting a chain of trainee dealer principals. Although Don Gibbons was a director, and later chairman, of Colonial Motor Company, he continued to live in Waipukurau for many years.

The name of the company was no longer applicable, and the new geographically apt name of Ruahine Motors Limited was chosen and approved in August 1969, reflecting as it did the ranges to the west of the dealership. The new Ford corporate 'blue band' signwriting completed an outstanding makeover.

The old workshop was modernised and a 'Diagnosis Centre' added to make it the

smartest in Hawke's Bay. A new 'smoko' room was built in the corner of the workshop. Under its concrete floor are buried many obsolete early model Ford parts, cleared from the parts shelves. To obtain a write-off and retrieve sales tax, parts had to be 'destroyed'. To satisfy Inland Revenue, burying them under the concrete floor meant they were effectively 'destroyed.'

Customers approved of the new image and found it very conducive to drop into the revamped premises. Staff members were delighted with all the sprucing up, and set to work with vigour. The company had always enjoyed a following of loyal customers who preferred to support local businesses, and this gave a solid nucleus to the dealership which performed well. This all happened as the market shifted, and the supply and sales of new cars expanded.

In 1968, when Alda Anderson broke the CMC record, by balancing her debtors' ledger first time for 14 consecutive months, manager David Bodley, with accountant Robin Astridge watching, presented her with a cheque.

In 1969, when David Bodley transferred to Te Awamutu as manager, Roger Gardner shifted from sales manager at Te Awamutu to be Ruahine Motors' manager.

In the 1960s farming subsidies created new opportunities. One of Ruahine Motors' customers, Jack Stoddart, used old 4x4 army trucks to spread fertilser. With the lift in business he purchased a new D750 truck in 1966, with fertiliser bin and 4WD front axle added by Moore and Heaven from Wellsford. The truck worked so well that when his son, Ron, started work he bought another, and they were seen all over central Hawke's Bay spreading fertiliser. With subsidies, many rough and remote farms were cleared and sown in new pastures and, with the use of fertilisers and new farming methods, farm productivity increased dramatically.

The large numbers of sheep bred in the area could not be handled in a one day sale, and subsequent huge sales occurred every week for up to six weeks. The annual January breeding ewe fairs were something of a legend from the 1950s through to the early 1970s, with over 100,000 two-tooth ewes regularly sold at auction in one day at Waipukurau. The rise in popularity of sheep following the wool boom in 1951, and the later government subsidies, created huge demand, with buyers from all over New Zealand attending.

The logistics of transporting and cataloguing these sales were immense, many stock starting their journey the day before. Often, up to 50 stock transporter trucks at a time would be backed up, waiting for space to unload. On the fall of the hammer, stock would start the journey to their new owners, sometimes taking two days to arrive.

The cattle sales were later each year, and although stock numbers sold were not as large, the amount of money exchanged was, with buyers coming from all over New Zealand.

Smaller farmers were often one-man operations, and tried to counter price drops with increased efficiency. But it was still necessary to make hay and plant crops, so agricultural contractors found a steadily increasing demand for their services.

Motorbikes caused a small farming revolution following the oil crisis of 1973, and were quickly adopted as the best method of getting around stock. Far faster than Land Rovers and tractors, they used a fraction of the fuel. Working dogs found it hard to keep up, and often hitched a pillion ride!

In early 1974, Roger Gardner was transferred to Fagan Motors, Masterton, and Brian Willis came from Lower Hutt to take over for several months, before shifting to Te Kuiti as manager. In August

Top left: Roger Gardner became manager in November 1969.

Above right: J W (Jim) Oliver was presented with his 25 year gold watch by Peter C Gibbons.

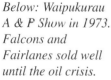

Below: Waipukurau A & P Show in 1973. Falcons and Fairlanes sold well until the oil crisis.

1974, Ken Mullan arrived from Timaru to be manager. He had worked at many CMC Group companies around New Zealand, firstly on the accounting side and for nearly 10 years in sales.

Meanwhile, as fuel costs rose Ford was well placed with the Cortina and Escort cars which saved the day when the government introduced differential tax on cars in 1975 and Falcon sales, traditionally about 60%, fell to 15% overnight.

In June 1975 Stan Watson married Alma Jolly, the Waipawa chemist, and joined Ruahine Motors as sales manager, having been sales manager of Auckland Motor Company. Born in Wellington, he started as a motor apprentice, later moving to sales before shifting to Auckland, but he found the transition tricky: "I remember the first month we only sold one used car, and being used to selling about 30 a month in Auckland, this worried me until I got the scale of things.

" We were flooded with new cars then; there were huge shipments of new Falcons arriving – I think 23 arrived in one week –

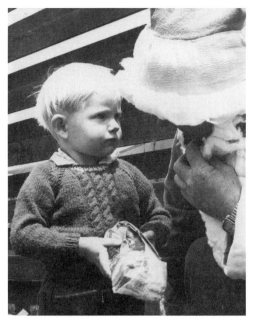

which made it hard going. We steadily got through them though, and were soon looking for more."

In 1975 Terry Boswell transferred from Fagan Motors to be accountant, after a succession of accountants had only stayed for a short while.

At this time, there was a very real threat that fuel might be rationed, so when natural gas became available in Hawke's Bay many vehicles were converted to use Compressed Natural Gas (CNG) fuel. CNG conversion was never as effective with smaller engines as Liquid Petroleum Gas (LPG), a much better and cleaner fuel. In 1979, with the second 'oil shock', government regulated 'carless days' allowing petrol engine vehicles to operate only six days each week. This further stimulated gas conversions.

In 1982 Terry Boswell shifted to Avery Motors and Stan Watson became administration manager, as well as handling the accounting and selling vehicles. At the same time Buster Gay joined the sales force, using his very good local knowledge and sales experience to advantage.

In April 1984, Ken Mullan transferred to Hawke Motors, Morrinsville and John Blyth was appointed manager. Starting with CMC Group at Invercargill in 1966, he later shifted to New Plymouth, and came from Timaru Motors where he had been sales manager.

When the new Labour government swept into power in 1984, with its new 'market force' policies, one of the first affected areas was farming. The removal of subsidies changed the industry overnight and farmers immediately shed labour and costs, in an attempt to control their budgets. From a farming perspective, bank managers became fearsome people with the ability to control your future and, if your balance sheet looked bad, sell you up. Central Hawke's Bay suffered less than many areas, but the effects on service industries were severe, and many were cut back or wound up.

Although Ruahine Motors managed to get through the downturn well, many of the other franchise dealers, branches of Hastings or Napier businesses, were closed to protect their main offices. This

Kanui Station collected a new DT 2418 truck and a new Ford County tractor on the same day in 1982.

The staff farewelled Ken Mullan in 1985. From left standing: Tom Bell, Gay Reid, Wayne Ewing, Buster Gay, Robin Ellen, Sandra Arlidge, Stan Watson, Michael Hook, Ken Mullan, John Ferguson, Don Kinnaird, John Ward, plus customer Joe Mita.
In front: Rod Wilson, Norm Hook, and Paul Shanks.

In 1987, Jim Robb, watched by his winning team, received the prize of a trip to Europe with Ford, from zone manager Nigel Harris. From left: Nigel Harris, Ford; Jim Robb, manager; Stan Watson, accountant; Don Kinnaird, service manager; Buster Gay, sales manger; and Wayne Ewing, parts manager.

strengthened Ruahine Motors.

When John Blyth was transferred to Panmure Motors in 1986 after two and a half years, Jim Robb was manager for two years before returning to Auckland as manager of New Lynn Motors. Jim Gibbons, great grandson of Hope Gibbons, who was at Newlands Motors, Johnsonville, took over in February 1989.

The staff at Ruahine Motors has always been customer focussed and when Ford introduced the President's Awards, recognising dealers who had quality customer care, Ruahine Motors was amongst the early dealers to receive recognition. This has continued and the dealership has won many Ford awards for customer service and sales market leadership.

By 1990 economic conditions were becoming extreme in the cities, just as the country areas were starting to recover. However, it was not a good time for rural Ford dealers who firstly lost tractors, and then heavy trucks, as Ford tried to rationalise. Many smaller dealers did not sell large quantities of either, but the mix of tractors, trucks and cars was important to their service and parts business, and did wonders for their bottom line.

Fortunately, the overheads of Ruahine Motors were comparatively low. The Braithwaite buildings of the 1920s were quite sound, but did need maintenance and changes to keep them current. Major changes were made to the offices in the early 1990s. At this point the interior partitions were shifted and rebuilt with the office, parts and service reception becoming one combined area, greatly helping the smaller staff to overlap and job share when business got hectic.

In September 1992 Jim Gibbons transferred to manage Phillipps Motors, New Plymouth. Stan Watson stayed to manage the business until David Tobin shifted from Christchurch, where he had been parts manager, to become dealer

Top: Stan Watson was sales manager in 1975.

Below: Kiwi Host played an important part in 1995, and these staff members all bought into the scheme. From left standing: Dave Tobin, manager; Janine Legarth, Phil Gray, Corry Waihape, Wayne Ewing, Don Kinnaird, and Mike O'Brien. In front: Paul Shanks, Don Carter, Dick Waren, Peter Brown, and Wayne Halligan.

Left: When Ruahine Motors turned 60 in 1998 Nigel Wark, Ford managing director, presented this commemorative plaque for the company to Dave Tobin.

Right: In 1999, Wayne Ewing received his 25 year gold watch from Graeme Gibbons, CMC's CEO.

Below: Michelle Halford completed her apprenticeship in 2000, gaining distinction by being that year's runner-up in the Motor Trade Association 'Apprentice of the Year' awards.

principal in November 1992.

Stan Watson had joined the company in 1975 and, once David Tobin became established, decided to retire. He had been an important mentor for staff and managers over 18 years, able to turn his hand from sales to administration and back again, and providing a cohesive element in the company.

When Don Kinnaird, service manager for 16 years, left, Paul Shanks took over the roll.

In 1998 Wayne Ewing celebrated 25 years service to the company, and was rewarded with his gold Omega watch. At the 60th anniversary dinner of Ruahine Motors, Ford m-d Nigel Wark presented the

company with a special commemorative plaque.

Buster Gay left the sales force for a short period, when he was attracted back to another business. However, this did not last and he was soon back as a contract salesman. In the interim, Ian Large arrived from radio advertising and quickly shifted his sales skills to Ford cars. Jeffery Irving also took over as accountant.

In November 2001 David Tobin died after a long battle with cancer. When he lost all his hair with early treatment, many of the staff had No.1 haircuts, showing him great respect and support.

In February 2002, Roger Taylor transferred from sales manager at Dunedin City Ford to be manager, staying for 12 months, before returning to Dunedin as dealer principal. He took with him Jeffrey Irving, who has become business manager at Dunedin.

Hamish Jacob, who grew up in Ashburton, before moving to Avon City Motors in Christchurch, where he was sales manager, was appointed manager in 2003.

Today, the management team at Ruahine Motors comprises Ian Large, sales manager; Wayne Ewing, parts manager; and Paul Shanks, service manager. Phil Ryan is business manager for both Ruahine and Fagan Motors, and lives in Masterton.

Ruahine Motors has been a very successful dealership, with loyal customers and a dedicated staff, and continues to nurture first time managers who have successfully moved to other Colonial Motor Company dealerships as dealer principals.

Ruahine Motors staff in 2000. From left: Duncan Harding, Hayden LeCompte, Wayne Ewing, Buster Gay, Pam Drylie, Jeffrey Irving, Ian Large, Michelle Halford, Marcus Avery, Dave Tobin, Yvonne Monk, Alan Basher, Gaynor Ramsay, and Paul Donghi.

Below: Ruahine staff raise their glasses to Ford's 100th birthday in 2003. From left: Duncan Harding, Ian Large, Phillip Tidswell, Paddy McCloskey, Michelle Halford, Krystina Fredrics, Paul Donghi, Casey Lancaster, Brad Sturm, Gaynor Ramsay, Amy Campbell, Hayden LeCompte, Wayne Ewing, Marcus Avery, and dealer principal, Hamish Jacob.

Lyttle's garage became a Ford sub-agent to Gordon Hughan, Carterton, in 1915. The premises were in Queen Street, opposite the present swimming complex.

Lyttle and Hughan shared a stand at the A & P Show. From left: J H (Jim) Lyttle; Arthur W Petherick, CMC; Gordon Hughan; and an unidentified customer.

CHAPTER TWENTYONE
WAIRARAPA –
FAGAN MOTORS

Masterton is the commercial centre and principal market town of the Wairarapa region, a farming district with sheep and beef grazing and some dairying. The region is also renowned for high quality wines, olives, apples and other horticultural products. There are an unusual number of schools in the region as well as enterprises as diverse as electronics and fruit packing. There is also wood processing, following large plantings of exotic trees by the NZ Forest Service and others. Limestone is quarried nearby at Gladstone, Weraiti, Tauweru and Mauriceville.

Formerly, Borthwick's large meat freezing works operated from 1909, Donald's wool presses were made in Masterton for over 100 years, Master Industries manufactured white goods, and the Government Printing Office was set up as a regional development initiative. These, plus many light industrial ventures, jointly employed some 1,500 people. All closed down in the 1980-90s, as government policies and priorities changed.

Golden Shears, the world's premier sheep shearing competition, conceived by Federated Farmers' chairman R E (Bob) Chamberlain and committee to improve the quality of shearing, has been held annually since 1961. A shearing museum is now being established in relocated historic woolsheds to commemorate this event and the Wairarapa's place in the history of sheep farming in this country. The first successful commercial aerial topdressing flight took place at Wairere Station, using a converted Grumman Avenger aeroplane in 1947, spawning an industry. The National Wildlife Centre for endangered bird species is nearby to the north, and has successfully reared many endangered breeds.

Masterton was founded in 1854 by Joseph Masters, prime mover in the Small Farms Association which purchased some of the land bought from local Kahungunu Maori by Sir Donald McLean, on behalf of Governor Grey. Access at the time was across the newly formed Rimutaka track, or around the coast from Orongorongo to Ocean Beach and thence to Featherston. A track had been started across the Rimutaka Range in 1846 and by 1853 was open for wheeled vehicles. Today the main road follows this same route. The first settlers arrived in 1854 and 1855, many walking across the Rimutakas, then up the valley, a four day journey.

Greytown, in the middle of the valley, was established by the Small Farms Association a few weeks before Masterton. Featherston and Carterton developed around convenient coaching stops. Martinborough was established later in the 1870s; a sleepy, rural servicing town for decades, it has grown spectacularly since the first vineyards began producing their quality wines in the 1970s.

By 1866 a travel service operated between Masterton and Wellington, using coaches manufactured by William Black in Courtenay Place. In 1873 the town was declared a borough. The railway opened between Masterton and Wellington in 1880, using a unique Fell cog drive locomotive section across the Rimutaka Incline. This existed until a tunnel of 6.2 kilometres was driven through the range in 1955. Five commuter trains now operate daily during the week, to and from Wellington.

The first motorcars appeared early in the 20th century, using the coach roads from Wellington to Hawke's Bay. By 1907 there was a Ford dealer, Gordon Hughan, in Carterton. In 1914, sub-branches of Gordon Hughan had been formed – at Martinborough by Evans & Woodley, who traded on for a few years; and by T Wrigley in Masterton for a short time. A year later in Masterton, J H (Jim) Lyttle started the Ford garage situated in Queen Street North, near where the Horseshoe Bar is today. His brother, Ted, joined him after serving overseas in the war. Ted Lyttle's son, Graeme, later worked for Fagan Motors as business manager.

In June 1919, Gordon Hughan's Carterton premises burnt down one night with the disastrous loss of his blacksmith

Top: F R Bridges' premises in mid-1931, in Queen Street south, next to Anstice's bakery (where Tranzit Buses are today). From left: B Lock, F R Bridges, Jimmy Anderson, G Hood, J Kiddle, Nancy McEwen, and C Wakelin.

Bottom: In November 1933, Fagan Motors took over Foreman's stables on the corner of Dixon and Bannister Streets, converting them to "magnificent new premises". In 1938, Ingley and Morris' service station and workshop next door in Dixon Street was taken over, staff and equipment included.

shop, cycle shop and garage, all the plant, records, and 33 cars. The garage was rebuilt, but when the business was under pressure in 1922 brothers H B and R B Gibbons, of Colonial Motor Company, stepped in to help Gordon Hughan, taking a shareholding in the newly formed limited liability company. The 'Masterton Ford Motors' agency was changed to McDonald, when Lyttle's moved to Chapel Street and took on the Maxwell agency, in the new Daniell's building, behind today's district library. McDonald was not successful and in 1927 the dealership sold to F R Bridges, a former sales manager at Ford Sales and Service, Wellington. The company was then at 292 Queen Street, renting premises from Anstice's bakery where Tranzit Coachlines are today.

The Depression caused havoc for undercapitalized F R Bridges, and the bank appointed Patrick Feltham Fagan as receiver, on Armistice Day, November 11 1931. Colonial Motor Company bought the business from the receiver early in 1932, when it was reformed and registered as Fagan Motors Ltd. Pat Fagan was appointed manager, having moved from John W Andrews, Auckland, where he was used car manager.

Times were very tough at the end of 1931. While there were only six on the staff, no-one was laid off. Staff worked 44 hours a week, including Saturday morning, and the manager attended all after-hours calls. Standard pay rate for a mechanic was 1s 3d per hour (£2 15s 0d per week). Trading had started to improve when, in June 1932, school leaver T B (Dick) Eliot, was hired as a helper in the workshop at 10s per week; he stayed for 44 years, later becoming sales manager. He remembered: "We even traded in a horse and cart on a used car. One of the salesmen had already arranged a sale for the horse, and we sold the cart at the next week's cattle sale, at a profit of course."

When business improved and larger premises were needed the lease on Foreman's Stables at the corner of Bannister and Dixon Streets was taken over. After a considerable make-over, with truckloads of old harness, gigs, chaff, straw and other horse age 'rubbish' consigned to the dump, "the magnificent new premises" were opened in November 1933. Here, with 10,000 sq ft, and the new Ford V8 available, business progressed rapidly to the point where additional premises on the corner of Chapel and Perry Streets were leased to sell used vehicles.

Outside the workshop at 'smoko' time in 1941. From left, standing around the Model A workshop car: Norm Norris, Dick Eliot, Jack Leete, Pat Hancock, Alan Henderson. In front: not known, John Morris, Doug Ranston, Roy Price, Trevor Jones, Les Wales, and Cyril Smith. The workshop was reputed to be like the South Pole in winter despite the waste oil heater.

In 1936 the old company with its £1,000 capital was wound up, and a new Fagan Motors Ltd was incorporated with £12,000 capital. Business expanded and there were soon 34 on the staff.

The leased premises were purchased in 1938, and a month later an offer was made, and accepted, to purchase as a going concern, the next-door service station of Ingley and Morris Ltd. The building was new and ideally suited to Fagan's, and a purpose built workshop of 10,000 sq ft, complete with trained staff, meant the whole business could be reorganized and greater services made available to customers straight away. Brothers John and Roy Morris continued to work at Fagan Motors until retiring in the 1970s.

At the outbreak of the Second World War in 1939, many staff members joined up to serve their country. War seriously disrupted all business and Fagan's had to make do as best it could. The severe Wairarapa earthquake in 1942 caused much structural damage to the building, and Fagan Motors was one of the first to repair and reinforce its buildings to new earthquake standards.

After the war, most of the staff returned, and business resumed and continued to develop as farming expanded. New assisted immigrants arrived in New Zealand and Fagan's found jobs for two of them, George Elrick from Scotland, and David Laban from London.

Many returning war servicemen took up balloted rehabilitation farms in the back-blocks of Wairarapa. Much of the Wairarapa was still covered with manuka scrub and, with the return of the Fordson franchise to Ford dealers in 1946, many tractors were sold fitted with wide steel spade lugged wheels, and a front crushing bar for clearing scrub. They literally pushed the scrub over, much of it 3-4 metres high, and crushed it under the steel wheels. After a drying out period, the scrub was then burnt and grass sown for pasture. Thousands of acres were 'broken in' in this way, with hundreds of tractors sold to make their contribution to the process. In 1947, Len Daniell pioneered commercial aerial topdressing at Wairere Station, and proved its practicality for developing pasture on hill country farms.

It became clear farming was going ahead, and Colonial Motor Company looked at likely future expansion needs. Fagan Motors purchased a property in Dixon Street in 1951, and a modern workshop with display space beside it was erected to handle tractors and equipment. Bill Grieg joined the company then as a tractor salesman and in the next 25 years sold over 500 of them. Early Fordson County tractors, firstly crawlers, and then with 4 wheel drive, were fitted with steel wheels and often a bull blade and, with their greater traction and weight, found a natural application in Wairarapa hill country, doing far more than the smaller Fordsons.

Over the next few years, properties adjoining the tractor workshop in Dixon Street were bought up as they became available. The principal property, a substantial two-storey house belonging to Dr Palmer,

A tractor field day in 1947 with an E27N tractor. While Dick Eliot refuels, farmers study the mole plough behind.

was built in 1879 by James Macara who drove between Wellington and Masterton in 1867, using coaches built by William Black at Courtenay Place, Wellington. The enterprising Macara later bought the coach run and operated the Sample Rooms across the road in William Street, backing onto his stables on the corner of Bannister and Dixon Streets. Today the stables are gone, William Street no longer exists, being built over by The Warehouse, and the Sample Rooms have been relocated to Wrigley Street. Properties at the rear of Fagan Motors, adjoining Hessey Street, and a carrier's yard with a lane, were also purchased.

Today Fagan Motors occupies about two hectares with access to both Dixon and Hessey Streets. Some of James Macara's original plantings remain, the mature trees and gardens adding to the ambience of the dealership. A new workshop of 10,000 sq ft, with part mezzanine floor, was constructed in 1964. The steel portalled building, with a special hard-surfaced concrete floor, has north opening doors under a canopy for quick service. The many roof and wall light panels create well-lit working areas, sheltered from the cold southerlies but with flexible ventilation in the summer. Illuminated pit sub-floors and a large drive-over lubrication and inspection pit were very much 'best practice' in 1965.

Martyn Spencer designed a number of similar style workshops for other CMC Group companies around New Zealand. Many have been adapted to meet current needs, but all have stood the test of time, proving their sound original design. The pit sub-floors have been filled and replaced by two pole hoists – today's best practice.

A former maternity home on the property was given a facelift and shifted beside the new workshop, becoming the parts merchandising building, with staff cafeteria, and PABX exchange. Today it houses heavy truck parts.

In 1965 the dealership staff of 37 shifted from Bannister Street across the road to the new Dixon Street site. The offices were situated in James Macara's former house with a used vehicle display extending from the house to the tractor workshop further along the street.

In 1964, when Ford introduced its new tractor with Select-O-Speed transmission that had to be re-worked, Fagan Motors lost thousands in warranty costs, but even more in reputation. Fortunately the manual gearbox model was reliable.

After 40 years working for CMC Group, 35 of them managing Fagan Motors, Pat Fagan retired. He had seen the company, after a shaky start, firmly established and now relocated into a central site with space to park trucks, tractors and cars. His replacement, Randal Thomson, was a local man who had joined Colonial Motor Company audit team in 1954 and worked

at Wellington, Timaru, Te Kuiti and Otahuhu.

Randal Thomson encouraged selling of No Remittance cars to supplement the sparse allocation of new cars available, and was able to show the sales team the latest methods from Auckland. It was clear that the industrial and commercial side of the business was increasing with the expansion of Masterton, and a 10 acre block of industrial land on the main south road at Waingawa, adjacent to Borthwick's freezing works and Masterton stock saleyards, was bought for future development.

In the late 1960s and early 1970s, governments were encouraging industry to decentralise to the provinces, with regional suspensory loans and development grants. The Government Printing Office shifted some of its operations from Wellington, and the NZ Land Tax office was established in Masterton. Several high-tech industries started, making buttons from milk powder, plastics, and pre and post-stressed concrete products, and a cigarette factory was opened. Masterton was expected to reach city status.

All the industrial changes brought more work for Fagan Motors with diversified tractor applications at their peak. The rear mounted diggers fitted to the new Ford

Dr Palmers's house, bought in 1960, served as an office for several years. It was built in 1879 by James Macara, owner of the coach run and Sample Rooms, and many trees planted by him have survived. The house was subsequently sold and relocated to Colombo Road.

In 1965 a new 10,000 sq ft workshop was built. It is still in use today, although the pits have been filled in and two-pole hoists are used.

The staff outside the new workshop offices in November 1965. Back left: Roger Fairbrother, Russell Fenwick, Ken Barnes, Dennis Morgan, L Barnes, L Shute, Richard Mercer, Graeme Fisher, D Magill. Third row: Jim Asplet, P Moss, Bill Greig, Rex Nicholls, Frank Snodgrass, Ian Skeet, J Taylor, George Elrick, Alan Lambourn. Second row: Jim Welsh, G McKay, Dave Lawrence, P Davidson, Jim Parker, G Hunter, Dennis Shaw. Front: Roy A Morris, Norm F Norris, M Foot, J Stuart, Graeme N Lyttle, Pat F Fagan, T B Dick Elliot, John T Morris, Cyril B Smith, Les D Wales, Norm A Hipwell.

Right: Omega 25 year club, 1965. Standing left: Roy Morris, Cyril Smith, Les Wales, Norm Norris. Front: Dick Eliot, Pat Fagan, John Morris.

tractors found a ready market on building sites, and were particularly good at digging and maintaining agricultural drains. A mini motor scraper, a local innovation built for the Fordson County tractor, was very effective for cleaning hill country dams, as well as building farm tracks and general contracting.

Administration and sales had been operating from James Macara's former house since 1965 with no showroom, and it was now time to complete the dealership.

Tractor repairs were shifted into the main workshop and the 1951 workshop on Dixon Street was extended in 1972 and converted to become a showroom and administration offices. James Macara's 90 year old two-storey house was sold and transported to Colombo Road where it was converted to four flats, and the area sealed for used vehicle display.

The new English D Series range of trucks introduced in 1966, put Ford into contention with commercial operators and

were very popular. A new turbocharged engine was introduced in 1969, and was an excellent performer in certain applications such as buses and main line haulage. However in some slower, full load applications it could not disperse heat and seized. The dealership had to live through these problems, but sales people became very wary of their reputations and service people had to mop up the mess again.

When Randal Thomson shifted to manage Timaru Motors' operations at the start of 1974, Roger Gardner transferred from Ruahine Motors at Waipukurau, as manager. There were 47 on the staff, and it was the time of the first oil crisis, with speed limits reduced to 90kph. There were

subsidies to adapt cars to natural gas or LPG use. Many other artificial dampers were put in place by the government to conserve fuel imports, and the first 'Think Big' projects were started, aiming to make New Zealand independent of imported oil. Motorcycles became very popular on farms, and tractor sales reduced as farmers cut costs.

After a nightmare first week, when six new turbo engine trucks belonging to Transport Wairarapa seized up, Roger Gardner decided the problem had to be solved. After discussions with Bill Hargreaves, m-d of Transport Wairarapa, his company was sold into the larger V8 Cummins engine DT2418 model. This did perform well, and Fagan's became established with the Ford DT2418 200hp light tandem, selling 10% of Ford's New Zealand supply. Only one further turbo engine D Series was sold, and used turbo trade-ins were sold out of the district.

Much of this business depended on the support of the parts and service team, who recognized the owner's need to keep trucks working as their responsibility. Many midnight hours were worked getting trucks back on the road, but the service paid off with customers appreciating the extra help to keep them operating.

After the shock announcement in the 1975 Budget, where differential taxation was applied to car registrations, Falcon sales that had accounted for 50-60% of car sales, suddenly dropped to 15%, and stock agents who had been a large user group of Falcons, and previously Zephyrs, were forced by their management into smaller cars to save fuel. They hated smaller cars

Left: Randal Thomson was manager from 1965-73.

Ben Iorns, then 93 years old, was 'grounded' in 1976. Fagan's sold the one year old 1936 V8 coupe to him for £85, and took it back to sell again 39 years later. It was tendered and, instead of $1,000, Ben Iorns got $2,600. He hands over the keys to G M Taylor, who has restored the car to mint condition on Auckland's North Shore.

The workshop lined up in 1985. From left: Neil McKay, Steve Howard, Mark Mahood, Doug Parkinson, Robert Unsworth, Ian Bradley, Gavin Henwood, Brian Callister, John Scott, Errol Krivan, and foreman Ken Howard.

and saw them as a loss of face. When Alex Clark was delivered a new Cortina 2 litre, he remarked to Roger Gardner, "I'm going to kill this car". He was a high mileage stock auctioneer and to his credit, after completing 100,000 very hard, trouble free kilometres, he came back and said "You know, this is not a bad car". He left the stock industry, but had become a loyal customer, purchasing many Ford vehicles.

Fagan Motors integrated their parts and service into one operation in 1981, with Keith Goodall the first parts and service manager in New Zealand. This integration was a key factor in achieving satisfied customers. For years, service and parts managers had fought over costs, affecting the profit generated in each department. Having a foot in both camps, Keith Goodall short-circuited barriers, achieved harmony that benefited all, and presented a united front to customers.

Masterton's expansion faltered in the

1980s when the new Labour government introduced wide-ranging 'free market' policies. Many large businesses in the district were re-located, and Borthwicks freezing works was sold and a short time later closed down. Suddenly the workforce did not have enough jobs. The population of Masterton stagnated at 20,000 people, then receded as workers moved away to find jobs. This had an effect on all car dealers and registration numbers dwindled for the next decade.

The English Ford D Series trucks ended in 1983, and Ford decided not to bring in the Cargo replacement. When Ford struck a deal with the Japanese Hino truck factory to re-badge the truck Ford N Series and market it in New Zealand, Fagan's sold them well to their existing customers. They were a good reliable truck with very few operational problems.

Trucks became an expanding market, as regulations against competing with rail

Fagan Motors in 1985.

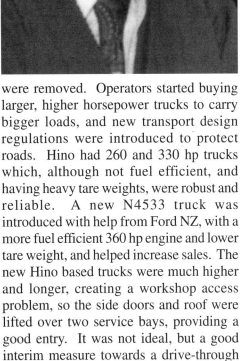

Left: Graeme Lyttle retired after 40 years in 1987.

Right: Keith Goodall, first parts and service manager.

were removed. Operators started buying larger, higher horsepower trucks to carry bigger loads, and new transport design regulations were introduced to protect roads. Hino had 260 and 330 hp trucks which, although not fuel efficient, and having heavy tare weights, were robust and reliable. A new N4533 truck was introduced with help from Ford NZ, with a more fuel efficient 360 hp engine and lower tare weight, and helped increase sales. The new Hino based trucks were much higher and longer, creating a workshop access problem, so the side doors and roof were lifted over two service bays, providing a good entry. It was not ideal, but a good interim measure towards a drive-through system, and did give weather protection for mechanics.

When he retired in 1987 Graeme Lyttle had been business manager for 26 years. He started in the office in 1954, and had been accountant at Te Kuiti for a year before returning to Masterton. Born and bred in Masterton, his father Ted and uncle Jim had held the sub-agency to Gordon Hughan and were Ford agents in Masterton between 1915 and 1923. Graeme Lyttle's integrity and quietly strong personality had helped to back up management with an accounting assurance second to none. His outside interests in St John's saw him awarded the top honour of Serving Brother, and for many years he was a borough councillor.

When the new Labour government took office in 1984 little changed initially, but by 1987 farming had been dealt a new hand. Subsidies were removed, with the new free market approach; incomes dropped sharply; and many farmers stopped buying. Masterton was quickly affected, and service industries withered further, many closing down. When import restrictions were removed and tariffs reduced steadily, Japanese used cars flooded into the country, collapsing prices and further stressing dealers. Fagan Motors was no exception, and restructured, leasing off part of the premises to other businesses. Staff was reduced to around 30 people to match needs. Despite all these handicaps, the staff rose to meet the challenges of change, and market leadership belonged to Fagan Motors. New computer systems helped, giving quick cost analysis at the press of a button.

"With the changed import controls, we decided to try importing our own vehicles, including a number of 'used' Ford Sierra cars from England," says Roger Gardner. "They were in fact new cars that had been registered in England, but had only travelled about 50 miles and were 'tax-free'. At the same time a used Ford Capri, Range Rover and some Mercedes trucks were imported, but the venture ended up with very little margin, plus the truly used vehicles had rust problems from salted English roads, made worse by being

Roger Gardner receives the third President's award from Ford Asia Pacific president Bob Spavero in 1992, with Jim Miller, Ford NZ managing director, watching. Jim Miller came to Masterton and took the staff out to dinner.

Achiever Awards as runners-up, plus numerous sales awards for market leadership.

In 1993 the company was entered in the first Business Development Awards. "It was to see how we compared when benchmarked across all industries," said Roger Gardner. "After a comprehensive assessment by a high-powered panel, Fagan Motors received one of two local Quality Awards. I had not told the staff we were entering, and came back from the presentation by the Minister of Business Development and presented it to the staff. They were stunned to silence and we were all delighted. The recognition of their collective quality actions in looking after customers has given all the staff a great deal of satisfaction – it is something intangible, and hard to quantify, but it creates a very good bond. People like working here."

In 1991 Ford rationalised truck dealers for the whole of the country and ceased to allow Fagan Motors to be a truck dealer despite the dealership's strong volumes and performance. "It was a bitter blow. Ford said there was logic in the move but it was lost on us. With heavy trucks, service really does count, and the core of our commercial business had been built around truck service," said Roger Gardner. "We persisted with the service and parts for trucks, and held our customers, but it wasn't quite the same. To make matters worse, Norwood's decided to take the tractor franchise away, giving it to their own Masterton branch. I could see big holes in

shipped through the tropics. It was decided there was little to be gained, so the project was stopped."

In 1990 Fagan Motors were awarded the Ford President's Award for delivering best customer satisfaction. The award is judged by customers and measured on a comprehensive group of standards, with awards made to the top New Zealand dealers in four size groups. "That was one of the highlights of my career, and reaffirmed the emphasis on customer service that our team had developed," says Roger Gardner. The company went on to win three President's Awards, and has also received a number of Distinguished

Long time customer Charlie Bannister was an agricultural contracting legend. He preferred mid size 2 W D Fordson Major and Ford 4000 tractors, taking them on hills which made your hair stand on end. He said: "Two wheel drive with steel spade lug wheels gives you a much better feel for your limit than 4WD." [Photo: Alan James]

This page bottom: Mark Mahood and Alan James discuss the merits of a new N1521 turbo engine in 1989.

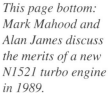

Opposite bottom: Third President's Award winning staff of Fagan Motors in 1992: From left back: Gavin Henwood, Andrew Tutty, Mark Mahood, John Scott, Erroll Krivan, Ken Howard, Ian Bradley, John Simons, and Fred Mason. Middle: Warren Adam, Derek Williams, Mark O'Hara, Neil McKay, Doug Parkinson, Elwyn Priday, Keith Goodall, Rose Alexander, Tony On Hing, Faye Taplin, Keith Allen, and Allen James. Sitting: David Miller, Roger Gardner, Steve Lyttle, Bill Hintz in front, and Sharon Compton, right. Away: Wayne Babbington. [Photo: Peter Nikolaison]

our business developing quickly, and we had no control over what was happening. Then to top it off, Transport Wairarapa, our biggest commercial customer, was liquidated. It was a black time."

In October 1991 Gordon Hughan Ltd, the oldest Ford dealership in New Zealand, closed down. Roger Gardner remembers: "Bill Worsfold, who owned Gordon Hughan Ltd, phoned to tell me that he had received an offer for the land and buildings, and was going to close down. Ford agreed we could take over his territory, and suddenly it was looking a little better. We managed to retain most of Hughan's customers, and probably got a few more to replace any we lost. It also made our vehicle volumes a much better size, without having to add a lot of extra overhead. There had been the lowest new vehicle registrations for 23 years in 1991. By then, service intervals had grown larger and vehicle quality had improved hugely, which meant our car servicing had reduced a lot. Hughan's closing helped fill some of the gaps "

Between 1990 and 1993, government services in the Wairarapa were reduced, and removed in some cases, putting considerable strain on many businesses. Masterton had reverted to being an agricultural service town, but it consolidated, and gradually many city people have relocated to the better country lifestyle, and commute to work in Wellington.

Keith Goodall retired in 1994, having contributed a great deal to the training of young staff in both parts and service. His last 14 years in charge of parts and service had been an immense success for the company and the idea of merging the two areas had spread to other Ford dealers.

In 1994, the extra heavy truck franchise was reviewed, following the takeover of Southpac Trucks by Colonial Motor Company, and Fagan Motors were offered the Kenworth and Foden franchise for the lower North Island. This was a whole new challenge and involved the stocking and wholesaling of parts, and the employment of an outside salesman, Tom Kerr, at Napier. As it was in contravention of the Ford franchise arrangement, a new sales company, Fagan Trucks Ltd, was formed.

Very quickly, the reducing car parts

business was topped up with big truck parts. The old maternity home parts building, was given a facelift and looked terrific. Roger Gardner said: "With the customer satisfaction training, the team were able to increase results with ease. It was an interesting period, with new customers from all over New Zealand phoning in for spare parts, and even sometimes from Australia. If a big truck is off the road, owners will go to extraordinary lengths to find a part, which our parts team was able to do."

With big rigs, big space is needed to manoeuvre them. When a drive-through 22 metre bay workshop became available in 1996 at the old Transport Wairarapa depot, it was decided to move big trucks there, and Mark Mahood shifted to Solway to manage the truck shop. Heavy duty truck parts stayed at Dixon Street with Mark O'Hara shifting from heavy truck mechanic to be the champion of heavy truck parts. Ford Louisville extra heavy trucks for the Lower North Island were also rationalised as part of the Masterton operation.

Trucks have been a significant contributor to Fagan Motors' profit over a long period, with most of the success based on customer service. However, Ford cars have always been the prime focus of the company, and Ford is the predominant name in the Wairarapa. The staff drive customer service, and it's not surprising that Fagan Motors has the largest service workshop in the Wairarapa.

Roger Gardner retired at the end of 1998, handing over to sales manager Steve Lyttle. At the same time heavy truck sales changed and now operates as a branch of Southpac Trucks in Auckland with Mark O'Hara shifting from his parts sales role to sell Kenworth, Foden and DAF trucks from the south corner of Fagan Motors.

Farming has had several very good years at the beginning of the new millennium, and Steve Lyttle and his team – Phil Ryan, business manager; Keith Allen, sales manager; Mark Mahood, truck service manager; and David Millar, parts and service manager – are carrying on very successfully the traditions of the past –looking after the transportation needs of their customers by giving good service.

A particularly innovative Masterton initiative was the first sheep shearing competition in 1961. R E (Bob) Chamberlain, a long time customer of Fagan Motors, and chairman of Federated Farmers, developed the idea with a committee of volunteers, as a means to improve the quality of shearing. The first Golden Shears Championship was a success and the competition has contributed to the very high standard of shearing in New Zealand. Today, it is regarded as the world's premier shearing competition, with the world championships being held in Masterton every four years. Interestingly, the most successful open shearing champion, and also world champion is a nephew of Pat Fagan, David Fagan, who at last count had won 16 open titles, and the world championship five times. David and John Fagan operate an agricultural supply business from the building where Te Kuiti Motors once operated. Fagan Motors has been a sponsor of Golden Shears since 1961. Seen in the 1992 photo are David Fagan, open champion, Roger Gardner and Edsel Forde, runner-up. The connection with Edsel Forde is more esoteric. [Photo: Mike Warman]

Top: Hayes & McKeage were the first Ford agents in Lower Hutt about 1909. Hayes is in the driver's seat of the Model T on the right about 1911.

Right: In 1928, CMC built on the corner of Queens Drive and Main Hutt Road, and appointed Ward and Rawnsley Ford dealers.

Above: The original premises were extended and modernised in 1951 by Keith Cook, of King, Cook and Dawson. It was known as the 'porthole building'.

Right: The dealership consolidated into a smaller operation further up High Street in 1990, lowering costs.

CHAPTER TWENTYTWO

HUTT CITY – STEVENS MOTORS LTD

Hutt City is the combination of Lower Hutt, Wainuiomata, Eastbourne and the former borough of Petone, bordering Wellington Harbour. The city lies in the valley between the foothills of the Rimutaka and Akatarawa Ranges. Today a memorial building stands by the seashore where the first settlers of the New Zealand Company landed in 1840. A year before, a preliminary expedition arrived on the *Tory*, under Colonel William Wakefield, and bought land for the new settlement from Ngati Awa Maoris. Colonel Wakefield named the river and area Hutt, after Sir William Hutt, a former chairman of the New Zealand Company. Petone, 'End of sands', was called Britannia by the first settlers.

The valley had long been occupied by Maori and was named Heretaunga after their homelands in Hawke's Bay. It had rich, fertile soil much covered by bush and was a very good hunting and fishing ground. A number of pa sites were established but then abandoned when the river flooded and changed direction, and after being sacked by other Maori tribes.

The New Zealand Company planned to settle the valley, but constant flooding and, in 1846, a severe earthquake, drove many settlers to Thorndon and Te Aro on the other side of the harbour. The Hutt Valley was rich in timber and mills were set up there, together with market gardens and farms to feed the growing town of Wellington where climate and soils were less accommodating. Access to Wellington was by boat until the 1855 earthquake when a strip of land lifted three metres, allowing the Hutt Road to be formed.

Regular coach services began operating to the Wairarapa in 1866, using coaches built by William Black at Courtenay Place. The railway connected Hutt Valley with Wellington in 1874 and carried on across the Rimutakas to Masterton in 1880, using a unique Fell cog drive engine to cross the Incline.

As Wellington grew, so did the Hutt Valley; Lower Hutt was constituted a borough in 1891 and a city in 1941. After river stop banks were built in the early 20th century, Lower Hutt developed as the industrial centre for the region, and the Railway Workshops were opened at Woburn in 1929. The mouth of the Hutt River was stabilized at Seaview, and cheap rental state housing was constructed in the 1930s to attract labour. Many new industries were established – General Motors commenced assembly of vehicles at Petone in 1926 and Ford Motor Company at Seaview in 1936, with the majority of all car assembly for New Zealand centred in the Hutt Valley from 1938. Wool stores and bulk oil and fuel terminals were located on reclaimed land beside the harbour, and a number of government research institutes and laboratories were established through the valley.

Today much of the original industry has moved away, or closed down with changes in government policies, but the area has consolidated to become the distribution centre for the Wellington district.

Motor vehicles arrived in the country at the beginning of the 20th century, and Wellington was one of the first places to see them. Hayes & McKeage, engineers at Lower Hutt, was the first Ford agency in the Hutt Valley about 1909, but by 1915 most Ford vehicles in the area were sold directly by Colonial Motor Company from Courtenay Place in Wellington. In 1922, Ford Sales and Service Wellington Ltd was set up as a separate dealer, with sales at Courtenay Place and service in Ebor Street.

In 1927, the $^3/_8$ acre corner site of Main Hutt Road (later High Street) and Queen's Drive was sold by F N R Meadows to Colonial Motor Company, and a contract was let to Abingel Concrete Block Company for £3,026 to erect a garage premises using concrete blocks, a new and virtually untried building method. This site had a government valuation of £1,159 with Hutt River Board rates of £1 10s 9d a year.

Ward & Rawnsley Ltd became the Ford

dealer and rented the premises from Colonial Motor Company in September 1928. The Model A Ford had just arrived in New Zealand and the public demand for this car was considerable, assuring the new dealer a fast start in business. The two partners had been employed by Colonial Motor Company, Tom Ward as a salesman, and Jack Rawnsley as Wellington assembly manager. The adventurous Rawnsley had also been a fighter pilot in the Royal Flying Corps in the First World War, and after returning home, climbed Mt Cook, before joining Colonial Motor Company in 1923.

Another Ford dealer, Howell Motors Ltd, was established at Trentham in March 1932.

Like many dealers, Ward and Rawnsley found business very difficult during the Depression of the early thirties and in 1935 they decided to end their partnership and sell to Colonial Motor Company. Jack Rawnsley later became a prominent wing commander in the RNZAF during the Second World War.

The new company of Stevens Motors took over, with John Victor (Jack) Stevens as manager. Jack Stevens had previously been assistant manager at CMC's Auckland branch, and Timaru branch before that. Gordon Darnell, newly certified 'A' grade mechanic, was one of the six staff of Ward and Rawnsley to transfer to Stevens. Peter G Patton transferred from Avery Motors and was service manager; Claude F Draper was parts manager; R G (Bob) Gower was the first accountant, having been trained as a member of H N Scrimshaw's audit team for several years. In 1936, the premises were extended under the watchful eyes of the company's architects, King, Cook and Dawson.

When Bob Gower decided to go farming, H N Scrimshaw wrote to C Lennox Henderson, who worked for an accountancy firm in Wellington, to see if he was interested in becoming accountant at Stevens Motors. It wasn't a chance letter as F H (Toddy) Johnston, a director and former general manager of Colonial Motor Company, had previously met Lennox Henderson at a dinner party in Wellington. Before accepting, he decided to have a closer look at the business and set off one Sunday to do this. He quizzed the petrol station attendant Wattie Longman, with all sorts of questions about Stevens Motors. Next day the attendant told Bob Gower: "A

long lofty fellow was here yesterday asking a lot of questions." Lennox accepted, and from then was known as 'Lofty'.

The new job included buying Bob Gower's bicycle for 27s 6d. As Lofty put it: "Lofty bought Bob's bicycle, and Bob went farming". Bicycles were quite useful in those days, especially with wartime petrol rationing, and when Lofty was called up to the army in 1940, he sold his bicycle to Gordon Darnell for 27s 6d. When he returned from the war, Lofty bought it back for 27s 6d, and later sold it to an apprentice for 27s 6d. " It was always 27s 6d." Why was it 27s 6d? Was it a coincidence that his first week's wages were, yes, 27s 6d?

Under Jack Stevens' able direction, Stevens Motors grew. However, it was hard going at first, because of the aftermath of the Depression, and then the war years, when the supply of motor vehicles dried-up completely, and technical manpower was extremely short.

Gordon Darnell became service manager in 1940 when Peter Patton went into the army. Working with only a limited staff, he put in very long hours to service Ford vehicles in the area, as well as maintaining all Army vehicles in the district. He also instructed night classes in vehicle maintenance, these including many women keen to do their bit for the war effort. This led to Gordon Darnell's involvement with the Apprentice Training Board as well as personally overseeing the training for over 80 apprentice mechanics during his time with Stevens Motors.

Jack Stevens retired in 1942, and E F (Fred) Emmerson became manager, but there were no vehicles to sell, and hardly any parts available, so the business was barely ticking over outside the service department.

Many staff members returned after the war to take up their old jobs. It was obvious Stevens Motors would soon have to be substantially enlarged to cope and keep pace with the rapid expansion taking place in the Hutt Valley. But there was no possibility of building extensions in the immediate post-war years due to delays with building permits and regulations.

Cars slowly became available, but import restrictions were severe, and only a few arrived. This meant there were not enough to supply the demand, causing frustrations all around. Trucks and tractors were available so all the sales effort was applied to these. With the growth of

The first workshop and parts building of 20,000 sq ft was built in 1958, across the road in High Street.

industry in the valley, many sales were made to businesses, and Stevens Motors built a considerable customer bank.

In 1951, the original building with arched verandah was modernised, a service station was added, and the distinctive port-hole façade design incorporated into the building under the direction of Keith Cook, who lived nearby, of King, Cook and Dawson, architects.

Meanwhile, due to the land sales control regulations, a great deal of difficulty was experienced buying suitable property for future expansion. Seventeen land transactions were entered into in a frustrating land search saga. In one case, A J Webster's wood, coal and cartage business was bought as a going concern further out on west High Street. Stevens then had the added problem of operating another organisation as well as its motor business, and W A (Bill) Maclaren remembers being assigned the job of managing Webster's soon after he joined the company in 1948 as a clerk. Later, having got the merchant back into a sound condition, the business was sold off for re-location and the land retained.

Fred Emmerson left at the end of 1951, and Lennox Henderson became manager the next year.

After 30 years of protracted negotiating, much of it with the city council which changed street alignments, and the

Inside, the new workshop was naturally well lit and equipped with the latest tools.

Above: Workshop and parts were extended by another 10,000 sq ft and the service station shifted across the road in 1965.

Right: The new administration building was finally commissioned in 1967, directly across High Street from the parts and service departments.

demolition of eight old houses, Stevens Motors had acquired two continuous blocks of property facing each other across High Street.

New building construction was still restricted when the first service and parts two-storey building was proposed, and lengthy negotiations occurred with the building controller before it was finally occupied in June 1958. Built by W M Angus & Co, this building of 20,000 sq ft, had a new single-storey workshop, extensive parts department on two floors, cafeteria and offices.

The old premises, on the corner of High Street and Queen's Drive, continued as the sales centre for new and used vehicles, accounting and administration offices and heavy truck repairs. A number of CMC Group personnel were trained at Stevens, including Bill Maclaren, Max Caigou, George Daniel, Brian Willis, Ken Mullan and Jim Gibbons – all of them later became dealer principals. Peter Cederman moved from Lower Hutt where he was accountant, to be assistant managing director of Avery Motors, then manager and later general manager at Colonial Motor Company.

In November 1965, Stevens commissioned its second building of 10,000 sq ft, alongside and integrated with the 1958 building, for heavy truck service, wheel alignment and lubrication, while vehicle sales and petrol still remained at the original site on the corner of Queen's Drive.

When the project was started, Martyn Spencer, the design engineer, discovered the foundations were unstable and it was decided they should be taken down to a solid base. Excavation of a huge 15ft hole unearthed the reason for the instability – a large, dried up streambed with huge logs blocking what had been its entrance to the Hutt River some long time before.

Two years later in December 1967, the new 9,200 sq ft sales and administration centre was completed immediately across the road from the service and parts centre, and the original premises from 1927 were finally sold. Those original premises of 4,000 sq ft, with six employees, had grown in 40 years to 40,000 sq ft and 77 staff. It had been a long haul to meet the needs of the dealership, which was now CMC Group's show place, able to supply complete motoring and transport needs for all Hutt customers.

1966 Omega club and part of the management team. From left: Brian Willis, parts manager; Gordon Darnell, service manager; H T Anderson, sales manager; Alan Davidson, business manager.

After the Second World War, motor industry suppliers were given tariff protection for making components such as heaters, radiators, exhausts, radios, springs, seats, paints and a host of smaller components, and the number of these in the Hutt Valley grew significantly. New immigrants arrived from England and Holland under the 'Ten Pound Pom' and similar schemes in the early 1950s, many settling in the Hutt. Stevens welcomed a number, who stayed many years, giving excellent service.

Vehicle sales grew significantly with the range of Ford vehicles available after import restrictions were lifted in the 1970s. The years of training and grooming of staff by Lofty Henderson were paying off and profits increased. He was appointed a director of Colonial Motor Company in 1973. In 1978 Lofty Henderson retired after 41 years at Stevens Motors, 36 as dealer principal.

Randal Thomson shifted from Timaru to become general manager, after extensive experience with the CMC Group, managing both Masterton and Timaru. Stevens now had a staff of 90, and a large volume of commercial business with fleet and truck operators in the Hutt Valley. Randal Thomson had excellent backup from his key people, who included Alan Davidson, business manager; Peter Mather, new vehicle manager; Ray Abbott, used vehicle manager; Jim Gibson, commercial vehicle manager; Brian Willis, parts manager; John Leeney, marketing manager; and Gordon Darnell, service manager. Gordon Darnell retired soon afterwards, having completed over 46 years with Stevens Motors, and 52 years in the motor industry since the start of his apprenticeship. Malcolm Orr was

Two new R series buses were delivered to Eastbourne-Days Bay Bus Co in 1971. Handing over are John Gibson and Lofty Henderson on the right.

Jock Dunlop was presented with his 25 year gold watch by Lofty Henderson.

Below right: Gordon Darnell delivered gifts and spoke at Lofty Henderson's retirement after 41 years, 36 as dealer principal of Stevens Motors. He was also a director of CMC.

Below: One of the surprise gifts for Lofty Henderson, unwrapped by his wife Margaret, was a new set of golf clubs, which no doubt cost 27s 6d.

appointed service manager.

On August 8 1985, disaster struck, swiftly and almost completely. About 9pm, fire razed the 20 year old sales and administration block of Stevens Motors, fortunately empty of people. The fire was one of the largest in Lower Hutt's history and was a raging inferno within 10 minutes. Petrol tanks in the showroom display cars exploded in the heat, making conventional fire fighting impossible, but the fire was contained and left to burn out. It was thought to have been arson. After Gordon Hughan in Carterton lost all his records by fire in 1919, Colonial Motor Company had suggested a policy of protecting records, each dealer constructing a fire delay storage room. This paid off, with all sales, service and accounting records remaining intact.

As it turned out, the fire was possibly Stevens Motors' saviour. The new government's free market policies had thrown the motor industry into turmoil and Stevens Motors had been in a vulnerable position with the industry rationalisation as the space needed for service and parts was diminishing. Consequently, it was decided not to rebuild the administration and sales building, as this would over-capitalise the dealership and make it uncompetitive.

Left: Ray Abbot spent many years as used car manager.

Right: Randal Thomson was appointed CEO in 1978.

Below left: Malcolm Orr became service manager in 1978.

Below: Norah and Gordon Darnell. Retiring as service manager in 1978 after 50 years in the industry, he kept working as supervisor of truck and tractor repairs. Gordon Darnell started with D C Motors in 1928, shifted to Ward & Rawnsley in 1935, and Stevens Motors in 1936. He served on the Motor Trade Association for 10 years, the Trade Certification Board, and the Wellington district Motor Trade Apprenticeship committee. He was an active vintage car enthusiast in his spare time, and rescued the 1903 Model A Fordmobile.

Instead, the existing workshop and parts building was modified to include the showroom and a used car display beside this in what had been a service car park. The company had nearly one hectare of land on that site, and it was used much more efficiently with some rearrangement. The fire site was redeveloped for multi-storeyed office space and retail shops.

The 1985 to 1991 period was a very critical one for the motor industry, deregulation introducing immense change after a 50 year period of severe restriction. Land values had also altered dramatically with Lower Hutt's expansion, and commercial land was now retail. This was a great concern as motor vehicle sales and service cannot survive the costs associated with high value land.

Ford Motor Company was also making massive changes and had decided its Lower Hutt plant at Seaview would be closed, and all operations shifted to Manukau City. With Japanese used cars now being imported in huge numbers, the assembly industry was in danger.

When Foodstuffs made an offer of $6.5 million for all the land and buildings, in 1989, alternatives were investigated. Liquorland's premises further along High Street were available plus adjoining land and, although tight, it was thought the dealership could be relocated. This would cost $2.5 million. Agreement was reached and the dealership relocated in May 1990. Some additional land was leased nearby, and the company shook down into an attractive new location. The lower

The new Courier inspected closely by sales staff when it arrived in 1981. From left: Manuel Lopez, Ray Abbot, Jim Gibson and unidentified staffer. Behind the group is the new Econovan, introduced at the same time.

Right: Don Waugh, parts manager, checking some of his parts figures that Robyn Saunders has machined on the new Burroughs AE501 data capture machine in 1978. The machine was a punch card sorter, which pre-dated computers.

Below: Stevens' Omega club grew by three in 1979. From left: Alan Davidson, Trevor Evans, Anton Rosenberg, John Leeney, Don Waugh, Peter Mather, Lennox Henderson, Gordon Darnell and Jock Dunlop.

Opposite bottom: John Leeney and his father Bill. Bill Leeney started at Timaru CMC in 1923, shifted to CMC assembly in 1932, and transferred to Ford at Seaview in 1936. John Leeney started his mechanical apprenticeship in 1954. In 1958 he was new vehicle service supervisor; then had a number of positions until he was new vehicle sales manager in 1980, later operations manager, and relieving dealer principal.

operating costs helped Stevens to cope with the new trading conditions at a time when rationalisation of the industry was the key to survival or failure.

Randal Thomson retired in October 1992 after 36 years work with the CMC Group. In his 27 years as a dealer principal, he had been involved in relocating three dealerships and had worked in many CMC Group locations.

Malcolm Davison, who owned the major share of Maidstone Motors, Upper Hutt, sold the business to Colonial Motor Company, and was appointed joint dealer principal of both Stevens Motors and Maidstone Motors from January 15 1993. The synergy helped both companies to progress, but Malcolm Davison's resignation in June 1994 was unexpected.

John Leeney acted as relieving dealer principal for a period until a new appointment was made. He started in the

workshop at Stevens in 1957 and had been service receptionist, in parts marketing, used vehicle manager, new vehicle

Above: After the fire in 1985, sales and administration was incorporated into the parts and service building, significantly reducing operating costs.

Left: Peter Mather delivers a new Laser Sport to high profile Tony Nightingale, of Resene Paints, in 1991.

manager and operations manager.

On September 3 1994, S H Hutchison was appointed chief executive. He had been in the motor industry for 12 years, but found the transition to a Ford dealership difficult, and resigned in May 1997.

It was decided the Wellington area CMC Group companies – Maidstone, Stevens, Newlands and Avery Motors – would work as a Ford Retail Network under Ian Duncan, chief executive of Avery Motors. This meant that most functions were shared, with common accounting by one staff group. A similar approach was used in vehicle sales, service, parts and finance. There were also the advantages of joint purchasing power for advertising and utilities. The FRN certainly stripped a lot of cost out of the combined operations, but the individual parts didn't seem to retain their own distinctive character.

When Ian Duncan resigned on November 30 2001, the dealerships were split into two parts, with Stevens Motors operating Ford and Mazda for the Hutt Valley from High Street, Lower Hutt. The

Stevens Motors received the new Ford corporate signage in 2003, in time to celebrate the Ford centenary. Standing from left: Paul Jackson, Sandy Jackson, Barbara Patterson, Kris Wyszynski, Vincent Cox, David Brooke, Fred Harding, Darren Kipa, Joe Hall, Tyler King, Ray Liew, Ian Wimms, Justin MacKay, and Cliff Clamp. Sitting: Rob Morris-Jenkins, Stacey Reid, Tom Ninness, Rex Howard, Deborah Hawkins, Stuart Gibbons, dealer principal, Paul Bond, Cameron Osbourne, and John Cook.

common functions and purchasing were still shared with Avery Motors.

Stuart Barnes Gibbons was appointed chief executive officer in February 2002. Great grandson of Hope Gibbons, he was previously general manager of East City Ford, Auckland, and had worked for CMC Group since 1982, at Hawke Motors, Morrinsville, Energy City Ford, New Plymouth, South Auckland Motors and West Auckland Motors.

CHAPTER TWENTYTHREE
WELLINGTON

Wellington, the capital city stands on the south western tip of the North Island beside one of the most attractive harbours in the world, and takes its name from the Duke of Wellington who supported the 'Wakefield Scheme' for the colonisation of New Zealand.

Preceding the signing of the Treaty of Waitangi, a 'New Zealand Association' was formed in 1837 by Edward Gibbon Wakefield with the altruistic aims of colonizing and then self-governing the country, but the British government rejected the plan because they had plans to make a treaty with the natives.

Wakefield anticipated the British government would then have a sole right to any land acquisition so, without telling them, he changed the organisation to the 'New Zealand Company' and, with the express purpose of making a profit, dispatched his brother, Col William Wakefield, on the *Tory*, to purchase land for settlements at Wellington and other places. Settlers were then quickly recruited, by 'selling' land with a rebated passage. Four ships had sailed with settlers before Wakefield had even arrived in New Zealand on the *Tory*, let alone bought land.

When Col Wakefield arrived in the Marlborough Sounds he met whaler 'Dicky' Barrett who guided the *Tory* back to Port Nicholson. There they met 18 Maori chiefs and, with Barrett's poor interpretation, 'bought' land much to the chiefs' later surprise, leading to later land wars. As the first settlers arrived, Governor Hobson was on his way from Sydney to Waitangi to negotiate the Treaty.

Long before 1839, chief Whatonga had moved from Whakatane to Mahia and then Wellington, where his sons, Tara and Tautoki, built a pa on Matiu (Somes Island) and then Motu Kairangi (Miramar Island). The Ngai-Tara (Tara's descendants) increased in numbers and built other pa sites around the harbour. Many battles were fought between tribes in the southern North Island and over time other tribes settled nearby.

When settlers arrived, some Maori thought their presence would help keep peace among the tribes, but two Ngati Toa chiefs, Te Rauparaha and Te Rangihaeata, ensured

this did not happen. There were many battles and skirmishes over land purchases, and 22 settlers were massacred at Wairau in the north of the South Island.

There were more ructions when a massive earthquake of Richter 8+ occurred near Wellington in 1855. Settlers were terrified, and when after-shocks made this worse, many left New Zealand. Virtually every masonry structure in the area was damaged, and parts of Wellington Harbour were lifted, including a shelf along the hills from Ngauranga to Petone where the Hutt Road and motorway run. A fault line 90kms long lifted three metres at the eastern base of the Rimutaka Ranges, and gave coastal access from Orongorongo to the Wairarapa.

When it was created the capital of New Zealand in 1865, Wellington had a population of nearly 10,000 people. William Black's coach building factory had been in Courtenay Place for six years, where Colonial Motor Company stands today. Like other businesses, Black's coach building surged ahead with the town's new status and the many new residents who were attracted there.

William McLean MP imported two Benz cars in 1898, the first cars to reach New Zealand. Finding he was unable to use them, he took a private member's bill to Parliament which subsequently passed The McLean Motor-car Act in 1898.

Rouse & Hurrell Ltd (renamed Colonial Motor Company in 1911) distributed Ford cars from 1908, with selling done from 89 Courtenay Place, in Wellington. Agency agreements were made with various garages around New Zealand in strategic service and population centres. Getting around was difficult in many areas and the development of roads, and bridges particularly, depended upon the attitude of the local councils. Much of the country was serviced by sea or rail.

Colonial Motor Company was re-formed in 1919, and greatly expanded, when the Gibbons family gained control. In 1921, the construction of the 100ft high nine-storey assembly plant started, the first vehicle 'factory' in New Zealand, and then the tallest building in Wellington.

The sheer volume of business being done dictated the company be split into departments: head office, assembly, manufacturing, retailing, parts and service. Vehicles were sold from Courtenay Place, the showroom the same one that had displayed carriages back in 1886. New vehicles and demonstrators were parked perpendicular to the street during the day. The service department on the corner of York and Taranaki Streets was sold in 1922 to Dunlop Tyre Company, and new workshops built later at Ebor Street.

FORD SALES & SERVICE WELLINGTON LTD

The retailing of vehicles and service was incorporated separately as Ford Sales and Service Wellington Ltd in March 1923. The general manager was Colonel (later Brigadier) H E Avery; Harris Daw was sales manager; James Walker, service manager; G C Boyes, accountant; Vic Frost, parts manager and Bert Rogers the first foreman. Jim Hughes was one of the first employees and later became service manager.

The new art deco Ebor Street workshop was opened in No 2 bay during 1924, when Len Morrison started as an apprentice, with 24 other servicemen. At that time, Ford Model Ts accounted for approximately one in every three vehicles, and were by far the largest presence in the New Zealand market. Petrol was 9 pence a gallon with no tax, and you could buy a new Model T for £170. Wages by contrast, were £5 for a journeyman working 47 hours per week (2s 11d. per hour or $8.22/hr in 2000 terms).

In 1926 the Model T was coming to the end of its run and sales were slowing as people decided it wasn't so fashionable any more and other makes were catching up. In August 1927 Henry Ford announced that a new car would replace it soon, but it was August 1928 before the Model A arrived, and Pete Petersen had succeeded James Walker as service manager. Sales had just got going again, with G H Tomline as sales manager, when the Great Depression hit in 1930, a year later than in the United States.

People who did not live through this period have difficulty in comprehending how serious conditions were. More than 20% of the working population was out of work (and men under 18 and women were not counted!). Wages dropped more than 20%, sales generally fell 60%, and for new vehicles, the reduction was over 80%. Used vehicles were almost sale proof, and values worse because people were more concerned with the basics of enough food and clothing.

By 1933 things started to improve and a new small Ford became available from England. The 8hp Model Y was very popular, selling for £215, a much smaller look-alike version of its big brother Ford V8. Business picked up quickly with the new Ford 10hp in 1935, and staff numbers grew to 50. Pete Peterson went to Morrinsville as manager, and Jim Power became service manager. He had previously been on H N Scrimshaw's audit team.

Colonel H E Avery, first manager.

AVERY MOTORS LTD

When Ford Motor Company decided to set up its own assembly and distribution in New Zealand, the Colonial Motor Company had to re-name dealerships with 'Ford' in their title. Consequently, Ford Sales and Service Ltd was re-named Avery Motors Ltd in 1936. The sales operation was still in Courtenay Place on the ground floor at Colonial Motor Company and the workshops were at Ebor Street.

Two acres of land originally set aside for the Anglican Cathedral were leased to Avery Motors in Taranaki Street in 1936, opposite the end of Ghuznee Street and backing onto Ebor Street, beside Standard Motor Bodies. Petrol pumps and a lubrication service bay were built during 1937, but buildings of 30,000 sq ft were held up awaiting city council planning consent. The petrol station was a very popular place, with six brands on offer: Atlantic, Big Tree, Europa, Plume, Shell and Texaco. The new site was vacant, waiting for building consent, and parking was let out at 1s a day, 5s a week, or £1 per month, but there were few takers.

Managing director Colonel H E Avery retired and was seconded to Army HQ towards the end of 1936. W A (Bill) Fraser, who had been manager of the Wellington branch of Colonial Motor Company, took

over as general manager. His deputy was J A (Jack) McInnes, who had been with CMC Auckland branch. Staff increased to nearly 70 people, but they were at a number of locations, including part of the now disused assembly building.

With the continuing expansion of car sales, it was decided to shift retail operations to Taranaki Street in 1938. Used cars were displayed innovatively on an open-air lot. 'The Car of the Week' had a special display stand with a striped canopy over it. Finally, the city council gave approval to build but, because of road planning provisions, permanent materials could not be used. Building commenced in 1938 and continued until September 1939, the month the Second World War began.

Right across the country, the motor industry stopped almost overnight. Many staff joined up, and sadly far too many did not return, paying with their lives to defend their country's freedom. The Army leased the new building for the duration of the war plus six months, as a distribution centre.

The government requisitioned all 1938 and 1939 used cars for military use, and new vehicles ceased production. Strict petrol rationing meant that few vehicles, other than those related to the 'war effort',

Motor mechanic Len Morrison in 1930 on his Harley with a mate.

Above: Taranaki Street 1937: lubritorium on left, petrol station middle, and sales office right. The petrol station collected parking fees of 1s per day, 5s per week, or £1 per month.

Right: Started in 1938, the main building was finished as war was declared.

were in use. Petrol rations were worked on three engine sizes to allow about 150 miles per month. There was very little to sell, parts were scarce, service did not have enough mechanics, and the business struggled to break even again, for the second time in 10 years.

W A (Bill) Fraser died suddenly just before the end of the war, and his estate was the first to claim under the new staff superannuation scheme. J A (Jack) McInnes was appointed general manager. Bill Fraser's brother, George, returned from active service and was made assistant general manager. The Army eventually moved out of the building and the showroom and offices were then completed. Walter Harvey returned from the services and was appointed the new parts manager in 1949, after Phil Young resigned.

In 1945, after the end of the war, there was a welcome return of many of the staff, but trading was difficult, with petrol and food still rationed. New cars were kept under tight licensing for 25 years afterwards as New Zealand paid the price of the war. Demand was high for cars, and there was a ready sale in used vehicles,

which in many cases fetched more than when new. Newspapers were scanned for used cars for sale as soon as they hit the streets, with eager buyers immediately telephoning or even knocking on doors. Surplus army vehicles were snapped up although they, of course, needed repainting. Service work increased to keep the used cars on the road, but this was difficult with the shortage of mechanics.

Many new immigrants arrived after the war with assisted passages offered by the government. Nick Zoet, a qualified mechanic, stepped off the boat from Holland in 1953 and into a job at Avery's, unable to speak any English. Guy Walker came from England as a salesman in 1958 and was soon new car sales manager. Peter Mather came from England in 1953, and joined as a salesman, becoming used car manager in 1958. Tony Muollo, born in Greece, joined in 1951 on the petrol station, becoming cashier in 1960. Jim Papanicolau, also from Greece, joined Napier Motors in Dunedin in 1958, completed his apprenticeship and joined Avery Motors, later becoming foreman of apprentices.

Left: Bill Fraser was appointed manager at the end of 1936.

Right: Jack McInnes became manager when Bill Fraser died.

Left: George Fraser was fourth manager in 1954.

Right: Wally Harvey was appointed parts manager in 1949, working until he died in 1982. Outstanding in his job, he trained many apprentices, and others who successfully followed his lead.

Left: Guy Walker emigrated from Britain, becoming sales manager in 1964.

Right: Peter Mather was No Remittance manager in 1962, later transferring to Stevens Motors as sales manager.

A group of long serving key people was able to guide the new arrivals. Bill Drew was assistant manager; Jim Flannery, chief accountant; Jim Hughes, service manager; Vern Neville, accountant; and Len Morrison, new car service foreman.

New Zealand was short of managers, and if you needed someone, the easiest way to get them was by pirating another business. Jack McInnes resigned in 1954 and went to Dominion Motors. George Fraser became general manager, but two years later also went to Dominion Motors. J R G (Jim) Jack, from Selwyn Motors Palmerston North, transferred to become general manager in July 1956, but decided he did not like the city, and in June 1958 bought a service station at Taumarunui. Ian G Lyons, at Hawke Motors, Te Aroha, was promoted to general manager in March 1959.

Commercial vehicles were not in as short supply as cars, and truck sales expanded when the Thames Trader arrived in 1957, helping Avery Motors to develop a very strong commercial division. Fred England, who returned from the Air Force and got a job as petrol station manager with Avery's, saw the opportunities and was soon selling the popular Traders. He became commercial sales manager in 1964, selling hundreds of trucks, many with Standard Motor Bodies built bodies. The Ford D Series in 1966 further improved sales.

No Remittance car sales expanded in the 1960s with Peter Mather focusing on the opportunities. These were given a boost when Ford introduced the bonus scheme, of an extra allocation unit for every No Remittance licence. The No Remittance scheme, for all the criticism and abuse, certainly produced results for Avery's.

With the increasing business, more suitable space was hard to find, and land at Taranaki /Ebor Streets was overpriced for motor vehicle repair and sales. When the former stock sale yards at Johnsonville were offered for sale in 1956, the company bought the 2 1/4 acres within 48 hours. The area was adjacent to the new motorway from Johnsonville to Porirua and had become part of Wellington City. Getting the zoning changed was another saga, and took nearly three years. The land was re-contoured, removing a ridge and improving the drainage.

By 1961 a contract had been let for a workshop and parts building. The foundations had to be laid a certain way to cope with the plasticity of the clay, and the 9,000 sq ft building was in three butting sections to allow for any movement. Cleverly, it looked like one building from the outside. Considered very modern at the time, the side-opening workshop with roller doors, was lit naturally by the translucent roof and wall panels, and designed to take the new Thames Trader trucks. After a number of hold-ups the branch was opened in April 1963. Most of the new vehicle pre-delivery and truck service was shifted to Johnsonville, easing the pressure at Taranaki Street.

Ian Lyons was head-hunted to Auckland in 1964, and M L (Max) Caigou returned

Fred England (right) congratulates salesman Des Mines on another sale. He started as service station manager when demobbed from the Air Force after the war in 1946, sold Thames Traders in 1957, and became commercial manager. Fred England had sold well over 1,000 new trucks for Avery Motors when he decided to retire 40 years later.

to his hometown to be general manager. He had started at Colonial Motor Company head office in 1952, and transferred to Te Awamutu, Lower Hutt, Waipukurau, Masterton, then was manager of Macaulay Motors, Invercargill.

By 1965 Ford wanted the branch made into a new dealership and separated from Avery's, and so Newlands Motors opened on June 13 1965, with Alan Hodges, assistant to the managing director of Avery's, appointed as manager.

Avery Motors was now faced with an entirely new problem; it had spawned its own competitor! Although the two companies worked in some harmony they were, nevertheless, vying for some of the same customers, which was exactly what

Ford wanted. Avery Motors did not have a pre-delivery and truck workshop any more, and 120 people were competing for space at Taranaki Street.

The main building was given a welcome renovation in 1968, with a new look glass-fronted entrance to the showroom for vehicles and parts, and a new, wide, service reception portico. Internal alterations to offices were made and the workshop gained a little more space. When service manager Jim Hughes retired, after serving 45 years, the new service manager, Joe Feasey, introduced new ideas to help internal communication between parts and service which reduced the amount of foot traffic, and enabled mechanics to stay on the job with parts and materials brought to them. He also concentrated on bringing through new apprentices, sometimes as many as 12 in a year.

Jim Flannery, chief accountant for many years, shifted to CMC head office in 1967, becoming secretary, and Jack Harland took over as business manager.

Truck servicing was still a problem, as the building was not equipped for it, so No 3 bay of the Ebor Street workshop next to Standard Motor Bodies was used for this purpose.

All these things helped to make the place less congested, but there still wasn't enough space. There was also the worry that the city council may extend Ghuznee Street right through the dealership buildings so Standard Motor Bodies' woodwork and paint shop was taken over and converted to a 9,000 sq ft workshop, with a 110ft sub-floor pit accommodating 12 cars. Ross Telford became service manager technical and Reg Stephen service

Max Caigou was appointed managing director in 1964, after experience with five CMC Group companies. After a serious heart attack he became CMC secretary in 1973.

The Omega club in 1966. Standing left: Vern Neville, accountant; Len Morrison, pre-delivery foreman; Charles Smith, wheel alignment; Jack Harland, sales administrator. In front: Jim Flannery, chief accountant; Bill Hawley Drew, assistant manager; Jim Hughes, service manager.

Above: Avery Motors' stand at the Wellington Trades Fair in 1969. On display: Escort 1300, Capri 2000XL hatch, MkIV Zephyr V6, Cortina MkII 1600 Super, Falcon XW Utility and Escort 1100 van.

Below: Avery Motors had a facelift in 1969, with a new showroom and service reception area opening up the business to customers.

manager for administration, both having joined as apprentices.

Any residential Jessie Street properties backing onto Standard Motor Bodies which came onto the market were bought to provide more space. Finally, suitable flat land was found in Adelaide Road in February 1971, when a former timber yard and joinery and six houses were purchased for $204,500. The old stuctures were demolished and a new double storey building was designed and built with a workshop and showroom on the ground floor and offices above. The building, tendered at $156,477, was set to the back of the property, which bordered Oxford Lane, Oxford Street and Adelaide Road, allowing direct rear access to the workshop. The 30ft deep by 120ft frontage to Adelaide Road provided excellent display space for

vehicles, and Newtown branch manager Richard Kilkenny, and his 10 staff, got away to a fast start in October 1972.

By 1971, new vehicles were more freely available, and Ford was well positioned with smaller Escort and Cortina cars when the oil crisis hit at the end of 1973. With Wellington on piped natural gas, the compressed natural gas (CNG) conversions helped to keep larger Falcon sales going. Avery Motors was training between six and 10 new apprentices each year.

In 1973 Max Caigou was appointed secretary to the CMC Group at Colonial Motor Company head office. He had managed to regroup and re-house parts of the company, creating much more space which helped increase productivity. George Daniel shifted from Sockburn Motors, Christchurch, to become general manager

Adelaide Road branch was opened by Sir Francis Kitts, Wellington's mayor in 1973. From left: Martyn Spencer, building designer; Peter Gibbons, CMC managing director; Sir Francis Kitts, Norm Wilson, Ford NZ; Richard Kilkenny, manager; and Max Caigou managing director.

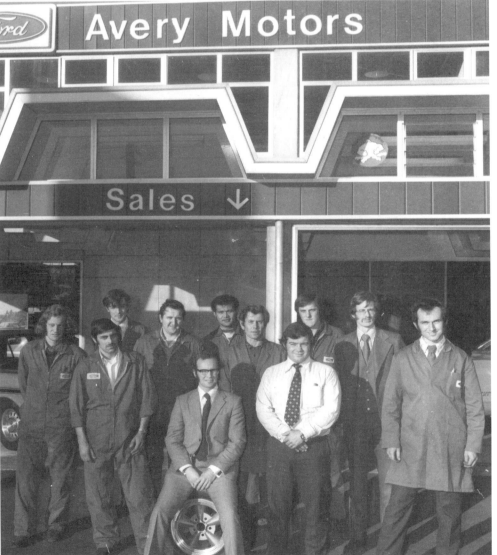

Avery Motors' Adelaide Road staff. From left: Monty Spencer, Tony Muollo, Glen Palmer, Roger Humphries, Richard Kilkenny, Toma Faavanga, Don Law, Darryl Sturgess, Jim Gush, Rick Stevens, and Roy Hobson.

George Daniel was appointed managing director in 1972. He had started in the office at £4 per week in 1946, and shifted to several CMC Group companies before managing Sockburn Motors for five years.

Stephen Eagles, with service manager Joe Feasey, won the Polytechnic Trust Norwood Award, for best all round apprentice in the Wellington area, and Avery's cup for Apprentice of the Year in 1972.

of Avery Motors, where he started work for CMC Group as an office boy in 1946 at £4 per week.

Len Morrison completed 50 years in the service department at Avery Motors in 1974. He had started in No 2 bay at Ebor Street as an apprentice in 1924, and became pre-delivery foreman after the war.

Richard Kilkenny was transferred to be assistant manager of Newlands Motors in 1976, and Ted Clay was appointed sales and branch manager at Newtown.

The lease of the Avery Motors site was renewed with the Diocesan Trust Board at the end of 1978. With inflation, the value of the land had increased substantially and the lease rental was now $95,250 per year plus outgoings.

When the city council required all CBD owners of masonry buildings to meet new earthquake standards, or demolish them, negotiations proceeded through a third party with Challenge Corp, owners of the two properties on the south boundary of Avery Motors, and next to Standard Motor Bodies. After two years negotiation, Challenge Corporation sold both sites on the corner of Jessie and Taranaki Streets.

The large five-storey building at 97 Taranaki Street was not economic to bring up to seismic standards and was demolished. The building next to it was a different matter. Major structural and exterior changes were made, and in March 1983 Avery Motors moved into its new home. More space was taken over from

Standard Motor Bodies, and the Newtown branch was closed and shifted to town.

The new dealership was still tight for room, but it was a commanding site and dovetailed well with the established workshop. As well, there were no longer worries about Ghuznee Street extensions.

The Magix computer system introduced in 1986 made significant changes automating cross entry systems, with many mechanical clerical jobs eliminated. However, many more fundamental changes occurred with the new Labour government's 'more market' policy changes in 1985 which the industry was not prepared for. These affected licensing and progressively changed the industry. The share market crash in 1987 further darkened

the business scene. The challenge to survive, which started in agriculture, had filtered into the city by 1989. One of the worst aspects was the importation of used cars. Throughout the country, used car sales plummeted when 'Jap Imports' arrived, having been artificially depreciated to low values in Japan.

Cut-backs were inevitable and Avery Motors was quick to act, although it had already done much of what was necessary with the Wellington rationalisation and closure of the Newtown branch.

George Daniel retired on March 31 1990 after 44 years with CMC Group, and had the satisfaction of seeing the company relocate to a permanent home. Pat Cody transferred from Timaru Motors to become managing director.

Meanwhile, rationalisation was still occurring in the Ford NZ network, with the tractor business sold off worldwide in 1988. Truck sales were rationalised to the main dealers, and Avery Motors supplied surrounding dealers' clients from Wellington with N Series Hino Fords until they ran out in 1993. Avery's also became a Ford Louisville extra heavy truck dealer to Ford Australia. When the protection for rail was lifted in 1988, after 50 years of cartage of goods limited to 30 miles, and later to 150km, the heavy truck market picked up rapidly after deregulation, and the demand for extra heavy models has kept increasing ever since.

Richard Kilkenny resigned as manager of Newlands Motors in August 1993. After discussion with Ford it was decided to rationalise the market area, and Newlands Motors became a branch of Avery Motors again from September 1 1993, after 28

years as a separate dealership.

Pat Cody retired on June 30 1995. Since starting as a truck salesman at Macaulay Motors in 1958, he became general sales manager, and was transferred to Timaru as manager in 1978. Pat Cody came to manage Avery Motors in March 1990, and was appointed a director of Colonial Motor Company in November 1992.

Ian J Duncan was appointed chief executive from July 1 1995, having been new car sales manager at John Andrew Ford in Auckland. Soon afterwards, Avery Motors started the process to become ISO 9002 certified in quality assurance which was fully awarded in 1996. Early on, the extra heavy Louisville trucks were reassigned to Fagan Motors and Avery's concentrated on new and used cars and light commercials. With all the deregulation, the Government Stores Board had been sold and no longer had preferred access to Ford

Reg Stephen became service manager administrative in 1976. He started his apprenticeship with Avery's in 1951, and here receives his 25 year gold watch from P C Gibbons.

Avery Motors shifted next door in 1983. The new showroom, parts department and administration centre gave a new style to the business, and concentrated all staff in one place.

Left: Ross Telford became service manager technical in 1976, having started at Avery's in 1956. Outside work he was a keen and successful yachtsman.
Right: When he retired Jack Harland had worked 50 years for the company – mostly in Wellington, but also at Invercargill and Kaikohe. He saw many changes to nearly every aspect of the business, particularly with the introduction of computers.

Below: Managing director Pat Cody presents Gerard Arthurs with his Top Technician Award following his Ford registered technician examinations.

vehicles. Avery Motors' fleet department was beefed up and actively chased government fleet sales.

It was decided that the Wellington area CMC Group companies, Maidstone, Stevens, Wellington Mazda and Avery Motors at Taranaki Street and Johnsonville, would work as a Ford Retail Network, under chief executive Ian Duncan. This meant many functions were shared, with common accounting by one staff group.

Similarly, there was a sharing of functions with used vehicle sales, service, parts and finance, plus the advantages of joint purchasing power for advertising, and utilities. The FRN certainly stripped a lot of cost out of the combined operations, but the individual parts lost some of their original character and culture.

When Ian Duncan resigned on November 30 2001, the dealerships were split into two parts, with Stevens Motors operating Ford and Mazda for the Hutt Valley from High Street, Lower Hutt, and Avery Motors the Wellington sites, including Wellington Mazda and Jack Patterson Panelbeaters. They still shared common accounting and purchasing functions.

Grant Daniel moved from being general manager at Colonial Motor Company to be chief executive of Avery Motors in December 2001 and has remained there since. Grant Daniel, whose father George was managing director until he retired in 1990, started with the CMC Group in 1974, and has been at audit, Timaru Motors, Hawke Motors, Fairhall Motors as manager, Hutchinson Motors as general sales manager, Phillipps Motors as dealer principal, and at Colonial Motor Company from 1990. His key people are: Conrad Healy, new vehicle manager; Gary Loughran, used vehicle manager; David Lavington, service manager; long serving parts manager, Martin Shaw; and Brett Winley, financial services manager.

JOHNSONVILLE – NEWLANDS MOTORS LTD

Johnsonville takes its name from original settler Frank Johnson, who arrived on the *Adelaide* on March 7 1840. In the New Zealand Company ballot for sections held in England on August 1 1839, Johnson drew 100 acre Lot 11 Kinapora, 11 miles north of Wellington. When he arrived at Petone, there was no access to the sections, and a bridle path was pushed through, but not for wheeled vehicles. Johnson took possession of his land in June 1841 and settled there. His house was beside the Johnsonville Stream where Trafalgar Street is today. Much of the area was covered in heavy bush, mostly totara. Johnson set up a mill and began cutting timber, and the place became known as Johnson's Clearing, and later Johnsonville. Much of the totara was used for building and roofing shingles (selling at 14s per 1,000) in Wellington.

When a military road was built northwest from Kaiwharawhara up Ngaio Gorge, and across to where it joined the Bridle Track to Porirua at Broderick Road, reaching Paekakariki in 1849, Johnsonville became a resting point where horses were changed, and traffic increased accordingly.

In 1846, Johnson started selling off sections of his land, and left the area, having disposed of them at a handsome profit. Hotels and stores were soon built, and in 1871 a post office was established. On November 16 1874 elections were held to form the first town board. Johnsonville remained a small town for a long time, largely servicing the surrounding small farms. The first railway – from Wellington to Palmerston North – was built in the 1880s.

When the very narrow, tortuous Ngauranga Gorge Road was rebuilt in 1939, it closed for a year during construction. After the motorway, announced in 1949, was built, motor traffic increased dramatically. Johnsonville town board held its last meeting on March 19 1953, the area becoming part of the Onslow district in Wellington.

In 1887 Freeman R Jackson, of Wanganui, purchased two acres of land in Broderick Road to sell stock from. However, the sale yards' smell and noise became a bone of contention with residents who, 60 years later, petitioned the town board for its removal. The sale yards were moved to Raroa, and the land sold to Alex Harvey and Sons. In 1956, when the land was offered for sale, it was bought by Colonial Motor Company.

Newlands Motors Ltd started operations on June 13 1965, the nearby suburb named after ship's boy Thomas Newland who began farming there in the 1850s.

Alan Hodges was appointed manager, with a staff of 24. For two years prior to this the company had operated as a branch of Avery Motors, Wellington. Alan Hodges joined Avery Motors as assistant to the manager in late 1964. He had grown up in Invercargill where he worked in sales and administration in the transport industry. The two-year-old buildings were purpose built for servicing cars and Thames Trader and new D Series Ford trucks. Alan Hodges

The staff at the beginning were nearly all from Avery Motors. From left standing: R Love, J Crawford, H Snow, J Duncan, R McNab, R Shaw, M Clarke, W Brown, D Andrews, E Anderson, and M Fogarty.
Sitting: T Syron, W Nott, Evelyn Hutchins, Alan Hodges, Ivy Pycroft, M Ensor, Tom Hutchins and G Beaver. Absent: K Hedges, M Martin, P Batten, E Porter, and R Mercer.

*Above: Newlands
Motors 1965.*

*Above: Newlands
Motors backed onto
the railway and was
beside the new
shopping mall.*

*Right: The workshop
was full of natural
light.*

Left: Alan Hodges was the first manager.

Right: Evelyn Hutchins was a full time driver.

also handled all sales for a period. Much of the service work was new vehicle pre-delivery initially, done under contract to Avery Motors. In those days vehicles were driven or railed from the factory to dealers and Evelyn Hutchins, wife of parts manager Tom Hutchins, was employed full time delivering cars from the Ford factory at Seaview to Newlands Motors and on to Avery Motors. Evelyn Hutchins shifted on average 1,000 new cars and commercials each year, and in her 'spare' time, used vehicles, and new car swaps with other dealers.

The dealership territory was most of the Onslow district, from Ngaio to Newlands and north of Johnsonville to Tawa, a rapidly growing part of Wellington. No Remittance

sales helped to increase the number of new cars which were still in very short supply. Alan Hodges also knew a lot about buses from his Invercargill days, and when the new Ford R 226 bus chassis was introduced, he recognised a winner, quickly selling several to the two local operators, Newlands Coach Services and Meehan Coachlines.

As the dealership was growing, N A (Norm) Hipwell transferred from Fagan Motors in 1968, as sales manager, selling new and used cars. Most new car customers were from Onslow and Tawa, but used cars were sold to a much larger Wellington catchment. The large Johnsonville shopping mall next door brought in a great deal of traffic to the area at weekends

Alan Hodges resigned in 1971 after

Newlands had a new manager, Norman Shorter, when this 1972 photograph was taken. Standing left: B Meredith, A Sutorius, T Hughes, R Gillespie, J Sinclair, J Darrell, G Liddell, R Crabtree, I Fraser, C Parfitt, W Williams, G O'Hara, R Smith, R Dunn, D Ross, Martin Powell and B Griffin. Sitting: Evelyn Hutchins, M Ensor, R Davenport-Brown, Norm Hipwell, Norm Shorter, R Jackson, P Mann, Tom Hutchins, H Juchnowicz, J Tickner. Absent: W Brown, T Toomer, G Fifield, S McCarthy.

Above: Bob Holden, and co-driver Hon John Dawson-Daimer, had a back-up crew of Mike Martin and Keith Pfeffer in the 1972 Heatway Rally. Australian Bob Holden won most of the special stages in his twin-cam Escort. The back-up crew was delighted that its preparation was also successful, as the car arrived only seven days before the start.

Middle: When gas arrived in Wellington, Newlands Motors was one of the first to have CNG, LPG and petrol, all selling in volume.

Right: LPG required strict handling procedures and there was a special compound for the storage cylinder.

Ian Lambie was general manager from 1977 to 1981.

getting the dealership well established in the area, which had increased in population by more than 50% in five years. N R (Norm) Shorter was appointed general manager, transferring from Te Kuiti Motors. He was secretary of Battersby Motors for many years prior to joining CMC Group in 1963.

New car supply had now increased with the freeing up of license, and new vehicle volumes increased quickly. Johnsonville continued to expand, with the town becoming the commercial hub of the area, and the service station was increased in size to cope with the large throughput of fuel.

When Norm Shorter retired in 1977, Ian Lambie, who had been at Avery Motors for six months, and previously managed Fairhall Motors at Kaikohe, was appointed general manager.

With the second oil crisis, it was decided to sell liquid petroleum gas (LPG) and compressed natural gas (CNG). The LPG installation required significant safety measures for the nine tonne storage cylinder which was isolated in its compound at the rear of the property. Staff were also trained and qualified in the installation of gas conversions to vehicles. Demand for the conversion kits was high as people tried to combat the restrictions placed on petrol use – 'carless days' and price hikes – and the dealership had

difficulty in keeping up with the demand.

In 1981 Ian Lambie was transferred to Napier Motors, Dunedin, and Richard J Kilkenny, who was assistant manager, was appointed manager. He had been in the CMC Group for a number of years, and had an immense amount of experience from his many postings around New Zealand. His grandfather and father had been the Ford

Richard Kilkenny was appointed manager, and receives his gold watch from Peter Gibbons in 1991. It was a Mickey Mouse watch as the Omega had not arrived!

dealer at Westport from the 1920s until selling out in 1960.

Newlands Motors was one of the first volume service stations selling all fuels – petrol, diesel, LPG and CNG. Petrol volumes were over one million litres, and LPG was selling nearly $^1/_2$ million litres equivalent per year, which was very high. The station was well positioned to catch all main road traffic from the motorway.

When the Ford Laser was launched in 1981, it was the top selling new car on the market, with excellent fuel economy amongst its attributes. However, with the introduction of the new government's 'more market' policies in 1985, marketing changed dramatically, and Newlands Motors concentrated on retailing used vehicles at a profit, which was very difficult as values fell rapidly with the huge volumes of 'Jap Imports'.

The Johnsonville Mall was expanded in 1987 and part of the original Newlands Motors land, kept for later development beside the mall, was sold to allow this. With multi fuels still selling in volume, and new deregulation of oil and petrol prices, it was decided to shift the service station to the side, giving Newlands Motors a more effective used car display area. A new service station was built, and leased to Caltex.

Richard Kilkenny resigned at the end of August 1993 and, with the rationalisation of the motor industry taking place, it was decided that management of the site would revert to Avery Motors.

Today, Avery Motors' Johnsonville branch is still performing with distinction, serving the Onslow district well, and providing Taranaki Street with a safety valve of workshop space.

CHAPTER TWENTYFOUR

STANDARD MOTOR BODIES LTD & COLMOCO ENGINEERING EBOR STREET, WELLINGTON

During the 1920s, Colonial Motor Company steadily acquired one acre town blocks of property at Te Aro, Wellington behind York Street and between Taranaki and Tory Streets. A large part of Ebor Street, where the service workshops were sited, was included in these acquisitions.

With the ever-expanding number of Model T Fords and the need for specialised uses, another company, Standard Motor Bodies Ltd (SMB) was formed on December 5 1925. This was located in the end bays of the Ford workshops, at the top of Ebor Street, principally to build commercial bodies on the Model T chassis and repair damaged vehicles. A variety of 'standard' body designs were made for Ford vans and trucks in particular.

John Hunt, a master coachbuilder and wheelwright, who came to New Zealand in 1895 from High Wycombe, England, was the first manager, bringing a wealth of practical experience. He quickly set up the business.

John Hunt had worked previously at Munt Cottrell, Wellington carriers who built their own drays, as did Bob McCluggage, who joined him as accountant in March 1926. Bob McCluggage worked exactly 50 years, retiring in 1976. Accounting initially was very basic, involving an exercise book and cheque butts, but the office ran quite smoothly. He worked with John Hunt for 36 years until John died, and had this to say:

"John was a tough old rooster, but he was a soft touch as well. He had the interests of his workers at heart and had a word with them all each day right to the end. He got good co-operation from them because he was fair. And he knew his stuff too; he was a master wheelwright and coachbuilder and had learnt his craft in England. There was a good atmosphere in the workshop, he saw to that, but you had to be up to the mark. Like his foremen, he carried a four-foot ruler all the time and if you played up you were likely to get a clout with it. He was also a good businessman. His maxim was 'don't price yourself out of the business'.

"But in the beginning, the company concentrated on designing and building standardised commercial bodies on Ford Model T chassis. At that time the country was in the transition period from horse-drawn to motorised vehicles, but horses still provided the bulk of the power.

"Motor trucks were available but were mostly about three tons capacity and much too big and expensive for many trades. Butchers, grocers, bakers and milkmen still delivered door to door and preferred the horse. The Model T provided a chassis on which a cheap, light body could be built. The basic truck was a simple job, a cab and a flat tray. The tray was made with Southland silver beech runners and crossbars with a white pine floor. The cab was framed with beech; the back of light tongue and groove matai; the sides of white

Staff in 1926. John Hunt is eighth from left in the centre row.

pine. The roof of three ply was covered with light canvas, well painted. Shatterproof glass was unknown then and the screen was $1/4$ inch plate glass. Seating was an un-sprung cushion, with a padded board across the cab as backrest. The cushion had to be easily removed because the petrol tank was under the seat.

"There were not many petrol pumps then and fuel was in four-gallon tins which were quite hard to manage. The body was quite basic, but it had to be because our price was £32 at the factory door and the retail price was £40. Extras were tail and sideboards, rear mudguards, and storm curtains on the side.

"Van bodies were just as basic and were panelled in kauri, panel steel not being in vogue then. These sold for £40, and retailed for £50. Colours were basic too – red, blue or green, mixed in the paint shop with raw materials mostly from England.

"The factory equipment was far behind the standards of today. The common set-up was one prime mover, a coal gas engine, or an electric motor, and this drove a long overhead shaft that had pulleys from which machines could be belt driven. Electric motors at that time were all very bulky and quite unsuitable for individual machines. At SMB the main power was an enormous 15hp electric motor driving the main shaft, with fast and loose pulleys above each machine. The loose pulley was not keyed to the shaft and when a machine was not being used its driving belt was shifted to the loose pulley."

Despite some of the old fashioned methods, by today's standards, SMB was a leader in new techniques and processes. In 1927 they started using compressed air tools. Spray painting was only beginning

Below and following page: Body shop in 1930, showing virtually every stage of body building work. It is interesting to study in conjunction with Harold Gower's commentary in the text.

and they re-painted Mr Virtue's car – 20 coats, but they all had an orange peel effect. Finally, a hand-brushed coat of clear lacquer produced a wonderful result and a very happy customer.

Bob McCluggage said: "Compressed air was just coming in and the compressor was driven from a cross-shaft which was driven by a Model T engine and exhausted into a tank. Machines in use were a crosscut saw, a 'buzz' planer and a band saw plus a few air drills. Every tradesman of course provided his own tool chest, and it was customary to look over his tools when he arrived to form an opinion of his standing.

"Conditions of employment were different too. Hours of work were $8^{1}/2$ hours each week day and $4^{1}/2$ hours on Saturday. The award rate for 47 hours was 2s 3d per hour or £5 5s 9d per week.

SMB introduced windscreen wipers in the late 1920s as a sales incentive. "They were hand operated of course, but the opposition accused us of unfair trade practices – told everyone only cissies needed windscreen wipers. Even doors and windows on trucks didn't come in until later; a real man wasn't supposed to need them."

It was almost true that Standard Motor Bodies could make anything. Certainly, they were able to adapt the uses of all manner of vehicles and made very successful buses, fire engines, concrete mixer trucks and mobile workshops, to name but a few of the non-standard types of Ford vehicles. They produced the first Model A school bus for the Education Department in 1930. In the early stages, all the bodies were wooden framed, using Southland beech and kauri, which were mounted to the chassis.

Everything was done in the Ebor Street workshops by their own blacksmiths, wheelwrights, coachbuilders, painters, panel beaters and engineers. Early on they built large wooden trailers for the Public Works Department. These were adapted from horse trailers and had wooden wheels with steel tyres. Truck cabs were quite spartan in those days with no doors, let alone wind-up side windows.

In 1928, NZ Insurance Company entered into an arrangement that Standard Motor Bodies would repair damaged vehicles; this meant an immediate expansion into the neighbouring area at Ebor Street. A year later, on June 16 1929, the day of the Murchison Earthquake, work started on SMB's new larger repair workshops. Today these workshops are still in use as Avery Motors' service department.

When SMB built the first petrol tankers in the early 1930s, Atlantic ordered 32 of them. Bob McCluggage remembered: "Each tanker had to have a coat of shellac varnish on the inside and apprentices were sent in to do the job. One joker flaked out with the fumes and we only just got him out in time."

Harold Gower, an apprentice body builder in 1928, retired after 41 years in 1969. He recalled some of the early days:

"There were two types of roof construction; the more square type was gradually replaced with the rounded corners .... The rounded corners were made up with wooden slats about 1 inch wide and $^1/_2$ inch thick, and were made in a similar manner to the planking on the sides of boats, glued together, rounded with a plane and finished with a wood rasp, then covered with a fabric, mostly black hoodite, but sometimes if it was a cheaper type, with canvas. The back corners were made from a solid block and rounded by hand.

"Painting was also a coach builder's art handed down, with all the paint applied by brush, one coat of primer, one coat of colour with a final coat of carriage varnish, smoothed out with a camel hair brush, and they were always wanted out yesterday. There was no drying room in the paint shop and quite often during winter the varnish was still tacky the next morning, but the remedy was simply to run it out in the air and throw a bucket of icy cold water over the whole vehicle, and when the air had dried off the water, the varnish had set enough for a delivery to be made. Hand brushing was replaced by spray painting, at first using 'Egyptian Lacquer'; when Hope Gibbons Ltd imported an enamel called 'Glyco' the whole procedure changed and meant that bays had to be built with fans to take away the over spray, but it meant a big saving in time.

"We had at that time strict supervision from the 'Boss' and it wasn't unusual to have our attention drawn to any shoddy workmanship with a resounding thump across the backside with his four foot rule from the other side of the job, or perhaps the words, 'Harold, Joe doesn't want to talk to you, he is very busy'.

"The repair shop was quite different. Seldom did we have a chassis to repair; when a car had a bad smash there was literally nothing left but a pile of matchwood. The body maker got what he could out of the bits and pieces to get a body shape to work to.

"We had to cut all the wood shapes ourselves, put them together and then make or repair the doors before the panels were applied (sides only as the roof was covered

Fire engines were a major development with the Ford V8 in the mid 1930s. Under the skin they were quite a complicated piece of engineering.

with black 'hoodite'). An accident sometimes damaged the wooden wheel spokes and it was the body man's job to replace these with ones made from hardwood. We rigged up a sort of lathe from the horizontal borer in the machine shop and had tables for the angles of the base that fitted onto the hub, according to the number of spokes.

"In those days we had the weekly

inspection of the plant by old Hope B Gibbons who knew the names of all the staff and would often say a few words about the work they were doing.

"We built vans and cabs (bodies) to a jig and they were sent by rail to Auckland to be fitted by Colonial Motor Company Auckland branch. They would be collected by dray, pulled by two Clydesdale horses. On one occasion there was a lot of noise

when men were lifting a van body onto the dray. They had got the front part onto the rear edge of the dray when the horses took fright and bolted, eventually coming to a halt when the dray collected some cars further down Ebor Street. The van body was damaged and 'Old John's' four-foot rule worked overtime on that occasion."

Fire engines had been built by the Colonial Motor Company since the mid 1920s, firstly on the Model T, and then Model A, chassis, and were made by the dozens for fire-fighting all over New Zealand. They were simple, fast and reliable, providing a quick response and, of course, they were much cheaper than the specialised English units. Nearly every fire brigade in New Zealand was equipped with a Ford 'Flyer', the first response fire engine.

With the arrival of the Ford V8 a whole new opportunity opened up because its engine was both powerful and compact and could provide the muscle for pumping water. The Ford V8 became the new 'Flyer' for most brigades in New Zealand.

In 1936 Standard Motor Bodies was restructured and Colonial Motor Company opened a new Colmoco Engineering Works in Ebor Street in the brick workshops alongside SMB. At the same time Avery Motors was established and buildings were constructed fronting Taranaki Street, but running back to Ebor Street, which became a large industrial area.

When Ford Motor Company set up an assembly plant at Seaview, Lower Hutt, the Colonial Motor Company's nine-storey assembly plant was no longer necessary. A number of staff transferred to Ford, and those remaining with CMC were placed with the engineering division. Under the manager, Jack Manning, all kinds of new ventures were started, dovetailing with Standard Motor Bodies. A cam and roller hydraulic lift hoist for tipping truck bodies, winches and fire fighting pumps, were amongst the early ones.

Larger Ford V8 trucks were now available, together with other makes, and Standard Motor Bodies became a large supplier of tip truck bodies and fire engines, with many of the components manufactured and supplied by Colmoco Engineering.

Fire pumps were developed for a range of applications, and CMC had raw brass castings made at Penfolds in Christchurch and Crittals in Auckland. Alloy Steel Ltd in Christchurch made the steel castings. These were all machined and mated at Ebor Street into highly efficient, either single or two stage, centrifugal pumps. They operated at 4,000 rpm and could be directly coupled to the compact Ford V8 engine which gave an adequate 'specific speed' for pumping. Machines were available as front, mid and rear mounted pumps for both tractors and trucks and independent trailer-pumps. The pumps were not only used for fighting fires; they could be adapted to pump large volumes of storm water to help control flooding.

Jack Manning's style was very different from John Hunt's, but he was good with words and his tongue could be just as effective as John Hunt's four-foot ruler, and he wouldn't tolerate any slackness either. He had been a senior instructor in the service department, teaching mechanics from all around New Zealand, the new service methods for all new Model A and Ford V8 vehicles prior to Ford taking over assembly. Jack Manning was always able to look at new ideas in a practical way, to see how they could be done. He also organised family picnic outings for his staff.

In 1934, Mick Allison started as an apprentice panelbeater aged 14. Pay was 10s per week, and together with a working foreman, a tradesman and 16 other apprentices they toiled away under the watchful eye of John Hunt. Mick Allison looked back in 1983:

"He was a hard old buggar that one, but he was fair and I got on with him alright. His glass-fronted office was walled with mirrors, cunningly placed so he could watch just about every corner of the workshop."

After about a year he called Mick Allison into his office: "Now listen, I've been watching you, you're not doing badly, and you're learning. I'm going to give you another 2s 6d a week, but whatever you do, don't tell the other apprentices." Mick returned to the shop floor swelling with pride and with renewed enthusiasm for his job. Some time later he discovered all apprentices had got the same raise.

"John used to give us overtime nearly every night, even when we were supposed to be going to night school. He reckoned that keeping up production was more important than book learning. We used to get tea and biscuits – plain biscuits – during the 10 minute break in the evening shift.

The 1946 Ford V8 'jail bar' (because of the grill) arrived as a chassis/cowl, which meant the engine, gearbox and chassis with body panels from the windscreen forward. All the white body behind was made by SMB. This body, with a side hatch, carried a ton of payload.

Below: A tradesman teaching an apprentice how to draw and roll guards and flare the edges. These may be used on a trailer or as part of the wheel arch in a body. With curving they become much stronger.

My mate Roy Reid made two huge pots of tea and threw the biscuits down to us."

There was no staff cafeteria in those days; they ate their lunch sitting on a bench or standing up. No social functions either, apart from football matches against other firms on Saturday afternoons, and a family picnic at Christmas.

Mick Allison finished his apprenticeship in 1939, earning £2 5s a week. Like most of the others he left because John Hunt wouldn't pay any more. He went to General Motors for £6 0s 3d a week.

When the Second World War began, many of the men left to fight overseas and, initially, work reduced in volume.

In 1941, after the disastrous loss of men and equipment during battles in Crete and Greece, the government ordered 400 new truck bodies to be built by the end of February 1942. These were the MT2 and MT4 personnel carriers that were bolted directly onto a Ford or Chevrolet truck chassis. They were a well-side design with steel framed canopy covered with canvas.

This was a large order on top of other work, making fire pumps and other military goods, but was started immediately. Then the shipping dates were altered and the bodies had to be ready a month earlier at the end of January. At the beginning of December 1941 the pressure was really on,

The blacksmith was a very important part of the business. Tom Montague could fashion all sorts of brackets, frames and housings, make bolts and pins, levers, springs or rods, and put in any sorts of cranks, or twists, in a piece of steel.

Below: Tom Montague swings the hammer.

SMB made a variety of basic workshop equipment. Left, a mechanic's tool trolley and a battery trolley. They also made 'creepers', a low trolley on castors, which a mechanic could lie on, and roll, creeping with his feet, underneath a vehicle.

then came the order that the truck bodies had to be ready by the end of December. The staff set to, broke all records and had the last body ready to ship on Christmas Eve, more than two months ahead of schedule. Christmas Day was a well-earned rest for the staff with their families, exhausted but well pleased with their efforts for the troops in Egypt.

The trimming department was also kept busy with war work for the New Zealand and US armies. It turned out canvas 'kit' bags, machette cases, pistol holsters, and specialised leather gun site and range finder cases and holdalls.

SMB and CMC were declared essential war industries in 1942. Trailer pumps continued to be made at the rate of about 60 per month, and were shipped all over the world as well as around New Zealand. The United States had now joined in the war and Liberty P and K class ships were coming down into the Pacific but, in their haste to build the ships, mainly for the Atlantic convoys, no provision had been made for fire fighting. Consequently, when a ship called into Wellington harbour to pick up troops, there would be a phone order to install fire pumps and, under Frank Anderson the foreman, they would be built to requirements within hours, often through the night. This done, the pumps had to be fitted to the ship, often in time to sail again the next day. They were similar to the trailer pumps, but had to be adapted to fit the lower revving Gray marine diesels.

Petrol engines were not allowed because of the higher risk of fire.

The company also developed special NZ Forest Service fire engines using Beaverette 4x4 Ford V8s, with a large rear mounted water tank which could be driven across country to a fire.

In all, more than 3,000 trailer fire-pumps and 200 other types were built for the war effort, an outstanding effort for such a small operation.

John Hunt's son, Peter, was discharged from the army after being wounded in Libya and a long period of convalescence. He went to work for Ford at Seaview for a period, but came to Standard Motor Bodies in 1944 to help out in the office. Over a period he took over much of his father's work. John Hunt had started at Standard Motor Bodies in 1925 and was now in his 70s.

After most of the men returned from the war, there were about 100 working at SMB. Although Standard Motor Bodies and Colmoco Engineering were separate businesses, they had a common interest in helping each other on large jobs. A decision was made that they could also work on other than new Ford new vehicles.

Much of Standard Motor Bodies' work was repairing damaged cars, and specialised chassis straightening and wheel alignment equipment was installed in 1959. Many new fire engines and truck and van bodies were still being built, including the first all steel and all alloy ones in New

Standard Motor Bodies retail shop and trim department was on the corner of Ebor and Tory Streets. SMB made seats cushions and roof coverings for vehicles, and a variety of other goods. During the war this included roll up stretchers, holdalls for equipment, officers' kit. Later there were sheepskin seat covers and John Hunt's famous leather travel bags, which he presented to the Tractor Banner award winners. SMB would re-upholster anything, including a DC3 aircraft in leather for the Queen's tour.

Zealand. Ford E83W 10hp trucks came in as chassis cowls, and SMB still made the cab and rear deck, but the era of wooden cabs was over. Vans were nearly all steel now, and making a chassis cowl into a steel van became too expensive.

A number of unusual jobs were also done at Ebor Street. A DC3 aircraft was re-trimmed in leather by the trim department, for the Royal Tour in 1953, drawing much very favourable comment. SMB made the steel sleds towed behind tractors for Sir Edmund Hillary's dash to the South Pole.

The Sno-Cats used in the Trans-Antarctic crossing were overhauled at Ebor Street. SMB still had a blacksmith, Tom Montague, who made many of the steel brackets, hinges, bumpers and equipment needed for industrial use.

On May 3 1957, a fire broke out at 3 am, gutting the bodybuilding bay, and the firm was lucky not to be completely burnt out. A temporary roof was built over the area and work continued during re-building. A new staff cafeteria and office was added.

Far left: John Hunt, founding manager, was tough but fair.

Left: Peter Hunt took over much of his father's work after the war.

Above: This 4-pole electro-hydraulic vehicle hoist was made in the 1960s and sold in good numbers.

Opposite top: Thames Traders offered new opportunities. This truck was fitted with 4-wheel steering in 1959, so the payload could be increased, and an eight-yard body fitted, all at SMB.

Opposite bottom: Fire engines were still being made and shifted to alloy bodies to save weight.

Panel beating and crash repair was a key component of the business from 1930. Chassis straightening was a major part of vehicle repair. Three chassis pullers at work in the 1960s.

The Omega club in 1966. Standing left: George Guise, Mick Connolly, Bob McCluggage, I (Kreuge) Howard. Sitting: Ray Hunt, Jack Manning, Martin Butler.

Colmoco's engineering department was busy manufacturing fire pumping equipment, and making vehicle hoists to lift truck bodies and also pole hoists for servicing in workshops. In 1958 they made a sump eductor for cleaning out street drain sumps and a street sweeper. Both these specialised units were built onto trucks for the city council. They were highly complicated, but successful, and were also built on other than Ford vehicles. When Coca-Cola came to New Zealand, the company built a special pinch chassis that allowed a low loading V-deck body to be built on the truck.

Jack Manning retired at the end of 1961,

The Omega club in 1972. Standing left: Ray Hunt, George Guise. Sitting: Tom Montague, Duncan Skinner and Bob McCluggage.

Goods distribution changed in the 1960s, making new demands. This 'pinch' chassis and body was built for a Coca Cola low loading truck, getting a maximum number of bottle crates aboard.

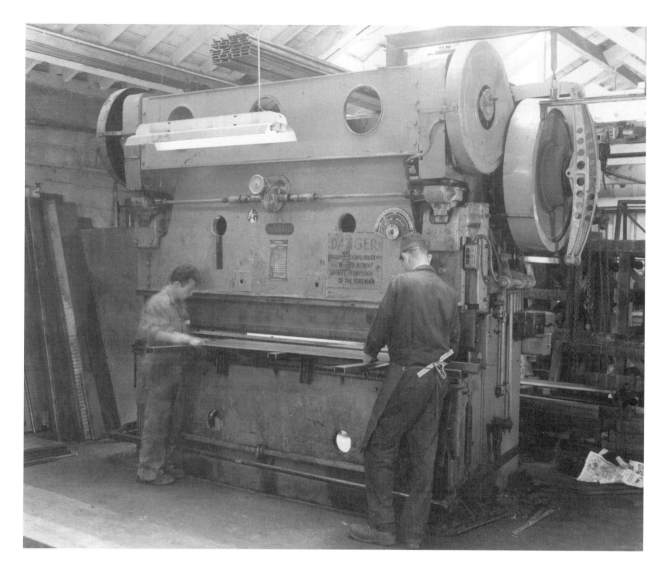

having worked for CMC Group for 33 years. His ability to visualise how a new piece of equipment would work, and then get it built, had been a great asset to the company.

John Hunt was 88 when he died in March 1962. Right up to the end, he had been in the office each day, but his son, Peter, was doing most of his work. John Hunt left his stamp on the business, which was now a very large and diverse company. Standard Motor Bodies could build or fix almost anything, and easily qualified for a motto such as 'You name it, we'll make it'.

Peter Hunt became general manager and Colmoco Engineering was merged with Standard Motor Bodies, with Martin Butler managing the truck conversions and bodies.

The company functioned as it had and was still busy, but was increasingly subjected to competition. A number of tenders were lost to small specialist companies, and very few fire engines were now made. Much of the pumping equipment could be bought 'off the shelf' from specialist suppliers in England and United States and, with their large volumes, prices were lower.

In 1969, after Peter Hunt resigned and left Wellington to go farming, severing 45 years of family association with the company, R G (Bob) Tunley, a long serving foreman in the panel department, was appointed manager.

Rent was increasing quickly with the rise in land value in the Te Aro area, and when more business in heavy truck bodybuilding was lost to tenders because

of the high overheads, a decision was made to close that part of the business, and shift the panel repairs into Ebor Street No 1 Bay. The trim department, which operated from the Ebor and Tory Streets corner, relocated into one of the Jessie Street houses owned by Colonial Motor Company, and the corner was leased for retail shopping. This freed up a complete workshop area which was taken over by Avery Motors, now under considerable pressure for such space. The savings in overhead were considerable, and took some pressure off SMB.

Above: The trim shop moved to Jessie Street in 1970. From left: Barry Southgate (back to camera), Noel Heyworth, Martin Olsen, Charlie Smith and Paul Tunley. Apart from vehicle trimming, they could re-upholster hotel chairs and furniture.

Left: Bob Tunley was manager after Peter Hunt retired.

Opposite top: This Sonntag heavy press was able to bend or guillotine plate steel for truck bodies, and press to 100 tonnes. With good equipment, time and money were saved, and the finished job was done to a higher standard.

Opposite bottom: SMB could do almost anything. When was the last time you had a Tucker Sno-cat in for repairs? "Well, actually, in 1958, we had four in after the Trans Antarctic Crossing."

*Frank Butler
clocked up 40 years
and is congratulated
by Peter Gibbons.*

Following the changes made by government in 1985, another of the Ebor Street bays was vacated by SMB and leased to the Automobile Association for a workshop and inspection unit, and the wheel alignment unit was moved to Avery Motors.

After fire broke out at Standard Motor Bodies shop at No 2 Ebor Street, gutting the entire building, and damaging those buildings each side, it was decided to close down the remaining parts of the business and transfer the staff and any work to Avery Motors.

*Ebor Street walls
are still there today
and, with their art
deco styling, have
city heritage
registration. SMB
was absorbed into
Avery Motors in the
1980s after the fire
in No.2 (middle) bay
gutted the building.
Today, it is a
parking precinct.*

Standard Motor Bodies has a proud history to look back on. When Ford arrived in 1936, the company had adapted and continued building specialist bodies. Through the Second Word War the company carried the day for Colonial Motor Company, making a good profit, and a very large contribution to the war effort. After the war new ventures were successfully undertaken, and it supported all the subsidiary companies with expertise and innovation. The motor industry is noted for one thing, and that is change. Every objective Standard Motor Bodies had been set in 1925 had changed and, despite reinventing itself several times, its time had now come.

CHAPTER TWENTYFIVE

NELSON AND BLENHEIM – M S FORD 1998 LTD

Nelson is the 'capital' of the province of the same name, and Blenheim is the principal town of Marlborough. Combined, the two areas cover the top 20% of the South Island. Both areas are regarded as desirable places to live, with plentiful sunshine, excellent beaches, waterways and national parks.

NELSON

On December 25 1642, when Dutch explorer, Abel Tasman, anchored in the bay that takes his name, and received a hostile reception from Ngati Tumatakokiri who killed four of his crew, he named the area Moordenaers (Murderers' Bay), and set sail again. Maori tribes from the north successively sacked the area, despatching any defenders and depleting the population. Waitaha Maori had first settled there, but were driven out by Ngati Mamoe who suffered the same fate from the Ngati Tumatakokiri. Captain James Cook was there in 1770, and in 1827 d'Urville, the French commander, spent several days exploring the area.

Named after Admiral Lord Horatio Nelson, Nelson had its beginnings as a European settlement on October 9 1841 when the New Zealand Company's first settlers arrived on the *Whitby*, *Will Watch* and *Arrow*. They discovered Nelson Haven 11 days later and decided to make their settlement beside its sheltered inlet waters. The New Zealand Company offered settlers 1,000 allotments – a town acre, a suburban block and 150 rural acres for £300. Within a short time 2,000 settlers had arrived. The settlement fell on hard times for a period following the suspension of New Zealand Company business in 1844, which halted capital works. A total of 300 men were unemployed and, with no cash, they bartered amongst themselves for their basic needs. By 1853 the town had recovered and was capital of the very large provincial district of Nelson, stretching down to Greymouth and across to North Canterbury.

In 1858, Queen Victoria issued letters-patent creating the Diocese of Nelson, and proclaiming 'the said Town of Nelson shall be a City'. It was the first to reach city status in the country and had a bishop but did not qualify as a borough until 1874.

Today, it is a charming cathedral city of 42,000, renowned for its equable climate and wonderful golden beaches. All manner of farming activities abound in the area: tobacco, hops, pip and berry fruits, grapes, vegetables and forestry. There is an international port and fishing industry, with canning, bottling and preserving plants; there are wineries and light industries. Many of the original buildings remain, creating a unique charm, and there is a thriving art and crafts community. With the nearby national parks, it has become a tourist mecca.

[The following passage, describing early Nelson Ford dealers, is part of an article written in 2002 by Denis LeCren, for the Nelson Vintage Car Club magazine The Crank Case. *He has generously allowed these extracts, and some of his photographs, to be reproduced.]*

"The company of W G Vining Ltd was set up on the May 26 1914, in Trafalgar St, taking over the business previously run by W G Vining on his own. During this early period he sold Cadillacs and later obtained franchises for Hudson, Essex, Chevrolet and Rover cars. He did sell one new Ford Model T in 1915, the same car bought second hand from R Wright & Son in 1925 by Arthur Waterhouse, and subsequently sold to Denny King.

In May 1919 The Nelson Universal Car Company Ltd was formed as 'District Agents for Ford Cars' with a capital of £1,800. Two of the many objects of the company were:

a. to acquire and take over as a going concern the motor business and premises of Frank Rupert Hallam in Hardy St. Nelson;

b. to carry on the business of

Top: G M Smart Ltd, dealers in 1930.

Middle: The first day M S Motors opened in 1938. The buildings had doubled in size since 1930.

Bottom: M S Motors opened up the front of the premises in 1950.

manufacturers of, importers of, dealers in, agents for, repairers, cleaners, storers, and warehouses of automobiles, motor cars, motors, motor cycles, bicycles, velocipedes and carriages of all kinds.

The shareholders were listed as: Frank Rupert Hallam, Thomas Harrison Horrax, Charles John Harley, Philip Best and Harold Leon Harley.

The number of Fords sold is unknown but Account No 661 dated June 14 1920 indicates the sale of one Ford touring car to Mrs Kerr, Miss Manssen and Mr Barnes. This car was complete with the following extras:

2 gallons benzine @ 4s 6d per gallon,
4 gallons of oil @ 3s 6d per gallon,
1 inner tube, 5lbs grease and 2 spark plugs.

Registration and number plates cost ten shillings!

On March 10 1920 the capital was increased by £1,600 and on October 15 1925 F R Hallam was appointed as liquidator for a voluntary winding up of the business.

By 1926 the Ford agency had changed to R Wright & Son and on April 12 1926 a second hand Ford car engine no 45003 was sold for £40 to Mr Arthur Waterhouse of Stoke and on July 6 1927 Mr Kerr of Atawhai bought a second hand Ford ton truck for £85. The premises of this firm opened onto Victoria Avenue later called Achilles Ave about where Briscoes are today.

G M Smart Ltd took over the premises formerly occupied by R Wright and Son a

corrugated iron building in Victoria Ave, which had a workshop, petrol station and a showroom facility for one car! Used cars were housed inside at night but during the day were displayed on either side of Victoria Ave.

With the closing of G M Smart Ltd, M S Motors Ltd was established by Dick Stevenson and Bob McKegg on August 1 1938 and continued to trade for nearly 60 years. Difficult times were experienced during the war years but once over, the company grew with the buoyant years that followed. Bob McKegg sold out in 1957 after which three generations of Stevensons had the control of the company. Ford cars have always been their only franchise. During this period the site was extended into Halifax St.

As the business premises could not be expanded further and a large customer base had been formed in the Richmond area, the company bought an acre of land in Richmond in 1965 and early in 1967 commenced selling Fords from these new premises."

The Stevenson family has been active in the business for over 60 years from 1938 and, after Bob McKegg sold out to Dick Stevenson in 1957, there have been two further generations involved; Dick Stevenson's son, Bernie, was managing director for many years; and his grandson Rob for the last five years. The business was sold to Colonial Motor Company in April 1998.

The Colonial Motor Company set up M S Ford 1998 Ltd, buying the trading company, plant and stock of M S Motors Ltd in April 1998. All 27 staff transferred to the new company. John Flanagan, previously dealer principal of Avon City Ford at Christchurch, was appointed chief executive, and took over on June 2 1998.

The trading company was located in Halifax Street, but was relocated to premises acquired at Haven Road, formerly used by the GM dealer, which had closed down.

Ken Mullan, the CMC internal auditor, was there to assist John Flanagan the first day, and helped to organise stock take and asset inventories. The main asset, 27 staff members, all had to have new employment contracts, and there were a myriad of details to be gone through. At the end of the month the transfer to Haven Road was accomplished, with the company continuing to trade right through.

To make the business more effective, John Flanagan decided to set up outlying service points, together with fuel. BP agreed to lease service station sites to M S Ford at Haven Road, Richmond, Washington Road and Blenheim. Two have Service Lane quick service points attached, to give customers convenient choices. The Washington Road BP outlet closed recently due to changes on the main south route but Annesbrook has been added.

The service stations are run as a cluster by M S Ford's service station manager, Kate Motley, with assistance from business manager Michael Harte, and are proving to be very popular. They employ 46 people on a full time basis.

Vehicle sales, under sales manager Daron Graham, and specialised service, operate from the main Haven Road Ford dealership, next to one of the BP operations.

M S Ford head office in Haven Road.

With the increasing volumes of service work from the Service Lane outlets, employment has nearly doubled since 1998. Service manager Craig Brett and parts manager Steve Toms are both delighted with the extra business achieved.

Customer satisfaction has been the driving force at all locations. Standards have been introduced, together with training. This has worked well, and in 2003 the dealership achieved Ford's highest acknowledgement, the President's Award.

John Flanagan is pleased with the progress of his whole team and branches

Above: Some of M S Ford's key people at Haven Road. From left: Paul Carnegie, Andrew Siddells, Glen Scrimgeour, Kellie Cockerell, Michael Harte, Andrea Martyn, Colin Roach and Daron Graham.

Right: BP 24 hour at Haven Road. From left: Quentin Rewi, Ellie Martyn, Kate Motley and John Flanagan.

Richmond Service Lane staff. From left: Steve Martyn, John Andrews and John Silke.

to date and says that profitability has been boosted by getting the service and 'customer focus' culture and standards working properly. He adds: "There is still a lot to do, and it's early days yet. Now, we must consolidate on our good work and turn this into volume customer business, to provide total customer satisfaction to more people." The future is looking good.

BLENHEIM

Marlborough is renowned worldwide for its wine industry, established over the last 30 years around Blenheim which, with over 2,600 hours of sunshine each year, deserves its title of 'the Sunshine Capital'.

About 1826, visiting sealers named the inlet north of Cloudy Bay, Port Underwood. The area on the southern side of Cloudy Bay, at the confluence of the Opawa and Omaka rivers, was a safe ford and landing place, and future site of Blenheim. It was then a marshy low-lying area, not good for habitation, but close by the Wairau Plain.

Captain John Blenkinsopp, master of the whaler *Caroline*, claimed to have bought the whole of the Wairau Plain from Te Rauparaha and other chiefs during the 1830s. After he sold his dubious title to the New Zealand Company, who started surveying the area, Maori resisted, claiming the land was theirs and had not been sold; this led to the Wairau massacre in 1843 and the survey was abandoned.

In March 1847, Sir George Grey succeeded in buying the Wairau and Awatere Plains from Maori, and later more land to Kaiapoi, enabling settlement to go ahead mainly by sheep farmers.

When Wynen's store at Beaver Station opened in 1852 James Sinclair built a hut there, and the town of Beaver was laid out

soon afterwards on 300 acres, owned jointly by Henry Seymour and Alfred Fell.

The 1855 earthquake deepened the Opawa River two metres, enabling schooners to ply right up to Beaver, and direct shipping was now possible.

In 1857, Governor Gore Browne named the new province, on the top eastern corner of the South Island, Marlborough, after John Churchill, Duke of Marlborough, and the Beaver settlement was renamed Blenheim after one of Marlborough's greatest battle victories. Blenheim became the provincial capital in 1865. Many small industries grew up nearby – a cheese factory, brick and tile works, meat abattoir and salt harvesting. There was also intensive pip, stone and berry fruit growing, and market gardening, as well as sheep farming. The railway reached Picton in 1875, helping to get produce to the markets, but did not push through to Christchurch until 1945.

Blenheim consolidated and progressed but it was not until the grape vines planted in the 1970s proved so successful that the area mushroomed with intensive viticulture. The town now has a population of 25,000, with 40,000 in the region.

Early motorists were able to follow the coach roads along the east coast to Christchurch, around to Nelson, and through the Wairau Valley to Murchison and the West Coast. The first Ford dealer, Edward Parker, a general trader, took on the franchise about 1913. About 1920, Dix and Sons obtained the franchise and shifted to dedicated motor garage premises. However, when they took on Chevrolet in 1927, they lost the Ford franchise which went to Lucas Brothers. Ed Lucas, and his brother Fred, had started a service garage

Above left: Washington Road Service Lane staff. Left: Matt Fry, Ricky Barneo, Kyle Egan.

Above right: BP Annesbrooke and Service Lane staff. From left: Bill Thompson, Ian McNabb, Jason Ilton, Steven Mitchell and Grady Stevens.

Above: Lucas Brothers built a very smart new dealership in 1929.

Below: In 1933, Phil Phillipps was dropped off in Blenheim by H N Scrimshaw to help Lucas Brothers, and was accountant for five years.

at Seddon in 1919, and shifted to leased premises in Blenheim to operate the Ford garage, still keeping their branch at Seddon.

In 1929, Lucas Brothers borrowed money and shifted to very smart new premises in Alfred Street. The Depression hit in late 1930, and caused them considerable financial stress but, with assistance from Colonial Motor Company, they managed to trade out of the situation. Phil Phillipps was sent in by H N Scrimshaw to advise the company and became accountant for five years before going to New Plymouth to head Phillipps

Motors in 1938.

When Ed Lucas retired in 1958, his son Ted took over the business, which he ran for another 33 years. Ted Lucas remembers the day he made his biggest ever sale, to Montana Wines in 1973. He delivered 26 new Ford tractors, together with a large variety of equipment: ploughs, cultivators, loaders and water tankers. How could he forget a sale like that! As well, he sold Montana five more tractors a year later.

In September 1991 Ted Lucas retired and sold the dealership to Stephen Overton who had farmed near Christchurch and, after five years running Overton Ford, decided to sell and return south. Peter Grace was dealer principal of the new company, Marlborough Ford, which later became part of the Ford rationalisation of dealers.

In 1998, Colonial Motor Company purchased Marlborough Ford which they run as a branch of MS Ford Nelson. MS Ford Marlborough is at 5-7 Nelson Road, and Carl Doocey is branch manager with a staff of 11, operating a full range of Ford service, parts and vehicle sales. Recently, Dick Munsey, who worked with John Flanagan in Christchurch, retired after helping to re-establish the vehicle sales side of the business in Blenheim.

One of M S Ford Nelson's cluster of BP service stations is at Blenheim. BP Express Blenheim maintains a very important 24 hour service for travellers as well as a Blenheim and surrounding districts clientele.

M S Ford Marlborough staff outside the Nelson Road premises. Left row: Gordon Robinson, Matt Rose, Carl Doocey, Shelley Thompson, Brent Boyd, Brady Price, and Andrew Dawson, David Newman, David Harper and Darrell Bate.

BP Express Blenheim day staff. From left: Ray Eden, Jo Lonsdale, Belinda Finlay and Michael Hall.

Outside Henry Ranger's premises about 1911, a chauffeur and Model T Landau deVille wait for the owner to return. A number of conversions were made to Model Ts, to accommodate owners' requirements. Some had wire spoked wheels. [Photo from Steffano Webb Collection, Alexander Turnbull Library]

Below: Ford Motors Rifle Club 1929. Back left: D Collins, W Henry, W Etwell, A Cameron, A Hughes, L Willis, J Lake. Front: J Haworth, A J Bruning, C Cochrane, L McCallum, J Allen. Absent: L Salkeld, L Morgan, E Vincent.

CHAPTER TWENTYSIX

CHRISTCHURCH – HUTCHINSON MOTORS LTD / TEAM HUTCHINSON FORD

After the arrival of the French at Akaroa on Banks Peninsula in 1840, the British took a greater interest in the area. Colonel William Wakefield asked that the New Zealand Company's proposed Nelson settlement be established at Lyttleton, but the presence of the French stopped this. The New Zealand Company had successfully established settlements at Wellington and Wanganui, before being thwarted by Lt. Governor Hobson who ruled no further land sales be made south of Wellington, as too many land claims on Banks Peninsula were unresolved. Hobson offered Warkworth for settlement instead.

In 1846, following a bungled crown land deed agreement with Ngai Tahu, the incoming Governor George Grey waived the Crown's right to pre-emption over Maori land in the South Island, making way for private land purchase. Grey also made money available to the Canterbury Association.

The Association was formed in London, following a partnership between Edward Gibbon Wakefield, Col Wakefield's brother, and John Robert Godley in 1847-48. Its aims were to form "the most Church of England country in the world", and its 53 members included two archbishops, seven bishops, 14 peers, four baronets, and 16 members of parliament.

The Canterbury Pilgrims' and Early Settlers' Association founded the South Island settlement, with the first ship of 'Canterbury Pilgrims' arriving aboard the *Charlotte Jane* on December 16 1850 at Port Cooper (Lyttelton). The *Randolf* arrived the same afternoon, the *Sir George Seymour* next morning, and the *Cressy*, which had sprung a foremast, on December 27. The 782 settlers who arrived then walked on the Bridle Path over the Port Hills to find their allotments.

Three towns had been turveyed – Lyttelton, Sumner and Christchurch – and Jollie, the surveyor, laid the plans in front of Captain Joseph Thomas, the Association surveyor, who pulled out his *Peerage*, and read out likely street names. When Jollie agreed, the name was written on the street, and it was baptised. Lyttelton was first, followed by Sumner, and finally Christchurch took what was left over.

There were already 1,000 or so settlers in the area, known as 'Pre-Adamites', the first of whom, William Deans, settled at Dean's Bush in 1843.

The centre of Christchurch is marked by the magnificent cathedral, commenced in 1864 and consecrated 40 years later. Today, the city has a population approaching 400,000, and has expanded to be the South Island's principal commercial centre through which flows the rich primary produce of the Canterbury district. The city is noted for its beautiful gardens, fine buildings, and an essentially English culture, with museums, art galleries and university.

Henry J Ranger started the first Ford agency in Christchurch about 1910, in Chester Street. Many of the early Model T Fords he sold had special bodies made locally in Christchurch to customer requirements. The bodies were often quite different from those made by Ford, with luxurious leather seating and even 'Landau' bodies, so the chauffeur could sit separately from his passengers. Wire spoke wheels were an option. The area had comparatively good roads by New Zealand standards and Christchurch was one of the first places to have an Automobile Association.

When Henry Ranger retired, he sold out to Bob Jay and Bob Wright, who formed the Canterbury Motor Company Ltd about 1920. After the 1921 recession this company shifted to premises at 94 Tuam Street, and was then known as Jay & Wright Ltd. However, the premises were not really satisfactory and sales and service suffered as a result.

Jay & Wright Ltd was finally bought out in May 1925 by Colonial Motor Company. The dealership moved to larger leased premises at 162–166 Tuam Street, and the company was renamed Ford Motors (Canterbury) Ltd. George Duncalf, manager of Colonial Motor Company Timaru branch, was transferred to take over the dealership. Within a short time the 'New Beauty' Model T was introduced, and more than 50 people were working at the enlarged dealership.

Tractors, which ran on kerosene, formed a major part of the operation in the early years, with sales averaging one a day. This kept two full time servicemen busy, travelling around farms to carry out repairs and servicing.

When Williams, Stephens & Co, timber and hardware merchants, sawmillers and joiners, offered their Tuam Street property for sale in September 1929 it was bought by Colonial Motor Company. The extensive two acre property, which ran between Tuam and St Asaph Streets, offered more scope than the leased property, and had substantial buildings set back from the Tuam Street frontage, making it ideal for vehicle display.

Over a year after taking possession, and many alterations – building a petrol station, lubrication bays, offices, parts and service facilities and a vehicle ramp to the second floor – Ford Motors Canterbury moved in. Although the Depression was at its worst point and trading was very tough, the services offered were of a sufficient standard to carry the business through this difficult period. Nevertheless, staff numbers dropped to 34.

Clarrie Cochrane became service manager in 1932, having started at Jay & Wright in 1924 and working his way up to service foreman. In 1973 he remembered that, in early 1932, the second floor at Tuam Street was set up as a modern spray painting shop. Prior to this, painting was carried out with a brush. The first gas analyser in New Zealand was installed in 1933, taking the guesswork out of carburettor tuning. An electrical workshop was added in 1933. By then the business was offering a very comprehensive range of services, including new and used car, truck and

Williams, Stephens & Co's substantial premises and two acres of land were purchased for Ford Motors (Canterbury) in 1930. After considerable changes, the business opened there in 1931.

tractor sales, parts and petrol bowser sales, lubrication, tune-up, overhaul and reconditioning, trimming, electrical, tyres, minor panel repairs and vehicle painting, plus vehicle recovery and farm servicing. The first Ford V8 cars and trucks arrived in 1932.

Business started to recover by the mid-1930s and, when George Duncalf retired in June 1934, Ormond Hutchinson, who had been Colonial Motor Company branch manager at Timaru, shifted to Christchurch as manager. He was one of the most experienced persons in the motor industry, having started with Colonial Motor Company in 1920 as first road organiser,

Left: Reconditioning engines was common; new rings, bearings and a rebore took eight hours for a 4-cylinder, 12 hours for a V8.

Below: Repainting in 1933 was usually done by hand. Ford Motors had the latest spray equipment.

The lube bay 1933.

Olympia skating rink was bought for used car retailing. A competition, with a vehicle as the prize, brought a crowd to the opening.

with a territory from Kaikoura to Invercargill. Orm Hutchinson pioneered tractor sales in New Zealand, holding demonstrations all over the eastern South Island. (In those days the West Coast and Nelson and Marlborough were serviced more easily by boat from Wellington.)

Orm Hutchinson was very innovative and loved new challenges. In 1936 he helped his staff achieve a groundbreaking fleet deal with Gold Band Taxis in Christchurch. The 52 new Ford V8s Fordor models, factory painted in fleet colours, were delivered to the Gold Band stand in Cathedral Square, and 52 Whippets traded in. No cash changed hands, the cars operated 24 hours a day, and weekly hire purchase payments were made. At the end of three years the cars, having covered 300,000 miles, were traded back for new

ones, again with no cash deposit, and just weekly hire purchase payments. The otherwise unpaid drivers received about 33% of their takings on each shift.

When Ford moved to New Zealand in 1936 and took over assembly and distribution from Colonial Motor Company, all dealers had to remove 'Ford' from their names, and Ford Motors Canterbury Ltd became Hutchinson Motors Ltd. Ford also removed the Fordson tractor franchise from all dealers, claiming they had not achieved full sales potential, and believing greater sales would be achieved with a specialist organisation. However, Ford had not taken account of the effects of the Depression and sales fell further with the new distributor.

New vehicle sales increased quickly in

the mid-1930s, but used cars were a problem. Hutchinson Motors, which then had 30 salesmen and 30% of new vehicle market share, had difficulty keeping used car stock numbers below 150 units. Other dealers had the same problem – many cars were not refurbished, or displayed properly. A decision was made to form a separate used car sales division and, after an interminable hunt for premises, the former Tuam Street Olympia skating rink was bought a little east of the dealership, and Olympia Used Cars Ltd set up.

A competition was staged to launch the new business using a Ford V8 light delivery, put up on blocks and set running in gear, with a mask over the dash. The person who was closest to guessing the speedometer reading at the end of 24 hours won the vehicle. This was too good to be true, and a huge crowd blocked Tuam Street, filled the building, and delayed Mayor Robert McFarlane from opening the new business.

Olympia Used Cars' building was 200ft deep with 100ft frontage and displayed 80 used cars, greatly increasing sales rates and, with this competitive advantage, Hutchinson's sold more new cars.

After the Second World War began in 1939, there were virtually no new cars for six years and the government immediately requisitioned all 1938 and 1939 used cars. Petrol was severely rationed, 4 gallons per month for small cars, 8 gallons for large, which meant many people walked, cycled or took the infrequent bus.

A large proportion of Hutchinson's staff members volunteered to serve with the armed forces, with many wounded in action and two tragically killed. It was a very trying time for management who had great difficulty making ends meet. However, Hutchinson's was one of the few businesses to keep everyone employed and operated at a profit right through the war.

During the war Olympia Used Cars was closed down and the building leased to the RNZAF. After the war, with all the shortages, it was decided to sell the building to Champion Motors who began assembling Standard cars there for New Zealand.

An innovation during the war was the 'gas bag' developed for small cars, and gas producers for larger cars. Although neither gave a great range, and slow starting problems were annoying, it meant that people could continue to go about their

business without using petrol.

During the war, the Christchurch City Council was short of omnibuses, and Hutchinson's adapted 21 standard Ford V8 trucks to forward control buses, which operated very successfully for many years. After the end of the war, Canadian V8 bus chassis were some of the first commercial vehicles assembled and the council increased its fleet with a number of these.

Nearly all staff returned from overseas, and the business picked up again. New cars were to remain short for another 25 years, so it was particularly fortunate that the Fordson tractor franchise reverted to Ford dealers. In 1946 the new E27N Fordson was introduced with petrol, kerosene and diesel options, and tractor sales took off. Sales were further aided by the 18hp Ford Ferguson introduced in 1947 but, after Henry Ford argued with Harry Ferguson, production of these ceased. Field days were successfully held in many Canterbury locations and tractors once again sold at

Six staff enlisted in the RNZAF in 1940 and visited the Centennial Exhibition in Wellington. From back left: Alec Hughes, L Williams and Keith Mann. Front: Jack Walker, Charlie Barker and Max Snook. Thirty years later five were still on the staff.

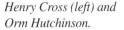

Henry Cross (left) and Orm Hutchinson.

Tractors were a major profit centre in 1957.

nearly one a day for a period.

With New Zealand's labour shortages after the war as industry developed, the government encouraged selected immigrants from England and Europe, a number of whom Hutchinson Motors employed, finding nearly all of them to be of a high calibre, keen to help and work. Their imported skills helped the business immensely.

Many of the staff members who went away to the war had seen new machines and industrial processes; some had driven cars and trucks for the first time and most returned with new ideas. Max Snook, who had served in the Air Force, developed new ideas for using tractors, including a way of fitting the hydraulic clamshell, patented by Henry Cross, to an E27N Fordson so that one man, using the 'Pelican' loader, could quickly unload railway wagons of bulk materials. This helped ease the country's labour shortage, and nearly every railway yard and contractor in New Zealand bought one.

In 1947 Orm Hutchinson was asked to join the Colonial Motor Company board

of directors in recognition of his marketing and administrative skills and experience. He had served in the First World War as a gunner in France, and after his experiences in harnessing horses before dawn to tow the guns, he was determined he would never be involved with horses again. Returning home, he replied to a CMC advertisement in 1920 and joined the motor industry. Tractors were better than horses and much easier to catch. Ironically, he later developed an interest in harness racing, and was involved with the national administration of this sport. In the 1960s, having turned down a major award, he was awarded the Order of the British Empire in recognition of his services to harness racing.

Sales of tractors continued through the 1950s. In 1952, the new 40hp Fordson Major sold very strongly, including to the Chatham Islands, and made Hutchinson Motors a lot of money. Max Snook pioneered the Chatham Islands market, and a serviceman would fly over every six months, sometimes for a week, servicing and repairing the Fordson tractors and machinery on the islands.

However, tractors created tremendous pressure on the Tuam Street facilities, as overhauling a tractor can take up the space of four cars. Finding a solution became a headache for Orm Hutchinson. In June 1954 the first $1\frac{1}{2}$ acres of land was purchased at Sockburn beside the Main South Road. In all, 10 adjoining parcels of land were bought, making five acres in total. Needless to say, it all took time. The land provided a relief valve and plans were submitted to Ford and the council for approval in 1956. Getting the necessary permits slowed everything down.

There was life-long commitment to Max Snook from Chatham Island customers.

However, construction of the first 120ft x 65ft workshop started in April 1957.

As soon as this was ready, tractor sales and service were moved out to the new location. Stage two then commenced, adding another 5,000 sq ft. The sales offices were in a former grocer's shop on the corner of Epsom Road and the staff cafeteria and facilities in another one of the remaining residential houses taken over in the land purchases.

A property in Tuam Street belonging to Combined Co-op Distributors, beside the council car park and next to Hutchinson Motors, had been bought in 1952 and was used for tractors until they shifted to Sockburn. This was converted for car display, greatly improving used vehicle sales, and was known as 'the egg floor'.

With the introduction of the very popular Thames Trader truck range in 1957, trucks sales put pressure on Tuam Street, as trucks also took up a lot more space than cars so Sockburn stage three, a separate workshop of 7,000 sq ft, was proposed. The large cash input required was putting further pressure on resources, but a prefabricated building 40ft x 30ft was found and erected for storage as an interim measure. There were now 200 people working at Hutchinson Motors.

Meanwhile, new cars were still in very short supply, with severe import restrictions. It was quite difficult to allocate cars because, for every car that arrived, there were 10 buyers, and deciding priorities always offended the other nine who missed out.

Left: Tuam Street about 1958. The external vehicle ramp to the second floor had been removed.

Below: The 'egg floor' was converted to a very smart used car display in 1960, 100 yards from the main premises.

Above: The Omega club in 1965 was the biggest in the country. Standing left: C A Barker, R N Burgess, Max Snook, Bill Adorian, A M Britten, A E Ragg, Keith Mann, Charlie Witty, F J Matthews, Colin Lake. Front: Alec Hughes, Charlie Cochrane, Ormond Hutchinson, Miss R M Bowlker, and H A R N Burgess.

When the government introduced the No Remittance Scheme, allowing private imports of new cars using funds held overseas, salesmen from Hutchinson Motors became adept at tracking down Christchurch people with connections with England. Many new cars were sold this way!

Because the company could not get enough new cars to satisfy its customers, it was actively buying in and refurbishing used cars for resale. However, display space wasn't large enough, nor was the location. Used cars were better displayed on open lots, where the public had access.

By 1964 car volumes had increased significantly, with No Remittance sales now contributing to a third of new car volumes. There was an incentive from Ford of 1 for 1; for every No Remittance order sold, the dealer received an additional new allocated car. Hutchinson's salesmen did well, and the volume of No Remittance sales increased significantly as many new ways of creating licences were exploited.

New cars still required considerable servicing in the post-war period, partly because of design, but mostly because of poor New Zealand assembly. Progress was now being made with rust treatment at the

Charlie Witty and Charlie Cochrane, with Ormond Hutchinson (middle), had served 44 and 48 years when they retired.

factory, but it was not unusual for a car to be semi-rebuilt by dealers, taking hours, and often days. Pre-delivery not only cost money, but took up more space, and was competing with retail servicing work.

Ford had now added a number of new dealers in metropolitan areas where populations were expanding. Christchurch had similarly expanded, and after discussion with Ford, it was decided to create Sockburn branch as a separate dealership.

Sockburn Motors Ltd began trading on September 1 1965.

Business was now different, and the allocation of new cars, commercials and tractors was split between the companies. Christchurch was split into two territories, and customers had to decide where they wished to trade. Most of the staff at Sockburn Motors was originally from Hutchinson Motors, and there was still a good deal of co-operation between the companies. Hutchinson Motors' Tuam Street facility was again under pressure for space. Orm Hutchinson did his homework on traffic flows and population trends, and the Papanui suburb showed up as the likely place for another branch. That was one thing; finding suitable land was another.

Papanui branch was launched in November 1968, following the purchase of a small workshop and one acre of land on the corner of Blair Avenue and Papanui Road, the main northern outlet from the city. A smart new workshop was built for the opening, and used vehicles were displayed beside this. The workshop was kept filled from town and much of the new vehicle preparation was also handled there.

Tuam Street was still overloaded, particularly in the workshop and with used cars. The Mark IV Zephyr, introduced in 1966, was a very innovative design with many new features such as disc brakes, but it was also having a nightmare run and giving extensive warranty problems, causing further crowding in the workshop.

Papanui Road branch was working well, but had no room to expand, so the answer was another branch. More homework showed Sydenham as a likely site. The development of the new Lyttleton road tunnel would shift the rail marshalling yards to Middleton, and free up land in Sydenham for industrial development. A check of traffic densities and registrations showed that the area was a good one. The hunt for a site was on, and the Ace Service Station was purchased, followed by further residential properties alongside, providing nearly an acre in total.

Opposition leader and local MP, the Hon Norman J Kirk, opened the new branch in 1970. After the houses were removed, the display site was further developed into two tiers, giving excellent visibility for cars on display.

More land was purchased and rezoned beside the Papanui branch and the building was extended, and a service station added in 1970. This brought in a great deal more traffic and sales and repairs increased.

From 1970, the new car market freed up following government changes to import licensing and, as more cars became available, the prices of used cars fell. For the first time in 30 years, an ordinary New Zealander could buy a new car, and the market became very competitive, creating new opportunities for Hutchinson Motors.

However, the first oil shock of 1973 brought a new dimension to trading, and the rapid escalation of petrol prices. New Zealand had good, cheaper natural gas supplies and the government quickly

Papanui branch was started in 1964.

Hon Norman Kirk opened the Sydenham branch, which was in his electorate, after Orm Hutchinson had handed him the key.

encouraged gas conversions. The South Island had no natural gas (CNG), but liquefied petroleum gas (LPG) was transportable, and gas conversions kept workshops busy.

Ormond Hutchinson retired at the end of March 1973. He had worked for

Colonial Motor Company since 1920, and his 53 years of service, including his 39 year leadership of Hutchinson Motors, were outstanding. He was recognised for his innovation and pioneering spirit and lauded by the motor industry, every Ford dealer, and many overseas, as a great industry figure. Known by his staff as 'The Chief', he had encouraged many of them to develop their talents and, despite a gruff exterior, was loved and revered by them all.

His son, Ormond Alexander Hutchinson, was appointed manager of Hutchinson Motors. Later, on November 18 1973, he was appointed a director of Colonial Motor Company.

In 1974, when Ford opened another assembly plant designed to build Falcon, at Wiri, it now had more production capacity than any other car manufacturer in New Zealand. Ford cars were also being imported from England and Australia in large quantities. That the public preferred buying the cars built overseas, because the finish was superior, sent a very strong message to Ford and worker unions about

Christchurch A & P Show in 1969 had a variety of product on display, including a Hamilton jet boat powered with a 3 litre V6 Zephyr engine.

their standards.

Tuam Street premises had a major upgrade in 1978, designed by Christchurch architect, Sir Miles Warren. Most of the administration was moved to the upper floor, allowing customers access to sales, parts and service from Tuam Street. The frontage gave a much more modern and unified appearance to what was still a 19th century building.

The work was hardly finished when the second oil crisis hit, and government legislated 'carless days', with motorists having to decide which day of the week their cars would stay in the garage. This produced another wave of LPG conversions, and petrol increased in price again, to 41.5 cents per litre, over four times as high as 1972's 10.12 cents per litre.

After the 1981 introduction of the Ford Courier Utility and the Laser car range, the staff could not get over the different assembly standards with these Japanese-sourced Fords. When Telstar replaced Cortina in 1983 it was the same and, within a short time, the amount of rectification and warranty work had significantly reduced. Customer acceptance of the new vehicles was high, and Laser shot to No.1 spot in the NZ market within its first year.

In 1985 Ford decided the Christchurch market territories would be split in a different way. A line was drawn, giving Sockburn Motors a large part of Hutchinson Motors' territory, including Papanui branch. Hutchinson's staff couldn't believe they would lose a high number of their best customers. Maurie Burrows was then service manager, and recalls 'Hutch' Hutchinson's endeavours to get Ford to see reason. "Hutch hired a helicopter, and flew Ford representation manager Ash Waugh over the city, counting swimming pools in given areas, and then comparing this with the changes, as a measure of customers' disposable income." However Ford was resolute, and Sockburn Motors took over Papanui branch on August 1 1985.

Soon afterwards Hutchinson Motors decided to include the whole staff in their new trading name – Team Hutchinson Ford. Used cars were successfully consolidated at the main dealership and the 'Egg Floor' was sold.

The late 1980s were a turbulent period for the industry, with the government's new 'free market' policies in force. Market conditions were turned upside down, and imports liberalised. Following the

sharemarket crash in 1987, restructuring for survival was necessary. Sydenham branch was transferred to a smaller site at Lincoln Road and the service station and surplus land sold to Mobil.

The Magix Computer system was introduced in 1986, with large reductions in office staff, as repetitive clerical work was eliminated. Service was still a major strength, as many customers decided to hang on to their existing vehicles. Staff numbers dwindled but the company quickly adjusted to the new conditions.

Hutch Hutchinson, now also known as Orm, retired from day-to-day affairs in June 1990, while remaining a director of

Above: Maurice Burrows started as an apprentice, became service manager and later, operations manager. Hutch Hutchinson presenting his 25 year gold watch in 1981.

Below: They retired together in 1980. Colin Lake, parts manager, worked 45 years; and Keith Mann, foreman, 50 years.

Don Haberfield, the witty editor of the staff magazine, hid behind the nom de plume of 'The thin man', and enjoyed salmon fishing.

excellence award for customer service, based on established quality standards, and measured by the dealership's own customers, it was almost as if the President's Award and Distinguished Achiever's Award had been written for Team Hutchinson Ford. The dealership had a culture of looking after customers and had never tolerated any poor practices. After a bad start, when Ford set the wrong sales targets, the dealership excelled, winning seven President's Awards in a row, and has been in the winner's circle for the past 14 years.

Team Hutchinson Ford applied for ISO9002 certification, as a positive reinforcement of their quality attitude. ISO (International Standards Organisation) guarantees certain specific quality standards, and certification was completed in 1995, after 12 months preparation.

As a part of facility renewal, the interior of Team Hutchinson Ford's main premises were re-designed, using Paul Goldsmith Architects. The stunning new showroom and customer facility combined large historic photo murals with new vehicle display, emphasising the proud history of the company. Ford managing director Tony Brigden, and Orm Hutchinson, newly elected chairman of Colonial Motor Company, jointly launched the renewed facility in 1995, with all NZ Ford dealers attending.

Ormond A Hutchinson became chairman of Colonial Motor Company in 1995 and also a director of Tower Corporation. In 2000 he died suddenly, closing another large chapter in the company's history. His son,

Colonial Motor Company. Hutch had worked at Tuam Street since 1953, joining as assistant accountant. He became accountant, assistant manager, manager, and was managing director from 1973.

Russell J Lange was appointed chief executive on July 1 1990. He joined Hutchinson Motors in 1982 as new vehicle manager, and became general sales manager in 1985. In 1987 he was transferred to Phillipps Motors, New Plymouth as manager, returning in 1989 to become manager of Team Hutchinson Ford.

In 1989, when Ford introduced a new

Bottom left: Bill Adorian retired in 1978, a top salesman for 44 years.

Bottom right: Long serving business manager Graeme Payne.

Team Hutchinson Ford looking very smart with the new Ford corporate livery in 2002.

John Hutchinson, is new vehicle sales manager at Team Hutchinson Ford. He started there in 1993. In 2003, three generations of the family had delivered 110 years of commitment to the Colonial Motor Company, a truly remarkable achievement.

Today, Team Hutchinson Ford goes forth as a united group, who adhere to their own high quality standards that are also recognised internationally. Their objective is to make their customers completely satisfied. CEO Russell Lange says: "This is a never ending task, but we are well along this road. We have 85 dedicated staff members, sell top quality products, and have the best facility in New Zealand."

There is no doubt 'The Chief' would approve.

In 2004, Team Hutchinson Ford was delighted to win their eighth President's Award.

*Building of the first
workshop at
Sockburn started in
1957.*

*Sockburn Motors at
its new premises on
the main arterial
route south from
Christchurch.*

CHAPTER TWENTYSEVEN

CHRISTCHURCH SOUTH –
SOCKBURN MOTORS LTD /
AVON CITY FORD

On September 1 1965 Sockburn Motors Ltd commenced trading from new premises on the Main South Road, bounded by Racecourse and Epsom Roads at Sockburn. Although it was a new dealer and newly formed company, it had been started as a branch of Hutchinson Motors Ltd. After a complicated series of land transactions, with the key site being purchased from the Hill Estate, and nine subsequent transactions with other parties, the five acre site was bought in 1954. It is opposite the southern roundabout of Blenheim Road, which today is the main arterial route to the south, and has the highest density traffic flow in the South Island.

Orm Hutchinson Snr said that tractors had been a critical element in choosing the Sockburn site. "Fordson tractors had had a checkered time in the past. In 1936 the franchise was taken away from Ford dealers, and given to Booth MacDonald Ltd. When they failed to get a satisfactory market share it was given to Gough, Gough & Hamer, who had John Deere and Caterpillar tractors, but they failed to perform. In 1946 Ford gave it back to Ford dealers, and with the new Fordson E27N and Ford Ferguson tractors, there was an immediate boost in sales. However, with conflict between Ford and Ferguson, the small Ford Ferguson was withdrawn, creating doubts about the future. When Henry Ford II was appointed, the company had renewed vigour and enthusiasm.

"We were behind our competitors with facilities and it was obvious that the city centre was not the right place to market and service tractors. After an intensive study, Sockburn was settled on as the right location, closer to many of our farmer and industrial clients, and large enough to provide for at least 50 years ahead. We received assurances from the district

Orm Hutchinson and R B Gibbons planted a commemorative tree at the opening of the new buildings in 1965.

commissioner of works and Main Highways Board on the exact location of the proposed new bridge over the railway to make sure it didn't conflict with our five stage development plan prepared by Martyn Spencer in Wellington.

"Land purchases were completed in 1954, except for the house and dairy on the corner. The owners still had seven years of their 10 year lease to run, and were only prepared to sell on the most favourable terms. We decided to wait until the lease expired, and started on the first workshop.

"The next year the Main Highways Board was disbanded and replaced by the National Roads Board. Their new purchasing officer came to see me on Christmas Eve in 1955 to tell me that they would be buying a strip of land back from us that would effectively divide our property in two and make it useless for our plans. This was stunning news and a great Christmas box!

"We made immediate representations to National Roads Board, showing them our consultation with their predecessors, and how seriously this change would affect our plans. We suggested that by moving the intersection slightly, both developments would still work. Fortunately they saw reason, but we lost 20ft of land on the south side with the realignment of Racecourse Road."

W A (Bill) Goss was appointed dealer principal when the dealership opened in September 1965. A qualified accountant, he started work with an accountancy firm during the Depression and then joined up during the Second World War, serving in the army in England after he had been very ill. After the war he worked in his family's timber business, before joining Hutchinson's in 1955, later becoming commercial sales manager. He was involved in the development of Sockburn branch from an early date. All 43 staff members, mostly in the workshop, came from Hutchinson's, so the transition was one of management rather than establishing a new business, and Sockburn Motors still worked closely with Hutchinson's. Initially, the sales and administration offices and parts were operated from a former house on Epsom Road, with a staff cafeteria in the next house.

Sockburn Motors got off to a very fast start with all the commercial activity and tractors, but new cars were scarce, and rationed by the government's import restrictions. Many of the new car sales were made using the No Remittance scheme, and for every sale made using overseas funds, another new car was received on allocation. Buildings were still being constructed but, as the site developed, it was an eye-catching area, very suitable for used car, truck and tractor display.

With the volume of work available a

Left: Bill Goss was appointed first manager of Sockburn Motors in 1965.

Right: Ian Lambie, accountant.

Left: Trevor Jupp, service manager.

Right: Vern Newcombe, parts manager.

new panel and paint shop was built at the rear of the site, which quickly boosted business. The paint booth was one of the first in New Zealand to have full air conditioning, controlling temperature and filtering air to keep dust out, thus ensuring a perfect finish.

The tractor workshop was very busy, not only doing normal overhaul and repair work, but also with warranty. The introduction of the new Ford tractors in 1965 brought the revolutionary transmission known as Select-O-Speed, which had 10 forward and three reverse gears, all engaged hydraulically, and able to shift from neutral to drive, and between gears without a clutch. It was brilliant – until the gremlins arrived and tractors mysteriously lost some of their gears again and again. It was a very embarrassing time for both customers and dealers and kept workshops through the country busy, with

David Burn created prize winning gardens.

Left: Max Snook was tractor sales manager.

Right: Max Snook demonstrating the gold medal winning trencher.

sales affected. Fortunately, the manual gearbox models were trouble free and kept the tractor range going.

The gardens of Christchurch are justly famous. Consequently, it was a considerable achievement for Sockburn Motors to win first prize in the commercial section of the Canterbury Horticultural Society's annual contest in 1968. It certainly showed the dedication of the dealership's handyman gardener, David Burn, one of the '£10 Pom' immigrants, who arrived from Yorkshire in 1952. He started at Sockburn in 1966 with a landscape plan and raw patches of kerbed

seal and earth and created an immaculate vista of garden beds and lawns complementing the dealership's appearance. His dedication was respected by all staff members who kept the large area tidy and well presented.

Sockburn Motors helped develop many new industrial equipment items. Max Snook adapted Henry Cross' patent design of the Pelican loader to the Fordson E27N tractor. The patent was bought and the

Max Snook talking to Governor-General Sir Denis Blundell about the trencher.

Pelican developed to fit the E27N, the new Fordson Major, Ford tractors, and then trucks. A rear loader and chain trencher were also developed. When tractor safety requirements were introduced by the Department of Agriculture, Max Snook was consulted to make sure the regulations were practical, and a 'Safe-T-Frame' was developed.

Max Snook first visited the Chathams in 1952, when at Hutchinson Motors, travelling a day and a half each way by the 600 ton steamer *Port Waikato*. There were few roads and he used a horse to get to many remote farms and a tractor to others. He convinced farmers that tractors would develop pastures and roads on the islands.

Tractors were exported to the Chatham Islands from Hutchinson's and Sockburn Motors, helping the islanders with solutions to their problems. A rear hydraulic crane was made, enabling a tractor to back into the sea to load and unload two tonne shipping containers from lighters. At the airstrip, formed using a Fordson and front-end loader, a forklift was mounted on the rear of a Fordson and used to unload freight from Bristol Freighter planes, which serviced the islands for years. About 50-60 Fordson tractors were in use there in the 1970s when Max was made an honorary Chatham Islander for his years of help.

The company was also involved with C W F Hamilton & Co Ltd, which developed the jet boat using marine converted Ford engines. The Ford Zephyr engines were particularly suitable for their sports runabout which was able to navigate shallow Canterbury streams, rivers or sea waters, and resulted in huge export orders.

At the end of 1969 Bill Goss, poor health resulting from his war service, could not continue to manage the dealership and moved to a more suitable position at Hutchinson Motors, and George Daniel, assistant manager there, shifted out to become manager.

Truck sales and service increased steadily with the 1966 introduction of the Ford D Series range of English trucks. They were a modern version of the Trader trucks introduced in 1957, having many improvements, and a new tilt cab design making it much easier to get in and out. The 2-8 tonne range was extended with two tandem models, a turbocharged six and a V8 Cummins model, plus a bus chassis. The new trucks were very popular with customers and large numbers were sold to

councils, carriers, companies, construction industries and farmers. A key factor to these sales was the excellent backup service.

The company had been operating for some time without proper administration and sales facilities, from converted houses and the converted corner store from 1967. In 1973 a new showroom and administration area were built onto the original workshop and parts building. New cars were starting to become more plentiful in New Zealand, and sales volumes increased quickly, particularly with Australian Falcons. The new showroom faced Main South Road and had a two-tiered display area. The oil crisis in late 1973, and escalation in petrol prices, checked Falcon sales, but LPG conversions were soon available, and many were converted to run on petroleum gas.

When George Daniel was transferred to Avery Motors in Wellington at the end of 1973 the business had nearly doubled in eight years – staff numbers had increased to 65, nearly half in the workshops, nine in parts.

Noel Simons had started at Hutchinson Motors in 1954 as a garage attendant, later moving to used vehicle sales. In 1970 he was appointed manager at Papanui branch, and manager of Sockburn Motors in January 1973, retaining the close ties between the two Christchurch dealerships.

In 1975 the fuel crisis prompted the government to make changes to registration charges. On the surface these seemed to be minor, but the effect it triggered was not. Also influenced by escalating fuel costs,

Second manager, George Daniel, presents John Hooper with his 25 year gold watch.

the public switched from large to small cars almost overnight. Falcon sales fell to about 15%, but fortunately Ford Cortina became the country's No 1 seller.

When Japan became an important export market and cars started to be imported from there, Ford, with their investment in Mazda, was well positioned to take advantage. In 1981 the first Japanese Fords appeared, the Ford Courier utility (alias Mazda B Series). It was an immediate success. Soon afterwards, the Ford Laser car range (alias Mazda 323), was a spectacular success, and moved to No 1 spot in the New Zealand market, displacing Cortina. Many people would not buy a Japanese car, but a Ford was not considered to be one.

Following the 1973 oil crisis, tractor volumes had reduced and Ford decided to quit their Mowbray Street tractor assembly unit, getting Sockburn Motors to contract assemble for them. This change helped both parties and kept the Sockburn site fully occupied as a result.

On the truck front, Ford D Series finished in 1983, and Ford did not continue with the replacement English Cargo. Instead, Ford NZ established an alliance with Hino Japan and the starved NZ Ford truck dealers quickly established the Hino-Ford after a worrying 18 months with no heavy trucks.

In the mid-1980s, Ford altered Sockburn Motors' franchise territory,

taking in the northern Papanui area of Christchurch. Morrie Burrows, service manager at Hutchinson's, remembered staff were very unhappy, thinking the bulk of their 'spending' customers had been removed. Ford people were, however, resolute despite spirited opposition. In order to deal with their changed and expanded role in the city, a new name was chosen to convey the changes. Ford said Hutchinson Motors' Papanui branch must now adopt the name of Sockburn Motors, and on August 1 1985, the 'old' Sockburn Motors became Avon City Ford Ltd, a name synonymous with the city of Christchurch.

On November 30 1986 Noel Simons retired and Paul Jordan was appointed manager. He had been manager of Avon City's Papanui branch. He started at Hutchinson Motors in 1961, went out for a period selling used cars on his own, and then joined New Lynn Motors, before returning to Christchurch in 1985.

When the change in government in 1984 brought massive changes to New Zealand, with new 'free market' policies, and a floating dollar, tractor sales crashed as farmers tried to contain their spending. This was followed by the sharemarket crash in 1987 and labour market policy changes, and very quickly the motor industry was in turmoil. Added to this, import licence tendering was introduced and 'Jap Imports' commenced. Many NZ franchise dealers failed financially at this time.

Avon City Ford felt the changes as keenly as other dealers, and looked for new ways to fill the sales gaps. Encouraged by Ford, dealers fought each other for the

reduced new vehicle sales numbers. Neighbouring Ford dealers became enemies as they picked each other off, and 'red ink' flowed.

When, in 1988 Ford decided to sell out of tractors worldwide, and Ford NZ sold to C B Norwood, local distributors for New Holland, Fiat and Kubota tractors, Avon City assembly ceased. Tractor sales and service remained, but on a very different scale as Norwood's had their own branch operation at Templeton.

Paul Jordan, experienced with used cars, sought out new opportunities with Jap Imports, and Avon City Ford tendered for licence. It brought in many imports from Japan, making a new profit centre from this business. Used Cargo trucks from England were also imported and rebuilt with NZ bodies.

At the same time new trucks were changing and the number of truck dealers was reduced to 18 nationally. By 1990 the Ford-Hino partnership was in doubt, and

Ford NZ looked at other options, but they never eventuated.

Amidst all the turmoil of changes, Ford introduced their new retail excellence system in 1989 – the President's Award, a measure of quality standards by the dealership's own customers. Christchurch had been built on the culture of looking after customers, a legacy from Ormond Hutchinson that succeeding management of both dealerships were committed to. In 1990 and 1991, Avon City was runner up for the President's Award, receiving Distinguished Achiever awards.

In 1993 Ford began importing North American Ford Louisville extra heavy trucks, which were being built with right hand drive by Ford Australia. Avon City Ford, as the logical truck centre of the South Island, became one of four dealers nationally handling Louisville. However, sales of this truck in the South Island were not great, with most being sold through

Top: Ford tractors were assembled under contract at Sockburn.

Lower: In May 1980, the world ploughing championships were held at Lincoln, near Christchurch, and over 30% of contestants used Ford tractors, prepared and supplied by Sockburn Motors.

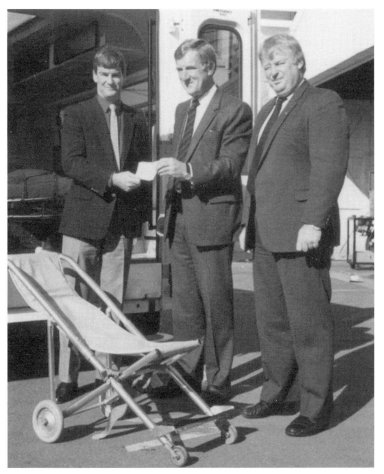

Hutch Hutchinson and Paul Jordan, manager of Avon City Ford, in a joint promotion.

introduction of the Magix system in the mid-1980s. The many repetitive cross entries between parts and service had been eliminated, and all new cars were now ordered 'on-line' from Ford. However, new and used cars and light commercials were still being sold eyeball to eyeball, and finance sales commissions had increased to become a significant profit centre. Workshops had changed with new high-tech computer based tools which analysed problems and adjustments. Vehicles had improved to such a degree that warranty had reduced and service intervals had extended. There was now no need for the Papanui branch workshop, and this was transferred back to Sockburn, with plans to lease the service station to BP.

The dealership had now been operating for 20 years and was in need of renovation. Paul Goldsmith Architects re-designed the frontage, interior and appearance, without major structural changes, giving a spectacular new image to the dealership, and ensured its now commanding presence dominated the Main South Road.

Quality awards started to flow in 1994, and have done every year since then, as the customer-focussed staff work to a common goal. Standards had always been important, and, with a staff largely trained on site, results were assured.

When the Rangiora Ford dealership ceased to operate in 1996, Avon City took over this area, leasing a two bay workshop to service local customer vehicles. Business was slow at first, but when locals found the new people were genuinely keen to help them, the business snowballed and today the branch has six staff.

On June 30 1998, John Flanagan transferred to take over the Nelson and Blenheim Ford dealerships, now called M S Ford, and purchased by Colonial Motor Company.

John W Luxton was shifted from Macaulay Motors, Invercargill to become CEO on July 1 1998. A horticulture graduate, he started at Hutchinson Motors in 1990 in vehicle sales, and became fleet sales manager. In 1993 he was transferred to Te Awamutu as dealer principal, then became CEO of Macaulay Motors in 1995.

Pre-employment training became available to accredited Ford dealers in 1998 and looked a likely winner for the dealership. Service manager Bruce McCoubrey, who had worked for Avon City since leaving school and starting his diesel

Timaru Motors. In 1994 Ford gave the franchise to Timaru Motors.

Ford tractors went in 1993, when C B Norwood took over sales and service at their Templeton branch. This directly affected a long established group of Ford and Fordson tractor owners, but Ford was no longer involved and the Ford name was removed from the product.

When Paul Jordan resigned from Avon City Ford on October 31 1993, to return to the used car business, John A Flanagan took over management and was appointed CEO in February 1994. He had spent 15 years with his father in the motor business before joining Avon City Ford in 1985 as a salesman, later becoming sales manager. Also a rugby league coach, John Flanagan was a strong motivator of people, encouraging them to use their collective skills in the company's interests.

The business was now very different from the one he had started in eight years before. Staff numbers had reduced significantly, and heavy trucks had ended with the Louisville and the N Series Ford Hino. Trader trucks from 1.5 to 4 tonnes remained, but they were really only light units.

Computers had significantly reduced the number of office people since the

apprenticeship in 1977, took on the responsibility of getting this scheme off the ground. Employing their own trainer, the courses of 10 students have been popular, and classes have expanded, with students working towards their NZQA exams. The scheme also gives Avon City first selection choice for apprentices.

Business manager Craig Fuller has responsibility for all Avon City accounting and oversees two regional dealerships. Parts Manager Paul Leary started at Sockburn Motors in 1971 and today has combined responsibility for Ford parts operations in Christchurch.

Avon City Ford was one of the dealerships to pilot the new Ford Worldwide appearance identification upgrade, further enhancing an already impressive image.

John Luxton said: "In order to retain and satisfy our customers we must strive to be the very best we can in all areas of our business – at Avon City Ford we collectively seek improvement."

Avon City Ford in 1990.

Avon City Ford has been consistently winner or runner up in the President's Awards over the last 15 years. Here the 2001 management team hold their seven President's Awards. Left: John Luxton, CEO; Paul Leary, parts manager; Bruce McCoubrey, service manager; Sean O'Farrell, used vehicle manager; Hamish Jacob, sales manager; and Craig Fuller, business manager. They have since won an eighth President's Award.

CMC Timaru branch about 1917.

Timaru Motors in 1966 occupied most of the CMC branch administration, parts and distribution buildings. The original branch is in the centre.

CHAPTER TWENTYEIGHT

TIMARU –
CMC SOUTH ISLAND /
TIMARU MOTORS LTD

Timaru City is nestled on the east coast of the South Island at the southern edge of the Canterbury Plains. The prosperous principal city of South Canterbury, with a population of 30,000 people, it is 160 km south of Christchurch, and 200 km north of Dunedin. Timaru has two livestock freezing works, considerable light industry, and services the surrounding country area and Mackenzie Basin, by air, road, rail and sea. The artificial port of Timaru receives international shipping, and was established with a concrete breakwater in the 1880s. This was extended on the northern side to make a safe harbour in 1906. The nearby Caroline Bay beach is a holiday resort attracting thousands to its annual summer carnival.

The name has two possible meanings: Timaru (the shady cabbage tree) and Te Maru (place of shelter), as it was a favourite haven for travellers.

The first Maori in the region lived in limestone caves and rock overhangs, ancient rock drawings suggesting they were probably moa hunters. Rapuwai, and later Ngati Mamoe, followed the cave dwellers. During the 17th century, the warlike Ngai Tahu, who settled near Temuka, drove the Ngati Mamoe south.

A whaling station was established at Patiti (Jack's) Point in 1837, and another at Whaler's Creek, but they were later transferred to Banks Peninsular. When the area between the Ashburton and Waitaki rivers was opened up for settlement, the brothers George and Robert Heaton Rhodes took up 'The Levels' sheep run, between the Opihi and Pareora rivers. The government retained a reserve for a town at Timaru, and the Rhodes brothers shrewdly freeholded 50 hectares next to this on what they considered better land, subdividing this and selling it before the government land was sold.

There were no port facilities and ships stood off, or were moored in the open roadstead, and wrecks were frequent. A landing service was initiated in 1864 by the provincial government, but this was also hazardous, and subsequently a groin was formed which led to the breakwater. The harbour board was established in 1877.

Settlers arrived from the 1860s onwards, and a borough was proclaimed in 1868. At first the town struggled without regular communications, but went ahead in tandem with the railway in 1877, and Timaru became a city in 1948. The soils in the area proved very fertile, with good cropping and grazing providing a solid foundation to the region's prosperity.

The first Ford dealer in Timaru was Kingham & Andrews, operating from premises in Latter and North Streets about 1908. Kingham & Andrews are also believed to have engaged the first motor mechanic apprentice in Timaru. By 1914 Andrews had left the partnership and H H Kingham remained the dealer. Charlie Baker took over in 1919 and moved the dealership to Barnard Street, to a site near the Drill Hall. In 1922 Cecil Wood Ltd took over the dealership, relocating to the corner of Sefton and Theodosia Streets. In 1927 Dunnett and Downey took over as Ford dealers and were located opposite the post office in King George Street.

Timaru was a key place for Colonial Motor Company because of its port which could accept large overseas ships carrying new Model T Fords directly from Ford Canada. With wheels off, hood and windscreen removed and packed inside, each car fitted into a surprisingly small, wooden, packing case.

Colonial Motor Company decided to establish a South Island branch in 1916, appointed J B Murphy to manage it, and instructed him to find suitable land for a depot and warehouse near the port at Timaru. He located land in Sophia Street, midway between Strathallen and Canon Streets, which was bought for £1,400. The

warehouse was designed by Timaru architect Herbert Hall, and a tender of £2,910 from builders Shillito Brothers was accepted. The 8,000 sq ft building had room for secure storage of cased cars, with space to unpack and assemble them. Even in those days there was a myriad of paperwork; customs declarations, excise payments, shipping and rail manifests, invoicing for orders and distribution documents. Spare parts were also held here.

Newly assembled Model T cars were railed to the south as far as Invercargill, and north to Christchurch and Kaikoura. The West Coast was serviced from Wellington by coastal freighters which plied regularly between Greymouth, Westport, Nelson and Wellington.

In 1917, land neighbouring the branch was bought, with a 33ft frontage and 165ft deep, and further building extensions were made at a cost of £2,000. In 1918, the first shipment of Fordson tractors arrived, and in 1919 one ton Model T trucks.

J B Murphy resigned in 1920 and was replaced by Walter Ingles. The extra stock requirements were starting to put pressure on space and, in 1920, Miss A Smith sold her adjoining property to the company for £2,350, giving a considerably larger area for storage.

When Ormond Hutchinson joined Colonial Motor Company in 1920, he was sent to Timaru branch, becoming the first road organiser in New Zealand, with a territory from Kaikoura to Invercargill. He visited dealers every month, making sure they were maximising the opportunities available with tractors, trucks and cars. He also spent time with sales people, showing them how to demonstrate tractors, and speaking to groups of farmers about the benefits available from using tractors instead of horses. Once the first tractor was sold in an area, it usually bred more sales, as neighbours observed how it worked, but the conversion from horses to tractors was often difficult until a farmer actually operated the Fordson himself.

The Gibbons family acquired the majority shareholding in Colonial Motor Company in 1918 and, after the war ended, turned their attention to a higher percentage of car assembly to save shipping space, which was at a premium throughout the Pacific, because of large losses in the Atlantic during the war. In 1920 the shortage of shipping space actually restricted the number of cars that could be sold in New Zealand.

The new assembly plant, the first in the country, was built at 89 Courtenay Place, Wellington, behind the head office. The plant was fully operational in 1922, lowering the shipping freight cost per unit, and further reducing the price of the Model T. Sales expanded rapidly, and George Duncalf became branch manager after Walter Ingles left in 1922.

With this success, it was decided to set up smaller plants in Auckland and Timaru, further saving internal freight. More land at 157 Sophia Street was bought from M O'Meehan in 1924, and major extensions planned by Herbert Hall. Shillito Brothers won the contract at £6,597 for the two-storey south building, and £6,746 for the two storey north building, giving nearly 40,000 sq ft of floor space in total.

One of the first of the new assembly staff members was interviewed in 1979. William (Bill) Leeney joined in 1923, having been Mrs Elworthy's chauffeur prior to this. He was paid 2s 2d per hour, which was good money in those days. (CPI converts to about $15.00/hr in 2000.) He was also paid a bonus of 2d per hour as a tester, when he took each car on a 3 mile run to make sure everything was working properly. At first, the cars came as before, one car per case, semi knocked down. When the new assembly buildings were finished, the 'New Beauty' model arrived fully knocked down, and the production line started. Body and smaller components were assembled and put together on the top floor, and chassis parts assembled on the ground floor. As assembly of the chassis was completed, the body was lowered through a bay in the top floor, onto the chassis. Guards, running boards and wiring were added, and the completed car started and test run by Bill Leeney.

One test drive he never forgot occurred soon after he started smoking a pipe he had won at the Dunedin Exhibition. Smoking was banned in the factory, so Bill lit his pipe on a test run, but didn't notice a cinder that flew out and into the 'hoodite' roof fabric. "I wondered why everyone was waving to me, but I just thought they were being friendly. I turned the corner and with a different wind direction, had the smoke blow directly to me. I jammed on the brakes, ripped off the smouldering roof, and put the fire out."

George Duncalf transferred to manage

Ford Motors (Canterbury) Ltd, which started in Christchurch in May 1925, and Ormond Hutchinson was appointed branch manager.

By now the Auckland, Wellington and Timaru plants were on an equal assembly footing, so Hope B Gibbons devised a competition to see which one could build a car the fastest. Rules were laid down, and a team at each plant selected to build a 'New Beauty' Model T Phaeton. Each car had to be able to be driven around the block afterwards.

Official timekeepers were at each plant as the teams started. In Timaru chassis parts were riveted together, springs, axles, wheels, engine and gearbox fitted, body lowered on. The radiator, running boards and windscreen screwed on. Electrical fittings positioned and wired, bonnet on and the car was fired up 52 minutes after starting.

Bill Leeney remembered: " I took the car out to the kerb and tightened the wheel nuts, because I couldn't remember anyone doing this, before starting off. When I turned the first corner all four doors flew open, and when I got back I said it had to be rebuilt. The whole car felt strange on the road.

"We got a cable from Mr Hope B Gibbons congratulating us on bringing home the bacon, so the boss, Orm Hutchinson, sent us home with a pound of bacon and a dozen eggs as a bonus. I'll admit we cheated a bit, but we were only a minute ahead of Wellington, and 90 seconds ahead of Auckland, and I don't think their efforts were any better than ours. And besides, it took three hours to build a 'New Beauty' properly." When the car was stripped down, it was only half assembled, with 102 rivets missing from the chassis alone!

Like all Colonial Motor Company employees, at Christmas the Timaru branch staff received a bonus of one day's pay for every three months' service, with a minimum of £1, and a maximum of 10 working days pay. As Bill Leeney put it, "Pretty generous for those days." [About $611 for 10 days in 2000]

By now, there were a number of specialists at Timaru who travelled around dealers, helping them with any problems. One was W Stanley Smart, sales and service manager. (His mother was a Hurrell, and niece of Henry Hurrell.) He transferred from Timaru to be service manager at John W Andrew and Sons, Auckland in September 1930, taking over from his cousin Jack Broun, who became NZ service manager at Colonial

Motor Company. Sadly, Stan Smart died less than a year later.

The assembly plant switched to the Model A in 1928, and cars were trans-shipped from Ford Canada via Vancouver. Shipping arrivals were irregular; 200 cars would arrive, and all registered assembly workers would be called in to assemble the stock. Then, if another boatload had not arrived, they would be stood down until the next shipment arrived. Assembly workers were paid much more than other workers, so people were always available. With the huge run down in sales during the Depression, the plant was closed in 1932 when the V8 arrived. The V8 required new body jigs which were expensive and, with the low sales volumes, it was decided to cut costs and assemble them in Wellington. Bill Leeney was one of those offered a job at Courtenay Place, and moved to Wellington, and later Ford, when Seaview opened at the end of 1936.

Joe Roseveare was an unofficial messenger boy after school in 1932. "Once a week the men would pass the hat around, and if I was lucky I'd get up to a shilling for doing the week's messages, which was a good bit of money in those days," he recalled. His father, Joe Senior, started with Colonial Motor Company in 1915, assembling cars at Courtenay Place, Wellington, and shifted to Timaru when assembly started in the 1920s. One of his jobs was to help pick up the cases of knocked down parts from the ship. Cases were swung straight out of the ship's hold onto the company's trucks, which then drove to the plant. The company paid the bond and wharf rates, as if they had gone through the rail system, but avoided the normal delays. Timaru Motors accepted Joe Junior's application to be an apprentice mechanic in 1935, and he turned up for work in short pants. He remembered: "After two weeks work at 15 shillings a week, I had saved 7s 6d, enough to buy my first pair of long pants."

Timaru branch continued with Orm Hutchinson as manager until 1935, when he transferred to Ford Motors (Canterbury) in Christchurch. R U (Bob) Macaulay became branch manager until the branch closed in 1936, when Ford Motor Company started distribution from Seaview. He then became manager at Invercargill.

Timaru Motors was incorporated in June 1931, after Clifford Atkinson's appointment by the receivers for Dunnett and Downey Ltd. The Depression was having a disastrous effect on businesses all

over the country, and there was no possibility of finding buyers, so Colonial Motor Company had to take over if they were to have representation in Timaru. With the economic difficulties at the time, the dealership operated from the assembly plant building.

P S (Sid) Enting, assistant branch manager, was appointed first manager of Timaru Motors in June 1931. He was at Wellington branch as a road organiser covering the lower North Island before coming to Timaru in 1930, after Stanley Smart went to Auckland. In 1979, he recalled: "Those were trying times for the industry with the country deep in the Depression period. Rather than create unemployment, the company asked all staff to take a reduction of 10% in wages and salaries. We had about 20 new cars in stock, which was a big figure then, and 40 odd second-hand vehicles, which was far too many."

Turning down a transfer Sid Enting left Timaru Motors in 1933 and later went into a real estate business on his own account in Timaru.

In June 1933, when D S (Don) Mullan, 25 years old, took over as manager, it was completely by chance. He and CMC auditor Neil Scrimshaw, were at Timaru branch for a period after assembly work ended, and he was left behind to finish the accounting work. In the event, he stayed

Don Mullan happened to be in Timaru when Sid Enting resigned, and became manager in 1933.

37 years until he retired. "With the close down in production, we took over more of the assembly plant to use as our office and showroom, as well as storage for new stock." Besides the manager, Timaru Motors had an accountant, service manager, five mechanics, a lubrication attendant, and four salesmen.

Being a salesman then was no cakewalk. Acording to Don Mullan, salesmen had to keep their demonstrators in 100% order at all times. "Every morning they had to take their demonstrator out for inspection, and both car and salesman went through a regimental going over by the manager, making sure everything was spotless, even under the mudguards. And if either didn't make the grade, it all had to be done again.

"Timaru Motors took over the north building, with the administration office and ramp up to the first floor for the storage of new cars – this became the showroom. Of course it was pretty flattering, because the stock for the South Island was held there prior to despatch to dealers, and there could be 60 new vehicles there.

"By 1933, we began to pull out of the down period, and sold about two or three new cars a month, and up to six used cars. Our stock of used cars grew quite significantly to about 60 or so as the operation stepped in to assist other firms who were really feeling the pinch.

"The market improved in 1935 with the introduction of the new Centrepoise V8, and really stepped up in 1936. Changes were made to the buildings – the workshop was set up in the old assembly area, and parts was in the centre building.

"Timaru's traditional trade with farmers suffered a severe set back when Ford took tractors away in 1936, giving Booth MacDonald and later Gough, Gough and Hamer the entire tractor franchise."

Staff numbers built up to 35, but with the outbreak of war in 1939, dropped to 10. Don Mullan recalled: "The pressure was really on us as we were regarded as an essential industry. The service crew worked seven days a week and three nights, and we even had to black out the skylights in the workshop so nothing showed at night. On top of this, the lads were nearly all put in the Home Guard, and required to do things that we regarded as time wasting – such as digging holes in the beach. This was most frustrating, as we were being worked to the limit to try to keep all the trucks running, to keep the community going."

The old assembly plant's southern building was leased to the army as Home Guard headquarters and truck pool for the National Military Reserve. "This posed further problems as they sent all their trucks to us for repair, but wouldn't let any of the mechanics they'd taken from us work on them, even though they were some of our best men." The north building was used during the war to store wool, taking up to 1,000 bales at 3d. per bale per week rental.

Ford returned the tractors to dealers in 1946. "A lot of tractors were sold at this time as the farming community recovered from the war period. We held a large demonstration at the Fairview farm of Bill Stafford (the local Department of Agriculture superintendent). Hundreds came from all over the South Island to see the new Fordson Major E27N, the first

The 1950s panel shop was tucked into part of the old plant.

The new area for used cars and underseal was only a transition move.

In 1955, Washdyke was still a country village. Timaru Motors branch is opposite the intersection, where the bottom centre road from the Mackenzie Country joins Highway No.1, about two kilometres from the centre of Timaru.

Washdyke branch was attractively planted, with plenty of space.

tractor available in numbers after the war. The brown kerosene-powered unit with 9 inch tyres marketed at £345, and we thought we were made when eight sold that afternoon." However, new cars remained very scarce with import restrictions for the next 25 years.

In 1953 No. 81 Sophia Street was bought and the brick house pulled down with the old bricks used to make the back wall of a lean-to for marketing used cars. Timaru Motors bought the franchise to steam clean and apply underseal to new and used cars, and this operation was set up using open-air ramps behind the used cars.

All new cars for delivery to Ford dealers were treated after they had been uplifted from the port, before despatch to their destinations. Road noise was reduced, and the treatment also helped make up for factory deficiencies, blocking holes underneath and making cars more water and dust proof.

Tractors were the only product in free supply and were selling very well, but the old assembly plant was not a suitable sales outlet and there was nowhere to display used tractors or equipment. When Ford introduced the new Fordson Major 40hp diesel and petrol tractors in 1952, and sales took off with the wool boom, a study of the perimeter of Timaru city led to the decision to relocate tractors to Washdyke, then a small village three miles north of Timaru, at the main road intersection of Highway 44 to Lake Tekapo and the Mackenzie Country. Fourteen acres of land were purchased in 1953 and, with a Highway 1 frontage of 300 ft, Washdyke branch started.

The land ran back towards the sea, and was cleared of gorse, with three acres kept for the branch operation beside the road. This area was quite low lying, so fill was brought in and spread. A number of heavy trucks, like the Shell tanker, helped

consolidation by 'arranging' to drive over it. Trees were planted, and gardens established with roses planted along the rear fence.

A five bay workshop of 30 ft span, with tilt doors opening north, and sheltered from the southerly, was finished in 1955. Tractors and equipment for sale were displayed beside the road. The 'farm' at the rear was harrowed and sown in linseed, producing a profitable crop worth £258 the first year and providing useful tractor training for salesmen.

Joe Roseveare rejoined the company after working for five years in Nelson. He became a tractor salesman, and said the working hours were often quite long: "In those days we used to deliver the tractors ourselves, and I remember taking an E27N to Warter and Williams' farm in Middle Valley near Fairlie. I started out at 7am with my lunch, a packet of cigarettes, and a bottle of oil, to replace what I burnt on the journey, touring at the handsome speed of 8kph (top speed of a 4.3 Green Spot 'Cast Iron Clarice').

"Unfortunately I was given the wrong directions and didn't get to the farm until about 5pm, nearly frozen through, and with no cigarettes left. I was picked up by Don Mullan who, as they hadn't heard from me

for hours, had set out on the road and see if anything had happened to me."

Washdyke proved an excellent site, and the tractor and workshop business improved quickly in the very attractive 'country' environment. Although a lot of servicing was done on farms, diesel required more stringent conditions and workshop servicing increased. Cross and Pyke's service station next door came up for sale in 1958, and was promptly bought. There was room for expansion and it was a valuable place for storing and displaying equipment, wheels, power take-offs and tractor parts. When Ford Trader trucks were introduced in 1957, they were marketed alongside the tractors. Levels County Council bought six new Trader dumpers and were able to have them serviced in the county, at Washdyke.

Tractors still provided a major opportunity, but its territory extended 105km inland on the Opihi River to the Two Thumb Range above Mt Cook, 125km down the Southern Alps to Omaramara, and 100km out to the coast along the Hook River – some 7,500 sq km in total – and many of the operators were miles away from Timaru.

Colin Neill was a tractor mechanic at Washdyke, having served his

Timaru won the Champion of Champions tractor banner in 1954. From left: Not known; Bill Toomey, Ford NZ; Cyril McKay; Randal Thomson; not known; Wattie Falloon; Dave Douche, Alliance Finance; not known; George Weston; Alister Rosevear; Fred Fisher; Brian Faith.

Colin Neill and his wife Joan managed the Fairlie branch.

apprenticeship at Fairlie, 60 kilometres inland. After receiving some management training he established Fairlie branch in 1956 at his home, using a V8 van as mobile workshop, and carrying everything with him to the tractor requiring servicing. When Timaru Motors bought an old abandoned garage in Princes Street, Fairlie, in 1958, it, in Colin's words, "gave me somewhere to store parts and work out of the wet". With a backyard of 7,500 sq km he needed it. The building was old and leaked, snow blew under the doors and around corners in winter, but it was a public base. He was the only mobile serviceman in an area that had very few service stations, and few people lived in the Mackenzie basin. A great many passed through, however, and Colin had to contend with breakdowns at all hours, but he never

turned down anyone who needed help.

Colin Neill's wife, Joan, did most of the branch bookwork, tidying up invoices and charge sheets so Colin could get on with the job. Together they ran the branch for more than 25 years.

Meanwhile, the company was still looking for space with good street visibility to relocate their vehicle sales operations. The city milk treatment station on the north corner of Sophia and Canon Streets, was bought in 1965 and, after major conversions, it opened as a new and used vehicle sales centre.

A breakthrough came in 1969, with the purchase of half an acre from Prosser's wood and coal yard on the south corner of Canon and Sophia Streets. This was beside 81 Sophia Street, where the used cars and underseal plant was located, and gave the company a chance to develop a more effective business site. The section was brought up to Sophia Street level using attractive split stone retaining walls, with planter gardens and an attractive stairway to Canon Street, and a petrol station was incorporated into the site together with expanded used vehicle display.

Don Mullan, in Timaru nearly 40 years, retired in December 1970. He was also a director of Colonial Motor Company from May 1962 until February 1973. Wattie Falloon, who had also joined Timaru Motors in 1933, was now appointed general manager. He had started as a boy at Maude Brothers in Oamaru, then worked at Callendar's at Waimate, both Ford agents, before coming to Timaru, and working his way up to service manager, and latterly

assistant to Don Mullan.

Trucks were also a large part of Timaru Motors business, with the new D Series Fords introduced from 1966. These included the popular new turbo engine R Series bus chassis, and one of Wattie Falloon's first jobs was to hand over the keys for the first of eight new Timaru City Council buses.

When Wattie Falloon died in September 1973, his sudden death shocked everyone. He had spent 40 years with Timaru Motors and another 10 prior to that with other Ford dealers, and knew how to look after customers. Randal Thomson was appointed general manager, moving from Fagan Motors, Masterton. He had spent time at Timaru Motors in the 1950s, and knew many of the staff and customers, although a large number of staff members were now reaching retirement age and there were many more new, younger faces around the premises.

The company operated from five locations, was overcapitalised, and needed rationalising. Most of the land needed for redevelopment had been secured, but selling the old assembly plant remained a problem for the dealership. The workshop and administration offices were still in the old building, and Inland Revenue had leased the top floor soon after the war. Many considered buying it, but none did. When Hamilton Motors in Canon Street came on the market, it was bought, then the final piece of wanted land – the McCelland two-storey building in Canon Street – was bought in 1977.

Relocation of the dealership was now a priority and, after Randal Thomson finally convinced the council that the city needed the assembly plant for car parking, the sale went through in 1976. This paved the way for a new building on the corner of Canon and Sophia Streets. The sales centre was converted to the Timaru Tyre Centre which now employed four men besides the manager Frank Hoare, who had started by himself five years earlier, where the underseal plant had been. Plans were finalised for the new dealership building and the service department was shifted to the rear of the Tyre Centre, also using the Hamilton Motors site. The contract for construction of the new sales showroom, administration and parts building was let to Prosser Ltd, from whom the corner site had been bought in 1969.

Timaru about 1962. The assembly plant is the large building in the middle. Along Sophia Street, two properties to the left, is the used car and underseal area. Next left, and on the corner of Canon Street, is Prosser's yard. The port, above, was close to the assembly plant and has been extensively developed since.

Above: Don Mullan, with his wife Orma, in 1975.

Right: Wattie Falloon became general manager.

When Randal Thomson was transferred to Stevens Motors, Lower Hutt, in May 1978, Pat Cody who had been sales manager at Macaulay Motors, Invercargill, was appointed manager. He had plenty to occupy him: the new building to finalise; a number of new staff members to train; and the problems of the NZ vehicle market, with finance controls, and the shift to smaller cars as fuel prices escalated. John Blyth, previously at Macaulay Motors and then Phillipps Motors as accountant and then vehicle sales, joined him as sales manager.

Tractors sales had slowed, but trucks were still strong, and there were plenty of opportunities, but they had to be chased. Timaru Motors now employed 40 people in town and 15 at Washdyke.

The 1980s were a difficult time, with the government's new free market policies bringing many changes, but Timaru Motors did well, consolidating on its corner site. Although servicing requirements for new cars declined, a new workshop was built, where the used car lean-to had been at the south end, and the Tyre Centre building was sold. Computers were introduced from the

Wattie Falloon delivering the first of eight new Ford R228 50 seat omnibuses to the city council in 1971.

The Omega club in front of the old assembly plant before it was pulled down in 1976. Back left: Ted Hanifin, Bill Watson, Les Mahoney, Len Spurdon, Geoff Tollin, George Williams, Pat Cody (manager). Front: Jim Watt, Alister Rosevear, Ed Candy, Joe Rosevear, Cyril McKay, Alan Sherson, Alistair Cotterell. Absent: Colin Neill and Brian Faith.

In 1976 Timaru lost the solid silver Macaulay Motors Cup, which they had held for 35 years, to Hutchinson Motors. They were all smiling at the end, but some more than others. From left back: A Rosevear, A Cotterell, A Sherson, J Rosevear, J Bower, C Mackay, W Watson, R Thomson. Sitting: C Lake, V Newcombe, J Airey, O Hutchinson, I McGill, A Oliver, D McGill, W Weatherhead.

mid-1980s, reducing the need for as many office staff.

In 1990 Pat Cody was transferred to Avery Motors, Wellington and Russell Marr, who had been sales manager, was appointed manager in July. He had trained as a diesel mechanic, joining the company as tractor salesman in 1980, and had a passion for trucks and customer needs.

However, the market was in a state of flux with the Hino-Ford alliance in doubt. With the changes in road haulage regulations, which allowed competition against rail, line haul operators increased and started looking at extra heavy trucks. Ford Louisville trucks were introduced to New Zealand, with four specialist truck dealers designated. There was a ready sale of the new extra heavy Ford Louisville trucks, many for line haul and others to off-road users. Russell Marr sold one to Bill Richardson in 1989, owner of Allied Concrete, and he was sufficiently impressed to start buying several each year as his business expanded. In a very short time, the Washdyke operation had expanded considerably in truck service and sales.

Meanwhile, in town, the car and light commercial market was improving and, when space became very tight, some of the service work was shifted to Washdyke and a mini bus was used to ferry customers and drivers. However, it was obvious the current trend was likely to continue and three new bays were added at the rear of

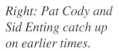

Right: Pat Cody and Sid Enting catch up on earlier times.

Below: Pat Cody farewelled to Wellington in 1990. Back left: Winsome Cody, Ed Candy, Trish Adelman, Ken Adelman, Pat Cody. Front: Edna Candy, Garfield and Bev Andrew, Wendy and Russell Marr.

the Washdyke workshop in 1993.

In 1991 Timaru Motors won its first Distinguished Achievement Award, introduced by Ford in 1989, together with sales and service quality standards, and measured by the dealer's own customers. Four size groups were awarded President's Awards, presented by Ford Asia Pacific president and runners up received Distinguished Achievement Awards. Since 1991 Timaru Motors has won four more Distinguished Achievement Awards and three President's Awards, in addition to many more for their truck operations.

By the end of 1993 Timaru had sold over 30 Ford Louisville new trucks and was asked to take over their sales and servicing for the South Island. Now that the Hino-Ford trucks had run out, Colonial Motor Company was looking for a replacement truck, and when the PACCAR franchise came on the market, it bought the major share of this business from Carter Holt Harvey. Timaru Motors took on the South Island agency for Foden and Kenworth brands on January 1 1994, and a new company, Timaru Trucks Ltd, was formed to keep these trucks entirely separate from the Ford franchise. Timaru Motors decided it would no longer handle tractors as these had become very specialised and could not be sold and serviced in tandem with trucks.

Truck operations had extended considerably from the original Washdyke branch, and sales just kept on growing. In most cases, servicing of trucks was handled by specialists in key locations, but keeping in touch with customers from Nelson to Invercargill was now a major task, with one salesman on the road full time.

The split operation of city and branch was not entirely satisfactory as Timaru was always under pressure to cope, and more and more work was transferred to

The new dealership was much more compact, and more suited to vehicle sales.

Trucks became increasingly dominant at Washdyke. Here, in 1984, with the N 1117 Ford-Hino bus are, from left: Chris Rodley, not known, Chris Johnson, Russell Marr and Ed Candy.

All operations at Washdyke in 1996. Truck sales and service are on the left hand side; and car sales and service are in front and to the right. A truck panel and paint business is leased at the rear.

Below: Cathy Cliff (right) is showing Colleen Hawke how to get the figures out in 1977.

Below right: Russell Marr, CEO.

Washdyke, which had changed considerably and was now known by its road name, Hilton Highway. The small village had disappeared, and been replaced by a number of retail outlets. After the new bypass route was built to the west, it was evident that much of the commercial area was shifting to Hilton Highway which had effectively become part of Timaru. When an offer was made to buy the Sophia and Canon Streets corner in May 1997, it was accepted and Paul Goldsmith Architects was asked to redesign the dealership. The spectacular result was opened in February 1998.

Andrew Garfield, long time parts manager, and Cathy Cliff in the office, who received her 25 year Omega gold watch in 2002, both think that the new dealership is an amazing place to work in.

When Ford US sold its heavy truck

division to Freightliner Corporation in 1998, this presented a problem to Timaru, which had now sold more than 150 Louisville trucks, mostly to Allied Concrete. Both Kenworth Australia, and German Motor Distributors, the new NZ agent for the Louisville, were concerned about the competitive situation with the two brands so, as Allied preferred to run with the Louisville replacement, Sterling, and now had 100 operating, Timaru Motors decided to give up Kenworth and Foden.

In 1999, Timaru Trucks changed its name to Trucks South Ltd and has the GMD franchises–Sterling and Mercedes Benz trucks. Their new truck franchises have worked well for them, with sales of more than 100 each year.

Mazda, Ford's international partner, was no longer represented in Timaru, and after some negotiation, the franchise went to Timaru Motors.

Today the partnerships with all franchises are operating well under a united staff group at Timaru Motors' Hilton Highway dealership. It is winning customer quality awards as a top dealership for all its distributors.

Trucks South was formed in 1999. Gerald Stanley and Serge Terry from German Motor Distributors are with Russell Marr (centre).

Timaru Motors have won three President's Awards and five Distinguished Achievement Awards from Ford and several more from GMD. The 2001 staff, clockwise from left: Russell Marr, Wayne Hitchcock, Brian Grace, Kevin Ryan, Garfield Andrew, John Neale, Julie King, Gavin Beech, Dean Brown, Kevin Heywood, Brad McSweeney, Wayne Pateman, Lloyd Cross, Neil Holwell, Doug Harvey, Derek Mayne, Ted Best, Callum Scott, Jeff Henderson, Sam Dupont, Jason Fowler, Tony Firman, Graham Woods, Terry Fraser, Graham Campbell, Ann Donovan, Rana McNeill, Kathy Cliff, Melissa Paterson, Kimberly Blakemore and Julie Shand.

*Ford Motors
(Dunedin) Ltd,
1923.*

*Sales prizes were
common in the
1920s. This gold fob
watch was awarded
to F O'Neill for
winning the prize for
the most sales
between May and
July 1927.*

CHAPTER TWENTYNINE

DUNEDIN –
NAPIER MOTORS /
DUNEDIN CITY FORD

Dunedin City lies in a beautiful amphitheatre at the head of Otago Harbour, some 24km from the Pacific Ocean at Taiaroa Head. The city has spread across the flat lands and nearby hills, and across the isthmus to the Otago Peninsula. Over the years much land has been reclaimed from the harbour for use by industry and business.

Ngai Tahu and Ngati Mamoe, who both occupied the Otago peninsula during the 18th century, had little in common. When Ngai Tahu, jealous of the fishing prowess of Ngati Mamoe, spoiled their fishing grounds and damaged their canoes, the passive Ngati Mamoe bided their time before seeking retribution, capturing Ngai Tahu chief Tarewai, attacking him with cutting stones and slicing his flesh. After a minor diversion, Tarewai escaped, and waited for utu (revenge). Ngati Mamoe paramount chief Te Raki-ihia was taken, killed and eaten, and his bones used to make fish hooks by Ngai Tahu – the ultimate desecration. In return, Te Raki-ihia's son took his warriors to collect firewood near the Ngai Tahu kaika (village), Otakou, and killed many Ngai Tahu. Attacks and counter attacks continued for years.

After Daniel Cooper, captain of the sealer *Unity*, found and used the safe harbour in 1809, it became known as Port Daniel. When a brig, *Matilda,* anchored there in 1813, and one long boat and crew disappeared, it was thought they had drowned, until it was discovered they had been killed and eaten by Maori incensed at the sealers' cruelty.

In 1817, when one of his party was recognised as a trader in preserved, tattooed Maori heads, sealer Captain James Kelly and his men were attacked while trying to trade iron for potatoes, losing three men. When Kelly and the rest of his party made it back to the *Sophia*, to find another Maori group trying to trade with the brig's crew, Kelly and his crew attacked them with sealing knives, slaughtering them, and then killed more Maori (over 70 in total), smashed canoes, and razed their village, which they named 'City of Otago'. Today the place is still known as 'Murdering Beach'. (The Ngati Mamoe pa 'Otakou' was pronounced 'Otago' in the more guttural Ngai Tahu accent, and was officially spelt this way following a ruling from Sir George Grey on December 26 1848.)

Maori in the district suffered greatly from the diseases brought by the sealers and whalers, which decimated considerable numbers at Otakou pa, reducing it to a population of 110 in 1847.

Meanwhile, Scotland was in the grips of depression in 1840, with about 25% of the working population unemployed, and even those in work barely surviving. When Scottish MP George Rennie formed the 'New Edinburgh' Plan, for a New Zealand settlement, Rev Thomas Burns insisted it be an exclusive Free Church settlement, easing Rennie out. Captain William Cargill and Rev Burns assumed leadership and gave the movement its special settlement character.

On May 18 1843, Rev Dr Chalmers stormed out of the established Kirk of Scotland with 400 ministers, split the congregation, and formed the Free Church of Scotland to cater for Presbyterians wishing to choose their own ministers. Chalmers endorsed Burns' plan to form the new settlement, giving it the necessary impetus.

The New Zealand Company agreed to cede some of its land so a Scottish settlement could be established. Edward Gibbon Wakefield entrusted surveyor Frederick Tuckett with laying out the Otago site, and Governor Fitzroy waived the Crown's right of pre-emption to this land.

In November 1847, the emigrant ships *John Wickliffe* and *Philip Laing* set sail for Otago Harbour with 344 passengers, arriving on March 23 1848. Surveyor Charles Kettle surveyed the plan of

Dunedin, choosing names for the main streets and suburbs to associate the link between the 'Old' and 'New' Edinburgh. The ships *Blundell* and *Bernicia* added 200 more and by the end of 1849 another 500 settlers had arrived.

In 1861 the discovery of gold by Gabriel Reid caused the first of several rushes. After Gabriel's Gully came rushes to the Dunstan diggings and the Shotover River – 'the richest river in the world' – only to be outdone by William Fox's group who found a fortune in the Arrow River. Most of the able-bodied men raced to the diggings but, once the town recovered, Dunedin's economy leapt ahead.

Gold made Dunedin, giving it a wealth that produced many fine buildings and monuments and making it the only Victorian city in New Zealand. Gold also provided the very strong economic base which made Dunedin the commercial capital of New Zealand with traditional Scottish skills of banking and engineering endowing the city with great benefits. With its Scottish ethos, Dunedin is recognized as the 'Edinburgh of the South'.

Very much a part of the city, Otago University was established in 1878, New Zealand's first, with distinctive, slate-roofed, bluestone buildings. Many other magnificent bluestone churches, schools, libraries, galleries and buildings, give the city solidity unique in the country.

The deepwater harbour was developed early, encouraging major late 19th century industrial growth, with freezing works, woollen and flour mills, consumer goods, heavy and precision engineering, fertiliser, cement and pottery manufacture in the city and nearby towns of Green Island, Mosgiel and Port Chalmers. Much of the city's electric power is self-generated from the Waipori River. Opened in 1863, the first railway between Port Chalmers and the city was purchased by government 10 years later. By 1879 the railway connected Dunedin with Bluff and Lyttleton. Dunedin Airport opened in 1962.

G W Woods & Co was the Otago and Southland Ford franchise holder from about 1910. They were stock and station agents in close contact with the farming community and had branches throughout the area. While they did a very good job, they were not car specialists, and had many agencies for other products, and W J P McCulloch was appointed the Ford dealer

in Dunedin about 1912, with premises in the Octagon.

McCulloch sold out in 1917 to Todd Brothers, Ford dealers at Heriot and Roxburgh. Charles Todd had become a fellmonger at Heriot in 1884 with his son Charles. Later, they began the Heriot trading store, which was the centre of the rabbit fur trade in the late 19th century. In 1915 Charles Jnr moved to Dunedin, and formed a stock and station agency, Todd Brothers Ltd, for his four sons. Soon there were branches in many parts of Otago, selling Ford cars and later trucks and tractors.

In 1923 Todd Motor Company was formed to handle the motor franchise portion of Todd Brothers, and they decided to expand their range of franchises. When they added Overland cars in 1923, Henry Ford's dealer policy of exclusivity was contravened and Colonial Motor Company was forced to cancel their franchise.

New Ford dealer service points were formed to replace Todd's: Alex Pringle at Milton; John H Stevenson at Balclutha; D R Jones at Lawrence and Roxburgh; Alex Smith at Ranfurly; R E Haywood at Cromwell; G W Woods & Co at Heriot and Tapanui; H Herson at Alexandra; and J F Warren at Palmerston.

After difficulty finding a Dunedin dealer replacement, H B & R B Gibbons formed Ford Motors (Dunedin) Ltd, with John Grendon Phillips as dealer and shareholder. John Phillips had worked for Colonial Motor Company since 1907, when he started as an office boy, and resigned as manager of the CMC Auckland branch to start the Dunedin dealership.

Having relinquished its licence and being vacant, the Newmarket Hotel was purchased, on the corner of Hope Street and Manor Place, facing Princes Street. The showroom was in the former bar, with the sales manager and manager sharing an office in the old dining room on the first floor, and the general office next door in a former bedroom. Most of the ground floor had the partitions stripped to provide workshop and parts areas. New petrol pumps, or 'bowsers', were set up on the footpath with petrol tanks in the cellar where beer had been stored. The two-storey brick building was impressive, especially as a sign proclaimed: 'Open continuously, expert mechanics in attendance day and night'.

Model T Fords were everywhere in

those days, with sales further stimulated as prices kept coming down. A standard Model T Phaeton tourer cost £170, and you could buy a chassis for £125, a runabout for £154, coupe for £248, town sedan for £270, and a truck chassis for £154. Joe Spiro was the accountant, starting in January 1924. Stan King joined as a message boy in August that year.

In 1926, architects Coombs & White revised plans, prepared by them in 1923, for a grand, four-storey building of 16,800 sq ft per floor. But the plans were shelved again when John Phillips resigned with personal difficulties in 1926.

When H B & R B Gibbons appointed G W Massingham manager in December 1926, the Model T was close to being withdrawn and competition was forcing changes. The 'T' was still the most popular car on the market, but it was hard selling against the Chevrolet Nationals and Dodge 4 with their new 'popular' features.

The Model T ran out in late 1927, and there was a year with no cars, when Chevrolet managed to get market leadership. The Model A was a great success when it arrived in August, regaining leadership, but trading was tough, with dealers making very little money.

In 1930 G W Massingham resigned, and his deputy B Allison was appointed. The Depression hit at the end of 1930, a year after the Wall Street crash, and used cars became a nightmare as they fell to a fraction of their book value. Losses mounted, staff

numbers reduced. B Allison resigned in 1933. It was a difficult time.

When J L (Les) Napier was appointed manager in 1934, trading was improving rapidly with the popular Ford V8s available and the Depression ending. He had served in the First World War as a bugler in the NZ Forces band. When he entered in a competition to find the best bugler, and won, he was pronounced the best bugler in the British Forces, and King George V presented him with a silver bugle. With this prized possession, he formed a bugle band after the war, and was called on every ANZAC Day to play 'The Last Post'.

When, in 1936, Ford Motor Company set up in New Zealand and insisted 'Ford' be removed from all dealer names, Colonial Motor Company decided that subsidiaries would take their manager's name, so the company became Napier Motors Ltd. Les Napier resigned in July 1936, joining the Austin dealer, Vickery's.

A C (Mac) McPherson was appointed manager of Napier Motors in September 1936. A keen rugby player, he was in the vintage 1930 Wellington representative team. After joining Colonial Motor Company in 1926, as head office cashier, he shifted to production and wholesale, before a transfer as assistant manager Auckland branch and, then in 1936, to become CMC branch manager at Timaru.

His humour and canny administration skills brought stability to the Dunedin dealership and, very soon, the staff at

Joe Spiro was accountant for 28 years from 1924.

A C McPherson brought unity and teamwork to the company when he arrived in 1936.

Con Berry, gold medallist.

Napier Motors was moulded into a team. Business expanded quickly, and it was obvious more space was going to be required, so Mac McPherson kept an eye on nearby properties. The old hotel's stable yard was now roofed to provide much needed workshop space, and part of the old workshop on the ground floor was used to house the increasing parts stock needed by the expanded model range.

Over a period of 15 years the company was successful in buying all the adjoining properties up to the Rugby Hotel in Hope Street, converting these for parts, staff facilities and off street parking for workshop reception.

In 1939, Con Berry transferred to Napier Motors as parts manager. Starting at CMC Timaru branch in 1925, he later became South Island parts manager, until Ford took over in 1936. He was the last employee left at the branch, locking up and giving the keys to Don Mullan, and then working for Timaru Motors. His knowledge and skills were imparted to many new trainees over the years.

After Ford set up in New Zealand the volume of new cars increased quickly as they sought an improved market share, so

The hotel was modernised and integrated with parts and the workshop in Hope Street.

used cars quickly became a problem for all dealers, and the gross retained on new vehicles declined. When the Second World War was declared in 1939, imports stopped and the government requisitioned all 1938 and 1939 used cars, leaving dealers in a weak position.

The war was a difficult period, and with a number of its staff members joining up, Napier Motors was left short-handed. A surprise of note occurred in 1941, when Mac McPherson, seemingly a confirmed bachelor, left the office for a week's holiday. On the Monday, Jessie Elmslie, the vivacious typist and an Otago badminton representative, was not about either. Both Jessie and Mac returned to the office a week later. They had married, been on honeymoon for a week, and not one person in the office had any inkling of the romance.

Mac McPherson was a true Scot with his dedication to conserving expenditure. His office overlooking Manor Place never got sun, and was freezing in winter, when he wore a stout woollen coat to keep him warm. Visitors from anywhere north of Dunedin always thought his office was like the South Pole. When asked if they were cold, and there was no clear reply, conversation was in an icy atmosphere with an early conclusion. If they said it was cold, Mac McPherson got out an antique electric heater and plugged in the dodgy looking cord. The very meek ray of warmth did not encourage visitors to stay any longer than necessary. The main office was bathed in sun from the Hope Street windows and pleasantly warm.

After the war, staff returned from the services, and several new immigrants were taken on, bringing new skills and ideas. The service department, and tractor and used cars sales, were the dealership's mainstays, because of licence restrictions. In 1946, the premises were given a makeover, the white Art Deco look helping to connect up the disparate buildings.

Joe Spiro had been accountant for 28 years when he retired in 1952. After seeing the company through a depression and war, he was able to hand over books that showed a credit balance after all the losses during the difficult years. He was replaced by C C (Mac) McDermott who had emigrated from London in the 1920s, completing his accountancy qualifications after navy service in the war, and was a shipping company secretary before joining Napier Motors as accountant.

In 1947, the new Fordson E27N was the first post-war tractor available in volume, and farmers bought them to develop their farms. In 1952 the new Fordson Major 40hp was a huge success, arriving as farmers were achieving record returns with the wool boom of 1951. The new tractors increased the volume of diesel servicing, which needed specialised treatment and training.

When it became clear Hope Street was not going to have enough space, detailed studies suggested Anderson's Bay was a likely commercial centre as there was no spare land in the city. Napier Motors needed to get closer to its farmer clients so land was bought at Green Island for a tractor branch. Residential houses were bought in Anderson's Bay Road, followed by more properties in Macandrew Bay Road. After the corner site had been secured, a commercial workshop was planned, and erected in 1958.

In 1964 a new sales centre costing £21,340 was built on the corner of Anderson's Bay and Macandrew Bay Roads. The building, known as the 'cathedral' by some, and 'rocket centre' by others, was a landmark. Napier Motors pioneered vehicle sales in the area, but

Anderson's Bay workshop was built in 1958.

Top: The 'rocket centre', or 'cathedral', 1964.

Middle: The Omega club in 1965. From left, standing: Bob Manson, service reception; Ces Maker, pre-delivery; Keith Maxwell, engine sales; Colin Challis, service foreman; Win Smith, new car service; Rod Culling, lube manager; Jim Walker, commercial sales manager. Sitting: Con Berry, parts manager; Len Keogh, service manager; Mac McPherson, managing director; Stan King, sub-accountant; and Perc Williams, sales manager.

Below: Anderson's Bay headquarters.

within a short period other franchises could see the benefits and followed. Today it is the motor trading centre of Dunedin.

In 1968, after two years negotiation, the company bought Steelway Industries' relatively new building adjoining the workshop and sales centre, in Macandrew Bay Road, giving the company a two acre site. The interior of the building was redesigned and the north and west walls fitted with display windows to provide a highly visible showroom. A second 10 bay car workshop was incorporated into this building and, in May 1969, the administration, sales and parts sections moved in.

A C 'Mac' McPherson retired in 1969 after 43 years with CMC Group. Mac McPherson had moulded the staff into an effective team who did things properly, won the trust of customers and made money. A great raconteur, he encouraged the staff social club, with its entertainment evenings, 'representative' trips away playing sports against other dealers, family outings and car trials. It had taken until 1952, and considerable determination, to get the company out of the red after the Depression and the Second World War, and it must have been satisfying for Mac McPherson to retire knowing the company was well positioned and going ahead.

W R (Bill) Blackburn was appointed manager. Mac McPherson's assistant for a number of years, he arranged much of the redevelopment at Anderson's Bay, where

The girls' rally team, 1964. Left: Diane Hislop, navigator, Helen and Linda Stewart (sisters and support crew), and Gaye Napier, driver.

he had grown up. He started at Hope Street in 1946 in parts, and after a two year stint farming in the Maniatoto, returned to parts wholesaling in 1952, then No Remittance sales, later becoming vehicle sales manager.

After the administration shifted to Anderson's Bay, the old hotel at Hope Street was demolished and the site converted to sell used cars. The former lube bay had one wall removed and became a covered service station and sales depot, keeping the town base open. The parts operation stayed at Hope Street, with a smaller depot and retail display at Anderson's Bay.

In 1969 an existing garage was bought at Factory Road, Mosgiel, from Michael

Left: W R (Bill) Blackburn.

Right: Michael Eaves.

The Newmarket Hotel was demolished and converted to a sales centre and service station.

Eaves who stayed on as branch supervisor for a year, with four mechanics, a cost clerk and a salesman, to operate the business. Alan Lion, who was supervising tractor operations, managed the branch for two years, getting tractors properly established. This branch gave Napier Motors the opportunity to get closer to their farmer clients and the business quickly expanded. The premises were enlarged in 1972, adding an eight bay workshop, parts and sales office.

Alan McElroy joined the company as branch manager in 1972, and the front yard was sealed, giving display space for new and used vehicles and tractors. After lengthy negotiations with the Motor Spirits Licensing Board, a petrol seller's licence was obtained in 1977 and pumps and a canopy were added, bringing a steady flow

Hope Street parts and wholesale was parts HQ.

Alan McElroy, manager of Mosgiel branch, in 1972.

of people to the branch. This left insufficient room to display vehicles, so Alan McElroy convinced a neighbour to sell his property, and soon there was room for 30 vehicles. After 10 years the branch had a staff of 14 people, mostly living nearby.

Mosgiel branch serviced farms from Waitati in the north to Waihola south, and inland to Hyde. With the steady development of tractors, this extended to Outram and Middlemarch. The branch was very successful, achieving over 30% Ford penetration for new vehicles into the district, and selling tractors and used cars profitably.

In 1975, on the 50th anniversary of starting work for Colonial Motor Company, Con Berry was picked up for work by Win Winfield, fleet sales manager, in his 1924 Model T Ford. Starting at CMC Timaru branch in 1925, Con Berry became South Island parts manager, and was the last person on the staff when the branch closed down after Ford took over distribution in 1936. He transferred to retail parts at Timaru Motors then, in 1939, went to Dunedin as parts manager for Napier Motors. Ford Motor Company twice awarded him Gold Medallions for outstanding performance (only one other medallion award has been made in New Zealand). Stepping down from parts manager in 1973, Con Berry ran training seminars in parts management for CMC Group. Such service today is rare, and even in 1975 was a remarkable and celebrated event.

After being diagnosed with cancer, Bill

Blackburn retired in September 1981 and, sadly, died soon afterwards aged 52. He had been a stalwart of Napier Motors, and had seen it grow substantially in his 12 years at the helm, and 33 years service with the company.

Ian D Lambie was appointed general manager in September 1981. Starting from school as an office boy at Hutchinson Motors, he became accountant at Sockburn Motors, transferring to Te Kuiti Motors, then to sales at South Auckland Motors. In 1971 he was manager of Fairhall Motors, Kaikohe, then Newlands Motors, Johnsonville.

When the new 'market forces' Labour government turned New Zealand upside

Ron Wilson checks a Ford 7710 prior to delivery at Mosgiel.

On the 50th anniversary of his starting work for CMC, Con Berry was collected from home by Win Winfield in his 1924 Model T.

down in the mid-1980s, Ian Lambie's experience came to the fore. Changes were necessary to survive and, as Anderson's Bay was now the motor centre, a decision was made to close Hope Street. When Ford sold out of tractors in 1988, Mosgiel branch was no longer viable. Rationalisation was taking place in the industry, and many dealers failed, as they had done in the 1930s, and Mosgiel was sold.

Concentrating the dealership at Anderson's Bay had immediate benefits. It removed duplication and the introduction of the Magix computer system in 1986 helped to slim expenses, with many cross-entry clerical jobs in parts and service removed. With less administration, staff members were much more productive.

Stan King and Bill Blackburn.

Finding the breakeven point was the key to survival.

When Ford introduced new quality standards to sales and service, to raise customer service levels and satisfaction, with the presentation of a President's Award and Distinguished Achievement Awards, to many Ford dealers this meant no change from existing practices, and Napier Motors received the Distinguished Achievement Award in the first year. The company had always had a culture of treating customers well, but the 'official' recognition was much appreciated by all the staff. Since then the company has been in the winning circle seven times, despite increased competition from other dealers, and higher performance scores.

The name 'Napier' Motors had for many years caused confusion for obvious reasons, and so when Ford agreed to allow the use of their name again, a change was considered. After much discussion, everyone agreed that 'Dunedin City Ford' had a good ring to it and ended any confusion. The company changed to its new name in 1992.

Trucks had been an important part of the business for 60 years and when Ford did not renew their N Series contract with Hino in 1992, and there were no longer heavy trucks available, there was a significant gap. Only cars and light commercials were left, but Ford now opened up the range of vehicles, with their

Above: The management team at the Laser launch in 1981. From left, standing: Ray Cuthbertson, service manager; Jack Joyce, parts manager; Ian Lambie, dealer principal; Michael Eaves, commercial sales manager; George Molloy, general sales manager; Cyril McDermott, business manager; Merv Marshall and Des Ferguson, salesmen. Front: Alan McElroy, Mosgiel manager; and Roger Hall, accountant.

Middle: Dunedin City Ford had consolidated to one site in 1995.

Left: Dunedin City Ford welcomed its first President's Award in 2000, after being Distinguished Achiever five times.

multiple sources, and could take advantage of currency pricing differences.

Rationalisation of Ford dealers started, with the realisation that representation relied on profit as much as market share, and by the mid-1990s many of the 83 Ford dealers in 1981 had disappeared. Ford advised many small dealers they could become Ford service dealers, and draw their parts and vehicles from main dealerships. Robb's Garage at Roxburgh, Warren's Garage at Palmerston and, after David Sterritt Motors sold the business, Oamaru became service dealers for Dunedin City Ford. The effect was to enlarge the dealership territory to cover the region from the Waitaki River in the north to Milton in the south and inland to Alexandra, Cromwell and Wanaka.

Dunedin City Ford remains strong, its customers well satisfied with the excellent service. In 2003, Ian Lambie retired from the company, but was elected a director of Colonial Motor Company.

Roger Taylor, who had worked at Dunedin City Ford since 1993, has returned as CEO after a year as dealer principal of Ruahine Motors, Waipukurau, committed to continue the tradition of sound management and top customer service.

Dunedin City Ford staff salute the 1903 Fordmobile in 2003. Standing left to right, front to back: Brian Cleary, Laurie Troy, Ron Gill, Doug Marshall, Simon Taylor, Harold Offen, Brent Mulqueen, Andrew Aitken, Bryce Thompson, Phillip Rohmets, Roger Taylor, Jenny Wragg, Heather Mason, Tracey Williams, Paulette Wilson, Ray Boyes, Sid Jackways, Steve Simpson, Ron Wilson, Brian McCracken, Noel Perry, Alan Rogers, Robert Bain, Chris Stichman, Lindsay Phillips, Paul Lamond. In front:Michael Williams, David Mclea, Michael Walters, Andre Waho, Michael Shum, Geoffrey Sachtler, Ken Ward, Robbie Dick, Gordon McKenzie.

CHAPTER THIRTY

INVERCARGILL –
MACAULAY MOTORS LTD

Known by the Maoris as 'Murihiku', the tail end of the land, New Zealand's southernmost district of Southland had its beginnings with the government's purchase of 2.8 million hectares of land in August 1853.

The Waitaha tribe, original occupiers of the south, lived off the abundant food of birds and fish in the area. Otago's Ngati Mamoe invaded the south, conquering and absorbing the Waitaha and then, a short while later, suffered the same fate at the hands of the Ngai Tahu.

In 1855, John Kelly, an Irish seaman and whaler, who had settled earlier at Ruapeke Island, married a Scottish widow in Dunedin. They sailed to Bluff, and became the first settlers at the site of Invercargill, which became known as Kelly's Point. By October 1856 there was a sizable settlement of people, most living under canvas.

The ship *Star* arrived at New River estuary on November 6 1856 with 30 new settlers. A post office was established there and on March 20 1857, the first town sections were sold. Governor Gore Browne named the settlement Invercargill, after Captain William Cargill, superintendant of Otago,

With more than 1,000 people living in the area in 1861, it became the province of Southland, with Invercargill as its capital. About the same time, many residents left to seek their fortunes following the discovery of gold in Otago. Various schemes to find gold in Southland failed, as did the wooden track railway linking the goldfields.

The young province had its financial difficulties for several years until Sir Julius Vogel's public works scheme brought huge sums of money and settlers to the colony in 1869 and 1870. Many settled in the south, helping Invercargill to get going again. The town grew quickly, becoming a borough in 1871, and electing its first town council.

The climate can be decidedly cool, and records are held for the least hours of sunshine in New Zealand, but the annual rainfall of 1,000mm is spread evenly and pastures never dry out in summer. This makes for quite outstanding grass growth. Predominantly a sheep grazing area, there is also cropping, forestry, and dairying which has increased rapidly with the high returns possible at the end of the 20th century. Industry is dominated by meat freezing works established in the 1880s, and the huge aluminium smelter at Tiwai Point, built in 1970, that manufactures aluminium from imported alumina, using cheap electricity from Manapouri. Industry has developed in support of the primary producers, whose export harvest is mostly shipped from the port of Bluff.

The first Ford dealer, G W Woods and Company, was established in 1911, in premises originally a livery and bait stables, and also the horse auction centre for Invercargill.

However, the Dee Street premises, situated up a lane behind the Grand Hotel, were damaged by fire on the night of December 16 1916, killing caretaker John McIvor, who slept there. The roof fell in and 40 cars were lost with damage estimated at £20,000, but the building was not affected structurally so a new roof was fitted to the existing walls and the business carried on.

In the early days, rabbits were a major crop in Central Otago, and G W Woods, financed by one of the stock and station agents, helped set up a daily truck service, collecting rabbits from all over the region.

In 1936 G W Woods and Company had serious financial difficulties, largely because of the Depression, and Colonial Motor Company took over the business. On December 4 1936 the business re-opened as Macaulay Motors Ltd, the new manager, R U (Bob) Macaulay. At the time there were 16 people on the staff. The service manager was paid £6 12s 6d per 44 hour week, and mechanics were paid 2s per hour. A new Ford 'C' 10 hp car cost £310.

One of the first challenges faced by Bob Macaulay was the congestion. Business

G W Woods premises about 1919, in the lane behind the Grand Hotel, Dee Street.

had started to go ahead after the Depression, and Ford Motor Company, which had just taken over distribution from Colonial Motor Company, wanted the business to have more space and occupy a better position. The city was already crowded so this was not an easy task.

As a temporary measure, additional premises were leased to store vehicles and recondition used cars but, while this eased the congestion, a better location was still needed.

Used cars were cheap in those days, and before Warrant of Fitness tests came in, a car could be bought for as little as £2 10s. The records show some very cheap vehicle

sales: Ford grey tourer £3; Ford T coupe £3 10s, Ford T tourer £5, Oakland tourer £7 10s.

Les McDermott, then sales manager, remembered: "Customers often asked, 'What guarantee is there with this car?' They were informed that it was guaranteed until it was off the premises. And then you prayed that it would actually get that far without mishap. One £10 car was driven on a complete tour around the South Island without a breakdown; another didn't reach the owner's home less than a mile away.

Right: Bob Macaulay had a detailed appreciation of tractors, and got them going again in 1947.
Far right: Les McDermott had a fantastic recall of people's vehicle transactions.

In October 1937 we sold a Ford T, an Oakland and an Overland tourer at £8 for the three cars. About that time a good Ford T was worth £25, but in 1936 we sold a Ford T Fordor for £60."

Business went ahead and by 1940 the staff had increased to 40. Everything was on hold during the Second World War however; more than half the staff were in the armed forces, leaving only twelve in the business. Bob Macaulay took on the accountant's job as well, Les McDermott looked after parts in addition to sales, and Harold Murphy was service manager.

Les McDermott started as an office junior with G W Woods about 1920, working his way up to be assistant manager at Macaulays. He had a remarkable

memory, and quickly became a most efficient salesman, with the ability to recite to customers all the details of their vehicle and tractor purchases since the Model T days, together with the prices paid for both vehicles and trade-ins.

Harold Murphy employed Les Myers as an apprentice in 1941, at 16s 10d per week. A week later Les turned 16 and had to pay Social Security Tax that immediately reduced his pay to 15s 2d. When Harold Murphy found service work piling up during the war, because they were short-handed and couldn't get trained staff, he employed two girls as mechanics. "They were very good, and adapted quickly to the work, and they were also some of the first women in the country to work in a male

Above: Macaulay Motors staff, 1936. Back, from left: Stan Lyzmoor, Morris Galt, Fred Byers, Alex Jordan, Doug Sheriffs, not known, apprentice from Bluff, not known, Roy McMillan, John Welsh, not known, Doug Dixon, Gordon Simpson, Gavin Currie. Sitting: W J Watson, J R Haworth, R U Macaulay, L R McDermott, H C Hurrell, Margery Fortune.

Betty Brice, tune-up specialist, in 1942, with Harold Murphy on left and Bob Macaulay, right. The Ford laboratory test unit was one of the first pieces of mandatory equipment, putting Ford ahead of competitors.

dominated industry."

Les Myers, later service manager, recalled when the girls were taken on: "In those days we only had a staff of three mechanics and two apprentices, and we had to operate about 11 hours a day, six days a week patching up cars, as we had no supply of parts. I remember the raised eyebrows amongst our customers at the time, but soon Betty was well accepted as she did a first class job. Besides, we had the only Ford test set in Invercargill, and all Ford users and other car owners came here to get their cars synchronised."

In 1942, new, large, Dee Street premises were purchased from the Ward Estate, plus a block of buildings fronting Dee Street. The re-design of these buildings was delayed because of restrictions during and after the war, and they were not finished until 1953 but, after a £20,000 refit, the dealership had a new showroom, offices, parts and staff facilities in high profile Dee Street.

After the war, staff returned, but business took time to pick up, with the continuing frustration of rationing and import restrictions as New Zealand paid off its war debt.

However, tractors were classed as essential goods so there were no import restrictions, and the tractor franchise was given back to Ford dealers in 1946.

The new Fordson E27N tractor had rear hydraulic lift arms and kerosene, petrol and diesel engine options. Ford's new tractor manager, Bill Toomey, offered salespeople and dealers competitions and prizes to get the market moving, and when sales took off, Macaulays were soon selling between 50 and 100 new Fordson tractors a year.

When the new 40hp Fordson Major tractor arrived in 1952, tractors became the major part of Macaulay Motors' business. The wool boom of 1951 meant farmers had some real money in their pockets for the first time since the Depression, and tractors and cars were on the shopping list. However, the new Consul and Zephyr 6 cars were very hard to get which was particularly frustrating for customers who could afford a new car, possibly for the first time.

Tractors required two workshop bays and more space to park, so the existing workshop, behind the hotel, was inadequate. After considering all the factors, it was decided tractors should be located near the edge of the city. Macaulay Motors purchased five houses at Avenal in 1954, on the northern outskirts of the city and had them re-zoned industrial. The houses were removed and a new truck and tractor sales and service facility was built, including a modern lubrication bay.

Les McDermott was in his element with tractors and, at the sales peak in 1957, Macaulays sold 108 of them. The team

At the Industries Fair in 1956, Macaulays had a cut-away Anglia, showing the component parts.

won the coveted 'Grand Champions of Sales' in 1949 and 1955. It was a team effort, aided by servicemen, including Martin Short.

Martin Short had started with G W Woods in 1912, but his apprenticeship was interrupted in 1915 when he sailed for Europe to fight in the First World War. He was twice wounded in France but returned in 1919, in 1936 and again in 1948. He became one of the first tractor mechanics, and revelled in hard work. He would set off at 7.30 in the morning to a job 50 kilometres away, 'split' the tractor, rebore the engine, fit new pistons and rings, reassemble and run the tractor, and be home before nightfall, all on his own. The same

job could take some people 10-15 hours in a workshop.

Martin Short had legendary strength, despite his slight, wiry body. He used an extended crank handle to turn over tight engines and, some of the older hands insisted, he would at times lift the whole front end and wheels of the tractor off the ground with his efforts.

Martin Short also acted as a spotter for Les McDermott. "Les used to sell the tractors from his office and I delivered and demonstrated them. I used to carry them on an old 1936 Ford V8 that had been traded in by a sawmiller, who had used it as a log transporter.

"We used to call the old truck 'the

Avenal I was constructed in 1958, shifting tractor and truck work from town.

On farm tractor service was demanding, and really took off when radio-telephones came in. Trist Atkins was at Macaulays for a period, and knew Nevile Lodge who did this cartoon.

Macaulay management in 1965. Standing left: G C Hawes, tractor foreman; H Bennett, service foreman; L P Denton, used car manager; G R Soulsby, truck manager; H R Holden, Avenal foreman; R Johansen, electrical foreman; P A Cody, new car manager; J Soutar, Avenal foreman. Sitting: W S Henderson, tractor manager; W D Maclaren, manager; R U Macaulay, managing director; L D Myers, service manager; E D Jackson, accountant. Inset: A B Dunn, parts manager; C W Clark, panel foreman.

When Bob Macaulay retired in 1965, Bill Maclaren gave him his own trumpet to blow. R B Gibbons, CMC, and Harold P Ralph, Ford, enjoyed being there.

wrecker' and I developed a close affection for it. In the course of its career, we must have put at least two engines in it, running up a total of more than 350,000 miles. That old truck used to know the best turnip paddocks and the best watering holes in the district.

"Up until the time I retired in 1965, we used to constantly put in the best sales figures in the country, topping the New Zealand figures for about five or six years, which wasn't bad, considering the population we serviced."

Tractors became a huge operation at Macaulay Motors and, with 100 tractors a year being sold, it was more than a one-man job to keep them operating. Tractor servicing grew and grew on the farm, using service vans, or trucks, and a mechanic. Keeping in touch was vital and, in the late 1950s, radio telephones were pioneered in the service vans. Les Myers said it was hard convincing Bob Macaulay the cost would be justifiable. "Very few people operated R/Ts then and farmers were sometimes astonished to see a van and serviceman turn up minutes after they had phoned for help. The R/Ts certainly helped the efficiency and there were many more productive

hours."

Sadly, Les McDermott died suddenly in 1960, having worked at the dealership since 1920, mainly as sales manager.

Bob Macaulay knew the premises would have to expand, and in the light of the success of Avenal 1, more houses and an existing garage across the road were purchased, even though the zoning hadn't been confirmed. The existing garage complied with zoning, so an immediate start was made on Avenal 2 with a 21 metre span workshop and open, used vehicle display which opened in 1964 and, as they became available, the corner dairy and four more houses in Fox Street were purchased. Finally, after the balance of the land in the block was bought by J J Limited, a

established, with a two-storey house on site converted to a sales facility and staff cafeteria for the 25 staff. Another two-storey house at the corner of Liffey and Fox Streets, adjoining the Avenal II workshop, was converted for service reception, accounting and administration. These were interim measures anticipating the eventual closure of Dee Street.

Bob Macaulay had now carried through a great part of the plan begun in 1954. He had met the challenges of a very busy and frustrating time in the motor industry. He had found the initial building in Dee Street and given the company a professional base and image. He had seen the need for and planned the expansion to Avenal, gone through the protracted acquisition of land, and finally made it all happen. Bill Maclaren arrived in 1964 as manager, anticipating the retirement of Bob Macaulay in May 1965, after working for the CMC Group for 39 years.

Bill Maclaren now had to consolidate the operation, and develop new markets to sustain the growth of the company, with the help of the very strong young management group he had inherited.

No Remittance selling of new cars was at its height, and one opposition dealer was setting the pace, aided by a loophole in regulations. But the loyal farming base stuck with Macaulays in the main, and the company continued to expand.

Ford introduced the new Ford tractor range in early 1965 and they were a considerable improvement on the previous Fordsons. Not all was perfect however, and the revolutionary Select-O-Speed transmission was not fully tested for 'farming'. Unusual gremlins taxed the service technicians and all transmissions had to be 'reworked' progressively, causing a lot of customer grief and staff frustration, and considerable cost for the dealership.

These problems were exacerbated the following year with the introduction of the Zephyr Mark IV, an amazing new car that had gremlins caused by New Zealand fuel. Again, despite the new car's good points, there were plenty of heartaches for dealers and customers. The Falcon car range came built up from Australia, and was very popular with No Remittance sales.

When it was announced that Comalco was to open a huge aluminium smelter at Tiwai Point, 30 kms south of Invercargill, on an arm of Bluff Harbour, Macaulays was determined to be in on the ground floor with

neighbouring garage, the City Council relented and granted commercial zoning for the whole area.

Subsequently, Macaulay Motors needed a 0.3 metre strip to fit their new 21 metre workshop floor and J J Ltd agreed on a lease in perpetuity to allow this. No set amount was arranged but from time to time payments are made. These are consumed on site by both parties – with the aid of water and soda, plus the payment of one shilling!

After the houses along Fox Street were removed the Avenal III workshop was begun, designed to eventually house the main town facility. A 21 metre deep structure, to match the other buildings, with a large north side canopy, it stretches 35 metres along the street, with sub-floor maintenance bays, modern lubrication and staff facilities. To beat the Southland winters, the roof, with 20% natural lighting, and walls, were insulated, gas heating fitted, and the opening north side sheltered from the bitter, prevailing Antarctic winds. Another parts depot was set up in the new building, specifically to cater for tractors and trucks which were rapidly growing in volume.

At the same time, a used car centre was

Opposite bottom: This 8,000 lb forklift, made for the aluminium smelter, had special solid tyres and a heat shield for shifting crucibles of molten aluminium from furnace to moulds.

Right: Macaulay Motors basketball team in 1973. From left: Don Leighton, Ross Middlemiss, Stan Sanders, Tony Johns, Mike Kelly, John Stenntjes, and Paul Tuatini.

Below:This 'piggy-back' forklift was developed by the tractor team to help the brewery driver deliver pallets to customers quickly.

vehicle supply. The new vehicle manager, Pat Cody, eventually found the key person and arranged a meeting with Kaiser Engineers and Constructors Inc., the engineering firm which built the smelter.

Like most companies which were not resident in New Zealand, Kaiser could not comprehend the vehicle market shortages at the time, but was eventually convinced to purchase six No Remittance Falcons and five Escort vans. In the next 15 months they purchased another six No Remittance vehicles and 12 light commercials including a Transit Ambulance.

These transactions were to be a key factor in the tender for vehicle supply to

NZ Aluminium Smelters, the operating company. After convincing the new NZAS company to let them tender, Macaulays blanched at the tender invitation of 100 pages that arrived. Doubtful they would be considered, Macaulays was prodded by Kaisers to 'have a go' and, after a huge amount of work and legal advice, the tender bid was sent to Melbourne.

Subsequently, when the smelter opened in 1970, New Zealand Aluminium Smelters took an initial delivery that included one Fairlane, nine Falcons, Escort Vans, 30 tonne trailers, 15 tonne forklifts, trucks and tractors. In total there were 42 units with a value of $306,000. At the time Falcons were selling for $3,100 and Escort vans were $1,769, and many smaller dealers would have been happy to do that much business in a year. It was certainly something for the Macaulays team to crow about.

The smelter brought new diversification for the business in the industrial equipment applications possible using Ford tractors, many of which were local innovations. First, there was a forklift able to withstand the heat and to lift and shift 3.5 tonnes of molten aluminium in crucibles, from the furnace to the moulds. Another was able to load and stack moulded sows of aluminium, ready for shipment.

Tractor sales manager, Peter Tait, became the industrial adaptor and headed the 'heavy lifting brigade' trio with Ray Swale and Paul Drummond. One of the units they pioneered was the piggy-backed fork lift, mounted on a small parking tray and ramp at the back of a large truck and trailer unit, so the driver was able to load or unload pallets of beer into the customer's warehouse. This innovation is used today by other companies all over the country.

After all the shortages of vehicles, especially cars, it was good to be able to supply what people wanted. Macaulays certainly got their share of what was being sold and, in 1972, were presented with a plaque commemorating their inclusion in the top 50 Ford tractor dealerships world-

Above: In 1972, Macaulay Motors was acknowledged by Ford International, as being one of the top 50 tractor dealers in the world. It is thought to be the only dealer in New Zealand to receive this award.

wide, which was a considerable achievement.

In 1973, Bill Maclaren set Peter Tait a target of 100 tractor units – if he delivered them in the year, he would be able to have a Falcon GT as a company car. He ended up two units short when tractor stock ran out. "We had really pushed the sales along and I saw the target as being in my grasp, when we just ran out of stock and couldn't get any more units in." The frustrations of the motor industry have always been too little or too much stock.

With all these tractor units and adaptions being sold around Southland, the service team had ever increasing workloads, sometimes in the remote outlying areas of Fiordland or Stewart Island. While there are boats plying freight in and out of these areas, breakdowns can demand urgent attention and, many times, service people are flown to remote areas by float plane, then sometimes find the weather closes in and that they cannot get home for several days.

Avenal III was finalised in 1977, with a link building being constructed between it and Avenal II, and the total operations were moved from Dee Street. For the first time in 20 years all 84 staff were together as a cohesive unit and the managerial difficulties of split sites vanished. One very happy service manager, Les Myers, well remembered the difficulties of running three service shops. "When we operated servicing units at Dee Street in the city centre, with the tractor and truck supporting units at the three Avenal sites, life was just chaos," he said. "I ran up a pretty big mileage just travelling between the sites. I'd say that I was the most relieved man in the dealership when we finally consolidated

The Invercargill City Council ran a scheduled service over one of the toughest routes anywhere, the Boreland Pass (3,300 ft), in Fiordland. This Ford R1014 40 seater, with an exhaust brake retarder, the only vehicle allowed on the south arm road of Lake Manapouri, managed easily.

Delivering vehicles to Deep Cove took time. After catching this barge, it is a half day to the power station inside the tunnel.

our operations."

Before long the Avenal I workshop was doubled in size to 7,000 sq ft with an apron covering the northern side for quick service, and consolidated into one tractor and truck workshop and sales unit.

In 1978 Rex Dowling was appointed parts manager. With a staff of 16 at the time, he had one of the largest parts operations in the South Island. One of his first jobs was to centralise the operation at Avenal. "Prior to this we had been working under some difficulty, with virtually three departments operating, which gave us difficulties in stock ordering and administration. Under the new system we have a completely different operation. First of all, it's obviously far more efficient with parts for car, truck and tractor stored in one area and run by one department. Because of this we have been able to reduce stock a little, and the new layout has been designed to give us plenty of space which allows for easier stock management."

Because of its remoteness and therefore erratic supply, Invercargill needed to carry more stock and they had to work on a three week lead time as opposed to about a week for most North Island dealers. Subsequently, in 1978, Macaulays joined the Ford Dealer Service Bureau and with the daily update and weekly ordering, they were able to keep customers happy with less stock.

To assist with tractor parts, tractor wrecking started in 1976 with Adrian Parry running this operation from a converted house. 'Half-a-Mo', as Peter Tait nicknamed him, because it was his stock

Top left: Peter Tait, chief of the heavy lifting brigade, nearly won a Falcon GT company car.

Top right: David Jackson was business manager for many years.

Below: Parts manager Rex Dowling, and technician Jimmy Johnstone received their 25 year gold watches from Graeme Gibbons in 1991. Rex Dowling, who has unique computer skills, later became a key person in developing the Magix parts and service system for dealers at Automotive Computer Systems (ACS).

Below right: Used tractor wrecking was very profitable, as 'Half-a-mo', Adrian Parry proved.

remark to a customer while he went to have a look for the part, was able to save thousands out of damaged or obsolete tractors. In the late 1970s, he said: "I still get asked for parts for 1940 vintage tractors, but they are getting progressively rarer nowadays." He was able to rebuild tractors from several wrecked ones in the yard. "This not only gives a farmer a good cheap back-up unit but also provides us with a tidy profit."

One morning Peter Michels was passed a message to say that the boss wanted to see him. Apprehensive, he knocked on the door and went in to be told by business manager Dave Jackson, and Bill Maclaren, that Les Myers was retiring soon and they would like him to take over as service manager. "Well, you could have knocked me over with a feather," said Peter Michels, who imagined he had done something wrong. "It just blew me away – I thought I wasn't up to such a job. Les had been a good boss and friend to me, but to step into his shoes was something I thought it was beyond me." However,

Invercargill is renown for its cool weather. In 1985 it was cold.

the 'bosses' persisted and he took over in due course. Les Myers retired in 1985, having worked at Macaulays for 44 years, during which the staff grew from 12 employees to 112.

Bill Maclaren was also approaching retirement and, in January 1986, Alan McElroy joined the team as assistant manager. Prior to this he had been at Sockburn, had started at Napier Motors and been manager of the Mosgiel branch in 1972. He had a good knowledge of tractors and used vehicle trading. Used vehicles were by then more plentiful and provided an important profit centre when handled well.

Macaulays was now going through a different stage of development. The economic scene had changed with the 'more market' policies introduced by the new Labour Government in the mid-1980s. Farmers no longer received any subsidies, and progressive deregulation of industries and sale of government trading operations was causing economic stress, particularly in agricultural areas. Cars, tractors and trucks were affected in Invercargill, but not as seriously as in some areas.

When Bill Maclaren retired, on September 30 1988, he had worked 40 years for Colonial Motor Company. He and his wife Daphne moved to Arrowtown, where they had a holiday cottage they extended and modernised, and Alan McElroy was appointed dealer principal.

Later in 1988, Ford Motor Company

Invercargill's Dee Street runs north-south between Macaulay's two properties at Avenal, with Bluff Hill on the horizon. The two earlier properties are ringed in downtown Dee Street.

John Scott (left) was top New Zealand tractor salesman in 1990, and Macaulay Motors top dealers. He is with customer Colin Ward who has 10 Fords on his farm.

sold the tractor franchise to C B Norwood Ltd, and the company was now dealing with different masters, but fortuately the strength of Macaulays was appreciated. The change brought more complexities and different systems. In the same year, used vehicles became exempt from import licensing, and New Zealand was suddenly flooded with Japanese used cars which placed enormous pressure on dealers. Within two years most Ford dealers in New Zealand were reeling with the changes and some closed. Macaulays, under Alan McElroy, responded by opening an import used car outlet away from the dealership.

About this time, Ford was also winding down its involvement in heavy trucks and, knowing the supply contract with Hino would not be renewed, tractors and heavy truck operations were merged and brought back to the Avenal III site. The original

Gaye and Alan McElroy.

Avenal I site was sold, and the company adjusted to the new 'lean' trading conditions where everyone went faster and faster to stay in the same place.

Out of the blue, in 1993, the new Commerce Commission took a case against Macaulays, over changes made to a new vehicle. The Commission, it is fair to say, was 'looking for a dealer' to make an example of. Alteration of speedos on Jap imports was rife throughout New Zealand. Importers often wrongly specified new vehicles, and components needed to be swapped around to meet customer demand. New vehicle sales were often so hard to get that dealerships went to extraordinary lengths to make sales, often swapping over gearboxes or engines to suit a customer.

The Commission did not want to prosecute a small dealer, which might not be able to pay, but Macaulays presented an ideal target. At the last minute, a staff member likely to be personally affected, turned crown witness in exchange for immunity.

The resultant trial damaged the reputation of both Macaulays and its chief executive, Alan McElroy, both of whom were in an invidious position and could not win. They had trusted an employee, who had let them down and then turned against them. A reserved judgment was issued, penalising the company for the conduct of its officers and employees. Even though Alan McElroy was found not guilty, Ford would not allow him to continue as Ford dealer principal.

The case considerably affected some staff and they left. Alan McElroy, as chief

in the same position.

Subsequently the company was restructured with Macaulay Motors running Ford cars and light trucks under new dealer principal John Luxton, who was transferred from Craik Motors, Te Awamutu, on September 18 1993.

Southland Tractors Ltd, with Alan McElroy as chief executive, was formed to sell and service New Holland, Ford, Fiat and Kubota tractors and equipment for the whole of Southland.

Grant Price, who started at Macaulays as an apprentice technician in 1985, served his time on cars, trucks and tractors. He transferred from mobile tractor service to vehicle sales, and later started the Queenstown branch. He became vehicle sales manager at Macaulays and finally dealer principal on June 1 1998, when John Luxton was transferred to Christchurch.

Today the tractor business is as strong as ever. Alan McElroy decided to retire in 2001, and Grant Price is now chief executive of both companies. John Scott, who also started as a tractor apprentice, is operations manager of Southland Tractors.

The decision to cut back, by selling Avenal I in 1989, was prudent at the time,

Grant Price became dealer principal of Macaulay Ford in 1998, and Southland Tractors in 2001, when Alan McElroy retired.

Some of Southland Tractors staff in front of their new facility. Standing left: Craig Maclellen, Grant Caughey, Graham Franke, John Scott (operations manager), Jamie Robson, Matthew Kells, and Grant Price. In front: Roger Mckay and Ant Scurr.

executive and dealer principal, had to take responsibility for what had happened, but he and the company were the victims of circumstances. Just about any dealer in New Zealand at that time could have been

Some of Macaulay Motors staff outside their newly Ford corporate identity dealership. From back left: Bruce Woodd, Joel Ropiha, Mark Smith, Aaron Smith, Alister Swan, Sheldon Beckett, Neil Madden, Tony Mackenzie, Mike Lane, Darren Robbie, Davie Timothy (obscured), Adam Blanks. Front: Greg Peters, Craig Hall, Ken McArthur, Peter Michels, Colin Clark, Arron Cooper, Rob Kelly, Robert Macaulay, Stephen Snoep, Ricky McDermott, Carolyn Graham, Chris Broad, Mike Lane, Nicola Scott, Tracy Ward, Jeff Shaw, Quinton Thompson, Nathan Davis, and Grant Price.

but the business is stronger today as the rural economy has recovered. Tractors have a new location, still in Dee Street, the main north road, but seven kilometres further out of Invercargill, opposite the stock sale yards.

Macaulay Motors is still the southernmost Ford dealer in the world. It also operates three used vehicle outlets away from the main dealership, each catering to different market sectors, and has a branch at Queenstown Airport. The total staff numbers 69, and the company's objectives are to meet and, if possible, surpass the needs of their many customers.

PART THREE – TRACTORS AND TRUCKS

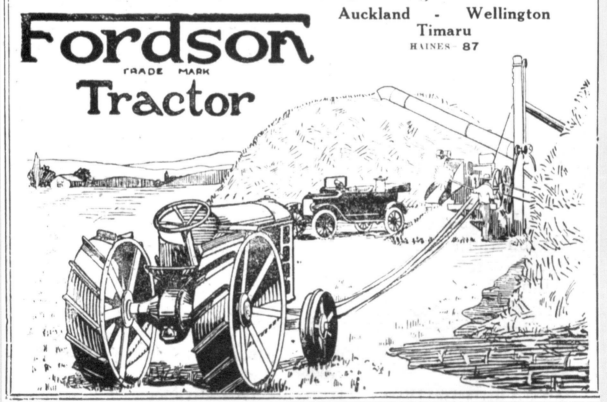

Plenty of Power for Threshing

The Fordson Tractor will undertake any job you can reasonably ask of it.

Its engine is of 22 horse-power at 1000 revolutions. Will draw a weight of 9 tons. Works 24 hours a day if necessary.

Fordson farming is the modern, progressive way. Enquire to-day.

Price £325 F.O.B. WELLINGTON

THE COLONIAL MOTOR CO., LTD.

Auckland - Wellington
Timaru

HAINES - 87

Fordson
TRADE MARK
Tractor

An advertisment from 1922.

Henry Ford driving his first experimental tractor in 1907.

A trusty Fordson F ploughing at night by the light of a bonfire. During the First World War, Britain was very short of food, and often work was done at night, as golf courses and pasture land were converted to produce enough crops to feed a nation at war. This occurred again 20 years later in the Second World War, using very similar Model N tractors.

CHAPTER THIRTYONE

FORDSON TRACTORS

The importance of Fordson tractors cannot be underestimated. The Fordson was introduced to New Zealand at the end of 1918, but supplies were quite erratic until the early 1920s due to production and shipping difficulties through the First World War. The concept of the tractor as a work tool was new, and its capability was unknown. However, Colonial Motor Company executives realised the Fordson's potential and set about a campaign to establish it, not only on farms, but also in industry, where it had the capability to do far more than a man with a pick and shovel.

The following article was written by G Hugh Sumpter and Associates for CMC Group staff, and appeared in their in-house magazine, *IMPACT*, in two parts in 1974 and 1977. It has been included to give a perspective of the tractor's importance to the Colonial Motor Company and the development of New Zealand. The Fordson tractor had a parallel partner, the Model T Ford. Both created a paradigm shift in people's thinking, and added immensely to the lives and opportunities of ordinary people.

IN THE BEGINNING...
THE EARLY 1900s

Henry Ford branched out on his own, trying out engines and building improved models on the principle of his first car. It was in this period that he gave serious thought to the invention of tractors for the farmers, although 15 years were to elapse before he had them out on the market. In fact, the tractor idea had been in the back of his head since he became interested, as a young boy, in a clumsy road engine propelled by steam and used for operating sawmills and threshing machines.

From the time he started making automobiles there was not a year in which he did not make experiments looking toward the tractor. In 1907 he made what has been called the first Ford tractor, but, as he later remarked, "the public was more interested in being carried than in being pulled; the horseless carriage made a greater appeal to the imagination. And so it was that I practically dropped work upon a tractor until the automobile was in production. With the automobile on the farms, the tractor became a necessity. For then the farmers had been introduced to power."

In Henry Ford's usual way, the Fordson grew into shape through constant experimentation, not only in the workshop but on the farm, and that he might get the experiences from various soils and conditions which face the farmer, he gradually acquired a farm numbering several thousand acres. Here the Fordson tractor was developed as a Henry Ford and not a Ford Motor Company enterprise. Henry Ford & Son was formed as a Michigan corporation in 1917. In 1920 it became part of the 'new' Ford Motor Company.

THE FIRST WORLD WAR

While Ford had been experimenting with farm tractors since 1902, he did not produce them until the outbreak of the First World War. The Allies' food emergency in 1917 caused him to send the first of these tractors to England. Officers of the British government later expressed doubt whether it would have been possible to meet the crisis without them.

The Fordson tractors were operated mostly by women who ploughed up golf courses and landed estates for the raising of crops, without taking men away from the battlefronts.

As there were not enough draft animals in Britain to cultivate crops to replace foodstuffs sunk by German submarines, the British investigated power farming. Only steam tractors were known in England, and there were few of them; all the factories were busy making munitions and could not stop to produce farming machinery.

Experiments with a number of tractors, including two Fords, were conducted. The judges were impressed with the American

machines, and Percival Perry, in charge of Ford affairs in Britain, cabled Edsel Ford on April 7 1917, asking his help. Henry Ford himself replied that he would lend his drawings of the tractors' plans so that the manufacturing and assembling could be done in England; also, he would ship as many men as were needed to get the work under way, with Charles F. Sorenson, the general superintendent of the Ford Motor Company as director of the job.

It was soon found that many of the necessary materials could not be got in England, so the tractors had to be made and shipped from Dearborn.

The lowest price Ford could quote was US$1,500 for a tractor that should have been delivered for US$700 under normal conditions. Sorensen was apologetic over the seemingly exorbitant figure, but the British promptly asked for 5,000 machines. That order established Ford in the tractor business.

By April 1918, the entire British order, raised to 7,000, had been fulfilled despite the problems encountered in shipping materials over then submarine-infested oceans.

Thus England was introduced to Fordson tractors a year before the United States, although actual production in Britain was only 7,600 units between 1919-22 when production ceased there and all tractors were once again produced in the United States.

CORK

In 1928 the Fordsons ceased production in Detroit and tractor operations were transferred to Cork in Ireland. In 1929 the Cork model, an advanced Fordson, came out. Incidentally, Fordsons were being assembled at Cork from July 1919.

In 1933, two years after the opening of the Ford factory at Dagenham, production

of tractors was transferred to England and the 'improved' Fordson was manufactured at Dagenham for the world. The improvements included an engine governor as standard equipment; counter-balanced crankshaft; larger size radiator; improved driving position, stronger differential, worm and worm wheel, bigger air cleaner and a bigger bore – $4^{1}/_{8}$ inches as against 4 inches.

LIGHT v HEAVY-WEIGHT

The Fordson from the very start looked like a tractor! This may sound pretty self evident in the light of what we see about us today. But the Fordson appeared at a time when the youthful tractor industry was producing an assortment of machinery that varied from the practical to the weird and wonderful.

With a few exceptions, many of them were very heavy in relation to the horsepower produced.

The Fordson helped change all that. At 22 cwt., its weight was only 1 cwt. per horsepower, compared with the 3 or 4 cwt. per horsepower of some of the heavier machines then on the market.

Looking at photos of the first Fordson, it is hard to escape the conclusion that this was the basic design that set down once and for all the standards to be followed by other tractor manufacturers!

One tractor authority in Great Britain was later to describe the Fordson as the "near ideal" in farm tractors.

A handbook on the farm tractor produced during the First World War in Britain compares a large variety of machines – including oil and steam tractors designed for working on farms. It had particular praise for the Fordson.

Referring to weight, it said that "if

These 1924 'Cork' tractors were photographed at Ratana, near Wanganui, ploughing 800 acres to grow wheat for Maori prophet Wiremu Ratana, an early advocate of 'Fordson farming'.

sufficient tractive grip can be obtained by a powerful tractor weighing less than 25 cwt., then the 22 cwt. Fordson represents a type which is approaching the ideal: for, be it remembered, weight is not necessary for any other purpose but to aid adhesion and give strength.

"Strength, however, can be had without exceeding a ton, by the combination of good material and good workmanship.

"In addition to anticipating the probable future developments in the matter of weight, the makers of the Fordson appear to have got ahead of rival firms in general design. In seeking to improve a complicated piece of machinery, a good engineer endeavours to dispense with some part of it, whilst a bad one adds something to it.

"The former principle, which has apparently been adhered to very closely by the designer of the Fordson, has resulted in the production of an efficient little tractor that is the embodiment of simplicity: and simplicity must have a greater influence in making the tractor popular than any other factor; first, because it makes possible low cost of production and low selling price, and thus appeals to the farmers as a profitable investment; and, secondly, because the average farmer has not acquired that confidence in machinery possessed by the manufacturer and the average townsman; consequently, the simpler a machine is the more readily he will take to it."

Prophetic words these! Because the points made by this writer – economy, simplicity and ease of operation – would have been among the vital factors that must have clinched many a 'deal' for Fordson salesmen.

In 1922 an engineer representative from one of the companies supplying the Ford Motor Company, Detroit, managed to buttonhole Henry Ford while he was in the tractor plant. Mr Ford never had an office but spent all his time about the factory.

The object of the interview was to persuade Mr Ford to fit an engine governor to the, then, five-year-old Model N Fordson. Mr Ford listened as long as his patience would allow and then replied: "Young man, your idea of improving the Fordson tractor is to add something to it. My idea of improving it is to take something OFF!"

So power farming got a very simple start: an engine and transmission bolted together, (the first unit construction and universally copied since) four wheels, steering gear etc., with no frills. It also had the first 'solid state' ignition system complete with flywheel magneto and tremblers.

TRACTOR v HORSES

The superiority of the tractor over the horse seems so self-evident in this technological age, that we may well wonder why early tractor salesmen ever had any bother in selling their wares. But they did. And the answer lay mostly in the fact that they were selling a new concept in farming. Persuading people to give up the traditional for something new, is no easy task. The farmer was no exception.

The horse was still king, whether ploughing or trotting to town between the shafts of the family gig.

The farmer knew it, the tractor salesman knew it. But in acknowledging this, he was one jump ahead of the man tilling the soil.

The man promoting the Fordson tractor was part of a skilled marketing campaign. He knew what a Fordson could do. He had a mass of facts and figures to prove it. Given the opportunity, he would put theory into successful practice but it was a long grind.

Demonstration followed demonstration, resulting in many a paddock ploughed for naught before the advantages of greater output and the drudgery of looking after horse teams started to convince farmers in significant numbers.

At about £175 only the most progressive farmers took the plunge and even then they could not all afford implements designed for tractor use. It was not uncommon to see a Fordson ploughing with the farmer on the seat and his wife running along behind controlling a swing plough by the handles! The more gallant farmers may have taught their wives to drive the tractor while they took over the plough, but if so they have gone unrecorded.

Current farming literature of that period makes it clear that the Fordson's simplicity of operation played no small part in completing a successful sale.

The salesman's next job was to convince the farmer that the Fordson was far and away cheaper to own and run than horses.

Advertisements and articles in early farming magazines punch home this point time and time again.

One widely read New Zealand farming magazine was *Fordson Farming in New Zealand*. It carried photos and stories of satisfied Fordson farmers. And they were not just articles of fulsome praise. They contained facts and figures showing what was what!

In case the reader missed the point, there appeared at the foot of each page a slogan. Examples include: 'Flies don't worry the Fordson in the hot season', 'I've got a Fordson working for me – she's replaced six horses and two farm hands', 'Fordson steps in where horses fear to tread', 'Give her a drink of water, some kerosene and oil, and she'll toil 24 hours a day', 'I take only 20 minutes to feed and groom my Fordson', 'She does every job on the farm except wean the calves'.

Easily assimilated, they would have made an immediate impression on the prospective buyer of a Fordson. And when he wanted to get down to the nitty gritty, he was confronted with a wealth of farming data that must have convinced even the most sceptical. Much of it still makes fascinating reading today.

Equally fascinating was the approach of the Ford Motor Company in publishing sales and service data for dealers and salesmen. A 1923 edition is a mine of information and covers every conceivable point that a prospective Fordson tractor owner would need to know. It must have made the salesman a veritable walking encyclopaedia of information.

First off, he had some excellent general points to make. Here are some of them:

"The harness and whiffletrees for an eight-horse team cost more than a Fordson tractor, yet the eight won't do more work."

"The eight horses cost double the price of the Fordson, and that at the low price of horses."

"Grooming eight horses once a day at 14 minutes a horse takes two hours. Watering and feeding another hour. Harnessing and un-harnessing, hitching up and unhooking, leading from barn to implement etc., take yet another hour. Four hours' work has been lost without expenditure of any energy in productive work."

"A Fordson can be filled with water, fuel and oil, and thoroughly gone over in half an hour."

"A Fordson can be worked continuously day and night through all the seasons of ploughing, seeding, haying, harvesting."

"Horses cannot be humanely worked more than eight hours in the heavier operations, or ten in the lighter."

"It takes a few hours to make a Fordson; it takes three years' time and three years' care (some horsemen say five years) to make a work horse. At any time in those three years the colt may die and be a total loss."

"A Fordson eats only when it is engaged in productive work – horses eat 365 days a year."

"A Fordson makes every acre of the farm a source of profit – an eight-horse team withdraws 40 acres from the farm's return to feed itself."

Pressed for finer detail, the salesman could talk about the number of acres that could be ploughed in one day of 10 hours (7.6 acres) based on a driving speed of $2^3/_4$ miles per hour, the proper ploughing speed for a Fordson tractor. He could talk about the variation in draft in different soils, the varying speeds on Fordson tractor pulley at 1000 rpm, belt lengths needed for balers, grinders, pumps, saws, chaff cutters and so on. He could talk about a Government ploughing test during the First World War between a Fordson tractor and an eight-horse team. The cost per acre with the Fordson was 9/-; the horses 15/-. Final figures showed that Fordson-ploughing cost one-third less than horse-ploughing.

The Fordson tractor went round the field two and one-half times to the horse-drawn gang ploughs' once. Incidentally, the Fordson cost £440 (by 1923 the price had dropped to £365) compared with £600 for the eight-horse team.

Faced with these facts, it was inevitable that the farmer would bow to the obvious and buy a Fordson tractor. The farming revolution was under way!

THE GLORIOUS TWENTIES

COLONIAL MOTORS INTRODUCE FORDSON FARMING IN NZ

The introduction of the Fordson tractor in New Zealand was due to the enthusiasm of Hope Gibbons and two of his sons, Hope B and Robert B Gibbons. They not only saw the immense possibilities of mechanised farming; they had the courage to put their ideas into practice.

The wheels of the first Fordson to be landed in this country had scarcely started

to turn before the two brothers were bringing in the Oliver range of implements, designed specially for Henry Ford's brilliant new tractor.

All this was backed up with a dynamic marketing campaign that generated real enthusiasm among the dealers. It is also to Mr Hope and Mr Robert Gibbons that the credit goes for introducing the industrial tractor. Running parallel with the promotion of the Fordson for agriculture was the Industrial Fordson 'For any Pull, Push, Lift or Carry'.

Selling tractors in the immediate post-First World War years was very much an ideal. Tractors were an entirely new concept. The new breed of Fordson salesmen had to use their imagination. They had to look where a tractor could fit in. They were literally on ground where no tractor had ever been before. An even bigger challenge, however, was money.

Farmers by and large had little or no ready cash. Quoting a price of £325 for a Fordson in 1919 (the price had dropped to £166 by the late 1920s) may well have been a little like asking for the moon. Apart from the money, there was the business of getting to grips with what a tractor was all about.

Faithful old Dobbin was something the farmer understood. He had grown up with the horse, as had his father and grandfather before him. He knew what to expect of a horse. He had enough horse 'lore' inside his head to sink a ship.

During his farming life the only likely intrusion upon traditional ways might be the introduction of a new implement. The motive power remained just as nature had first fashioned it. Confronted with a newfangled tractor, the farmer might decide against any change when all seemed to be going well.

What he often did not fully appreciate, however, was the cost and the time involved in maintaining a team of horses. This was considerable but its true economic significance was not seen till the arrival of the Fordson tractor. Some of the sturdier sons of the soil may well have felt that a working comparison between their horses and a Fordson bordered on blasphemy! But there were some equally sturdy salesmen around and they never let up on hammering away at this very point. There were no tricks. They had facts and figures to show they were talking sound economic sense.

Progress at first was slow but by sticking to their guns they began to make headway.

The results, when they did come, were impressive.

In three years, 1923, 1924, 1925, the Fordson had revolutionised farming in New Zealand yet the development of tractor power on the farm was still only in its infancy.

The *New Zealand Official Year Book* for 1926 showed that in 1923 247 Fordsons were sold; in 1924 473; in 1925 997; in 1926 1047. By 1926 there were more than 2,700 Fordson tractors working in the country and the number was still increasing. No matter how isolated a farming community, word of any new development soon gets around. And that is how it was with the new Fordson...

Once a farmer had taken the plunge and bought a Fordson, he found that his costs were going down and production was going up, and he wasted no time in spreading the good news!

Often as not, he would put pen to paper and send to a farming magazine a glowing account of his Fordson's achievements. If he was keen, and many farmers were, he would even include photos showing the Fordson at work on a variety of tasks.

It all made very good reading particularly for those whose job it was to advertise and publicise the Fordson as widely as possible.

They formulated a marketing campaign which would do credit to the seventies. They generated real enthusiasm among dealers and salesmen.

The contents of those early advertisements may today seem quaint or even naïve. It might seem stating the obvious, that tractors did not need hay or oats or only needed to be given water once a day. But as already indicated, the salesman had to get across to the farmer that the Fordson tractor, compared with horses, was a far better all-round proposition. And the best way to prove that was through his pocket. *Fordson Farming in New Zealand* published by The Colonial Motor Company Limited, was packed with success stories.

An editorial in a 1926 issue summed it all up: "The New Zealand farmers' watchword for 1926 is economy – more production at less cost. You can't make the land yield more than a certain amount. There is only one way left to cut down the cost of farming so that every bit of produce you obtain brings you bigger profit.

"What is the biggest item you can cut

out? It is horses. Replace your teams with a Fordson.

"The Fordson tractor will do all jobs your horses do. It will do them quicker and cheaper. The Fordson runs on kerosene, the cheapest fuel there is. Its running expenses are just about half what your horses cost. Horses are an expense to the farmer every day of the year. The initial cost of the Fordson is half as much as horses. It is no expense when idle."

Farmers found these words were no idle boast. A North Otago farmer said he had found the Fordson a great boon. Fifty acres, which would have been used for horse feed, was now being put to productive use. He also saved 800 sacks of oats and chaff each year and had been able to dispense with a ploughman and five horses.

An Ashburton farmer ploughed 100 acres, grubbed 80 acres, rolled 80 acres and harrowed 150 acres and in all this work tractor repair expenses had been nil.

A Central Otago farmer found that after buying his Fordson he was able to dispose of all his horses, which previously were idle for eight months of the year. He was now always well ahead with his work and in the two years he had owned the tractor, which included a lot of contract work, his only working expenses had been three commutators, a few coil points and a new set of valves.

A Lyndhurst farmer, having owned a Fordson for a similar length of time, had not had a single breakage or mechanical stop.

Wood-sawing problems helped sell a Fordson to another farmer. "Before I bought the Fordson I had a portable sawmill and was unable to get the kind of power to run this as I wanted, so when the dealer asked me for a chance to demonstrate the Fordson I told him he might put it to work on the sawmill. This he did, and the result was that I purchased the tractor on the spot.

"In addition to doing general farm work, I can saw on an average 15 cords of wood a day and cost of operation is low. My reason for choosing the Fordson, when I decided to buy a tractor, was the low cost of operation, and ease of handling and service, for all of which the Fordson is so widely known.

"I am more than pleased with the Fordson tractor, and feel that it is one of the best investments a farmer can make."

And that is what more and more farmers were doing – selling their horses and buying Fordson tractors. When a farmer could be shown, for instance, that a Fordson mowed 15 acres in a 10-hour day for 1s 11d. an acre, against horses mowing seven acres in the same time for 3s 4d. an acre; that the cost of fodder for his horses, the cost of wages and harness, veterinary attention and the land set aside for grazing all added up to a princely sum, then a new Fordson client was on his way!

One of the outstanding features of the early Fordson was its mechanical reliability. Its record here was quite remarkable and would stand comparison with similar machinery of today. What

On the Model N, introduced in 1927, the bore was increased ¹/8 inch, increasing power from 20 to 23hp. Spade lugs were fitted to the rear wheels, and front wheels were made of cast iron. In 1933 production shifted from Cork to Dagenham, and tractors were now painted dark blue with orange wheels.

makes this all the more notable is that it was achieved by working land a great deal more rough than would be found on many farms today, farms that have long since had their bumps and hollows all ironed out....

Fordson tractors brought in new land that no horse team could ever hope to tackle. They converted heavy swamp to productive pasture. They did this by drawing an Oliver swamp plough turning a furrow 24 inches wide by 12 inches deep, no mean accomplishment in those days. They cleared thick scrub and bush. They dragged out heavy tree stumps. Their versatility was quite endless. Draining, harvesting, threshing, as well as hundreds of belt jobs – all were signal proof of Fordson's all-round importance in New Zealand's developing farming industry.

Farmers of that era, once having bought their Fordsons, worked them long, hard hours. This is a recurring theme of articles written in the 1920s. A 10-14 hour day seemed to be quite commonplace with many a farmer working his Fordson 19-20 hours a day; though not, of course, for 365 days a year! But when the pressure was on the Fordson was not spared.

All this, of course, was eloquent testimony to Fordson's designers and the excellence of its engineering.

It was a good tractor, there was no doubt of that. But, like the thoroughbred it was, it had one or two idiosyncrasies, which although eventually accepted as part of the tractor's character, could sometimes be a little 'off-putting'.

The Fordson was never the easiest of tractors to start, especially in cold weather. It used to be a long-standing joke among the Fordson-owning fraternity that if you wanted to make a man out of a boy you sent him out to crank up a Fordson on a cold and frosty morning. There were then no self-starters nor anti-freeze. The radiator held 10 gallons of water, which had to be drained every night in winter.

Apart from its 23 to 1 reduction, much of the trouble lay with the 21 gallons of engine oil and 3 gallons of heavy gearbox oil. This was nothing like the refined product now in use. The Fordson's flywheel used to turn in thick black goo; that is about all it could be called. Gearbox oil was like butter. This heavy oil was used right up to and including the Second World War.

The knowledgeable often resorted to sundry tricks to get things cracking. One was the use of a blowtorch to heat up the hot-place in the manifold exhaust, which went around the intake tube.

W. (Wattie) Falloon, late general manager of Timaru Motors, recalled the starting difficulties of the early Fordson. He put it thus: "Starting the engine was one of the major problems with the first Fordsons. In the early twenties it was considered that 'heavy duty oil' was a heavy oil as thick as treacle and Valvoline Heavy Duty was like that. The only light oil in widespread use was in the Model T transmission, where Valvoline Light was the popular oil.

"The thick oil in the Fordson sump became so heavy in cold weather that cranking the engine was often a nightmare for the owner, who would then resort to calling his Ford dealer for help.

"A small fire using pieces of dry gorse or other firewood was often lit under the sump to warm up the oil. This would ease the drag against the oil in the crankcase, and hopefully the tractor would start.

"The arrival in 1925 of the high tension magneto conversion was claimed to be the end of most starting problems, and so it was, but only after the Ford magneto was replaced with the then much more efficient Bosch one in 1929. To achieve this improvement, a campaign was run throughout New Zealand, probably one of the first of its kind for Ford dealers."

Because of its worm drive the Fordson could never be towed, thus precluding the use of another tractor to get it started. On the other hand, being in constant mesh with nothing to wear, the transmission proved to be very long lasting; as, indeed, was the tractor as a whole.

Mr Orm Hutchinson, of Hutchinson Motors summed up during an interview for this history, when he described the Fordson being somewhat like the Model T in that it remained basically the same throughout its manufacture: "There were some minor changes but these didn't alter the tractor to any great degree. The Fordson was accepted on its merits from the day it first arrived in this country and it did a wonderful job.

"There were never any parts problems. Parts were fundamental and there was nothing basically wrong with the tractor. It is not like today where everybody wants to change everything each year."

The early days of mechanised farming provided their share of interesting anecdotes and for this story of the Fordson,

CMC have been fortunate in being able to call upon the reminiscences of [three] men who helped play an important part in the Fordson's pioneering role, ... whose long working association with CMC and their combined knowledge of the Fordson, would be hard to rival. They are Messrs O (Orm) Hutchinson, R U (Bob) Macaulay and W J S (Bill) McCurdie.

Mr Hutchinson began his long career with CMC in September, 1920. He was appointed manager of the Timaru assembly operations in 1925 and took over the operation of Ford Motors (Canterbury) Ltd, in 1932. Today he is a director of CMC.

Mr McCurdie, now living in Britain, recently spent some months in New Zealand on an extended holiday and the opportunity was taken to discuss his career while he was visiting Wellington. In 1927 he went to Queensland as sales manager for the Fordson state distributors. In 1931 he went to Britain, joining the Ford Motor Company, Dagenham, where he worked for 20 years. Resigning, he went to South Africa as managing director of Howard Rotavator S A, Durban, where he was responsible for Southern Africa to the Congo. He later returned to Britain as the company's group liaison officer for the United Kingdom and the Continent.

Mr Macaulay joined CMC in Wellington in 1929, followed by an appointment to Auckland and thence Timaru in 1934, taking over from Mr Hutchinson who had been appointed manager at Christchurch. December 1935 saw the establishment of Macaulay Motors at Invercargill with Mr Macaulay taking over the assets from Ford dealer G W Woods & Co.

Mr Hutchinson recalls that in the late 1920s, about 1926 or 1927, the total sales of the Fordson then exceeded the best sales of Ford in later years. It was in excess of 1200 units in one season.

Tractors were assembled in Auckland, Timaru and Wellington. Mr Hutchinson and his salesmen went out and sold them on the farms.

"We used to transport the tractor on a Model T truck. At that time the only implements available were those designed to be horse-drawn. These were attached to the tractor drawbar. With a two-furrow plough, for example, a man used to have to walk with it to control the depth.

"Those early selling days were hard work. We had to take the tractor to the farmer and show him what it could do. That was the way it was done.

"Initially, there were no enquiries; we had to get out and find our buyers. We had to be able to show the farmer that cultivation of his land could be done more economically and better than if it was done by horses.

"One of the points we always emphasised to the farmer was the amount of land he had to leave 'tied-up' to feed his horses. We showed him that by selling his horses and buying a tractor, that land could be cultivated for extra produce.

"Operating the Fordson was comparable to knowing the facts of a Model T car and that was a good selling point. The first tractors we had were highly successful and up to 80 percent of the market were Fordsons. Henry Ford did a terrific job in producing this one.

"I remember a demonstration at Pleasant Point where I drove the tractor while Bill Marsden (foreman of the assembly plant) handled the implements. It took us a whole day. The farmer we were hoping to sell to had not had any previous acquaintance with tractors. It was a case of going straight from horses to a tractor. As things turned out, he bought the Fordson.

"Tractors sold in Canterbury were used extensively for crop work, mainly wheat. Normal mowers were used for cutting the wheat and the threshing was done by steam traction engines. Mr Clarke at Levels had a team of traction engines and it was his job to carry out the threshing. The paddocks in those days were much bigger than what they are now, at least 200 acres.

"A large proportion of the tractors sold by CMC were sold in Southland. G W Woods and Co in Invercargill, and their successors, Macaulay Motors Ltd., did a very good job here.

"CMC thought they should have a dealership in Gore and not a branch of G W Woods and so they appointed Dave McKenzie as their dealer there. He had a big area. It went to about Edendale in the south and up to Balfour in the north. He was of course also a Model T dealer. Dave later decided he wanted to go north so Vic Lattey (a roadman with CMC) was appointed the dealer in Gore.

"In those days, the late twenties, the normal tractor dealer was expected to carry at least a month's supply of stock and he did.

"James Rule & Company of Ashburton

sold a lot of tractors. He later went to Raetihi and Bert Holmes, his son-in-law, was appointed dealer in Ashburton.

"Bill Halley, Temuka, was one of the first Ford dealers in New Zealand after Gordon Hughan. He retired in Christchurch and his son Albert (A D) carried on the business.

"The tractors initially shipped out to New Zealand came in cases made of beautiful timber and we did quite a good business in selling this wood. Today we use pre-built cases that are disassembled and used several times and quite a lot of our export trade to Australia is based on these New Zealand-made cases."

Motorists with a competitive spirit often take considerable pleasure in comparing their car with another, even one of similar make, and claiming they have the better vehicle. It would seem that this sort of thing is just not limited to motorists.

Mr Macaulay remembers that at Pukekohe some years ago, two adjoining farmers both owned Fordsons. The tractor serviceman went out and found that one farmer was particularly keen on getting his tractor to go faster! So the neighbours had a tractor race to discover the Fordson's racing capability.

The most important event in the 1930s as far as tractors were concerned was the change from the steel-wheeled tractor to the pneumatic-tyred machine. That was in 1935 when CMC imported two pneumatic-tyred tractors (referred to as land utility tractors) as an experiment.

CMC, in a bid to try and interest farmers, supplied one unit on consignment to the Invercargill dealership. The tractor was taken to a well-known Southland tractor owner, Mr J E MacIntyre, of Longbush. After trying it out he was convinced that the rubber-tyred tractor was a sound practical unit. The other unit went to Cambridge dealer Wilkinson & Co.

Gradually pneumatics outsold the steel-wheeled units. They were both available, but the rubber-tyred version became the norm before the Second World War.

There was, at first, a loss of traction with rubber-tyred tractors but this was overcome by filling the rear wheels with water.

Mr Macaulay recalls: "I can remember a tyre traveller coming to me and he was very jubilant because they had discovered that filling the tyres with water on a tractor near Lumsden, solved the problem of traction. Prior to this it was quite common to sell wheel weights for the rear wheels to increase grip. Filling tyres with water was a great deal cheaper and a great deal more satisfactory.

"Tractors were usually delivered on the dealer's truck. I can remember a tractor actually being sold from Invercargill city. Our method of delivery was to drive the tractor to the Invercargill Railway Station, load it on to a railway truck and then ring up the farmer and tell him the tractor had

Special wheels were made for mowing the golf course at Miramar in Wellington. A sickle bar mower is mid-mounted and driven from the belt pulley for mowing the rough, with fairway gang mowers towed behind.

been loaded and he could collect it ex-rail.

"We used to include £5 delivery charge in the price of the tractor, and in those days that easily covered railage to the farmer's nearest railway station which usually had a loading bank where he could unload the tractor and drive it to his farm. A salesman would then go out and show him how to operate it.

"Farmers never seemed to have any particular mechanical problems with their tractors. The older farmer was very self-reliant and if he had a Ford car he would learn how to use a Fordson tractor.

"Mechanics would go out and attend to tractor repairs in the field and that is where they were mainly done – out in the open. It was not often that tractors were brought into the garage.

"In Southland for many years we had a farmer tractor salesman who could deal with all the problems or questions which a farmer would raise when thinking of purchasing a tractor. He would talk from his own experience, which was appreciated by his prospective buyers.

"The techniques altered somewhat after some farmers' sons had been sent to Lincoln and Massey and had learnt quite a bit about mechanised farming.

"Some of the salesmen were sometimes a little non-plussed when asked highly technical questions about draw-bar pull of tractors and certain technical data which they never knew existed. But these were just the changing times and we had to adapt to it.

"At one stage in the forties, Ford in England supplied the Fordson major half-track. Quite a few of these were sold, compared with the Ford County crawler which came later. The half-track unit was used quite a lot for pulling mole-drain ploughs.

"Farmers would sometimes buy County crawlers on a price basis when they should have perhaps bought something a good deal heavier. They were put into work for which they weren't meant to be used, sometimes on very heavy country.

"This sort of thing was very noticeable in the Model T days when people used to be able to buy all sorts of attachments to go on to a Model T truck which was used far beyond its capacity and the same thing happened with crawler tractors.

"There was very little problem with tractor supplies. Occasionally there were shortages but not for long. They were nothing like the problems we had to face with motor vehicles which, as far back as I can remember, was always a feast or a famine, but with tractors, the supplies were reasonably good.

"In the 1930s, when a farmer bought a tractor, it cost him £220 delivered. This would have been a steel-wheeled tractor in 1936-37. The price was £215 F O B in Timaru but £220 delivered. The original rubber-tyre tractor we received in 1935 was £260.

"In the early sixties, we were one of the first firms in Southland to introduce two-way radio equipped service vans and I can remember shortly after, a farmer ringing to say he was having trouble with his tractor and wanted a mechanic immediately. By sheer coincidence, our mechanic was on an adjoining farm and we got him on the radio. He arrived at the farmer's door just as he was walking out from the telephone!

"Stewart Island came within our orbit, but no farming as we knew it on the mainland was done there. About 10 years ago I don't think there were more than two or three farms. However, the Agriculture Department records showed the island had a certain number of farm holdings and I can remember the Ford Motor Company expressing concern because we didn't appear to have sold many tractors, if any, there. We were able to reassure the company that the farms were all heavy bush and not workable.

"I used to have all Macaulay Motors' tractor purchases and sales information from the time we started until one day we got a particularly enthusiastic accountant who sent the whole lot to the destructor! Present-day accountants will do well to remember that some records are useful in the years ahead."

Mr McCurdie, who can look back on a colourful and extensive career in both the motor and agricultural industries, remembers well his early days with CMC.

His first job was with the Tourist Motor Company in Hastings but his preference was working with cars and tractors. His chance soon came. In 1922, at the age of 21, he joined CMC and not long after, began specialising in selling Fordson tractors. This was really a two-pronged affair. Not only was he promoting tractors for use on farms; he was also helping to spearhead the Fordson on the industrial front, especially Fordson-powered road-making machinery.

"I came down to Wellington to be interviewed," said Mr McCurdie, "It was a pretty searching affair but I got the job and was asked to start on Monday morning. The first thing that happened was my being told to learn the spare parts book of the Model T

off by heart! Well, I worked on that book night and day and at a subsequent meeting succeeded in answering some very probing questions from Mr F H ('Toddy') Johnson who was general manager. That effort brought me quick promotion.

"Bill Taylor, who was then in charge of head office spare parts department, was promoted to assistant branch manager at Auckland and I took his place in Wellington. The Fordson was beginning to establish a hold and the whole thing just fell into my lap. I was most interested in tractors and things really started getting underway by 1923.

"We were forging ahead on the farms and notching up corresponding achievements on the industrial side. This was especially so with road-making machinery.

"When we sold a tractor to a farmer we could count on selling anything from a quarter to a half of its value in agricultural equipment. On the industrial side we could sell three or four times the value of a tractor. For example, the Miami scoop sold for £130 compared with £175 for the tractor. A Wehr grader sold for £600 plus or minus according to the equipment.

"There was definitely some wonderful farm equipment in those days. For example, there was the Oliver No. 8 plough, 10 or 12 inch. This was very good as were the Oliver disc harrows. Made by the predecessors of today's Oliver Company, they were all imported by CMC. In those days there were no import licences to bother us.

"The Oliver equipment had a wonderful name. Apart from workmanship, the secret of their success was that they were able to buy high quality steel at a reasonable price.

"Interestingly enough, there is a parallel here in the Ford T. The steel in its frame was so good it was used for cutters in lathes. The axle shafts were also of high quality steel and these were highly sought after by engineering shops.

"Talking of farming equipment, I remember the late Jack Kilkenny of Westport importing in the 1930s, the Ferguson bolt-on plough for the Model N Fordson. Strangely enough, it turned out to be a failure and yet this same plough was destined to be the foundation of the great Ferguson empire.

"Although Fordsons sold well, we didn't have it all our own way in the 1920s. We had stiff competition from the International 10/20 and Case Model C. These were both very popular as was the Allis Chalmers which

came not long after."

Using films in promotional work is taken for granted these days but Mr McCurdie recalls an occasion early in the piece when appearing before the camera caused him some initial apprehension.

"Mr B L Dallard, director of prisons, asked if we could help clear the bog oak from the swamp at Wi Tako. Prison labour at 8/- a day or £25 an acre was proving very expensive. We used a Fordson fitted with the Trackson Full Crawler equipment. We also made a big tripod to pull out the logs. This was quite something as it was the first logging arch to be used in New Zealand.

"I was on the tractor as overseer and my overalls were similar to those of the prisoners.

"One day a government publicity team came along to film the operation. I wasn't very keen about appearing as I felt that anyone knowing me and seeing me in the film, would immediately think I was one of the inmates! So I put my fears to one of the film crew. 'Oh, don't worry about that,' he said. 'We're not allowed to show prisoners' faces and as we will be able to film yours, people will know you're all right!'

"That film was eventually sold to Metro-Goldwyn-Mayer and shown all over the world."

In 1927 Mr McCurdie left CMC and went to work in Queensland, still selling Fordson tractors. After three years, he went to Great Britain and joined the Ford Motor Company.

HIGH PRAISE FOR CMC FROM FORD

When Mr McCurdie arrived in Australia he was immediately offered a position with Motors & Tractors Ltd., Sydney, the New South Wales Fordson distributors. A few days later he was sent an expenses-paid invitation to go to Brisbane.

Eventually it transpired that the reason for this enthusiastic welcome was the build-up given to the Colonial Motor Company Ltd., by Ford, Detroit.

CMC had been held up as an example to the rest of the world-wide Ford organisation for selling the highest ratio of Fordson tractors to cars and trucks – far in excess of any other Ford branch or national distributor. This was 1,047 Fordsons to just over 12,000 cars and trucks.

FORDSON CRAWLERS

Not long after the steel-wheeled Fordson was introduced, Ford developed a full crawler but dealers in this country were at first reluctant to take on anything so new. Mr Orm Hutchinson has a good story to tell on this: "One of the first Fordson Full Crawlers imported by CMC went to the Timaru branch and, as most dealers were reluctant to stock one of these, we had to motivate sales activity.

"I arranged with a very good friend of mine, the late Allan Grant of 'Strathconnan', Fairlie, to send the crawler to his station. Here we carried out our demonstration and left the tractor for a trial period of about two months on the basis that if it operated to his satisfaction he would buy; if not, we were to take it back.

"During the trial period I received a very tough assignment from the late Mr Hope B Gibbons. He had built a beautiful home at Lyall Bay, Wellington, on quite a sizeable piece of picturesque land through which ran a delightful little stream. He proposed to stock this with the best possible goldfish, which he said came from South Canterbury. My assignment was to produce the goldfish.

"I thought of Allan Grant, whose home was situated in several acres of gardens and parkland in which there were small streams and an artificial lake teeming with goldfish. I told him my problem and he invited me to his place to take as many as I wanted. This was just before the end of the Fordson crawler trial period.

"Equipped with two acclimatisation fish-carrying cans, I arrived at 'Strathconnan' at about 8.30 one morning. Allan, his manservant and I began fishing for goldfish but this was too slow. So Allan, who was a bachelor, sent his manservant inside to get a couple of big curtains and with these we successfully netted the required number.

"Then it was down to business and when I finally took my departure about 8 pm, I had with me two cans of goldfish and orders for one Fordson Full Crawler, one Ford truck and one Ford sedan which Allan wanted to give to his station manager for doing such a good job of managing the place while he was on a trip to Britain. As well as this, the back seat of my car was laden with roses from his beautiful rose garden. For me it was a very memorable day.

"In the twenties the Hermitage at Mount Cook was operated by the Mount Cook Motor Company Ltd, and this company also operated the motor coach service from Timaru to the Hermitage and on to Queenstown. During the snow season the buses had difficulty on occasions in negotiating the road from Birch Creek to

An impressive conversion kit was available for the Model F, making it competitive with the Caterpillar 2 ton but, at half the price, the ordinary Fordson sold better.

the Hermitage, so I interested the late Mr Rudolph Wigley, managing director of the company, in a Fordson Full Crawler to which was attached a mechanical snow plough we had imported.

"Mr Wigley, who was a good friend of mine, was a very keen business man. The deal was that we were to give a demonstration with the combination. If it cleared the road and operated satisfactorily, he would buy; otherwise, we were to take it back. I sent the combination to Mount Cook at the beginning of the winter and awaited the snow, which was a long time coming.

"One Friday late in August, 1925 I was on one of my periodic visits to the Christchurch Ford dealership, when I had a telephone call from our Timaru headquarters stating that it was snowing heavily at Mount Cook. I returned to Timaru very late, but immediately made arrangements with Bill Marsden and a press reporter to accompany me to the Hermitage early on the Saturday. The last 15 miles provided very tough going for our Model T sedan, even though we had chains fitted.

"Sunday morning broke beautifully fine with about two feet of snow at the Hermitage. We then started on the big adventure not knowing, but hoping, that the Fordson Full Crawler would operate on the top of the snow. With the snowplough attached, we cleared many miles of the road. The result was an order from Mr Wigley for the combination, which did yeoman service for many years clearing snow from the main road and also from the Ball Hut Road.

"Later, the Ministry of Works took the responsibility of clearing the roads, and until some 15 years ago, the remains of the old combination were to be seen in its last resting place overgrown with scrub at the back of the garage at Mount Cook."

FINAL CHECK...

Mr McCurdie relates the following incident illustrating the difference between CMC marketing methods in the twenties and those developed by Ford of Britain.

It was the practice in Britain to ship out one or two Fordson tractors to selected dealers, without the formality of an order and then follow up their arrival with a visit from the area representative whose function was to collect payment in the form of a bank draft – dealers' cheques were not acceptable.

On one occasion two tractors were shipped to the dealer in Aberdeen which resulted in the following telegrams: – "General Manager, Ford Motor Co. Ltd., Trafford Park, Manchester. Ford representative Russell found dead in lavatory of Palace Hotel Stop Wire instructions."

To which the Ford General Manager replied: – "Search him for tractor drafts and pull chain."

The Fordson was destined to play a part as universal as the Ford car and commercial vehicle. Its adaptability as a haulage unit

Orm Hutchinson demonstrating the Trackson F and snow plough, and clearing the road at Mt Cook in 1925.

and as a stationary power-plant quickly made it the automatic choice of municipalities, borough and county councils, other public bodies and contractors.

Looking at early literature publicising the Fordson's all-round capabilities, it seems there was virtually little that this nuggety tractor could not do.

As a stationery power-plant it was used to operate air compressors, asphalt and concrete mixers, cranes, drainage pumps, elevators, electric lighting plants, hoists, machine tools, pile drivers, pumps of all descriptions, quarrying machinery, rock drills, stone crushers, threshing machines, winches, wharf work and macadamising.

Nor was its versatility anything less on the highways and by-ways where it was used for draining, excavation work, furniture removal, golf course cutting and rolling, grading, road rolling, shunting, street cleaning, tar spraying, timber hauling, travelling crane and winch, locomotive work on railways and haulage of all kinds.

Just as farmers were quick to sing the praises of their Fordsons, so too were local body engineers and contractors and county clerks. Wrote one road engineer: "I had seen the tractor perform and had read of its achievements. It took some persuasion to convince my superiors that the Fordson was what we needed, but I finally got one in on demonstration.

"That demonstration period paid the cost of the tractor before we had even purchased it. It convinced everyone that we could not afford to get along without the tractor for another day.

"It is a tremendous time-saver; it has cut my costs 20 percent. It will pull anything, it seems. I haven't come across anything yet that has stopped it. And after six months' use the repair costs have amounted to just a few shillings."

This was no isolated song of praise. Letters from satisfied owners flowed in a steady stream to CMC headquarters in Wellington. Here are excerpts:

"Wanganui City Council owns two Fordson-Wehr graders; one has been in operation for the past 18 months, during which time it has done excellent work in the maintenance of suburban streets. It travels an average (estimated) distance of 260 miles per month, at a cost, including all overhead charges, of 2/8 per mile."

Mr Crofton Staveley, city engineer: "It is light in repairs, easy to manipulate, and has proved a valuable addition to our plant."

Public Works Department: "The Fordson-Wehr grader is used by the Public Works Department. In making the deviation over Mount Cargill, near Dunedin, they used a 1924 model Wehr with great success. This sort of work is a real testimonial to the efficiency and design of this outfit. Even on a job such as the above mentioned, one man controls the whole machine. If it can be done on Mount Cargill, it can be done anywhere. The Department has since purchased five more Fordson-Wehr graders."

The Amner Lime Company Ltd, Napier: "About 14 months ago we purchased one of your Fordson tractors. Since then it has had the most constant work, principally taking four-ton loads of lime from our lime works to Port Ahuriri railway station down an incline of one in seven, and usually bringing back loads of varying weights.

"Last week, the tractor was taken to pieces for inspection, and to our great surprise showed practically no sign of wear. We think this is remarkable, considering the hard, gruelling work which it has been doing."

Mr B C Basstain, engineer to the Southland County Council, said that each of their one-man operated Fordson-Wehr graders replaced at least one six-horse grader and two men and was giving entire satisfaction.

One firm said it had replaced seven 4-ton lorries with Fordsons and trailers. It told CMC that "the initial cost of the entire tractor and trailer equipment was insignificant compared with the large investment necessary for each heavy motor truck.

"Several months' experience with the Fordson outfits has shown a cut in transporation cost of approximately 50 percent for the work to which they have been assigned."

The Pukekura Park Board at New Plymouth hit upon a rather novel use for their Fordson tractor: "One of the lakes in the park had become badly silted up with some hundreds of tons of mud, washed down by the stream which feeds the lake. The Board decided to remove this silt. A derrick was erected on the bank of the lake and the Fordson was commissioned to act as a winch to haul out buckets of mud from the bottom of the lake. The tractor was

jacked up off the ground and large wooden blocks placed under the front axle and the rear axle housing, thus keeping the whole outfit firm and rigid. The end of the drag cable was tied to a rear spoke and the slack cable was wound on the wheel itself. By using the low gear and reverse, the tractor made a most satisfactory winch and the work proceeded at a rapid rate."

Front-end loaders, earth scoops and so on arouse no particular comment in this age of mechanisation. Indeed, the very size and power of some of these units – particularly giant earth movers – tend to make it seem all so new. But this is not the case. What is being used today is merely a progressive development of equipment that first saw the light of day nearly 50 years ago, often as not from machinery first made for operation with a Fordson tractor. Indeed, this power equipment, so ably promoted by CMC, anticipated by some years the eventual mechanisation of the then Public Works Department by the Minister of Works, Mr Semple.

Mr McCurdie recalls this equipment well. "What you see about you today are really just variations on an old theme. The real difference is that everything is so much bigger with, of course, greatly improved performance. Even so, the equipment used in the 1920s for road building and similar work was truly excellent for its time. Examples that readily come to mind are the Fordson-Miami earth scoop, the Fordson-Lessman front-end loader and the FordsonWehr graders. These did wonderful work. In fact, those front-end loaders were the first ever made.

"About 1924 the newly constituted Main Highways Board held its first full-scale meeting. I was then a young man with CMC and I invited Mr F W Furkett, the chief engineer of the Public Works Department, and the delegates to come and see the range of Fordson-powered road-making machinery at CMC in Wellington. There were 63 members attending the meeting and Mr Furkett, in accepting the invitation, asked that cars be sent to pick them up. His parting words to me were: 'We'll ring you at 3.45'.

"As it turned out, I was only given a quarter of an hour's warning. After a fine old scramble I managed to round up the right number of cars and drivers and we had the board members around at CMC by 4.15 pm.

"Mr R B Gibbons was there and he said to me, 'Well, get up on the tractor and say something!' It was a pretty tough assignment for a 22-year-old but an order is an order and without any further ado I got up on a tractor and said 'something'.

"My little speech must have proved satisfactory to my audience of experts because the whole thing turned out very well indeed."

The Fordson-Wehr grader was a success from the moment it arrived in this country. When CMC first imported these, one was landed at Timaru for the branch there. Orm Hutchinson was manager and he immediately got in touch with councillors and engineers of the local and contiguous counties.

"The Waimate County Council was the first we were able to interest," he said, "and we arranged for a demonstration on one of the main county roads.

"The Wehr grader was operated by the late Bill Marsden, foreman of the CMC assembly plant, and the demonstration was so impressive we were successful in getting an order.

"When this grader was being operated by the council we were able to arrange, with the co-operation of several South Island dealers, for a number of county engineers to come to South Canterbury and see the Waimate grader operating under country conditions.

"The results were quite good, and progressively sales were made to the following county councils: Southland three graders; Vincent two; Waimate two; Dunedin one. All of these graders operated most successfully for many, many years."

RAILWAY APPLICATIONS

Among CMC's many enterprising activities in the sale of Ford products over the past 50 years, few were as novel as the company's successful effort in 1924 to get Fordson tractors accepted as shunting units by the New Zealand Railways.

The outcome was a remarkably ugly duckling of the iron road, which came to be tagged officially as 'TR 1' or, to give it the full title, the Adamson-Fordson tractor with four king-sized steel wheels adapted to run on rails and inter-connected fore and aft by coupling rods. It was the first tractor to be converted for this work in New Zealand.

There were, of course, many other

This Fordson F was converted to a NZ Railways TR1 shunter in 1924. With a special ballasted frame, transmission and coupled cast steel wheels, it could shift a large rake of wagons, and gave 24 years service.

modifications such as transmission, and dead weights at front to maximise front wheel traction.

TR 1 was powered by a standard 22 hp Fordson tractor motor coupled to a gearbox giving three speeds in each direction, and installed in a patent under-frame. This was imported by CMC from the Adamson Motor Company of Birmingham, Alabama, USA.

Mr Ernest Fay, the equipment engineer for NZ Railways, had a great ambition to have a Fordson locomotive at each of the busier stations so that the goods train could be made up by the station foreman and so speed the main line locomotive on its way.

Mr K I Bullock, of the Auckland Railway Enthusiasts' Society, has recalled that as a piece of machinery TR 1 was 'rather a horror'.

However, TR 1 was in fact the fore-runner of today's fleet of diesel shunting locomotives in the service of the Railways Department.

The early-days Colonial Motor Company was very active in introducing Fordson tractors to the New Zealand scene. And at the same time the need for light shunting units in the New Zealand railways was arising.

Already in use, was a small petrol engine inspection trolley purchased from an American maker in 1896, an English-built Alldays and Onions motorcar fitted with flanged wheels, and a small railcar powered by a McEwan-Pratt petrol engine.

Up to this stage, however, no one had thought of employing the internal combustion

engine in a light-shunting unit. By 1922, experiments to ascertain whether Westinghouse and Thomas petrol-electric railcars would be suitable for light shunting were being made in Wellington. However, they were found to be too slow and cumbersome.

Two years later CMC made the breakthrough by adapting the 22hp Fordson tractor for use on rails. It was one of six initial tractor-rail conversions by the company. The other five were sold to serve as sawmill tramway locomotives, a role in which they gave yeoman service.

TR 1 gave early promise in its trials. Surprisingly heavy loads of up to 136 tons were hauled without, as a report at the time said, 'splutter or fuss'.

TR 1's trials were performed at the Railways Department's bush tramway at Erua, near National Park; at the railway sawmill at Frankton; at the Penrose maintenance depot; at Mamaku station in the Rotorua district, and thence to a not very illustrious career at Petone railway workshops.

TR 1 was not popular with steam-experienced railwaymen. They claimed the plucky little tractor unit was too slow, too light and that her gearing could not withstand the heavy surges characteristic of railway hauling.

Before long TR 1 was relegated to Putaruru and here the little shunter was more fortunate. She found herself in the hands of a

man prepared to study her different ways and to coax the best performance from her. She responded with good service.

After a short time at Paeroa, where her reputation was restored, TR 1 was transferred to Te Aroha, which was supposed to be her last working district. But TR 1 surprised her critics and continued to give faithful service until March 31 1948, when she was officially retired after 24 years of haulage and shunting.

With the comparative success of TR 1, the New Zealand Railways dispatched an order to Muir-Hill Equipment Ltd, Manchester, in 1928, for two small units suitable for Fordson power plants.

This followed the success of a similar tractor supplied by Muir-Hill for use on a light railway of 60 cm gauge on the Mulifanua rubber plantation in Western Samoa. This unit eventually found its way into service in New Zealand in 1940 and became TR 40.

The two Muir-Hill locomotives were of similar design to the Samoan tractor but were larger and heavier. Each was powered by a Fordson petrol engine, developing 22hp at 1400rpm driving through a multiple-disc clutch, three-speed gearbox and an axle-shaft, with chain transmission to both axles.

Known as TR 4 and 5, they were described by Mr P R Angus in 1932 as "having a Fordson engine that is sound, simple and economical, while cheap and easy to run."

These two rail tractors were in service only a few months when it was decided to purchase two more. A & G Price Ltd, Thames, who received the contract to build the two extra units, copied closely the original Muir-Hills, but they replaced the tall sentry box cab of the originals with a wider, six foot one which provided better visibility for the driver.

TR 6 and 7 were the first A & G Price locomotives to be powered by internal-combustion engines. In tests carried out at Wanganui in 1932, these little rail tractors proved they could haul a load of 55 tons on short grades of 1 in 82, and the same load could be shifted on the level at more than 6 mph.

Both units stayed in service, giving very little mechanical trouble for more than 20 years and were scrapped only when the diesel engine had made its appearance.

There was also the Fordson-powered bush locomotive, which extended the power from the prime mover to the log-carrying bogies both ahead and astern. These were a success on many wooden tramlines in the bush and much safer than steam as there was no fire hazard from sparks. They also had excellent traction for holding the load going down to the mill and climbing back into the bush empty.

An early shunter shifting a rake of wagons on a private quarry rail track.

DEPRESSION YEARS

After the boom years of the late 1920s the world wide Depression hit New Zealand in the early thirties, bringing with it financial disaster and ruin to many people from all walks of life.

The motor industry was no exception and when the better times came in the middle and late thirties, many motor businesses, well known in say 1930, were no longer in existence, or had been through liquidation procedures and reformed with different capital structures.

Farmers were amongst the worst hit and the following table taken from Colonial Motor Company records shows how tractor sales plummeted:

Sales to	1930	1931	1932	1933	1934	1935
Dealers	194	38	44	47	88	88

The Colonial Motor Company Limited suffered too and as an example (following a January shipment of 120 units), 40 tractors arrived on the *Otaki* in February 1930. Of these 40 tractors none were sold in 1930, 1 was sold in 1931, 22 in 1932, and the remainder in 1933.

An even longer wait was suffered by the tractors on the *City of Khartoum* that berthed in July 1930. They were not delivered to dealers until between May and October, 1934.

For the whole of New Zealand, total tractor imports from 1932-1935 were only 1,348 units. In 1936 the total imports numbered 1,484 tractors.

Needless to say, mechanised farming made few strides during the early thirties, but by the end of the thirties there were 9,500 tractors in use in New Zealand.

FRANCHISE LOST

When the Ford Motor Company was established at Seaview in 1936, it cancelled the tractor franchise within months and appointed Booth McDonald Ltd., a firm dealing in agricultural implements.

Then, once again, they took it away and allocated it to Gough, Gough and Hamer Ltd. That was in 1938. The following year the Second World War broke out and not many tractors came out in that period.

However, Ford took the tractor franchise back again and returned it to the dealers in 1946.

AFTER THE WAR - E27N

In 1946 Ford dealers came back into the Ford tractor business with the introduction of the post-war E27N Fordson Major. Using the same engine as the Model N Fordson it superseded, the E27N offered many improvements based on Ford's considerable tractor experience in Britain where 94 percent of all tractors made during the war were Fordsons. Four models were available in petrol or kerosene. All had three forward and one reverse gear but gear ratios differed to give various working speeds for particular jobs.

Like the earlier Fordson, which was available with standard gears (green spot) or lower ratio ploughing gears (red spot), the gear ratios were classified:-

4.3 Green spot standard ratio,
4.3 Red spot special ratio,
7.5 Green spot standard ratio,
7.5 Red spot special ratio.

The 4.3 Green was the standard agricultural version with speeds of 2.54, 3.85, and 5.37mph at 1200 engine rpm. The 4.3 Red spot had a low first and second gear for specialised jobs; speeds being 2.02, 3.06, and 5.37mph. The 7.5 Green, used mainly by contractors who required a faster road gear, produced 2.73, 3.85 and 9.65mph and the 7.5 Red spot produced 2.16, 3.06 and 9.65mph. These figures relate to pneumatic-type versions; steel wheel equipped models were somewhat slower.

Hydraulic three-point linkage, steel wheels, Darlington overdrive, half-track kits and other items could be supplied as optional extras. At a later date Ford also supplied a full range of Ford Ransome implements and Howard rotary hoes as part of an idea to enable dealers to sell a complete range of equipment to farmers.

It was after the Second World War, when freer imports of tractors became possible, that competition from opposition tractors grew stronger. There had already been experience of this in the 1930s with International Harvester, Allis Chalmers, McCormack Deering and Lanz tractors which were good machines and provided real opposition in some parts of the country.

The E27N was affectionately known as 'Cast-iron Clarice.' This was no misnomer as she would take on virtually anything and could be bedecked with all manner of weird and wonderful contraptions, many of a Heath Robinson nature designed by

The first major change came with the E27N, which had a dual range gearbox, three more powerful engines running on kerosene, petrol or diesel, and three point linkage hydraulics available.

budding engineers who had many grievous failures but some successes. Like its famous predecessor, the new Fordson was quick to make its mark whatever the conditions.

Early in 1951 in the most easterly Ford territory in New Zealand, a Fordson Major diesel tractor with 16 inch Country Full Tracks completed the arduous job of creating rich pasture from 40 acres of soggy swampland.

The swamp was on the property of Mr S H Burdett at Ngawhatutu, north of Wairoa. Before work commenced, the land was to all intents and purposes, useless. In summer, cattle could graze in the drier parts, but as soon as the first rains came, the animals were completely bogged. It was decided that with proper draining and filling, the land could be converted to its full productivity.

The bringing in of 40 acres of swampy and useless land created considerable interest amongst the farming community, both European and Maori. A start was made in June 1951, on seven acres of the driest portion. The results hoped for were achieved, and at one stage the seven acres were carrying 20 lambs to the acre. The cultivation of the remaining 33 acres was commenced later in the year.

A contemporary report said the improved condition of the land "is a striking example of what can be achieved with the use of mechanical equipment, the correct cultivation and the improvement of the land by the use of green feed crops for autumn and winter."

The exceptionally low tread pressure of the Fordson Major tracks was an important feature responsible for the completion of this job. In the extremely soft conditions experienced, the pressure of 31lbs per square inch was instrumental in maintaining a steady pace throughout.

Similar accounts of Fordson Major achievements could be repeated almost without end. Joe Rosevear, of Timaru Motors Limited, tells such a story here:

"One of the more pleasant installations in recent times was on November 15 1972, the day we delivered a new Ford 3000 to the 'Grampians Station' of 48,000 acres in the Mackenzie Country, 75 miles from Timaru.

"As it was on the eve of Mr Don Mullan's retirement, Colin Neill (Fairlie) and I thought it a good farewell gesture to pick up Don at Lake Tekapo and take him along to help with the installation and collect the cheque; Don was very good at that and over the years we were educated accordingly.

"This turned out to be a day to remember for all concerned. Over a cup of tea in the men's quarters, Don recalled the time he and our popular and very knowledgeable general manager, the late Mr Wattie Falloon, delivered an E 27 N Fordson Major petrol (4.3 Green Spot) up this self-same road to the next door station (only eight miles further on in 1947-48). First, the tractor had to be railed to Fairlie (the train only ran three times a week) and

then driven in hourly shifts averaging four mph up the 43 miles of dusty, rough road. There were no sealed roads then, very few bridges and numerous streams to cross. In comparison with the modern means of transport with good roads and everything laid on, they had to work long hours for every sale."

Following the introduction of the E27N, dealers soon realised that not only did they have a good tractor for agricultural purposes selling at a low price, they also had the answer to a growing demand for mechanisation by contractors, local bodies and government departments. Everything hinged on the ability of obtaining the necessary equipment suitable for this new opportunity. This was soon forthcoming and the Fordson took to its new industrial role like a duck to water.

CMC's engineering division, for example, developed a simple and efficient power take-off-driven winch for rear-mounting on the E27N and this, in conjunction with a Christchurch-produced logging arch, gave the Fordson an entry into the logging industry. A modified version of the winch is still being sold to power authorities and some contractors.

Further examples of the development of this kind of machinery can be found in the section given over to post-war industrial equipment.

The E27N had a most successful run and was not phased out until 1952 when the new Fordson was introduced.

FORD FERGUSON

The Ford Ferguson tractor (it is more correctly known as the Ford tractor with Ferguson system and hydraulics) was introduced to New Zealand in 1947. Its hydraulic system was a major advance in hydraulic implement control and created a lot of interest. It meant that mounted implements could be used without land wheels.

Many of the engine components followed Ford's principle of inter-changeability. Valve assemblies were the V8 type, pistons were Mercury and so on. It was a wonderfully versatile tractor that could outperform many of the larger competitors.

There was only one real Ferguson tractor and it was made by David Brown, called the Ferguson-Brown (correctly known as the Ferguson). It was produced

from 1936. Rated at 12hp it weighed just 14 cwt. It was Ferguson's idea to keep the weight down. Ferguson demonstrated one of these models to Henry Ford in October 1938, and a gentleman's agreement between the two men was made. The 9N as it was known was first sold in the United States in 1939. The 8N produced in 1947 by Ford alone was similar to the tractor marketed by Ferguson. His was the first three-point hydraulic system and patents dated back to 1934. These finally ran out in 1949.

Ford salesmen had to learn about hydraulic attachments on tractors, and at Invercargill, for example, Macaulay Motors ran tractor schools.

Dealers were most enthusiastic about Ford Ferguson tractors as they were a very good little unit. District ploughing competitions were very popular for demonstrating tractors and the Ford Ferguson quickly became a firm favourite.

One of the first demonstrations given by Macaulay Motors Ltd, Invercargill, was at a ploughing competition near Heddons Bush on a Mr McDonald's farm. Mr R U Macaulay recalls that occasion with wry amusement: "We had only just received a Ford Ferguson tractor and unfortunately, on the day, it developed a fault in the automatic depth attachment. This made the plough go deeper, much to the amusement of the farmers and to our discomfort.

"Some months later the owner of the farm came in specially to tell me that the wheat grown on the strip where the plough went haywire had given the best yield of any wheat in the entire crop!"

Harry Ferguson and Ford unfortunately 'fell out' and this broke up their joint manufacturing arrangement to produce the Ford Ferguson tractor. It was 10 years before another small Ford tractor was produced. The lack of such a tractor was a blow to the North Island particularly, where 70 percent of sales at that time were in the small tractor class.

FIRST DIESEL

The E27N was fitted with a Perkins P 6T 6cylinder diesel engine in 1949. This model sold for £786 and was the Ford dealer's first introduction to diesel in the Ford tractor field.

The P6T was de-rated to 45hp by fitting cast pistons and holding maximum rpm to 1,500. With a maximum drawbar pull of

5,300 pounds it was claimed to have the working capacity equivalent to a 14-horse team. In spite of its 12volt electric starter, it was not the best of starters in colder climates, especially on a frosty morning. Max Snook, manager of Sockburn Motor's tractor division, remembers many an occasion when he had to fill the radiator with hot water for some extra heat after the cold starting procedure didn't bring any result.

However, this was the dawn of the diesel-powered tractor era and it was largely due to the Fordson influence that tractor power was converted from mainly petrol/kerosene to diesel. This was not surprising, because in addition to low maintenance requirements the reliability of diesel engines is excellent. Fuel cost was low and fuel usage varied from 1/2 - 3/4 gallon on light work and from 3/4 - 1 gallon per hour on heavy work.

The lugging power from the diesel enabled much greater workloads than farmers with petrol/kerosene units had been used to, so it was not surprising that diesel became the fuel for the future, especially on larger tractors.

BOOM YEARS

The 1950s were the boom years for tractor sales. On only four occasions has

New Zealand imported more than 10,000 tractors in a year – 1951, 1952, 1954 and 1957.

By 1950 there were 27,000 tractors in use; from 1950-59 the number increased to over 75,000. At the end of 1969, the equivalent total was 95,500 of which diesel tractors represented probably close to 50 percent.

NEW FORDSON MAJOR

The official Ford presentation in New Zealand of the new Fordson Major in 1952 was held in the Majestic Cabaret in Wellington. A new tractor was dismantled and re-assembled in the ballroom. This was then covered by a haystack in readiness for the unveiling.

Bill Toomey, then the tractor manager for the Ford Motor Company, had to guarantee that there would not be any oil spillage on the carpet. He did a very good job and the occasion of the unveiling will no doubt be remembered by many of the older CMC members.

With a choice of three completely new overhead valve 4 cylinder engines – petrol, diesel, kerosene – six forward speeds and two reverse speeds, modern styling and hydraulics, the new Fordson Major was a

The Ford-Ferguson system was a new smaller petrol 18hp tractor with rear hydraulic lift arms, and a spring top link valve, enabling draft control. Harry Ferguson and Henry Ford developed this in 1938, but war delayed its full release and after disagreement over patents, it was withdrawn.

The Fordson Major 40hp petrol and diesel engines had three point linkage hydraulics. It was a vastly improved tractor which sold very well.

major step forward in tractor design. By using many parts common to the petrol and kerosene engines, buyers were able to acquire a diesel engine tractor at a comparatively low price.

The DDN and DKN series proved winners, particularly the diesel with its direct injection fuel system. It was renowned for its easy starting although, for a year or two after its introduction, there were problems with the starter itself – a pin sometimes came adrift and then became enmeshed with the ring gear, causing considerable damage. This problem was reported to Dagenham who replied that they were having no problems of that sort.

When Mr Jack Broun, service manager of Ford New Zealand, visited Dagenham he was somewhat concerned that no remedy had been provided and they insisted that the problem did not arise in the UK. This was quite true, he discovered, because self-starters were not standard equipment on home market tractors!

POWER MAJOR

Following the success of the Fordson Dexta, which filled the lower horsepower range, Ford uprated the Fordson Major engines by 10 bhp to 51.8 maximum bhp in 1958. Strengthened transmission, improved hydraulics, easier rear wheel track adjustment and the throttle lever located under the steering wheel all contributed to yet further advance by Ford's tractor range to meet the demand for increased power.

SUPER MAJOR

Three years later, in 1961, significant improvements to the Fordson Major/Power Major line were announced under the new name of Super Major. Single lever control hydraulics and the new flow control valve improved the efficiency of implements operated by the tractor's hydraulics and enabled rapid changes from category 1 to category 2 implements.

Differential lock was a helpful aid in wet or soft conditions and the introduction of rear wheel disc brakes made the driver's lot easier by reducing pedal effort.

DEXTA – THE MAJOR GETS A WORKMATE

After 40 years of manufacturing tractors, the Fordson Dexta was announced in October 1957. Designed to meet the need for a lighter tractor, the Dexta was equipped with a 3 cylinder 32hp diesel engine. This engine provided a high torque at lower engine speeds so that the tractor performed well on slow speed work and ploughing, yet had a high top speed of 17mph (27kph).

The hydraulics on the Dexta represented a further advance in simplified operation. Draft Control (Qualitrol) enables an implement to operate at a fixed depth but if an obstruction, or heavy patch of soil, is encountered, the hydraulics raise the implement and transfer weight to the rear wheels of the tractor, thereby giving increased wheel grip. The implement is

then automatically repositioned at its former depth. Set in Position Control, the driver puts an implement at a position relative to the tractor and this position is maintained irrespective of changes in soil resistance.

Live power take-off (PTO) and live hydraulics were available as an option, which was already offered on the Major, and can be used independently of forward movement of the tractor. Thus the tractor can serve as a second engine to operate trailed equipment.

The Dexta quickly established a big following, although the years of virtually undisputed leadership in the light tractor market by Massey-Ferguson gave Dexta salesmen no walkover. Well specified, the Dexta was backed up by numerous Ford selling aids particularly in comparisons with other tractors.

Improvements were made to meet the markets. In 1960 a new gearbox was introduced, offering a lower first gear speed yet retaining a high top speed of over 15mph.

A petrol engine Dexta was announced in New Zealand in 1961. With its competitive price it was planned to cater for the smaller farm unit as well as helping to meet the need for a second tractor on larger farms. It became a valued addition to the tractor range.

Following the Super Major in 1962, an additional Dexta model was announced – the Super Dexta – but too late to affect the 1962 tractor sales figures in New Zealand. Although tractors were still subject to import licensing the competition was strong.

For 1962 Ferguson just retained the unit sales lead with 1,120 units, Fordson sales were 1,112, International 657, David Brown 594 and Nuffield 348. That year the highest number of units sold by a Ford dealer was 62, an impressive total even by 1974 standards.

COLOUR CHANGE

In 1963, Fordson tractors were accepted as being painted in Fordson blue, with orange wheels. The 'New Look', announced in October 1963, incorporated a new blue-grey colour scheme for the entire Fordson range.

The basic colour remained Fordson blue, but wheels, fenders, seat, radiator grille and headlights were in light grey.

Concurrent with the New Look introduction, engine power on the Super Dexta was increased to 44.5bhp. Headlights on all models were set into the grille of the

The new small 32hp Fordson Dexta was an instant hit in 1958.

tractor, whereas in the past they had been mounted on the outside of the radiator cowling.

Final changes occurred on the Super Major at this time. Increased PTO horsepower, a double acting top link, and a double action clutch for the live PTO completed the Fordson Super Major line.

POST-WAR INDUSTRIAL EQUIPMENT

THE PELICAN

As farming got under way after the Second World War, the demand for bulk fertiliser and lime increased enormously. Handlers were faced with the problem of unloading railway trucks. Bulk fertiliser was loaded in the old type LA trucks and to unload these the central door was removed. A front-end loader then unloaded the central area of the wagon through the opening. When this was removed it was then necessary to hand-shovel the contents of both ends of the wagon into the centre for the front-end loader.

Max Snook and his Sockburn team had a close look at this and wondered whether it would be possible to produce some means of unloading from over the top of the wagon:

"I knew a Mr H G Cross who manufactured foundry coke in Christchurch. The coal for his coke came into a siding at the factory in LA wagons and was unloaded into bins from an overhead gantry using a special clamshell bucket. He held the patent on this.

"With some misgivings, I suggested we use this bucket mounted on a jib and fitted to the rear of the tractor, thereby reducing front axle loading and increasing traction on the rear wheels.

"He agreed and after some trials and problems, No. 1 clamshell loader, aptly named the Pelican, was produced.

"Our first public demonstration was held in the railway yards at Leeston. This drew a big crowd and on that first morning, local contractors ordered two units. We found we could handle four tons in five minutes from wagon to truck and, of course, this was a great selling point.

"Little did we realise that morning that we would still be selling the Pelican in 1974 with over 240 sales throughout New Zealand to date.

"Over the years the unit has been modified and developed to suit confined areas and speed up handling.

"The slewing model with extending jib overcame the necessity of having to drive the tractor back and forth to unload and so reduced loading time.

"With the phasing out of the E27 model, the Pelican was modified and fitted to the DDN series.

"A problem arose with the dry plate clutch as loader work called for constant use and 'riding' the clutch. We again experimented and overcame this by converting the clutch to a wet unit. So far, I would say we have carried out this modification some 300 times for a multitude of uses, besides giving details of this to other dealers to better overcome the problem.

"Enquiries came from all over New Zealand for the Pelican and we demonstrated at field days, machine fairs and to Government departments.

"I well remember demonstrating an early version to the Railways Department and coal merchants in the Wellington marshalling yards. It was necessary to drive along the Quay to get there and I created quite a stir driving this old girl through the heavy traffic, and was very relieved to arrive in one piece!

"At this time there was also a big demand for aerial sowing and this again presented problems with the loading of aircraft. Once again the Pelican was modified and a special loader bucket replaced the clamshell and worked successfully.

"The Pelican clamshell and aircraft loaders were exhibited at the Canterbury A & P Shows and were awarded Gold and Silver medals for units contributing most to helping in this field."

TRENCHING

Sockburn Motors scored another success with their development of the 'Socmote' Trencher. Designed to fit Ford tractors, it was constructed largely from readily available Ford parts. Robust design and construction contributed to its outstanding reliability.

Leading on from the experience gained in such equipment, in September 1974 Sockburn Motors announced a successor, the hydraulically driven 'Impact' Trenching Machine, which is built round the Ford 3550 Industrial tractor.

When digging, the tractor is driven by

a hydraulic motor and gear reduction box so that its speed can be varied from zero up to 30 feet per minute.

The fully hydraulic-powered trencher can dig trenches from five inches to 10 inches wide and up to five feet deep. With no mechanical drives, gearbox or bevel gear drives, the trencher is readily adjustable to the prevailing digging conditions, thus providing a very high safety factor and reducing overall wear and maintenance to a minimum.

The first units have been sold and the modern design, together with their practical experience, will keep Sockburn Motors Limited to the fore in this field.

The growth in the industrial applications of tractors has been phenomenal. In this review, it is impossible to do more than skim the surface.

LOADERS AND DIGGERS

A number of companies have specialised in producing industrial attachments for tractors. In addition to those already mentioned, the most common are the front-end loaders, rear or side mounted diggers, (backhoes), grader blades and fork-lift truck applications. Well known manufacturers of these items include Belcher Built Equipment Ltd, Massey Engineering Co. Ltd, Lees Industrial Ltd, David Taylor Hydraulics Ltd, Tractor Equipment Co Ltd, Trackweld Ltd, and CWF Hamilton & Co Ltd.

Thanks to the development of the diesel-engined tractor and the many refinements to its hydraulics, tractors are well established in many industrial and contracting applicators. Ford tractors have retained their very large share of this specialised market and recent moves helped to improve their share even more.

INDUSTRIAL TRACTORS

The introduction to New Zealand of the Ford 4500 Industrial tractor in 1969 enabled buyers to choose from a much wider range of industrial type tractor-mounted equipment. Equipped with the same diesel engine as the 4000, the 4500 was sold in New Zealand with torque converter transmission. In applications such as loading which requires numerous forward/backward movements, the torque converter enables a great saving in time.

Prior to the introduction of the 4500 and in many uses still, the Ford 5000 was the main industrial workhorse,

In 1973, Ford introduced the 50 hp Diesel 3550 Industrial tractor. This uses the same engine as the Ford 3000 tractor. Like the 4500, it is supplied from Britain. Models sold in New Zealand have dual range transmission giving six forward speeds and four reverse speeds through a manually operated shuttle-type transmission that is designed for loader work.

This 3550, the latest in the New Zealand industrial tractor field, will help keep this important part of the tractor market very much alive.

THE PAST 10 YEARS

By 1964 production of tractors from

On display at the Christchurch A & P Show in 1969, the new Ford tractors had 10 base models in various sizes to choose from.

This smaller Ford County 4004 4WD has dual water ballasted rear wheels, and was very useful in adverse conditions for towing feed trailers on farms.

Ford in Britain and the United States had well exceeded 3,000,000 and Ford was then, as now, the world's largest tractor and vehicle maker. It was with considerable anticipation that over 5,000 selected dealers from all over the world, including 20 from New Zealand, were taken to New York in November 1964 for the dealer introduction of the new Ford tractors at Radio City.

FORD TRACTORS

The Ford 2000, 3000, 4000 and 5000 tractors were introduced to New Zealand in March 1965, and bring this review up to the present. The modern looking all-new

tractors brought the Dexta, Super Dexta, Major and Super Major model names into one worldwide range referred to as the 6X range. Fordson was dropped and Ford became the tractor brand.

In line with the new model, new production procedures were employed and different parts of the tractors were made in various countries, thus making a truly international tractor. It was designed also as an interchangeable range because more than 40 percent of the parts are common to each tractor.

In addition to the new over-square engines, a hydraulically shifted

This tiny Ford 1200, seen spraying vines, was designed for horticultural use. It was fully equipped and had 4WD.

transmission was offered as an option on the 3000, 4000, and 5000 tractors. The Select-O-Speed transmission enabled the driver to change gear on the move and offered a choice of 10 forward and two reverse gears. The possible fuel savings, time savings and longer engine life as a result of no clutch, no stop, gear changes plus the simple selection of the correct gears for each job was a big selling feature.

Tractors fitted with Select-0-Speed were sold in considerable numbers. Unfortunately, problems arose with a few of the first of these transmissions and the ill repute so gained took some time to overcome, but for most users Select-0-Speed was a boon.

Sales of the new tractors met with ready response from the tractor-buying public. However, all was not plain sailing – supply and production delays, improved models by competitors, and import licensing made the dealers' selling task more difficult. The problems were not insurmountable of course. In 1966 the Ford market penetration percentage was 24 percent in March that year, but swept steadily upwards to record more than 40 percent of the market in the latter months.

Progress continued and in August 1968, a new updated range of Ford 2000, 3000, 4000 and 5000 tractors was brought out. These improved tractors are referred to as the 6Y range and are those sold in New Zealand at present. Changes at that time included the up-rating of the 4000 from 56 horsepower to 62hp and the 5000 from 67hp to 77hp.

In the agricultural tractor range there has been an increasing trend towards higher-powered tractors. In some cases the cost of extra horsepower is outweighed by the ability either to pull a heavier implement (perhaps an extra furrow on a plough) or to use existing equipment and travel faster.

High-speed farming is growing and to cater for it the Ford 7000 tractor was introduced in 1973. Equipped with a 256 cubic inch, 83 horsepower turbocharged diesel engine and 8 speed transmission, it is also supplied with what Ford claims is 'the greatest advance in tractor hydraulics since the 3-point hitch the Load Monitor draft control system'. This is a device that monitors the torque in the tractor's main driveline between transmission and the rear axle. When torque changes, the system operates quickly to effectively maintain the correct draft, not only with fully mounted and semi-mounted implements, but also with trailed implements. A further move in this direction is evidenced by the recent introduction of the Ford 8600 tractor of 116hp.

Thus Ford has equipped dealers in New Zealand to offer the agricultural community a range of six basic tractors to meet the challenges of the seventies, a far cry from the famous Fordson of the 1920s.

SAFETY FRAMES

Max Snook and Hutchinson Motors were early in the field with research into tractor safety frames. "We worked in closely with Lincoln College from the early days of their entry into the agricultural engineering field," said Mr Snook.

"The late Mr A W Ridolls, a lecturer in engineering at the college, was the driving force in this area and he fought hard for an agricultural engineering research institute at the college.

"Through discussions with him and Mr C Crosbie, engineer for the Department of Agriculture, Christchurch, it was obvious that legislation covering tractor safety would be introduced.

"Some early experimental work with our assistance had been carried out with safety frames for our tractors. Two frames for Fordson Majors were imported from Sweden with the right to manufacture under licence in New Zealand.

"There was a lot of opposition from farmers and various organisations who claimed that frames were not necessary, that they worked on flat country, that the frame would impede the operator's movements and so on. However, we went ahead and produced a simple 2-poster.

"Working in conjunction with the engineering institute, we used an old tractor and conducted a live test on hill country rolling the tractor over 30 times. From this we developed the 'Safe T' safety frame fitted with impact discs also developed from tests.

"By the time legislation was introduced in 1970, we had a full range of 'Safe T' frames for all model Ford tractors, including the old E27N and DDN series.

Parts of Southland are off the beaten track. Peter Tait and Pat Cody delivered this County 1124 tractor with winch and dozer blade to Cecil Peak Station in 1970. At Kingston wharf, the wheels and blade were removed, making it light enough for the Earnslaw *boat crane to lift it aboard. It was later reassembled further up Lake Wakatipu.*

Ford County tractors were large and heavy enough to give more traction. This impressive 754 model is towing a massive trailer load of aluminium sows. It was fitted with a bulldozer blade for use in emergencies at the Tiwai Point smelter.

"We know of two lives saved with our frames and we feel we have at least some satisfaction for our efforts. Today frames are held in Auckland for quick despatch to North Island centres and in Christchurch for the South Island."

THE FUTURE

Tractor reliability has been established, hydraulics are efficient and simple to operate. It would seem that for a country such as New Zealand, the agricultural tractor will continue to grow in importance. Operator comfort and convenience, already good, is bound to advance. Air-conditioning and stereo equipment are popular extras amongst tractor users in the United States so the advent of 'pop tunes while you plough' may be near for tractor operators in New Zealand. Ford makes larger horsepower tractors overseas. Perhaps some of these will be sold here as the market requires them, a fact which Ford would greet happily as for many years Ford tractors have been leaders in the 50hp plus class and, with their dealers, obviously intend to remain as such.

Three new tractor manufacturing plants in Brazil, Turkey and in the United States are opening in 1974, and will produce at least 40,000 more tractors annually to supplement the main Ford tractor production at the Basildon plant in England. This will help alleviate tractor shortages, which have been felt keenly in the past year.

In New Zealand, CMC has continued its policy of up-dating its companies'

premises and training staff to make the most of the products available from Ford for the benefit of all concerned – manufacturer, dealer, the tractor buyer and user and thereby the country. At the end of 1973, a total of 264,430 tractors of all makes were registered plus many more which are not registered as they never travel on public roads.

It is reasonable to conclude that Ford tractors have been a major factor in our economic well being – and that they will continue so in the future.

The Ford name has now changed to New Holland, and Southland Tractors is the only subsidiary company still selling tractors. Operations manager, John Scott (right), is one of New Zealand's top salesmen and the company, one of the top tractor dealers.

New Zealand agriculture drifted in the 1970s with the world energy crisis and the effects of Britain's entry to the European Common Market and New Zealand government policies. In industry, many new manufacturers entered the market, making highly specialised equipment. Tractor sales declined from 1975 as many farmers shed labour and used contractors for much of their seasonal work.

Ford, in their wisdom, decided to amalgamate their tractor division with New Holland and Fiat, and in 1988 sold their interests in tractors worldwide, to concentrate their resources on the production of cars and trucks.

Today, only one subsidiary, Southland Tractors Ltd, sells tractors. They operate in conjunction with Macaulay Motors at Invercargill, servicing Southland province, a major cropping area.

Two of Fonterra's new Foden Alpha 8x4 units towing 4 axle trailers, which have Caterpillar C12 450hp engines and 18 speed Roadranger gearboxes, carting 42,000 litres of milk each.

DAF CF 8x4 430hp curtainsider B trains of TNL Transport have 50 tonne ratings.

CHAPTER THIRTYTWO

THE PACCAR CONNECTION – SOUTHPAC TRUCKS LTD MANUKAU CITY

Southpac Trucks started trading on January 1 1994, but negotiations on its new ownership and structure had been going on for several months. The previous company, South Pacific Trucks, was a subsidiary of Carter Holt Harvey whose main business was timber, forestry and paper. Carter Holt Harvey was taken over by International Paper, which decided in February 1993 that South Pacific Trucks was not a core part of their business and should be sold.

South Pacific Trucks was New Zealand agent for Foden and Kenworth trucks, selling about 90 custom-built trucks a year, and providing the parts and service back-up for owners. The company operated from a workshop and parts facility in Wiri Station Road at Manukau City. The suppliers, PACCAR Inc based at Seattle in the United States, became involved in finding a replacement for its franchise.

Vance Bingham and Dave Cast from PACCAR Inc, together with Joe Rizzo and Harry Samson from PACCAR Australia, conducted interviews in Auckland to find interested parties to take on the franchise. Vance Bingham recalls that after they advertised for expressions of interest, bidders were selected for these interviews. "There were six parties: other suppliers, transport operators, another sales company, a team from South Pacific, and Colonial Motor Company, and we gave each party an opportunity to submit their interest and reasons for wanting the franchise.

"Initially we discarded Colonial, because they needed a cab over (forward control) replacement for the Hino-Ford trucks that were no longer available, and they also handled Ford Louisville which was a competitor to Kenworth and we saw a conflict with this.

"At the time we recognised there was a core team of people at South Pacific who, we thought, were a key to the future continuity of the franchise, and they had a good business plan. Colonial were primarily interested in Foden, but we wanted the two makes to be kept together.

"From past experience, we really didn't want transport operators involved with the franchise. After reflection on the interviews, we thought the team at South Pacific probably wouldn't have the financial backing on their own, but asked them and Colonial to come back in a month with a firmer proposal. It worked, and Southpac Trucks was formed."

In the interim, Carter Holt co-operated by retaining some key people on the payroll, although a number were made redundant and found alternative jobs. When the new company was formed, a number returned.

Southpac Trucks Ltd was set up as the main New Zealand distributor, with five sales agents and 10 parts and service agents. The leased premises of South Pacific Trucks at Manukau City was taken over and the parts stock and service operation transferred. There were 15 people on the staff, with Mike Corliss the CEO.

With all the key people in place, Southpac Trucks' first task was to consolidate their sales distribution, and service and parts sub-agents. From Mike Corliss' perspective, customer service was the most important driving factor for the new company. Ten, and later two more, parts and service agents were appointed to make a national chain of 'ALLRIG' dealers, responsible for supporting all PACCAR products in New Zealand. By dialling a single 24 hour access number, breakdown and parts service customers are directed to the nearest ALLRIG dealer, who has a person and vehicle on standby, ready to assist the Kenworth, Foden or DAF owner.

Ford NZ was advised early in the negotiations, and agreed that the new company could be part of CMC, provided it was seen as separate and did not compromise any of the Ford operations. Because three of the CMC Group

MIKE CORLISS

Mike Corliss, now on 12 months health leave, was the founding CEO.

Mike Corliss grew up in the heavy truck industry in Christchurch, where his father was sales manager for International Trucks, and later truck manager of Canterbury Farmers, who were Bedford agents. He became a fitter/welder with Canterbury Transport Engineering, before taking an adult apprenticeship with Andrews and Beavan as fitter and turner. He then joined the Andrews and Beavan drawing office and completed his NZCE(Mech). In 1986 he joined Specialist Transport Equipment (STE) in Christchurch who were Foden sales agents.

Mike Corliss went to Australia for further experience, where he worked for Caterpillar and later as regional sales manager for Freightliner and Mercedes-Benz trucks. He returned in late 1992 to manage South Island sales of Foden and Kenworth for South Pacific Trucks. When Carter Holt Harvey announced their intention to quit trucks, he expressed interest, along with Maarten Durent and Steve Slipper. When Southpac was formed, Mike Corliss became a key shareholder in the new company with Colonial Motor Company and, with his wide experience in heavy trucks, the logical person to be CEO.

companies were involved, three new entities were formed to handle sales: South Auckland Trucks Ltd at Manukau City, Fagan Trucks Ltd at Masterton and Timaru Trucks Ltd at Timaru. Each of the three Ford dealerships was also handling Ford Louisville. The other two independent sales agents were: Continental Heavy Commercials (CHC) under Dave Parsons at Manukau City; and K W Trucks at Rotorua under Kevin Wells.

At the time, a number of PACCAR trucks were entering New Zealand as parallel imports, and being converted to right hand drive. PACCAR was not happy with this, believing it would undermine the New Zealand agent. They decided to take legal action to stop infringement of their franchise (intellectual property). Parallel imports slowed immediately, and have now almost ceased. Other imports from Europe were generally poorly specified, and thus non-competitive.

After a shakedown period, Southpac Trucks progressed well with sales of trucks and parts growing rapidly. A Kenworth Roadshow was mounted in early 1995 and toured New Zealand, promoting the company and PACCAR products. Customer goodwill and acceptance was very high and Southpac soon found they were way ahead of their budget forecasts.

This growth continued, with a spectacular first year result which highlighted the urgent need to find more space. After looking at other options, it was decided that 96 Wiri Station Road was the best location. There were negotiations with the owners, and the head lease for the whole building was taken over in April 1997.

Extensive refurbishment plans were drawn up by Paul Goldsmith Architects and, five months later, when Southpac was offered the option of buying the building, this was taken up by Colonial Motor Company. The building was leased back to Southpac, safeguarding CMC's position, a standard policy with most subsidiaries. The builders moved in and the barn shed was transformed into a much more attractive and functional operation.

Each PACCAR brand has its own market niche and customer following, and Southpac have worked hard to maintain this individuality and brand following.

Kenworth has an enduring reputation for being tough and reliable, both on and off road. Built to cope with Australian conditions, it is regarded as the premier quality custom-built heavy truck in Australasia. Owners can build in unique detail specifications to their own requirements, and as Kenworth say – 'quality doesn't cost money, it saves money'.

Foden was bought by PACCAR in 1981, after the Foden works in England were liquidated, following the loss of a large

Maarten Durent, new CEO and former national parts manager, with Vance Bingham, PACCAR export sales manager, discuss engine re-powering options at the truck rebuild centre.

military contract when the new British government reneged. The truck factory was being rebuilt on the outskirts of Sandbach at the time, and PACCAR completed the new assembly line as if it were for Kenworths. Slowly the brand has been re-established as the premium English cab over custom-built truck brand, using top quality driveline components.

When DAF Trucks at Eindhoven, Holland, was up for sale in 1995, PACCAR bid for the medium and heavy truck division of this very successful European truck manufacturer. PACCAR did not want to merge the Foden and DAF brands, believing that while companies would not compete they would retain their current market stances, and it was decided to share manufacturing opportunities to achieve economic gains. As a result, DAF now make the distinctive Foden Alpha cabs by adapting a medium DAF cab. These are

Original staff members: Matt Lamb, new national parts manager; Richard Gordon, Foden product manager; and Maarten Durent in the main parts warehouse.

A classic bonneted Kenworth T904 620hp Cummins Signature 6x4 tractor unit and multi axle low loader, with a GCW of 130 tonnes, belonging to Durhams in Christchurch.

shipped to Sandbach, and save Foden considerable cost, as well as reducing the DAF cab manufacturing unit cost.

DAF, which marketed their trucks in New Zealand in the late 1980s for a short period, is unlike other PACCAR affiliates and makes all its own engines and most of the driveline. DAF engineers visited the country to study the requirements, and are now building standard New Zealand specified models for several applications, but they are not custom-built like Foden and Kenworth.

Any truck is only as good as its back-up service and, in keeping this at the top level, Southpac added support staff as volumes increased. Dave Prosser arrived from Foden in UK and became fleet sales manager. He was well liked by customers and salesmen, providing a key link with Foden UK, but returned to England after only a short period. A new parts depot was established at Rotorua in 1998 to back up the service agent. Later, when Timaru Trucks decided to relinquish PACCAR in 1998, Southpac set up its own parts

Cameron Quarries bulk loading 29 tonnes of fertiliser into their new Foden Alpha 8x4 and trailer, which runs a Caterpillar C12 450hp engine.

Opzeeland operate several DAF CF 480hp 8x2 and 8x4 130m3 curtainsider B trains able to cart 27 tonnes of freight on line haul.

operation in Christchurch to back up South Island service agents, as they had done in Rotorua.

Several other moves occurred at the same time. When KW Trucks was taken over, South Auckland Trucks closed down, and Fagan Trucks sales operation was taken over. Most salesmen were absorbed by Southpac: Kevin Wells in Rotorua, Tom Kerr in Napier, Mark O'Hara in Masterton and Mike Gillespie in Timaru, and have become an integral part of Southpac at Manukau City. Kevin Wells was appointed fleet sales manager but, sadly, died a short time later. CHC Group, under Dave Parsons, cover sales in the upper North Island, and have shifted their operation from Wiri Station Road to Rosscommon Road beside the new Western Motorway.

Because the New Zealand market is relatively small in international terms, nobody designs trucks specifically for local conditions. Other countries have their own requirements, often very different from New Zealand's. Here, the regulated axle weight limits are very low to prevent damage to our inferior roading, together with a 44 tonne total weight limit for each unit.

Foden and Kenworth trucks can be custom-built to suit customer requirements and local conditions. This does not mean their factories will actually build exactly what you order, because they will not compromise their own standards, but once the local need is understood, they have become much more sympathetic.

As Mike Corliss says: "The problem we have here is that there is nobody building trucks specifically for our market. Australia builds trucks for its unique requirements, the same for the USA, the UK and Europe – they all have manufacturers designing and building trucks for their own domestic markets. Yet our environment makes unique demands. We cover quite long distances, not by Australian or American standards certainly, but significantly more than is typical in Europe; we have a small population, so not a lot of money has been spent on roading networks; and of course with all our rivers and streams, we have hundreds of rickety old bridges with their low axle load limits.

"As a result, we're unique in that we want to put a lot of axles on the road, but we don't want our rigs to weigh much. In Europe, logically, if you put more axles on a truck, it's because you want to load more weight on it. And so when we say to a maker in Europe, as we did when we were introducing DAF, 'We want an eight-wheeler to pull a four-axle trailer' they look at all the axles and say, 'It must be running at about 80 tonnes GCW'. 'No, we have all those axles because the government requires it, to reduce point loading.'

"So we end up with a truck with a lot of

Dave Tennant, national service manager, discussing details of a new truck with Aaron Headington, DAF product manager. Both have been with Southpac since day one.

axles, which means we can get away with comparatively light frame rails and suspension. We have a moderate weight limit of 44 tonnes, but we're carting it through hilly terrain, so we need a high engine output. On the other hand, we're not Africa or Australia, so there's no need for a tropical radiator system.

"The point is, because we don't have anybody who builds a truck specifically for our market, it's really good to be able to mix and match from what PACCAR has available, to try to come up with the right product for the particular applications. What we end up with you probably wouldn't find anywhere else in the world.

"When you can offer trucks to customers that are properly suited to New

Mike Lambert Ltd's Kenworth K104 500hp Caterpillar C15 8x4 logger and trailer, able to haul 44 tonnes on road, and 65 off road.

Zealand conditions it makes a large difference to their performance and efficient operation."

Getting the right truck specifications for a client is a good start to having a satisfied customer. Making sure the trucks keep performing to their potential requires dedication, and staff at Southpac are very carefully selected and trained. Many of the key people have been there for a long time. Maarten Durent, now CEO, was national parts manager and has been in truck parts since he started work. Dave Tennant is service manager and started as a Foden apprentice over 27 years ago.

So how has the company performed? In the 10 years it has been operating, more than 1,500 new trucks over 300 hp have been sold, a significant share of the extra heavy truck market. Annual volumes are now approaching 300 units. Service has expanded significantly, with service staff trebling. Parts sales have moved from $200,000 per month to more than $1.2 million. Staff numbers have grown from 15 to over 70. Forecasts of 10 years ago now look very conservative compared to the growth actually achieved.

And customers? Fonterra is now the largest Foden Alpha fleet owner in the world with over 140 units operating. Mike Lambert Ltd has over 100 Kenworth trucks carting wood, Pacific Haulage nearly 50 units. Mike Corliss has led several customer tour groups to visit PACCAR factories and suppliers in the US, UK, Europe and Australia.

Southpac Trucks say that they aim to supply customers with the most cost effective solutions to their transport needs, whether it be parts, service or truck sales. Mike Corliss says: "If our customers are successful, we're successful." The increasing presence of Kenworth, Foden and DAF trucks on our roads is testament to the success of Southpac Trucks.

Kauriland Tanker on a Foden Alpha 8x4, with Cat C12 430hp engine, fitted with ABS braking, and used with a 4 axle trailer tank for rural delivery.

Original staff of Southpac Trucks in January 1994. From left: Alie Boxem, Beville Johnston, Maarten Durent, not known, Matt Lamb, Kevin Smith, Aaron Headington, Dave Tennant, Richard Gordon, Steve Slipper, Mike Corliss, Nicky Holden.
Absent: Patrick Howard and Ken –.

Southpac staff, 2004. From left: Glen Harvey, Sean Gilbert, Terry Carter, Matt Drayson, Carl Forbes, John Jones, Damian Hooper, Allan Kaiuha, Bill Wheeler, Noel Bloem, Bob Kitcher, Steve Buckley, Vaughan Brophy, Dave Tennant, Shane Mitchell, Dave Woods, Bob Bridgette, Dave Anderson, Brian Tennant, Steven Waldek, Vincent Alexander, Errol Riley, Maarten Durent, Mike Corliss, Frances Piper, Tracey Proffitt, Matt Lamb, Marc Linstrom, Janet Bridgette, Hayden Balfour-Bary, Gail Reeve, Glenda Lowe, Justin Wheeler, James Hemphill, Phil Erceg, Jansen Godsmark, Justin Woodcock, Paul Morgan, Mitchell Corliss and Luwayne Lowe. Another 17 were away.

THE APPENDICES

*One of America's big moments – the arrival of the Model T Ford in 1908
– as depicted by artist Norman Rockwell.*

Reproduced from The Ford Road, 1903-1978 *by Lorin Sorensen.*

CONSUMERS PRICE INDEX (CPI)

The reader may wish to compare historical prices against 2000 values. This can be done simply by dividing the historical price by the index for that year. i.e. a Model T cost £205 in 1912 – therefore its approximate comparative price in 1999 is £205 ÷ 0.018 = £11389 ($= 11,389 x 2 = $22,778). If you then compare what you got with what you would get today, it will give a value guide; however not all things are equal, due to taxes, quality, and changed methods – apples are not oranges.

YEAR	INDEX	CHANGE	YEAR	INDEX	CHANGE	YEAR	INDEX	CHANGE
			1921	0.034	3.0	1961	0.067	1.4
			1922	0.031	-8.8	1962	0.069	3.3
			1923	0.030	-3.2	1963	0.071	1.9
			1924	0.031	3.3	1964	0.073	3.0
			1925	0.031	0	1965	0.075	3.6
			1926	0.031	0	1966	0.078	3.3
			1927	0.031	0	1967	0.083	6.4
STATS.			1928	0.031	0	1968	0.086	3.6
START.			1929	0.031	0	1969	0.090	5.2
			1930	0.030	-3.2	1970	0.095	5.2
1891	0.015	0	1931	0.028	-7.8	1971	0.106	11.0
1892	0.015	0	1932	0.026	-8.1	1972	0.113	7.4
1893	0.015	0	1933	0.024	-5.1	1973	0.122	7.6
1894	0.015	0	1934	0.025	2.0	1974	0.134	10.0
1895	0.015	0	1935	0.025	2.8	1975	0.154	14.9
1896	0.015	0	1936	0.026	2.5	1976	0.181	17.7
1897	0.015	0	1937	0.028	7.4	1977	0.207	14.0
1898	0.016	6.7	1938	0.029	3.5	1978	0.232	12.3
1899	0.015	--6.7	1939	0.030	3.4	1979	0.261	12.4
1900	0.016	6.7	1940	0.031	4.7	1980	0.308	17.9
1901	0.016	0	1941	0.033	3.9	1981	0.354	15.1
1902	0.017	6.2	1942	0.033	2.6	1982	0.415	17.0
1903	0.016	--6.2	1943	0.034	2.6	1983	0.449	8.3
1904	0.017	6.2	1944	0.035	2.0	1984	0.470	4.7
1905	0.016	-6.2	1945	0.036	1.3	1985	0.548	16.6
1906	0.017	6.2	1946	0.036	1.0	1986	0.605	10.4
1907	0.018	5.6	1947	0.036	0.9	1987	0.720	18.9
1908	0.018	0	1948	0.040	10.6	1988	0.766	6.3
1909	0.017	-5.6	1949	0.040	1.1	1989	0.800	4.4
1910	0.018	5.6	1950	0.042	5.0	1990	0.861	7.6
1911	0.017	--5.6	1951	0.047	11.1	1991	0.885	2.8
1912	0.018	5.6	1952	0.051	8.6	1992	0.894	1.0
1913	0.018	0	1953	0.053	4.1	1993	0.905	1.3
1914	0.019	5.3	1954	0.057	5.9	1994	0.915	1.1
1915	0.021	10.5	1955	0.058	2.3	1995	0.957	4.6
1916	0.022	4.8	1956	0.059	2.6	1996	0.976	2.0
1917	0.024	8.3	1957	0.061	2.8	1997	0.987	1.1
1918	0.027	11.1	1958	0.062	2.3	1998	1.004	1.7
1919	0.030	11.1	1959	0.066	5.7	1999	1.000	-0.4
1920	0.033	10.0	1960	0.066	0.4	2000	1.053	2.0

The Rouse & Hurrell Carriage Building Company Ltd was formed on 12 August 1902, and became The Colonial Motor Company Ltd, on 15 August 1911.

Directors, General Managers and Secretaries

	DIRECTORS	APPOINTED	RETIRED	
*	Henry Arthur Hurrell	28 Aug 1902	1908	
	William Murphy	28 Aug 1902	1908	
	Edward Wade Petherick	28 Aug 1902	1909	
	James Ranson	28 Aug 1902	27 Jul 1908	sold to Meadows
+	Francis Sidey	28 Aug 1902	1909	
	Thomas Bevan Jnr.	28 Aug 1902	27 Jul 1908	sold to Meadows
+	Alexander Veitch	12 Sep 1902	1912	
+	Charles Boyd Norwood	29 May 1905	17 Oct 1913	went to Dominion Motors
+	Frederick N R Meadows	27 Jul 1908	27 Mar 1936	
	R Pearson	27 Jul 1908	17 Oct 1913	went to Dominion Motors
	Dr William E Collins	21 Oct 1912	10 Apr 1918	
*	Charles Corden Larmour	21 Oct 1912	12 Dec 1918	
	Michael Myers	2 Dec 1913	25 Mar 1926	
* +	Hopeful Barnes Gibbons	26 Apr 1918	9 Dec 1955	died aged 73
+	Hopeful Gibbons	21 Mar 1919	9 Jun 1947	died aged 91
* +	Robert Barnes Gibbons	16 Dec 1919	26 Jul 1973	died aged 84
+	Alfred Barnes Gibbons	16 Dec 1919	16 Nov 1961	died aged 76
	Norman Barnes Gibbons	25 Mar 1926	Sep 1950	died aged 63
	Frederick Hills Johnston	27 Mar 1936	30 Apr 1962	
	J M McLean	25 Mar 1931	18 Mar 1947	died aged 91
	Ormond Hutchinson	1 May 1947	12 Nov 1975	
	Fredrick Norman Gibbons	May 1948	14 Nov 1984	
	Alfred Barton Gibbons	1 Mar 1951	18 Nov 1980	
+	Gordon Hope Gibbons	26 Sep 1956	18 Nov 1992	
* +	Peter Craig Gibbons	26 Sep 1956	29 Nov 1995	
	Leslie Claude Gladding	16 Feb 1962	31 May 1979	
+	Gerald Barton Gibbons	1 May 1962	8 Dec 1983	
	Donald Sinclair Mullan	1 May 1962	7 Feb 1973	
	Colin John Cliff	1 Apr 1970	21 Nov 1990	
	C Lennox Henderson	7 Feb 1973	11 Nov 1981	
+	Ormond A Hutchinson	12 Nov 1975	1 Oct 2000	died aged 70
	Michael Hume Gibbons	20 Jun 1979	18 Oct 1995	resigned – sold to GPG
	C John Emery	18 Nov 1980	21 Nov 2002	
	WD (Bill) McLaren	11 Nov 1981	18 Nov 1989	
	John Greville Gibbons	8 Dec 1983	18 Oct 1995	resigned – sold to GPG
+	John Alexander Wylie	14 Nov 1984		
	PA (Pat) Cody	15 Nov 1989	25 Nov 1995	
	John A Blyth	21 Nov 1990		
	James Picot Gibbons	18 Nov 1992		
	AI (Tony) Gibbs (GPG)	18 Oct 1995	1 Oct 1997	GPG
*	Graeme Durrad Gibbons	29 Nov 1995		
	Maurice W Loomes (GPG)	29 Nov 1995	1 Oct 1997	GPG
	Gary H Weiss (GPG)	29 Nov 1995	1 Jul 1998	GPG
	C K Poh (Sun Motors, MBM)	1 Oct 1997	1 Jul 2003	MBM
	Dato' Rahim Halim (Sun Motors, MBM)	1 Oct 1997	1 Jul 2003	MBM
	Peter D Wilson	1 Jul 1998		
	Ian D Lambie	21 Nov 2002		

+ served as Chairman
* served as Managing Director

Article 76 added to Company Articles on 15 Nov 1979 stating Directors to retire at age 70

GENERAL MANAGERS	APPOINTED	RETIRED
Frederick Hills Johnston	18 Oct 1918	31 May 1936
Leslie H Clarke	19 May 1950	31 Jan 1960
Peter V Cederman	1 Feb 1961	29 Feb 1980
Graeme Durrad Gibbons	1 Sep 1987	30 Jun 1990
A Grant Daniel	1 Sep 1992	

SECRETARY	APPOINTED	RETIRED
Arthur Wade Petherick	12 Aug 1902	11 May 1909
Charles Corden Larmour	11 May 1909	10 Apr 1918
Hopeful Barnes Gibbons	10 Apr 1918	16 Dec 1919
Frederick Hills Johnston	16 Dec 1919	31 May 1936
Raphael Vincent Jones	31 Jul 1936	16 Oct 1936
R W (Pat) Stewart	16 Oct 1936	31 Jan 1961
H F (Frank) Perkins	1 Feb 1961	31 May 1964
W J Calder	1 Jun 1964	31 Dec 1966
C J L (Jim) Flannery	1 Jan 1967	31 May 1974
Maxwell L Caigou	1 Jun 1974	13 Nov 1996
Visteurs Altments	14 Nov 1996	20 Sep 1998
J G (Jack) Tuohy	21 Sep 1998	

11/11/2004

Colonial Motor Company Group Subsidiary Managers

NAME	COMPANY	Date	Left	Remarks
Auckland branch mgr	Universal Motor Co	1 Jan 1920	28 Feb 1925	Separate Manager appt
Col H E Avery	Ford Sales & Service (Wlgton) Ltd	Feb 1923	1936	Resigned - to Army HQ
John G Phillips	Ford Motors(Dunedin) Ltd	May 1923	Nov 1926	resigned
George Duncalf	Ford Motors (Canterbury) Ltd	May 1925	Jun 1934	retired
John E Hunt	Standard Motor Bodies Ltd Wlg	Sep 1925	Mar 1962	died
R M (Tex) Rickard	Universal Motors Ltd, Auckland	1 Mar 1925	31 Dec 1926	merged with JWAndrews
I E (Jack) Rawnsley	Ward & Rawnsley, Lower Hutt	Oct 1928	Jun 1935	resigned
Hector Brodie	Brodie Motors Ltd, Kaikohe	Aug 1930	Dec 1938	retired
G W Massingham	Ford Motors (Dunedin) Ltd	Dec 1927	Oct 1930	resigned
B Allison	Ford Motors (Dunedin) Ltd	Nov 1930	Mar 1933	resigned
J (Jim) Thornton	Northland Motors Ltd, Kaitaia	Jul 1931	May 1940	died
P S (Sid) Enting	Timaru Motors Ltd, Timaru	Jun 1931	May 1933	resigned
P F (Pat) Fagan	Fagan Motors Ltd, Masterton	Nov 1931	31 May 1966	retired
D S (Don) Mullan	Timaru Motors Ltd, Timaru	Jun 1933	Dec 1970	retired
L Napier	Napier Motors Ltd, Dunedin	1934	Aug 1936	retired
O (Orm) Hutchinson	Ford Motors (Canterbury) Ltd, Chch	Jun 1934	Nov 1975	retired
J (Jim) Craik	Craik Motors Ltd, Te Awamutu	Dec 1934	Mar 1948	resigned
J V (Jack) Stevens	Stevens Motors Ltd, Lower hutt	1Feb 1935	1942?	retired
Roy E Hawke	Hawke Motors Ltd, Te Aroha	Mar 1936	31 Dec 1948	retired
W A (Bill) Fraser	Avery Motors Ltd, Wellington	1936	Sep 1945	died
A C (Mac) McPherson	Napier Motors Ltd, Dunedin	Sep 1936	1969	retired
R U (Bob) Macaulay	Macaulay Motors Ltd, Invercargill	Dec 1935	1964	retired
J H (Jack) Manning	Colmoco Engineering, Ebor St,Wlg	Mar 1936	1962	retired
F M Cordery	Cordery Garage Ltd, Waipukurau	Nov 1938	1942?	retired
P L (Phil) Phillipps	Phillipps Motors Ltd, New Plymouth	Dec 1938	Jun 1968	retired
Harry (Fairy) Fairhall	Fairhall Motors Ltd, Kaikohe	Dec1938	6 Sep 1939	resigned
George M Fraser	Fairhall Motors Ltd, Kaikohe	6 Sep 1939	1940	called up
H Percy Ferguson	Northland Motors Ltd, Kaitaia	Aug 1940	1966	died
Ellis P Smith	Fairhall Motors Ltd, Kaikohe	Jul 1941	Jun 1950	tfr to Te Aroha
E F (Fred) Emmerson	Stevens Motors Ltd, Lower Hutt	1942?	Dec 1951	resigned
L E (Lou) Dodd	Cordery Garage Ltd, Waipukurau	1942?	Sep 1951	resigned
J A (Jack) McInnes	Avery Motors Ltd, Wellington	1945	31 Aug 1954	resigned
L H (Les) Clarke	Te Kuiti Motors Ltd, Te Kuiti	1946	Jan 1948	tfr to Te Aroha
L H (Les) Clarke	Hawke Motors Ltd, Te Aroha	Feb 1948	May 1950	tfr to CMC
W J (Jim) Ambler	Craik Motors Ltd, Te Awamutu	Mar 1948	Jul 1962	died
M W (Merv) Dineen	Te Kuiti Motors Ltd, Te Kuiti	Feb 1948	Oct 1962	tfr to Te Awamutu
G H (Don) Gibbons	Fairhall Motors Ltd, Kaikohe	Jun 1950	Sep 1956	tfr to Waipukurau
Ellis P Smith	Hawke Motors Ltd, Te Aroha	Jun 1950	1969	retired
J R (Jim) Haworth	Cordery Garage ltd, Waipukurau	23 Jul 1952	Sep 1956	resigned
C L (Lofty) Henderson	Stevens Motors Ltd, Lower Hutt	Aug 1954	Apr 1978	retired
L C (Les) Gladding	South Auckland Motors, Otahuhu	Sep 1954	Aug 1966	retired
George M Fraser	Avery Motors Ltd, Wellington	Jul 1956	Jun 1956	resigned
John R G Jack	Avery Motors Ltd, Wellington	Sep 1956	Jul 1958	resigned
G H (Don) Gibbons	Cordery Garage Ltd, Waipukurau	Sep 1956	Mar 1968	retired
J L (Jack) Harland	Fairhall Motors Ltd, Kaikohe	Jul 1958	1961	tfr to Wellington
Ian G Lyons	Avery Motors Ltd, Wellington	Mar1959	May 1964	resigned
H John Holder	Fairhall Motors Ltd, Kaikohe	Mar 1962	1965	tfr to New Lynn
Colin J Cliff	New Lynn Motors Ltd, New Lynn	Oct 1962	1985	retired
M W (Merv) Dineen	Craik Motors Ltd, Te Awamutu	Jul 1962	7 Oct 1969	died
T S (Trist) Atkins	Te Kuiti Motors Ltd, Te Kuiti	Aug 1962	Oct 1964	tfr to Panmure
Peter C Hunt	Standard Motor Bodies Ltd, Wlg	Mar 1962``	1969	resigned
T S (Trist) Atkins	Panmure Motors Ltd, Panmure	Jun 1964	1986	retired
N R (Norm) Shorter	Te Kuiti Motors Ltd, Te Kuiti	Jun 1964	1971	tfr to Johnsonville
W D (Bill) Maclaren	Macaulay Motors Ltd, Invercargill	30 Jun 1964	30 Sep 1988	retired
M L (Max) Caigou	Avery Motors Ltd, Wellington	30 Jun 1964	1973	to Secretary CMC
Barry C Wisneski	Fairhall Motors Ltd, Kaikohe	1965	1969	tfr to Morrinsville
Alan Hodges	Newlands Motors Ltd, Johnsonville	13 Jun 1965	Jan 1971	resigned
W A (Bill) Goss	Sockburn Motors Ltd, Christchurch	1 Sep 1965	31 Jan 1970	tfr to Hutchinson Mtrs
Randal J Thomson	Fagan Motors Ltd, Masterton	Jun 1966	Jan 1974	tf to Timaru
C John Emery	South Auckland Motors, Otahuhu	Aug 1966	Mar 1987	retired
A C (Alex) Trail	Northland Motors Ltd, Kaitaia	1967	1987	retired
David W Bodley	Cordery Garage Ltd, Waipukurau	Apr 1968	Nov 1969	tfr to Te Awamutu
Royce J Cox	Phillipps Motors Ltd, New Plymouth	Jun 1968	Oct 1984	retired
R G (Bob) Tunley	Standard Motor Bodies, Wellington	Jan 1969	1987	retired
W R (Bill) Blackburn	Napier Motors Ltd, Dunedin	Jun 1969	1981	died
Barry C Wisneski	Hawke Motors Ltd, Morrinsville	Oct 1969	Oct 1974	to CMC Int Auditor
David W Bodley	Craik Motors Ltd, Te Awamutu	Nov 1969	Jun 1993	retired

Colonial Motor Company Group Subsidiary Managers

NAME	COMPANY	Date	Left	Remarks
A Roger M Gardner	Ruahine Motors Ltd, Waipukurau	Nov 1969	Jan 1974	tfr to Masterton
A Ian Morgan	Fairhall Motors Ltd, Kaikohe	1969	1972	resigned
George Daniel	Sockburn Motors Ltd Christchurch	1 Feb 1970	1973	tfr to Wellington
Peter J Craig	Te Kuiti motors Ltd, Te Kuiti	Dec 1970	1974	tfr to Morrinsville
NR (Norm) Shorter	Newlands Motors Ltd	1971	Aug 1977	retired
W J (Wattie) Falloon	Timaru Motors Ltd, Timaru	1971	Oct 1973	died
Ian D Lambie	Fairhall Motors Ltd, Kaikohe	1Feb 1972	1 Feb 1977	tfr to Johnsonville
George Daniel	Avery Motors Ltd, Wellington	1973	31 Mar 1990	retired
Noel J Simons	Sockburn Motors Ltd, Christchurch	1973	31 Dec 1986	retired
OA (Orm) Hutchinson	Hutchinson Motors Christchurch	Nov 1973	30 Jun 1990	retired
Randal J Thomson	Timaru Motors Ltd, Timaru	Feb 1974	May 1978	tfr to Lower Hutt
A Roger M Gardner	Fagan Motors Ltd, Masterton	Feb 1974	31 Dec 1998	retired
Peter J Craig	Hawke Motors Ltd, Morrinsville	Aug 1974	Mar 1984	resigned
Brian P Willis	Te Kuiti Motors Ltd, Te Kuiti	Aug 1974	1980	resigned
K S (Ken) Mullan	Ruahine Motors Ltd, Waipukurau	Aug 1974	Mar 1984	tfr to Morrinsville
K Stuart Holm	Fairhall Motors Ltd, Kaikohe	Feb 1977	1978	resigned
Ian D Lambie	Newlands Motors Ltd, Johnsonville	Sep 1977	Sep 1981	tfr to Dunedin
Randal J Thomson	Stevens Motors Ltd, Lower Hutt	May 1978	Jan 1993	resigned
P A (Pat) Cody	Timaru Motors Ltd	May 1978	Apr 1990	tfr to Wellington
Richard J Kilkenny (act)	Fairhall Motors Ltd, Kaikohe	1980	1980	tfr to Wellington
Peter J Lloyd	Fairhall Motors Ltd, Kaikohe	1980	1984	tfr to New Plymouth
D J (Don) Hodgson	Te Kuiti Motors Ltd, Te Kuiti	Mar 1981	Dec 1984	tfr to Highland Park
Ian D Lambie	Napier Motors Ltd, Dunedin	Sep 1981	31 Jan 2003	retired
Richard J Kilkenny	Newlands Motors, Johnsonville	Sep 1981	31 Aug 1993	resigned
W J (Jack) Pearce	New Lynn Motors, New Lynn	Jun 1983	Mar 1989	tfr to Manukau City
K S (Ken) Mullan	Hawke Motors, Morrinsville	Mar 1984	1 Sep 1997	tfr CMC Internal Auditor
John A Blyth	Ruahine Motors Ltd, Waipukurau	April 1984	Dec 1986	tfr to Panmure
Peter J Lloyd	Phillipps Motors Ltd, New Plymouth	Nov 1984	Nov 1986	died
A Grant Daniel	Fairhall Motors Ltd, Kaikohe	Dec 1984	Mar 1987	tfr to Christchurch
Garry S Jackson	South Auckland Motors, ManukauC	6 May 1986	Mar 1990	resigned went to Ford
Neville W Goldsworthy	Te Kuiti Motors Ltd, Te Kuiti	Jan 1985	Jan 1987	tfr to Kaikohe/Kaitaia
John A Blyth	Panmure Motors Ltd, Panmure	Jan 1986	1 Mar 1999	to AAC merger
Paul A Jordan	Sockburn Motors Ltd, Christchurch	Jan 1986	Oct 1993	resigned
Trevor C Green	Highland Park Autos E Auckland	1 Mar 1987	30 Aug 1987	closed tfr to Panmure
Neville W Goldsworthy	Northland Motors Ltd, Kaitaia	Apr 1987	2001 closed	retired
J W (Jim) Robb	Ruahine Motors Ltd, Waipukurau	Feb 1987	Jan 1989	tfr to New Lynn
Russell J Lange	Phillipps Motors Ltd, New Plymouth	Apr 1987	31 Dec 1988	tfr to Christchurch
J P (Jim) Gibbons	Ruahine Motors Ltd, Waipukurau	Feb 1989	Sep 1992	tfr to New Plymouth
Neville W Goldsworthy	Fairhall Motors Ltd, Kaikohe	Apr 1987	Dec 1998 closed	retired
Alan C McElroy	Macaulay Motors Ltd, Invercargill	Oct 1988	Oct 1995	to Southland Tractors
A Grant Daniel	Phillipps Motors Ltd. New Plymouth	Dec 1989	14 Sep 1992	tfr to CMC Gen Mgr
W J (Jack) Pearce	South Auckland Motors, ManukauC	May 1990	31 Jul 1991	retired
PA (Pat) Cody	Avery Motors Ltd, Wellington	Apr 1990	Jun 1994	retired
Russell J Marr	Timaru Motors Ltd, Timaru	July 1990		
J W (Jim) Robb	New Lynn Motors, New Lynn	1 July 1990	1 Mar 1999	to AAC merger
Russell J Lange	Team Hutchinson Ford, Christch'ch	1 Jul 1990		
Matthew W Newman	South Auckland Motors, ManukauC	1 Aug 1991	1 Mar 1999	to AAC merger
J P (Jim) Gibbons	Phillipps Motors Ltd, New Plymouth	14 Sep 1992		
David W Tobin	Ruahine Motors Ltd, Waipukurau	2 Nov 1992	2 Nov 2001	died
Malcolm Davison	Stevens Motors Ltd, Lower Hutt	15 Jan 1993	Jul 1994	resigned
John W Luxton	Craik Motors Ltd, Te Awamutu	Aug 1993	Aug 1995	tfr to Invercargill
John Flanagan	Avon City Ford. Christchurch	Jan 1994	Jun 1998	tfr to Nelson
Ian J Duncan	Avery Motors Ltd, Wellington	May 1994	Dec 2001	resigned
S H (Steve) Hutchison	Stevens Motors Ltd, Lower Hutt	Sep 1994	May 1997	resigned
K S (Ken) Mullan (act)	Craik Motors Ltd, Te Awamutu	Sep 1995	Jan 1996 close	CMC Internal Auditor
John W Luxton	Macaulay Motors Ltd, Invercargill	Sep 1995	Aug 1998	tfr to Christchurch Sth
Alan C McElroy	Southland Tractors, Invercargill	Oct 1995	30 Jun 2001	resigned
John Flanagan	MS Motors (1998) Ltd, Nelson	1 Jul 1998		
John W Luxton	Avon City Ford, Christchurch	1 Jul 1998		
Grant N Price	Macaulay Motors Ltd, Invercargill	1 Jul 1998		
S W (Steve) Lyttle	Fagan Motors Ltd, Masterton	1 Jan 1999		
A Grant Daniel	Avery Motors Ltd, Wellington	Dec 2001		
Roger Taylor	Ruahine Motors Ltd, Waipukurau	Feb 2002	Jan 2003	tfr to Dunedin
Stuart B Gibbons	Stevens Motors Ltd, Lower Hutt	Feb 2002		
Roger Taylor	Dunedin City Ford, Dunedin	Jan 2003		
Hamish Jacob	Ruahine Motors Ltd, Waipukurau	Feb 2003		

FORD DEALERS & SERVICE AGENTS 1929
MAIN DEALERS HIGHLIGHTED

NORTH ISLAND		SOUTH ISLAND	
Auckland	**John W Andrew & Sons**	**Alexandra**	**Alexandra Motor Co**
	G A Haydon Ltd	**Ashburton**	**Ashburton Motors Ltd**
Cambridge	**Wikinson & Co**	**Balclutha**	**John H Stevenson Ltd**
Carterton	**Gordon Hughan Ltd**	**Blenheim**	**Lucas Bros Ltd**
Dannevirke	**W L Roberts & Co**	Cheviot	Cheviot Motor Eng Co Ltd
Dargaville	**Smith & Bradley**	**Christchurch**	**Ford Motors Canty Ltd**
Eketahuna	**Herbert's Ford Motor Co Ltd**	**Dunedin**	**Ford Motors (Dun) Ltd**
Eltham	**C C Stanners**	**Gore**	**David S Mackenzie Ltd**
Feilding	**Kingston Motors Ltd**	**Greymouth**	**Greymouth Motors Ltd**
Gisborne	**Bignell & Holmes**	**Invercargill**	**G W Woods & Co**
Hamilton	**Ford Sales & Service**	Kaikoura	P Curran
Hastings	J E Peach & Co Ltd	Lawrence	D W McIntosh
Hawera	**H R Kemp**	**Milton**	**Milton Motor Cycle Co**
Helensville	J F Lambert & Sons	**Nelson**	**G M Smart Ltd**
Inglewood	H Derby & Co Ltd	**Oamaru**	**Maude Bros Ltd**
Kaikohe	**Dalgety & Co Ltd**	Otautau	R Buchanan J
Kaitaia	**Northland Ford Service**	**Palmerston South**	**J F Warren**
Kawakawa	N H G Munro	**Ranfurly**	**Alex Smith & Co**
Levin	**J C Milnes**	**Rangiora**	**Johnston's Motor Co Ltd**
Lower Hutt	**Ward & Rawnsley Ltd**	Seddon	Lucas Bros Ltd
Marton	C A Rofe	**Temuka**	**A Halley**
Masterton	**Masterton Ford Motors Ltd**	**Timaru**	**Dunnett & Downey Ltd**
Matamata	D McL Wallace Ltd	**Waimate**	**Callender's Ltd**
Maungaturoto	Maungaturoto Dairy Co Ltd	**Westport**	**John Kilkenny Ltd**
Napier	**J E Peach & Co Ltd**	Winton	G W Woods & Co
New Plymouth	**H Derby & Co Ltd**		
Ohakune	Goe Sargeant		
Ohura	Kallil Motors		
Opotiki	A J Anderson		
Opunake	H Parkes & Co		
Otaki	J C Milnes		
Otorohanga	**Otorohanga Motors Ltd**		
Pahiatua	Herbert's Ford Motor Co Ltd		
Palmerston North	**Ford Motors Manawatu Ltd**		
Papakura	M J Dobbing		
Pukekohe	John W Andrew & Sons Ltd		
Rotorua	**Rotorua Ford Garage**		
Stratford	**Kleeman & Bishop Ltd**		
Taihape	**Austin Hayman**		
Taumarunui	**Ray Winger Ltd**		
Tauranga	**F N Christian & Co**		
Te Aroha	**D McL Wallace Ltd**		
Te Awamutu	**Ford Sales & Service**		
Te Kuiti	**Mackay & Jones Ltd**		
Te Puke	Bostock & Vercoe		
Thames	D McL Wallace Ltd		
Tokomaru Bay	Bignell & Holmes		
Waipawa	F R Furminger		
Waipukurau	**J L Braithwaite**		
Wairoa	**Wairoa Motor Garage Co Ltd**		
Wanganui	**Merewether Motor Co Ltd**		
Warkworth	**Civil's Garage**		
Wellington	**Ford Sales & Service Ltd**		
Whakatane	**Armstrong & Co**		
Whangarei	**Whangarei Engineering Co Ltd**		
Woodville	**R Munro**		

FORD DEALERS & SERVICE AGENTS 1936

DEALERS HIGHLIGHTED

NORTH ISLAND		SOUTH ISLAND	
Auckland	**John W Andrew & Sons**	**Alexandra**	**Alexandra Motor Co**
	G A Haydon Ltd	**Ashburton**	**Ashburton Motors Ltd**
Cambridge	**Wikinson & Co**	**Balclutha**	**John H Stevenson Ltd**
Carterton	**Gordon Hughan Ltd**	**Blenheim**	**Lucas Bros Ltd**
Dannevirke	**Huggins Motors Ltd**	Cheviot	Cheviot Motor Eng Co Ltd
Dargaville	**Smith's Garage**	**Christchurch**	**Hutchinson Motors Ltd**
Eketahuna	**Herbert's Motors Ltd**	Cromwell	Alexandra Motors Ltd
Eltham	**C C Stanners**	**Dunedin**	**Napier Motors Ltd**
Feilding	**Feilding Central Garage Ltd**	**Gore**	**A V Latty Ltd**
Gisborne	**Bignell & Holmes**	**Greymouth**	**Greymouth Motors Ltd**
Hamilton	**Armstrong Motors Ltd**	**Invercargill**	**Macaulay Motors Ltd**
Hastings	J E Peach & Co Ltd	Kaikoura	P Curran
Hawera	**H R Kemp**	Lawrence	Tuapeka Motors Ltd
Helensville	McLeod Motors	**Milton**	**Milton Motor Cycle Co**
Huntly	T Furniss	**Nelson**	**G M Smart Ltd**
Inglewood	H Derby & Co Ltd	**Oamaru**	**Maude Bros Ltd**
Kaikohe	**Brodie Motors Ltd**	Otautau	J H Mills & Co
Kaitaia	**Northland Motors Ltd**	**Palmerston South**	**J F Warren**
Levin	**Faloon Bros Ltd**	**Ranfurly**	**Alex Smith & Co**
Lower Hutt	**Stevens Motors Ltd**	**Rangiora**	**Johnston's Motor Co Ltd**
Marton	**Ward Motors Ltd**	Seddon	Lucas Bros Ltd
Masterton	**Fagan Motors Ltd**	**Temuka**	**A Halley**
Matakana	**Matakana Garage**	**Timaru**	**Timaru Motors Ltd**
Matamata		**Waimate**	**Canterbury Farmers CALtd**
Maungaturoto	Maungaturoto Dairy Co Ltd	**Westport**	**John Kilkenny Ltd**
Napier	**J E Peach & Co Ltd**	Winton	G W Woods & Co
New Plymouth	**Len Nicholls Motors Ltd**		
Ohakune	Geo Sargeant		
Ohura	Kallil Motors		
Opotiki	M O Kidd Ltd		
Opunake	Kleeman & Bishop Ltd		
Otaki	J C Milnes		
Otorohanga	**Otorohanga Motors Ltd**		
Pahiatua	Watts & Lawry Motors Ltd		
Palmerston North	**Selwyn Motors Ltd**		
Papakura	**M J Dobbing**		
Pukekohe	Stan Andrew Ltd Ltd		
Rotorua	**Rotorua Ford Garage**		
Stratford	**Kleeman & Bishop Ltd**		
Taihape	**Austin Hayman**		
Taumarunui	**Ray Winger Ltd**		
Tauranga	**F N Christian & Co**		
Te Aroha	**Hawke Motors Ltd**		
Te Awamutu	**Craik Motors Ltd**		
Te Kuiti	Te Kuiti Motors Ltd		
Te Puke	Te Puke Motors Ltd		
Thames	Hawke Motors Ltd		
Tokomaru Bay	Bignell & Holmes		
Trentham	Howell Motors Ltd		
Waipawa	F R Furminger Ltd		
Waipukurau	**J L Braithwaite Ltd**		
Wairoa	**Wairoa Motor Garage Co Ltd**		
Wanganui	**Merewether Motor Co Ltd**		
Warkworth			
Wellington	**Ford Sales & Service Ltd**		
Whakatane	**Armstrong & Co**		
Whangarei	**Whangarei Engineering Co Ltd**		
Woodville	**R Munro**		

FORD DEALERS 1970 CONFERENCE
CMC Group companies highlighted

Auckland	John W Andrew & Sons	Bob Greenfield
Cambridge	Wilkinson & Co	Bill Wilkinson
Carterton	Gordon Hughan Ltd	Bill Worsfold
Dannevirke	KB Motors	Graeme Bell and Jack Kearse
Dargaville	Dargaville Motors	Keith Louden
Eketahuna	Herberts Motors	Bert Rogers
Eltham	CC Stanners Motors	Ilay and Tom Stanners
Feilding	Feilding Central Garage	Alan and Geoff Rosoman
Gisborne	Holmes Motors	Dave Hewlett
Greenlane	McMillan Motors	Bob McMillan
Hamilton	Fairview Motors	Herbie Dyke
Hastings	Hastings Motors	Paul Jones
Hawera	Spinax Motors	Jim Keegan
Huntly	Smith Brothers	Ted & Dudley Smith
Johnsonville	Newlands Motors	Allan Hodges
Kaikohe	**Fairhall Motors**	**Ian Morgan**
Kaitaia	**Northland Motors**	**Alex Trail**
Levin	McMinn Motors	Don Colquhoun
Lower Hutt	**Stevens Motors**	**Loftie Henderson**
Marton	Forward Motors	Stan Tattle
Masterton	**Fagan Motors**	**Randal Thomson**
Maungaturoto	Central Motors	Ron Cullen
Morrisville	**Hawke Motors**	**Barry Wisneski**
Napier	South Pacific Motors	Barry Hannan
New Lynn	**New Lynn Motors**	**Colin Cliff**
New Plymouth	**Phillipps Motors**	**Royce Cox**
Ohura		
Opotiki	Opotiki Service Motors	Pat Borrie
Otahuhu	**South Auckland Motors**	**John Emery**
Otorohanga	Birch Motors	Ces Birch
Pahiatua	Terry's Garage	Les Terry
Palmerston North	Selwyn Motors	Bill Gibbons & John Livingston
Panmure	**Panmure Motors**	**Trist Atkins**
Papakura	Lees Bros	Rowley and Ted Lees
Porirua	Lynskey Motors	Brenden Lynskey
Pukekohe	D&W Motors	Gerry Davies & Jess de Willimoff
Putararu	Grange Motors	Garry Grange
Raetihi	Reynolds Motors	Trevor Reynolds
Rotorua	Lakeland Motors	Graham Laing
Stratford	Mountain Motors	Laurie Bond
Taihape	Hayman Motors	Harry Hayman
Takapuna	Lyon Motors	Gerry and Roger Lyon
Taumarunui	Taumarunui Motors	Arthur Allen
Taupo	Johnstone Motors	Doug Bowden
Tauranga	Tappenden Motors	Doug and Bill Tappenden
Te Awamutu	**Craik Motors**	**David Bodley**
Te Kuiti	**Te Kuiti Motors**	**Norm Shorter**
Te Puke	Te Puke Motors	Neil Brownlee
Thames	Goudie Motors	Colin Goudie
Upper Hutt	Tom Croft Motors	Tom Croft
Waipukurau	**Ruahine Motors**	**Roger Gardner**
Wairoa	DeLuxe Sevice Station	Bill Richards
Wanganui	Wanganui Motors	John Dyke
Wellington	**Avery Motors**	**Max Caigou**
Wellsford	Noel Kelly Motors	Noel Kelly
Whakatane		Lester Alley
Whangarei	Whangarei Engineering	Doug Smallbone
Woodville	Dickson & Horne	Noel Dickson
Alexandra	Alexandra Motors	Clarry Rooney
Ashburton	Gluyas Motors	John Gluyas
Balclutha	John H Stephenson	John McKenzie
Blenheim	Lucas Motors	Ted Lucas
Christchurch	**Hutchinson Motors**	**Orm & Hutch Hutchinson**
Dunedin	**Napier Motors**	**Bill Blackburn**
Geraldine	North End Garage	Bryan Warsaw
Gore	AV Latty	Bob & Denis Latty
Greymouth	Greymouth Motors	Jim Kennedy
Invercargill	**Macaulay Motors**	**Bill Maclaren**
Kaikoura	West End Motors	Dick Lee
Lawrence	Cross Motors	Stuart Cross
Milton		
Nelson	MS Motors	Bernie Stevenson
Oamaru	Knights Motors	Jim Craik
Palmerston Otago	Warrens Garage	Max Service
Ranfurly	Pringle Motors	Bob Pringle
Rangiora	Palmer & Doak	Richard Palmer
Roxburgh	Robbs Garage	Don Robb
Sockburn	**Sockburn Motors**	**George Daniel**
Timaru	**Timaru Motors**	**Don Mullan**
Waimate	Waimate Motors	Jack Dineen
Wanaka	Mansons Wanaka Motors	Jim Manson
Westport	Kilkenny Motors	Alva Hansby

FORD 60TH ANNIVERSARY IN NEW ZEALAND 1996

Ford Motor Co of New Zealand celebrated its 60th Anniversary at Puketutu Island on November 29 1996. The celebration marked the end of the large dealer groups as rationalisation started.

1. Barry Hoffman, Dannevirke
2. Brent Greig, Pukekohe
3. Jeff Copsey, North Shore
4. Mike Stevens, Cambridge
5. Ted Stone, Gisborne
6. Joe McAleese, Napier
7. Barry Holland, Stratford
8. John Cross, Wanganui
9. Brian Tappenden, Otorohanga
10. Greg Goudie, Silverdale
11. Jim Robb, West Auckland
12. Ian Duncan, Wellington
13. Richard Williams, Taupo
14. Herby Dyke, Dyke Group chmn
15. Orm Hutchinson, CMC chmn
16. John Dyke, Tauranga
17. Jim Gibbons, New Plymouth
18. John Luxton, Invercargill
19. Philip Hoffman, Pahiatua
20. Bill White, Greymouth
21. Colin Robb, Roxburgh
22. Ken Mullan, Morrinsville
23. Michael Brown, Whakatane
24. Rob Stevenson, Nelson
25. Ross Moore, Whangarei
26. Neville Goldsworthy, Kaitaia
27. Steven Hutchison, Lower Hutt
28. Trevor Walmsley, Auckland
29. Ian Lambie, Dunedin
30. Ian Redshaw, Wairoa
31. Peter Grace, Blenheim
32. Gordon Harrop, Hawera
33. Ian Shorter, Thames
34. Matthew Newman, Manukau
35. Paul Isaac, Taumarunui
36. Russell Lange, Christchurch

37. Gordon Powley, Levin
38. David Tobin, Waipukurau
39. Dennis Sexton, Hamilton
40. Lindsay West, Dargaville
41. Peter Gluyas, Ashburton
42. Don Stenhouse, Geraldine
43. Keith Taylor, Rotorua
44. Stuart Bowater, Auckland
45. John Flanagan, Christchurch Sth
46. Russell Marr, Timaru
47. David Sterritt, Oamaru
48. Peter Reese, Papakura
49. Ron Peterson, Kaikoura
50. Grant Daniel, CMC g-m

51. Roger Gardner, Masterton
52. Bob Stanners, Eltham
53. John Blyth, Panmure
54. Paul Jones, Hastings
55. Bob Rankin, Palmerston Nth
56. Eoin Service, Palmerston Sth
57. Tony Brigden, Ford NZ m-d
58. Nigel Wark, Ford NZ sales dir

Absent:
Noel Radd, Maungaturoto
Stephen Dyke, Porirua
Stewart Abernethy, Gore

FORD DEALERS, BRANCHES AND SERVICE AGENTS 2004

Ford Main Dealer points highlighted	Main Dealers are highlighted	Dealer Principals highlighted
Auckland	**John Andrew Ford**	D Ross Moore
Botany	South Auckland Motors branch	
Cambridge	Fairview Motors branch	
Dannevirke	**KB Motors**	Richard Gatward
Dargaville	**Dargaville Motors**	Lindsay West
Feilding	Courtesy Ford branch	
Gisborne	**Gisborne Motors**	Tim Macphee
Hamilton	**Fairview Motors**	Dennis Sexton
Hastings	Bay Ford branch	
Henderson	John Andrew Ford branch	
Hawera	**Tower Ford**	Gordon Harrop
Johnsonville	Avery Motors branch	
Kaitaia	Northland Mtrs (Pacific Motor Grp)	
Kerikeri	Pacific Motor Group branch	
Levin	Courtesy Ford branch	
Lower Hutt	**Stevens Motors** ¤	Stuart B Gibbons
Manukau City	**South Auckland Motors**	Matthew Newman
Masterton	**Fagan Motors** ¤	SW (Steve) Lyttle
Matamata	Fairview Motors branch	
Napier	**Bay Ford**	J (Joe) McAleese
New Plymouth	**Energy City Ford** ¤	JP (Jim) Gibbons
Ohakune	Wanganui Motors branch	
Pahiatua	**Hoffman Motors**	Philip Hoffman
Palmerston North	**Courtesy Ford**	Gordon Powley
Paraparaumu	Metro Ford	
Porirua	**Metro Ford**	Steven Dyke
Rotorua	**Carson Taylor Ford**	Keith Taylor
Silverdale	North Harbour Ford branch	
Stratford	**Mountain Motors**	Barry Holland
Taihape	Wanganui Motors branch	
Takapuna	**North Harbour Ford**	Alan Kirby
Taupo	**Central Motor Group**	Richard Williams
Tauranga	**Ultimate Motor Group**	John Cross
Te Awamutu	Fairview Motors branch	
Thames	Ultimate Motor Group branch	
Upper Hutt	Stevens Motors branch	
Waipukurau	**Ruahine Motors** ¤	Hamish Jacob
Wairoa	**DeLuxe Ford**	Ian C Redshaw
Wanganui	**Wanganui Motors**	Steven Dyke
Warkworth	North Harbour Ford	
Wellington	**Avery Motors** ¤	Grant Daniel
Whakatane	**Brown Bros Ford**	Michael Brown
Whangarei	**Pacific Motor Group**	Hamish Sheard
Ashburton	**Gluyas Motor Group**	Peter Gluyas
Balclutha	Regional Ford branch	
Blenheim	MS Ford branch	
Christchurch	**Team Hutchinson Ford** ¤	Russell J Lange
Christchurch South	**Avon City Ford** ¤	John W Luxton
Dunedin	**Dunedin City Ford** ¤	Roger Taylor
Gore	**Regional Ford**	Stewart Abernethy
Greymouth	**Greymouth Motors**	W (Bill) White
Invercargill	**Macaulay Motors** ¤	Grant Price
Nelson	**MS Motors**	John Flanagan
Queenstown	Macaulay Motors branch	
Rangiora	Avon City Ford branch	
Timaru	**Timaru Motors** ¤	Russell J Marr

Ford Service Agents

TOWN	COMPANY	MANAGER
Eltham	Stanners Motors	Keith Stanners
Huntly	Alf Wykes & Sons	Paul Wykes
Marton	Tasker Automotive	Wayne Tasker
Maungaturoto	Noel Radd Motors	Noel Radd
Morrinsville	Udy Automotive	Ivan Udy
Otorohanga	Brian Tappenden Motors	Brian Tappenden
Pukekohe	Pukekohe Motors	Geoff Lovegrove
Taumarunui	Paul Isaac Ford	Paul Isaac
Te Aroha	Axis Automotive	Paul Hammond
Tokoroa	Barry Wood Motors	Barry Wood
Alexandra	Brian Luff Automotive	Brian Luff
Kaikoura	West End Motors	Ron Peterson
Oamaru	Mortimer Auto & Marine	Paul Mortimer
Palmerston Otago	Warrens Garage	Eoin Service
Roxburgh	Robbs Garage	Colin Robb

CMC Group companies ¤

INDEX

What Will You Do For Help?

FARM help is scarce, but this condition can be relieved to a marked degree by using machines that accomplish more work in a given time with less man power

Why should the farmer cling to horses—a slow, expensive means of power—when every other business is adopting the truck and thereby reducing the cost of hauling, speeding up deliveries, and saving for human needs the food that the horses would otherwise consume?

The motor driven truck can work constantly at maximum load under the summer sun or in the coldest weather. Unlike the horse it needs no rests while working, it eats only while in actual use, and when the day's work is done it requires very little attention, and leaves you free for other jobs about the place. Then, it can be housed in one quarter the space of the horses, wagon and harness, it replaces.

It is a mistaken idea that a truck is useful only for driving upon paved roads. The Ford can be driven all over the farm, and used for hauling grain, potatoes, fruit, roots, fertilizer, wood, stock, milk, or any other product. The speed it travels, the time it saves, and its low upkeep cost appeal very strongly to all users of the Ford Truck. If you need help, order your Ford One Ton Truck to-day from the nearest Ford dealer.

Truck Chassis
complete with Solid rear tyre equipment,
£235
f.o.b., Wellington.

The Colonial Motor
Company, Limited
WELLINGTON   AUCKLAND   TIMARU

Truck Chassis
complete with Pnuematic, 34 x 4½ rear tyre equipment (quick detachable)
£235
f.o.b., Wellington.

siderably exceeded if the engine is accelerated. The low-speed-gear introduces a further reduction in the ratio of about 3 to 1, so that when it is employed the normal speed of the car is about 7 miles per hour.

The System of Control.

The control of a "Ford" car is very simple, the various levers and pedals for which are clearly shown in Fig. 8. To the right of the driver's seat is the change-speed lever, M^6, which lies in a central position when the car is at rest. To start the car—by introducing the low-speed-gear—this lever is pressed rearwardly, and, if moved as far as it will go, it will remain there. When starting, however, it is only necessary to press it back sufficiently to get under way, and it can then be moved forwards to bring the top-speed into play. When running normally it may be left in its forward position, or, when travelling in traffic, the clutch can be allowed to slip to a certain extent by exerting only the requisite pressure on the lever.

The foot-pedal, P^2, which lies just to the left of the steering-pillar, is that by which the "reverse" gear is introduced, and this, of course, is only used when the hand-lever, M^6, is in its neutral position.

To the left of this pedal is the brake-pedal, D^2, which actuates the internal expanding-brake, on the back axle.

The third, and smaller, pedal, G^7, is operated by the right foot, and it controls the throttle valve. The speed of the car on the road is therefore controlled for the most part by means of it, the speed increasing as it is depressed. When completely released, the engine can only obtain sufficient mixture to run quite slowly when the car is at rest.

The hand lever, J^6, on the steering pillar is that which regulates the time of ignition, and should, in consequence, be moved from the vertical position (in which it is in our illustration) downwardly, as the speed of the engine is allowed to increase. As shown, the ignition is "retarded" to the extent necessary for starting, and it assumes a horizontal position for full "advance." Relating also to the ignition system, is the two-way switch, J, which is fitted just below the seat. This switch allows either battery of cells to be brought into use, alternatively, or the current to be entirely cut off. The switch is also fitted with a detachable contact plug, J^5, which can be removed to prevent the car being started when the driver leaves it.

The body is constructed so that all the various parts of the mechanism can be readily got at when occasion demands. The front seat can be lifted up for replenishing, and the woodwork forming the front of it is hinged so that the coil can be exposed to view. The floor, too, both in the tonneau and in front of the driver, can be lifted out, so that there is no part of the mechanism to which access cannot be obtained quickly and conveniently. The front portion of the body forms a low dash, which is so constructed as to constitute a sufficiently large tool-box, in which even such comparatively large accessories as jacks and tyre pumps can be accommodated. The petrol tank holds about $4\frac{1}{2}$ gallons, which is found to be sufficient for running a distance of about 135 miles. As we have already said, the 4-seated car is made in such a way that the tonneau is detachable; when this is removed, a sloping back is substituted.

A NEW FIELD FOR THE PETROL MOTOR.

The Royal Horticultural Society's Show, which has been held during last week at the Botanical Gardens, Regent's Park, was, perhaps, hardly the place at which one might expect to find the latest application of the petrol motor. Nevertheless, visitors had hardly entered those pretty grounds before they were greeted with the unmistakable sound of the internal combustion motor at work. There has been a good deal said lately about parks and pests

FIG. 1.—The Merryweather "general purposes" pump at work in the Grounds of the Botanical Gardens.

FIG. 2.—Portable Petrol Motor-Driven Hop Washing Plant, constructed by Messrs. Merryweather and Sons.

connected in parallel. This radiator appears to be sufficiently effective to prevent any loss of water by evaporation when the car is running normally and continuously.

The flywheel, F¹, is of large diameter, and is sufficiently heavy to ensure steady running. It is mounted close up to the crank-chamber, and the crank-shaft projects through it right across the chassis to the right side, the change-speed-gear being mounted on it. The crank-shaft at its extreme end, just outside the bearing, E¹, is fitted with a pin, F⁵, to receive the starting handle, and it will be observed, in Figs. 1 and 5, that the handle is introduced through a hole in the side of the body. As a matter of fact, it is possible to start the engine from the driver's seat, and, as a comparatively low compression is arranged for in the cylinders, it is not difficult to turn it round. Usually, however, the engine is started from the ground.

The engine is capable of developing about 10-h.p., and it actually gives, we understand, 9-b.h.p. at about 800 revs. per min., which is considered to be the normal speed. In practice it runs at any speed up to about 1,400 revs. per min., and appears to do so without setting up any objectionable vibration.

The Change-speed-gear.

The type of change-speed-gear used on the Ford car is sufficiently similar to that employed on other American vehicles to render superfluous any very full description here, but it differs from others, inasmuch as no internally-toothed gear-wheels are used in it. Mounted freely on the crank-shaft, close up to the flywheel, F¹, is the sprocket-wheel from which the power is taken to the back axle by the chain, C. This sprocket is formed with deep flanges on either side, and the gear ratio

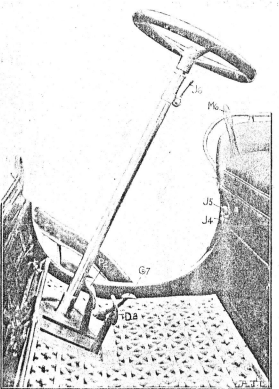

Fig. 8.—View showing the Regulating Levers and Pedals on the "Ford" Petrol Car.

between it and the back axle is about $3\frac{1}{8}$ to 1. Fixed rigidly to this sprocket is a spur-wheel, immediately outside which are two other spur-wheels that are also concentric with the crank-shaft. The central spur-wheel is somewhat smaller than the other two, and it is rigidly fixed to the shaft, whilst the outer wheel is free to revolve upon the crank-shaft but is rigid with the brake-drum which is held to give the "reverse." Engaging with all these three spur-wheels are two sets of corresponding planet wheels which are free to revolve upon pins fixed, on opposite sides of the crank-shaft, to the shell forming the low-speed brake-drum. Each set of three planets have their wheels fixed to one another, so that when the low-speed brake-drum is held stationary, they resemble the "back-gear" of an ordinary lathe.

Normally the whole of this gear (which is seen in Fig. 7) is "locked"—so that it runs as one piece with

the crank-shaft—by the disc-clutch which forms a part of it, and then the power is transmitted direct from the crank-shaft to the back axle. The clutch is formed by the disc, M¹, which rides upon a feather on the shaft, and can be forced up against the side of the "reverse" brake-drum when the cone, M, is caused to slide inwards along the shaft. The cone, M, engages with three toggle levers, M², and causes them to act in the well-known manner upon the sliding disc, whilst the clutch can be adjusted by screwing the bracket which carries the levers, M³, either inwards or outwards, and locked when adjusted, by a set screw. The clutch is operated from the rock-shaft, M⁴ (seen in Fig. 7), through the pivoted bell-crank, M⁵, and this same shaft also controls the brake-band, N, which acts on the low-speed brake-drum, so that both these speeds are controlled through the connecting-rod, M⁶, by the same hand-lever.

The low-speed-gear is introduced by tightening the brake-drum, N, about its drum, and then the pins upon which the planet wheels revolve are held stationary, so that a double reduction gearing is introduced between the crank-shaft and the sprocket. Provision is made by the set-screw, N², on the tightening lever, N¹, for adjusting the brake-band, N; the actual tightening action is obtained by cams on the rock-shaft, M⁴.

The "reverse" gear is not quite as satisfactory, from a mechanical point of view, as the low-speed-gear, although it is sufficiently so to suit its purpose; this is, to a great extent, shown by the fact that it is not so silent in action. When the brake-band, P, is tightened the spur-wheel attached to it is held stationary, and then the sprocket-wheel is driven in an opposite direction to the crank-shaft by virtue of the differences in diameter of the various planets and of the wheels with which they engage. The brake-band, P, is operated by a rod, P¹ (Fig. 3), which lies on the underside, and the adjustment-nut for the brake is also situated beneath the brake-drum; this gear is controlled by a foot-pedal.

The entire gear runs in oil, which can be introduced to it through a plug-hole fitted between the two brake drums. It contains sufficient oil for running a considerable distance without attention, but should be filled up occasionally to replenish what may have escaped. It will have been realised that it only contains nine spur-wheels in all, and it will be seen from our illustration that the case enclosing it is very compact. When the top-speed is in use, the gear ratio between the engine and the road-wheels is such that the car will travel at about 21 miles per hour when the engine is running at 800 revs. per min., though this speed can be con-

FIG. 6.—The "Ford" Engine, as seen from the "near" side of the chassis.

The commutator, J, is fitted just outside the crank-chamber on the projecting end of the cam-shaft, where it lies at the side of the car in a very convenient position. It has but one contact spring inside it, and is used in conjunction with a single trembler coil, which is fixed beneath the front seat on the left. The cam operating the commutator has two opposite projections, so that the low-tension circuit is completed to the coil twice—at equidistant points—during each revolution of the cam-shaft. The high-tension coil has both its terminals insulated, and the two high-tension wires are led to the two ignition plugs, J[1]. Electrically, therefore, the ignition plugs are in series with one another, and the spark occurs in both cylinders simultaneously, although only required in one at a time. The idle spark in the other cylinder merely takes place towards the end of the exhaust stroke, and therefore does no harm. The advantage of this arrangement, which is already known to our readers—as, for instance, in the twin-cylinder Chenard-Walcker car—is that one coil serves for two cylinders, and that perfect synchronism between cylinder and cylinder can be ensured. The commutator is, as usual, so mounted that it can be rocked about the cam-shaft, for varying the time of ignition in the cylinders, and this "timing" is controlled from a hand-lever on the steering pillar.

The type of carburettor, G[2], employed, is of the float-feed spray variety, and it is fixed (Figs. 2 and 3) almost centrally in the car just in front of the engine. It is of very simple construction, and with it is combined a throttle-valve that is connected by a system of levers, G[3], with a foot-pedal. The throttle-valve is normally held almost closed by a spring, but can be opened to any desired extent by depressing the pedal correspondingly. The float itself, in the carburettor, is made of cork, and is varnished to prevent any disintegration. The valve which cuts off the petrol feed to the car-

burettor is fixed direct to the upper side of the float. An adjustment, in the form of a needle-valve above the spray jet, is provided for enabling the richness of the mixture to be determined initially, and there are also adjustable screw stops by which the range of movement of the throttle-valve can be limited in both directions. The throttle-valve is so made that an approximately constant richness of mixture is maintained by it, for it not only controls the flow of the mixture to the engine but also of the air to itself. The entering air is in no way warmed, but is drawn straight in beneath the mixing chamber.

A comparatively long, branched induction pipe, G[4] (Fig. 3), leads the explosive mixture, on the underside of the engine, to both inlet-valves, and this pipe is designed in such a way as to ensure both cylinders obtaining an equal volume of charge.

The exhaust-pipe, H[1], lies alongside the induction-pipe, G[1], underneath the engine, and into it the exhaust gases from both cylinders are led direct. This pipe is clearly visible in Fig. 6, where it will be noticed that the gases have but a very short distance to travel to the exhaust box, H[2]. The exhaust-box appears to be very effective, although comparatively small for an engine of this power; it is constructed with four concentric tubes that form annular spaces into which the gases are successively led through rows of $\frac{5}{16}$-in. holes.

The circulating-pump, K[2], which is of the centrifugal type, is driven direct off the left end of the crank-shaft. It draws its supply of water from the bottom of the tank, K, and forces it up through the radiator, K[3], on its way to the cylinder-jackets. The water enters the bottom of each jacket, and is led back again from the top of each to the tank, K. The radiator is constructed of eighteen finned tubes which are arranged in six rows of three, placed one above the other. The water enters the bottom, and passes through each row of tubes in succession to the top, the tubes in each individual row being

FIG. 7.—The Change-speed-gear on the "Ford" Car, as seen from the "off" side of the chassis.

THE "FORD" PETROL CAR.

(Concluded.)

The Engine.

A SIDE-VIEW of the engine, fixed in place on the car, is given in Fig. 6, and this illustration, taken in conjunction with those of the chassis already referred to, will enable its construction to be clearly understood. It has two horizontal cylinders, F, which are bolted, slightly out of line with one another, on opposite sides of the crank-chamber. Each cylinder casting forms a large valve chamber beneath the cylinder proper, and there is a large water-jacket around the entire combustion-chamber. Although the cylinders are not in line with one another, yet their valve-chambers are so arranged as to be quite opposite, and the valves, being horizontal and pointing towards one another, can therefore be operated by the same cams. The inlet and exhaust-valves in each valve-chamber lie alongside one another, in such a way that the inlet-valve, G^6, of the one cylinder is in line with the inlet-valve of the other, and the two exhaust-valves, H^3, are also in line. Inspection plugs, G^5 and H, respectively, are screwed into the valve-chambers opposite to the inlet and exhaust-valves, so that any valve can be readily got at for grinding in when necessary; the inspection-covers, G^5, have the ignition-plugs, I^1, screwed through them. All four valves are normally held on their seats in the usual way, by helical springs, and they are operated by horizontal push-rods that pass through the base of the crank-chamber and engage with the two cams on the cam-shaft lying therein. The cylinders have a bore of $4\frac{1}{4}$ ins., and the stroke is 4 ins.

The crank-chamber proper is formed of two castings, F^1 and F^2, the joint between which is horizontal, and lies above the crank-shaft bearings. The lower casting, F^1, is slotted at each side to receive the bearings, which are made in two parts—divided vertically—and are forced up together by a wedge which can be tightened up against them from outside. The upper casting, F^2, is provided with a flat cover plate, F^3, to which is fixed a large sight-feed lubricator, L, which feeds the engine at six different points. The crank-shaft has two crank-pins arranged opposite one another, with only a thin cheek

Fig. 5.—Another View of the "Ford" Petrol Car, fitted with its Tonneau.

between them, and the two connecting rods, acting upon them, are quite straight. The reciprocating parts are in this way mechanically in balance, and the two pistons reciprocate in opposite directions to one another. The valves are so set that the two cylinders do not fire at the same time, but work alternately, and thus an impulse is given to the crank-shaft at the same moment during each revolution, thus also securing balance so far as regularity of impulse is concerned.

The crank-shaft is carried in bearings of large size, which are kept as near together as the cranks permit, but there is a spur-wheel between the crank and the bearing on the right side for driving the cam-shaft, which lies immediately below the crank-shaft. The cam-shaft and the spur-wheels driving it are thus kept well lubricated, since they lie inside the crank-chamber, and, as we have already said, the cam-shaft has only two cams formed on it, the one for actuating the two inlet-valves, and the other the two exhaust-valves.

The connecting rods have adjustable bearings at both ends, and their big-ends are so formed that only one bolt is required for holding the cap in place, the cap being hinged to the connecting rod on the underside.

The lubricator, L, is of larger size than usual, and is fitted with a filler cap, L^1, which—like the caps, G^1 and K^1, for the petrol and the water respectively—are readily accessible at all times for replenishing. There is a passage formed between the crank-chamber and the top of the lubricator, through the fitting which holds the latter in place, and a non-return valve is introduced in this passage. By this means a certain amount of pressure is, whilst the engine is running, maintained on the oil, because the two pistons tend to compress the air in the crank-chamber when travelling inwards, and to draw in a fresh charge of air when travelling outwards. Since the pressure is only maintained whilst the engine is running, its lubrication is to a great extent automatic. Each of the six feed pipes, leading from it, has a separate adjustment, and the oil to each drops through a short length of glass tubing. Two of the pipes feed the two pistons, two of them lead to the main-crank-shaft bearings, and the other two drip on to the connecting rods.

MW00737334

A R M Gardner
P O Box 779
Masterton 5840
New Zealand

3 December 2007

Carlton O Pate III
285 Forest Lane
Glastonbury
CT 06033
United States of America

Dear Carl,

Enclosed are a copy of *Ford Ahead-A History of The Colonial Motor Company Ltd* for your library together with a cd of photographs, all of which you may use, and unless specified otherwise below, should be attributed to The Colonial Motor Company Ltd and me. Also two copies of publications; a 1904 description in The Automotor Journal (UK?); a 1989 Road Test in the The Wairarapa Times-Age, Masterton; and quotes should be attributed to publications.

Cd photographs as follows:-

- Image 001.JPG-Page 11 from Geoff Easdown's book *A History of Ford Motor Co in Australia*. Any quote should be attributed to Geoff Easdown.
- Model A 1903 1a.doc.jpg-publicity shot of the CMC car after restoration in 1987. CMC photo
- Model A 1903 5.doc.jpg-Vintage buff, Gordon Darnell, Service Manager at Stevens Motors who saved the car and started the restoration. CMC photo
- Model A 1903 6.doc.jpg-Bernie Cheer and wife Natalie driving in the Centennial parade for the Carterton Borough in 1987. Bernie Cheer worked for Gordon Hughan Ltd, Carterton, is a Model T buff and did most of the mechanical restoration work and helps maintain the car today. Photo must always be attributed to G E Nikolaison, Photographer, Masterton.
- Model A 1903 7,doc.jpg- Bill Worsfold, MD of Gordon Hughan Ltd, surveys the re-building in 1970s. CMC photo
- Model A 1903 8a.doc.jpg-November 1951 at Ford Zephyr launch. Un-restored car on Model T wheels. Clockwise from front right; J A (Jack) McInnes, MD, Avery Motors, Wellington; Jack Jones, Salesman Avery Motors; L A (Les) Clarke, GM, Colonial Motor Co; Harold P Ralph, Gen Sales Mgr Ford Motor Co NZ (later MD Ford NZ). CMC photo.
- Model A 1903 10.doc.jpg- car after restoration at Gordon Hughan Ltd. CMC photo.

It is my hope that you will enjoy reading the history, which will give some insite into New Zealand transportation as well as Colonial Motor Company and its subsidiary companies. There are a few errors of course (p11,p52 +), but not knowing ones at the time.

Best wishes for a Happy Christmas and a fulfilling 2008, with completion of your book,

Regards

Roger Gardner

Tel + 64 6 370-1696   Mob +64 27 233-9032   e-mail to   roger.gardner@xtra.co.nz